ENGLISH-PUSHTO
PUSHTO-ENGLISH
COMBINED
DICTIONARY

STAR PUBLICATIONS (Pvt.) Ltd.
4/5 Asaf Ali Road, New Delhi-110002

ENGLISH-PUSHTO
PUSHTO-ENGLISH
COMBINED
DICTIONARY

Compiled and edited by:

HENRY WALTER BELLEW

ISBN : 81-7650-225-1

Published by : **STAR PUBLICATIONS (PVT.) LTD.**
4/5 Asaf Ali Road,
New Delhi-110002

This edition : 2006
Originally edition 1867

Printed at : Lahooti Offset Press, Delhi.

FROM THE PUBLISHERS:

We have planned to bring out a series of dictionaries compiled by prominent scholars in different languages of the world.

THIS DICTIONARY is one in that series, and we hope readers will find it useful.

This is our humble contribution in bringing various languages of the world together and closer to English.

FROM THE EDITOR

In compiling this Dictionary of the Pushto Language (English-Pushto and Pushto English), I have experienced considerable difficulties in deciding upon the words of foreign origin, principally Arabic and Persian, but of common use in Pushto that should find a place in these pages.

As a rule, words of the Arabic and Persian that are used in an unaltered form in the Pushto have been omitted, excepting only those of very common or general use ; for to have given place to all the words of those languages used in an unchanged form by Pashtoon authors, would have added unnecessarily to the bulk of the work without, in return, being of any practical utility in the study of the language, since their use is almost solely confined to literary works or to discussions on theological subjects.

Of the words purely Pushto, the most, it will be observed, are derived from the Persian. In most instances I have endeavoured to point out their sources in those languages, by quoting in brackets with each word the original form from which it may be derived, with a preceding capital letter for the initial of the language to which each belongs.

In some instances the changes are very slight, in others more complex, and in a few complete, but still in general accordance with the regular laws of philology, which in Pushto are variously illustrated according to the diverse vocal and phonetic peculiarities of the different tribes, composing the Afghan nation.

I have not had leisure to follow out this enquiry as fully as the subject demands, owing to the scant opportunities at my disposal in the intervals between my professional and military duties. I have considered it necessary, however, to allude to the subject, and to note in brief some instances that have attracted my attention, in the hope that they will, whilst serving as illustrations of the changes which words from the Persian and Indian languages undergo on becoming Pushto, at the same time suffice to guide the student desirous of a further investigation of the subject.

The letters of cognate sound with *j,* viz. *j* and *z,* in Pushto are often replaced by *g* and *dz* respectively, as in *kog.* (crooked) from *kaj, gala-i* (hail) from *jãlah,* and *nmūndz* (prayer) from *namãz.* By some tribes, as the Yusufzais and Eastern Afghans generally, the letters *j* and *g* are habitually pronounced, and generally also written as *j* and *g* respectively.

The letter *d* in words introduced from a foreign source, in the Pushto generally becomes replaced by *L,* as in *las* (ten) from the Hindi *das,* and *lerver* (husband's brother) from the Hindi *dervar,* and in *lãs* (hand) from *dast, lūm* (a net) from *dãm, plãr* (father) from *padar, plandar* (stepfather) from *padandar, lur* (daughter) from *dukhtar, lenvanai* (mad) from *diwãnah, lwashal* (to milk) from *doshidan,* etc., all from the Persian.

The letters *rd,* when coming together without an intervening vowel, are rendered in Pushto by *ṛ,* as in *wṛal* (to carry) from *burdan, rãwṛal* (to fetch) from *ãwurdan, khwuṛal* (to eat) from *khurdan, mṛal* (to die) from *murḍan, kṛal* (to do) from *kardan, sparal* or *spardai* (to undo) from *saparda, maṛanai* (manly) from *mardãnah,* etc. ; all from the Persian.

The letter *sh* is generally changed in Pushto in *kkh* or *ksh,* as in *pokkhal* or *pokshal* (to cover) from *poshidan ; bakhkkhal* or *bakhkshal,* sometimes contracted to *bakkhal* or *bakshal* (to give), from *bakhshidan* ; *kkhkal,* or *kakshal* or *kkshal* (to draw), from *kashidan* ; *kkhkandzal* or *kshakandzal,* often contracted to *kanzal* (to abuse), from *shikanjidan* (to torture) ; *tskkhal* or *tsakshal,* sometimes contracted to *tskal* or *skal* (to sip, drink), from *chashidan* ; *kkhkãrah* or *kkshãrah* (apparent) from *ashkãrah* ; *kkhkãr* or *kkshãr* (sport) from *shikar,* etc., etc., all from the Persian, Sometimes the letter *j,* taking the sound of *sh* in Pushto, undergoes the same change as that letter, as in *gwãkkhedal* or *gwãkshedal,* sometimes written *gwãkkhal* or *gwãkshal* (to chide), from the Persian *gwãjidan.* In one instance the *sh* becomes rendered in Pushto by *ts* as in *tsãtsedal* (to drop, distil), from the Persian *shãshidan.*

More complete changes are illustrated in the following examples of Pushto verbs derived from a Persian source. Generally such verbs undergo changes in the present and past tenses corresponding with those of the originals from which they are derived, as is shown in the following examples, viz., *khatal, khej.* (to rise), from *khãstan, khez-* ; *ghokkhtal* or *ghokshtal, ghwãṛ-* (to ask) from *khwãstan, khwãh-, ãghustal, ãghund-* (to wear, put on), from *ãghastan, ãghand-* etc., etc. And so *laral* (to have, possess), from *dãshtan, dãr-, karal* (to sow) from *kãshtan, kãr-* ; *rajedal* (to be scattered) from *rekhtan, rez-, zghaledal* (tc run) from *gurekhtan, gurez-*, etc., etc.

The word *kojdan* or *kojda* (a betrothal) is another instance of similar transformation, being derived from the Persian *khwastan* (to ask), or *khwast* (a request), through *ghokkhtal* or *ghokshtal,* and *ghokkht* or *ghoksht,* from the latter forms of which are derived *ghokshtan* or *kojdan-ghokshta* or *kojda.* And so on with many other words, whose originals in be Persian and Hindi will be found noted in their proper places in the text.

In compiling this Dictionary of the Pushto language, at the end of which I have added a reversed part in English and Pushto. My acknowledgments are due for the aid derived from Raverty's Dictionary, though, in many instances, we differ in meanings of certain words, such as *tsakkhkūrai, mãndah, kishor,* etc., etc., as well as in more important particulars respecting the family and structure of the language.

With the view to economising space, the present, active, and passive participles have been generally omitted from the first part of the work, as also have derivative adjectives and verbs, the rules with examples for forming these several parts of speech having been fully detailed in the Grammar.

Such as it is, however, I trust it will be found useful, especially as regards the second or English and Pushto part ; and with the Grammar and the Exercises and dialogues added to it, be serviceable in facilitating the study of Pushto (called as *Pukshto*) the language of the Afghans, and paving the way to the easy acquisition of a practical knowledge of the Pushto colloquial.

PART - I

ENGLISH–PUSHTO

Aback, ad. *biyarta, wrusto, pastana.*

Abaisance, s. *salām, sijda, t'az̤īm.*

Abandon, v.a. *pregdal, prekkhodal, prekkhawul, preyakkhal*; *tark k.*

Abandoned, a. *prekkhodalai, preyakkhai* or *prīkkhai.*

Abandonment, s. *prekkhodana, prekkhawuna.*

Abase, v.a. *spukawul.*

Abased, v.n. *spukedal.* a. *spukawulai, spukedalai.*

Abasement, s. *spuk·wālai, spukedana.*

Abash, v.a. *sharmawul.*

Abashed, v.n. *sharmedal.* a. *sharmsār, sharmindah*; *pakkhemān*; *sharmedalai.*

Abate, v.a. *kamawul, la-ag k.* v.n. *kamedal, la-ag ked.*

Abatement, s. *kamedana, kam·wālai, kam·tiyā, la-agedana, la-ag·wālai*; *chūk.*

Abbreviate, v.a. *landawul.*

Abbreviation, s. *land·wālai.*

Abdicate, v.a. *tark k. pregdal.* (Abandon).

Abdicator, s. *tark kawūnkai, prekkhodūnkai, tārik.*

Abdomen, s. *geda, kheta.* (hypogastrium) *spokhdza, spokhz.* (hypochondrium) *ta·ashai, dada.*

Abet, v.a. *madad warkawul, pushtī k.*; *lamsawul.*

Abetment, s. *madad, pushtī, komak*; *lamsūn.*

Abettor, s. *madad-, pushtī-, komak-,* etc. *warkawūnkai*; *lamsūnai.*

Abide, v.n. *osedal, āstedal, pātedal, pātai ked. wudaredal.*

Abject, a. *khwār, dūn, sperah·kai, sperah·makh.*

Abjectness, s. *khwārī, tabāhī.*

Ability, s. *qābiliyat, ṭāqat, was, yarz*; *qābil·tob.*

Abjure, v.a. *munkiredal.*

Able, a. *qābil, tuwānā.* v.n. *shwal, tuwānedal.* v.a. *tāqat-, zor-, wāk-, was-,* etc. *laral.*

Ablution, s. *ghusl,* (ceremonial) *āwdas, wazū, taimūm* or *tebūn.*

Abode, s. *dzāe, astoga, astogana, ṭīkāo, mīshta, kor, makān, kilai, deṛa, borjal.*

Abolish, v.a. *bandawul, mauqūf-, man'a-, mansūkh-,* etc. *k.*

Abominable, a. *bad, palīt, nā-pāk, stūkh, murdār.*

Abominate, v.a. *bad manal, chinjawul, kraka ākhistal, nafrat k., ghandal, kagal.*

Abort, v.a. *geḍa ghurzawul, ziyān k.*

Abortion, s. *da geḍe ziyān.* (in animals) *piyāza.*

Abortive, a. *be-fā-ida, 'abaṣ, bāṭil, nā-kār.*

Above, p. *pās, dapāsa, bānde, dabānde, porta, pahūrta.*

Abound, *wadānedal, ziyātedal, ḍeredal.*

About, p. *chāpera, chauper; dapāra, bābat; nizde* or *niȷ̂de, qarīb, tsakha* or *khatsa; lagiyā, mashghūl; pa andāz, pa ḥisāb.*

Abrade, v.a. *sūlawul, garawul, gargal, gasiyā k.* v.n. *sūledal, blodal, blosedal, gasiyā ked.*

Abrasion, s. *sūda, blos, gasiyā; blosedana, sūledana.*

Abreast, ad. *barābar, tsang pa tsang.*

Abroad, ad. *bahar* or *bāhir, pa pradī mulk* (or *dzāe*) *kkhke.*

Abrupt, a. *garandai, za-ar* or *zir, jalt; zīg, lwāṛ.* s. *ḍoghal, kand, gaṛang, kamar.*

Abruptly, ad. *nā-tsāpa, nā-gūmān, nāgāh, sam da lāsa.*

Abscess, s. *kharai, kkhanza, shīnai, nanaka-ī, kkhlūna, lūna.*

Abscond, v.n. *puṭedal, takkhtedal, firārī ked.*

Absence, s. *biyal-tūn, judā-ī, hijrān; nisht-wālai, ghair ḥāẓirī.*

Absent, a. *ghā-ib, nishtah, ghair ḥāẓir; biyal, judā; ghāfil, be-khūd, pa fikr kkshe ḍūb.*

Absolve, v.a. *pulawul, bakkhal* or *bakhkkhal.*

Absolved, a. *bakkhalai, pulawulai, khalāṣ, m'uāf.*

Absolute, a. *pūrah, sarāsar, amānī, tamām, ṭol, mutlaq; khpul-sar* or *khapsar, wāk-dār, mukhtār.*

Absolutely, ad. *amānī, sarāsarī, tamāmī.*

Absolution, s. *bakkhana, khalāṣī, puṛ* (or *pa-al*), *najāt.*

Absorb, v.a. *tskkhal* or *tskal* or *skal, wuchawul.*

Absorbed, v.n. *wuchedal, jaẕb ked.*

Abstain, v.a. *parhez-, pāl-,* etc. *k. lāṣ-, dzān-,* etc. *bāsal—yastal, lās-, dzān-* etc. *sātal.*

Abstemious, a. *parhez-gār, kam-khwurāk, pārsā.*

Abstinence, s. *pāl, parhez; roȷ̂a; pārsā-ī.*

Abstract, s. *mujmal, khulāṣa.*

Abstract, v.a. *bāsal—yastal, kāgal—kkhkal; biyalawul, judā k.*

Abstruse, a. *bārīk, narai, puṭ; grān, mushkil.*

Absurd, a. *'abaṣ, be-hūdah, wuch puch, yāwah, khushai, prat, harzah.*

Absurdity, s. *be-hūdagī, be-wūqūfī, kam-'aqlī.*

Abundance, s. *ḍer-wālai, wadānī, ābādī, frewānī, ziyāt-wālai.*

Abundant, a. *ḍer, ziyāt, frewān, ṭal.*

Abuse, s. *kkhkandzal* or *kanzal, peghor.* v.a. *kkhkandzal* or *kanzal, kanzal-, ruswā-,* etc. *k. peghor warkawul; bad sulūkī-, be-hurmatī-,* etc. *k.*

Abusive, a. *jiba-war, kanzal kawūnkai.*

Abyss, s. *gaṛang, kanda, ḍoghal, jawara.*

Accede, v.a. *manal, qabūlawul.*

Accent, s. *lahja, qirāt, ẓarb, ghag, makhraj.*

Accept, v.a. *manal, qabūlawul; ākhistal; khwakkhawul, pasandawul, kkhah ganral.*

Acceptable, a. *khwakkh, ghwarah.* v.n. *pasandedal, khwakkhedal, qabūledal.*

Access, s. *dakhl*; *rāsha darsha, nanawātah.*

Accession, s. *khātah, khatana.*

Accident, s. *āfat, wāq'ia, ḥādīsa, balā.*

Accidental, a. *qazā-ī, qismatī.*

Acclamation, s. *zwag zūg, hāhū, chīgha*; *āparīn, shābāsh.*

Accommodate, v.a. *dzāyawul*; *khidmat k. atsanral, hawārawul.*

Accommodation, s. *dzāe*; *khidmat.*

Accompany, v.n. *malgarai ked*; *khatsa tlal.*

Accomplice, s. *mal, malgarai, sharīk, yār.*

Accomplish, v.a. *tamāmawul, pūrah k. pa dzāe rāwṛal*; *kawul, kṛal.*

Accomplished, a. *tamām shawai* or *-karai, pūrah*; *qābil, pohānd, hunar-man, kāmil.*

Accomplishment, s. *tamāmī, anjām, taiyārī*; *hunar, qābil-tob, kāmil-tob.*

Accord, s. *rogha, joṛa, pakhulā-tob, āshtī*; *barābarī, nisbat.* (of own-) *pa khpul.* (of one-) *yak jihat, yak dil, yo shān.* v.n. *yak sān-* or *yo shān-, barābar-,* etc. *ked. lagedal.*

According to, p. *pa—sara.* (-custom) *pa dastūr sara.*

Accordingly, ad. *la de na, dzaka.*

Accost, v.a. *pukkhtedal, salām k. pukkhtana k. wayal, khabare k. nāre wahal.*

Account, v.a. *ganṛal, pohedal, shmeral,* s. *ḥisāb, shumār*; *qiṣṣa, bayān, naql, tazkira*; *dzawāb* or *jawāb, khabara.*

Accountable, a. *zāmin*; *tāwān-* or *dzawāb warkawūnkai.*

Accoutre, v.a. *mlā taṛal, drasta-* or *wasla āghostal.*

Accrue, v.n. *ḥāṣiledal, paidā ked.*; *khatal.*

Accumulate, v.a. *gaṭal, ṭolawul, yodzāe-, jam'a-, ambār-,* etc. *k.* v.n. *ṭoledal, jam'a-, yodzāe-,* etc. *ked.*

Accuracy, s. *rikkhtīn-tob, rikkhtīnī, jukht-wālai.*

Accurate, a. *rikkhtīnai, sūchah*; *jukht, barābar, rikkhtiyā.*

Accusation, s. *tuhmat* or *tomat, d'awa, malāmat, peghor, tor.*

Accuse, v.a. *d'awa-, faryād-,* etc. *k. tuhmat taṛal* or *-wayal* or *-pore k. peghor warkawul, tor pore k.*

Accuser, s. *d'awa-* or *tor pore kawūnkai, mudda'ī.*

Accustom, v.a. *āmokhtah-, 'ādat-,* etc. *k. rugdawul.*

Ache, s. *dard, khūg, randz, zakhm.* v.n. *khūgedal, dardedal.*

Acid, a. *trīw* (f.) *tarwa.*

Acidity, s. *trīw-tob, trīw-wālai.*

Acknowledge, v.a. *manal.* v.n. *qā-iledal.*

Acknowledgment, s. *manūn, qabūl*; *ḥujjat, rasīd*; *shukrāna.*

Acorn, s. *kwarai.*

Acquaint, v.a. *khabarawul, pohawul, āgāh k.*

Acquaintance, s. *pejand-galī, āshnā-ī*; *āshnāe, pejāndah.* (f.) *āshnāya, pejandala.*

Acquainted, v.n. *khabaredal, pohedal, āgāh-, wāqif-,* etc. *ked.*

Acquire, v.a. *gaṭal, mūndal, paidā-, ḥāṣil-, sagah-,* etc. *k.*

Acquit, v.a. *pulawul, bakkhal, wa-aṛ k.*

Acrid, a. *trīkh.* (f.) *tarkha.*

Acridity, s. *trīkh-wālai, trīkh-tob.*

Across, ad. *pore, pore ghāṛe.*

Act, v.a. *kawul, kṛal, pāzah-, 'amal-,* etc. *k.*

Action, s. *kār, kṛah, 'amal, ḥarkat, pāzah, chār.*

Active, a. *chālāk, chust, takṛah, tund, tez.*

Actively, ad. *pa chālākī sara.*

Activity, s. *chālākī, chustī, tund-wālai.*

Actor, s. *kawūnkai, kṛūnai, fā'il, 'āmil.* (in a play) *naṭ, pekkhe-gar, toq-mār, swāng kawūnkai* or *swāngai*

Actually, ad. *rikkhtiyā, pa wāq'i, qaṭ'aī.*

Acute, a. *tez, terah, sakht ; hokkhyār, pohānd.*

Acuteness, s. *tez·wālai, terah·tob, sakhtiyā ; hokkhyār·tiyā, hokkhyārī, pohānd·wālai.*

Adage, s. *matal, miṣl, miṣāl.*

Adapt, v.a. *joṛawul, dzāyawul, hawārawul, atsanṛal, samawul, drust-, barābar-, etc. k.*

Add, v.a. *joṛawul, lagawul, gaḍawul.*

Addition, s. *mīzān, hisāb ; joṛawūna, gaḍawūna.*

Additional, a. *ziyāt, nor, bul.*

Addle, a. *skhā, gandah, wrost.*

Address, v.a. *sawāl-, tapahūs or tapos-, etc. k. wayal, pukkhtedal ; sar·nāma līkal or kāgal—kkhkal darkhwāst k. salām k.*

Adept, s. *ustāz, kārī·gar, pokh, pūrah, hunar·man.*

Adequate, a. *bas, pūrah, kāfī.*

Adhere, v.n. *lagedal, nkkhatal, chaspedal ; grohedal.* v.a. *laman niwul, tāb'i·dārī k.*

Adherent, s. *tāb'i·dār, mlā·taṛ, ṭaraf·dār, para·dār, wābastah ; charekār, hamsāyah, faqīr.* a. *slekkht·nāk, bokkht, chaspān ; nkkhatai, lagedalai.*

Adhesion, s. *pewastagī ; chasp ; nkkhatūn.*

Adhesive, s. *slekkht·nāk, bokkht, barwai, chaspān.*

Adieu, s. *da khudāe pa amān, salām.*

Adjourn, v.a. *nāgha-, barkhwāst-, mauqūf-, etc. k.*

Adjust, v.a. *tartīb-, durust-, barābar-, etc. k. samawul, joṛawul, atsanṛal, hawārawul ; pūrah-, faiṣal-, ārāstah-, etc. k.*

Admirable, a. *nādir, 'ajīb, gharīb.*

Admire, v.n. *grohedal.* v.a. *kkhah ganṛal, stāyal.*

Admission, s. *dakhl, nanawātah, rāsha darsha ; manana, qabūledana.*

Admit, v.a. *dakhl- or lār warkawul ; manal, qabūlawul.*

Admonish, v.a. *pand-, naṣīhat-, tambīh-, etc. k. malāmatawul, ṭaqawul, traṭal, raṭal.*

Adopt, v.a. *khwakkhawul, pasandawul, ikhtiyārawul ; ākhistal.*

Adore, v.a. *parastī-, 'ibādat-, sijda-, etc. k.*

Adorn, v.a. *psolawul, singārawul, sāzawul, kkhewa k. kkhāyastah k. joṛawul.*

Adulation, s. *khushāmad, chāplūsī, ḍirpalī.*

Adulator, s. *khushāmad·gar, chāplūs, ḍirpal.*

Adult, s. *dzawān, zalmai, zalmoṭai, bālugh.*

Adulterate, v.a. *gaḍawul, nāsarah k.*

Adulteration, s. *gaḍūn, qalp·wālai.*

Adulterer, s. *kāsir, zinā·kār.*

Adultery, s. *kāsirī, zinā.*

Advance, v.n. *wṛānde tlal or -ked.* s. *pór, qarz, peshagī ; taraqqī ; gāndah.*

Advantage, s. *kkhegaṛa, gaṭa, sūd, fā-ida, bih·būdī, naf'a ; barai, ghalaba, fatḥa, wa-aṛ·wālai.*

Advantageous, a. *sūd·man, ghwarah, kkhah.*

Adventure, s. *kār, chal, chār, wāq'ia.*

Adventurer, s. *lawand, gashtai ; chaṭ, lūtsak.*

Adversary, s. *dukkhman, mudda'ī.*

Adversity, s. *tangī, tangsiyā, kam·bakhtī, bad·bakhtī, sakhtī, shāmat ; dukkhmani, mukhālifat, kharkhashī.*

Advice, s. *maṣlahat, mashwarat, pand, ṣalāḥ, naṣīhat ; khabar, iṭṭilā'a.*

Advise, v.a. *pand-, naṣīhat-, etc. -warkawul ; maṣlahat kawul ; khabarawul.*

Advisable, a. *munāsib, lāzim, lā-iq, ghwarah.*

Advocate, s. *wakīl, mukhtār.*

Adze, s. *tarkkhadza, tesha, sūza.*

Afar, ad. *lire, la warāya.*

Affable, a. *halīm, mihrbān, makhawar, khūsh sulūk, khūsh·goe.*

Affair, s. *kār, khabara, chār, muqaddama, mu'āmala, amr.*

Affect, v.a. *kār-, aṣr-, 'amal-, pāzah-, tāsīr-, etc. k. (feign) bāna-, makr-, etc., k.*

Affectation, s. *nāz, nakhra, makez, nakhra-bāzī; bāna, chal, fareb, makr, ḥīla.*

Affected, a. *chal·bāz, makr·jan, bāna·khor, farebī, ḥīla·bāz; nakhra·bāz.*

Affection, s. *mīna, muḥabbat, 'ishq, mihr, tapāk; mayan·tob, khwā khogī, ulfat.*

Affectionate, a. *mayan, mihrbān, khwā khogai.*

Affinity, s. *nisbat, 'alāqa; khpul·walī, rishta-dārī, ragai, wābastagī, sar·rishta.*

Affirm, v.a. *wayal, iqrār, k. lal* or *lawdal, gawāhī lal.*

Affirmation, s. *qaul, lafẓ, qarār, iqrār, iṣbāt.*

Afflict, v.a. *āzārawul, zaḥīrawul, randzawul.*

Afflicted, a. *randzūr, gham·jan, dard·man.*

Affliction, s. *randz, gham, dard, āzār, paskhāk* or *pakhsāk, mīrtsī, :akhtī.*

Afford, v.a. *warkawul, khartsawul, da warka-wulo ṭaqat laral.* v.n. *shwal, kedal, tu-wānedal.*

Affront, s. *khwā·badī, mānrai; spuk·tiyā, be-izzatī.*

Afoot, a. *palai, pa kkhpo, piyādah.*

Afraid, v.n. *weredal* or *yeredal.* (in animals) *tarhedal, bugnedal.*

After, p. *pas, b'ad, wrusto.* (year after year) *kāl pa kāl.* (-to-morrow) *pas ṣabā.* (following-) *pase.* a. *wrustai, wrustanai, wrustīnai, pasīnah.*

After all, ad. *ākhir.*

After-birth, s. *prewān.* (caul) *obanra.*

Afternoon, s. *dwah·pahār.* (early) *pekkhīn, māspekkhīn.* (late) *dīgar, māzdīgar.*

Afterwards, ad. *pas, ākhir, biyā, b'ad.*

Again, ad. *biyā, dubāra, bul her, bula plā, bul wār.* (-and again) *biyā biyā, wār pa wār.*

Agape, a. *ching, wīt, wāz.*

Age, s. *'umr, san.* (æra) *daur, daurān, dahr, zamāna.* (old-) *zor·tiyā, zor·wātai.*

Aged, a. *zor, būḍā.* (-man) *spīn·gīrai.* (-woman) *spīn·sara.*

Agent, s. *peshkār, nā-ib, wākīl, dīwān, kārdār.*

Aggravate, v.a. *wārawul, ṭaqawul, raṭal; batar k. ziyātawul.*

Aggregate, s. *ṭol, ṭol·ṭāl, jumla, wārah.*

Aghast, a. *hak·pak, ḥaq·ḥairān.*

Agile, a. *chālāk, garandai, tak·lāstaī, jalt.*

Agility, s. *chālākī, chustī, sam·dastī.*

Agitate, v.a. *tsandal, khwadzawul, laral, kkhorawul, shanawul.*

Agitated, v.n. *rapedal, khwadzedal; eshedal; kkhoredal.* a. *tsandalai, laralai.*

Agitation, s. *larza, rapedana; eshnā, josh.*

Ago, ad. *pakhwā, lar ghūne.* (long-) *lār ghah, lire lār ghah.*

Agony, s. *dzān·kandan; 'azāb, dard.*

Agree, v.a. *manal, qabūlawul, iqrār k. rogha-, jora-,* etc. *k. hokai wayal,* or *k.* v.n. *pakhulā-, rāẓī-, yo zṛah-, yo jihat-,* etc. *ked.*

Agreeable, a. *khwakkh, pīrzo, khwand·nāk, kkhah, kkhāghalai, manzūr, ghwarah.*

Agreeably, ad. *pa mūjib, pa ḥukm sara; khwand sara, khwakkhī sara.*

Agreement, s. *jora, rogha; sharṭ, wāda, lafẓ, qaul, qarār; neṭa, taṛa, oe.*

Agriculture, s. *kar, īwe,* or *yawe, zamīn-dārī, baz·garī, zirā'at,.dihqānī, charekārī.*

Agriculturist, s. *kar·kawūnkai, zamīndār, kikkht·gar, dihqān, charekār, baz·gar.*

Ague, s. *saṛa taba, saṛa lawe* or *saṛa lare, wāreza.*

Ah! in. *wā-ī! wūe! ākhkkh! wākhkkhe! hāe! wāh! wāwailā! daregha!*

Ahead, ad. *wrānde, pa makh kkshe.*

Aid, s. *kumak, madad, pushtī, yāwarī.*

Ailing, a. *randzūr, nā·jor, nā·rogh, bīmār, māndah.*

Ailment, s. *randz, nā·jor·tiyā, nā·rogh·tiyā, bimārī, maraẓ, māndagī, dard, āzār.*

Aim, s. *niyat, maṭlab, qaṣd, gheraẓ, irāda; naẓ̣ar; nakkha, tsalai, mukha.* v.n. *niyat-, qaṣd-,* etc. *k. naẓar taṛal* or *lagawul.*

Air, s. *bād, hawā.* (musical-) *badala, wazn, trang, sarod.* (assumed-) *nāz, nakhra, shokh.* (mien) *wajha, tsihra, ḍaul, chāl, chalan, ṣūrat.*

Alarm, *khof, yera* or *wera, tars, bāk*; *dagh-dagha, hāhū, ghāl-o-ghūl, shor-shaghab, zwag-zūg, hāṛa-hūṛa, chagh-chugh, ghoghā.* v.a. *werawul, tarhawul*; *baidār-, khabar-dār-,* etc. *k.* *ḍamāma-, naghāra-, ḍolkai-,* etc. *wahal.*

Alarming, a. *khof-nāk, tars-nāk, haibat-nāk.*

Alas! in. *hāe-hāe! wāe-wāe! armān dai!*

Alchemy, s. *kīmiyā.*

Alchemist, s. *kīmiyā-gar.*

Alert, a. *baidār, khabar-dār, hokkhyār*; *chā-lāk, chust, tak-lāstai.*

Alertness, s. *baidārī, hokkhyār-tiyā*; *chālākī.*

Alias, a. *nūmāndai, nūmedah, 'urf.*

Alien, a. *pradai, begānah, gharīb.*

Alight, v.n. *kūzedal, nāziledal.*

Alike, a. *gund, barābar, yo-shān, yo-rang, siyāl, makhai.*

Aliment, s. *tskkhāk-khwurāk, t'aām, shūma.*

Alimentary, a. *khwurākī, da khwuṛalu.*

Alive, a. *jwandai, baidār.*

Alkali, s. *kkhora, shkār.*

All, a. *ṭol, wāṛah, amānī, kul.* (-day) *kara-ī wradz.* (-night) *kara-ī shpa.* (at-) ad. *kruṭ, la sara.*

Allay, v.a. *kamawul, saṛawul, la-agawul.*

Allegiance, s. *tāb'i-dārī.*

Allegory, s. *misl, miṣāl, matal.*

Alliance, s. *joṛa, para, janba, joṛikkht*; *khpul-awī, khweshī.*

Alligator, s. *nahang, nāka.*

Allot, v.a. *weshal, hisk āchawul.*

Allotment, s. *wesh, brakha, hisk, wanḍ, pcṭai.*

Allow, v.a. *manal, qabūlawul*; *pregdal—pre-kkhodal*; *rawā laral*; *bakkhal, kkhandal*; *ijāzat-, ḥukm-,* etc. *warkawul.*

Allowance, s. *mawājib, tankhwāh rizq.* (in weight) *daṛa, ṭūṭankai.*

Allure, v.a. *ghulawul, darghalawul, fareftah-, mayan-,* etc. *k.*

Allurement, s. *fareftagī, ghuledana, mīna.*

Alluvium, s. *lāha, khaṭa, chīqaṛ.*

Ally, s. *mal, malgarai, yār*; *kumakī, sharīk.*

Almighty (the), *khudāe ta'ālā, ḥaqq ta'ālā.*

Almond, s. *bādām.*

Almonry, s. *langar, langar-khāna.*

Almost, ad. *nijde, qarīb.*

Alms, s. *khairāt, zakāt, ṣadqa, sarsāya, qurbānī*; *shukrāna.* (-house) *langar-khāna.*

Aloft, p. *pās, porta, bar.*

Alone, a. *yawādzai, tsaṛah, biyal, tanhā.*

Aloud, a. *pa ūchat āwāz sara.*

Alphabet, s. *paṭa-ī.*

Already, ad. *lā, os, la wṛūnbī na, larghūne.*

Also, c. *hum, aw, wa, o.*

Altar, s. *da qurbānī dzāe* or *-dunkācha.*

Alter, v.a. *badlawul, āwukkhtal.* v.n. *bad-ledal, girzedal.*

Alteration, s. *badal, tabdīl*; *girzedana.*

Altercation, s. *jagṛa, takrār, kharkhakkha, qīl-o-qāl, steza, qaẓiya, qatārai.*

Alternative, s. *chāra*; *wāk, ikhtiyār.*

Although, c. *agarchi, siwā la de na, ziyāt la de na, sara la de.*

Altogether, ad. *amānī, sarāsar, bilkul, ṭol-ṭāl, wāṛah, srup.* (in comp.) *tak-, ṭap-.* Ex. *tak spīn* (altogether white), *ṭap rūnd* (altogether blind).

Alum, s. *khāwra-ī, spīna khāwra.*

Always, ad. *mudām, har-kala, hamesha, tal, tar-tala.*

Amalgam, s. *qala-ī.*

Amass, v.a. *gaṭal, ṭolawul*; *yo-dzāyawul.*

Amaze, v.a. *hariyānawul, rabṛawul, sar gardān-, hekkh-, sarāsīmah-,* etc. *k.*

Ambassador, s. *āstodzai, elchī.*

Amber, s. *kah rubā.*

Ambergris, s. *'ambar.*

Ambiguous, a. *shakk·dār, shakk·man.*

Ambition, s. *himmat, zṛah, tam'a, dam.*

Amble, s. *yarg̱ha.* v.n. *pa yarg̱ho tlal.*

Ambuscade, s.) *puṭ·gana-ī, pasūnai, tsawai,*

Ambush, s.) *dak̲hma, kamīn.*

Amen, ad. *āmīn, hase di wī.*

Amenable, a. *eman, pos, narm ; da qābū lāndi ; da tāwān pīrzo.*

Amend, v.n. *rag̱hedal, joṛedal.*

Amendment, s. *kkhegaṛa, rag̱hedana.*

Amends, s. *tāwān, badal, nāg̱ha, būnga.*

Amiable, a. *nek, mihrbān, ḥalīm.*

Amicable, a. *nek·k̲hwāh, k̲hair·k̲hwāh.*

Amidst, p. *pa mandz kkhke.*

Amiss, a. *k̲haṭā, g̱halat ; bad, nā·sāz, nā·lā-iq, nā·munāsib.*

Amity, s. *rog̱ha, joṛa, dostī, āshtī.*

Ammoniac, s. (gum-) *ṣamāg̱h, oshāq.* (sal-) *noshādar.*

Ammunition, s. *da jang kālī, -sāmān, -asbāb ; dārū mardak ; golā bārūt.*

Amongst, p. *pa mandz kkshe* or *kkhke.*

Amorous, a. *mayan, 'āshiq.*

Amount, s. *mablag̱h, jam'a, jumla, kul, ṭol·ṭāl, wāṛah.*

Amour, s. *āshnā-ī, yārī, 'āshiqī, 'ishq·bāzī.*

Ample, a. *arat, plan, psorawar, sara·war ; der.*

Amplify, v.a. *aratawul, planawul ; derawul, ziyātawul.*

Amputate, v.a. *prekawul* or *prekṛal.*

Amulet, s. *t'awīz, tāwītak, amel, dawā.*

Amusement, s. *tamāsha, nandāra, loba.*

Analogy, s. *miṣāl ; nisbat.*

Anarchy, s. *patna, balwā, yāg̱hī·garī.*

Anathema, s. *kkhera, l'anat* or *n'alat.*

Ancestor, s. *nīkah, plār nīkah.*

Ancestry, s. *peṛa-ī, aṣl, pusht, rag, noga.*

Anchor, s. *langar.*

Anchorite, s. *zāhid, qalandar, gokkha·nishīn.*

Ancient, a. *zoṛ, pak̲hwānai, kuhand.*

Ancients, s. *pak̲hwānī 'ālam* or *-k̲halq.*

Anciently, ad. *pak̲hwā, lire larg̱hūne.*

And, c. *aw, wa, o.*

Anecdote, s. *qiṣṣa, naql, riwāyat, k̲habara.*

Anew, ad. *biyā, nawi.*

Angel, s. *pirikkhtah, malak.*

Anger, s. *qahr, g̱huṣṣa, g̱haẓab, k̲hapagī.*

Angle, s. *g̱ūṭ, grut, dwa·kkhāk̲ha.*

Angry, a. *k̲hapah, broṣ.* v.n. *k̲hapah ked.*

Anguish, s. *'aẓāb ; swai.*

Angular, a. *kog, krīng, g̱ūṭlai, kālkūc̲han.*

Animal, s. *dzanāwar, ḥaiwān.* a. *dzān·dār, gawai, wagaṛai.*

Animation, s. *jwand, jwandūn, dzān, sā ; baidārī, c̲halākī ; k̲hūsh·ḥālī.*

Animosity, s. *kīna, dukkhnī, 'adāwat, badī, ṭaka, k̲huṣūmat, bug̱hz.*

Ankle, s. *kkhangarai, kkhatgarai ; gīṭa-ī.*

Annals, s. *tawārīk̲h, ak̲hbār ; shajara.*

Annex, v.a. *lagawul, taṛal, joṛawul ; lāndi k. āk̲histal.*

Annihilation, s. *nā·būdī, halākat, fū·fanā.*

Announce, v.a. *k̲habarawul, wayal ; tsargand-, kkhkārah-,* etc. *k. munādī k. jār wahal.*

Annoy, v.a. *pārawul, zoral, rabṛawul k̲hapah k.*

Annual, a. *kālanai, har kālah.*

Annually, ad. *kāl pa kāl.*

Annul, v.a. *bandawul, man'a-, mauqūf-, mansūk̲h-,* etc. *k.*

Annular, a. *g̱hūnḍ* or *g̱hūnḍ·man, tsark̲han, tsalai.*

Anoint, v.a. *g̱hwaṛawul, mugal—mukkhal.*

Anomalous, a. *be·tartīb.*

Another, a. *bul, nor, bul tsok, nor tsok, bul tsa, nor tsa, bul yo, nor yo.*

Answer, s. *dzawāb, pāsukh.* v.a. *dzawāb-, tāwān-,* etc. *warkawul.*

Ant, s. *megai, mor.* (black-) *tor megai.* (red-)

sūr megṟɩ. (white-) *oenah.* (-hill) *megatūn,*
kkhor.

Antagonist, s. *dukkhman, muqābil ; raqīb, be-*
lak ; dzawāb, makhai.

Antecedent, a *pakhwānai, wrūnbanai, pekkhīn.*

Antechamber, s. *dālān, dahlīz, mandaw.*

Antelope, s. *osai, chikārah.*

Anterior, a. *wrāndīnai, pakhwānai, wrūn-*
banai, pekkhīn.

Anticipation, s. *pesh·dastī, pesh·bandī.*

Antidote, s. *tiriyāk, 'ilāj.*

Antimony, s. *rānjah, surma, kuhal.* (-box)
rānjaṛūma, ranjūnūna. (-bodkin) *salā-ī.*

Antipathy, s. *kraka.* (to food) *sekan.*

Anvil, s. *sandān, pa-alk ; tsaṭ.*

Anxiety, s. *gham, andekkhnā, wiswās, fikr ;*
gram.

Anxious, a.˷ *gham·jan, andekkh·man, wiswāsī,*
fikr·man ; gram·nāk.

Anus. s. *kūna, supra.* (prolapsus ani) *būra-ī*
(pruritus ani) *mawekkhe.*

Any, a. *tsok, tsa.*

Apart, a. *biyal, judā, yawādzai.*

Apartment, s. *khūna, koṭa, dzāe.*

Apathetic, a. *be·parwā, be·khabar, kāhil ; laṭ,*
shaṭal or shalaṭ, sust, ṭas mas.

Aperture, s. *sūṛa, khula, spam or swam.*

Apex, s. *sar, peza, pitska, tsūka.*

Apologize, v.a. *'uzr ghokkhtal ; minnat k.*

Apoplexy, s. *tsaṭ waṭ, sakta.*

Apostatize, v.a. *īmān-, dīn-, etc. bāelal.* v.n.
dīn-, īmān-, etc. na jārwatal.

Apostle, s. *rasūl, astādzai, paighāmbar.*

Apothecary, s. *pansārai.*

Apparatus, s. *sāz, sāmān, kālī, asbāb.*

Apparel, s. *āghūstan, pokkhāk ; jāme, zaṛūkī,*
kālī, nwarī.

Apparent, a. *tsargand, kkhkārah, bar̄ser,*
awtsār, bewrah, zāhir or jār.

Apparently, ad. *bartseran, pa jār, zāhiran.*

Appeal, v.a. *ghokkhtal, minnat-, sawāl-, etc. k.*

Appear, v.n. *tsargandedal, kkhkārah-, bartser-,*
etc. *ked. ; m'alūmedal.*

Appearance, s. *ṣūrat, wajha, tsihra, rang,*
shakl.

Appease, v.a. *saṛanul, pakhulā-, raẓā-, etc. k.*

Appetite, s. *ishtihā, lwaga, khwā, liwāl·tob,*
zṛah ; raghbat, shahwat, mīna.

Applaud, v.a. *stāyal, shābāshī-, āparīn-, etc. k.*

Applause, s. *shābāshī, stāyana.*

Apple, s. *manṛa, seb.* (crab-) *mānrū.* (-of
eye) *lema, kasai, bātor, torai.* (Adam's-)
stūnai.

Applicable, a. *munāsib, sazāwār, durust,*
jukht, joṛ.

Application, s. *mihnat, kokkhikkh, lagiyā·tob ;*
'arz, sawāl, darkhwāst.

Apply, v.a. *lagawul, pore taṛal ; sawāl-, 'arz-,*
darkhwāst-, etc. k. v.n. *barābar-, jukht-,*
etc. *lagedal ; joṛedal, lagedal.*

Appoint, v.a. *kkhkenawul or kenawul, mu-*
qarrar k. wulāṛawul, wudrawul. (-a time)
wāda k. neṭa taṛal.

Appointment, s. *dzāe, 'uhda ; lafz, sharṭ ;*
wāda, neṭa, taṛa.

Appraise, v.a. *bai'a-, qīmat-, nirkh-, etc. taṛal.*

Apprehend, v.a. *nīwul, giriftār k.* v.n. *po-*
hedal ; m'alūmedal ; weredal, andekkhedal,
wiswāsī ked.

Apprehension, s. *nīwah, giriftārī, gīr ; poha,*
khiyāl ; khof, andekkhnā, wiswās, wera.

Apprentice, s. *shāgird.*

Apprize, v.a. *khabarawul, āgāh k.* ͵

Approach, v.n. *nijde kedal.*

Approbation, s.⎞ *pasand, khwakkh, pīrzo,*
Approval,   ⎠ *raẓā, manẓūrī, qabūlī.*

Appropriate, v.a. *khpulawul, dzān ta ākhistal,*
rānwul, lānde k.

Approve, v.a. *khwakkhawul, manẓūr-, pasand-,*
etc. k., *manal, qabūlawul, kkhāghal.*

Apricot, s. *zardālū, makhranai.* (preserved-)
khubānī. (dried-) *kishta, ashāṛai, māmū-ī.*

April, s. *wisāk* or *baisāk*. (-shower) *wasa*.
Apropos, a. *jukht, joṛ, barābar*.
Apt, a. *munāsib*; *qābil, lā-iq*; *kārī-gar*.
Aqua-fortis, s. *tez āb*.
Aquatic, a. *ābī, dariyābī*.
Aqueduct, s. *nāla, wāla, lakkhtai, nāwa, pūl*; *tarnāo*; *kārez*; *trai*.
Arable, a. *sādīn, shudiyār*; *da kar, da karalo*.
Arbitrary, a. *zorāwar, khapsar* or *khpul-sar*.
Arbitrate, v.a. *gwākkhal* or *gwākkhedal*; *gwākkh-grandai-, jirga-, munṣifī-, inṣāf-, 'adālat-*, etc. *k*.
Arbitration, s. *gwākkh, jirga, munṣifī, m'arika*.
Arbitrator, s. *jirgatū, gwākkh-grandai, munṣif*.
Arbour, s. *chopāl, jūṛgaṛa, tsapar, manah, dāṛa, kūḍala, kūḍa-ī*.
Arch, s. *qubba, gunbata, ṭāq, miḥrāb, kamān*.
Archer, s. *līndai, līnda-kakkh, ghash-lāstai, rasā-līndai, kamān-kakkh, tīr-andāz, bar-kakkh*.
Archery, s. *kamān-kakkhī, tīr-andāzī*.
Architect, s. *rāj, m'imār, joṛawūnkai*.
Archives, s. *daftar, shajara, tawārīkh*.
Ardent, a. *tod, garm*; *tund, tez*; *mast*.
Ardour, s. *tod-wālai, todūkha, garmī*; *tezī, tund-wālai*; *mastī, tapāk*.
Arduous, a. *sakht, grān, mushkil, drūnd*.
Area, s. *maidān, sama, zmaka*; *anganr, gholai, jawas*.
Argument, s. *baḥs, ḥujjat, munāẓara, dalīl, wāsṭa*.
Arid, a. *wuch, sawai, sokṛah, sokhtah*; (as land) *chol, lallam*; *tosand*.
Aridity, s. *wuch-wālai, khushkī, sokhtagī*.
Arise, v.n. *pātsedal, khatal, walāṛedal, porta ked.*; *wudredal*.
Aristocracy, s. *khān-khwānīn, khānawādah khalq, firqa da ghaṭo khalqo*.
Aristocrat, s. *khānawādah saṛai, da ghaṭ-*, or *da loe kor-*, etc. *saṛai*.

Arm, s. *lās*. (above elbow) *gardai-lechai, tor-gharai, ma-aṭ*. (below elbow) *tsangal, lecha* or *letsa*. (cubit bone) *linda-ī*.
Arm, v.a. *mlā taṛal, wasla-, drasta-*, etc. *āghostal*; *dzān sambālawul*.
Armistice, s. *rogha, joṛa*; *gwākkh*.
Armful, s. *ghūzai, gheg*.
Armour, s. (chain) *zghara, zira*. (steel) *juba, baktar, jaushan*. (clad in) *zghar-yālai, baktar-*, etc. *āghostai, zira-, baktar-*, etc. *pokkh*.
Armpit, s. *trakh, tkharg, aṛkh, baghal*.
Arms, s. *wasla, drasta, da jang kālī, -sāz, -asbāb*, or *-hatiyār*.
Army, s. *lakkhkar, fauj*.
Aromatic, a. *khūshbū-dār, bū-ī-nāk*.
Around, ad. *chāpera, khwā o shā, girdā gird, chār chāpera*.
Arouse, v.a. *wīkkhawul, pātsawul, baidārawul*.
Arrange, v.a. *sambālawul, tartīb k., tanḍal, atsanṛal, lagawul, joṛawul, khundiyal*.
Arrangement, s. *tartīb, dzerma, bandobast, khundī-tob, joṛikkht*.
Array, s. *para, tsīṛa, para-bandi, ṣaff, qaṭār*; *libās, āghūstan, pokkhāk, zaṛūkī*. v.a. *poslal, pokkhal, āghostawul, zaṛūkī āgho-stal*; *para-*, etc. *taṛal* or *wudrawul*.
Arrears, s. *bāqī, pātī*.
Arrest, v.a. *nīwul, giriftār-, gīr-, band-, qaid-*, etc. *k*.
Arrival, s. *rātag, rātah, rasedah, dakhl, āmad, rātlana, rasedana*.
Arrive, v.n. *rātlal—rāghlal, rasedal*.
Arrogance, s. *kibr, bād, maghrūrī, khāntamā, gusṭākhī*.
Arrogant, a. *kibr-jan, bādī, maghrūr, gharah, gustākh*.
Arrow, s. *ghashai, tīr*. (-flight) *tīr-partāb, tīr-ras*. (wing place of-) *par-khāna*. (blunt-) *toqa, tuqqa*. (barbed-) *shata-ī*. (iron tip of-) *tūbrai*. (shaft of-) *lānga*,

tila-ī. (notch of-) *ghwākkhkai.* (wing of-) *banra, wazar.*
Arsenal, s. *silāḥ-khāna, jabba-khāna.*
Arsenic, s. *senkiyā, hartāl.*
Art, s. *hunar, ḥikmat, chal*; *kasb, pesha, ṣan'at, ustādī, pand, kārī-garī, dast-kārī.*
Artery, s. *rag.* (of the pulse) *nabẓ.*
Artful, a. *ḥikmatī, hunar-man*; *farebī, chal-bāz, chalwalai, ḥīla-bāz.*
Article, a. *kālai, shai, tsīz.*
Artifice, s. *chal, ḥīla, bāna, fareb, ṭagī, makr, palma, lamghaṛa-ī, hira-ī.*
Artificer, s. *kasb-gar, kārī-gar, pesha-war.*
Artificial, a. *jūṭah, nāsarah, naqlī*; *kasbī, hunarī*; *joṛ kaṛai, sākhtah.*
Artillery, s. *top-khāna.*
Artisan, s. See Artificer.
Artist, s. *ustād, kārī-gar, hunar-man*; *naqqāsh.*
Artless, a. *sādah-dil, rikkhtūnai, karah.*
As, c, *laka, hase.* (-if) *laka chi, ganre.*
Ascarides, s. *kīkkhai, chinjai.*
Ascend, v.n. *khatal, porta ked., pātsedal.*
Ascent, s. *khātah, khatana*; *taraqqa-ī, lwaṛa.*
Ascertain, v.a. *m'alūmawul, zdah-, taḥqīq-,* etc. *k.*
Ascetic, s. *zāhid, faqīr*; *malang, darwesh, qalandar.*
Ascribe, v.a. *nisbat lagawul, pore taṛal, pore k.*
Ashamed, a. *sharmindah, sharmsār, pakkhe-mān.* v.n. *sharmedal, pakkhemān ked.*
Ashes, s. *īre, khākistar.* (hot-) *skhwakkhtan, khoglan.* (cold-) *saṛe īre.*
Aside, ad. *biyal, pa ḍaḍe, pa trats.*
Ask, v.a. *pukkhtedal, ghokkhtal, sawāl-, tapos-, pukkhtana-, pursān-,* etc. *k.*
Aslant, a. *trats, tratskan, sangzan, kṛīng*; *shewah, sar-dzawar, sar-lwaṛ, pa rewand.*
Asleep, a. *ūdah, bīdah, khob-wṛai.*
Aspect, s. *makh, ṣūrat, tsihra, rang, shaki, rūe.*
Asperity, s. *zīg-wālai, lwāṛ-tiyā, zmokh-tiyā.*
Asperse, v.a. *peghor warkawul, tor pore k. tuhmat wayal, ghandal, kagal.*
Aspire, v.a. *tam'a, ārzū-, umed-,* etc. *laral.*
Ass, s. *khar.* (-colt) *bachrai, kūṭai, kūchai.* (wild-) *gorah khar, ghyarah.* (-load) *kharwār.* (-play) *khar-mastī, khar-khāṛai, khar-tīza.*
Assafœtida, s. *hanj, hanja.*
Assail, v.a. *halla-, dāṛa-, tsoṭ-, yūrush,* etc. *k.*
Assassin, s. *qātil, khūnī, marg kawūnkai.*
Assassinate, v.a. *wajal* or *wajlal, muṛ k., khūn-, marg-,* etc. *k.*
Assault, s. *halla, guẓār, tsoṭ, yūrush.*
Assemble, v.a. *ṭolawul, yo-dzāe-, jam'a-,* etc. *k.* v.n. *ṭoledal, yo-dzāe-, jam'a-,* etc. *ked.*
Assembly, s. *ṭolai, majlis, ḍala, jam'iyat*; *jirga.*
Assent, s. *raẓā, qabūl, hokai, oe.*
Assert, v.a. *wayal, lal* or *lawdal.*
Assertion, s. *wayai, wayana, khabara, lafẓ, lana, qaul, d'awa.*
Assessment, s. *kkhkewaṭ, māliya, bāj, ikhrāj.*
Assiduity, s. *kokshiksh* or *kokkhikkh, miḥnat, sa'ī, tapāk.*
Assiduous, a. *miḥnatī, sā'ī, kokkhikkhī.*
Assign, v.a. *neṭa taṛal, muqarrar k.*; *barāt warkawul.*
Assimilation, s. *gundi-tob, makhī-tob, hum-shaklī, hum-rangī.*
Assist, v.a. *komak-, madad-, mrasta-, pushtī-,* etc. *k., lās warkawul* or *nīwul.*
Assize, s. *'adālat, maḥkama*; *nirkh, rai.*
Associate, s. *mal, malgarai, āshnāe, yār*; *rafīq, sharīk.* v.a. *malgīrī k.*; *yārī-, āshnā-ī-,* etc. *k.*; *kilai k.*; *ṣuḥbat k.*; *sharīkī k.*
Association, s. *malgīrī, malgar-tiyā, sharīkī.*
Assort, v.a. *chunral, atsanral, tartīb k.*
Assortment, s. *tartīb, chīnda.*
Assume, v.a. *ākhistal, ikhtiyār-, d'awa-,* etc.

k. (airs) *nāz-, nakhra-,* etc. *k.* v.n. *nā-zedal.*

Assumption, s. *khpul·sṛrī, ᴂorāwarī, bādī·tob, kibr ;* wāk, *ikhtiyār ; ākhistana.*

Assurance, s. *bāwar, i'tibār, sā·wīsā, yaqīn, tawwakul ; gustākhī, be bākī.*

Assuredly, ad. *be·shakh, be shubha, albatta.*

Asthma, s. *sāh-* or *sā landī, kotāh sāhī.*

Asthmatic, a. *sāh landai, kotāh sāh.*

Astonish, v.a. *hariyānawul, rabṛawul, hekkh-, sargardān-, hak·pak-,* etc. *k.*

Astonishing, a. *'ajab, 'ajībah, 'ajūbah.*

Astonishment, s. *hariyānī* or *hairānī.*

Astray, a. *wruk, gumrāh, be lār.*

Astringent, a. *qābiz, ṭīng, klak, zmokht, stagh.*

Astrologer, s. *rammāl, najūmī.*

Astrology, s. *ramal, 'ilm da najūm.*

Asunder, ad. *biyal, judā.*

Asylum, s. *āsra, panāh, nanawātah, aman.*

At, p. *pa, pa kkhke.* (-home) *pa kor kkhke.* (-least) *hargora, kho.* (-once) *yak lakhta, pa ṭakī.* (-last) *ākhir.* (-length) *bāre.* (-me) *rā bānde.* (-most) *pa ḥadda.* (-all times) *har wakht, har kala.* (-how much) *pa tsomra.* (-all) *hado, bekhī.* (-present) *pa dā sā'at* or *-wakht* or *-mahal.* (-hand) *nijde, khatsa* or *tsakha.* (-first) *wṛunbe, awwal.* (-all events) *khwāh nā khwāh.* (-times) *kala kala.* (-sight) *pa līdah, pa kātah.* (-night) *pa shpe.*

Atheism, s. *ilḥād, inkār, zindīqī, gumrāhī.*

Atheist, s. *mulḥid, zindīq, munkir da khudāe.*

Athlete, s. *pahlawān, kaṭah.*

Athletic, a. *pahlawān, kaṭah, zor·man.*

Atmosphere, s. *bād, hawā.*

Atom, s. *pūṭai, pītsānṛai, ṭoṭai, zarra, chūr, reza, shama, daṛa.*

Atone, v.a. *tāwān-, badal-, 'iwaz-,* etc. *war-kawul ; kafārat k. dzār-, ṣadqa-, qurbān-,* etc. *k.*

Atrocious, a. *bad sakht, bashpaṛ.*

Atrophy, s. *narci randz, karedana, wuch·klak·wālai.*

Attach, v.a. *laganul, taṛal, pore k. khpula-wul, pewastah-, grohedah-,* etc. *k.*

Attachment, s. *pewastūn, taṛūn, band ; mīna, mayan·tob, muḥabbat, grohedana.*

Attack, v.a. *halla-, ḥamla-, guzār-, tsoṭ-, dāṛa dopa-, happa dapa-, yūrush-,* etc. *k.*

Attain, v.a. *mūndal, biyā·mūndal ; gaṭal, paidā-, ḥāṣil-,* etc. *k.* v.n. *rasedal, shwal.*

Attainable, a. *mūndūnai, shwūnai, da mūndalo.*

Attainment, s. *gāṭah, biyā·mūnd ; mūndana, rasedana.*

Attempt, s. *qaṣd, āzmekkht, zor, kokkhikkh, was, s'aī.*

Attend, v.a. *āwredal, ghwag bāsal—yastal* or *-adal—īkkhodal, nghwatal, ghaur-, fikr-,* etc. *k. ; khabar ākhistal, khidmat-, madār-,* etc. *k.* v.n. *malgarai ked. ḥāzir osedal.*

Attendance, s. *khidmat, nokrī.*

Attendant, s. *khidmat·gār, nokar, mulāzim ; mal, malgarai ; mlā·taṛ, jalaw·dār, nafar.*

Attention, s. *liḥāz, fikr, s'aī, kokkhikkh, baidārī, khabar·dārī, hokkhyārī.* (to a guest) *melmastiyā, mezmānī, madār, makh.*

Attentive. a. *hokkhyār, baidār, khabar·dār.*

Attest, v.a. *gawāhī lal* or *lawdal, shāhidī warkawul* or *lal.*

Attestation, s. *gawāhī, shāhidī ; gawāhī lana* or *warkawūna.*

Attire, v.a. *zaṛūkī-, nwarī-, pokkhāk-, libās-, jāme-,* etc. *āghostal ; poslal, āghostawul.*

Attitude, s. *wajha, daul, ṣūrat, shān, ḥāl.*

Attorney, s. *wakīl, mukhtār.*

Attract, v.a. *rākāgal—rākkhkal ; grohedah-, ✓areftah-,* etc. *k. ghulawul ; mayan k.*

Attracted, a. *rākkhkalai ; grohedalai,* etc. v.n. *grohedal, mayan ked.*

Attraction, s. *rākkhkana, kakkhikkh ; mīna, mayan·tob ; dil·barī, dil·farebī ; grohe-dana.*

Attribute, s. *khūe, khaṣlat, ṣifat, khāṣṣiyat.*
Audacious, a. *be bāk, nā·tars*; *be adab, gustākh.*
Audacity, s. *be bākī*; *be adabī.*
Audience, s. *majlis, dalbār*; *āwredūnkī, sām'iān.*
Auditor, s. *āwredūnkai, sām'i.* (of accounts) *muḥāsib, ḥisāb kawūnkai.*
Augment, v.a. *ziyātawul, ḍerawul.*
Augmentation, s. *ziyāt·wālai, ḍer·wālai*; *ziyātedana, ḍeredana.*
Augur, s. *pāl-* or *fāl katūnkai, fāl bīn, fālī, fāl yastūnkai.*
Augury, s. *fāl katana, fāl yastana, fāl bīnī.*
August, a. *ghaṭ, loe.* (the month) *bādro.*
Aunt, s. (father's or mother's sister) *tror.* (father's brother's wife) *tandor, tandyāra, kāka-ī.* (mother's brother's wife) *māma-ī.*
Auspicious, a. *iqbāl·man, bakhtawar, nek·bakht, mubārak.*
Austere, a. *sakht, zīg*; *trīw, zmokht*; *sūṭ, sūṭ·būṭ.*
Authentic, a. *rikkhtiyā, rikkhtīnai, taḥqīq.*
Author, s. *muṣannif, kitāb kkhkawūnkai*; *joṛawūnkai, kawūnkai, wayūnkai,* etc.
Authority, s. *wāk, ikhtiyār, was*; *maqdūr, zor, qudrat, ḥukūmat*; *ḥukm, farmān, sanad.*
Authorize, v.a. *ḥukm,- wāk-, ikhtiyār-,* etc. *warkawul.*
Autumn, s. *manai, khizān, kharīf.*
Auxiliary, a. *komakī, madad·gār, janba·dār.*
Avail, v.a. *fā-ida-, naf'a-,* etc. *rasawul.* v.n. *chaledal, pakār ked.* or *-rātlal.*
Avarice, s. *ḥirṣ, tam'a, bakhīlī.*
Avaricious, a. *bakhīl, ḥirṣ·nāk, ḥāriṣ, tām'i.*
Avaunt, in. *lire sha! biyarta sha!*
Avenge, v.a. *badal-, qiṣāṣ-, tāwān-,* etc. *ākhistal.*
Averse, a. *nā·rāẓ, mukhālif, khwā bad.*
Aversion, s. *kraka, chinjedana, kagana, ghandana.*

Avert, v.a. *man'a-, daf'a-,* etc. *k., girzawul, jārbāsal—jāryastal.*
Avidity, s. *tam'a, lwāl·tob, shauq, raghbat.*
Avocation, s. *kār, kasb, pesha.*
Avoid, v.a. *parhez k., dzān sātal.*
Await, v.n. *muntaẓir osedal, wudredal, pātedal.*
Awake, a. *wīkkh, baidār.* v.n. *wīkkhedal, pātsedal, baidār ked.*
Aware, a. *khabar, āgāh, wāqif*; *zdah.*
Away, ad. *lire.* in. *lire sha, biyarta sha.*
Awe, s. *khof, wera* or *yera, tars, bāk, ḥaibat, tor.*
Awful, a. *khof-, tars-, sahm-,* etc. *-nāk,* etc.
Awhile, ad. *drang sā'at, la-ag sā'at.*
Awkward, a. *kāwāk*; *lwāṛ.*
Awl, s. *nīra* or *rīna.*
Awning, s. *chatrai, siwrai, shāmiyāna, sāewān*
Awry, ad. *pa trats, kṛīng pṛīng, kog wog.*
Axe, s. *tabar,* (battle-) *tabar·zīn, gurz.*
Axis, s. *quṭb, ghashai.*
Axle, s. *laṭ, tīrak, tsākkhai.*
Aye, ad. *ho, āre, kkhah.*
Azure, a. *shīn.*

B.

Babble, v.a. *bak bak-, baṛ baṛ-,* etc., *k.* v.n. *ṭaredal.*
Babbler, s. *bak bakai, baṛ baṛai, ūnai, ṭarai,*
Babe, s. *bachai, tankai, tandai, m'aṣūm* or *māshūm, tai rawai, pa-ī rawdūnkai, wrūkai.*
Bachelor, s. *lawand, tsaṛah, mujarrad.*
Back, s. *shā.* ad. *biyarta, biyā, wrusto, pastana, pas.* (behind one's-) *pase shā.*
Back, v.n. (go-), *pastana-, wrusto-, biyarta-,* etc. *ked., stūnedal* or *stanedal.* v.a. (aid) *panāh-, komak-, pushtī-,* etc. *-warkawul, ḍaḍa lagawul.*
Backbite, v.a. *chughlī-, ghībat- ghammāzī-,* etc., *k.*

Backbiter, s. *chughlkhor, ghībat kawūnkai, mawās, ghammāz.*

Backbone, s. *mlā tīr, shamdza-ī.*

Backdoor, s. *da chane war, da kor da shā war.*

Backside, s. *kunāṭai, kūna, ghara, dumbāla; wrustai, shā.*

Backward, a. *nā-rāẓ, laṭ, ṭas mas, nā-rāst; sust, pasīnah.* ad. *wrusto, pastana, biyarta.*

Backwards, ad. *pa biyarta, wrusto.* a. *naskor, aṛawulai, apūṭah.*

Bad, a. *bad, nā-kārah, kharāb, nā-sarah.*

Badge, s. *nakkha* or *nakhkkha, nikkhān, togh, 'alāmat.*

Badger, s. *tor-lamai, gor-kakkh.*

Badly, ad. *pa bad shān sara.*

Badness, s. *kharābī, badī, 'aib.*

Baffle, v.a. *rabṛawul, ghulawul, wār khaṭā k., be fā-ida-, 'abaṣ-,* etc., *k.*

Bag, s. *ṭaila-ī, dzola-ī.* (clothes-) *katsoṛa, būtskha, buqcha.* (money-) *hamiyānī, badra.* (letter-) *kharīta.* (grain-) *tsaṭa, ghūndai.* (tent-) *gharāra.* (trinket-) *butskhakai.* (leather-) *bana-ī, gūḍai.* (ammunition-) *kīsa, kisbat.* (leather water-) *mashk, chāgul,* (leather air-) *shināz, zik, ĵai.* (baggage-) *malaw.*

Baggage, s. *asbāb, rakht, sāmān, partal.*

Bail, s. *ẓāminī, ẓamānat.* (the person) *ẓāmin.* (to give-) *ẓamānat-, ẓāmin warkawul.* (to take-) *ẓamānat-, ẓāmin ākhistal.*

Bailiff, s. *muḥaṣṣil, patwāṛī, kārdār, sazāwal.*

Bait, v.a. *tsar-, wākkhah-, khwāṛah-,* etc. *warkawul; bāolī warkawul; nahārai-, tāmba* or *ṭa'ām-, khwurāk-,* etc. *warkawul.*

Bake, v.a. *pa tanūr kkhke pakhawul; kaṛawul, wrītawul.*

Baker, s. *nānwā-ī, nān paz.*

Balance, s. *tala, tarāzū.* (the beam) *ḍānḍa-ī.* (the scale) *pala.* (the tongue) *ĵiba.* (of an account) *bāqī.* v.a. *talal, jokal; bāqī pūrah k., ḥisāb barābar k.*

Balcony, s. *bālā-khāna.*

Bald, a. (from age) *kal.* (from disease) *ganjai, suḍar, lenḍah, chatrai, pa-akhai.*

Bale, s. *anḍai, panḍ, peṭai.* (of grass) *geḍai.* v.a. *sandzal, toyawul, lawastal.*

Baleful, a. *bad, muẓirr, tāwānī, ziyānī.*

Balk, v.a. *wār khaṭā k., 'abaṣ k., wrānawul.*

Ball, s. *panḍos, panḍoskai, manḍos; gola-ī, mardakai; ghunḍūrai; nāch, gaḍedana.*

Ballad, s. *sandara, lanḍa-ī, chār bait, ghazal, ṭapa, miṣr'a, stāyana.*

Ballast, s. *langar.*

Ballot, v.a. *qur'a-, hisk-, pucha-,* etc. *āchawul.*

Bamboo, s. *bans.*

Balustrade, s. *kangura.*

Band, s. *paṛk, ṭolai, ṭolgai, ghol, tamba; firqa, janba; khel, cham.*

Bandage, s. *paṭa-ī, band, taṛūnai.* (for the head) *sar-pechak, sar-taṛūnai, tsapūṭkai, sar-basta.* (for clothes) *tanra-ī.* (a child's-) *seznī.*

Bandbox, s. *tawang.*

Banditti, s. *ghlah, shūk-mār, dāṛ, tāṛ, qazāk.*

Bandy, v.a. *radd badal k., qīl-o-qāl k., chaghawul.* a. *kog.* (-legged) *kage kkhpe.*

Bane, s. *zahr; nuqṣān, tāwān, ziyān.*

Baneful, a. *zahr-dār; nuqṣānī, muẓirr, moẓī,* etc.

Bang, v.a. *ṭakawul, wahal, ṭak-, daz-, ṭas-,* etc. *wahal.*

Bangle, s. *bāhū, wakkhai, chūrā, kaṛai, ma-aṭkai.*

Banish, v.a. *shaṛal, be waṭan-, jilā waṭan-,* etc. *k.*

Bank, s. *pūla, wand, band.* (river-) *ghāṛa.* (high-) *kamar.* (opposite-) *pore ghāṛa.* (-of clouds) *gūp, kha-aṭ.* (for money) *khizāna, koṭa-ī.*

Banker, s. *ṣarrāf, khizānchī, seṭ.*

Bankrupt, s. *nā-dār, dewāliyā, tabāh, khwār.*

Banner, s. *nakkha, janḍa, bairaq, tūgh.*

Bannock, s. (plain) *tsapaṭa-ī, kakoṛa.* (oiled-) *weshala.* (buttered-) *parāṭa, lūcha.* (sweet-) *amrasa.*

Banquet, s. *ẓiyāfat, melmastiyā, mihmānī.*

Banter, v.a. *ṭoqa-, washta-, maskhara-*, etc. *k.*

Bar, s. (cross-) *hūl* (upright-) *aṛam, aṛamai.* v.a. *bandawul, hūl-, aṛam-*, etc. *lagawul.*

Barbarian, s. *dzangalī, jāhil, banṛ·mānṛū.*

Barbarity, s. *be raḥmī, dzangalī·tob, jāhil·tob.*

Barbarous, a. *be raḥm*; *jāhil, dzaban, lwāṛ.*

Barbed, a. *shaṭa-ī-* or *biyak larūnkai.*

Barber, s. *nā-ī, gulābī.*

Barberry, s. *korai, karwara, zirishk.*

Bard, s. *mīrāṣī, ḍum, shā'ir.*

Bare, a. *barbanḍ* or *barmanḍ, lūts*; *ta-ash, khālī.* (-faced) *be makh, be ḥayā, be sharm, be parda.* (-footed) *abl, pkkhe·able.* (-headed) *sar·tor.* (-backed) *lūts, barbanḍ.*

Barely, ad. *surup, ta-ash, khālī, faqaṭ, ṣirf.*

Bargain, s. *sharṭ, wāda, iqrār, lafẓ, neṭa, taṛa, 'ahd.* v.a. *sharṭ-*, etc. *k.* or *taṛal*; *saudā-, bai'a-* etc. *k., chana wahal.*

Barge, s. *beṛa-ī, kishta-ī.* (-pole) *singāwanṛ.*

Bark, s. (tree-) *paṭ, poṭ, poṭakh, postakai, khwar.* (dog's-) *ghap, ghapā, ghāp.* v.a. *poṭ-*, etc. *kāgal—kkhkal* or *-bāsal—yastal*; *ghapal, ghap wahal.* v.n. *ghapedal.*

Barley, s. *orbūshe.* (a grain of-) *orbūsha.* (husk of-) *sharhata.*. (-bread) *orbūshīna.* (-gruel) *oghṛa.* (-grits) *dal, baṭa.*

Barm, s. *khamīra, toma* or *tomna, māya.*

Barn, s. *khirman, dīrmand, ambār·khāna.*

Barrack, s. *spāhī·khāna, urdū, ḍal.*

Barrel, s. *nal, nalī, shpela-ī.* (-bellied) *gagar, geḍa·war, kheṭa·war.*

Barren, a. (animal or tree) *shanḍa.* (land) *ḍāg, ūjāṛ, shāṛ.* (saline) *kkhoran.* (sandy) *shīglan.*

Barrenness, s. *shanḍ·wālai, shanḍ·tob.*

Barricade, s. *sangar, bāṛa, kūtsa·bandī.*

Barrier, s. *pūla, brīd* or *brīt, ḥadd.*

Barter, s. *adal·badal, plor, chana, saudā, lāgī, pīral·ploral, rākṛah·warkṛah.* v.a. *adal·badal-, plor-*, etc. *k., chana wahal.*

Base, a. *palīt, murdār, dūn, ḥarāmī, bad·ẕāt, kam·aṣl, be nog.* (-coin) *nā·sarah, jūṭah.*

Base, Basis, s. *āra, wekh, kūnsaṭ, būnsaṭ bunyād, pāya, pkkha, sar.*

Baseness, s. *dūnī, ḥarāmī·tob, bad·ẕātī*, etc.

Bashful, a. *sharm·nāk, ḥayā·nāk* or *ḥayā·dār, ghairat·nāk* or *ghairat·man.*

Basin, s. (of wood) *kanḍai* or *kanṛai, būgh.* (of pottery) *kanḍol, kanḍolai.* (kneading-) *kkhānak.* (beggar's-) *kachkol.* (wash-hand-) *tasht, lagan.* (dog's-) *chaṭ.*

Bask, v.a. *piṭāo-, nwar-, or-*, etc. *ta kkhke-nāstal.*

Basket, s. *ṭokra-ī.* (flat-) *shkarai* or *shkorai* or *shker, kkhkarai.* (fruit-) *kawāra, kāra.* (winnowing-) *chaj, tsap.* (safe-) *tsakai.* (clothes-) *tawang.* (bread-) *sawada.* (withy-) *keṛa.*

Bass, a. *bog, ḍaḍ.*

Bastard, s. *ḥarāmī, ḥarām·zādah, khaṭā·zowulai.*

Baste, v.a. *wahal, ṭakawul, kūṭal, atsanṛal.* (sew) *ganḍal, pezal, bezal.*

Bastion, s. *bruj, morcha, ḍamdama.*

Bat, s. *kkhāperak, shoparak.*

Batch, s. *gundī*; *nughd, ẕāt.*

Bath, s. (cold-) *ghusl.* (vapour-) *ḥammām.*

Bathe, v.a. *ghusl k., lanbal.* v n. *lanbedal.*

Baton, s. *amsā, lawaṛ, koṭak.*

Battalion, s. *palṭan.*

Batter, v.a. *wahal, ṭakawul, kūṭal, naṛawul, daṛ·daṛ-, chūr·chūr-, kanḍ·kapaṛ-*, etc. *k.*

Battery, s. *morcha, damdama.*

Battle, s. *jang.* (-array) *tsīṛa, para·basta, ṣaff·taṛah.*

Battlement, s. *kangura.*

Bawl, v.a. *naṛal, chighawul, nārə-, chighe-*, etc. *wahal.*

Bay, a. *sūr*. (at-) *jah*. (to stand at-) *jah ked*.
Bayonet, s. *sīkhcha, sangīn*.
Be, v.n. *kedal, shwal, osedal*.
Beach, s. *ghāṛa*.
Beacon, s. *nakkha, nikkhān, munāra, tsalai*.
Bead, s. (stone) *mara-ī*. (glass) *mashkanra*. (jet) *shaba*.
Beak, s. *makkhūka, tsūka, shūka*.
Beam, s. *bensh, lakaṛa, lahaṛai, paṭera, barga*.
Bean, s. *lobiyā*.
Bear, s. *yag, melū, khirs*.
Bear, v.a. *wṛal, rāwṛal*; *zghamal, petsal*. v.n. *sahal, sahedal*. (-young) *zegedal, zowul*.
Beard, s. *gīra, rīsh*. (of grasses) *banbal, lasha, shoṛa*. (grey-) *spīn·gīrai*. (-less) *chaṭ*.
Bearer, s. *wṛūnkai*; *zghamūnkai*, etc.
Beast, s. *dzanāwar, ḥaiwān*. (wild-) *waḥsh* (-of prey) *dad*. (-of burthen) *bār·kakkh, sutūr*. (quadruped) *tsārwai, dāba*.
Beastliness, s. *gandagī, palītī, murdārī*; *ḥaiwān·tob, ḍangar·tob*.
Beastly, a. *gandah, palīt, murdār*.
Beat, v.a. *wahal, ṭakawul, kūṭal*; *pa-aṛ-, māt-, lāndi-*, etc. *k., barai mūndal* or *gaṭal*.
Beaten, a. *wahalai, ṭakawulai, kūṭalai*; *pa-aṛ, māt*.
Beater, s. *wahūnkai*, etc.; *pa-aṛ-*, etc. *kawūnkai, wa-aṛ, barai mūndūnkai* or *gaṭūnkai*.
Beating, s. *wahal, wahana, kūṭana, kūṭal, ṭakawul, ṭakawūna*; *pa-aṛ kawūna*, etc.
Beau, s. *ṭatai, ṭainchī, bānkiyā, ḍaulī*.
Beautiful, a. *kkhāyastah, kkhkulai, khūb ṣūrat, pa-ī-* or *peǰ·makhai*.
Beautify, v.a. *kkhāyastah k., kkhāyast warkawul, andzorawul*. (-oneself) *singār-, kkhewa-*, etc. *k*.
Beauty, s. *kkhāyast, kkhāyast·wālai, joṛāb, kṛah·wṛah, pa-ī makh·tob*.

Because, c. *dzaka, ska, la de wa, la kabla*.
Beckon, v.a. *ishārat k., lās tsanḍal*.
Become, v.n. *shwal, kedal, osedal*; *pīrzo-, lā-iq-, munāsib-*, etc. *ked*.
Bed, s. *bechānra*. (-stead) *kaṭ, pālang, manj*. (-coverlet) *bṛastan, liḥāf*. (-mattress) *tolā-ī, nihālī, taltak*. (-cushion) *bālikkht, bālīn, bālikkhtak*. (-sheet) *tsādar, pālang pokkh*. (-time) *mākhustan* or *māskhutan*. (-ridden) a. *zmol, zam·zambolai* or *zam·zmolai*.
Bee, s. *macha-ī*. (honey-) *ghlauza* or *lauza, mach·machai*. (black-) *baurā*. (-hive) *gabīna, garbīnai, kkhor*.
Beet, s. *chughandar* or *chuqandar*.
Beetle, s. *gūngaṭ, ghozai, ghozakarkai, khaaṭak, chānrī*. (mallet) *ḍabalai, baghdar, tsobāṛai*.
Befall, v.n. *nāziledal, prewatal, rasedal, wāq'i ked*.
Before, p. *pakhwā, wṛūnbe, wṛānde, qabl, dwṛānde, makh kkhke*
Beforehand, ad. *awwal, wṛūnbe, peshtar*.
Beg, v.a. *gadā-ī k., khair ghokkhtal*; *minnat-, sawāl-*, etc. *k*.
Beget, v.a. *zegawul, zowul, blārbawul, ḍakawul, paidā k., shigāra k*.
Beggar, s. *gadāe, paqīr, muflis, kangāl, nesṭ·man, khwāṛ*.
Beggary, s. *gadā-ī, gadā·tob, paqīrī, khwārī*.
Begin, v.a. *shurū'-, ibtidā-, darak-*, etc. *k*.
Beginner, s. *shurū' kawūnkai, mubtadī*.
Begone, in. *dza! lire sha! wruk sha! chikhe!*
Behalf, s. *wāsiṭa, khāṭir, dapāra, pa ḥaqq*.
Behave, v.a. *sulūk k*. v.n. *chaledal, ramedal*.
Behaviour. s. *chāl, chalan, ṭarīqa, sulūk*.
Behind, p. *wrusto, dumbāl, pastana, pa shā*.
Behold, in. *gora! wu·gora! wu wīna!*
Behove, v.n. *lāzim-, wājib-, munāsib-*, etc. *ked*.
Belch, s. *agramai, argai, ḍakār, ṭegh*. v.a. *agramai-*, etc. *bāsal—yastal* or *-k*.
Belief, s. *bāwar, i'tibār*; *īmān, dīn*.

Believe, v.a. *bāwar-*, etc. *k.* or *laral*; *īmān-*, etc. *rāwṛal.*

Believer, s. *bāwar kawūnkai*; *īmān-dār, mūmin, m'utaqid.*

Bell, s. *zangola, zang, jaras, gingṛai, julājil.*

Belle, s. *nādira, nāznīna, pa-ī makha.*

Bellow, v.a. *naṛal, naṛā-, nāre-*, etc. *wahal.* v.n. *ghuṛunbedal, ghurchedal.*

Bellows, s. *bana-ī, pūgar.*

Belly, s. *geḍa, kheṭa*; *nas.* (-ache) *kānga.* (-fretting) *qur-qurai.*

Belong, v.n. *lagedal, nisbat ked., kedal.*

Beloved, a. *maḥbūb, mayan.*

Below, ad. *kkhkata, kkhkiya, lānde, kūz, lar.*

Belt, s. *tasmu, rog, band.* (waist-) *kamar-kīsa.* (sword-) *paṭa.* (shoulder-, ornamental) *banda-ī.*

Bench, s. *takhta, dunkācha.*

Bend, v.a. *ṭīṭawul, kagawul.* v.n. *ṭīṭedal, kagedal, kālkūch-, kaglech-*, etc. *ked.*

Beneath, p. *lānde, dalānde, kkshata, kkshiya.*

Benediction, s. *du'ā, du'ā da khair, tabarruk.*

Benefactor, s. *da n'imatūno bakkhūnkai, kkhegaṛa kawūnkai, khairāt warkawūukai.*

Beneficent, a. *bakkhana kawūnkai, faiẓ-*, or *n'imat rasawūnkai.*

Beneficial, a. *kkhah, fā-ida-, sūd-, naf'a-*, etc. *-man.*

Benefit, s. *kkhegaṛa, gaṭa, sūd, bihbūd, fā-ida.*

Benevolent, s. *sakhī, sakhāwatī, khairātī, mihrbān.*

Bent, a. *ṭīṭ, kog.*

Benumbed, a. *qaṛqechan, maṛghechan, ūdah.*

Bequeath, v.a. *hiba-, mīrāt-*, etc. *k.*

Bequest, s. *mīrās* or *mīrāt, hiba, tarka.*

Bereave, v.a. *ākhistal, shūkawul, lūts k.*

Berry, s. *dāna.*

Beseech, v.a. *minnat-, d'uā-*, etc. *k.*

Beside, ad. *tsakha* or *khatsa, nijde, pa tsang, pa aṛakh, pa ḍade.*

Besides, p. *siwā, ziyāt, 'alāwa, nor.*

Besiege, v.a. *ḥiṣārawul* or *īsārawul, ger k.*

Bespeak, v.a. *numaṛ k.*

Best, a. *ghwarah, ḍer kkhah, la ṭolo na kkhah.*

Bestow, v.a. *bakkhal, warkawul, kkhandal.*

Bet, v.a. *shart taṛal.*

Betimes, ad. *wakhtī.*

Betray, v.a. *ghulawul, ṭagī-, pudūli-*, etc. *k. parda porta k., khwāla wayal.*

Betroth, v.a. *koĵdan k.*

Betrothal, s. *koĵdan, koĵdana, koĵda.*

Betrothed, a. (-youth) *changhol.* (-maid) *changhala.*

Better, a. *ghwarah, awlātar, bihtar.*

Between, ad. *pa mandz* (or *myandz*) *kkshe.*

Beverage, s. *sharbat, tskkhāk.*

Bevy, s. *sail, ghol*; *poṛk, ṭolai*; *khel.*

Bewail, v.a. *wāwailā-, zārī-, faryād-*, etc. *k.* (-the dead) *wīr k., wainā wayal.*

Beware, v.n. *pohedal, khabar-dār-, hokkhyār-, baidār-, āgāh-*, etc. *osedal* or *ked.* v.a. *parhez-, pahm-*, etc. *k.*

Bewilder, v.a. *ḥariyānawul, rabṛawul, sargardānawul, hekkh-, hak-pak-, hak-ḥairān-*, etc., *k.*

Bewitch, v.a. *naẓar lagawul, siwrai āchawul, koḍ k., ghulawul, fareftah-, mayan-*, etc. *k.*

Beyond, p. *pore, lire, hagha khwā, pore ghāṛa, bāhar, warā* or *warāya.*

Bias, s. *khwā, mīna, zṛah, mrasta, rujū'a.* v.a. *khwā girzawul, lamsawul, mā-il-, ma-ilān-, grohedah*, etc. *k.*

Bible, s. *kitāb.* (Pentateuch) *tauret.* (Psalms) *zabūr.* (Gospels) *anjīl.* (Muhammad's) *qurān, furqān.*

Bicker, v.a. *chighawul, raṭal, traṭal, dāṛal, qaẓiya-, jagṛa-*, etc. *k.*

Bier, s. *tābūt, da muṛī takhta.*

Biestings, s. *wargah.*

Big, s. *loe, ghaṭ, kaṭah, star.*

Bile, s. *trīkhai, zahra, ṣafrā.*

Bilious, a. *ṣafrā-ī.*

Bill, s. (bird's) *makkhūka*. (account) *ḥisāb*. (note) *ḥujjat, tamassuk*, (-of exchange) *hunḍa-ī*. (-of sale) *qibāla, bai'a·nāma*.

Bind, v.a. *taṛal, lagawul, joṛawul*. (a book) *juz·* or *jild·bandī k*.

Binder, s. *taṛūnkai, taṛūnai*. (in comp.) *-band*.

Binding, s. *taṛūn, wandanai*. (book-) *jild·bandī*.

Biography, s. *tazkira, rawāyat*.

Bird, s. *marghah, marghai*. (-catcher) *mashkār, kkhkārī*. (-lime) *slekkh*. (-net) *ḍām, ḍaba-ī, jāl, dwa·gaza*. (-noose) *ghunḍārai, lwīna, lūma, lūmaka*. (-springe) *laṭ, talaka, kuṛka-ī*. (-trap) *paṛka, honṛā*.

Birth, s. *zowah, zowūna, zegedah, zegedana, tawallud, paidā-ish*. (-place) *waṭan, da paidā-ikkht*: *dzāe*. (-day) *da tawallud wradz*. (-right) *ḥaqq da masharī*.

Biscuit, s. *kak, kakoṛa*. (sweet-) *amrasa*.

Bit, s. *ṭoṭa, ṭoṭai, khatsosa*. (of food) *nwaṛa-ī, ṭūk*. (of a horse) *mlūna, qā-iza, dahana*.

Bitch, s. *spa-ī*. (-in heat) *spayama* or *spa-ema*.

Bite, v.a. *chīchal, khwuṛal, dāṛal, chak lagawul*.

Bitter, a. *trīkh, talkh*.

Bittern, s. *baglai, kablai*.

Bitterness, s. *trīkh·wālai, trīkh·tob, trīkh·tiyā*.

Bitumen, s. *qafr ul yahūd*.

Black, a. *tor*. (jet-) *tak tor*.

Blacken, v.a. *torawul*. v.n. *toredal*.

Blackguard, s. *charlanḍ, chaṭ, chulur, bad·m'ash, laṛalai, ḥarāmī, lūch lawanḍ, laṛo tsaṭo, kachar*.

Blackish, a. *tor·shān*.

Blackmail, s. *būnga*.

Blacksmith, s. *lohār, āhangar*.

Bladder, s. *pūkanṛa-ī*.

Blade, s. *palka, tegh*. (of grass) *khalai*. (of scissors) *para, pal*. (of plough) *pāla, saspāra*.

Blame, s. *malāmat, 'aib, taqṣīr, quṣūr, wabāl, gunāh*. v.a. *malāmatawul, raṭal, traṭal*.

Blameable, a. *malāmatī, taqṣīrī, gunah·gār*.

Blameless, a. *be gunāh, be quṣūr, be malāmat*.

Blamelessly, ad. *nā·ḥaqq, be sabab, be gunāh*, etc.

Bland, a. *post, narm, khog, mulā-im*.

Blandishment, s. *nāz, nakhra, karashma, makez*; *kkhewa, singār, ḍaul*.

Blank, a. *ta·ash* or *t·ish, khālī, spīn, sādah*.

Blanket, s. *shaṛa-ī, krāsta*.

Blaspheme, v.a. *kufr wayal*.

Blast, s. (breath) *pūk, pūkai*. (wind) *sīla-ī, jakaṛ, chapa*. (sound) *bāng, āwāz, ghag*.

Blast, v.a. *ālwūzawul, fanā k., barbādawul, wrukawul*; *kkhere k*.

Blaze, s. *lūkhaṛa, lanba, bāmbanṛa, ḍānḍa-ī, baṛānḍa, ghaṛānḍa*. v.a. *lūkhaṛa-*, etc. *k*.

Bleach, v.a. *spīnawul, spetsal*.

Bleak, a. *soṛ, yakh*.

Blear, a. *obĵan, dund, khīran, lechan, zawlan*.

Bleat, v.a. *bregan-, me me-*, etc. *k*. v.n. *bāngedal*.

Bleed, v.n. *wīnedal, wīne bahedal*. v.a. *rag wahal, wīne bāsal—yāstal*.

Blemish, s. *'aib, quṣūr, dāgh, tor, rakhna*.

Bless, v.a. *d'uā-, tabarruk-*, etc. *k., barakat warkawul*.

Blessing, s. *d'uā da khair, barakat, tabarruk*.

Blight, s. *torka-ī, surkha-ī*.

Blind, a. *ṛūnd*. (stone-) *ṭap ṛūnd*. (night-) *shamkor* or *shokor*. v.a. *ṛandawul, nā·bīnā k*. v.n. *ṛandedal*.

Blindfold, v.a. *starge puṭawul*. (-cattle) *kholai taṛal*. (-hawks) *ṭopa-ī pasarawul*.

Blindness, s. *ṛūnd·wālai, ṛunḍ·tiyā*. (night-) *shamkor·tiyā*.

Blink, v.a. *starge wahal, dzezme rapawul, dzanbal* or *dzamal*.

Blister, s. *tanrāka, pūla-ī, maṭāka*.

Blithe, s. *kkhād, khūsh·dil, khandā·rūe*.

Bloat, v.a. *paṛsawul.* v.n. *paṛsedal.*
Block, s. *tsaṭ, mūnḍ, garga, kunda.*
Blockade, v.a. *ḥiṣārawul* or *īsārawul, band-awul.*
Blockhead, s. *gedī-khar, khar, pūhaṛ, dūzai.*
Blood, s. *wīne.* (-shed) *khūn.* (breed) *ẕāt, rag, aṣl, nog.* (-stained) *pa wino habatah.*
Bloom, v.n. *ṭūkedal, zarghūnedal, ghwaredal.*
Blossom, s. *ghūṭa-ī, gul.* v.n. *khwaredal, spaṛedal, spaṛdai ked., ghwaredal,* etc.
Blot, s. *laka, ṭakai, dāgh; 'aib, nāmūs, tor.*
Blow, s. *guẕār.* (of fist) *gasa, ḍab, sūk, ṭas.* (of breath) *pūk, pūkai.* (of wind) *sīla-ī.*
Blow, v.a. (a fire) *pūkal, pūk wahal.* (as wind) v.n. *ālwatal, chaledal.* (as a flower) *ṭūkedal, ghwaredal, spaṛedal, spaṛdai ked.* (a bugle) v.a. *ghagawul.* (-out) *muṛ-, soṛ-,* etc. *k.* (-down) *ringaṛai k.*
Bludgeon, s. *koṭak, lawaṛ, ḍāng.*
Blue, a. *shīn-, nīl-, āsmānī-,* etc., *-rang.*
Blunder, s. *khaṭā.* v.a. *khaṭā k.*
Blunderbuss, s. *gharābīn, ṣaff-shikan.*
Blunt, a. *pa-ats* or *p-uts.* (-ness) s. *pa-ats-wālai.*
Blur, s. *dāgh, 'aib, tor, laka, ṭakai.*
Blurt, v.a. *parda prānatal, khwāla wayal.*
Blush, v.n. *sharmedal.*
Bluster, v.a. *lāp wahal, ṭar-ṭar k., dam wahal.*
Blusterer, s. *lāpak, ṭarai, ḍūzak, daz.*
Boar, s. *sarkūzai, kharbishoe, khūg.* (wild-) *soḍar, matah.*
Board, s. *takhta.* (writing-) *lauḥ, paṭa-ī.* (food) *tskkhāk khwurāk.*
Boasting, s. *lāpa, lāp shāp, dam.*
Boast, v.a. *lāp-, lāpa-, dam-,* etc., *wahal* or *k.*
Boat, s. *beṛa-ī, kishta-ī.* (bridge of-) *pul, jisr.* (-man) *mānrgai, mahanrah, mallāḥ.*
Bodkin, s. *salā-ī, sīkhcha, stan, dūk.*
Body, s. *tan, juṣṣa, ṣūrat, wujūd, jism.* (in comp.) *andām.* (of men, etc.) *ṭolai, ṭolgai, ghol, paṛk, khel, tanba, firqa.*

Bog, s. *bokkht, bokkhtana, yala, taramna, palanda.*
Boil, v.a. *eshawul* or *yashawul, khūṭ k.* v.n. *eshedal* or *yashedal, khūṭ ked.*
Boil, s. *dāna, nanaka-ī.* (blackhead-) *tora-dāna.* (acne-) *dzwānaka.* (heat-) *garmaka.* (whitlow) *kharai, shīnai.* (carbuncle) *kkhandza.* (abscess) *kkhalūna, lūna.*
Boiler, s. *khum, kaṛahai, ḍeg, dechka.*
Boiling, s. *eshnā, khūṭkai; yashānd* or *eshānd.*
Boisterous, a. *tund, tez, mast.*
Bold, a. *maṛanai, zṛah-war, tūrzan, bahādur, dilāwar, be bāk; gustākh, chūnkai, wītak.*
Boldness, s. *maṛāna, zṛah-war-tob. tūrzan-tob, bahādurī, maṛanī-tob, be bākī; gus-tākhī, shokhī, chūnkī-tob, be makh-tob, be ḥayā-tob.*
Bolster, s. *bālikkht, bālīn, takiya.*
Bolt, s. *hūl, mekhchū, bala-ī, jaranda-ī, aṛamai.*
Bond, s. *band, dzolana, dzel, kaṛa-ī, zandzīr.* (note) *hujjat, tamassuk.* (union), *pewand, band, jorikkht.* (blood) *ragai, khpulawī, rishta, wābastagī.* (compact) *wāda, taṛūn, taṛa, bandanr, lafẓ.*
Bondage, s. *qaid, band, bandī-tob; bandagī, ghulāmī, mra-e-tob.*
Bondmaid, s. *wīndza, kanīza, barda.*
Bondman, s. *mra-e, ghulām.*
Bondsman, s. *ẓāmin, yarghamāl* or *yarghamal.*
Bone, s. *haḍ, haḍūkai.*
Bonfire, s. *dūna, alāo, ḍānḍa-ī.*
Bonny, a. *kkhāyastah, kkhkulai, pa-ī-makhai* or *pej-makhai, pa-ī-makh.*
Bony, a. *haḍawar.*
Booby, s. *sādah-dil, pūhaṛ, gedī-khar, kam-'aql.*
Book, s. *kitāb.* (bound-) *jild.* (unbound-) *juz.* (-stand) *rahel.* (in comp) *-nāma.* (-binding) *juz-* or *jild-bandī.* (-boards) *kānṭa-ī.* (-binder) *jild-gar, ṣaḥḥāf.*

Boon, s. *ghanīmat, n'imat, barakat, bakht*; *in'ām, bakhkshiksh, bakkhana*. a. *khūsh-dil, kkhād, khandā-rūe. khūsh-ṭab'a.*

Boor, s. *gawār, ghunḍāyah, lwāṛ, pūhaṛ, dzaban.*

Boot, s. *moza, chakma.* (for women) *jista.* (to-) ad. *pa gaṭe, pa weṛiyā, pa ziyāt, junga.*

Booth, s. *tsapar, kūḍala, mana, jūngaṛa.*

Bootless, a. *'abas, be fā-ida, nīma-khwā, nīmgaṛai.*

Booty, s. *lūṭ, gaṭa, shūka, tāla, ghārat.*

Borax, s. *tanrakār.*

Border, s. *ḥadd, brīd, pūla*; *ghāṛa, morga*; *tsanḍa, tselma, ja-ī, laman.*

Bore, v.a. *barma-, sūṛai-*, etc. *k., sīkhal, petsal.*

Born, a. *zowulai, zegedalai, paidā shawai,* (in comp) *-zādah, -zai, -dzoe.*

Born, v.n. *zegedal, zowul, paidā ked.*

Borrow, v.a. *por-, qarẓ-*, etc. *ākhistal.* (a thing to be returned) *'āriyat-ākhistal.*

Borrower, s. *porawuṛai, qarẓ-dār.*

Bosom, s. (embrace) *gheg, ghūzai.* (chest) *ṭaṭar.* (breast) *sīna.*

Both, a. *dwāṛah, dwah-wāṛah.*

Bottle, s. *kkhīkkha.*

Bottom, s. *wekh, tal, mūnḍ*; *kūnsaṭ, būnsaṭ.*

Bottomless, a. *be pāyān, nā-pāyāw* or *nā-pāyāb.*

Bough, s. *tsānga, khrānga, lakkhta.* (large-) *kkhākh, khanḍ, ṭāl.*

Bound, v.a. *dangal, ṭop wahal, traplal.* v.n. *trapedal, ghwurzedal.* (ricochet) v.a. *ṭīndak wahal.* (limit) v.a. *pūla-, brīd-, ḥadd-*, etc. *taṛal.*

Boundary, s. *pūla, ḥadd, brīd.*

Boundless, a. *be ḥadda, be anda, be shāna, be nihāyata, be qiyāsa.*

Bountiful, a. *sakhī, sakhāwatī, faiẓ-rasān, kkhandanī-, bakkhana-*, etc. *kawūnkai.*

Bounty, s. *sakhāwat, sakhī-tob, bakkhana.*

Bow, s. *salām, adab*; *ṭīṭ-wālai.*

Bow, s. *līnda, līnda-ī, kamān.* (-string) *ĵa-ī.* (middle of-) *mūṭai.* (horn of-) *ghwagai, khām.* (notch of-) *zih-gīr.* (-for practice) *darwesha-ī.* (pellet-) *ghur-kamāna.* (pellet-cup) *pāṭa-ī.* (bar of cup) *panjakai,* (-of a fiddle) *kamāncha.* (rain-) *da būḍa-ī ṭāl, sara-shna kāsa.* (to bend a-) v.a. *ĵa-ī bānde k.* (to unbend a-) v.a. *ĵa-ī kūzawul.* (-maker) *kamān-gar.*

Bow, v.a. *ṭīṭawul.* v.n. *ṭīṭedal.*

Bowels, s. *laṛmānah, kulme.* (of ruminants) *ūjaṛī.*

Bower, s. *chopāl, jūngaṛa, tsapar, dzodz-khāna.*

Bowl, s. (pottery) *kanḍol, kanḍolai.* (glazed-) *zarghūn-kanḍol.* (china-) *chūna-ī* or *chīna-ī.* (wooden-) *kāsa, pīna, kunṛa-ī* or *kunḍa-ī.* (metal-) *kaṭorai.*

Box, s. *ṣandūq, ṣandūqcha.* (clothes-) *taunṛa-ī.* (band-) *tawang.* (trinket-) *haṛpa-ī.* (pill-) *dablai.* (in comp.) *-dān.* (blow) *tsapeṛa, ṭas.*

Boy, s. *halak, woṛkai.* (school-) *ĵanṛai.* (plough-) *ghunḍāyah.* (dancing-) *lakkhtai, lolai.*

Boyhood, s. *halak-wālai, wṛūk-wālai, ĵanṛī-tob.*

Brace, s. *taṛūn, tanṛa-ī, wandanai*; *lānga, piyāṛma, kakkha*; *joṛa, juft, qulba.*

Brace, v.a. *klakawul, tangawul, ṭīngawul, kāgal—kkhkal.*

Bracelet, s. (above elbow) *ma-aṭkai, bāzū-band.* (below elbow) *bāhū, bangrai.* (at wrist) *kanganr, kaṛai, wakkhai, gajrai.*

Bracket, s. *darai, raf*; *pushta, aṛam.*

Brackish, a. *mālgīn, kkhora-nāk*; *trīw.*

Braid, v.a. *odal.*

Brain, s. *māghzah.*

Brake, s. *karkanṛ, jāṛ, jāmbṛa.*

Bramble, s. *karkanṛa, jāṛa*; *aghzai, ghana.*

Bran, s. *sūṛī, būṭ·sūṛī, gadzārī.*

Branch, s. *kkhākh, tsānga, khana.* (family-) *kor, naṣl, pusht, alwād.*

Brand, v.a. *dāghawul, nughai gdalī—kkhodal; tor-, tuhmat-,* etc., *pore k., makh·torai k.*

Brandish, v.a. *tsandawul.*

Brass, s. *ziyaṛ.*

Brave, a. *maṛanai, zṛah·war, tūrzan, bahādur, takṛah, mazbūṭ, dilāwar.*

Bravery, s. *maṛāna, mardī, zṛah·war·tob,* etc.

Bravo, in. *shābāsh! āprīn!*

Brawl, v.a. *jagṛa-, qaẓiya-,* etc. *k., chighawul.*

Brawler, s. *jagṛāū, takrārī, jang·yālai.*

Bray, v.n. *hanredal.*

Breach, s. *chāwd, tsāk, darz; kandaw, jghand.*

Bread, s. *doḍa-ī.* (leavened-) *khamīra.* (unleavened-) *patīra.* (barley-) *orbūshīna.* (maize-) *sūkṛak.* (millet-) *khamacha, piyātsa.* (mixed meal-) *rāṛa, broṛa.* (dry-) *spora doḍa-ī.* (-of charity) *gharai, chaṛ.*

Breadth, s. *plan·wālai, arat·wālai, sor* or *psor.*

Break, v.a. *mātawul.* (-to atoms) *char·chūr-, daṛ·daṛ-, kanḍ·kapaṛ-, māt·guḍ-,* etc. *k.*

Breakfast, s. *nārai* or *nahārai, nāshta, tsākkhtī.* (-during Lent) *pesh·manai* or *·namai* or *·lamai.*

Breast, s. *sīna.* (nipple) *tai.* (-band) *tapor.*

Breastplate, s. *chaprās..*

Breastwork, s. *sangar, mard·raw, faṣīl.*

Breath, s. *sā* or *sāh, dam* or *dama.*

Breathe, v.a. *sā-, dam-,* etc. *ākhistal* or *rākāgal—rākkhkal.* (-upon) *damawul, dam k.*

Breeches, s. *paṛtūg, shalwār,*

Breed, s. *aṣl, naṣl, ẓāt, rag·rīkkha, nogai, ẓād·zawẓāt, rang.*

Breed, v.a. *pālal, parwaral; zegawul, naṣl·paidā k.* v.n. *langedal, zegedal; blārbedal, warla ked.*

Breeding, s. *pālana, parwarish; tarbiyai, t'alīm; langa, blārba, warla, ḍaka.*

Breeze, s. *hawā, bād, bādūkai, wagma.*

Brethren, s. *wrūnrah, 'azīzān.*

Brevity, s. *lanḍ·wālai ·lanḍ·ṭiyā.*

Bribe, s. *baḍa, rishwat, mok.*

Brick, s. *khakkhta.* (-bat) *ṭoṭa, roṛa.* (-dust) *surkhī.* (-kiln) *paja.* (-layer) *kullāl.*

Bridal, a. *nāweyat.*

Bride, s. *nāwe.* (bride's maid) *wrā·bānra-ī, wre-aza* or *wreyaza, mānja-ī.* (bride's female servant) *īnga.*

Bridegroom, s. *zalmai.* (bridegroom's man) *wrā·bānrai, jānjī, mānjī.*

Bridge, s. *pul.* (-of nose) *tindoṛai, tanbeza* or *tambūzai* or *tambūzak.* (of fiddle) *ṭaṭū, khargai.* (to make a-) v.a. *pul taṛal.*

Bridle, s. *wāga, mlūnz; jalab* or *jalaw.* (of cord) *gapī, pā-ī.* (camel's-) *pezwān.*

Brief, a. *lanḍ, kotāh.*

Brigade, s. *tuman, dasta.*

Brigand, s. *ghal, shūk·mār, qaẓẓāq.*

Bright, a. *rūnr, rokkhān, tāb·nāk; spīn, shīn.*

Brighten, v.a. *rūnrawul, spīnawul, pākawul, rokkhān k.* v.n. *rūnredal, dzaledal* or *dzal ked. brekkhedal; spīnedal, shīn-, pāk-,* etc. *ked.*

Brightness, s. *ranrā, brekkhnā, rokkhnā-ī.*

Brim, s. *morga, ghāṛa, tsanḍa.*

Brimstone, s. *gogar* or *gogil.*

Brindled, a. *brag, gag, chrag·brag, ablaq.*

Briny, s. *mālgīn.* (brine) *mālgīna oba.*

Bring, v.a. (-animate objects) *rāwustal.* (-inanimate objects) *rāwṛal.* (-forth young) *langedal.* (-off) *bachawul.* (-up) *pālal, parwaral.* (-under) *lānde k.*

Brink, s. *ghāṛa, morga, tsanḍa, ḍaḍa.*

Brisk, a. *chust, chālāk, takṛah, tund, gaṛandaī.*

Bristle, v.a. (as the hair or skin) *wekkhtah-, ghūnḍ-,* etc. *-zigedal* or *walāṛedal.* s. *da sarkūzī wekkhtah.*

Brittle, a. *nāzuk, mātedūnai, narai, spuk.*

Broad, a. *plan, arat, sara·war* or *psora·war.*

Broadcloth, s. *banāt.*
Broadness, *plan·wālai, arat·wālai, sor* or *psor.*
Brocade, s. *kimkhwāb, zar·baft, muqqaish.*
Broil, v.a. *wrītawul, kabābawul, teyal, talawul.*
Broken, a. *māt.* (-to bits) *māt·guḍ, kanḍ·kapaṛ, char·chūr, daṛ·daṛ.*
Broker, s. *dallāl.*
Bronchocele, s. *ghur.*
Brood, s. *zawzād* or *zauzāt, alwād, bachī.*
Brood, v.n. *ghamedal, nūledal, kaṛedal; fikr·man-, andekkh·man-, wiswāsī-,* etc. *ked.* (sit on eggs) *kuṛkedal, kuṛaka ked.*
Brook, s. *lakkhtai, nahar, arākh, wela, khwaṛ.* (dry bed of-) *kanda, kas, shela.*
Broom, s. *jārū.*
Broth, s. *kkhorwā.*
Brother, s. *wror.* (elder-) *mashar wror.* (younger-) *kashar wror.* (middle-) *mandzwai wror.* (foster-) *da tī-* or *da to wror.* (full-) *sakah wror.* (half-) *nā·sakah wror.* (-in law) *awkkhai.* (husband's-) *lewar.* (-hood) *wrorī, wror·walī, wror·galwī, wror·wālai.*
Brow, s. *wuchwulai* or *wucharlai, tandai, kolak.* (-of a hill) *kamar, tarai.*
Brown, a. *mushkai, bor, kha-aṛ.* (light-) *sperah.* (dark-) *sūr·bor.*
Browse, v.a. *powul.* (tend at-) *piyāyāl.* v.n. *tsaredal.*
Bruise, v.a. *blodal, sūlawul, dzabal; kuṭal, ṭakawul.* (-grain) *dal k.*
Brush, s. (weaver's-) *māla.* (fox's-) *lakai.* v.a. *jārū k.* (-clothes) *tsanḍal.*
Brushwood, s. *dzangal, jāṛ, jāmbṛa.*
Brutal, a. *be dard, be raḥm, sakht·dil, dzaban, ḥaiwānī.*
Brute, s. *ḥaiwān, dad, dzanāwar.*
Bubble, s. *bulbula* or *burbura, ghuiai, jakh.* v.n. *eshedal, khūṭ ked., khūtsedal.*
Bubo, s. *ghumba, ghunḍāṛai, stagh.*
Buck, s. *osai.* (-rabbit) *soe.*
Bucket, s. *boka, taghārai, satal; dalwa, gaḍhal; solāgha.*
Buckle, s. *kara-ī, gharabbai.*
Buckler, s. *ḍāl, spar.* (-handle) *lāstai, mūṭai.* (-cushion) *gaḍai.* (-boss) *patrai.*
Bud, s. *ghūṭa-ī.* (leaf-) *ghandal.* v.n. *ṭūkedal, ghwaredal, zarghūnedal.* v.a. *red-, qalam-,* etc. *k.*
Buffalo, s. *mekkh, gāwmekkh.* f. *mekkha.* (young-) *katai.* (two-year-old-) *joṭah.* (bull-) *sanḍah.*
Buffoon, s. *ṭoqī, ṭoq·mār, washtī, washt·mār, malanḍai, maskharāchī, pekkhe·gar.*
Buffoonery, s. *ṭoqa, washta, malanḍa, maskhara.*
Bug, s. *mungaṇr, kaṭmal.* (tree-) *khasak.*
Bugbear, s. *bāgū, bagalolai, bau.*
Bugle, s. *turai.* (Bugler) *turī·mār.*
Build, v.a. *joṛawul.*
Building, s. *kanḍar, māṇra-ī, koṭa, kor.*
Bulb, s. *ghūṭa, ghūṭa-ī.* (garlic-) *palai.*
Bulk, s. *ghaṭ·wālai, loe·wālai.*
Bulky, a. *ghaṭ, loe, nāpaṛ, star, khṛīs, gagar.*
Bull, s. *hīnḍah* or *mīnḍah.* (-calf) *skhai.*
Bullet, s. *mardaka* or *mardak, gola-ī.*
Bullion, s. *srah·zar, spīn·zar.*
Bullock, s. *ghwayai* or *ghwa-e ghutskai, ḍangar.* (steer) *zāṛai, skhwandarkoṭai, skhwandar.*
Bully, s. *zālim, zorāwar, luqah, ḍaz, zorūnkai.*
Bulrush, s. *lūkha, kahai, nal, baḍagāl.*
Bump, s. *pārsob, māṭūs, maṭāka, ghūnḍa, pūpaka, punḍ.*
Bunch, s. *ghotai, ghūncha, khosha.*
Bundle, s. *gāṭlai, peṭai, geḍai, panḍa, panḍūkai.* (-of hay) *beda, kalokkhta.*
Bung, s. *būja, ḍīḍa, khulborai, shoṛa.*
Buoyant, a. *spuk, pāyāwai.*
Bur, s. *jishai, kanḍala-ī.*
Burden, s. *bār.* v.a. *bār āchanul* or *k.; legdawul.*

Burdensome, a. *drūnd, ġrān, sakht.*
Burglar, s. *ghal, kanḍar-,* or *gūṭ mātawūnkai.*
Burglary, s. *ghlā, kanḍar-* or *gūṭ mātawūna.* (to commit-) v.a. *kanḍar-* or *gūṭ mātawul* or *k., naqb-zanī k.*
Burial, s. *khakkhawūna, khakkhedana.* (service) *janāza.* (-ground) *goristān, qabaristān.*
Burlesque, s. *toqa, malanḍa, mazākh.*
Burn, v.a. *swadzawul, sedzawul; balawul.* v.n. *swal, sedzal, baledal.*
Burning, s. *swai; sedzana; baledana; balawūna.*
Burnish, v.a. *rūnrawul, dzalkawul, rokkhān-, ṣaiqal-, ṣāf-, pāk-, brekkh-nāk-,* etc. *k.*
Burrow, v.a. *sūṛai-* or *sūṛa-, ghār-, surang-,* etc. *k.,* or *kanawdal,* or *kanal,* or *kanastal.*
Burst, v.n. *chāwdal, pṛak chāwdal, shledal, tsīredal, chāq ked.* (-into) *ḍūsa k.* (-out) *mātedal.* (-upon) *rā-māt ked.*
Bury, v.a. *khakkhawul.*
Bush, s. *būṭai, jāṛa, ḍakai.*
Bushel, s. *ogai.* (a quarter-) *kuṛai.*
Business, s. *kār, kasb, pesha, shewa.*
Buskin, s. *sugul; māsa-ī.*
Bustard, s. *tsāṛai, kha-aṛ-mor, ḥūbārah, tughdarī.*
Bustle, s. *chal-chalā, hatsa, tag-o-dau, tagā-pū.*
Busy, a. *lagiyā, mashghūl.*
But, c. *lekin, mangar, wale, balki, siwā.*
Butcher, s. *qaṣṣāb.* v.a. *ḥalālawul; wajlal* or *wajal, qatl-, marg-, khūn-, muṛ-,* etc. *k.*
Butt, s. *nakkha, mukha.* v.a. (-with the head) *ṭakar, ḍaghara* or *daaara, ṭakar-,* etc. *wahal.*
Butter, s. *kuch.* (preserved-) *ghwaṛī.*
Butterfly, s. *parakai, tārūgai, kambala-ī, bāmbīlakai.*
Buttermilk, s. *shomle* or *shlombe.* (sour-) *tarwe.*
Buttock, s. *kūnāṭai, surīn.*
Button, s. *ghoṭai.* (-loop) ***tanra-ī****, gūtma, pulghwākkha, ghaṛāsha.*
Buttress, s. *pushtī, aṛam.*
Buxom, a. *takṛah, chāgh, tāzah, khandā-rūe.*
Buy, v.a. *pīral* or *pīrawdal, pa bai'e ākhistal.*
Buzz, v.n. *bonredal.*
Buzzing, s. *bonr, bonrkai, bonredana.*
By, p. *pa.* (-day) *pa wradzi.* (-thousands) *pa zargūno.* (-hundreds) *pa ṣawūno.* (-all means) *pa har shān.* (-degrees) *pa ro ro, pa qalār.* (-no means) *pa hets shān, hechare, haḍo.* (-and bye) *pa drang, drang sā'at pas.* This preposition is often followed by *sara* (with), as *pa har shān sara,* by all means, etc.

C.

Cabal, s. *janba, para, gundī.*
Cabbage, s. *gobī, karamkala.*
Cabin, s. *koṭa; jūngaṛa, kuḍala, tsapar.*
Cable, s. *da beṛa-ī biyāstq,* or *-pa-aṛai,* or *-rasa-ī.*
Cactus, s. *ṭohaṛ, zaqūm, qūṛghandal.*
Cackle, v.a. *jak-jak-, chagh-chugh-,* etc. *k., chūqa wahal.*
Cadaverous, a. *sperah.*
Cadence, s. *wazn, āwāz, ghag, trang, badala.*
Cage, s. *pinjra, qafas.*
Cajole, v.a. *ghulawul, ṭagal.*
Calamitous, a. *bad-* or *kam-bakht, bad-naṣīb, balā-nāk, āfatī, ghaẓab-nāk.*
Calamity, s. *balā, āfat, nāzila, muṣībat.*
Calcine, v.a. *kushtah-, īre-,* etc. *k.*
Calculate, v.a. *shmāral* or *shmeral, ḥisābawul, ganral.*
Calculation, s. *ḥisāb, shumār* or *shmerah, andāza.*
Caldron, s. *khum, deg, saṭal; dechka, kaṛahai.*

Calendar, s. *patra, taqwīm.*
Calender, v.a. *batī-, kundī-, chāp-*, etc. *k.*
Calf, s. *bachai, chikorai.* (bull-) *skhai.* (buffalo-) *kaṭai.* (camel-) *jūngai, botai.* (stuffed-) *spandakh.* (-of leg) *paṛkai, gharai.*
Calico, s. *chīt.*
Calk, v.a. *chāwd-, darz-*, etc. *-bandī k.*
Call, s. *bāng, nāra.* (-for dogs) *tū·tū.* (-for cattle) *ṛī·ṛī.* (-for cats) *pa-ash·pa-ash.* (-for hawks) *qū·qū.* (-to drive cattle) *ta-arya·ta-arya.* (-to encourage dogs) *tap·tap.* (-to encourage fighting rams, etc.) *jig·jig, ḍrich·ḍrich.*
Call, v.a. *nāra wahal, bāng wayal, ghag k.* (summon) *balal, ṭalab k.* (name) *wayal, nūm ākhistal*; *nūm kegdal—kekkhodal* or *kkhkegdal*, etc. (-to mind) *yādawul.* (-back) *stūnawul* or *stanawul.* (-bad names) *kanzal k., kkhkandzal* or *kanzal.*
Called, a. *nūmāndai, nūmedah.*
Calling, s. *kār, kasb, pesha.*
Callous, a. *sakht, klak*; *be dard, be parwā.*
Callousness, s. *sakhtī, klak·wālai*; *be dardī.*
Calm, a. *āsūdah, hawār, ārām, band, walāṛ.* v.a. *walāṛawul, saṛawul, ārām warkawul.* s. *qalār·tiyā-* or *walāṛ·tiyā da bād.*
Calmly, ad. *pa qalār sara, pa ro ro.*
Calmness, s. *ārām-, qalār-, walāṛ-*, etc. *-tiyā*; *rāḥat, ṭāṭob.*
Calumniate, v.a. *tuhmat-* or *tūmat-, tor-*, etc. *-pore k. peghor warkawul, ghībat k.*
Calumny, s. *tuhmat, tor, peghor, ghībat.*
Camel, s. *ūkkh, shutur.* (young-) *jūng* or *jūngai, botai.* (rutting-) *baṛbaṛai.* (-driver) *sarwān, ūkkhbah.* (-saddle) *kata, pālān.* (-litter) *kajāwa.* (-bridle) *pezwān.* (-nose peg) *nata.*
Camp, s. *ḍera, muqām*; *urdū, ḍal.*
Campaign, s. *jang, ghazā, jihād*; *sama, maidān.*
Camphor, s. *kāfūr.*
Can, v.n. *shwal, tuwānedal.* s. *loṭkai.*
Canal, s. *nāla, wāla.* (small-) *lakkhtai.*
Cancel, v.a. *wrānawul, man'a k. bāṭil k.*
Cancer, s. *yaga, rasawla-ī, kkhandza, nāsūr.*
Candid, a. *rikkhtīnai, spīn, sūchah, ṣāf.*
Candidate, s. *umed·wār.*
Candle, s. *bāta-ī.* (-stick) *ḍīwaṭ.*
Candour, s. *rikkhtīn·tob, spīn·wālai, ṣafā-ī.*
Cane, s. *bet.* (sugar-) *ganna.* (-for eating) *ponḍa.* (-for the mill) *khū.*
Canister, s. *dablai, haṛpa-ī, ṣandūqcha.*
Cannibal, s. *saṛī-* or *ādam·khor, khūnāṛai.*
Cannon, s. *top, topa.* (-ball) *golā, gola-ī.*
Canoe, s. *kishta-ī.*
Canon, s. *qānūn, ā-īn, dastūr.*
Canopy, s. *chatr, sāewān, shāmiyāna, siwrai.*
Cant, s. *makr, riyā.* (-word) *takiya kalām.*
Canton, s. *tapa, cham, jam, khel.*
Cantonment, s. *urdū, ḍal, chāwnra-ī.*
Canvas, s. *biyasta-ī, ṭapṛa.*
Cap, s. *ṭopa-ī, khola·ī.* (padded-) *ṭūkhala-ī.* (-with ear flaps) *koṭakha, khūrjīna.*
Capable, a. *qābil, tuwānā, shwūnkai.*
Capacious, a. *arat, dzāyawar, kushād.*
Capacity, s. *tuwān, qābiliyat, qābil·tob, idrāk*; *arat·wālai, dzāe.*
Capital, s. *aṣl, māya, panga, saga.* a. *aṣlī, awwal, wṛūnbanai*; *da marg lā-iq* or *-sazā-wār.*
Capsicum, s. *sara·mrich.*
Caprice, s. *khiyāl, wahm.*
Capricious, a. *khiyālī, wahmī, nā·qalār.*
Captious, a. *ḥujjatī, takrārī, jang·yālai.*
Captivate, v.a. *ghulawul, fareftah-, mayan-, koḍ-*, etc. *k.*
Captive, s. *qaidī, bandī.*
Captivity, s. *qaid, band.*
Capture, v.a. *nīwal, ākhistal, giriftār k.*
Caracole, v.a. *top-, khartīza-, kharchaka-*, etc. *-wahal.*

Caravan, s. *kārwān, qāfila, sānga.*
Caravansary, s. *srāe, kārwān·srāe, rabāṭ.*
Caraway, s. *zīra, sperkai.*
Carbuncle, s. *kkhandza, dandārū, ghunḍārai.*
Carcass, s. *muṛai, lāsh.*
Card, s. *pāṇra, pata.* (playing-) *tās, ganjīfa.*
Card, v.a. *alājī-, tonbiyā-*, etc. *k.*
Cardamous, s. *ilāchī, hel.*
Carder, s. (cotton-) *alāj*; *nandāp* or *naddāf.* (his bow) *līnda.* (the beam) *ḍānḍat.* (the cord) *ĵa-ī.* (the beetle) *ḍabalai.* (the staff) *chūka.* (the comb) *alājī.*
Care, v.a. *fikr-, parwā-, ghaur-*, etc. *k., andekkhnā-, gham-*, etc. *k., khāṭir-, makh-, mulāḥiẓa-*, etc. *k., khabar·dārī-, tsoka-ī-*, etc. *k., sātana-, khundī-*, etc. *k.*
Career, s. *daur, daurān*; *manḍa, zghākkht.*
Careful, a. *khabar·dār, hokkhyār*; *fikr·man.*
Carefulness, s. *khabar·dārī, hokkhyār·tiyā.*
Careless, a. *be khabar, be parwā, be fikr, be gham, ghāfil, shānlai·wānlai.*
Caress, v.a. *nāzawul, nāz-, mīna-, dilāsa-*, etc. *k.*
Carious, a. *chinjan, wrost, skhā, shaṛhedalai.*
Carnage, s. *qatl, marg, khūn.*
Carnal, a. *nafsānī, shahwat·nāk, mast.*
Carnivorous, a. *ghwakkha·khor.* (-animal) *dad.*
Carol, v.a. *stāyal.* s. *stāyana.*
Carouse, v.a. *bad·masti k., sharāb tskkhal* or *tskal*; *nasha k.*
Carpenter, s. *tarkāṇr, darūz·gar.*
Carpet, s. *farsh*; *ghāla-ī, ghālīcha.* (cover for a-) *chāndānī.* (praying-) *saĵāda, muṣalla.*
Carriage, s. *gāḍa-ī*; *bār·bardārī, bār·kakkh*; *yūn, chāl, raftār*; *ḍaul, wajha.*
Carrier, s. *wṛūnkai*; *bār·kakkh. bār·bardār*; *harkārah, ḥammāl.*
Carrion, s. *murdār.*
Carrot, s. *gāzara, zardaka*
Carry, v.a. *wṛal, rāwṛal.*
Cart, s. *gāḍa-ī, arāba.* (-man) *gāḍa-ī·wān.*
Cartilage, s. *krachai, krachūnai, krapandūkai.* (-of the nose) *tandwai, tīndorai.*
Carve, v.a. *kanal* or *kanastal.* (-meat) *kūtal.*
Cascade, s. *tsādar, dāra, tandūra.*
Case s. *lifāfa, pokkh, ghilāf.* (sword-) *tekai, teka, miyān*; *kisbat, kīsa*; *ṣandūqcha, harpa-ī, ḥāl, ḥālat.*
Casement, s. *karka-ī.*
Cash, s. *naghd* or *naqd, rok.*
Casket, s. *dabalai, harpa-ī, ṣandūqcha.*
Cast, v.a. *wīshtal, āchawul. ghurzawul, lawastal.*
Cast, s. *kālbūt, ghālab* or *qālib.* (at play) *daw, guẓār.*
Caste, s. *rang, ẓāt, aṣl, qām* or *qaum, nog.*
Castle, s. *koṭ, qil'a, gaṛa-ī.*
Castor-oil, s. *da arhanḍo tel.*
Castrate, v.a. *khaṣṣī-, ākhtah-, malai-*, etc. *k.*
Casual, a. *qismatī, naṣībī, nā·gahān, nā·gūmān.*
Casualty, s. *āfat, kāna, nāzila.*
Cat, s. *pisho.* (tom-) *barghūṭ* or *narghūṭ.* (wild-) *pish·pṛāng.* (young-) *pishongaṛai.*
Catalogue, s. *siyāha.* (of men) *asāmī.*
Cataract, s *dāra, tsādar.* (of the eye) *parda, dund.*
Catarrh, s. *zukām, dūmai, sāṛa, yakhnī, nazla.*
Catastrophe, s. *balā, āfat, muṣībat, kāna.*
Catch, v.a. *nīwul, ākhistal, giriftār k.*
Catechize, v.a. *sawāl-, pukkhtana-*, etc. *k.*
Caterpillar, s. *pīsha-ī, chinjai.*
Catgut, s. *ĵa-ī, ĵaṇrai.*
Cattle, s. *tsārwai, ḍangar, māl, dāba.*
Caudle, s. *matar, lāwaṇr, kaṛa.*
Caught, v.n. *nkkhatal.* a. *nkkhatai.*
Caul, s. *obaṇra, da bachī parda.*
Cause, s. *sabab, jihat, kabl, bā-iṣ, wāsṭa*; *muqaddama.*

Cauterize, v.a. *dāghawul, dāgh lagawul.*
Cautious, a. *khabar-dār, hokkhyār, baidār.*
Cavalcade, s. *sparlī* or *swarlī ; jilaw.*
Cavalier, s. *spor* or *swor.*
Cavalry, s. *swārah, risāla.*
Cave, s. *smats* or *samist, ghār, kāz.*
Cavity, s. *doghal, ṭūbkai, jawara, kanda.*
Cease, v.a. *pregdal—prekkhodal—prekkhawul.* v.n. *ākhiredal, tamāmedal.*
Ceaseless, a. *mudāmī, dā-im.*
Cedar, s. *diyār.*
Cede, v.a. *pregdal, spāral, warkawul ; manal.*
Ceiling, s. *chat, bām, tsapar.*
Celebrate, v.a. *stāyal.* (-a day) *manal.*
Celebrated, a. *nūm-war, nām-dār, nāmer, mashhūr.*
Celebration, s. *stāyana ; manana.*
Celestial, a. *āsmānī, jannatī.*
Celibacy, s. *lawand-tob, tsaṛah-wālai.*
Cell, s. *khūna, koṭa ; gokkha, hujra.*
Cellar, s. *tah-khāna.*
Cement, s. *salekkh.* (mortar) *kūnai, gach.*
Cemetery, s. *maqbara, rauẓa ; qabristān, goristān, hadera.* (-of saints) *ziyārat, dargāh.*
Censer, s. *mujmir.*
Censor, s. *muḥtasib.*
Censure, v.a. *malāmat k., ṭaqawul, raṭal, traṭal.* (-oneself) *gram k.*
Cent, s. *sil.* (per-) *saikaṛa, pa sil, sil pase.*
Centipede, s. *zanza.*
Central, a. *miyānah, mandzai* or *mandzwai.*
Centre, s. *mandz* or *myandz.*
Centuple, a. *sil-bragh, sil-chand.*
Century, s. *sil-kāl.*
Cerate, s. *malham, paha, mom-roghan.*
Ceremony, s. *madār, khāṭir, makh, adab, taklīf, dastūr, rasm.*
Certain, a. *yaqīn, taḥqīq, ṣaḥīḥ, muqarrar.* (-one) *palānkai* or *falānai.*
Certainly, ad. *be shakk, albatta, rikkhtiyā.*
Certainty, s. *yaqīnī, zbād, taḥqīqī, iṣbāt.*
Certificate, s. *sanad, chīṭa-ī, kāghaẓ.*
Certify, v.a. *yaqīn-, zbād-, ṣābit-, taḥqīq-,* etc. *k.; khabar-, āgāh-,* etc. *k.*
Chafe, v.a. *blodal, sūlawul, mugal—mukkhal.* v.n. *blosedal, sūledal, sūdah ked.* (grieve) *ghamedal, sūledal, kaṛedal.*
Chaff, s. *būs, proṛ, sūṛī.* (of rice) *khamache.* (of corn, etc.) *drūze, gadzāre.*
Chagrin, s. *randz, khapagān, nūl, gram.*
Chain, s. *zandzīr.* (-link) *kaṛa-ī.*
Chair, s. *kursī, chaukī ; kaṭkai, peṛa-ī.*
Chalk, s. *spīna-khāwra.*
Challenge, v.a. *jang gokkhtal ; d'awa-,* etc. *k.* v.n. *gwākkhedal.*
Challenger, s. *mudd'a-ī ; jang joe ; gwākkhkai.*
Chamber, s. *koṭa, khūna.*
Chameleon, s. *karboṛai, tsarmakkhkai.*
Champ, v.a. *krapawul, chīchal.*
Champaign, s. *maidān, sama, ṣaḥrā.*
Champion, s. *pahalwān, tūrzan, bahādur.*
Chance, s. *naṣīb, qismat ; wār, puk ; daw.* v.n. *nāziledal, prewatal, wāqi'a ked.*
Change, v.a. *badlawul.* (-money) *māṭawul.* v.n. *badledal, āwukkhtal, girzedal.*
Changeable, a. *nā-pāedār, nā-qalār ; khūshai, nīma-khwā.*
Channel, s. *lār ; nāla, rūd-khāna, lakkhtai.*
Chant, v.a. *sarod-, sandara-, badala-,* etc. *wayal.*
Chaos, s, *tor-tam, ẓulmat.*
Chapter, s. *bāb, faṣl.* (of Qurān) *sūra.*
Character, s. *khoe, khaṣlat ; ṣifat, khāṣṣiyat ; nūm, nāmūs ; bashanj, pat.*
Charcoal, s. *skor.* (pl. *skārah*). (live-) *sarwaṭka* or *skarwaṭa.*
Charge, s. *amānat, spārah, sipurd, ḥawāla.* (order) *ḥukm, kariya, farmān.* (price) *bai'a. qīmat.* (expense) *kharts.* (onset) *halla, tsoṭ, guzār, brīd.* (advice) *maṣlaḥat.* (prohibitory) *qadaghan.*

Charge, v.a. *spāral, amānat-*, etc. *k.* **(order)** *farmāyal, ḥukm-*, etc. *warkawul.* (accuse) *d'awa k., tuhmat-, tor-*, etc., *-pore k.* (attack) *halla-*, etc. *k.* (load) *ḍakawul.* (enjoin) *tākīd-*, etc. *k., pohawul.* (in accounts) *kharts līkal.*

Charger, s. *jangī ās*; *tabākh, ghāb* or *qāb, tasht.*

Charitable, a. *sakhī, khairātī, sakhāwatī.*

Charity, s. *khairāt*; *zakāt, ṣadqa, sarsāya.*

Charm, s. *t'awīz.* (kind of) *mara-ī, tāwītah, amel, dawā, ṭilism.* (for snakes, etc.) *pāṛ.* (juggle) *mantar, koda, jādū, siḥr, hūda.*

Charm, v.a. *hūda-, dam-*, etc. *k.*; *pāṛawul*; *jādū-*, etc. *k., fareftah k., ghulawul.*

Charmer, s. *jādū·gar, koḍ·gar, siḥr·gar.* (snake-) *pāṛū.* (mistress) *dil·bar, dil·rubā, nāznīna.*

Charming, a. *kkhāyastah, khwakkh, khwand·nāk.*

Chart, s. *nakhkkha* or *naqsha.*

Charter, s. *sanad, 'ahd·nāma, iqrār·nāma.*

Chase, s. *kkhkār, ṣaid*; *pairawī, manḍa.* v.a. *kkhkār k., takkhtawul, zghalawul, pase manḍe·wahal.*

Chasm, s. *ḍoghal, ṭūbkai, gorhanda, gaṛang*; *kanda, chāwd, jawara.*

Chaste, a. *pāk·laman, ṇeko·kār, pākīzah, pāk.*

Chat, v.a. *kitī·pitī khabare k.*

Chatter, v.a. *bak·bak-, ṭar·ṭar-, chiṛ·chiṛ*, etc. *k.*

Chattels, s. *asbāb, kālī, sāmān, māl, bar·bast.*

Cheap, a. *arzān, wal* or *wel, spuk.*

Cheapness, s. *arzān·tiyā, wel·wālai.*

Cheat, s. *ṭag, farebī, darghal, sādū, makār, chal·bāz, chal·walai*; *ṭagī, droh, chal, makr.*

Cheat, v.a. *ṭagal, ṭagī-, fareb-, chal·bāzī-, darghalī-*, etc. *k., drohawul.*

Check, v.a. *hiṭālawul, ḥiṣārawul, man'a k., sambālawul, nkkhlawul, wudrawul.*

Cheek, s. *angai, anangai,* **koka-ī,** *bārkho.*

Cheer, s. *chigha, nāra*; *ārām, khwakkhī*; *'aish, khwand, maza*; *kkhādī*; *melmastiyā.*

Cheer, v.a. *chighe-*, etc. *wahal*; *tasallī-, dilāsa-*, etc. *k.*

Cheerful, a. *khwakkh, khūsh·ḥāl, kkhād, kkhādān, kkhād·man, khandā·rūe.*

Cheerless, a. *be dil, be ārām*; *khwār, lūts.*

Cheese, s. *panīr.* (soft-) *bagora, potsa.* (hard-) *qurut.*

Chequer, v.a. *brag-, gag-, rangīn-, chrag·brag-*, etc. *k.*

Cherish, v.a. *pālal, parwaral, nmāndzal*; *sātal, jghoral, khundiyal.*

Cherisher, a. *pālūnkai, parwarūnkai.* (in comp.) *parwar.*

Chess, s. *shatranj.* (-board) *bisāṭ*, (king) *shāh.* (queen) *wazīr.* (castle) *rukh.* (knight) *asp.* (bishop) *pīl.* (pawn) *piyādah.* (check) *kisht.* (checkmate) *māt.* (-player) *shatranj·bāz.*

Chest, s. *ṭaṭar, sīna.* (the cavity) *gargas, gogal.* (clothes-, etc.) *taunra-ī, ṣandūq.*

Chestnut, s. *banj, banj·pāṛ.* a. *surang.*

Chew, v.a. *chīchal, jowul, krapawul.* (the cud) *shkhwand k.*, or *-wahal*, or *-māṭawul.*

Chicken, s. *chirgūṛai, chūchai.* (-pox) *katswak.*

Chide, v.a. *raṭal, traṭal, peghorawul, dāṛal.*

Chief, a. *mashar, awwal, wṛūnbai.* s. *sardār, arbāb, khān, malik, ra-is, sarghanah, rāhīṭ.*

Chiefly, ad. *akṣar, wṛūnbe, awwalan.*

Chiefship, s. *khānī, sardārī, malikī.*

Child, s. *bachai, woṛkai, wṛūkai, māshūm*; *farzand, tūng.*

Childbirth, s. *langa, lang·wālai, langa·tob.*

Childhood, s. *halak·wālai, wṛūk·wālai, halkat, halkīna.*

Childish, a. *halak·shān*; *nā·dān.*

Childless, a. *lā·walad, be zawzāt, be farzand.* (by death) *būr.*

Chill, a. *soṛ, yakh.* s. *sāṛa, yakhnī.*

Chilliness, s. *soṛ·wālai, yakhnī, sāṛa*

Chime, v.a. *tarāne wayal, trangawul, tāl wahal.* v.n. *trangedal, granjedal.* s. *trang, tāl, tarāna.*

Chimney, s. *lū·kakkh, da lūgī sūrai.*

Chin, s. *zana, zanakh, zanakh·dān.* (double-) *ghab·ghab, jajūra.*

Chink, s. *chāwd, darz, rakhna, chāq.* (sound) *shrang, granj.* v.n. *shrangedal, granjedal.*

Chintz, s. *chīt.*

Chip, s. *ṭoṭa, ṭoṭkai, tūtankai, tarāza.*

Chipped, a. *būrai.*

Chirp, v.a. *chanr·chanr-, chir·chir-,* etc. *k.*

Chisel, s. *tswarlai, kkhatsulai* or *shatsurlai.*

Choice, a. *ghwarah, kkhah, khāṣṣ.* s. *wāk, ikhtiyār; khwakkh, pasand, razā.*

Choke, v.a. *khapah k., mara-ī khapa k.* v.n. *khapah ked.*

Cholera, s. *wabā.*

Choose, v.a. *khwakkhawul, chunral, laṭawul, anrawul, kkhāghal, pasand k.*

Chop, v.a. *kūtal, warĵal, ṭoṭa·ṭoṭa-, bĵa-,* etc. *k.*

Christ, s. *ḥazrat 'īsā, rūḥ·ullah.*

Christian, s. *'īsāwī, naṣārā; tarsā.*

Christianity, s. *'īsāwī mazhab* or *-dīn.*

Chronic, a. *der·pā, multawī.*

Chronicle, s. *tawārīkh; akhbār; roz·nāma.*

Chuckle, v.n. *khandedal, musedal.* (over enemy) v.a. *sakha k., wiyāral.* (as a fowl) *chugh·chugh k.*

Chum, s. *mal, malgarai; hānḍa-ī·wāl; ḥujra·wāl.*

Church, s. *masjid, jumā'at.*

Churl, s. *gawār, dihqān, ghunḍāyah; lwāṛ; bakhīl, shūm.*

Churn, v.a. *shā. bal.*

Churning, s. *shārbal.* (-stick) *manḍānrū.* (-tie) *barangai.* (-strap) *rog, tasma.* (-dish) *donra-ī.* (-cover) *barghol ai.*

Cinder, s. (cold-) *skor.* (hot-) *skarwaṭa, khuglan, skhwakkhtan.*

Cinnabar, s. *shingrap.*

Cinnamon, s. *dārchīnī.*

Circle, s. *tsarkh, churlai, chambar, dā-ira.*

Circuit, s. *daur, daurān; gakkht.*

Circular, a. *ghūnd* or *ghūnd·man, tsarkhai.*

Circulate, v.a. *chalawul, girzawul, jārī k.* v.n. *chaledal, girzedal, jārī ked.*

Circumcision, s. *sunnat, khatna.*

Circumspect, a. *hokkhyār, baidār, khabar·dār, pokh.*

Circumstance, s. *ḥālat, ḥāl; khabara.*

Circus, s. *jaulān·gāh.*

Cistern, s. *ḥauẓ, baha-ī, talāo, ḍanḍ.*

Citadel, s. *qil'a, koṭ, gaṛa-ī, arg, bālā·ḥiṣār.*

Cite, v.a. *balal, ṭalab k.; yādawal.*

Citizen, s. *kkhahr·wāl; daftarī.*

Citron, s. *nīmbū, triw nāranj.*

City, s. *kkhahr.*

Civil, a. *mulkī, dīwānī: makhawar, sulūkī, mihrbān.* (-court) *mulkī 'adālat.* (-war) *patna, khāna·jangī.* (-power) *'adālat.*

Civilian, s. *'āmmī; kasb·gar; ahl da qalam.*

Civility, s. *makhawarī, makh·tob, madār, adab, nek·sulūk, mihrbāngī.*

Civilize, v.a. *ābādawul, kkhāyastah-, ārāstah-,* etc. *k. sarī·tob chalawul.*

Claim, v.a. *d'awa-, darkhwāst-,* etc. *k.*

Claimant, s. *mudd'aī, dād·khwāh, d'awa·dār.*

Clammy, a. *bokkht, slekkht·nāk, barwai, chaspān.*

Clamour, s. *zwag·zwūg, shor·shaghab, ghoghā.*

Clamp, s. *patrai.*

Clan, s. *qām, khel, firqa, ulūs, ṭabar, cham.*

Clandestine, a. *puṭ, pinham, ghalai.*

Clangour, s. *shrang, granj, trang.*

Clap, v.a. (the hands) *tāl wahal; shābāsh k.*

Clapper, s. *ṭak·ṭakānrai, ĵiba, spai.*

Clarify, v.a. *pāk-, pākīzah-, spīn-, ṣāf-,* etc. *k.*

Clarion, s. *sarnāe.* (-player) *sarnāchī.*

Clash, v.a. *blodal, ṭakar-, ḍaka,-* etc. *khwuṛal.* v.n. *blosedal.*

Clasp, v.a. *pa ghegi nīwul; bargrandī k.*
Class, s. *aṣl, zāt, rang, nogai; ṭolai, cham, khel; darja, pāya.*
Classification, s. *tartīb, dzerma.*
Clatter, v.a. *trangawul, shrangawul, granjawul.*
Clause, s. *faṣl; shart.*
Clavicle, s. *grewa.*
Claw, s. *changul, mangul, panja, nūk.* v.a. *panja-*, etc. *wahal, nūkāra k.*
Clay, s. *maṭa-* or *maṭīna khāwra, khaṭa.*
Clayey, a. *maṭīn, khāwrīn.*
Clean, a. *pāk, pākīzah, ṣāf, spīn.* v.a. *pāk-*, etc. *k.*
Clear, a. *pāk, ṣaf; tsargand, kkhkārah, bartser, awtsār, bewrah; yalah, āzād, khalāṣ.* v.a. *spetsal, pākawul, spīn-*, etc. *k. tsargand-*, etc. *k. yalah-*, etc. *k.* (-the throat) *ghāṛa tāza k.*
Clearness, s. *pāk·wālai; tsargand·wālai*, etc.
Cleave, v.a. *chawul.* (asunder) *chaurang, k. prekawul.* (-to) v.n. *nkkhatal, lagedal, chaspedal.*
Cleaver, s. *ṭoqiyā, sāṭūl; prekawūnai.*
Cleft, s. *chāwd, chāq, wat, darz; kandaw, kand.*
Clemency, s. *ḥalīmī, shafaqat, raḥmat.*
Clement, a. *ḥalīm, mulā-im, raḥīm, narm.*
Clergy, s. *pādriyān, mullāyān, bāmbanrān.*
Clerk, s. *kātib, līkūnkai, kkhkawūnkai.*
Clever, a. *hokkhyār, pohānd, pokh; hunr·man, kārī·gar, qābil; kāgh, chirg.*
Client, s. *d'awa·gar, mudd'a-ī.*
Cliff, s. *kamar, tsaka, lākkh.*
Climate, s. *āb·o·hawā, hiwād, iqlīm.*
Climb, v.n. *khatal.*
Climber, s. *khatūnai.* (plant) *bel.*
Cling, v.n. *nkkhatal, chaspedal, lagedal.*
Clink, v.n. *shrangedal, granjedal.*
Clip, v.a. (hair, etc.) *skustal, kaṭeyal.* (cloth, etc.) *skakkhtal.* (dock) *ghūṭ k.* or *-prekawul.* (hair of head), *sar·kunḍai k.*

Cloak, s. *bārāna-ī; chogha, baraka.* (felt-) *kosai.* (fur-) *postīn.* (blanket-) *junga kiṛi shaṛa-ī.*
Clock, s. *gaṛī, sā'at.*
Clod, s. *lūṭa, chūm, gapa.*
Clog, s. *kanrāwa; haṭāl, nkkhata, bār.* v.a. *haṭālawul, kariyābawul, nkkhlawul.*
Close, v.a. *bandawul, joṛawul, lagawul, pewand k.; tamāmawul, khatm k.* (a door) *pore k.* (a book) *ṭapawul* or *ṭap wahal.*
Close, s. *ākhir, khatm; bāra, shpol, haḍera.*
Close, a. *nijdai; tang; pewastah; bakhīl, shūm; ṭīng, tat, ganr.* (as cloth) *ṭok.* (as stars) *jambaq.* (-cut) *ghūṭ, lanḍ.*
Closeness, s. *nijdekī; tang·wālai; pewastagī; bakhīlī, shūm·wālai; ṭīng·wālai.*
Closet, s. *ḥujra, khūna; gūṭ, gokkha.*
Cloth, s. *karbās, khāmtā; alwān, chīṭ*, etc. (woollen-woven-) *paṭū, baraka, shaṛa-ī, pashmīna*, etc. (woollen-unwoven-) *krāsta, lamtsai, kosai, namada*, etc. (broadcloth) *banāt.*
Clothe, v.a. *āghustawul, pokkhal, poslal; āghostal.*
Clothes, s. *zaṛūkī, nwarī* or *nmarī, pokkhāk, āghostan, libās, jāme.* (swaddling-) *oranrai.*
Cloud, s. *waryadz.*
Clout, s. *chīṛa, khartsoṛai, taghar.* (loin-) *lung, chotai, taṛāqa-ī.* (child's-) *kūna·starkai; taṛūnai.*
Clove, s. *lawang.* (-necklace) *lawang·hāṛ.*
Cloven, a. (cleft) *chāwd, chāq.* (-hoof) *swa.*
Clover, s. *speshtarai, shautal, speshtai.*
Clown, s. *ṭoq·mār, malanḍai, pekkhe·gar, maskharāchī; gawār, pūhaṛ, kāwāk, shāṛ.*
Cloy, v.a. *sekan k., kraka ākhistal.*
Club, s. *amsā, koṭak, lawaṛ, ḍāng.* (society) *cham, ṣuḥbat, jumā'at.*
Cluck, v.a. *kuṛ·kuṛ k.*
Clue, s. *belga* or *balga, darak.*
Clumsy, a. *kāwāk, bad·wajha, bad·ḍaul.*

Cluster, s. *wagai, khosha*; *ganr, tolai.*
Clutch, v.a. *pa mūṭ nīwul, ghoṭa-, chapa-*, etc. *nīwul* or *wahal.*
Coagulate, v.a. *ṭīngawul, klakawul, tomna-, māya-*, etc. *k.* v.n. *kangal-, khyam-*, etc. *ked.*
Coalesce, v.n. *gaḍedal, yo·dzāe ked.*
Coarse, a. *lwār, ghaṭ.*
Coast, s. *ghāṛa, ḍaḍa, tselma.*
Coat, s. *kurta, kadā-ī, khalqa, qādara-ī, lanḍa-ī, andraka.* (-for rain) *bārāna-ī.* (-of mail) *zghara, zira.*
Coax, v.a. *dam-, dam·dilāsa-, jāna-*, etc. *k.*, *jigī-jigī-, hāṛe·hāṛe-*, etc, *k.*
Cobbler, s. *mochī, tsamyār.*
Cobweb, s. *jāla-ī.*
Cock, s. *chirg.* (game-) *panḍāw·chirg.* (of a gun) *pāe, kajak.* (-crow) *charbāng* or *chirg·bāng.*
Cockade, s. *jogha, tūgh, zunbuk.*
Code, s. *shar'a.* (Afghan-) *pukkhtūn·walī.*
Co-equal, a. *siyāl, makhai, gund.*
Coerce, v.a. *zoral, lānde k.*
Coeval, a. *hum·dzolai, hum·'umr.*
Coffer, s. *khizāna.*
Coffin, s. *tābūt.*
Cog, v.a. *chāplūsī-, ḍirpalī-*, etc. *k.*, *ghulawul.* (of a wheel) s. *būṛai.*
Cohabit, v.a. *kilai-, kor-*, etc. *k.*, *kor·wālai k.*
Cohesive, a. *bokkht, barwai, slekkht·nāk.*
Coil, s. *pech, tāo, wal.*
Coin, s. *sika, paisa, naghd* or *naqd.* (counterfeit-) *jūṭah, nā·sarah.*
Coincide, v.n. *jukht-, barābar-, joṛ-*, etc. *lagedal.*
Cold, a. *soṛ, yakh.* s. *sāṛa, yakhnī*; *zukām, dūmai, nuzla.*
Colic, s. *bād·gola, sūda, shwala.*
Collapse, v.n. *drabal, aluwal·prewatal.*
Collar, s. *grewān.* (-of a dress) *grewa.* (neck-) *ṭauq.* (dog-) *ghaṛwandai.*

Colleague, s. *mal, malgarai.*
Collect, v.a. *ṭolawul, gaṭal, jam'a k.*, *laṭawul.*
College, s. *madrassa, maktab.*
Collision, s. *daka, ṭakaṛ*; *blos, blosedana.*
Colocynth, s. *maṛaghūnai, tarkha kakora.*
Colloquial, s. *da 'āmmiyāno jiba, wrāsha.*
Collusion, s. *joṛikkht, ṭagī, sāzish.*
Collyrium, s. *rānjah, surma, kuhal.* (-case) *rānjaṛūma.* (-bodkin) *salā ī.*
Colonize, v.a. *ābādawul, wadānawul.*
Colony, s. *bānḍa, nawū-ī*; *ābādī, wadānī.*
Colour, s. *rang, laun.* v.a. *rangawul.*
Coloured, a. *rangīn, rang kaṛai.*
Colours, s. *nakkha, janḍa, bairaq, togh.*
Colt, s. *bihānr.* (two-year-old-) *dwak.*
Column, s. *tsalai, munār, stan* or *sitūn.*
Comb, s. *gamanz* or *mangaz*; *shāna.* (honey-) *gabīna.* (cock's-) *chār·khwalak.* (curry-) *ghasho.*
Combat, s. *jang, muqaddama.*
Combatant, s. *jangī, mlā·taṛ, tūrzan.*
Combine, v.a. *joṛawul*; *gaḍawul, laṛal.*
Come, v.n. *rātlal—rāghlal, rasedal.*
Comedy, s. *malanḍa, pekkha, ṭoqa, swāng,*
Comely, a. *kkhkulai, kkhāyastah, pa-ī·makhai.*
Comet, s. *da jārū storai.*
Comfort, s. *ārām, mor·tiyā, ārām·tiyā*; *dilāsa, tasallī, ḍāḍ, khwā·khogī.*
Coming, a. *gāndah, āyandah.*
Command, s. *ḥukm, kariya, farmān, amr*; *wāk, was, qābū*; *farẓ.* v.a. *farmāyal, ḥukm-*, etc. *k.*
Commander, s. *ḥākim, sardār, sar·guroh.*
Commence, v.a. *ibtidā-, shur'ū-, darak-*, etc. *k.*
Commend, v.a. *stāyal, sipārish k.*
Commendation, s. *stāyana, sipārish.*
Commerce, s. *saudāgarī, wapār, lāgī, rākṛah·warkṛah.*
Commissary, s. *dāroghah*; *āstādzai.*
Commission, s. *sanad, 'uhda*; *parwāna, farmān*; *kār.*

Commit, v.a. *spāral, pāslawul, ,jumāral, ḥawāla-*, etc. *k.*; *kawul, kṛal.* (-adultery) *zinā-, kāsīrī-*, etc. *k.* (-robbery) *ghlā k.*
Committee, s. *jirga, m'arika, majlis.*
Commodious, a. *munāsib, lā-iq, pīrzo.*
Commodity, s. *māl, jins, saudā.*
Common, a. *'āmm, jārī, chalan.* s. *maidān, panḍ·ghālai, ḍāga, ṭikārkai*; *borjal.*
Commonly, ad. *akṣar, ziyātī.*
Community, s. *cham* or *jam, khel, ulūs*; *rāsha·darsha, gāwar ḍī·tob, malgar·tiyā.*
Compact, a. *ganr* or *gūr*; *tat, ṭīng.* (-cloth) *ṭoq.* (-crops) *ṭal.* s. *wāda, lafẓ, ṭaṛa, neṭa.*
Companion, s. *mal, malgarai*; *āshnāe, rafīq.*
Company, s. *majlis*; *ṭolai, paṛk, ghol*; *malgīrī, āshnā-ī*; *melmastiyā, ṣuḥbat.*
Comparison, s. *muqābala, miṣāl, nisbat.*
Compass, s. *qibla·numāe*; *chāper, gakkht*; *ḥadd, dzāe.* (reach) *partāb.* v.a. *ḥiṣārawul* or *īsārawul.*
Compasses, s. *pargār.*
Compassion, s. *dard, raḥm, zṛah·swai, tars.*
Compatible, a. *munāsib, pīrzo*; *barābar.*
Compel, v.a. *zoral, lānde k.*
Compensate, v.a. *tāwān-, nāgha-, badal-*, etc. *warkawul.*
Competence, s. *kifāyat, rozī.*
Competent, a. *qābil, lā-iq.*
Competition, s. *muqābala.*
Complacent, a. *ḥalīm, post, narm, makhawar.*
Complainant, s. *mudd'a-ī, faryādī, d'awa·gar*; *gila·man.*
Complaint, s. *nālish, māna, gila, faryād.*
Complaisance, s. *makh·tob, makhawarī, narmī, mihrbāngī.*
Complete, a. *pūrah, tamām, khatm, kāmil*; *bashpaṛ, amānī.*
Complex, a. *gaḍ·waḍ*; *grān, mushkil.*
Complexion, s. *da tsihre rang, charda, mizāj.* (dark-) *kaloṭ.*
Compliment, s. *madār, adab, salām, makh.*
Comply, v.a. *manal, qubūlawul.* v.n. *rāẓī ked.*
Compose, v.a. *joṛawul*; *tartīb-, ārāstah-*, etc. *k.*; *saṛawul*; *līkal, kāgal-kkhkal.*
Composition, s. *gaḍūn, gaḍedana, gaḍa.*
Compound, v.a. *gaḍawul.* a. *gaḍ.*
Comprehend, v.n. *pohedal.*
Comprehension, s. *poh, pahm, fikr.*
Compress, v.a. *chit k., drabawul.*
Comprise, v.a. *shāmil-, yo·dzāe-*, etc. *k.*
Compute, v.a. *ganral, shmeral, ḥisābawul.*
Comrade, s. *mal, malgarai, yār.*
Concave, a. *jawar, ḍoghal.*
Conceal, v.a. *puṭawul, pokkhal, ghalai k.*
Concealment, s. *puṭ·wālai, puṭedana, ghalī·tob.*
Concede, v.a. *manal, qabūlawul, bakkhal.*
Conceit, s. *khpul·sarī, bād, wiyāṛ, kibr.*
Conceited, a. *bādī, khpul·sar, kibr·jan.*
Conceivable, a. *shwūnkai.*
Conceive, v.n. *pohedal.* v.a. *fikr-, qiyās-*, etc. *k.*; *blārbedal, ḍakedal.*
Conception, s. *poh, pahm, fikr, qiyās, khiyāl*; *blārbedana, blārba·wālai, umed, ḍaka.*
Concern, s. *kār, m'amala*; *gham, fikr, parwā*; *andekkhnā, wiswās.*
Concerned, a. *gham·jan, fikr·man*; *wiswāsī, andekkh·nāk.*
Concerning, p. *bābat, ḥaqq.*
Concert, s. *ittipāq*; *malgar·ṭiyā*; *zamzama.*
Conciliate, v.a. *pakhulā k., gwākkhal.*
Concise, a. *lanḍ, kotāh.*
Conclude, v.a. *tamāmawul, ākhir-, khatm-*, etc. *k., khalāṣawul*; *m'alūmawul, ganral.* v.n. *pohedal.*
Concord, s. *rogha, joṛa, āshtī, ashtoka.*
Concourse, s. *ṭolai, jumā'at, ganr·'ālam.*
Concubine, s. *wīndza, 'aurata, sūryata.*
Concupiscence, s. *nas, mastī, shahwat.*
Concur, v.n. *yo·jihat-, yo·zṛah-, rāẓī-*, etc. *ked.*

Concussion, s. *ṭakar, ḍaka.*
Condemn, v.a. *bad manal, man'a k.*; *gunāh-, wabāl-, taqṣīr*, etc., *ṣābitawul* or *dzāyawul.*
Condescend, v.a. *mihrbāngī-, makh-, mulāḥiẓa-, madār-*, etc. *k.*
Condiment, s. *masāla.*
Condition, s. *ḥāl, ḥālat, ṣūrat, yang, shān*; *wāda, neṭa, lafẓ, sharṭ.*
Condole, v.a. *lās·nīwah k.*; *pātiḥa wayal, khwā·khogī k., pokkhal.*
Conduct, s. *chāl·chal, chalan, ṭarīqa*, etc.; *badraga*; *sulūk, madār, makh.*
Conduct, v.a. *badraga k., botlal—bīwul*; *rāwustal, rawānawul, chalawul.*
Confection, s. *ḥalwā, miṭiyā-ī, qanāt, shīrīnī.*
Confederacy, s. *para, janba, gundī.*
Confederate, s. *para·dār, janba·dār*; *mal.*
Conference, s. *jirga, maṣlaḥat, sawāl·dzawāb.*
Confess, v.a. *manal, khwāla wayal.* v.n. *qāiledal.*
Confidence, s. *bāwar, yaqīn, sāwīsā, khal, i'tibār.*
Confine, v.a. *band-, qaid-, ḥiṣār* or *īsār-*, etc. *k.*
Confirm, v.a. *rikkhtiyā-, zbād-, ṣābit-, taḥqīq-*, etc. *k.*
Confiscate, v.a. *nāgha-, ẓabṭ-, qurugh-*, etc. *k.*
Confluence, s. *gaḍedana.*
Conform, v.n. *yo·shān-, yo·ḍaul-, yo·makh-, yo·zṛah-*, etc. *ked.*
Confound, v.a. *gaḍ·waḍawul, laṛal, shārbal*; *ḥariyānawul, rabṛawul, sargardānawul, pareshān-, hak·pak-, hekkh-, huts-*, etc. *k.*
Confront, v.a. *makhā·makh-, muqābala*, etc. *k.*
Confute, v.a. *lā·dzawāb-, gram-, radd-*, etc. *k.*
Congeal, v.n. *ṭīngedal, kangal ked.*; *khyam ked.*
Congratulate, v.a. *mubārakī k.* or *wayal.*
Congregation, s. *ṭolai, jamā'at, majlis.*
Conjecture, s. *gūmān, 'aql, khiyāl.*
Conjugal, a *da tsakkhtan aw da kkhadze, da wādah karai aw da wadedali.*
Conjunction, s. *pewand, joṛ, taṛūn.*
Conjuncture, s. *wakht, neṭa, nobat, ṭāng.*
Conjure, v.a. *qasam-, saugand-*, etc. *warkawul*; *jādū-, koḍa-*, etc. *k.*
Conjurer, s. *jādū·gar, koḍ·gar, siḥr·gar.*
Connect, v.a. *joṛawul, lagawul, taṛal.*
Connexion, s. *joṛ, band, taṛūn*; *nisbat*; *ragai, khpulawī, khekkhī.* (carnal-) *gho, ghowūna, kor·wālai.*
Connive, v.a. *starge puṭawul.*
Connubial, a. See Conjugal.
Conquer, v a. *barai k.*, or *-mūndal, pa-aṛ k.*, etc.
Conquest, s. *barai, wa-aṛa, wa-aṛāna.*
Conscience, s. *īmān, diyānat*; *rikkhtīn·tob.*
Conscious, a. *khabar·dār, baidār, hokkhyār.*
Consecrate, v.a. *niyāz-, khairāt-*, etc. *k.*, or *-manal.*
Consent, s. *raẓā, qabūl, hokai, oe.*
Consequence, s. *natīja*; *pāzah.*
Consequently, ad. *dzaka, tro.*
Consider, v.a. *fikr-, pahm-, qiyās-*, etc. *k., andekkhnā-, hosh-*, etc. *k.*; *ganral.* v.n. *pohedal.*
Considerable, a. *loe, grān*; *ḍer*; *drund.*
Consign, v.a. *spāral, pāslawul, gumāral, ḥawāla k,*; *āstawul, legal.*
Consignment, s. *spārana, ḥawāla*; *asbāb, jins.*
Consist, v.n. *joṛedal, osedal, kedal, shwal.*
Consistent, a. *joṛ, sam*; *klak, ṭīng.*
Console, v.a. *tasallī-, dilāsā-, ḍāḍ-*, etc. *warkawul.*
Consort, s. *tsakkhtan, meṛah*; *kkhadza, artīna.* v.a. *kilai-, kor-, rozgār-, khasamāna-*, etc. *k.*; *yārī-, āshnā-ī-, malgīrī-*, etc. *k.*
Conspicuous, a. *tsargand, kkhkārah, mashhūr.*
Conspirator, s. *yāghī·gar, mufsid, pasātī.*
Conspire, v.a. *sāzish-, badī-*, etc. *k.*
Constant, a. *pāedār, qā-im.*
Constantly, ad. *har·wakht, har·sā'at.*

Consternation, s. *hariyānī, sargardānī*; *khof, yera, bāk, tor, tars, tarhara.*
Constipation, s. *qabz, qabziyat.*
Constituent, a. *aslī, zātī.*
Constitute, v.a. *joṛawul, wudrawul, paidā-, muqarrar-*, etc. *k.*, *wulāṛawul.*
Constitution, s. *mizāj, tab'a, khwā.*
Constrain, v.a. *zoral, sambālawul, ṭīngawul.*
Construct, v.a. *joṛawul, binā k.*
Consul, s. *wakīl, mukhtār.*
Consult, v.a. *jirga-, maslahat-, mashwarat-*. etc. *k.*
Consume, v.a. *sarf-, talaf-, kharts-*, etc. *k.*
Consummate, a. *pūrah, pokh, kāmil.*
Consumption, s. *kharts, sarfa*; *narai·randz, diqq, sill.*
Contact, s. *joṛ, lagedana*; *blos, blosedana.* (to come in-) v.n. *blosedal, jangedal, lagedal.*
Contagion, s. *wabā*; *gazak.*
Contain, v.a. *dzāyawul.* v.n. *dzāedal.*
Contaminate, v.a. *palīt-, nā·pāk-, skhā-, kakaṛ-, gazak-*, etc. *k.*
Contemn, v.a. *spuk ganṛal.*
Contemplate, v.a. *ghaur-, fikr-*, etc. *k.*; *nandāra-, tamāsha-*, etc. *k.*
Contemporary, s. *hum·dzolai, hum·wakht, kūl.*
Contemptible, a. *spuk, dūn, khushai.*
Contemptuous, a. *kibr·jan, bādī, be makh.*
Contend, v.a. *jagṛa-, qaziya-, takrār-*, etc. *k.*
Content, a. *rāzī, moṛ.* s. *razā, moṛ·tiyā.*
Context, s. *matan, 'ibārat, mazmūn.*
Contiguous, a. *nijdai, pewastah.*
Continent, a. *parhez·gār, pāk·laman.* s. *zmaka, barr, wucha.*
Contingent, a. *mauqūf*; *'ārizī.*
Continual, a. *pāedār, jārī, dā-im, pāyandah.*
Continuance, s. *pāedārī, mudāmī, dā-imī.*
Continue, v.n. *pāedal, osedal, pātedal.*
Contortion, s. *tāo, pech, wal, kālkūchaka.*
Contour, s. *makh, gūna, tsihra, shakl, ḍaul.*
Contract, s. *wāda, neṭa, bandanṛ, lafz*; *ṭeka.*
Contract, v.a. *tangawul, kāgal—kkhkal.* (a promise) *wāda-, neṭa-*, etc. *taṛal* or *k.* (a debt) *por ākhistal.* (a marriage) *wādah k., nikāh taṛal.* v.n. *kawt ked.*
Contradict, v.a. *khilāf wayal, radd-, darogh·jan-, hoḍ-*, etc. *k.*
Contrary, a. *khilāf, mukhālif, hoḍai.* s. *'aks, hoḍ.*
Contrast, v.a. *makhā·makh-, muqābala-*, etc. *k.*
Contrite, a. *tauba·gār, pakkhemān.*
Contrive, v.a. *band-, tadbīr-, hikmat-*, etc. *taṛal.*
Control, v.a. *sambālawul, qābū-, lānde-*, etc. *k., was chalawul.*
Controversy, s. *jagṛa, qaziya, radd·badal, bahs, hujjat, steza.*
Contumacy, s. *sarkakkhī, yāghī·garī.*
Contumely, s. *peghor, kkhkandzal, spuk·tiyā.*
Contusion, s. *blos, māṭūs, pūpaka, khūg, jobal.*
Convene, v.a. *ṭolawul, yo·dzāe k., balal.*
Convenient, a. *joṛ, pīrzo, khwakkh.*
Convention, s. *jirga, majlis, m'arika*; *wāda, taṛa, bandanṛ, neṭa.*
Conversant, a. *wāqif, āmokhtah, khabar·dār.*
Converse, v.a. *khabare k., sawāl·dzawāb k.*
Convert, v.a. *badlawul*: *murīd-, mutaqid-*, etc. *k.*
Convex, a. *ghūnḍ, gunbatī.*
Convey, v.a. (things) *āstawul, wṛal, legal.* (animals) *botlal—bīwul, rāwustal.*
Convict, s. *qaidī, bandī.*
Convict, v.a. *gunāh-*, etc. *zbād k.* or *sābit k.*
Convince, v.a. *qā-il k., gram k.*
Convivial, a. *khūsh·hāl, kkhād, khandā·rūe, melmah·dost.*
Convoke, v.a. *balal, ṭalab k., ṭolawul.*
Convoy, s. *badraga* or *badraqa.*
Convulsion, s. *ghoṭa, parghaz*; *balwā.*
Cook, v.a. *pakhawul.* s. *bāwarchī* or *barchī.*
Cool, a. *soṛ, yakh*; *be parwā*; *mānṛai·gar.*

Cool, v.a. *saṛawul, yakhawul.* v.n. *saṛedal.*

Coolness, s. *sāṛa, soṛ·wālai, yakhnī.* (pique) *marawar·tiyā, marawar·tob, mānṛai.*

Coop, s. (of leather) *daba.* (-maker) *dabāgh.*

Coping, s. *tsatsobai, bala-ī, parchaṭai, sarmātai, sharīfa.*

Copious, a. *ḍer, frewān.*

Copper, s. *tāmba.*

Copse, s. *jangai, darga, ghīl.*

Copulate, v.a. *ghayal—ghowul, kor·wālai-, gho-, jimā'a-*, etc. *k.*

Copy, s. *naql, namūna, nuskha*; *mashq.*

Coquetry, s. *nāz, nakhra, makez, karashma.*

Coral, s. *marjān.* (-diver) *marjīwanṛah.*

Cord, s. (thick-) *biyāsta, pa-aṛai, rasa-ī.* (thin-) *muzai, tār, spanṛsai.* (hair-) *antsa-ī, siyala-ī, wākkhkai.* (palm leaf-) *būnṛ.*

Core, s. *māghzah, zṛah, zaṛai.*

Coriander, s. *ḍaniya.*

Cork, s. (bung) *būja, ḍīḍa, khulborai.*

Cormorant, s. *kotān.* (glutton) *ghārai.*

Corn, s. *ghala, dāna.* (green-) *khwīd, khasīl.* (-stubble) *drūza.* (mowed-) *satrai.* (-sheaf) *geḍa-ī.* (-stack) *dala-ī.* (-bin) *kandū, koṭa-ī, khamba.* (-straw) *nāṛ.* (-broken straw) *būs.* (-treading floor) *dirmand, khirman.* (pile of trodden-) *wānṛa.* (of the foot) *baura-ī, rasaula-ī, kila-ī, mekh.*

Corner, s. *gūṭ, gokkha*; *dakhma.*

Corporeal, a. *jismānī.*

Corpse, s. *muṛai, lāsh, murdah.*

Corpulent, a. *tsorb, peraṛ, ghaṭ, punḍ.*

Correct, a. *joṛ, jukht, durust, barābar, sam, rikkhtiyā, kkhah.*

Correspond, v.n. *joṛ-, sam-, barābar-*, etc. *lagedal, makhai ked.* v.a. *chīṭa-ī-, kāghaz-*, etc. *līkal* or *kāgal—kkhkal* or *legal.*

Corroborate, v.a. *rikkhtiyā-, zbād-, ṣubūt-*, etc. *k.*

Corrode, v.a. *zang khwuṛal.* v.n. *zang ked.*

Corrupt, v.a. *bonṛawul, palītawul, kakaṛawul, skhā-, wrost-*, etc *k.*

Cost, s. *bai'a, kharts, qīmat*; *tāwān, nuqṣān.*

Costive, a. *qābiẓ, ṭīng, klak.*

Costiveness, s. *qabẓ, qabẓiyat.*

Costly, a. *qīmat·nāk, grān·bahā.*

Costume, s. *jāma, libās.*

Cot, s. *kaṭkai, kaṭolai.*

Cottage, s. *kaḍala, jūngaṛa.*

Cotton, s. *mālūch.* (-plant) *punba, kālaka.* (-seed) *pundāna.* (-stubble) *khirīz, khaṛanḍ.* (-stalks) *punbe·cho, kālak·cho.* (-pod) *ghoza.* (-picker) *panḍol·gar.* (his share) *panḍolī.* (-dresser) *naddāp, alāj.* (his mallet) *ḍabalai.* (his bow) *ḍānḍat.* (his gin) *alājī.* (carded-) *pāghunda.* (roll of-) *pūnṛa-ī.* (skein of-) *māshoṛa.* (-thread) *tonbiyā, aṭa.* (-reel) *aṭerān.*

Cough, s. *ṭūkhai, ṭūkha, ṭūkh·ṭūkh.* (hooping-) *pūkhalai, tora·ghāṛa, haba·ḍaba.* v.n. *ṭūkhedal.*

Council, s. *jirga, m'arika*; *dalbār, majlis.*

Counsel, s. *pand, naṣīḥat*; *maṣlaḥat, tadbīr, mashwarat*; *wakīl.*

Count, v.a. *shmeral, ḥisāb k.*; *ganṛal.*

Countenance, s. *makh, tsihra, bashra*; *mihrbāngī, mrasta, mulāḥiẓa.*

Counterfeit, a. *jūṭah, nā·sarah.* v.a. *bāna-, palma-, chal-, ṭagī-*, etc. *-k.*

Counterpane, s. *bṛastan, taltak.*

Counterpart, s. *joṛa, pala, makhai, dzawāb.*

Country, s. *mulk, hewād.* (own-) *waṭan.* (foreign-) *wilāyat.* (-man, etc.) *waṭanī.*

County, s. *pargana, tapa.*

Couple, s. *joṛa, qulba, juft*; *dwah.*

Courage, s. *maṛāna, mardī, zṛah, nar·tob, dilāwarī, tūrzan·tob, dzwān·mardī, himmat.*

Courageous, a. *maṛanai, zṛah·war, dilāwar, turzan, himmat·nāk.*

Courier, s. *qāṣid, chapar, āstādzai.*

Course, s. *zghākkht, manḍa*; *daur, daurān*; *yūn, chāl*; *lār*; *maidān.* (of-) ad. *albatta, be·shakk.*
Court, s. *dalbār, daulat·khāna.* (civil-) *'adālat, maḥkama.* (-yard) *gholai, anganr. jarvas.*
Court, v.a. *ghokkhtal*; *mīna-, 'ishq·bāzī-*, etc. *-k.*
Courteous, a. *makhawar, mihrbān, nek·khoe.*
Courtesan, s. *kachana-ī, lola-ī.*
Courtesy, s. *makh, mulāḥiza, adab, nek·sulūk.*
Courtier, s. *dalbārī.*
Courtship, s. *'ishq·bāzī, mīna, kkhpa·ārtūn, changhal·bāzī.*
Cousin, s. (father's brother's child) m. *tarbūr*; f. *tarla.* (mother's brother's child) *da māmā dzoe* or *lūr.*
Covenant, s. *wāda, taṛa, bandanr, 'ahd, qaul.*
Cover, s. *sar·pokkh, tekai, lifāfa.* (dish-) *bargholai.* (basket-) *kāra, sawada.*
Cover, v.a. *puṭawul, pokkhal.*
Covering, s. *pokkh, pokkhikkh, libās*; *miyān.*
Covet, v.a. *ṭam'a-. ḥirṣ-*, etc. *k.*
Covetous, a. *ṭam'a·jan, ḥirṣ·nāk, lirāl.*
Covey, s. *sail, ghol.*
Cow, s. *ghwā.* (-in heat) *ghwa-ema.* (milch-) *langa-*, or *pa-ī·wara ghwā.* (dry-) *zāṛa-ī.* (-pen) *ghojal.* (herd of-) *gohār.* (-dung) *ghoshoe.* (-dung fuel) *tsapiyāka,* (-dung stack) *gohāṭa.* (-keeper) *ghobah.*
Coward, s. *nā·mard, tuzan, kaṛū, sperkai, sperah·makh, taghan.*
Coy, a. *yer·man, sharm·sār, sharm·nāk, stāra prewatai.*
Crab, s. *kūnī·kabar, changākkh.* (-louse) *baṛora.*
Crack, s. *chāwd, darz, daṛa, rakhna.* (sound) *ḍaz, ṭas, trāk, khrach, ṭaq.*
Crack, v.n. *chāwdal, darz-.* etc. *ked.* v.a. *ḍaz-*, etc. *k.*, or *wahal.*
Crackle, v.n. *tsir·tsir-, sakkhā-*, etc. *ked.*

Cradle, s. *kaṭkai*; *zāngo, gahwāra.*
Craft, s. *kār, kasb, pesha*; *fareb, chal, ḥīla.*
Craftsman, s. *kārī·gar kasb·gar, pesha·war.*
Crafty, a. *chal·bāz, ḥīla·bāz, ṭag·bāz, farebī.*
Crag, s. *tsūka, kamar, garang.*
Cram, v.a. *manḍal, ḍakawu'.*
Cramp, s. *brekkh, tāo.*
Crane, s. *ḍing, zānrai, kulang.*
Crash, s. *khrach, khṛap, khṛas, drab,* v.n. *drabal, naṛedal.*
Crater, s. *garang, tortam, ḍoghal, kūhai.*
Crave, v.a. *ghokkhtal, minnat-, khwāst-*, etc. *k.*
Crawl, v.n. *tskhedal* or *tskedal, pa kharpotso tlal, ghūndzedal.*
Crazy, a. *lewanai, khushai, saudā-ī.*
Creak, v.n. *chingedal, trangedal.*
Cream, s. *perawai.*
Crease, s. *jūhaṛa, kṛaṭai, chīchaṛ, gundza.* v.a. *chunṛal, jung k., jūhaṛa-*, etc. *k.*
Create, v.a. *paidā k., joṛawul.*
Creation, s. *duniyā, naṛa-ī, khalq, makhlūq.*
Creator, s. *khāliq, paidā kawūnkai.*
Creature, s. *bandah, wagaṛai, ganai*; *ḥaiwān, dzanāwar*; *makhlūq.*
Credit, s. *por, qarẓ*; *nasiyah*; *bāwar, yaqīn. i'tibār.* v.a. *bāwar-*, etc. *k.* (buy on-) *pa por-*, etc. *ākhistal.*
Creditable, a. *mu'tabar*; *nām·war.*
Creditor, s. *porawuṛai.*
Creed, s. *īmān, dīn, mazhab*; *kalima.*
Creep, v.n. See Crawl.
Creeper, s. *bel*; *dzela, juṛang.*
Crescent, s. *myāsht, ḥilāl.*
Cress, s. *halam, tezak, tartezak.*
Crest, s. (bird's-) *chār·khwalai* or *chār·khwalak*; *zūnḍai.* (snake's-) *chaja.* (-of a hill) *kamar, ghākkhai*; *tsūka, peza.* (-of a helmet) *ṭurra, tāj.*
Crevice, s. *sūṛai, chāwd, darz, daṛa.*
Crew, s. *ghol, ṭolai*; *ḍala.* (ship's-) *jahāzī.*

Cricket, s. *kirṛai.*

Crier, s. *jārchī, munādī kawūnkai.* (-to prayers) *mu-azzin, mullā·bāng wayūnkai.*

Crime, s. *gunāh, wabāl, taqṣīr, khaṭā, baza. jurm.*

Crimson, a. *arghawānī, lāl, sūr.*

Cringe, v.a. *chāplūsī-, ḍirpalī-, khūshāmad-,* etc. *k.*

Cripple, a. *guḍ, kaṛam, zam·zmolai. shall, sukṛuk.* v.a. *guḍ-,* etc. *k.*

Crisis, s. *sā'at, ṭāng, nobat*; *kamāl.*

Critic, s. *ḥarf·gīr, 'aib·joe.*

Crockery, s. *lokkhī·largī, kaṭwī·kandolī.*

Crocodile, s. *magar, nahang.*

Crook, s. *kūnḍa.* (shepherd's-) *kūnṭai, aṛām-kai, machak.*

Crooked, a. *kog, kṛīng, tsoṛ, ṭīṭ, kālkūch.*

Crop, s. *faṣl.* (bird's-) *jajūra, ḥauṣila.* v.a. *tsaral*; *shūkawul*; *ghūṭ k.*

Cross, v.n. (-over) *pore watal* or *-tlal.* v.a. *lānde·bānde-, ore·pore-,* etc. *k.* (-breed) *rag gaḍawul.*

Cross, a. *sūṭ·būṭ, mānṛai·gar, marawar, khapah.* (-breed) *dwah·ragah.*

Crouch, v.n. *ghalai ked., puṭedal.* (cringe).

Crow, s. *qāghah* or *qārghah.*

Crow, v.a. (-over rival) *sakha-, wiyāṛ-,* etc. *k.*

Crowd, s. *ganṛ·'ālam, ḍala, lakkhkar.*

Crown, s. *tāj, khol.* (-of head) *ṭaṭar, ṭopal.*

Crude, a. *ūm, khām, kachah, nīmgaṛai, nīma·khwā, ūmghalan.*

Cruel, a. *ẓālim, be·raḥm, kānṛai·zṛah, sakht.*

Crumb, s. *ṭoṭai, pūṭai, chūr, reza.*

Crupper, s. (horse's-) *dumchī.* (bullock's-) *ghwa-e lang, piyāṛma.*

Crush, v.a. *chīt·pīt-, tsaplāk-,* etc. *k., da kkhpo·lānde k., paz wahal.*

Crust, s. *poṭ.* (scab) *khwar, waṛ, khīg.*

Crutch, s. *ṭāpoṛa.* (-of a sandal) *gaḍeka.*

Cry, v.a. *ĵaṛa'.* (-violently) *pa raṭ·raṭ ĵaṛal.* (call) *naṛal, nāre wahal, bāng wayal.*

Cry, s. *jaṛā*; *nāra, bāng.*

Crystal, s. *bilaur*; *qalam*; *gach.*

Cubit, s. *tsangal, lecha, hata.*

Cuckold, s. *dahūs, bagharai.*

Cucumber, s. *bādrang, tara, tarai.*

Cud, s. *shkhwand.* (-of hawks, etc.) *par muhra.*

Cuddle, v.n. *ghāṛa·ghaṛa-ī ked.*

Cudgel, s. *koṭak, dāng, lawaṛ.* v.a. *kūṭal, wahal, ṭakawul.*

Cuff, s. *tsapeṛa, ḍab, ṭas.* (-of a coat) *las-tūnṛai, piyākhla.*

Cuirass, s. *bakhtar, jaushan.*

Culinary, a. *pakhalai.*

Cull, v.a. *shūkawul*; *chunṛal.*

Culpable, a. *malāmatī, taqṣīrī.*

Culprit, s. *gunāh·gār, taqṣīrī.*

Cultivate, v.a. *ābādawul, wadānawul*; *kar-, īwe* or *yawe-,* etc. *-k.*

Cultivation, s. *ābādī, wadānī*; *kar, īwe* or *yawe, zarā'at.*

Cultivator, s. *zamīndār, kikkht·gar.* (hired-) *dihqān, charekār.*

Cumin, s. *zīra, zanka-ī.*

Cunning, a. *chal·bāz, farebī*; *kāgh, chirg.* s. *hunar, ḥikmat.*

Cup, s. (metal-) *kaṭorai, jām.* (pottery-) *kanḍol* or *kanḍolai.* (wooden-) *kunṛa-ī* or *kunḍa-ī, kāsa.* (china-) *piyāla, kāsa.*

Cupidity, s. *shahwat, mastī, naus*; *ḥirṣ.*

Cupola, s. *gunbat.*

Cupping-horn, s. *kkhkar.* (to cup) v.a. *kkhkar lagawul.*

Cur, s. *spai, kūtrai*; *qachar, lawanḍ.*

Curb, s. *kaṛa, zandzīra.* v.a. *sambālawul, qābū k.*

Curd, s. *māstāh, chaka*; *posta, matra, kha-areṛai.*

Curdle, v.a. *tomna-, māya-, ṭīng-,* etc. *k.*

Cure, v.a. *joṛawul, raghawul.* s. *'ilāj, raghawūna.*

Curious, a. *'ajīb, nādir* ; *ghwag·tsār.*
Curl, s. *wal, zulf, tsūnṛa.*
Current, a. *jārī, chalan, rawā.* s. *chalānda, dāra.*
Currier, s. *tsamyār, dabbāgh.*
Curry, v.a. *karāṛa k.* (tan) *dabbāghī k.* (-favour) *chāplūsī-, ḍirpalī-,* etc. *-k.*
Curse, v.a. *kkhere-, l'anat-, bad·d'uā-,* etc. *k.* s. *kkhera,* etc. ; *balā, āfat, wabāl, ghazab.*
Curtain, s. *parda, satra.* (-of a fort) *shīrāza.*
Curve, s. *ṭīṭa, kalkūch, kag·lech, wal, pech.*
Cushion, s. *bālikkhtak, bālikkht·goṭai.*
Custody, s. *amānat, ḥawāla* ; *qaid, band* ; *sātana, jghorana, khundī·tob.*
Custom, s. *dastūr, rasm, chāl, 'ādat, dod, rawāj.* (tax) *māliyā, khirāj, tāwān, bāj.* (-house) *tsoka-ī, ṭānṛa.* (-collector) *muḥaṣṣil, bāj·dār.*
Cut, s. *tsīra, parhār.* (-purse) *gan·kap.* a. *tsīralai, ghwuts, jobal.*
Cut, v.a. *tsīral.* (-off) *prekawul* or *prekṛal.* (-out clothes, etc.) *skakkhtal.* (wound) *jobalawul, ghwutsawul.* (-short) *ghūṭ prekawul, lanḍ k.*
Cutler, s. *āhan·gar, ṣaiqal·gar, lohār.*
Cycle, s. *daur, daurān, tsarkh, zamāna.*
Cylinder, s. *nal, shpelai.*
Cymbal, s. *zang, zangūla, jalājal.*
Cypress, s. *sarwa, ṣanobar.*

D.

Dab, v.a. *tapal.*
Daddy s. *bābū, dādā.*
Daffodil, s. *nargis, kangas.*
Dagger, s. *chāṛa. bihbūdī, pesh·qabza.*
Daily, ad. *rozmarra, har·roza, hara·wradz.*
Dainty, a. *khūsh·khwurāk* ; *khwand·nāk, maza·dār, tuḥfa.*
Dale, s. *dara.*
Dalliance, s. *nāz·o·nakhra, 'ishq·bāzī, 'āshiqī·m'ashūqī* ; *dirang, lārghak, sustī, multawī.*
Damage, s. *tāwān, n·uqṣān, ziyān, troṭ.*
Dame, s. *merman, bībī, korbana.*
Damn, v.a. *kkhere-, l'anat-, bad·d'uā-,* etc. *k., petī·mū k., gūna wri kawul.*
Damnable, a. *l'anatī, lā-iq da kkhero.*
Damp, a. *lūnd, tar, nam·nāk, zyam·nāk, ob·jan.*
Damsel, s. *peghla, jina-ī.* (betrothed-) *changhala.*
Dance, s. *gaḍeda* ; *nāch* ; *atanṛ, jihr.* v.n. *gaḍedal.* v.a. *nāch k. atanṛ-,* etc. *-āchawul.*
Dancer, s. *gaḍedūnkai, gaḍandai.* (rope-) *bāzī·gar, naṭ.*
Dangerous, a. *khaṭar·nāk.*
Dangle, v.n. *dzwaṛandedal, awezānd ked.*
Dapple, a. *brag, gag.*
Dare, v.n. *gwākkhedal.* v.a. *jah k., gwākkhawul.*
Dark, a. *tor, tārīk.* (-complexion) *kaloṭ.*
Darkness, s. *tyāra, tārīkī* ; *tortam, zulmat.*
Darling, s. *mayan, m'ashūq, dzān.*
Darn, v.a. *bezal* or *pezal, ganḍal* ; *rafū k.*
Dart, s. *shalgai, barcha, bala.* (iron) *sela.*
Dash, v.a. *wīshtal.* (-in pieces) *chūr·chūr-, ṭoṭe·ṭoṭe-, pūṭī·pūṭī-,* etc. *k.* (-water) *lawastal, toyawul.*
Dastard, s. *nā·mard, tuzan, kaṛū.*
Date, s. *tārīkh.* (fruit) *khajūr.*
Daub, v.a. *lewawul, akheṛal, akhāṛa k.*
Daughter, s. *lūr.* (-in law) *ngor.* (step-) *parkaṭa-ī, ba-anza-ī.* (brother's-) *wrera.* (sister's-) *khordza.*
Dauntless, a. *be·bāk, zṛah·war.*
Day, s. *wradz.* (to-) *nan.* (of to-) *nananai.* (-by day) *wradz pa wradz.* (every-) *hara wradz.* (-book) *roznāma.* (-light) *ranṛā wradz.* (-dawn) *chirg·bāng, ṣabā, sapede.* (by-) *da wradzi.* (-star) *sta·ga.* (all the-) *kara-ī wradz.*

Dazzle, v.n. *brekkhedal, dzaledal, dzal ked.*
Dead, a. *muṛ, muṛai.* (-as a tree) *mṛām* or *mṛāw.*
Deadly, a. *qātil.*
Deaf, a. *kūnr.* (-as a post) *ṭap kūnr.*
Deafness, s. *kūnr-wālai.*
Deal, v.a. *weshal, brakha k.*; *wapār-, lāgī-,* etc. *k.*; *lār-, rozgār-, lāg-,* etc. *k.* s. *da nakkhtar largai.*
Dealer, s. *wapārī, lāgī*; *saudāgar, parāchah, ṭaṭār.* (Hindu-) *banriyah, katrī, hindū.*
Dealing, s. *wapār, lāg, sūd-saudā*; *kārobār, rozgār, lār, 'alāqa.*
Dear, a. *mayan*; *grān.* (-me!) *hāe-hāe!* (my-) *dzāna, dzamā dzān!*
Dearth, s. *kākhtī, matrah, tangsiyā, ḍukāl.*
Death, s. *ajal, marg, qaẓā.* (early-) *dzwānī-marg.* (sudden-) *tsaṭ-waṭ*; *mafājāt.*
Debase, v.a. *spukawul, kamawul, la-agawul*; *be rūe-, be makh-,* etc. *k.*; *jūṭah-,* etc. *k.*
Debate, v.a. *bahs k.*
Debauch, s. *bad-mastī.*
Debauchee, s. *lawanḍ, kāsīr, bad-'amalī, chaṭ.*
Debauchery, s. *lawanḍ-tob, charcha, kāsīrī.*
Debility, s. *nā-tuwānī, kamzor-tiyā, māndagī.*
Debt, s. *por, qarẓ.*
Debtor, s. *porawuṛai, qarẓ-dār.*
Decant, v.a. *toyawul.* v.n. *toyedal* or *to-edal.*
Decay, v.n. *mṛāmedal, wrostedal, sharhedal*; *skhā ked.*
Deceitful, a. *chal-bāz, ṭag-bāz, farebī, droh-ūnai.*
Deceive, v.a. *ṭagal, ghulawul, ṭagī-, fareb-,* etc. *k.*
December, s. *poh* or *po.*
Decent, a. *joṛ, kkhah*; *munāsib, lā-iq.*
Decide, v.a. *faiṣal k.*
Decidedly, ad. *be-shakk.*
Decisive, a. *pūrah, kāfī-shāfī.*
Declaration, s. *iẓhār*; *gawāhī, shāhidī.*
Declare, v.a. *wayal, lawdal* or *lal.*
Decline, v.n. *prewatal, zawāl ked.*; *la-ag-, kam-,* etc. *ked.* v.a. *inkār k.*
Declivity, s. *ĵawara, tahana, rewand.*
Decompose, v.n. *wrostedal, skhā ked., sharhedal.*
Decorate, v.a. *joṛawul*; *andzorawul, singārawul, kkhāyastah-, ārāstah-,* etc. *k.*; *poslal, kkhewa k.*
Decorous, a. *joṛ, munāsib, kkhāyastah.*
Decoy, v.a. *ghulawul, ṭagawul.*
Decrease, s. *kam-tiyā, la-ag-wālai.* v.n. *kamedal, la-ag ked.*
Decree, s. *ḥukm, fatwā.*
Decrepit, a. *ṭap, khwār, zoṛ, kamzor.*
Dedicate, v.a. *niyāz-, ṣadqa-,* etc. *k.*
Deduct, v.a. *mujra ākhistal, stanawul, zwam k.*
Deed, s. *kār, kṛah, 'amal*; *sanad, qabāla.* (-of gift) *hiba-nāma.*
Deep, a. *ḍoghal, star, ĵawar, kand*; *pokh, hokkhyār.*
Deer, s. *osai.* (young-) *kablai.*
Deface, v.a. *wrānawul, habata k., kharāb k.*
Defame, v.a. *ruswā-, bad-nām-,* etc. *k., ghandal*; *tuhmat-, tor-,* etc. *pore k.*
Default, s. *khaṭā, taqṣīr.*
Defeat, v.a. *māt k., pa-aṛ k.*; *man'a k.*
Defection, s. *jārwātah*; *yāghī-garī.*
Defenceless, a. *lā-chār*; *be-panāh, khushai, ḍāga-ḍagalai.*
Defend, v.a. *bachawul, panāh k., ṣātal, gālal, ĵghoral, khundī k., madad k.*; *'uẓr-, dzawāb-,* etc. *k.*
Defendant, s. *asāmī, muddā-'alaih.*
Defender, s. *sātandoe, ĵghorai, bachawūnkai, panāh-, khundī-,* etc. *-kawūnkai.*
Defer, v.a. *lārghah-, dirangī-, sustī-,* etc. *k.*
Deference, s. *makh, mulāḥiẓa, madārā, liḥāẓ*; *bāwar, i'tibār.*
Deficient, a. *kam, la-ag*; *waṭah, troṭ, zwam.*
Defile, s. *tanga-ī, dara.*

Defile, v.a. *palītawul, kakaṛawul, nā·pāk-, murdār-*, etc. *k.*

Define, v.a. *pūla-, brīd-, ḥadd-*, etc. *taṛal; m'anā bayānawul.*

Definite, a. *muqarrar.*

Deflower, v.a. *bikr shlawul*, or *mātawul.*

Deformed, a. *bad·shakl*, or *·ḍaul*, or *·rang.*

Defraud, v.a. *drohawul, ṭagal, ghulawul.*

Defray, v.a. *kharts pūrah k., khejawul.*

Defy, v.a. *jang ghokkhtal, gwākkhal, d'awa k.*

Degenerate, a. *spuk, nā·kār, khwār, kam·aṣl.*

Degrade, v.a. *spukawul, makh·tor k.*

Degree, s. *pāya, dzāe, darja, martaba; qadr, ḥadd, andāza.*

Dejected, a. *gham·jan, dil·gīr, malāl, nūl·jan.*

Deign, v.a. *manal, qabūlawul, rawā·laral.*

Deism, s. *sūfī·garī.*

Deist, s. *sūfī.*

Deity, s. *khudāe, allah, rabb.*

Delay, v.a. *drangı-, lārghah-, dzanḍ-, sustī-, multawī-*, etc. *k.*

Delegate, s. *astādzai, wakīl; nā-ib, peshkār.* v.a. *āstawul, legal, rawānawul; spāral, ḥawāla k.*

Deleterious, a. *tāwānī, nuqṣānī, muẓirr.*

Deliberate, v.a. *fikr-, ghaur-, andekkhnā-*, etc. *k., maṣlaḥat-, tadbīr-, mashwarat-*, etc. *k.*

Delicacy, s. *bārīkī, narai·wālai; nāzakī, kkhkulī·tob; khwand, maza.*

Delicate, a. *narai, bārīk; nāzak, kkhkulai.*

Delicious, a. *khwand·nāk, maza·dār.*

Delight, s. *kkhādī, khwand, khūsh·ḥālī, khwakkhī.* (-over enemy) *sakha, wiyāṛ.*

Delighted, a. *kkhād, khūsh·ḥāl, khwakkh.*

Delineate, v.a. *kāgal—kkhkal, līkal.*

Delirious, a. *be·khūd, be·hokkh.*

Delirium. s. *be·khūdī, be·hokkhī, haẓiyān.*

Deliver, v.a. *spāral, ḥawāla k.; warkawul; khalāṣawul, āzādawul, yalah k; bachawul, wurhawul; bayānawul, wayal.*

Deliverance, s. *khalāṣī, āzādī, yalah·wālai.*

Delude, v.a. *ghulawul, fareftah k.*

Deluge, s. *sailāb, nīz* or *nyūz, chala, ṭughiyānī.* v.a. *gharqawul, ḍūbawul.*

Delusion, s. *khām·khiyāl, fareb, khaṭā.*

Demand, v.a. *d'awa k., ghokkhtal.*

Demeanour, s. *yūn, wajha, chāl·chalan.*

Demesne, s. *daftar, zmaka, wanḍ, ada-ī.*

Demolish, v.a. *naṛawul, wujāṛawul, wrānawul, nā·būd-, tālā-, kharāb-*, etc. *k.*

Demon, s. *dew, perai, rawai, ghūl.* (possessed of a-) *paṭ nīwulai.*

Demonstrate, v.a. *tsargandawul, bartser-, kkhkārah-*, etc. *k., kkhayal—kkhowul; zbād-, isbāt-*, etc. *k., dalīl rāwṛal.*

Demur, v.a. *drangī-, multawī-*, etc. *k.; andekkh-, shakk-, gūmān-*, etc. *laral.*

Demure, a. *ghalai, ghaṛand; drūnd, sūt.*

Den, s. *ghār, kāz; ghālai.*

Denial, s. *inkār, nahiya, munkir·tob; ibā.*

Denizen, s. *astogūnkai, osedūnkai.*

Denote, v.a. *kkhayal—kkhowul, kkhkārah k., bayānawul.*

Denounce, v.a. *ghandal, kagal, ruswā k., bad·nāmawul, malāmatawul, raṭal.*

Dense, a. *ganr, gūr.* (-crops) *ṭal, tat.* (-cloth) *ṭok.* (-liquids) *ṭīng.*

Dent, s. *jghanḍ, kandaw, wat.*

Denude, v.a. *barbanḍawul, poṭ-, tsarman-*, etc. *-kāgal—kkhkal* or *-bāsal—yastal.*

Deny, v.a. *inkār k.* v.n. *munkiredal.*

Depart, v.n. *tlal—lāṛal, lwukkhtal, rawānedal, drūmal; legdal—lekkhal.*

Departure, s. *tah, tlana, legdana, rawānagī, warṭag, pand.*

Depend, v.n. *dzwaṛandedal, āwezānd ked.; āsra-, umed-*, etc. *laral; mauqūf-*, etc. *ked.*

Dependence, s. *āsra, umed, takiya, bāwar; i'tibār; 'alāqa; tāb'i·dārī.*

Dependant, a. *dzwaṛanḍ; mauqūf.*

Dependent, s. *hamsāyah, tāb'i·dār.*

Deplore, v.a. *afsos-, tartāb-, gila-,* etc. *k.*
Deponent, s. *gawāhī lūnai, shāhid.*
Deportment, s. *yūn, chāl, chalan, taur.*
Depose, v.a. *gawāhī-, shāhidī-,* etc. *lal* or *lawdal; sharal; mauqūf k.*
Deposit, s. *amānat; graw.* v.a. *gdal* or *īgdal, yakkhodal* or *īkkhodal, yakkhawul* or *īkkhawul; spāral; amānat kegdal,* etc.
Deposition, s. *gawāhī, shāhidī.*
Depository, s. *ambār·khāna, koṭī.*
Depraved, a. *bad, kharāb, nā·kār, tabāh.*
Deprecate, v.a. *minnat-, d'uā-,* etc. *k., panāh-, 'uzr-,* etc. *-ghokkhtal.*
Depreciate, v.a. *spukawul, kamawul, la-agawul; kagal, ghandal, spuk ganral.*
Depredation, s. *lūṭ, nātah, tālā, tākht, tārāj.*
Depress, v.a. *lānde k., ghamawul; ṭīṭawul.*
Depression, s. *gham, khapagān, dil·tangī, da zṛah nūl; doghal, ĵawar, tahna, ĵawar·tiyā.*
Deprive, v.a. *ākhistal, shūkawul, man'a k.*
Depth, s. *ĵawar·tiyā, star·wālai.*
Deputation, s. *jirga, m'arika, astādzī.*
Depute, v.a. *jirga-,* etc. *āstawul* or *legdal; wakīl wudrawul.*
Deputy, s. *nā-ib, wakīl; jirgatū, astādzai.*
Derision, s. *ṭoqa, khandā, pekkha.*
Derive, v.a. *mūndal, gaṭal, paidā k.*
Derogate, v.a. *ghandal, kagal, spukawul.*
Derogatory, a. *spuk, ruswā, nā·kār, nāsāz.*
Descant, v.a. *bayānawul, wayal.*
Descend, v.n. *kūzedal, nāziledal, prewatal.*
Descendant, s. *alwād, zawzād, nasl, zurriyāt.*
Descent, s. *kūzedana, prewātah, nazūl; ĵawar, tahna; aṣl, ẕāt, peṛa-ī.*
Describe, v.a. *bayānawul, kkhayal—kkhowul.*
Description, s. *bayān, naql; ṣūrat, shān; rang.*
Desert, s. *ḥaqq, qadr, sazāwārī, lā-iq·wālai.*
Desert, s. *ṣaḥrā, maidān, maira, dakkht, chol, bāyābān.* a. *wairān, wujāṛ, ta-ash, dzangal.*
Desert, v.a. *pregdal, prekkhodal, prekkhawul, prekkhal, tark k.* v.n. *takkhtedal, puṭedal.*
Deserted, a. *wairān, ghair·ābād, khushai, ṛang, sunj; prekkhodai, prīkkhai, tark·karai.*
Deserter, s. *takkhtedūnkai.*
Deserve, v.a. *ḥaqq laral.* v.n. *lā-iq-, wājib-, sazāwār-, qābil-,* etc. *-ked.*
Design, s. *niyat, rūkh, qaṣd, irāda; mudd'ā, matlab; band, chal; nakhkkkha* or *naqsha.*
Design, v.a. *niyat-,* etc. *taral* or *laral; joṛawul.*
Desirable, a. *khwakkh, pīrzo, ghwarah.*
Desire, s. *ghokkht, armān, ārzū, murād, handa, hatsa, khwakkhī.* (carnal) *naus, shahwat.*
Desire, v.a. *ghokkhtal, armān-,* etc. *laral; farmāyal.*
Desolate, a. *wairān, wujāṛ, ṛang, sunj, chauṛ.* v.a. *wairānawul, wujāṛawul, tālā-,* etc. *k.*
Despair, s. *nā·umedī; gham, nūl.*
Desperate, a. *be·bāk, lewanai.*
Despise, v.a. *spuk ganral, bad manal, kagal.*
Despot, s. *ẓālim, zorāwar, khpul·sar.*
Despotism, s. *ẓulm, zorāwarī, zabardastī.*
Destination, s. *borjal. ṭīkāo, mazal.*
Destiny, s. *naṣīb, qismat, taqdīr, bakht; ajal.*
Destitute, a. *khwār, lā·chār, be·kas, muflis.*
Destroy, v.a. *wrānawul, habatah-, halāk-, tālā-, kharāb-, nā·būd-, fanā-,* etc. *k.*
Destruction, s. *halākat, kharābī, wrānī,* etc.
Destructive, a. *muẓirr, ziyānī. tārānī.*
Desultory, a. *be·tartīb, nā·qalār, be·sar.*
Detach, v.a. *biyalawul, judā k., lwuṛawul.*
Detached, v.n. *biyaledal, lwukkhtal, judā ked.*
Detachment, s. *ghol, dasta, ṭolai, ta'īnāt.*
Detail, v.a. *biyal·biyal-, judā·judā-, mufaṣṣal-,* etc. *-wayal* or *-bayānawul* or *-līkal.*
Detain, v.a. *man'a k., haṭālawul; khundiyal, sātal; stūnawul; bandawul, qaid k.*
Deter, v.a. *yerawul* or *werawul.*

Determination, s. *qaṣd, niyat*; *ḥukm, amr.*

Detest, v.a. *bad manal* or *ganral, kagal, chinjawul, kraka āḵẖistal.*

Detract, v.a. *ghandal, chughlī-, ghībat-,* etc. *k. tor pore·k., spukawul; kamawul, la-agawul.*

Detriment, s. *tāwān, ziyān, nuqṣān, ḵẖalal, budrī, troṭ.*

Devastate, v.a. *natal, wrānī-, lūṭ-, tālā-, paemālī-, tāḵẖt·tārāj-, chauṛ-,* etc. *k.*

Develop, v.a. *ziyātawul, wadānawul.*

Deviate, v.n. *girzedal, āwukkhtal, gharedal, gumrāh ked.* v.a. *girzawūl.*

Device, s. *band, tadbīr, ḥikmat, chal; nakkha.*

Devil, s. *shaiṭān; dew, rawai.*

Devious, a. *kag·lech, kālkūchan.*

Devise, v.a. *band taṛal, tadbīr-,* etc. *k.* (give) *bakkhal, hiba k.*

Devolve, v.n. *rasedal, prewatal, lāzim ked.*

Devote, v.a. *ṣadqa-, qurbān-,* etc. *k.; niyāz-,* etc. *manal* or *k.; bakkhal, wudrawul.*

Devotee, s. *zāhid, mūttaqid.*

Devotion, s. *'ibādat, bandagī; nmūndz; mashghūlā shughl, lagiyā.*

Devout, a. *nek, m'utakif, nmāndz·guzār.*

Dew, s. *pa-arkha.*

Dewlap, s. *jajūra;· ghab·ghab, ghuṭ·yālai, gharai.*

Dexterous, a. *chālāk, tak·lāstai.*

Dialect, s. *jiba, wrāsha.*

Dialogue, s. *sawāl·dzawāb, khabare.*

Diamond, s. *almās.*

Diaphragm, s. *prīnṛ, parda (da gede).*

Diarrhœa, s. *bahedana da dastūno.* (to have-) v.a. *rīḵẖ wahal.* (having-) a. *rīḵẖan.*

Diary, s. *roz·nāma.*

Dice, s. *qimār.*

Dictionary, s. *lughat.*

Die, v.n. *mṛal, muṛ ked.*

Diet, s. *ḵẖwurāk; pāl·parhez.*

Difference, s. *biyal·tūn* or *biyal·wālai, farq.*

Different, a. *biyal, bul, judā.*

Difficult, a. *sakht, grān, mushkil.*

Difficulty, s. *sakhtiyā, grān·tiyā, tangsiyā.*

Diffidence, s. *wiswās, andekkhnā; yera, wahm; stāra; shakk, shubha.*

Diffuse, v.a. *ḵẖwarawul.*

Dig, v.a. *kandal* or *kanal, kṇawdal, kanastal.*

Digest, v.a. *hazm k.*

Dignity, s. *pāya, martaba; qadr, 'izzat.*

Dike, s. *kanda, kāha-ī; ḵẖandaq; pūla, wand.*

Dilapidate, v.n. *naṛedal, wrānedal.*

Dilate, v.a. *planawul, aṛat k.; ūgdawul.* v.n. *ghwaredal, planedal, paṛsedal.*

Dilatory, a. *sust, laṭ, drang, nā·rāst.*

Dilemma, s. *balā, nkkhatai, sāḵẖa.*

Diligent, a. *miḥnatī, kokshiksh kawūnkai, sā'ī.*

Dilute, v.a. *mahīn-, narai-,* etc. *k.*

Dim, a. *dund.*

Diminish, v.a. *kamawul, landawul, la-ag k.*

Diminutive, a. *pūṭai, wṛūkai, waṛkoṭai, kuchanai, kachoṭai, ḵẖarmandai, woṛ, la-ag.*

Dimple, s. *kwata-ī; ta-apai.*

Din, s. *ghāw, zwag·zūg, shor.*

Dinner, s. *tsākkhtī; doda-ī; ḵẖwurāk.*

Dint, s. *zor, qunwat.*

Dip, v.a. *dubawul, gharqawul, ghoṭa-, ghūpa-,* etc. *-warkawul -wahal* or *-ḵẖwuṛal.* (-as bread in soup, etc.) *chūka k.*

Diploma, s. *sanad.*

Dire, a. *bashpaṛ, sakht; haibat·nāk.*

Direct, a. *sam, negh, barābar.*

Direct, v.a. *kkhayal—kkhowul; farmāyal, ḥukm·chalawul; nazar lagawul; sar·nāma līkal,* or *-kāgal—kkhkal.*

Direction, s. *lorai, ḵẖwā, rūḵẖ, maḵẖ, palaw; sar·nāma, nakkha; farmān, ḥukm.*

Directly, ad. *pa ṭakī, pa de sā'at, sam da lāsa.*

Director, s. *kkhowūnkai; kār kawūnkai; pīr.*

Dirge, s. *wīr* or *vīr, wainā.*

Dirt, s. *ḵẖīra, palītī, rash.*

Dirty, a. *ḵẖīran, khachan, palīt.*

Dis-, the particle of negation, is expressed by the prefixes *be-*, *nā-*, *lā-*, *bad-*, etc.
Disable, v.a. *lā·chār-*, *nā·tuwān-*, *be·ṭāqat-*, *be·maqdūr-*, *'ājiz-*, etc. *k.*
Disadvantage, s. *tāwān*, *ziyān*, *nuqṣān*.
Disadvantageous a. *'abaṣ*, *be·fā-idah*.
Disaffected, a. *yāghī*, *sar·kakkh*, *nā·rāẓ*.
Disagree, v.n. *nā·rāẓ-*, *mukhālif-*, etc. *ked.*
Disagreeable, a. *kagalai*, *bad*, *ghāndah*.
Disagreement, s. *jagṛa*, *steza*, *poṭ*.
Disappear, v.n. *puṭedal*, *wrukedal*, *ghā-ib ked.*
Disappoint, v.a. *nā·umed k.*
Disappointed, a. *nā·umed*, *malāl*; *mīkkh·mīkkh*.
Disapprove, v.a. *bad·manal*, *kagal*, *ghandal*.
Disaster, s. *āfat*, *bad·balā*, *randz*, *muṣībat*.
Disastrous, a. *bad·* or *kam·bakht*.
Disbelieve, v.a. *na·manal*, *bāwar na·kawul*.
Discard, v.a. *sharal*; *liri k.*
Discern, v.a. *pejandal*, *m'alūmawul*; *kaṭal*, *goral*, *līdal*.
Discerning, a. *hokkhyār*, *pohānd*.
Discernment, s. *poh*, *'aql*.
Discharge, v.a. *khalāṣawul*, *ta-ashawul*; *lire-*, *biyarta-*, etc. *-k.*, *dzawāb warkawul*; *ghurzawul*, *wīshtal*; *purah k.*, *pa dzāe k.*
Discharge, s. *khalāṣī*, *dzawāb*. (explosion) *ḍaz*, *shilak*. (-from debt, etc.) *rāẓī·nāma*, *faiṣal·nāma*.
Disciple, s. *murīd*, *shāgird*, *ṭālib*. (-of Christ) *ḥawārī*.
Discipline, s. *ā-īn*, *qā'ida*, *dustūr*.
Disciplined, a. *āmokhtah*, *el*.
Disclose, v.a. *prānatal tsargandawul*, *kkhkārah-*, *bartser-*, etc. *k.*, *parda porta k.*, *khwālā wayal*, *spekkhta āṛawul*, *pudūlī k.*
Discolour, v.n. *bad·rang-*, *dāghī-*, etc. *-ked.*
Discomfit, v.a. *lānde-*, *pa-ar-*, *māt-*, etc. *k.*
Discompose, v.a. *rabṛawul*, *ḥariyānawul*; *wrānawul*, *kharāb-*, *gaḍ·waḍ-*, *be·tartīb-*, etc. *-k.*, *wār·khaṭā k.*

Disconsolate, a. *gham·nāk*, *nūl·jan*, *dil·tang*
Discontented, a. *nā·rāẓ*, *be·ṣabr*.
Discontinue, v.a. *pregdal—prekkhodal*, *prekkhawul*, *prekkhal*, *tark k.*
Discord, s. *patna*, *pasāt*; *sākha*.
Discordant, a. *nā·sāz*, *be·ṭāng*.
Discover, v.a. *m'alūmawul*, *pejandal*; *tsargandawul*, *kkhkārah-*, *bartser-*, etc. *k.*; *kkhayal—kkhowul*; *mūndal*, *biyā·mūndal*.
Discount, s. *troṭ*, *waṭa*.
Discourage, v.a. *yerawul*, *zṛah chīngawul*.
Discourse, s. *khabare*, *qīl·o·qā'*, *gangosai*, *kkhkālwa*, *wayana*.
Discreet, a. *hokkhyār*, *pohānd*, *pokh*.
Discuss, v.a. *baḥṣ k.*
Disease, s. *bīmārī*, *maraẓ*, *āzār*, *nājoṛ·tiyā*, *nārogh·tiyā*, *randz*.
Diseased, a. *bīmār*, *marīẓ*, *nājoṛ*, *nārogh*, *randzūr*, *āzārī*.
Disembark, v.a. *kūzawul*. v.n. *kūzedal*.
Disengage, v.a. *āzādawul*, *khalāṣawul*, *yalah k.*, *prānatal*, *spaṛdal*.
Disfigure, v.a. *bad rangawul*, *wrānawul*.
Disgorge, v.a. *jārbāsal—jāryastal*.
Disgrace, v.a. *bad·nām-*, *ruswā-*, *makh·tor-*, *be·nang-*, *be·makh-*, etc. *k.*, *sharmawul*.
Disgraceful, a. *bad*, *nā·kkhanai*, *nā·lā-iq*.
Disguise, s. *bāna*, *libās*, *swāng*.
Disgust, s. *kraka*.
Disgusted, v.n. *chinjedal*.
Dish, s. (wooden-) *kkhānak*. (brass-) *tālai*. (iron-) *tabakhai*. (pottery-) *taba-ī*, *taghārai*. (china-) *rikebī*. (chafing-) *majmir*. (-of stone for baking on) *shokānrai*. (-of made food) *sālan*, *qatagh*, *ngolai*.
Dishearten, v.a. *zṛah chīngawul*, *nā·umed k.*
Dishevelled, a. *spaṛdalai*; *shānlai·wānlai*.
Dishonest, a. *be·īmān*, *nā·rāst*.
Dishonour, s. *be·'izzatī*, *bad·nāmī*, *makh·torī*.
Disjoint, v.a. *kūtal*, *band prekawul*, *bja k.*
Disk, s. *chakai*, *tsarkhai*, *ṭakai*, *qurṣ*.

Dislike, v.a. *bad manal, chinjawul, kagal, kraka ākhistal, ghandal.*

Dislocate, v.a. *be·dzāe k.*

Dismal, a. *khof·nāk, andekkh·nāk, tars·nāk*; *tor, tārīk*; *gham·jan, malāl.*

Dismantle, v.a. *naṛawul, wrānawul, shūkawul, barbandawul, spaṛdal.*

Dismay, s. *wera* or *yera, khof, tor, bāk.*

Dismiss, v.a. *rukhṣat k., dzawāb warkawul, lire-, biyarṭa-*, etc. *k.*

Dismount, v.n. *kūzedal.*

Disobedient, a. *yāghī, sar·kakkh.*

Disoblige, v.a. *wezār-, khapah-, randzūr-*, etc. *k., kaṛawul.*

Disobliging, a. *be·makh, be·muruwwat.*

Disorder, s. *be·tartībī, gaḍ·waḍ·tob, be·band-obastī.* v.a. *gaḍ·waḍ k.*

Disown, v.n. *munkiredal.*

Disparage, v.a. *spukawul, kagal, ghandal, tor pore k., ghībat k.*

Dispatch, v.a. *ástawul, legdal, legal*; *chalawul, rawānawul.*

Dispatch, s. *talwāṛ, tak·lāstai·tob, jalta-ī.*

Dispel, v.a. *khwarawul, lire k., wrukawul.*

Dispensary, s. *dawā·khāna.*

Dispense, v.a. *weshal, kkhandal.* (-with) *mu'āf k., pulawul.*

Disperse, v.a. *khwarawul, takkhtawul, tār·pa·tār k.*

Displace, v.a. *sharal, be·dzāe k.*

Display, v.a. *kkhkārah-, bartser-*, etc. *k.*

Display, s. *nandāra, tamāsha.*

Displease, v.a. *khapah-, marawar-*, etc. *k., kaṛawul, randzawul, wezārawul.*

Disposal, s. *wāk, qābū, rokh, ikhtiyār.*

Dispose. v.a. *tartībawul, sambālawul, gdal. īkkhodal* or *yakkhodal, īkkhawul* or *yakkhawul*; *kegdal* or *kkhkegdal, kekkhodal* or *kkhkekkhodal, khartsawul*; *warkawul, hiba k., bakkhal* or *bakhkkhal*; *kkhkenawul.*

Disposition, s. *tartīb, ḍaul*; *khwā, khoe, mizāj, lokkhai, salīqa, ṭab'a.*

Dispossess, v.a. *sharal, shūkawul, be·dzāe k.*

Disprove, v.a. *bāṭil-, darogh·jan k.*

Dispute, v.a. *jagṛa-, steza-, takrār-, qaẓiya-*, etc. *k.*; *baḥs k.*

Disreputable, a. *be·i'tibār, nā·lā·iq, ruswā.*

Disrespectful, a. *be·adab, be·makh.*

Dissatisfied, a. *nā·rāẓ, nā·khwakkh.*

Dissect, v.a. *tsīral, kūtal.*

Dissemble, v.a. *bāna-, lamghaṛa-ī*, etc. *k.*

Disseminate, v.a. *khwarawul, tār·pa·tār k.*

Dissension, s. *patna, jagṛa, steza, pasāt.*

Dissipate, v.a. *wrukawul, talaf-, ṣarf-, charcha-*, etc. *k.*; *mastī-, nasha·khorī-*, etc. *k.*

Dissolute, a. *chaṭ, lawand, qachar.*

Dissolve, v.a. (-by fire) *wīlī k.* (-by water) *oba k.* (-an assembly) *bar·khwāst k.*

Dissuade, v.a. *man'a k., khwā girzawul.*

Distance, s. *farq.* (-of time) *mūda.* (-of place) *lār, dzāe.* (respect) *adab.*

Distant, a. *lirai, prat.*

Distend, v.a. *parsawul, wīṛawul.* v.n. *paṛsedal, wīṛedal.*

Distention, s. *pāṛsob, waram.*

Distil, v.a. *tsātsawul.* v.n. *tsātsedal.*

Distinct, a. *biyal, judā.*

Distinction, s. *biyal·tūn, judā-ī, farq.*

Distinguish, v.a. *pejandal*; *zdah k., m'alūmawul, nāmer-, nām·dār-, nūm·war-*, etc. *k.*

Distort, v.a. *kog k.* or *kagawul, kṛīngawul, ṭīṭawul.*

Distract, va. *rabṛawul, ḥariyānawul, sargardān-, pareshān-, lewanai-*, etc. *k.*

Distress, s. *khwārī, tangsiyā, mīrtsī, randz.*

Distress, v.a. *tangawul, rabṛawal, āzārawul, zahīrawul.*

Distribute, v.a. *weshal, wesh-, brakha-, qismat-*, etc. *k.*

District, s. *tapa, pargana.*

Distrust, s. *gumān, shakk, shubha.*

Distrustful, a. *bad·gumān, shakk·man.*
Disturb, v.a. *rabṛawul, pārawul, khwadzawul, laṛal, kkhorawul.*
Ditch, s. *kanda, kāha-ī. kaḍa-ī.*
Ditty, s. *chār·bait, ṭapa, sandara, lanḍa-ī.*
Dive, v.a. *ghūpa-, ghoṭa-,* etc. *wahal* or *k.*
Diverge, v.n. *biyaledal, girzedal, lwukkhtal.*
Diverse, a. *biyal—biyal*; *dzane.*
Diversion, s. *nandāra, tamāsha, sail, loba.*
Divert, v.a. *girzawul, āwukkhtal*; *ghulawul.*
Divest, v.a. *barbandawul*; *shūkawul.*
Divide, v.a. *prekawul* or *prekṛal, tsīral, ghwutsawul*; *weshal, brakha-, qismat-, wanḍ-,* etc. *k.*
Dividend, s. *brakha, wesh, pucha, wanḍ.*
Divination, s. *pāl katara, koḍa, 'ilm da ghā-ib.*
Divine, a. *ilāhī, rabbānī, khudā-ī.* s. *faqīh.*
Divinity, s. *khudā-ī*; *fiqha.* (the-) *khudāe.*
Division, s. *wesh, brakha, ḥiṣṣa, wanḍ,* (-of land) *paṭai, līkai, wand, ada-ī.* (-of country) *tapa, pargana, khel.* (-of village) *kandai, mālat, cham, palaw.*
Divorce, s. *ṭalāq.* v.a. *ṭalāq k., pa kāghaz-, pa dreo kāṇro-,* etc. *ṭalāq·warkawul,*
Divulge, v.a. *tsargandawul, kkhkārah k., parda porta k., khwāla wayal, pudūlī k.*
Dizzy, a. *sargardān, akar·ĵan.*
Do, v.a. *kawul, kṛal, joṛawul, pa dzāe k.*
Docile, a. *el* or *īl, eman.*
Dock, s. (for vessels) *danḍ, ḥauẓ, ḍab.* (the plant) *shalkhai.*
Dock, v.a. (cut short) *lanḍ-, ghūṭ-,* etc. *prekawul* or *k.* (-the hair) *sar·kunḍai k.*
Doctor, s. *ḥakīm, ṭabīb.* (-of law) *faqīh.* (-of divinity) *maulawī.*
Doctrine, s. *mazhab*; *masla*; *'ilm.*
Dodge, v.a. *chal·wal-, lamghaṛa-ī-,* etc. *k.*
Doer, s. *kawūnkai, kṛūnai.*
Dog, s. *spai.* (terrier) *pishtai.* (pointer-) *khandai.* (greyhound-) *tāzī.* (mastiff-) *khaḍal.* (mongrel-) *kutah.* (-tick) *koṇr, kūnai, wradza.* (-fly) *manganr·mach.* (-in heat) *spiyama* or *spe-ama.* (-platter) *chaṭ.*
Doings, s. *kār, kṛah, kṛah·wṛah.*
Doleful, a. *gham·nāk, malāl, sūṭ·būṭ.*
Doll, s. *gūda-ī, lola-ī, nānaka-ī, nenzaka.*
Dolt, s. *pūhaṛ, gedī·khar, kawdan, kam·'aql.*
Domain, s. *mulk, daftar*; *wanḍ, ada-ī.*
Dome, s. *gunbat.*
Domestic, a. *āmokhtah, eman, el* or *īl.* s. *koranai*; *nokar, khāna·zād.* (-economy) *kormāna.*
Dominion, s. *ḥukūmat, sardārī, khānī.*
Donation, s. *bakhkshiksh, bakkhana, khwaṛa.*
Donor, s. *warkawūnkai, bakkhawūnkai.*
Doom, s. *ḥukm, fatwā*; *naṣīb, qismat*; *ajal.*
Door, s. *war.* (-frame) *darshal.* (-leaf) *pala, tamba.* (-heel) *chūṛ* (-keeper) *darwānchī, darwāza·wān, ghāwchī.*
Dose, s. *khwurāk.* (dry-) *paka* or *kapa.* (liquid-) *gūṭ, īnda, ghuṛap.*
Dot, s. *ṭakai, nuqta, pitsāṇrai, pūṭai.*
Double, a. *dwah·bragh, bgharg, dogānah.* (of a fox, etc.) *kālkūchaka.*
Doubt, s. *shakk, shubha, gumān.* v.a. *shakk-,* etc. *laral.*
Doubtful, a. *shakk·dār, shakk·man, gumānī.*
Doubtless, ad. *be·shakk, be·shubha, yaqīnan.*
Dough, s. *khamīra, ākkhalai.* (lump of-) *peṛa, ghunḍa.*
Dove, s. *qumrī, tatawa, spalama.* (ring-) *gūgushtū, kuṛkuṛa-ī.*
Dovetail, v.a. *ageyal.*
Dower, s. (portion) *dhadz, dūd, kulang.* (jointure) *mahr, kābīn.*
Down, p. *kkhkata, lānde, kkhke-a* or *kkhkiya.*
Down, s. *maidān, sama, maira.* (hair) *ghūna, tor·wekkhtah, zunba, waṛa-ī.* (-of beard) *khorma.*
Doze, v.a. *parnā-, khob-,* etc. *wṛal*; *ūdah-, bīdah-,* etc. *ked.*
Draft, s. *hunḍa-ī, burāt, ḥujjat.*

DRA	DRO

Drag, v.a. *rākāgal—rākkhkal, kashāla k.*

Dragon, s. *kkhā·mār, ajdahā, nihang.*

Dragoon, s. *turk·* or *chābuk·sawār, swor* or *spor.*

Drain, s. *mora-ī, nāla;* *lakkhtai.*

Drain, v.a. *wuchawul, rākāgal—rākkhkal.*

Dram, s. *dirham, misqāl;* *gūṭ, ghuṛap.*

Drama, s. *naql, swāng, pekkha.*

Draper, s. *bazzāz, parānchah.*

Drapery, s. *ṭūkai, zaṛūkai, pokkhāk.*

Draught, s. (gulp) *gūṭ, īṇda, ghuṛap, qurṭ.* (beverage) *sharbat, tskkhāk* or *skāk.* (wind) *wo, bāḍ;* *pū, tsapa.* (cattle) *bār· kakkh.* (copy) *naql.* (drawing) *nakhkkha.*

Draw, v.a. *rākāgal — rākkhkal.* (picture) *kāgal—kkhkal, līkal, kwekkhkal.*

Drawback, s. *'aib, stūnai.*

Drawers, s. *paṛtūg, shalwār, tambān.* (hem of-) *baḍa.* (hole of hem) *kustīj.* (tape of-) *paṛtūghākkh.* (leg of-) *pā-entsa.* (fork of-) *khakkhtagai.*

Drawing, s. *nakhkkha* or *naqsha;* *kakkhikkh, kakkha, kashāla.*

Dread, s. *yera* or *wera, bāk, khof, tars;* *wiswās, andekkhnā, gram.* v.n. *weredal* or *yeredal, andekkhedal.* v.a. *tars-,* etc., *laral* or *-khwuṛal;* *gram k.*

Dreadful, a. *khof·nāk, haibat·nāk;* *bad, bashpaṛ, sakht.*

Dreadfully, ad. *be·shāna, be·ḥadda.*

Dream, s. *khob.* (fancy) *khiyāl.* (nightmare) *khapasa.* v.a. *khob līdal;* *khiyāl k.*

Dreary, a. *wairān, wujāṛ, khushai, sunj.*

Dredge, v.a. (flour) *bornah k.*

Dregs, s. *khaṭbel.* (clotted-) *matra.* (-of vegetables) *gaḍzārai.* (-of metals) *khīra.*

Drench, v.a. *lūndawul, khushtawul, lūnd· khusht k.* (purge) *jullāb-, jāṛ-,* etc. *warkawul.*

Dress, s. *āghostana, pokkhāk, jāma, zaṛūkai, kālai, nmarai* or *nwarai.*

Dress, v.a. *āghostal, āghostawul, poslal, pokkhal.* (cook) *pakhawul.* (-a wound) *paha pore k.*

Dribble, v.n. *tsātsedal.*

Drift, s. (aim) *gharaz, maṭlab.* (rain and wind) *sīla-ī, jam·jakaṛ* (-wood, etc.) *kanga·khar, niyūz·nṛai.* (-mud) *laha, lāe.*

Drill, s. *barma.* (military-) *qawā'id.* v.a. *barma-, sūrai-,* etc. *k., tsekhal;* *qawā'id kkhayal—kkhowul.*

Drink, v.a. *tskal* or *tskkhal* or *skal.* s. *tskkhāk,* etc.

Drive, v.a. *chalawul.* (-cattle) *biyāyal— bīwul—botlal, ramawul.* (-a horse) *zoral.* (-away) *takkhtawul, sharal, raṭal, lire k.* (-a nail) *wahal, ṭakcwul, mandal.* (-into) *kkhke·mandal, dūsa k.*

Drivel, v.a. *lāṛa ghurzawul* or *toyawul.*

Drizzle, v.n. *pūna-, rangai bārān-, narai bārān-,* etc. *oredal.*

Droll, a. *'ajab, khandā·nāk.* s. *ṭoq·mār, washt·mār, maskharāchī, pekkhe·gar, malandai.*

Drollery, s. *washta, ṭoqa, maskhara, pekkha.*

Droop, v.n. *mrāmedal, kumanredal;* *kaṛedal, nūledal, ghamedal, malāl ked.;* *prewatal, ṭīṭedal.*

Drop, v.n. (distil) *tsātsedal.* (fall) *prewatal.* (-into) *kkhkewatal.* (slip) *khwa·edal* or *khwahedal.* (descend) *kūzedal.* v.a.(leap) *dangal.* (cease) *pregdal, prekkhodal* or *prekkhal.*

Drop, s. *tsātskai.* (a little) *chilka.*

Dropsy, s. *jahola, taghārak, istisqā.*

Dross, s. (-of metals) *khīra, maṭa.* (-of iron) *ospankharai.* (-vegetables) *gaḍzārai, drūza.*

Drought, s. *sūkṛa, khushk·sālī.*

Drove, s. *ṭolai, park.* (-of oxen) *gohār.* (-of buffaloes) *goram.* (-of sheep, etc.) *kandak, rama, ghela.*

Drover, s. (-of oxen) *gāhū, gorwān, gāharai, ghobah.* (-of buffaloes) *gūjar.* (-of sheep) *shpūn.*

Drown, v.a. *ḍūbawul, gharqawul, lāhū k.*

Drowsy, a. *khob-wrai, parnā-wrai.*

Drub, v.a. *wahal, ṭakawul, kūṭal.*

Drug, s. *dawā, dārū, darmān*; *būṭai.*

Druggist, s. *pansārī.*

Drum, s. *ḍol, ḍolkai, ḍamāma.* (kettle-) *ḍūmbakai, tanbal, naghāra.* v.a. *ḍol-*, etc. *wahal* or *-ghagawul.*

Drummer, s. *ḍol wahūnkai, ḍa-am* or *ḍum, naghārchī.*

Drunkard, s. *sharābī, nasha-khor, 'amalī, bangī, kaipī.*

Drunken, a. *mast*; *be-khūd, nasha-wrai.*

Dry, a. *wuch, khushk*; *tagai, tosand.* (-bread) *spora ḍoḍa-ī.* v.a. *wuchawul.* v.n. *wuchedal.*

Dryness, s. *wuch-wālai, khushkī.*

Duck, s. *baṭa.* (wild-) *hīla-ī.*

Duck, v.a. *ghūpa-, ghoṭa-*, etc. *wahal* or *-khwuṛal*; *sar ṭīṭawul.*

Ductile, a. *narm, post* or *pos, mulā-im.*

Due, a. *bāqī*; *wājib, munāsib.* s. *ḥaqq*; *qarẓ, por*; *maḥṣūl, chūngai, dastūr.*

Dulcimer, s. *sitār, rabāb, sārinda, ghachaka, chamtāra.*

Dull, a. *pa-ats, be-dam, be-āb*; *tīrah, dund*; *kam-'aql, gedī*; *sust, laṭ, shaṭal* or *shalaṭ.*

Duly, ad. *jukht, barābar.*

Dumb, a. *gung, lāl.* s. *gungai.*

Dun, v.a. *zoral, taqāẓa k.*

Dun, a. *samand.* s. *muḥaṣṣil, sazāwal.*

Dunce, s. *pūhaṛ, gūlī-khar, kam-'aql.*

Dung, s. (human-) *ghul.* (orbicular of sheep, etc.) *pucha.* (-of cows and buffaloes) *ghoshoe, ghoshāk.* (horse-) *kharshan.* (birds-) *paikhāl, rikh.* (-of kids, etc.) *poghla, pekhāṛa.* (-heap) *ḍerān, khadzala.* (mass of cow-) *sūṭa.* (fuel of cow-) *tsapiyāka.* (stack of fuel of cow-) *gohāṭa.*

Dung, v.a. *ghul k*; *khaṛal, loya baul-k., ḥājat ta kkhkenāstal.*

Dungeon, s. *qaid-khāna, zindān.*

Dupe, s. *ghulawulai*; *drohawulai, ṭīṭālai.*

Duplicate, s. *naql, joṛa.*

Duplicity, s. *palma, ṭagī, ṭīṭāl, chal-wal.*

Durable, a. *pāedār, maẓbūṭ, qā-im, ṣābit.*

Duration, s. *pāedārī, mūda.*

During, p. *tar—pore, hombra chī.*

Dusk, s. *mākkhām, shafaq.*

Dusky, a. *ṭor, mushkai, kha-aṛ, skāṇr.*

Dust, s. *dūṛa, khāwra, gard* or *garz, ghubār.*

Dust, v.a. *duṛawul.* (shake) *tsanḍal.* (dredge) *borqah k.*

Dusty, a. *garz wahalai, pa dūṛo ḍak.*

Dutiful, a. *farmān-bardār, khidmatī, manūnkai.*

Duty, s. *farẓ, sharṭ.* (office) *kār.* (military) *pahra, tsoka-ī.* (tax) *maḥṣūl, bāj, chūngai, ḥaqq.*

Dwarf, s. *chūnai, poṭai, mandarai, tsongai.*

Dwell, v.n. *osedal, āstedal, pātedal.* v.a. *mīshta-, astoga-, kilai-, ṭīkāo-. basiyā-*, etc. *k.*

Dweller, s. *osedūnkai, āstedūnkai, astogūnkai.*

Dwelling, s. *astoga, mīshta, dzāe, kor, makān.*

Dwindle, v.n. *kamedal, la-agedal, narai-, mahīn-, bārīk-, kotāh-*, etc. *ked.*

Dye, v.a. *rangawul, rang warkawul.*

Dyer, s. *dobī, rang-rez.*

Dynasty, s. *salṭanat, khāndān, rāj.*

Dysentery, s. *ra-ama, kānga, ṛap.* (to have-) v.a. *ra-ame-, ṛap, ghurzawul, kānga niwul.*

Dyspepsia, s. *bad-haẓmī*; *agheṛana, āṭerana.* (to have-) v.a. *agheṛal, aṭeral.*

Dyspeptic, a. *āgheṛalai, aṭeralai.*

E.

Each, p. *har·yo, yo·yo.* (-other) *yo·bul, dzabla.*
Eager, a. *tez, tod, garm; mayan; liwāl.*
Eagle, s. *bātūr, gargas.*
Ear, s. *ghwag.* (-of corn) *wagai, chala-ī.* (-ring) *chala, wālai, lakkhta-ī, barghwagai, ḍeḍa, barghoṭai, mandara-ī.* (lobe of-) *narma-ī, liraga-ī, būtska-ī.*
Earless, a. *būṛai.*
Early, a. *wakhtī.* (-crop) *mahīnah.* (-morning) *saḥār* or *saḥr, ṣubḥa.*
Earn, v.a. *gaṭal, paidā k., kamā-ī k., ḥāṣil k.*
Earnest, a. *garm, tod, sā'ī, pa jid.*
Earth, s. *khāwra; zmaka, zamīn; mulk, būm; duniyā, jahān, naṛa-ī.*
Earthen, a. *khāwrīn.*
Earthly, a. *jahānī, duniyā-ī.*
Earthquake, s. *zalzala, laṛza.*
Ease, s. *āsān·tiyā, ārām.*
East, s. *nmar·* or *nwar·khātah.*
Eastward, ad. *nwar·khātah khwā.*
Easy, a. *āsān; sam, spuk, halak; āsūdah, moṛ.*
Eat, v.a. *khwuṛal.*
Eatable, a. *khwurākī.*
Eater, s. *khwuṛūnkai, khwurindah* (in comp.) *-khor.*
Eaves, s. *bala-ī, sharīfa, sarmāta-ī, tsatso-ba-ī, parchata-ī.* (-dropper) *ghwag·tsārai.* (-dropping) *ghwag·tsārana.*
Eaves-drop, v.a. *ghwag tsāral.*
Ebb, s. *zawāl, prewātah, kamedana.*
Ebullition, s. *eshnā, khūṭkai, josh.*
Eccentric, a. *pa trats; kāwāk, lewanai.*
Echo, s. *ghag, kāngai, anga-ī, angāza, āwāz.*
Eclat, s. *raunaq, dabdaba.*
Eclipse, s. *tandar.* v.a. *tandar nīwul.*
Economy, s. *kormāna; tartīb.*
Ecstacy, s. *be·khūdī, be·shāna ḍera kkhādī.*
Eddy, s. *ghurzai, gird·āb; ḍab.*
Edge, s. *ghāṛa, morga, tselma, ja-ī.* (of a blade) *dam.* (to set on-) v.a. *ghākkh ṭaghawul.*
Edge, v.a. (sharpen) *tera k.* (instigate) *lamsawul.* (fringe) *jānja-ī lgawul.*
Edging, s. *jānja-ī, laman, palaw, trāṭa, maghzai.*
Edict, s. *sanad, raqam, farmān, jār.*
Edifice, s. *makān, mānṛa-ī, mina, ḥawela-ī.*
Edify, v.a. *pohawul, kkhayal—kkhowul, t'alīm k.*
Edition, s. *chāp, tālīf.*
Editor, s. *murattib, mu-allif.*
Educate, v.a. *pālal, lwalawul, tarbiyat-, t'alīm-,* etc. *k.*
Education, s. *pālana, tarbiyat, t'alīm.*
Eel, s. *mār·māhai, mār·kab.*
Efface, v.a. *wrānawul, habatah k., wrukawul.*
Effect, s. *'amal, pāzah, aṣar, kār.*
Effect, v.a. *kawul, kṛal, joṛawul, 'amal-,* etc. *k.*
Effects, s. *māl, asbāb, kālī, sāmān.* (-of deceased) *tarka, pāto.*
Effectual, a. *kārī, kāmil, pūrah, kāfī·shāfī.*
Effeminate, a. *kkhadzonak, nā·mard.*
Effervesce, v.n. *eshedal* or *yashedal, khuṭ ked.*
Effervescence, s. *eshnā, khuṭkai, josh.*
Efficient, a. *pūrah, kāmil, qābil, kār·sāz.*
Effigy, s. *but, tsera, ṣūrat.*
Effluvium, s. *būe, soṛ·bū-ī; bṛās.*
Effort, s. *zor, sa'ī, miḥnat, kokshiksh.*
Effrontery, s. *be·makh·tob, be·ḥayā-ī, be·sharmī.*
Effulgence, s. *ranṛā, rokkhnā-ī, brekkhnā.*
Effulgent, a. *rokkhān, dzalak·nāk, brekkh·nāk.*
Effusion, s. *rezish, toe, tuedana, bahedana.*
Egg, s. *haga-ī, hā.* (-plant) *bāṭīganṛ.*
Egotism, s. *khpulī, khūdī, manī.*
Egregious, a. *bashpaṛ, bad, sakht, ghaṭ.*
Egress, s. *wātah, khātah, barāmad.*
Eight, a. *atah.* (eighth) a. *atam.*

Eighteen, a. *atah·las.* (18th) *atah·lasam.*
Eighty, a. *atiyā.* (eightieth) *atiyā·yam.*
Either, p. *yā.* pr. *tsok, kūm, tsa.*
Eject, v.a. *sharal, bāsal—yastal, jārbāsal—jāryastal, pore·jane k.*
Ejection, s. *sharūn, yastūn, jāryastūn.*
Elaborate, a. *narai, mahīn; mushkil, grān.*
Elapse, v.n. *teredal.*
Elastic, a. *post, narm; damdār, mulā-im.*
Elated, a. *khwakkh, kkhād, kkhād·man; bādī, kibr·jan, maghrūr.*
Elbow, s. *tsangal.*
Elder, a. *mashar.* s. *spīn·gīrai; pīr, shekh.*
Elect, v.a. *khwakkhawul, chunral.*
Elegance, s. *kkhāyast, kkhāyast·wālai, jorāb, krah·wrah, spetsal·tob.*
Elegant, a. *kkhāyastah, nāzak.*
Elegy, s. *wīr, wainā.*
Element, s. *aṣlī shai.*
Elephant, s. *hātī, pīl.*
Elevate, v.a. *khejawul, porta k., pātsawul.*
Elevated, a. *ūchat, hask, lwar.*
Elevation, s. *ūchat·wālai, bulandai, taraqqai, khātah, hask·wālai; sarfarāzī.*
Eleven, a. *yolas.* (eleventh) a. *yolasam.*
Elicit, v.a. *kāgal—kkhkal, bāsal—yastal, m'alūmawul.*
Eligible, a. *ghwarah, lā·iq, khwakkh, pīrzo.*
Elixir, s. *aksīr, 'araq.*
Elk, s. *gāwuz.*
Elocution, s. *khula·warī, khula·war·tob.*
Elope, v.n. *puṭedal, takkhtedal.* (-as a woman) *maṭīza ked.* (-with a woman) v.a. *maṭīz k.*
Eloquent, a. *khula·war, khog·zabān.*
Else, p. *yā.* pr. *bl, nor.* (any one-) *bul·tsok, nor·tsok.* (anything-) *bul·tsa, nor·tsa.*
Else, ad. *kanra, kana, ganra.*
Elsewhere, ad. *bul·charta, nor·charta.*
Elucidate, v.a. *kkhkārah k., prānatal, bayān k.*
Elude, v.n. *puṭedal, bachedal, khalāṣedal.*
Elysium, s. *jannat, bihikkht.*
Emaciate, v.n. *wuchedal, kaṛedal, zahedal.*
Emaciation, s. *ḍangar·tob, wuch·klak·tob.*
Emancipate, v.a. *āzādawul, khalāṣawul, yalah k.*
Embalm, v.a. *muṛai pa maṣālo ḍakawul.*
Embankment. s. *pūla, wand, band.*
Embark, v.n. *pa beṛa-ī sparedal* or *khatal.*
Embarrass, v.a. *rabṛawul, ḥariyānawul, tangawul, sargardānawul.*
Embarrassed, a. *ḥariyān, sargardān.*
Embassy, s. *elchī·garī.*
Embellish, v.a. *joṛawul, andzorawul, ārāstah-, kkhāyastah-,* etc. *k.*
Embellishment, s. *andzor, zeba, kkhāyast, kkhāyast·wālai, ḍaul, kkhewa.*
Embers, s. *īre.* (hot-) *khuglan, skarwaṭa, skhwakkhtan, akhgar.* (cold-) *saṛe īre.*
Embezzle, v.a. *puṭawul. ghlā k., wrukawul.*
Emblem, s. *nakkha, nikkhān, 'alāmat.*
Embrace, s. *gheg, ghūza.*
Embrace, v.a. *ghāṛa·ghaṛa-ī-, baṛgaṛandai-, bara·gaṛa-, rogh·baṛ-,* etc. *k.*
Embrocate, v.a. *ghwaṛawul, mugal—mukkhal, tabal.*
Embrocation, s. *mālish, takoṛ, tab.*
Embroider, v.a. *bezal* or *pezal, būṭai gandal.*
Embroil, v.a. *nkkhlawul.*
Emerald, s. *zamarrud.*
Emerge, v.n. *watal, khatal.*
Emergency, s. *ẓarūrat; wāqi'a, ḥādiṣa.*
Emergent, a. *ẓarūr.*
Emery, s. *kurand.*
Emetic, s. *da bāka-ī-, da chāl-, da jāryasto-,* etc. *dawā, khwā·garzanai dārū.*
Emigrant, s. *musāfir, pradai.*
Emigrate, v.a. *kaḍa wṛal, legdal—lekkhal.*
Eminence, s. *ūchat·wālai, hask·wālai; khātah, taraqqai; ḍerai, ghunḍa-ī, kha-at, potai, rāsha, rashaka-ī; zbargī, loe·wālai; ḥaẓrat.*
Eminent, a. *ūchat; ghaṭ, loe; zbarg.*

Emissary, s. *jāsūs, tsārī, dzaraı, mukhbir.*
Emollient, a. *post, narm, mulā-im.*
Emolument, s. *gaṭa, sūd, naf'a, ḥāṣil.*
Emotion, s. *eshnā, khuṭkai; randz, dard.*
Empale, v.a. *pa sūla-ī khejawul; tsekhal.*
Emperor, s. *sulṭān, bādshāh, malik.*
Emphasis, s. *tākīd; ẓarb; dranāwai, drund-wālai.*
Emphatic, a. *tākīdī; drūnd.*
Empire, s. *salṭanat, rāj, bādshāhī.*
Employ, v.a. *mashghūlawul, lagawul; chalawul; kharts k., sātal, pa kār rānṛal.*
Employer, s. *khāwind, tsakkhtan, nāyak.*
Employment, s. *kār, khidmat, mashghūlā.*
Emporium, s. *bāzār, ganj, manḍha-ī, bandar.*
Empower, v.a. *wāk-, ikhtiyār-,* etc. *warkawul.*
Empty, a. *ta-ash, khālī, daḍ.*
Emulate, v.a. *sām sorai k., ghairat laral.*
Emulation, s. *ghairat, barābarī, samsorai.*
Emulous, a. *ghairat-man, himmat-nāk.*
Enable, v.a. *quwat-, ṭāqat-, zor-, tuwān-,* etc. *warkawul.*
Enact, v.a. *fārmāyal, ḥukm k.*
Enamel, s. *mīnā, jaṛāo, rang, āb.*
Enamour, v.a. *mayan-, 'āshiq-, fareftah,* etc. *k.; grohedah k.*
Encamp, v.a *ḍera-, muqām-,* etc. *k.*
Enchanter, s. *jādū-gar, koḍ-gar, siḥr-gar.*
Enchantment, s. *jādū, koḍa, siḥr.*
Enclose, v.a. *īsārawul* or *ḥiṣārawul, ger k.; shpol-, keṛa-, jal-, bāra-, pūla-,* etc. *taṛal* or *-k.; nghakkhtal, lifāfa k.*
Enclosure, s. *iḥāṭa, bāra, ḥiṣār, hadera.* (-for cattle) *bānḍa, shpol.* (-of a house) *jal, gholai.*
Encounter, v.a. *jang k.* v.n. *miliyā, ked. pekkhedal.*
Encourage, v.a. *dam-, dilāsa-,* etc. *warkawul.*
Encroach, v.a. *lānde k., dakhl k.*
Encroachment, s. *dakhl, gharaẓ.*

Encumber, v.a. *kariyābawul, dranawul, bār āchawul.*
End, s. *ākhir, khatm; anjām, tamāmī; ḥadd, sar-peza, tsūka.* v.a. *ākhir-, khatm-,* etc. *k.*
Endear, v.a. *mayan-, 'azīz-,* etc. *k., khpulawul.*
Endeavour, s. *miḥnat, was, sa'ī, kokshiksh, hatsa.*
Endless, a. *be-ḥadd, be-and; tal, mudām.*
Endorse, v.a. *ṣaḥīḥ-, dast-khaṭṭ-,* etc. *k.*
Endowment, s. *waqf, hiba; khairāt, niyāz, bakkhana; hunar.*
Endurance, s. *ṣabr, zgham, tāb, zor, ṭāqat.*
Endure, v.a. *zghamal, ṣabr k., sahal, petsal.* v.n. *pāedal, sahedal.*
Enemy, s. *dukkhman: mīrtsaman.*
Energetic, a. *chālāk, takṛah, maẓbūṭ.*
Energy, s. *zor, quwat, bram, tuwān.*
Enervate, v.a. *kam-zor-, kam-quwat-,* etc. *k.*
Enforce, v.a. *maẓbūṭ-, muḥkam-,* etc. *k., zoral, chalawul, rawā-, jārī-,* etc. *k.*
Engage, v.a. *mashghūlawul, lagiyā, k., sātal, lagawul, wāda-, neṭa-, sharṭ,* etc. *taṛal* or *k.*
Engaged, a. *lagiyā, mashghūl.*
Engagement, s. *iqrār, wāda, neṭa, sharṭ; kār, kasb, mashghūlā; jang, muqadamma.* (-in marriage) *koĵdan* or *koĵda.*
Engender, v.a. *paidā k., rānṛal.*
Engine, s. *kālai, hatiyār, ālat, ṣana'at.*
Engrave, v.a. *kandal* or *kanal, kanastal.*
Engraver, s. *muhr-kan.*
Enhance, v.a. *qīmat ziyātawul, nirkh kamawul* or *-la-agawul; khejawul, dranawul.*
Enigma, s. *ramūz, kināya.*
Enjoin, v.a. *farmāyal, k iya-, tākīd-,* etc. *k.*
Enjoy, v.a. *khwand-, maza-,* etc. *k.*
Enjoyment, s. *khwand, maza; kkhādī, khwakkhī.*
Enlist, v.a. *nokar k.; nūm līkal; mal-, malgarai-,* etc. *k.*

Enmity, s. *dukkhmanī, 'inād, 'aks, mīrtsī.*
Enormous. a. *ghaṭ, bashpaṛ, loe, star, nāpaṛ.*
Enough, ad. *bas, ḍer, kāfī, kifāyat.*
Enquiry, s. *sawāl, pukkhtana, tapos* or *tafahūs, pursān, pursish, shanana.*
Ensign, s. *nakkha, nikkhān, bairaq, janḍa.*
Ensnare, v.a. *ghulawul*; *nīwul, nkkhlawul.*
Ensue, v.n. *prewatal, khatal, kedal.*
Entangle, v.a. *arjal·barjal-, aṛang·baṛang-, tsapolai-*, etc. *k.*; *nkkhlawul.*
Enter, v.n. *nanawatal, dākhiledal.*
Enterprise, s. *muhimm, grān·kār.*
Enterprising, a. *himmat·nāk, zṛah·war.*
Entertain, v.a. *pālal, sātal, nmāndzal*; *melmastiyā-, ẓiyāfat-, mezmānī-*, etc. *k.*
Entertainer, s. *melmah·dost, korbah, sat kawūnkai.*
Entertainment, s. *melmastiyā, sat*; *tamāsha, nandāra*; *loba, sail.*
Enthusiasm, s. *sargarmi, mīna, 'ishq.*
Enthusiast, s. *saudā-ī*; *'āshiq, liwāl.*
Entice, v.a. *ghulawul, ṭagal, lamsawul, fareb-, targhīb-*, etc. *warkawul.*
Entire, a. *tamām, pūrah, sābat, kāmil.*
Entirely, ad. *amānī, sarāsar, surup.*
Entitle, v.a. *ḥaqq·man k.*; *nūm īgdal* or *gdal*, or *-kkhkegdal* or *-kegdal.*
Entrails, s. *laṛmānah.*
Entrance, s. *war, darwāza, khula, darak*; *nanawātah, dakhl.*
Entrance, v.a. *be·khūd-, fareftuh-*, etc. *k., damawul, hūda k., paṭ nīwul.*
Entrap, v.a. *nīwul, nkkhlawul, ger k.*
Entrapped, a. *nīwai, nkkhatai.* v.n. *nkkhatal* or *nkkhledal.*
Entreat, v.a. *minnat k.*; *ghokkhtal, du'ā k.*
Entreaty, s. *minnat, d'uā, darkhwāst.*
Entrenchment, s. *bāra, sangar, gaṛa-ī.*
Enumeration, s. *shmer, shumār, ḥisāb.*
Envelope, s. *lifāfa*; *poṭ, postakai.*
Envelope, v.a. *ngharal—nghakkhtal.*

Envious, a. *ḥāsid, ḥasad·nāk.*
Environs, s. *sawād, chār·chāper.*
Envoy, s. *elchī, wakīl, astā·dzai.*
Envy, s. *ḥasrat, ḥasad, rashk, wiyāṛ.*
Ephemeral, s. *fānī, teredūnai.*
Epicure, s. *geḍa·parwar, khūsh·khwurāk.*
Epidemic, s. *wabā*; *'āmm.*
Epilepsy, s. *mergai, mahergа.*
Epistle, s. *nāma, chīṭa-ī, khaṭṭ, kāghaz.*
Epitaph, s. *da qabr kitāba.*
Epithalamium, s. *kkhādiyāna, sandara.*
Epitome, s. *khulāṣa, mukhtaṣar, lanḍa.*
Epoch, s. *tārīkh, kāl, mūda, san.*
Equal, a. *barābar, makhai, gund, yo·shān*; *sam, hawārah.* s. *samsorai, humdzolai, siyāl, sārai, twal, makhai.*
Equality, s. *barābar·wālai, makhai·tob*; *sam·wālai.*
Equanimity, s. *qalār·tiyā, ṣabr.*
Equestrian, a. *sparlai, sparlanai.* s. *swor* or *spor.*
Equip, v.a. *tayār k., sambālawul, mlā taṛal, wasla-, drasta-*, etc. *warkawul, dzerma k.*
Equipage, s. *sāz, sāmān, asbāb, kālī.* (retinue) *swarlī* or *sparlī, jalab.*
Equitable, a. *'ādil, rikkhtīnai, rāst·man.*
Equity, s. *inṣāf, rāstī, niyāw, 'adl.*
Equivalent. a. *barābar, twal*; *badal, 'iwaẓ.*
Equivocal, a. *shakk·man, gumānī.*
Equivocate, v.a. *palma-, hira-ī*, etc. *k., aṛawale·khabare k., darogh·jane khabare k.*
Era, s. *tārīkh, kāl, san, mūda.*
Eradicate, v.a. *munḍ-, wekh-, būnsaṭ-*, etc. *bāsal—y istal*, or *-khejawul*, or *-kāgal—kkhkal.*
Erase, v.a. *wrānawul, qalam pre·kāgal.*
Ere, ad. *wṛunbe, awwal, lā*; *pakhwā, wṛāndе.* (-now) *lā tar osa.* (-while) *lā pakhwā.* (-long) *pa la-age mūde kkhke.*
Erect, a. *walāṛ, negh, lak, zīg, jig.*
Erect, v.a. *walāṛawul, wadrawul, khejawul.*

Err, v.a. *khatā k.*
Errand, s. *paighām.* (-boy) *harkārah.*
Erroneous, a. *ghalat.*
Error, s. *khatā, wabāl, gunā, taqṣīr.*
Erudition, s. *'ilm, qābil·tob.*
Eruption, s. *eshnā, khut, khutkai, josh.* (prickly heat-) *garmaka.* (acne-) *dzwānaka.* (small-pox) *nanaka-ī.* (measles-) *sharai.* (tooth-) *sara·makha.* (jet) *fawāra, dāra.*
Erysipelas, s. *surkh·bād.*
Escalade, s. *khātah pa kamandūno.* (-ladder) *kamand.*
Escape, s. *khalāṣī, tekkhta, bachāw, bach.*
Escape, v.n. *bachedal, takkhtedal, khalāṣedal, wurhedal, yalah ked.* (miss) *terwatal.*
Escheat, v.n. *lā·wāriṣ ked.*
Escort, s. *badraga* ; *jalab, sparlī.*
Especially, ad. *khuṣūṣan.*
Esplanade, s. *maidān, ḍāga, panḍ·ghālai.*
Espouse, v.a. *kojdan k., wādah k., nikāḥ taṛal.* (a cause, etc.) *ākhistal, bacharwul, komak warkawul.*
Essay, s. (attempt) *qaṣd.* (trial) *āzmekkht.* (endeavour) *kokshiksh, sa'ī.* (treatise) *risāla.*
Essence, s. *'araq, johar, aṣl.* (perfume) *'atr.*
Essential, a. *aṣlī* ; *zarūr* ; *sūchah.*
Establish, v.a. *muqarrar-, jārī-,* etc. *k., chalawul, rawānawul* ; *qā-im-, mazbūt-,* etc. *k., wudrawul, kkhkenawul, pāedār k.*
Estate, s. (land) *dawtar* or *daftar, wanḍ.* (fief) *jāgīr, jāedād.* (property) *māl, daulat, milk.* (hereditary) *mīrāṣ* or *mīrāt.* (deceased's) *pāto, tarka.* (rank) *pāya, martaba, darja.*
Esteem, s. *qadr, 'izzat* ; *mīna, tapāk.*
Esteem, v.a. *qadr-,* etc. *pejandal* ; *mu'tabar-, nek-,* etc. *ganral* ; *mīna-,* etc. *k.*
Estimable, s. *'izzat·nāk, mu'tabar, nek.*
Estimate, v.a. *shmeral, ganral.*
Estimation. s. *rāe, khiyāl, poha, fikr, nazar.*
Estrange, v.a. *marawar-, mānrai-,* etc. *k.* ; *pradai-, begānah-,* etc. *k.*
Estrangement, s. *mānrai, marawar·tob* ; *pradī·tob, begān·tūn, begānah·tob* or *begān·tob.*
Eternal, a. *abadī, dā-im, jāwīd* or *jāwīdān.*
Eternally, ad. *tal, tal·tala, tal·tar·tala, mudāman, hamesh.*
Eternity, s. *abad, azal, baqā.* (to all-) ad. *tar·abada, tar·azala.*
Ethereal, a. *āsmānī, hawā-ī.*
Ethics, s. *pand·nāma, naṣīḥat·nāma.*
Etiquette, s. *adab, makh, madāra.*
Etymology, s. *ṣarf* ; *peza-ī, hezagī.*
Eulogy, s. *stāyana, ṣanā, t'arīf.*
Eunuch, s. *hijrai, khunṣā.*
European, s. *farangai.* a. *farangī.*
Evacuate, v.a. *ta-asharwul, khālī-, khushai-,* etc. *k.* ; *jārbāsal—jāryastal.*
Evade, v.a. *palma-, bāna-, hira-ī-,* etc. *k.* ; *tagī-, chal·bāzī-,* etc. *k.* v.n. *bachedal, putedal, terwatal.*
Evanescent, a. *fānī, teredūnai.* (-colour) *om.*
Evaporate, v.n. *wuchedal.*
Evasion, s. *bāna, ḥīla* ; *palma, hira-ī.*
Evasive, a. *bāna·war, ḥīla·bāz.*
Even, a. *barābar, yo·shān.* (similar) *gund.* (-in weight) *twal.* (smooth) *hawārah, sam.* (odd and-) *juft·o·tāk.*
Even, ad. *hum, lā, hado, yara, kho.*
Evening, s. *mākkhām, begāh.* (to-morrow-) *ṣabā begāh.* (last-) *begāh.* (of last-) *begānai, baranai.*
Evenness, a. *barābar·wālai, sam·wālai.*
Event, s. *wāqi'a, chal, khabara, qiṣṣa,* (at all-) *hargora, kām·nā·kām, khwāh·makhwāh, kho.*
Ever, ad. *kala, chare.*
Everlasting, a. *dā-im, qā-im, lā·zawal.*
Evermore, ad. *hamesh, mudām, tar·abada.*

Every, a. *har.* (-person) *har·tsok.* (-thing) *har·tsa.*

Evidence, s. *gawāhī, shāhidī; dalīl; nakkha.* (to give-) v.a. *gawāhī-* or *shāhidī lal* or *-lawdal.*

Evident, a. *tsargand, kkhkārah, bartser, awtsār.*

Evidently, ad. *zāhiran, bartseran, pa jār.*

Evil, a. *bad, kharāb.* s. *'aib, kharābī; balā, āfat; gunāh, nabāl.* (-doer) a. *bad·kirdār, gunāh·gār.*

Ewer, s. *kūza, kūza·ra-ī, khum·ra-ī, kunja-ī.*

Exact, a. *jukht, kat·mat, jor, barābar.*

Exact, v.a. *zoral; taqāza k.*

Exaggerate, v.a. *ziyātawul, ūgdawul, mubālagha k.*

Exalt, v.a. *pāya pa porta k.; khejawul, pātsawul.*

Examine, v.a. *āzmāyal, āzmekkht k.; imtihān ākhistal* or *k.; latawul, shanal, katal.*

Example, s. *misāl, namūna; 'ibrat, siyāsat.*

Exasperate, v.a. *rabrawul, zoral; pārawul; khapah k., tongawul, tongāra k., ageyal.*

Excavate, v.a. *kanal, kanawdal, kanastal.*

Excavation, s. *kanda, doghal.*

Exceed, v.n. *ziyātedal.*

Excel, v.n. *pūrah-, kāmil-, ghālib-,* etc. *ked.*

Except, p. *siwā, baghair, be·la—na.*

Excess, s. *ziyātī, der·wālai; charcha.*

Excessive, a. *der, ziyāt, be·shān.*

Excessively, ad. *be·hadda, be·shāna.*

Exchange, s. *badal, 'iwaz; adal·badal; wata.*

Excise, s. *chūngai, sāw, mahsūl.*

Excise, v.a. *tsīral, prekawul* or *prekral.*

Excite, v.a. *pārawul; lamsawul; pātsawul, paidā k.; ageyal, tongawul.*

Excitement, s. *eshnā; pārawūna; lamsūn.*

Exclaim, v.a. *nāra wahal, bāng wayal, shor k., chighawul.*

Exclamation, s. *nāra, sūra, chigha, ghag, zwag; wāwailā, faryād.*

Exclude, v.a. *sharal, lire k., ratul.*

Excoriate, v.a. *garawul, sūlawul, nwarawul, sūdah k., nūkāre wahal.* v.n. *sūledal, sūdah ked.*

Excrement, s. *ghul.* (-of diarrhœa) *ka-ar, rīkh.* (-of dysentery) *ra-ama, rap.*

Excruciate, v.a. *khūgawul, 'azābawul, āzārawul.*

Exculpate, v.a. *pulawul, be·gunāh k., bakkhal.*

Excursion, s. *sail; gakkht.* (-foray) *dāra.*

Excuse, v.a. *pulawul, bakkhal; bāna-, hira-ī-, 'uzr-,* etc. *k., hujjat k.*

Execrable, a. *bad, l'anatī, makrūh.*

Execrate, v.a. *kkhera k.*

Execute, v.a. *kawul, kral, pa·dzāe k., jorawul, tamāmawul, pūrah k.; qatlawul, wajal* or *wajlal, mur k.; jārī k., chalawul.*

Execution, s. *kawūna, krah, jorawuna; qatl.*

Executioner, s. *jallād, qātil.*

Executive, a. *kār guzār; mukhtār kār.*

Executor, s. *wasī.*

Exemplary, a. *nek, sawābī; 'ibrat·nāk.*

Exemplify, v.a. *misal ākhistal,* or *-rāwral.*

Exempt, v.a. *pregdal—prekkhodal, āzādawul, pulawul, bakkhal, bachawul, khalāsawul.*

Exercise, v.a. *'amal k., chalawul, jārī k., lagawul, mashghūlawul.*

Exercise, s. *'amal, ist'imāl; mashghulā, kār; sail, gakkht.* (lesson) *dars, sabaq.* (horses) *jaulān, kartab.* (hawks, dogs, etc.) *sāolī.* (troops) *qawā'id.*

Exert, v.a. *kokshikkh-, sa'ī-, zor-,* etc. *k.; stam wahal.*

Exhalation, s. *brās, bukhār, dam, lū, lara, piyālkhla, wagma.*

Exhaust, v.a. *ta-ashawul, khālī-, khushai-,* etc. *k.; wrukawul, kharts-, sarf-,* etc. *k.; tamām-, pūrah-,* etc. *k.; starai-, be·dam-,* etc. *k.*

Exhaustless, a. *be·nihāyat, be·zawāl.*

Exhibit, v.a. *kkhayal—kkhowul, prānatal, kkhkārah-, bartser-, tsargand-*, etc. *k.*
Exhibition, s. *tamāsha, nandāra.*
Exhilarate, v.a. *kkhād-, khwakkh-*, etc. *k.*
Exhort, v.a. *pand, naṣīhat-*, etc. *warkawul.*
Exigency, s. *tangsiyā, lā-chārī, sakhtī, ẓarūrat.*
Exile, s. *jilā-waṭanī, be-waṭanī.* (the person) *pradai, begānah, be-waṭan.*
Exist, v.n. *shwal, kedal, osedal, maujūdedal.*
Existence, s. *shta-wālai, hastī, būd, ĵwand.*
Existent, a. *osan, osanai, maujūd.*
Exit, s. *wātah, watana, wartag.*
Exonerate, v.a. *pulawul, khalāṣawul.*
Exorbitant, a. *be-andāz, be-nihāyat.*
Exorcise, v.a. *damawul, hūda k., koḍ k.*
Exordium, s. *debācha, muqaddama.*
Exotic, a. *pradai, begānah, gharīb.*
Expand, v.n. *planedal, aratedal.* (swell) *parsedal.* (-as a flower) *ghwaredal, khwaredal.* (spread) *wīṛedal, pheledal.*
Expanse, s. *arat-wālai, plan-wālai, sor* or *psor.*
Expect, v.a. *lār katal, umed laral.*
Expectant, a. *umed-wār, muntaẓir.*
Expectation, s. *umed, āsra.*
Expedient, a. *munāsib, ghwarah, wājib.* s. *band, tadbīr, chāra, chal.*
Expedition, s. *chālākī, chustī, talwār.* (journey) *safar.* (military-) *chapāo, tākht.* (foray) *dāṛa, bota.* (against infidels) *ghazā, jihād.*
Expeditious, a. *gaṛandai, tak-lāstai, chālāk, chust, za-ar* or *zir, jalt.*
Expel, v.a. *sharal, lire k., pore-ĵane k., bāsal—yastal, raṭal, traṭal.*
Expend, v.a. *kharts-, ṣarf-*, etc. *k., lagawul.*
Expense, s. *kharts*; *qīmat, bai'a.*
Expensive, a. *khartsī, tāwānī*; *grān, qīmatī, qīmat-nāk.*
Experience, s. *poha, wuqūf*; *āzmekkht.*
Experience, v.a. *ĭidal, terawul, zghamal, khwuṛal, kāgal—kkhkal.*
Experienced, a. *āmokhtah, āzmūdah, pokh, wāqif, khabar-dār, zdah.*
Experiment, s. *āzmekkht, tajriba, imtiḥān.*
Expert, a. *kārī-gar, hunar-man, hokkhyār*; *chālāk, pokh.*
Expiate, v.a. *kafāra warkawul, tāwān warkawul.*
Expiration, s. *anjām, khatm, ākhirat.* (death) *dzān-kadan, marg.*
Expire, v.n. *mṛal, muṛ ked.*; *teredal*; *tamāmedal.* (breathe) *sā-, sāh-, dam-*, etc. *bāsal—yastal, -sharal, -pregdal—prekkhodal*, etc.
Explain, v.a. *bayānawul, pohawul, kkhayal—kkhowul, kkhkārah k.*
Explanation, s. *bayān, kkhowūna, m'anā, sharaḥ.*
Expletive, s. *takiya-kalām.*
Explicit, a. *tsargand, ṣāf, kkhkārah, ẓāhir.*
Explode, v.n. *pṛak-chāwdal, ālwatal.* v.a. *daz wahal, ālwūzawul.*
Exploit, s. *karāmat, ghaṭ-kār, zbargī.*
Explore, v.a. *laṭawul, shanal.*
Explosion, s. *ḍaz, ṭas.*
Export, v.a. *bul mulk ta āstawul* or *-legal.*
Expose, v.a. *kkhkārah-, bartser-*, etc. *k., parda porta k.*
Exposition, s. *sharaḥ, bayān.*
Expostulate, v.a. *takrār-, ḥujjat-*, etc. *k.*
Exposure, s. *kkhkārah-tob, barbanḍ-tob.*
Expound, v.a. *bayānawul, m'anā-kkhayal—kkhowul.*
Express, v.a. *wayal, lal* or *lawdal*; *nichoṛawul, nakkhtedzal, paz wahal, zbekkhal.*
Express, a. *tsargand, awtsār*; *khāṣṣ.* s. *qāṣid, chapar.*
Expression, s. *khabara, wayai, sukhan, kalām*; *nichoṛ, paz.*
Expressly, ad. *pa qaṣd, qaṣdan.*

Expulsion, s. _sharana._

Expunge, v.a. _qalam wahal, wrānawul._

Exquisite, a. _pākīzah, nā̆dir, matrah, ghwarah._

Extant, a. _osan, osanai, maujūd._

Extempore, ad. _sam da lāsa._

Extend, v.n. _rasedal, ūgdedal, ziyātedal._

Extension, s. _ūgd·wālai, ziyāt·wālai._

Extensive, a. _loe, plan, arat, ūgd, kushād._

Extent, s. _ūgd·wālai, plan·wālai ; qadr, andāza,_

Extenuate, v.a. _kamawul, la-agawul._

Exterior, a. _bāhir, wardzanai._

Extinct, a. _wruk, ter, nā·būd, nest, nishtah._

Extinguish, v.a. _mur-, sor-, gul-,_ etc. _k._

Extirpate, v.a. _prekawul, tsīral ; mund-, wekh-, būnsat-,_ etc. _khejawul, -bāsal— yastal, -kāgal—kkhkal._

Extol, v.a. _stāyal, stāyana k._ or _-wayal._

Extort, v.a. _shūkawul, pa zor ākhistal._

Extortion, s. _ziyātī, zulm._

Extract, s. _'araq, jauhar._

Extract, v.a. _bāsal—yastal, kāgal—kkhkal._

Extraction, s. _rag, nogai, zāt, asl._

Extraneous, a. _pradai, begānah._

Extraordinary, a. _'ajab, nādir._

Extravagant, a. _khartsī, tārānī, isrāfī, be· tartīb, chakhraba kawūnkai._

Extreme, a. _der, be·shān, be·hadd._ s. _hadd._

Extremely, ad. _be·hadda, be·shāna._

Extremity, s. _sar, tsūka, peza ; hadd, pūla, brīd ; rokh, dada, tselma, tsanda, palaw._ (distress) _tangsiyā, lā·chārī, mīrtsī._

Extricate, v.a. _prānatawul, āzādawul, khalāṣ- awul, spardal._

Exuberance, s. _frewānī, wadānī, der·wālai._

Exuberant, a. _frewān, wadān, der, ziyāt._

Exudation, s. _zyam, naw ; khwale._

Exude, v.a. _zyam-, naw-,_ etc. _k._ v.n. _watal, khwale ked., zyam-,_ etc. _ked._

Exult, v.a. _sakha k., wiyāral, kkhādī k._

Eye, s. _starga._ (-sight) _nazar._ (-ball) _lema,_

starghalai. (-socket) _starghālai, gogil._ (-pupil) _torai, kasai, bātūr._ (-iris) _lema._ (-brow) _wrūdza._ (-lid) _dzedzma_ or _dzegma._ (-lash) _bānra._ (-witness) _gawāh, shāhid._ (-of a needle) _swam_ or _spam._

Eye diseases, s. (opthalmia) _lccha._ (albugo) _gul._ (pannus) _nakhūna._ (cataract) _parda._ (sore eyes) _lechane·starge._

F.

Fable, s. _qiṣṣa, naql, hikāyat, matal, miṣāl._

Fabricate, v.a. _jorawul, tandal._

Fabulous, a. _darogh, wahmī._

Face, s. _makh, tsihra, bashra, mushāda, rūe gūna._ (-to face) _makhā·makh._

Facetious, a. _toq·mār, washtai_ or _washt·mār, malandai._

Facilitate, v.a. _āsānawul._

Facility, s. _āsān·tiyā._

Facing, a. _makhā·makh, wrāndai._

Fact, s. _wāq'ia, gharaz, matlab, kār, krah._

Faction, s. _para, janba, gundī ; putna, pasāt._

Factious, a. _pasātī_ or _fasādī, takrārī._

Factor, s. _kār kawūnkai, gumāshtah, dīwān._

Factory, s. _kār·khāna, kotī._

Faculty, s. _quwat, qudrat, tuwān ; khāṣṣiyat, lokkhai, khoe, tāṣīr ; 'aql, shu'ūr._

Fade, v.n. _mrāmedal_ or _mrāwedal, kumanredal, marghechan-, pezai-, malāl-,_ etc. _ked._

Fag, v.n. _rabredal, starai ked._

Fagot, s. _gedai, panda, bālanr._

Fail, v.a. _khatā k._ v.n. _kamedal._

Failing, s. _'aib, quṣūr, khatā, nuqṣān._

Faint, a. _māndah, tap, nā·tuwān, za'īf._ s. _parghaz, be·khūdī,_ v.n. _parghaz ked._

Fair, a. _gorah, spīn ; kkhāyastah, kkhkulai, pa-ī·makhai_ or _pej·makhai ; sāf, pāk, kkhah, jor._ (-sky) _shīn._

Fair, s. *mela*.
Fairly, ad. *pa rāstī sara*.
Fairy, s. *parī, perai*. (the fairies) *piriyān*.
Faith, s. *īmān, dīn, khal, kesh, sāwīsā, bāwar*.
Faithful, a. *īmān-dār, wafā-dār, rikkhtīnai*.
Faithless, a. *be-īmān, be-wafā*.
Falcon, s. (Royal-) *shahīn*. (Peregrine- or Falco Sacer) *chargh, charghelai, tsarkh*. (Tercel-) *bahra-ī-bach*. See Hawk.
Falconer, s. *bāz-wān, mashkār, kkhkārī*.
Fall, v.n. *prewatal, lwedal*. (-in) *drabal*. (-into) *kkhkewatal*. (slip) *khwa-edal* or *khwahedal*.
Fall, s. *prewātah, lwedana*; *drabai*; *khwai*. (foot-) *trapai*.
Fallacy, s. *darogh, ghalat, kizb*.
Fallen, a. *prewatai, prot, lwedalai*.
Fallible, a. *gunāh-gār, quṣūr-man*.
Fallow, s. *wad, shāṛ, banjaṛ*.
False, a. *darogh-jan, darghal, nā-rāst, kāzib*. (-coin) *jūṭah, nā-sarah*.
Falsehood, s. *darogh, kizb*; *palma, fareb*.
Falter, v.n. *ṭaparedal*; *budrī-, tīndak-*, etc. *khwuṛal*; *pa jibe nkkhatal*.
Fame, s. *nūm, āwāza*.
Famed, a. *nūm-war, nāmer, mashhūr*.
Familiar, a. *khamsor*; *m'alūm*. s. *āshnāe, yār, mal*.
Family, s. *kor, kaḍa, ṭabar*; *khānawādah, khāndān, tabār, nasl*.
Famine, s. *grānī, kākhtī, ḍūkāl, qātī*.
Famish, v.n. *da lwuge mṛal*.
Famous, a. *mashhūr, nūm-war, nāmer*.
Fan, s. *babozai*. (-for flies) *chawṛa-ī*. (-for sifting grain) *chaj, tsap*.
Fanatic, s. *muta'ṣṣib, lewanai, saudā-ī*.
Fancy, s. *qiyās, khiyāl, wahm, and*.
Fang, s. *ghākkh, dāṛa*.
Fantasm, s. *wahm, khiyāl*.
Fantastic, a. *wahmī, khiyālī*; *washtai, malandai, swāngī*.

Far, ad. *lire* or *liri*. (as far as) *pore* or *pori, tar—pore*. (-away) *warāya*.
Farce, s. *pekkha, ṭoqe, washta*.
Fare, s. *khwurāk, khwāṛah, sat*; *kreha, kirāha*. v.a. *khwuṛal, sat k*. v.n. *teredal, chaledal, guzrānedal*.
Farewell, ad. *da khudāe pa amān, salām*.
Farm, s. *paṭai, wanḍ, dawtar, zamīn, ada-ī*; *ijāra*.
Farmer, s. *zamīndār*; *ijāra-dār*.
Farrier, s. *n'al-band*.
Fart, s. *dau, ṭa-as, ṭar, tīz, pa-as, pa-aska-ī*. v.a. *aratal, tīz-*, etc. *āchawul, ṭar*, etc. *k*.
Farther, ad. *lire* or *liri, nor lire*.
Fascinate, v.a. *fareftah-, mayan-, koḍ-*, etc. *k*.
Fashion, s. *ḍaul, shān, shakl, rang, wajha, tarkīb, chāl, rasm, dod, dastūr*.
Fashion, v.a. *joṛawul, tanḍal*.
Fast, a. *jalt, tez, gaṛandai, talwārī, talwār-gandai, halwāk, za-ar* or *zir*; *maḥkam, mazbūṭ*; *ṭīng, klak*.
Fast, s. *roja*. v.a. *roja laral* or *-nīwul*.
Fasten, v.a. *taṛal, lagawul*; *ṭīngawul, klakawul*; *kāgal—kkhkal*; *mazbūṭ k*.
Fastidious, a. *bādī, kibr-jan, khāntamā*.
Fasting, a. *nahār*. (voluntary-) *nahwa, roja*.
Fat, a. *tsorb, peṛ, peraṛ, punḍ, tanḍ, ghaṭ, kharaṭ*. (-as a child) *khamaṭ, chāgh*.
Fat, s. *spīna, wāzda*. (kidney-) *ghoz*. (melted-) *roghan, mū, ghwaṛī*.
Fatal, a. *qātil, kārī*; *qazā-ī*.
Fatality, s. *naṣīb, qazā, qismat, taqdīr*.
Fate, s. *ajal, marg, maut*; *qazā, qismat*.
Father, s. *plār*. (-in-law) *skhar*. (step-) *plandar*. (grand-) *nīkah*. (great grand-) *wa-ar-nīkah*. (great great grand-) *lā wa-ar-nīkah*.
Fatherless, a. *be-plār, plār-muṛai, yatīm*.
Fathom, s. *wāzah*.
Fatigue, v.a. *rabṛawul, staṛai-, stomān-, ṭap-, haukah-, māndah-*, etc. *k*.

Fault, s. *'aib, khatā, taqṣīr, wabāl, gunāh, quṣūr.* (to find-) v.a. *malāmatawul, ṭaqawul, raṭal, traṭal, kagal, ghandal.*

Faultless, a. *be-gunāh, be-quṣūr, be-taqṣīr.*

Faulty, a. *'aib-nāk, quṣūr-man, gunāh-gār, taqṣīrī ; bad, nā-kārah.*

Favour, s. *mrasta, mihrbānī, mihrbāngī, sat, makh, sela, selwa.*

Favourable, a. *barābar, munāsib, pīrzo ; makhawar, mihrbān.*

Favourite, a. *khwakkh, ghwarah, kkhkulai.*

Fawn, v.a. *chāplūsī-, ḍirpalī-, khushāmadī-, falān dast-māl-, jig-jigī-,* etc. *k.*

Fealty, s. *wafā-dārī, tābi'-dārī, kālkhwāhī.*

Fear, s. *wera* or *yera, tars, khof, bāk, sahm, tara ; wiswās, andekkhnā.*

Fear, v.n. *weredal, tarhedal, bugnedal.* v.a. *tars-, tor-,* etc. *khwuṛal.*

Fearful, a. *tars-nāk, khof-nāk ; tarhūr, yerman.*

Fearless, a. *be-bāk, be-ḍar.*

Feasible, a. *shwunai* or *shwūnkai.*

Feast, s. *melmastiyā, ẓiyāfat, jashn.*

Feat, s. *kār, kṛah ; bāzī.*

Feather, s. *banra, banraka, par.*

Feature, s. *tsihra, shakl, ṣūrat.*

February, s. *pāganr.*

Fee, s. *shukrāna ; ḥaqq, ajr, miḥnat ; chūngai.*

Feeble, a. *nā-tuwān, ẓa'īf, kam-ṭāqat, ṭap, kam-quwat, kam-zor, 'ājiz.*

Feed, v.a. *khwuṛawul ; tsarawul.* (eat) *khwuṛal.* (graze) v.n. *tsaredal* or *tsaral.* (-cattle) *wākkhah āchawul.* (-birds) *tāmba warkawul.* (nourish) *parwaral, pālal, sātal, parwarish k.*

Feel, v.a. *laṭawul, lamsawul, masa k.* (suffer) v.n. *pohedal, m'alūmedal, zghamedal, kedal.* (bear) v.a. *khwuṛal, līdal, kagal—kkhkal.* (-pain) *khūgedal, dardedal.* (-the pulse) *nabẓ katal.* (-for others) *dil-sozī-, gham-khwārī-, zṛah-swai-,* etc. *k.*

Feeling, s. *poh, pahm.*

Feign, v.a. *bāna-, ḥīla-, makr-,* etc. *k.* ; *palma-, hira-ī-, lamghaṛa-ī-,* etc. *k.*

Felicity, s. *kkhādī, khwakkhī, khush-ḥālī, khwand ; barakat, bakhtawarī, nek-bakhtī.*

Fell, v.a. *prekawul, wahal, naṛawul.*

Fell, a. *sakht, kāfir, ẓālim, khūnāṛai.*

Fellow, s. *mal, malgarai, humdzolai, samsorai.* (match) *makhai, gund, dzawāb, joṛah.* (contemptuous-) *lawanḍ, chaṭ. qachar, dahūs, chulur.* (in comp.) *hum-,*

Fellowship, s. *malgar-tiyā, sharākat ; rogha, joṛa.*

Felon, s. *gunāh-gār, taqṣīrī, mujrim.*

Felt, s. *lamtsa-ī, krāsta, namada.*

Female, a. *zanāna, māndīna.* s. *kkhadza, artīna.* (covert-) *maṛokkha, sohāgan.*

Feminine, a. *zanānī, māndīna, kkhadza.*

Fen, s. *jaba.*

Fence, s. *bāra, panāh.* (thorn-) *shpol, jal.* (withy or twig-) *kera.* v.a. *bāra-,* etc. *taṛal.*

Fence, v.a. *ḍāl-bāzī-, gatka-bāzī-,* etc. *k.*

Fennel, s. *sowa, kāgah.*

Fenugreek, s. *malkhoza.*

Ferment, s. *khamīra, tomna, māya ; eshnā, khuṭkai, josh ; bāwā, patna.*

Ferment, v.n. *khamīra-,* etc. *ked.* ; *eshedal, khuṭ ked.*

Ferocious, a. *waḥshī, khūnāḷrai, ẓālim.*

Ferocity, s. *waḥshat, khūn-khwārī, zulm.*

Ferret, s. *nolai.*

Ferrule, s. *ghamai, ṭekai.*

Ferry, s. *gudar, paṭanr.* (-boat) *bera-ī.* (-man) *mānrgai, mahanrah.*

Fertile, a. *zar-khez, ghala-khez, lap-tsat, barakatī.*

Fertilize, v.a. (-land) *watar k., zor-, quwat-,* etc. *warkawul.* (-animals) *ḍakawul, blārba k.*

Ferula, s. *bet, dira, qamchī, karoṛa.*

Fervent, a. *tod, garm.*

Fervour, s. *tod-wālai, todūkha, swai, garmī.*

Fester, v.n. *zawlan-, gazak-*, etc. *ked., khūedal.*

Festival, s. *akhtar, 'īd.* (-after Ramazān) *wṛūkai akhtar.* (-of Abraham's sacrifice) *loe akhtar.* (-of a saint) *mela, 'urs.* (marriage-) *wādah.* (feast) *kkhādī.*

Festivity, s. *kkhādī, khūsh·ḥālī, khwakkhī.*

Festoon s. *laṛ, hāṛ, zundai, zunbak.*

Fetch, v.a. (things) *rāwṛal.* (animals) *rāwustal.*

Fetid, a. *skhā, gandah, bad·bū* or *bad bū-ī·dār, wrost.*

Fetter, s. *dzolana, karai, band, zandzīr.* (-for cattle) *shkel, wandar, palwākkha, ghaṛwandai.*

Feud, s. *patna, badī, khāna·jangī, mīrtsī.*

Fever, s. *taba.* (-and ague) *saṛa taba, saṛa lare, saṛa lawe.* (intermittent-) *wāreza taba.* (remittent-) *wāra·gara taba.* (continued-) *shebara taba.* (bilious-) *zyaṛa-ī taba.* (typhus-) *skārwa-ī taba.*

Feverish, a. *tab·jan, taba nīwulai.*

Few, a. *la-ag, kam, pūṭai, pitsānrai, tso.*

Fibre, s. *rekkha, rag, tār, pala.*

Fibrous, s. *rekkhan.*

Fickle, a. *nā·qalār, nā·pāedār, khushai.*

Fiction, s. *naql, joṛ karai.*

Fictitious, a. *naqlī, nā·sarah, jūṭah.*

Fiddle, s. *sitāra, sāringai, chamtāra, sārinda,* (-string) *tār.* (-bow) *kamāncha.* (-key) *ghwagai.* (-bridge) *ṭaṭū, khargai.*

Fidelity, s. *īmān·dārī, rāst bāzī, wafā·dārī, namak ḥalālī, rikkhtīn·tob.*

Fidget, v.a. *kūnāṭī khwadzawul.* v.n. *wiswāsī ked., pa mawekkho laṛamedal.*

Fief, s. *jāedād, jāgīr, aima, dawtar.*

Field, s. *paṭai, wand.* (crop) *kikkht.* (plain) *maidān, ḍāga.*

Fiend, s. *shaiṭān*; *perai, rawai*; *dukkhman.*

Fierce, a. *tund, sakht, ẓālim, qahr·jan.*

Fiery, a. *tod, tez, garm, tāw·jan, tund, jalt.*

Fife, s. *surnāe, shpela-ī.*

Fifer, s. *surnā·chī, shpela-ī·mār.*

Fifteen, a. *pīndzah·las.* (15th) *pīndzah·lasam.*

Fifty, a. *pindzos.* (-one) *yo·pindzos*, etc.

Fig, s. *īndzar.* (wild-) *gūlar.* (Banian-) *baṛgat.* (Sacred-) *pīpal.*

Fight, s. *jang, muqaddama.* v.a. *jangawul.*

Fighter, s. *jangī, jangawar, jang kawūnkai*; *jang·yālai.*

Figurative, a. *naqlī, shaklī, majāzī, tamṣīlī.*

Figure. s. *shakl, ḍaul, ṣūrat, rang, shān.*

Figure, v.a. *joṛawul, tanḍal*; *nakhkkha kāgai—kkhkal* or *-līkal.*

Figured, a. *būṭī·dār, rangīn.*

File, s. *sohān, chausār.* (row) *qaṭār, para.* (catalogue) *daftar, fard.*

Filings, s. *reza, chūr.*

Fill, v.a. *ḍakawul.*

Fillet, s. *paṭai, paṛūkai.* (-for the head) *sar·taṛūnai, sar·basta, tsapūṭkai.*

Fillip, s. *chūṭkī.*

Filly, s. *bihānra, biyāna.*

Film, s. *jāla-ī.* (-of the eye) *gul, nakhūna.*

Filter, s. *chānra.* v.a. *chānr k.*

Filth, s. *khīra, rash, chirk.*

Filthy, a. *khīran, palīt, nā·pāk, khachan.*

Fin, s. *wazar da kab* or *-da māhī.*

Final, a. *ākhir, wrūstai, akhīr*; *pūrah.*

Finally, ad. *ākhiran, alqiṣṣa.*

Finance, s. *mālguzārī, āmdanī.*

Find, v.a. *mūndal, biyā·mūndal, paidā k.* (-fault) *raṭal, traṭal, ṭaqawul, malāmatawul.*

Fine, s. *nāgha, tāwān, jarīmāna.*

Fine, a. *narai, mahīn, bārīk.* (-sky) *shīn, ṣāf.*

Finger, s. *gūta.* (thumb) *baṭa-* or *ghaṭa gūṭa.* (fore-) *miswāka gūta.* (middle-) *miyandza gūta.* (ring-) *khamacha gūta.* (little-) *kacha gūta.* (-nail) *nūk.* (-quick) *awra-ī.*

Finis, s. *tam·tamām, ākhir, khatm.*
Finish, v.a. *tamāmawul, pūrah-, khatm-,* etc. *k.*
Fir, s. *nakkhtar.* (-cone) *gūjal.* (-seed) *chalghozai* or *janghoza* or *zanrghoza.*
Fire, s. *or.* (-fly) *orakai.* (-place) *ngharai, orghālai.* (-wood) *bālanr, khashāk.* (-brand) *shūsha-ī.* (-poker) *or larūnai.* (-stone) *shokānrai.* (-works) *ātashbāzī.* (-worshipper) *gabar.* (-lock) *bandūkh, topak.*
Fire, v.a. *or pore k., balawul.* (-a gun) *chalawul, khalāṣawul.*
Firm, a. *mazbūṭ, klak, ṭīng, pāedar.*
Firmament, s. *āsmān, kursī, tsarkh.*
First, a. *awwal* or *awwulanai, wṛūnbai* or *wṛūnbanai.* (-born) *mashar.*
Firstly, ad. *awwalan, wṛūnbe, warkhata.*
Fish, s. *kab, māhai.* (-hook) *kunḍa.*
Fissure, s. *chāwd. darz, daṛa, chāq, rakhna.*
Fist, s. *mūṭ, mūṭai*; *sūk.*
Fistula, s. *nāsūr.*
Fit, s. *ghoṭa*; *nobat.* (fainting-) *parghaz.* (hysterical-) *da piriyāno ghoṭa.*
Fit, a. *wājib, munāsib, lāzim, lā-iq*; *qābil, joṛ, barābar*; *pīrzo, yarzan, dzāe·lar.*
Five, a. *pīndzah.* (fifth) a. *pīndzam.*
Fix, s. *nkkhatai, balā.*
Fix, v.a. *lagawul, taṛal, joṛawul, pore k.*; *wudrawul, walāṛawul, muqarrar-, klak-, mazbūṭ-,* etc. *k.*; *khakkhawul, njatal*; *khejawul, kkhkenawul.*
Flabby, a. *narm, post, sust*; *tsorb.*
Flag, s. *nakkha, janḍa, togh, bairagh.*
Flag, v.n. *ṭaparedal, pāte ked., staṛai ked.*
Flagrant, a. *tsargand*; *mashhūr*; *bad.*
Flake, s. *tsapak, tsaparkai.*
Flame, s. *lanba, shughla* (fire), *baṛānḍa, gharānḍa lūkhaṛa, gharghara, bāmbanra, ḍānḍa-ī.*
Flank, s. *ḍaḍa, aṛkh, tsang*; *tselma, tsanḍa*; *tashai.*
Flannel, s. *shaṛa-ī, pashmīna, waṛīna.*
Flap, v.a. *tsanḍal, khwadzawul, rapawul.* v.n. *tsapedal, tsrapedal, ṭrapedal, rapedal.*
Flare, v.n. *brekkhedal, rūnredal, dzaledal.*
Flash. s. *brekkh, brekkhnā, dzalk, palwasha.*
Flask. s. *kupa-ī, kupṛa-ī*; *kkhīkkha, khumra-ī.*
Flat, a. *sam, sat, hawār, barābar.* (pressed-) *tsaplāk, chīt.* (-taste) *be·khwand, be·maza, bilmagai, bilmangah.* (-on the back) *stūnī·stagh.* (-footed) *chapakh.*
Flatten, v.a. *samawul, hawārawul*; *chīt-,* etc. *k.*
Flatterer, s. *chāplūs, khūshāmad·gar, ḍirpal.*
Flattery, s. *chāplūsī, khūshāmadī, ḍirpalī.*
Flatulent, a. *bādī.*
Flavour, s. *khwand, maza, swād, tsaka.*
Flaw, s. *chāwd, darz, daṛa*; *'aib, laka, dāgh,*
Flax, s. *sanr.*
Flay, v.a. *tsarman-, poṭ-,* etc., *ākhistal, -bāsal—yastal, -kāgal—kkhkal.*
Flea, s. *wruga.*
Fleam, s. *nashtar* or *neshtar.*
Fleawort, s. *ispaghol* or *īsapghol.*
Flee, v.n. *takkhtedal, puṭedal.*
Fleece, s. *waṛa-ī, warg.*
Fleece, v.a. *shūkawul, lūṭawul.*
Fleet, a. *gaṛandai, jalt, tez, zghard, halwāk.*
Fleeting, a. *teredūnai, fānī.*
Flesh, s. *ghwakkha.* (body) *dzān.* (lust) *naus, shahwat.* (-brush) *khīsa.*
Flexible, a. *narm, post, mulā-im, ṭīṭedūnai.*
Flexure, s. *ṭīṭ·wālai, kog·wālai*; *kaglech, kālkūch*; *gūṭ, grut.*
Flight, s. *tekkhta.* (-of birds) *sail, ghol.* (-of an arrow) *partaw.*
Flighty, a. *khushai, khiyālī, saudā-ī.*
Flimsy, a. *spuk, halak, narai, nā·kārah.*
Flinch, v.n. *bugnedal, weredal, haṭedal.*
Fling, v.a. *āchawul, wīshtal, ghurzawul.*

Flint, s. *bakra-ī*. (steel) *punḍ*. (gun-) *chaqmaq*.
Flinty, a. *sakht, klak, kānrez*.
Flirt, s. *nakhra·bāza, lashmaka-ī, shatāha*.
Flit, v.n. *ālwatal*. v.a. *kaḍa wṛal*.
Float, s. *pāyāba* or *pāyawai*. v.n. *bahedal, lāhū ked., lānbo ked*.
Flock, s. *ramma*. (leader of-) *nar·kakkh*, (-of sheep, goats, or deer) *kanḍak, ghela. psa*. (-of birds) *sail, ghol*. (-of lambs, etc.) *olah* (a crowd of men, etc.) *ṭol. ṭolai, ṭolgai*.
Flock, v.n. *ṭoledal, yo·dzāe-, jam'a-*, etc. *ked*.
Flog, v.a. *wahal, karoṛe-*, etc. *wahal*.
Flood, s. *sailāb, niyūz* or *nīz*. (-of tears) *raṭ*.
Flood, v.a. *lāhū-, hūk-*, etc. *k., niyūz wṛal*.
Floodgate, s. *warkh, ghwagai*.
Floor, s. *zmaka, zamīn* ; *takhta·bandī*.
Florid, a. *sūr*.
Florist, s. *gul·kar*.
Flounce, s. *tsanḍa, jānja-ī*.
Flounce, v.n. *tsrapedal, ghurzedal*.
Flounder, v.n. *ṭrapedal, tsrapedal* ; *rghaṛedal*. v.a. *ghoṭa wahal*.
Flour, s. *oṛah, maidah*. (dredging-) *bornah*.
Flourish, v.n. *ābādedal, wadānedal, tāzah-, takṛah-*, etc. *osedal*. v.a. *tsanḍal, khwadzawul, rapawul*.
Flow, v.n. *bahedal, chaledal, rawānedal, jārī ked*.
Flower, s. *gul*. (-garden) *gul·shan*. (-bed) *gul·zār*.
Flower, v.n. *khwaredal, ghwaredal, ṭūkedal*.
Fluctuate, v. *chapa-, chalaka-*, etc. *wahal*. v.n. *be·ārām-, nā·qalār-*, etc. *ked*.
Fluent, a. *jārī, rawān*. (in speech) *khula·war*.
Fluid, a. *wīlī, oba, ābī, pakhsiyāh*.
Flummery, s. *pālūda, oghṛa. atob, daliya*.
Flush, v.n. *sūr·makh ked., sharmedal*.
Flute, s. *shpela-ī*.
Flutter, v.n. (-hover as a bird) *ṭrapedal, tsapedal*. (-as a leaf) *rapedal, shanedal*. (palpitate) *dṛazedal, paṛakedal, laṛzedal*.
Flux, s. *sailāb* ; *rezish, nazla* ; *nāstah, ra-ama, dast*.
Fly, s. *mach*. (horse-) *ghobāṛai, bhaganṛ*.
Fly, v.n. *ālwatal, wurzedal*.
Foal, s. *bihānr, biyān*.
Foam, s. *zag, kaf*.
Fodder, s. *wākkhah, giyāh, 'alaf*. (-of corn) *khasīl, khwīd*. (-of maize) *ṭānṭa*. (-of rice) *palāla*. (-of pulses) *kaṭī*.
Foe, s. *dukkhman, khaṣam*.
Fœtus, s. *bachai, kachandai*.
Fog, s. *laṛa* ; *ghubār*.
Foil, s. *gatka*. v.a. *wrānawul*.
Fold, s. *bāra, hadera*. (sheep-) *bānḍa, shpol*. (of a door) *tanba, pala*. (layer) *bragh, tah*. (crease) *gundza, chunṛa, kṛatai*. (-of a rope) *wal, tāw, pech*. (-on fold) ad. *pabla-, wabla-* or *zabla bānde*. (in comp.) *-bragh, -chand*.
Fold, v.a. *nghakkhtal*.
Foliage, s, *pānṛe, zarghūn·tob*.
Folk, s. *khalq, 'ālam, makhlūq*.
Follow, v.n. *pala·pase tlal*. v.a. *pairawī-, murīdī-*, etc. *k., manal, laman nīwul*.
Follower, s. *pairaw, murīd, tāb'i·dār*.
Folly, s. *nā·dānī, kam·'aqlī, nā·poha*.
Foment, v.a. *sekal, ṭakor k*. (stir up) *pātsawul, khejawul, porta k*.
Fond, a. *mayan*. (in comp.) *-dost, -parast*.
Fondle, v.a. *nāzawul, mīna k*.
Fondness, s. *mīna, shauq, zṛah, khwā*.
Fontanelle, s. *tandai*.
Food, s. *khwārah, khwurāk, shūma, qūt, ṭ'ām*. (-for a journey) *tokkha, tsawrai*. (-of cattle) *tsar, wākkhah*. (-of hawks) *tāmba*. (prepared-) *sālan, qatagh, ngholai*.
Fool, s. *nā·dān, kam·'aql, gedī·khar, lewanai*.
Foolish, a. *nā·dān, be·wuqūf, kawdan, pūhaṛ, ablah, palwanḍ*.

Foot, s. *pkkha* or *kkhpa*. (on-) *palai, pa kkhpo*. (-step) *qadam, mand, gām*. (-mark) *pal, mand*. (-fall) *trapai*. (-stool) *mora*.
Footman, s. *piyādah, harkarah*; *shātar*; *mlā·tar*.
Footpad, s. *rāh·zan, shūk·mār, lār·wahūnkai*.
Footpath, s. *tsara·lār* or *-wāt*.
Fop, s. *bānkā, daulī, tatai, tainchī*.
For, p. *dapāra*; *wāsta, khātir*. (-as much) *la de na, dzaka, ska*. (-instance) *pa misāl, laka*. (-the most part) *aksar*. (-what?) *tsa·la, wale*.
Forage, s. *wākkhah, gayāh, tsar*.
Foray, s. *dāra·dopa, hapa·dapa, bota, chapāo*.
Forbear, v.a. *zghamal, sabr-, pāl-, parhez-*, etc. *k*.
Forbearance, s. *sabr, zgham*.
Forbid, v.a. *man'a k*.
Forbidden, a. *man'a, harām*.
Force, s. *zor, quwat, was, tuwān, bram, tāqat*; *zulm, ziyātī, jabr*.
Force, v.a. *zoral, tezal*.
Forceps, s. *ambūr, nūtsai*.
Ford, s. *gudar, pai*. v.n. *pore tlal* or *-watal*.
Fordable, a. *payāw*.
Fore, a. *wrūnbai, wrūnbanai, wrāndīnai, pakhwānai, pekkhīn*.
Fore, ad. *wrānde, wrūnbe*.
Forefather, s. *nīkah*.
Forego, v.a. *pregdal—prekkhodal, tark k*.
Forehead, s. *wuchwalai* or *ucharlai, tandai*.
Foreign, a. *pradai, begānah, opwah*.
Foreknowledge, s. *'ilm da ghā-ib*.
Foreman, s. *peshkār*.
Forementioned, a. *mazkūr*.
Foremost, a. *wrūnbai, wrāndīnai, awwalanai, awwal*.
Forenoon, s. *pekkhīn, tsākkht*.
Forepart, s. *makh, sar, wrūnbai*.
Forerunner, s. *peshraw, wrānde tlūnai*.
Forest, s. *banr, dzangal, besha*.
Forestal, v.a. *pesh·dastī k*.
Foretell, v.a. *pāl-* or *fāl katal, ghā-ib wayal*.
Forethought, s. *dūr·andekkhī, pesh·fikrī*.
Forewarn, v.a. *wrūnbe khabarawul, āgāh k*.
Forfeit, s. *nāgha, tāwān, jurīmāna, qurq*.
Forfeit, v.a. *nāgha-*, etc. *warkawul, bā-elal*.
Forge, s. *lohār·khāna, bat*.
Forge, v.a. *jāl·sāzī k*.
Forget, v.a. *herawul*.
Forgive, v.a. *bakkhal, pulawul*.
Forgiveness, s. *bakkhana*.
Forgotten, a. *her, ter·her*.
Fork, s. *dwa·kkhākha*. (pitch-) *panj·ghākkhai*.
Forked, a. *kkhākh·dār*.
Forlorn, a. *be·kas, khwār, yawādzai, lā·chār*.
Form, s. *sūrat, shakl, shān, rang, tartīb*.
Form, v.a. *jorawul, tandal, tartībawul*.
Formal, a. *rasmī, chalanī, qānūnī*.
Formation, s. *tarkīb, sākht, jorawūna*.
Former, a. *pakhwānai, wrūnbanai*.
Formerly, ad. *pakhwā, wrūnbe*.
Formidable, a. *tars·nāk, khof·nāk*.
Formula, s. *nuskha*; *tarkīb*; *tartīb*.
Fornication, s. *kāsīrī, zinā·kārī, harām·kārī*.
Fornicator, s. *kāsīr, zinā·kār, harām·kār*.
Forsake, v.a. *pregdal—prekkhodal, tark k*.
Forswear, v.a. *qasam-, saugand-*, etc. *khwural*; *nā·haqq qasam-*, etc, *khwural*.
Fort, s. *qil'a, kot, gara-ī, bāra, hisār*.
Forth, ad. *wrānde*; *bāhir*.
Forthwith, ad. *os, pa takī, sam da lāsa, pa de sā'at, wasīka*.
Fortify, v.a. *mazbūt-, mahkam-*, etc. *k*.; *ār-, hisar-, bāra-, panāh-*, etc. *k*.
Fortitude, s. *sabr, zgham*; *zrah, himmat*.
Fortress, s. *kot, gara-ī*.
Fortuitous, a. *nāgahān, ittifāqī*.
Fortunate, a. *nek·bakht, barakatī, bakhtawar, sa'ādat·man, bakhtyār*.
Fortune, s. *bakht, nasīb, qismat*; *zamāna, rozgār*; *iqbāl, sa'ādat*; *māl, duniyā*,

daulat; *falak*, *tsarkh*. (-teller) *fāl·bīn*, *pāl·katūnkai*, *rammāl*, *d'awatī*.
Forty, a. *tsalwekkht*. (-one) *yo tsalwekkht*, etc.
Forum, s. *chauk*, *chārsū*, *bāzār*.
Forward, ad. *makhe*, *wṛānde*. a. *wṛāndai*, *makh*; *tayār*; *wīt*, *chūnkai*, *gustākh*.
Forward, v.a. *chalawul*, *rawānawul*, *āstawul*, *legal*, *rasawul*.
Foster, v.a. *pālal*, *nmāndzal*, *parwaral*. (-son) *pālalai dzoe*. (-daughter) *pālali lūr*. (-brother) *da tī* or *-to wror*. (-sister) *da ti* or *-to khor*. (-father) *plandar*, *pālūnkai plār*. (-mother) *dā-ī*, *pālūnki mor*.
Foul, a. *nā·pāk*, *palīt*, *murdār*, *kakaṛ*.
Foundation, s. *āra*, *wekh*, *bonsaṭ*, *kūnsaṭ*; *sar*, *aṣl*, *bunyād*. (pedestal) *pāya*, *asās*.
Fountain, s. *chīna*, *chashma*.
Four, a. *tsalor*. (fourth) *tsaloram*. (-fold) *tsalor·bragh*. (-footed) *chār·pā*. (-score) *tsalor shili*.
Fourteen. a. *tswārlas*.
Fowl, s. *chirg*. (water-) *hīla-ī*. (-of the air) *marghah* (p. *mārghah*), *marghai*. (Cochin-) *kulang*, *kurmang*. (game-) *panḍāw·chirg*.
Fowler, s. *kkhkārī*.
Fox, s. *lūnbaṛ*, *troṛa-ī*, *sperlam* or *spalam*.
Fraction, s. *kasr*, *ḥiṣṣa*, *ṭoṭai*, *ṭakai*.
Fracture, s. *māt*, *daṛa*, *chāwd*.
Fragile, a. *mātedūnai*, *narai*, *nāzak*.
Fragment, s. *ṭoṭa*, *reza*, *richa*, *chur*.
Fragrance, s. *'aṭr*, *khūsh·bū-ī*.
Fragrant, a. *khūsh·bū*, *bū-ī·nāk*, *khūshbū-ī·dār*.
Frail, a. *nāzak*, *nā·tuwān*, *ẓa'īf*, *kam·zor*, *nā·pāedār*, *fānī*.
Frame, s. *kināra*, *kāna*. (door-) *darshal*. (mould) *qālib*.
Frame, v.a. *joṛawul*, *taṛal*.
Frank, a. *spīn*, *ṣāf*, *sādah·dil*, *rikkhtīnai*.
Frankincense, s. *lobān*, *'ūd*.
Frantic, a. *lewanai*, *saudā-ī*.
Fraternity, s. *wrorī*, *wror·walī*.
Fraud, s. *ṭagī*, *fareb*, *droh*, *ghlā*, *chal*.
Fraudulent, a. *ṭag·bāz*, *farebī*, *chal·bāz*.
Fraught, s. *pūrah*, *ḍak*.
Fray, v.n. *sūledal*, *sūdah ked.*; *blosedal*.
Freak, s. *khiyāl*, *wahm*.
Freckle, s. *tarsarai*, *ta-apai*.
Free, a. *yalah*, *saṛah*, *wazgār*, *āzād*, *khalāṣ*. (-will) *wāk*, *ikhtiyār*, *raẓā*.
Freeze, v.n. *kangal-*, *khyam-*, etc. *ked.*, *yakhedal*.
Freight, s. *bār*; *bār·bardārī*; *kreha*, *maḥṣūl*.
Frenzy, s. *sarsām*, *lewan·tob*, *paṭ*.
Frequent, a. *ḍer*, *ziyāt*, *lagiyā*.
Frequent, v.a. *rāsha·darsha-*, *tlana·rātlana-*. etc. *k.* v.n. *osedal*, *pātedal*.
Frequently, ad. *akṣar*, *ziyātī*, *ḍer dzala*, *wār·wār*.
Fresh, a. *zarghūn*, *shīn*; *tāzah*, *takṛah*, *tayār*; *nawai*; *hosā*. (complexion) *skānr*.
Fret, v.n. *zahīredal*, *kaṛedal*, *nūledal*, *ghamedal*, *wiwāsī ked.* (-as cloth) *sūledal*. (as water) *tsapare-*, *pache-*, etc. *ked.*
Fretful, a. *khapah*, *wiswāsī*, *nā·qalār*.
Friction, s. *sūledana*, *sūda*; *mālish*, *masha*, *mukkhana*.
Friar, s. *miyā* or *mī-ā*, *paqīr*.
Friday, s. *jum'a*, *ādīna*.
Friend, s. *āshnāe*, *yār*, *dost*, *peẓandgalai*.
Friendless, a. *be·kas*, *khwār*.
Friendly, a. *mihrbān*, *khair·khwāh* or *kāl·khwāh*.
Friendship, s. *āshnā-ī*, *yārī*, *yārāna*, *khpul·walī*.
Fright, s. *yera* or *wera*, *tars*, *tor*, *khof*, *tara*, *ḍār*.
Frighten, v.a. *yerawul* or *werawul*, *tarhawul*, *torawul*, *ḍārawul*.
Frightened, v.n. *weredal*, *tarhedal*, *ḍāredal*. v.a- *tor khwuṛal*.
Frightened, a. *yeredalai*, *tarhedalai*, *tor·khwuṛalai*, *ḍāredalai*.

Frightful, a. *tars-, khof-, tor-, haul-*, etc. *-nāk.*
Frigid, a. *soṛ, yakh ; qaṛqechan, maṛghechan.*
Fringe, s. *tsanḍa, jāwja-ī, laman.* (frill) *sarwazana, zunḍa-ī, surkha-ī.*
Frisk, v.a. *traplal, top wahal, kharmastī-, tskhe-*, etc. *k.*
Fritter, v.n. *shaṛhedal.* (trifle) v.a. *jakh wahal.*
Frivolous, a. *spuk, halak, puch, khushai, nā·tsīz.*
Frock, s. *anga, khalqa, kāḍa-ī.* (quilted-) *andarka.* (long-) *qādara-ī.* (short-) *lanḍa-ī.* (woman's-) *pepna-ī, ganḍola-ī.*
Frog, s. *chīndakh, changakkh, shlānda.*
Frolic, s. *loba, mastī, ṭel·ṭāl, tskhe.*
From, p. *la, da, la—na.*
Front, s. *makh, wṛāndai.* (in-) ad. *wṛānde, makhā·makh, makh·kkhke, sāmnre.*
Front, v.n. *wṛānde-, makh-, sāmnre-*, etc. *ked.*
Frontier, s. *pūla, brīd, ḥadd.*
Frost, s. *kangal, yakh.* (hoar-) *parkha, ksa-ī.* (-bitten) a. *qaṛqechan, maṛghechan, kaskar.*
Frosty, a. *soṛ, yakh.*
Froth, s. *zag, kaf.*
Frothy, a. *zag·jan, kaf·dār.*
Froward, a. *ḥoḍai, sar·kakkh, sar·zor, ṭakanrai.*
Frown, v.a. *brandawul, starge brandawul.*
Frozen, a. *kangal-*, or *yakh·shawai.*
Fructify, v.a. *bārdār k.; blārba k.*
Frugal, a. *parhez·gār ; kam·khwurāk.*
Fruit, s. *mewa ; bār.*
Fruitful, a. *mewa·dār ; bār·dār.*
Fruitless, a. *be·mewa, be·bār, shanḍ.* (vain) *be·sūd, be·fā-ida, 'abas-, bar·bād, be·būd.*
Frustrate, v.a. *bāṭil-, 'abas-*, etc. *k., wrānawul.*
Fry, v.a. *talawul, teyal, wrītawul, alwoyal.*
Frying-pan, s. *taba-ī, tabakhai, teghna.*
Fuel, s. *bālanr, largai, khāshāk, khadzala, warkhaṛa.* (cowdung-) *ghoshoe.*
Fugitive, s. *takkhtedūnai.*

Fulfil, v.a. *tamāmawul, pa dzāe-, pūrah-*, etc. *k.*
Full, a. *ḍak, pūrah ; moṛ ; sekan.*
Fuller, s. *dobī, rang·rez.*
Fully, ad. *pa kkhah shān sara, qaṭ'a-ī.*
Fulness, s. *ṭamām·tiyā, ḍak·wālai ; moṛ·tiyā ; arat·wālai ; sekan·tob.*
Fulsome, a. *nā·khwakkh, kraka·nāk ; puch.*
Fumble, v.a. *wār·khaṭā-k., kāwākī k.*
Fumbler, s. *pūhaṛ, kāwāk, lwāṛ.*
Fumigate, v.a. *lū-, lūgai-, lūkhaṛa-*, etc. *k.*
Fun, s. *loba, mastī ; tamāsha, nandāra ; ṭoqa·washta, ṭel·ṭāl.*
Function, s. *kār, 'amal ; khidmat ; 'uhda.*
Fund, s. *sarmāya, saga, panga.*
Fundament, s. *būnsaṭ, kūnsaṭ ; kūna, ghara, supra.*
Fundamental, a, *aṣlī, bunyādī, ẕātī.*
Funeral, s. *janāza.* (burial) *khakkhawūna, dafn.* (-service) *fātiḥa, pātā.* (-condolence) *lās·nīwah.* (-food) *shūma, muṛ·shūma.*
Funnel, s. *tsūkkhka, nala ; jāba.*
Funny, a. *ṭoq·mār, washtī, wītak.*
Fur, s. *waṛa-ī, pashm.* (-skin) *postīn.* (-coat) *nīm·tanai, nīmcha, postīncha.*
Furbish, v.a. (metals) *ṣaiqal k.* (polish) *mugal—mukkhal.* (scrape) *togal.*
Furious, a. *qahr·nāk, bṛos, lewanai.*
Furl, v.a. *nghaṛal—nghakkhtal.*
Furnace, s. *tanūr.*
Furnish, v.a. *warkawul, rasawul, paidā k.; sambālawul, sāzawul, ārāstah k.*
Furniture, s. *rakht, asbāb, kālai, sāmān, sāz·sāmān, partal.*
Furrow, s. *līk, karkkha.*
Further, v.a. *madad-, komak-, mrasta-*, etc. *k.*
Fury, s. *qahr, ghaẓab, lewan·tob.*
Fuse, v.a, *wilī k., oba k.*
Fusee, s. *bāta-ī, patīla* or *falīta.*
Fuss, s. *chal·chalā, tak·o·pū, rabaṛ.*

Futile, a. *'abas̤, bāt̤il, khushai, be fā-ida, spuk, nā·tsīz, be·sūd.*
Future, a. *gāndah, makh, rātlana, āyandah.*
Futurity, s. *ākhirat, 'āqibat.*
Fye, in. *toba! petī·mū!*

G.

Gabble, v.a. *bak·bak-, baq·baq-, baṛ·baṛ-, ṭar·ṭar-, char·char-,* etc. *k.*
Gabbler, s. *baq·baqai, baṛ·baṛai, ūnai, ṭarai.*
Gad, v.a. *hujra·gardī k.* v.n. *girzedal.*
Gadfly, s. *bhaganr, manganr·mach.*
Gag, v.a. *būja pa khule kkhke mandal, khula bandawul.*
Gain, s. *gaṭa, sūd, fā-ida, naf'a.*
Gain, v.a. *gaṭal, mūndal.* (-over) *grohedah k.* v.n. (win) *wa-aṛ ked.* (a victory) v.a. *barai mūndal.*
Gainer, s. *gaṭa kawūnkai, wa-aṛ, barai mūndūnkai.*
Gainful, a. *sūd·man, fā-ida·man.*
Gainsay, v.a. *khilāf wayal, radd k.*
Gait, s. *yūn, chāl, tlana, chalan, raftār.*
Gale, s. *sīla-ī, bād, ṭūpān.*
Gall, s. *trīkha, zahra, s̤afrā.* (-bladder) *trīkhai.*
Gall, v.a. *sūdah-, gasiyā-,* etc. *k., sūlawul.*
Gallant, a. *maṛanai, dzwān·mard, tūrzan.*
Gallant. s. *'ishq·bāz, kāsīr; yār, āshnāe.*
Gallantry, s. *maṛāna, zṛahwar·tob, tūrzan·tob, zmarī·tob, dzwān·mardī; kāsīrī, 'ishq·bāzī; āshnā-ī, yārāna.*
Gallery, s. *bālā·khāna, shāhnishīn, dūnkācha, aiwān.* (mine) *surang.*
Gallop, s. *poya, tākht.*
Gallop, v.a. *pa·poyo-, pa·tākht-,* etc. *zghalawul.* v.n. *pa·poyo-,* etc., *tlal* or *-zghaledal.*
Gallows, s. *dār, sūla-ī, gahwāra.* (-rope) *tezanda-ī, zanda-ī, pā-ī.*

Galls, Gallnut, s. *māzū.*
Gamble, v.a. *jū-ārī-, jū-ā·bāzī-, qimār·bāzī-,* etc. *k.*
Gambler, s. *jū-ār·gar, jū-ā·bāz.*
Gambol, s. *ṭel·ṭāl, mastī, tskhe, loba.*
Game, s. *loba, bāzī.*
Gander, s. *baṭ, qāz; pūhaṛ, gedī.*
Gang, s. *ṭolai, dāṛa, paṛk, tāmba, ghol, cham.*
Gangrene, s. *skhā, gazak.*
Gaol, s. *zindān, qaid-, bandī-,* etc. *khāna.*
Gap, s. *kanḍāw, darghol, wut, gūṭ.*
Gape, v.n. *wītedal, chīngedal, wāzedal.* v.a *khula chīngawul, -wāzawul* or *-wītawul.* (yawn) *aswelai-, khamiyāza-,* etc. *k.* (stare) *ghaṭ·katal.*
Gaping, a. *wīt, chīng, wāz.*
Garb, s. *toga, shān, rāng; jāma, pokkhāk, libās.*
Garbage, s. *ūjrai, larai.*
Garble, v.a. *latawul, chunṛal.*
Garden, s. *bāgh, bāghcha.* (flower-) *gulshan, bostān.* (-of Eden) *jannat, 'adan.*
Gardener, s. *bāghwān.*
Gardening, s. *bāghwānī, bāghwān·tob.*
Gargle, v.a. *ghar·ghaṛa k.*
Garland, s. *hār, lar, amel.*
Garlic, s. *ūga.*
Garment, s. *āghostana, jāma, zaṛūkai, libās, nwarai.* (beggar's-) *gand* or *kind.*
Garner, s. *khamba, kandū, koṭa, ambār·khāna.*
Garnish, v.a. *joṛawul, andzorawul.*
Garrison, s. *qil'a, gaṛa-ī; da qil'e khalq.*
Garrulous, a. *baq·baqai, ṭarai, baṛ·baṛai,*
Gash, s. *parhār, tsīra, ghwuts, zakhm.* v.a. *tsīral, ghwutsawul, joblawul, zakhmī k.*
Gasp, v.a. *lanḍa sāh-* or *sāh pa·porta ākhistal.* v.n. *sāh khatal, sāh·lanḍah ked.*
Gate, s. *war.* (-way) *darwāza.*
Gather, v.a. *ṭolawul, jam'a-, yo·dzāe-,* etc. *k.* (select) *anṛawul, chunṛal, laṭawul.* (pluck) *shūkawul.*

Gathering, s. *ṭol, ṭolai.* (-of cloth) *jung.*
Gaudy, a. *rangā-rang, rangīn.*
Gauge, v.a. *mech-, kach-,* etc. *k.*
Gay, a. *kkhād, kkhād-man, khush-ḥāl.*
Gaze, v.a. *katal, ghaṭ katal, dzīr k.*
Gazette, s. *akhbār.*
Gear, s. *kālī, sāz-sāmān, asbāb.*
Geld, v.a. *khaṣṣī-, ākhtah-,* etc. *k.*; *malai k.*
Gem, s. *gauhar* or *jauhar.*
Gender, s. *jins, qism.* (masculine-) *nārīnah, nar, muzakkar.* (feminine-) *māndīna, kkhadza, muwannaṣ.*
Genealogy, s. *shajra, nasal, nasab, aṣl, peṛa-ī.*
General, a. *'āmm, jārī*; *shāmil.*
General, s. *sardār, sar-guroh, mashar.*
Generally, ad. *akṣar, ziyātī.*
Generate, v.a. *paidā k.*; *zegawul.*
Generation, s. *paidā-ikkht*; *peṛa-ī, pusht*; *alwād, zāwzāt*; *zamāna, daur.*
Generosity, s. *sakhāwat, sakhī-tob, sakhā, bakkhana.*
Generous, a. *sakhī, bakkhūnai.*
Genial, a. *joṛ, khwakkh, barābar, pīrzo.*
Genitals, s. *andām-nihānī, satar, ṣūrat, 'aurat.* (hair of-) *tor-wekkhtah.*
Genius, s. *khoe, khaṣlat, ṭab'a, khwā, mizāj, lokkhai.* (evil-) *perai, parī.* (capacity) *poha, pahm, idrāk.*
Genteel, a. *makhawar, spīn-robai, satar-pokkh.*
Gentility, s. *makhawar-tob, sharāfat.*
Gentle, a. *ḥalīm, aṣīl, ashrāf.*
Gentleman, s. *ṣāḥib-* or *ashrāf-zādah.*
Gently, ad. *ro-ro, pa-qalār.*
Gentry, s. *ra-isān, ashrāfān.*
Genuine, a. *sūchah, karah, aṣīl, khāliṣ, nughd, rikkhtīnai.*
Genus, s. *rag, qūm, qism, nogai, jins.*
Germinate, v.n. *ṭūkedal, zarghūnedal.* v.a. *red k.*
Gesture, s. *ḥarakat*; *shān.*
Get, v.a. *mūndal, gaṭal, paidā k.*
Ghastly, a. *sperah.*
Ghost, s. *rawai*; *perai.*
Giant, s. *ghaṭ-khṛīs, nāpaṛ-* or *gagar saṛai*; *dew, 'ifrīt.*
Gibbet, s. *dār, gahwāra.* v.a. *tezanda-ī warkawul*; *dzwaṛandawul.*
Giddiness, s. *sar-ghurzai, akar, sar-girzai.*
Gift, s. *bakhkshiksh, bakkhana. nazr, hiba.*
Gifted, a. *qābil, qudrat-man, zbarg.*
Gigantic, a. *khṛīs, nāpaṛ, dang-, star, ghaṭ, loe.*
Giggle, v.n. *khandedal, musedal.*
Gilding, s. *ṭilā-kārī.*
Gill, s. *wakkhkai.*
Gimlet, s. *barma, tswarla-ī.*
Gin, s. *dām, lwīna, lūma, lūmaka, paṛka, laṭ.*
Ginger, s. (green-) *adrak.* (dry-) *sūnḍ.*
Gipsey, s. *naṭ*; *kochī.*
Gird, v.a. *taṛal.*
Girder, s. *taṛūnai.* (-beam) *bensh, paṭera, tīr.*
Girdle, s. *mlā-taṛūnai, mlā-band, kamar-band.* (woman's-) *tapor.* (sash) *paṭka.*
Girl, s. *jina-ī.* (mature-) *peghla.* (betrothed-) *changhala.* (slave-) *wīndza.* (servant-) *mazdūra.* (kept-) *khidmat-gāra.* (dancing-) *lola-ī, kachana-ī.*
Girth, s. *paṭā-ī*; *tāng.*
Give, v.a. *warkawul, bakkhal, kkhandal.* (evidence) *lal* or *lawdal.*
Giver, s. *warkawūnkai, bakkhūnkai*; *lūnai.*
Gizzard, s. *shā-ṭinga.*
Glad, a. *khwakkh, kkhād, khush, khush-ḥāl.*
Gladtidings, s. *zera.* (bringer of-) *zera-garai.*
Gladiator s. *tūra-bāz, shamsher-bāz.*
Gladness, s. *khwakkhī, kkhādī, khush-ḥālī.* (-over a rival) *sakha, wiyāṛ.*
Glance, v.a. *nazar pa za-ar terawul.* (shine) v.n. *dzal kedal.* (fly off) v.a. *tīndak wahal.*
Gland, s. *stagha, ghudūd, ghūnḍārai.*

Glare, s. *ranṛā, dzalah, brekkhnā.*
Glaring, a. *kkhkārah, tsargand, awtsār.*
Glass, s. *kkhīkkha.* (-cup) *piyāla.* (mirror) *ā-īna.*
Glaze, v.a. *malma-,* or *mulamm'a k., rang pore k., kāshī k.*
Glazier, s. *kāshī-gar.*
Gleam, s. *partaw, palwasha.*
Gleam, v.n. *dzalkedal, brekkhedal.*
Glean, v.a. *anrawul, chūnral, drūze ṭolawul.*
Glee, s. *kkhādī, khwand.* (song) *ṭapa.*
Glimmer, s. *dzalak, palwasha.*
Glitter, v.n. *brekkhedal, dzalkedal, rūnredal.*
Globe, s. *duniyā, naṛa-ī, jahān.* (celestial) *tsarkh, falak, kursī.* (ball) *ghunḍai, manḍos, panḍos, mardak.*
Globular, a. *ghunḍ, ghunḍ-man.*
Globule, s. *gola-ī, mardakoṭai, ghunḍūrai.*
Gloom, s. *tyāra, tor-wālai, tor-tam; gham, nūl.*
Glorify, v.a. *stāyal, ṣanā wayal.*
Glorious, a. *mubārak; majīd; loe, jalāl; kkhah.*
Glory, s. *nang, nūm, iqbāl.*
Gloss, s. *rang.*
Glossy, a. *brekkh-nāk, dzalak-nāk.*
Glove, s. *dastāna, da lās joṛāba.* (gauntlet) *dast-gala.* (for hawking) *bela.*
Glow, v.n. *todedal, swal.*
Glow. s. *todūkha, swai.* (-worm) *or-orakai.*
Glue, s. *slekkh; leṭa-ī.*
Glutton, s. *geḍa-war, ghārai, ghārdal, ḥirṣ-nāk, rawai.*
Gnash, v.a. *ghākkh chīchal* or *-kṛapawul.*
Gnat, s. *māshai, ghamāsha, jak* or *jakh.*
Gnaw, v.a. *chīchal, kṛapawul.*
Go, v.n. *tlal—lāṛal, drūmal* or *drūmedal, chaledal, rawānedal; kūch k., legdal.*
Goad, s. *chūka, trāṭ, konṭa-ī.*
Goal, s. *ṭīkāo, mazal, borjal.*
Goat, s. *buz* or *wuz.* (he-) *psah.* (she-) *bza.* (-in heat) *wazema.* (kid) *warghūmai, chelai.* (yearling-) *serlai.* (-hair) *wajghūne.*
Gobble, v.a. *gaṛandai khwuṛal.*
Goblet, s. *kaṭorai, jām, shāh-kāsa.*
Goblin, s. *bāgū, bagalola-ī; rawai.*
God, s. *khudāe, allah, rabb.* (-forbid) *khudāe di na ka* or *-kāndi.* (-preserve us) *yā khudāya-* or *yā rabba khair ka.* (-knows) *khudāe khabar* or *-zdah.* (by-!) *khudāe go.* (good-!) *allahu akbar, subḥān allah.* (my-!) *yā dzamā khudāya.* (for God's sake) *da khudāe da pāra.* (-bless thee) *khudāe di wusāta* or *-wubakkha* or *-loe ka.* (-curse thee) *peṭī mū, pa tā n'alat, khudāe di mīrāt ka.* (-grant) *khudāe di wuka* or *-wukī.* (-protect thee) *da khudāe pa amān.*
Godliness, s. *dīn-dārī, taqwā.*
Godly, a. *dīn-dār, namāndzī, nmūndz-guẕār.*
Going, s, *tah, tlah, yūn, pand.*
Goitre, s. *ghur.*
Gold, s. *srah-zar, zar, ṭila.* (-smith) *zar-gar.*
Golden, a. *zarīn.*
Gonorrhœa, s. *sozāk.*
Good, a. *kkhah, nek, pakīzah, ghwarah.* s. *kkhegaṛa, fā-ida, sūd.*
Goodness, s, *kkhah-wālai, nekī.*
Goods, s. *asbāb.* (cattle) *māl.* (clothes) *rakht.* (furniture, etc.) *kālai.*
Goodwill, s. *nek-* or *khair-khwāhī.*
Goose, s. (domestic) *baṭa.* (wild-) *qāza.*
Gore, v.a. *pa kkhkar wahal.*
Gore, s. *pranṛ, jākai, malob, wīne.*
Gorge. s. *dara, tanga-ī; ghāṛa, mara-ī.*
Gormandize, v.a. *be-khrata-, be-prata-,* etc. *khwuṛal.*
Gospel s. *injīl; ḥaqq.*
Gossip, v.a. *khushe khabare k.; khabare-atare-, khabare-mabare k,*
Gourd, s. *kadū.* (-seed) *kadū-zarai.*
Gout, s. *bād, naqras.*

Govern, v.a, *ḥukūmat-, ḥukm-,* etc. *k.* or *chalawul.* (manage) *sambālawul.*

Government, s. *ḥukūmɔt, 'amal; sarkār, rāj; sardārī, khānī, malikī.*

Governor, s. *ḥākim, sardār, khān, malik.*

Gown, s. (man's) *chapan, qādara-ī.* (woman's) *peshwāz, pepna-ī.*

Grace, s. *mihrbāngī.* (favour) *mrasta.* (pardon) *bakkhana.* (beauty) *kkhāyast.* (manner) *nāz, karakkhma.* (by the grace of God) *da khudāe pa mihrbāngī sara.* (-before meals) *bismillah.* (-after meals) *d'uā, shukur.* (a form of-) *shukur alhamdu l illah, rabbā ṣanā tā lara.* (title) *ḥazrat.*

Graceful, a. *kkhāyastah, kkhkulai, nāzak.* (in comp.) *khūsh-.*

Gracefulness, s. *kkhāyast·wālai, kkhāyast, jorāb, krah·wrah.*

Gracious, a. *mihrbān.*

Graciously, ad. *pa mihrbāngī sara.*

Gradation, s. *darja, pāya, wār.*

Gradually, ad. *ro·ro, wār pa wār.*

Graft, s. *pewand, band, qalam.*

Grain, s. *ghalla, dāna.* (a single-) *dāna.* (bruised-) *dal.* (ground-) *orah.* (finely ground-) *maidah.* (parched-) *nīna, pūlah.* (mixed-) *gādera.* (-merchant) *saudāgar, ghalla·farosh, banriyā.*

Grammar, s. *ṣarf·o·naḥw.*

Granary, s. *anbār·khāna.*

Grand, a. *loe, ghaṭ, star.*

Grandee, s. *amīr, arbāb.*

Grandeur, s. *loe·wālai, ghaṭ·wālai; zbargī.*

Grant, v.a. *warkawul, bakkhal; manal, qabūlawul.*

Granule, s. *dāna; pūṭai, pitsānrai.*

Grape, s. *angūr.* (-vine) *tāk.* (wild-) *kwar.* (dried-) *watska, mewa.*

Grapple, v.a. *parzawul, nīwul.*

Grasp, v.a. *pa qabẓe-, pa panje-, pa mūṭe-, pa mungali-,* etc. *nīwul.*

Grass, s. *wākkhah, gayāh, 'alaf.* (varieties of-) *drab, dūp, kabl, shama, shāmukha, dīla, ghūndwagai, sargarai, sarbaga, wīga, mota, panai, malai, manaārū, dadam,* etc.

Grasshopper, s. *toqā, kha-argai; mlakh.*

Grate, v.a. *taghawul, brekkhawul; zdoyal.* v.n. *gharedal.*

Grateful, a. *shukur·guzār; khwand·nāk.*

Gratification, s. *khwakkhī; khwand.* (over another's misfortunes) *sakha, wiyār.*

Gratify, v.a. *khāṭir k., nāzawul, kkhāghal.*

Gratis, ad. *weriyā, mupt, hase.*

Gratitude, s. *shukur·guzārī.*

Gratuitous, a. *weriyā, mupt.*

Gratuity, s. *bakhkshiksh, in'ām, shukrāna, pekkh·kakkh, khwaṛa.*

Grave, s. *gor, qabr, maqbara.* (the niche) *lahad.* (-stone) *khadza* or *khāda.* (-digger) *qabr·kan, gor·kan.* (-badger) *gor·kakkh.* (-clothes) *kafan.*

Grave, a. *drūnd, grān; fikr·man, ghalai.*

Gravel, s. *kānr, gghal, ghaṭa·shiga.*

Gravitate, v.n. *kkhkenāstal, prewatal.*

Gravity, s. *drūnd·wālai, dranāwai.*

Gravy, s. *kkhorwā.*

Gray, a. *sperah, kha-ar, khākī.* (-hair) *brag.*

Graze, v.a. *piyāyal—powul.* v.n. *tsaral, tsaredal.* (abrade) *blosedal; sūledal.*

Grazier, s. *powūnkai.* (of cows) *ghobah.* (of buffaloes) *mekkhbah, gūjar.* (of camels) *ūkkhbak, sārwān.* (of sheep, etc.) *gadbah, shpūn, shpankai.*

Grease, s. *ghwarī, mū.* v.a. *ghwarawul.*

Greasy, a. *ghwar.*

Great, a. *ghaṭ, loe, star; zbarg.*

Greatly, ad. *nihāyat, der.*

Greatness, s. *star·wālai,* etc. *; zbargī.*

Greediness, s. *ḥirṣ, tam'a, liwāl·tob.*

Greedy, a. *ḥāriṣ, ḥirṣ·nāk, geda·war.*

Green, a. *shīn, zarghūn; ūm, kachah.*

Greens, s. *sāg, sābah, talkārī, tara.* (varieties

ot-) panerak, sharotal, warkhārai, chalwerai, tāndola, tsārmai, jawānrwān, etc. (cultivated-) pālak, malkhoza, āorai, mūlai, gāzara, ṭepar, etc. (dish of-) sāgīnrai.
Greet, v.a. mubārakī wayal; salām-'alaik-, joṛ-tāzah-, etc. k.
Grief, s. gham, randz, paskhāk or pakhsāk, nūl; gram.
Grievance, s. faryād; sakhtī, dzaur, jabr, ẓulm.
Grieve, v.n. nūledal, randzedal, kaṛedal, ghamedal, zahīredal. v.a. āzārawul, zahīrawul, etc.
Grieved, a. gham-jan, nūl-jan, randzūr, dil-gīr.
Grievous, a. gham-nāk; jabr-nāk, sakht, randz-nāk.
Grill, v.a. wrītawul, alwoyal, talawul, teyal.
Grim, a. sūṭ-būṭ, mushād; zīg, sakht, klak.
Grimace, s. pekkha, tsera, būṭ-urbūz.
Grin, v.n. musedal. v.a. dāṛe-, ghākkh-, etc. chīngawul.
Grind, v.a. oṛawul, anral, oṛah k.
Grindstone, s. psān. (-wheel) tsarkh. (-for corn) mechan. (-for spices) tīga, silāta.
Gripe, s. qabẓa, da mūṭī nīwah. (belly-) kānga, tāo, pech.
Gripe, v.a. pa qabẓe-, pa mūṭī-, etc. nīwul. (as birds and beasts) pa panje-, pa manguli-, etc. nīwul. (as the belly) v.n. kānga-, tāo-, etc. ked.
Gristle, s. krachai, krachūnai, krachandūkai.
Grit, s. kānr, shiga; dal, drūza, gadzārai.
Gritty, a. shiglan, kānran, kānrez.
Groan, v.a. zwergai or zgerwai-, angahār or hengahar-, etc. k.
Grocer, s. pansārī, banriyā.
Groin, s. mghāna.
Groom, s, shātar, jalau-dār, nafar.
Groove, s. kīla, karkkha.
Grope, v.n. ṭaparedal. v.a. laṭawul.
Gross, a. tsorb, peraṛ; ghaṭ, lwāṛ; nāpaṛ, star.
Gross, s. ṭol, ṭol-ṭāl, tamām, kull.
Ground, s. zmaka or mzaka, zamīn.
Groundless, a. be-mūjib, nā-ḥaqq.
Group, s. ṭolgai, tamba, tsīṛa, paṛk, jam.
Grouse, s. kha-aṛārai, kha-aṛai-kauntar, kha-aṛgaṭ.
Grove, s. jangai, banr.
Grovel, v.n. rghaṛedal—rghakkhtal.
Grow, v.n. (increase) ghaṭedal, ziyātedal, loe ked. (vegetate) ṭūkedal, zarghūnedal. (-old) zaṛedal. (become) kedal.
Growl, v.n. ghuṛunbedal, gṛanjedal.
Grudge, v.a. daregh k. (owe a-) dukkhmanī-, badī-, khwā-badī-, 'ināḍ-, kīna-, etc. laral.
Gruel, s. atob, oghra, daliya; āsh, shīra.
Gruff, a. sakht, tursh-rūe, suṭ-būṭ, qahr-jan.
Grumble, v.a. gila-, māna-, etc. k. v.n. gṛanjedal, ghuṛunbedal. (as the bowels) qur-qur ked.
Guarantee, s. ẓamānat. (person) ẓāmin.
Guard, s. pahra, tsoka-ī; pāswān, kashak; pahra-dār, tsoka-ī-dār. (over crops and cattle) kakkhai. (protector) sātūnkai, sātandoe, jghorai, pāslawūnai.
Guard, v.a. pahra-, etc. k.; pāswānī-, etc. k., gālal; kakkhī-tob k.; sātal, jghoral, pāslawul, khundī k., or khundiyal.
Guess, v.a. qiyās-, khiyāl-, aṭkal-, etc. k., pejandal, m'alūmawul.
Guest, s. melmah, mezmān.
Guidance, s. kkhowuna, hidāyat, murshidī.
Guide, s. balad, lār-kkhowūnkai, būmiyā. (spiritual) pīr, murshid, hādī, peshwā.
Guile, s. ṭag-bāzī, chal-bāzī, lamghaṛa-ī-tob. ṭagī, ḥīla, fareb.
Guilt, s. gunāh, taqṣīr; wabāl, baza.
Guiltless, a. be-gunāh, be-quṣūr, be-taqṣīr.
Guilty, a. gunāh-gār, taqṣīr, quṣūr-man.
Guise, s. ṣūrat, shakl, shān; bāna, libās; parda.

Guitar, s. *sitāra, chamtāra.* (Fiddle).

Gullet, s. *mara-ī, sra·ghāṛa.*

Gulp, s. *ghurap, gūṭ, īnda.* v.a. *nghaṛdal.*

Gum, s. *chīṛ, jāwla.* (of teeth) *ūra-ī* or *awra-ī.*

Gun, s. *bandūkh, ṭopak.* (-barrel) *nala.* (-stock) *kundāgh.* (-sight) *mach, zarai, dīdwān, ghūṭa-ī* (-match) *bāta-ī, patīla.* (-cock) *pāya.* (-trigger) *chajak.* (-priming pan) *kandol, māsha, ātash·khāna.* (-chamber) *khizana.* (-priming powder) *ranjak.* (-cleaning rod) *bargho, margholai.* (ramrod) *gaz, sīkh.* (-aiming rest) *sipāwa* or *sipāya.* (-powder) *dārū.* (-ball) *mardaka.*

Gunner, s. *ṭopak·chī, bandūkh·chī*; *top·chī.*

Gush, v.n. *pa·dāro watal* or *-bahedal.* v.a. *dāra wahal.*

Gust, s. *chapa, jakaṛ, sīla-ī.*

Gut, s. *kulma, laṛmūn*; *larai, ūjrai.*

Gutter, s. *nāwa, lakkhta-ī, wāla, tarnāo.*

Guttural, a. *ḥalqī.*

Gymnastic, a. *kushtī, pahalwānī.*

Gyves, s. *dzolana, pakhwandai, pāekara, pāela.*

H.

Haberdasher, s. *banjārī.*

Habit, s. *'ādat, yūn, 'amal*; *khoe, khaṣlat*; *mizāj, ṭabī'at.*

Habitation, s. *astoga, kor*; *dzāe, meshta, borjal.*

Habitual, a. *'ādatī, āmokhtah.*

Habituate, v.a. *'ādatī-*, etc. *k.*, *rūgdawul.*

Hack, v.a. *kūtal, ṭoṭa·ṭoṭa-, chūr·chūr-*, etc. *k.*

Hag, s. *zaṛa-ī, jāḍa-ī.*

Haggard, a. *tap, ḍangar, wuch·klak, tsoṛ.*

Hail, s. *jāla, gala-ī.* v.n. *jāle-*, etc. *oredal.*

Hail, v.a. *salām·'alaik-, joṛ·tāzah-*, etc. *k.*

Hair, s. *wekkhtah.* (dressed) *sar·kundai.* (lock or curl of-) *tsūnra, tsunraka, zulf, wal.* (braid or plait of-) *orbal, kontsa-ī, nghakkhai.* (top knot of-) *tsaṛai.* (-of pubes) *tor·wekkhtah.* (-of the body) *zunba, ghūna.* (goat's-) *ūjghūne.* (ribbon or braid for the-) *bachawai, pekawai, peyawai.*

Hairy, a. *babar, waṛan.*

Hale, a. *takṛah·tāzah, rogh·mot, joṛ, tandurust.*

Half, a. *nīm.* (-done) *nīmgaṛai.* s. *nīmai, nīmāyah.*

Hall, s. *dālān, khūna.* (public-) *hujra.* (-of audience) *dalbār, bārgāh.*

Halloo, v.a. *chigha-, nāra-*, etc. *wahal.*

Hallowed, a. *pāk, muqaddas.*

Halo, s. *hāla, shpol.*

Halt, v.n. *wudredal*; *guḍedal*; *jah ked.* v.a. *dera-, muqām-, ṭīkāo-*, etc. *k.*

Halter, s. *khapī* or *gapī, pā-ī, bāḍgol.* (headstall) *ter·sarai.* (hangman's-) *tezanda-ī, zanda-ī, pā-ī.*

Halve, v.a. *nīmawul, dwah·nīm k.*

Ham, s. (thigh) *wrūn, patūn.*

Hamlet, s. *bānḍa, kaloṭai.*

Hammer, s. *pa-alk, tsaṭak.* (wooden-) *baghdar, ḍabalai.* (washerman's-) *tsobāṛai.*

Hammer, v.a. *wahal, ṭakawul, trakawul, ṭak wahal.*

Hamper, s. *khalta, kawāra, ṭokra-ī, kāra, sawada.*

Hamper, v.a. *kariyābawul, haṭālawul.*

Hamstring, v.a. *pai k.*, or *-wahal.*

Hand, s. *lās*; *chaka, panja, mangul.* (-ful) *lapa* or *lapaka, paka* or *kapa.* (palm of-) *warghawai, khapaṛ.* (-breadth) *tsapak.* (closed-) *mūṭ.* (-in hand) *chak·pa·chak.* (-cuff) *karai.* (-held to receive) *mangul, changul.* (-held to take or seize) *panja.*

Handful, s. *chung, qawda.* (double-) *lapakai.*

Handkerchief, s. *rumāl, dast·māl.* (-for head) *sar·basta, sar·pechak, sar·tarūnai, tsapotkai.*

Handle, s. *mūṭai, lāstai, dasta.*

Handle, v.a. *lās lagawul, -warwral, -wahal,* etc., *laṭawul, nīwul*; *chalawul.*

Handmaid, s. *mazdūra, khidmat·gāra sahela-ī.* (brides-) *īnga.*

Handmill, s. *mechan.* (lower stone) *kkhkatanai pal.* (upper stone) *portanai pal.* (-handle) *lāstai.* (pivot or axle) *tīrak.* (axle bar) *ḍīḍa, kkhārag.* (-cup) *ghāṛa.* (-hopper) *ḍol, ganḍ.*

Handsome, a. *kkhāyastah, kkhkulai, pa-ī·makhai* or *pej·makhai.*

Handsomely, ad. *pa kkhah shān sara.*

Handsomeness, s. *kkhāyast, kkhāyast·wālai, kkhkulai·wālai, kkhkulī·tob, pej·makh·tob.*

Handy, a. *tak·lāstai*; *tayār*; *nijdai.*

Hang, v.n. *dzwaṛandedal, āwezānd . ked.* v.a. *āwezānd k., dzwaṛandawul.* (a criminal) *tezanda-ī warkawul, pa dār khejawul.*

Hangman, s. *jallāt, tezanda-ī warkawūnkai, dār·kash.*

Hank, s. *tranjūkai.* (ring) *karai.*

Hanker, v.n. *liwāl-, mayan-,* etc. *ked.* v.a. *mīna-, raghbat-, shauq-,* etc. *laral.*

Hapless, a. *kam·bakht, be·qismat, be·naṣīb.*

Haply, ad. *kkhā-ī, gunde*; *wī ba.*

Happen, v.n. *kedal, shwal, nāziledal, prewatal, teredal, waqi'a ked., pekkhedal.*

Happily, ad. *pa khair sara, pa kkhādī sara.*

Happy, a. *khwakkh, kkhād, kkhād·man.*

Harangue, v.a. *w'aẓ k., kalām wayal.*

Harass, v.a. *rabṛawul, āzārawul, tangawul, tongawul, ṭongāra k.*

Harbinger, s. *peshraw, astādzai.*

Harbour, s. *bandar*; *panāh.*

Hard, a. *klak, sakht*; *grān, mushkil*; *pokh, takṛah.*

Hard-hearted, a. *nā·tars, kānrai·zṛah, be·dard.*

Hardiness, s. *klak·wālai, maẓbūṭ·tiyā, ta·kṛah·wālai*; *zṛah·war·tob.*

Hardly, ad. *pa mushkil sara, pa rabaṛ sara*; *kamtar, mushkila, hīla.*

Hardness, s. *klak·wālai, sakht·wālai.*

Hardship, s. *tangsiyā, rabaṛ, sakhtī.*

Hardware, s. *da ospane kālī.*

Hardy, a. *klak, maẓbūṭ, zṛah·war, maṛanai, takṛah, ṭīng.*

Hare, s. *soe.* (hare's form) *soghālai.*

Harebrained, a. *khushai, lewanai.*

Hark, in. *wāwra! ghwag bāsa!* or *-nīsa!* or *-kegda!*

Harlot, s. *kāsīra, shatāha*; *lola-ī, kachana-ī.*

Harm, s. *tāwān, ziyān, nuqṣān.*

Harmful, a. *tāwānī, nuqṣānī, ziyānī.*

Harmonious, a. *barābar, yo·shān*; *khog.*

Harmony, s. *rogha, joṛa, āshtī*; *sarod, tarāna.*

Harness, s. *da ās kālī*; *sāz·sāmān.*

Harp, s. *barbaṭ.*

Harpoon, s. *biyak.*

Harrow, s. *ghākkhawar.*

Harsh, a. *trīw, trīkh*; *zīg, lwāṛ.*

Harvest, s. *faṣl.* (reaped-) *lau.* (gathered-) *khirman, dirmand.* (spring-) *oṛai.* (autumn-) *manai.*

Hash, v.a. *qīma k., ṭoṭe k.*

Haste, s. *talwār, talwal, jaltī, shitābī.* (to make-) *talwār-,* etc. *k.*

Hasty, a. *talwārī, talwalai, jalt.*

Hat, s. *ṭopa-ī, khola-ī-*

Hatch, v.n. *kuṛaka ked.*; *pa hago kkhkenāstal, bachī bāsal—yastal.*

Hatchet, s. *tabar.*

Hate, v.a. *bad manal, kagal, chinjawul, ghandal, kraka ākhistal.*

Hateful, a. *bad, kagalai, kraka·nāk, ghāndah.*

Hatred, s. *badī, khwā·badī, dukkhnī, kīna, khuṣūmat, ṭaka, ghach.*

Haughtiness, s. *kibr, bād, maghrūrī, khpul-sarī.*

Haughty, a. *kibr-jan, bādī, khāntamā.*

Haul, v.a. *rākāgal—rākkhkal.*

Haunch, s *kūnātai; ṭūṭa, ḍūḍa, patūn.*

Haunt, s. *borjal, meshta, astoga.*

Haunt, v.n. *osedal, āstedal.*

Hautboy, s. *sarnāe, tūrai.*

Have, v.a. *laral, darlal.*

Haven, s. *bandar, panāh.*

Havock, s. *tākht-tārāj, tālā, kharābi, wrānī.*

Hawk, s. *bāz.* (goshawk) *bāz, kaṭah-bāz, jurrah.* m. (varieties of-) *turmatai, bākkha, shaindai, lagar, jagar, regai, shikrai.* (-of the first year) *chūz.* (-of the second year) *khāna-kurīz.* (old-) *terīnāk.* (-from the nest) *shānī.* (caught-) *dāmī.* (-perch) *chakas.* (-bells) *gīngrai.* (-jessies) *tasme.* (-hood) *ṭopa-ī.* (-lure) *dalba.* (-drag) *bāolī.* (-glove) *bela.*

Hawk, v.a. *da bāz-* or *da chargh kkhkār k.*; (expectorate) *ghāṛa tāza k.* (sell) *banjārī k.*

Hay, s. *wuch wākkhah, wuch-giyāh, pashkālai.* (-of pulses) *kaṭī.* (coil of-) *beda.*

Hazard, s. *khaṭra, bāk, muhimm, andekkhnā.* (stroke) *daw, guzār.* (chance) *gumān.*

Haze, s. *dund, ghubār, ḍūp, laṛa, tyāra.*

He, pr. *haghah, dā, dah, de, di.*

Head, s. *sar, kala, koṭai.* (-band) *sar-pechak, sar-taṛūnai.* (-piece) *paṭkai, lūnga-ī.* (-stall) *ter sarai.* (-and tail) *shīr-khaṭ.* (crown of-) *ṭopal, ṭaṭar.*

Headlong, a. *aluwal; talwalai; naskor.*

Headstrong, a. *zorāwar, sar-zor, sar-kakkh, ṭakanṛai, khpul-sar, hoḍai.*

Heal, v.a. *joṛawul, raghawul.* v.n. *joṛedal. raghedal.*

Health, s. *rogh-wālai, joṛ-wālai, rogh-tiyā, joṛ-tiyā, tandrustī.*

Healthy, a. *rogh, joṛ, tandrust.*

Heap, s. *ṭop, kat, rāsha, rash.* (all of a-) *sūṭ-būṭ, aluwal, yak-lakhta.*

Heap, v.a. *tapal, ṭolawul, ḍera-ī-, kat-,* etc. *k.*

Hear, v.a. *āwredal; ghwag bāsal—yastdl, -nīwul,* or *-kegdal—kekkhodal.* (attend) *nghwatal.* (over-) *ghwag tsāral.*

Hearer, s. *āwredūnkai, sām'i.*

Hearing, s. *āwredana, sim'a.*

Hearsay, s. *āwredali khabara, afwāh.*

Heart, s. *zṛah, dil.* (-string) *māndara.* (-ache) *zṛah-swai, zṛah-nūl.* (-burning) *mānṛai, mīrtsī.*

Heartily, ad. *pa dwāṛo stargo.*

Hearty, a. *takṛah, tāzah, rogh-joṛ; zrah-war.*

Heat, s. *tod-wālai, todūkha, garmī, tāw.*

Heat, v.a. *todawul.* (warm) *taṛam k.*

Heathen, s. *but parast, kāfir.*

Heave, v.a. *khejawul; āchawul, ghurzawul, wīshtal.*

Heaven, s. *āsmān, falak; jannat, bihikkht.*

Heaviness, s. *drūnd-wālai, dranāwai.*

Heavy, a. *drūnd.*

Hedge, s. *bāra, shpol, keṛa, jal.*

Hedgehog, s. *shīshkai, zigkai.*

Heed, s. *parwā, fikr, poh, pahm, khabar.*

Heedful, a. *khabar-dār, baidār, hokkhyār.*

Heel, s. *pūnda* or *pūnḍa-ī.* (-of a door) *chūṛ.*

Heifer, s. *skhwandara, skhwandarkoṭa-ī.*

Height, s. *ūchat-wālai, hask-wālai.*

Heighten, v.a. *ūchatawul; ziyātawul.*

Heinous, a. *bad-sakht, bad-balā.*

Heir, s. *wāriṣ, ḥaqq-dār.* (-less) *lā-wāriṣ.*

Hell, s. *doghakkh* or *dozakh, jahannum, saqar.*

Hellebore, s. *kūtkī.*

Helm, s. *sīngāwanṛ, chapa.*

Helmet, s. *khol.*

Help, s. *madad, komak, pushtī, mrasta; tsāra, 'ilāj.* v.a. *madad-,* etc. *k.* or *-war-kawul; tsāra-,* etc. *laral.*

Helper, s. *madad-gār, komakī, yār, mal.*

Helpless, a. *lā·tsār, nā·tuwān, 'ājiz.* (-from wounds) *zmol, zam·zmolai, kand·kapaṛ.*

Helter-skelter, a. *gaḍ·wad, lānde·bānde.*

Hem, s. *laman, jāwja-ī ; trāṭa, maghzai.* (corner of a dress) *pitskai.*

Hem, v.a. *gandal, bezal.*

Hemp, s. *sanṛ.*

Hen, s. *chirga.*

Hence, ad. *la de na, dzaka ; la de dzāya.* in. *lire ! lire sha !*

Henceforth, ad. *wrānde.*

Her, pr. *hagha, dā, da, de, di.*

Herald, s. *jār·chī, munadī kawūnkai.*

Herb, s. *būṭai.* (pot-) *sāg.*

Herbage, s. *wākkhah, giyāh.*

Herd, s. *ramma, ṭol, ṭolai, ṭolgai, paṛk.* (-of cows) *gāhar, gohār.* (-of buffaloes) *goram.*

Herdsman, s. (-of oxen) *gāhū, ghobak.* (-of buffaloes) *gūjar, mekkhbah.* (-of sheep, etc.) *gaḍbah, shpūn.*

Here, ad. *dalta, dale, hīsta.*

Hereafter, ad. *la de na wrusto, biyā.*

Hereby, ad. *pa de, la de na.*

Hereditary, a. *mīrāṣī.* (-tenant) *mīrāṣ khor.*

Herein, ad. *pa de kkhke.*

Heresy, s. *rāfizī·tob, darogh.*

Heretic, s. *rāfizī, khārijī, darogh·jan.*

Herewith, ad. *de sara.*

Heritage, s. *mīrāṣ or mīrāt.*

Hermaphrodite, s. *kkhadzūnak, khunṣā, hijṛai.*

Hermit, s. *gokkha nishīn.*

Hernia, s. *tsūhra, khoṭa bād.*

Hero, s. *bahādur, maṛanai, turzan.*

Heroism, s. *maṛanī·tob, tūrzan·tob.*

Heron, s. *baglai.*

Hesitate, v.n. *wrānde·wrusto ked., stāra pre-watal, shakk·man-, wiswāsī-, andekkh·man-,* etc. *ked.*

Heterodox, a. *khārijī ; mukhālif.*

Heterogeneous, a. *gaḍ·wad, argajah ; mukhālif, 'aks, nā·munāfiq.*

Hew, v.a. *prekawul or prekṛal, kūtal ; tsaurang k.*

Hiccough, s. *haṭkai.*

Hidden, a. *puṭ, pinham.*

Hide, v.n. *puṭedal.* v.a. *puṭawuh*

Hide, s. *tsarman, poṭ, tsarm.*

Hideous, a. *bad, nā·kārah, haul·nāk.*

Hie, v.n. *drūmal, za-ar or zir-, gaṛandai-,* etc. *tlal—lāṛal.*

High, a. *ūchat, hask ; lwaṛ ; dang.*

Highlander, s. *rohīlai, kohistānai, da ghra saṛai, ghartsanai.*

Highly, ad. *ḍer, nihāyat, be·shāna.*

Highminded, a. *kibr·jan, bāḍī.*

Highness, s. *ūchat·wālai, hask·wālai ; lwaṛ·tiyā ; dang·wālai.* (title) *haẓrat.*

Highway, s. *bādshāhī lār, saṛak.*

Highwayman, s. *lār wahūnkai, shūk·mār, rāh·zan, ghal.*

Hilarity, s. *kkhādī, khūsh·hālī, khandā, mastī.*

Hill, s. *ghar, koh.* (low spur of-) *pukkhta, kha-aṭ.*

Hillock, s. *ghunda-ī, dera-ī, taraqqa-ī, pota-ī.*

Hilt, s. *mūṭai, lāstai, qabẓa.*

Hinder, v.a. *haṭālawul, kariyābawul, man'a k.*

Hinderance, s. *haṭāl, kariyāb, āṛ, harakat.*

Hindermost, a. *wrustai, wrustanai, akhīr, pastanai, ākhirīn.*

Hinge, s. *qabẓa, chūṛ.*

Hint, s. *ishārat, kināyat.*

Hip, s. *ṭuṭa, dūda.* (-bone) *kkhna.*

Hire, s. *ajr, ujrat, mihnat, mazdūrī, kreha.*

Hireling, s. *mazdūr.*

Hiss, v.a. (as snake, etc.) *pakh wahal.* (as meat on the fire) *sakkha-, dzadz-,* etc. *wahal.*

History, s. *tawārīkh, rawāyat, tazkira.*

Hit, v.a. *wahal, lagawul.* v.n. *jangedal, lagedal.*

Hither, ad. *dalta, rāhīsta, de khwā, de palaw.*

Hitherto, ad. *tar osa, tar osa pore.*

Hive, s. *kor, khūna.* (bees-) *gabīna, garbīnai.* (wasps-) *kkhor.* (ants-) *megatūn.*

Hoar, a. *sperah, brag, ẓpīn.*

Hoard, v.a. *ṭolawul, gaṭal, ambār-, jam'a-,* etc. *k.*

Hoard, s. *jam'a, panga, saga, anbār, māya.*

Hoarse, a. *bog, ḍaḍ.*

Hobble, v.n. *gudedal, pa kharpotso tlal— lāṛal; ṭaparedal.*

Hocus-pocus, s. *chal·wal, jādū, koḍ.*

Hodge-podge, a. *gaḍ·waḍ, aṛang·baṛang argajah.*

Hodiernal, a. *nananai.*

Hoe, s. *kodāla-ī, saspor, sakkhsora, kasha-ī.* (small) *rambai.*

Hog, s. *kharbīshoe, sarkūzai.* (wild-) *soḍar, maṭah.*

Hoist, v.a. *khejawul, ūchatawul, porta k.*

Hold, v.a. *nīwul.* (take) *ākhistal.* (-fast) *klak nīwul, ṭīngawul.* (contain) *dzāyawul.* (consider) *ganral.* (keep-) *sātal, sambā- lāwul, khundī k.* v.n. (remain) *osedal, pātedal.* (cling) *nkkhatal.* (contain) *dzā-edal.* (connect) *lagedal.*

Holder, s. *ākhistūnai; sātandoe, sātūnkai; dzāyūnkai, larūnkai.* (in comp.) *-dār, -gīr, -khor.*

Hole, s. *sūṛa, sūṛai.* (pit) *doghal, ṭūbkai* or *ṭublai, kanda.* (opening) *khula, swam* or *spam.*

Holiday, s. *akhtar, 'īd.*

Hollo, in. *o! ai! yā! yāe!* v.a. *nāra wahal.*

Hollow, a. *ta-ash* or *t-ish, khālī; ḍaḍ, kāwāk; khushai.*

Hollow, s. *tahana, jawara; kanda, kas.*

Holy, a. *pāk; nek, pārsā.*

Holy Ghost, s. *rūḥu l·quds, ruḥ·ullah.*

Homage, s. *tāb'i·dārī, salāmī.*

Home, s. *borjal, kor, dzāe, astoga, mīshta, ṭīkāo.* (country) *waṭan, mulk, wilāyat, dzāe·dzāegai.* (-made) *koranai, khānagī.*

Homeless, a. *be·kor, dar·ba·dar, khawre·pa- sar.*

Homely, a. *khamsor, sādah ;. lwāṛ.*

Homogeneous, a. *barābar, yo shān, yo jins.*

Hone, s. *belāw, belho, barjo, psān.*

Honest, a. *rikkhtīnai, nek, karah, sam.*

Honesty, s. *rikkhtīn·tob, nekī, rāstī.*

Honey, s. *shāt* or *shahad.* (-comb) *gabīna.*

Honeycombed, a. *zang wahalai, chinjī khwuṛalai.*

Honour, s. *nang, nūm, 'izzat, makh, abrū.*

Honourable, a. *nang·yālai,'izzat·nāk ; nūm· war; makhawar.*

Hood, s. *ṭopa·ī, khola·ī, kulāh.* (woman's-) *paṛūnai, oṛanai.* (snake's-) *chaja.*

Hoof, s. *sum.* (cloven-) *swa, kkhongarai.*

Hook, s. *kunda.* (flesh-) *nukhakkh.*

Hoop, s. *chambar, chak.*

Hoot, v.a. *chighawul.*

Hop, v.a. *tskhawul, tskhc k., tīndak-, ṭop-,* etc. *wahal.*

Hope, s. *umed, āsra; khal.* v.a. *umed-, etc laral.*

Hopeful, a. *umed·wār.*

Hopeless, a. *nā·umed.*

Horde, s. *ulas, tapa.*

Horizon, s. *ufuq.*

Horizontal, a. *prot, mlāst, sam.*

Horn, s. *kkhkar, kkhākh.*

Horned, a. *kkhkarawar, kkhākh·dār.*

Hornet, s. *danbara, dandāra, ghālbūza.*

Horrible, a. *bad sakht ; kagalai, ghāndah ; khof-, haul-. taṛs-,* etc. *-nāk.*

Horripilate, v.n. *ghūna zīgedal.*

Horror, s. *wera* or *yera, tor, tars.*

Horse, s. *ās.* (pack-) *yābū, ṭaṭū.* (ambling-) *yarghah.* (-dealer) *dallāl.* (-breaker) *chābuk sawār.* (-man) *spor* or *swor.* (-shoe) *nāl.*

Horticulture, s. *bāghwānī, gul karana.*

Hose, s. *joṛāba, moza.* (leather) *mīza·ī.*

Hospitable, a. *melmah·dost, doda-ī·mār.*
Hospital, s. *bīmār·khāna ; langar·khāna.*
Hospitality, s. *melmastiyā.*
Host, s. *korbah, melmah·dost ; merah, tsakkh-tan ; lakkhkar, ganr·khalq.*
Hostage, s. *yarghamāl.*
Hostess, s. *korbana, merman.*
Hostile, a. *dukkhman, mukhālif.*
Hostility, s. *dukkhmanī, badī, 'adāwat.*
Hot, a. *tod, garm.*
Hound, s. *tāzī-* or *kkhkārī spai.* v.a. *spī pase k.*
Hour, s. *sā'at, garai.*
Hourly, ad. *har sā'at, sā'at pa sā'at.*
House, s. *kor, khāna.* (storied-) *mānra-ī, angar.* (premises) *hawela-ī, mena.* (-holder) *korbah, dawtarī.* (-wife) *korbana, merman.* (-keeping) *kormāna.* (-hold) *tabar, kor, khāndān, khān·o·mān, kada.* (-tax) *lūgī·tāwān.* (-ruins) *kandar.* (-rent) *kreha, tāwān.* (-breaker) *ghal, gūt mātawūnkai, kandar kawūnkai.* (court of a-) *gholai.* (side of a-) *chana.*
Hovel, s. *jūngara, kadala, manah.*
Hover, v.n. *tsrapedal, rapedal ; girzedal.*
How, ad. *tsanga? tsa ranga? pa tsa shān?*
However, ad. *walekin, wale, mangar.*
Howl, v.a. *ghapal, angolā k., nāra wahal.*
Hubbub, s. *zwag·zwūg, chagh·chugh, nāre·sūre, hāra·hūra, dagh·dagha.*
Hue, s. *rang, laun.* (-and cry) *hūhā.*
Hug, v.a. *ghāra·ghara-ī k.*
Huge, a. *loe, ghat, star ; nāpar, khrīs.*
Hum, v.n. *bonredal.* v.a. *zwag k.*
Hum, s. *bonra.* (conversation) *gangosai, skālwah* or *kkhkālwah.*
Human, a. *basharī, insānī, nāsūt.* (-being) s. *wagarai, gawai ; bashar, insān.*
Humane, a. *nek·khoe, mulā-im, rahm·dil.*
Humanity, s. *sarī·tob, ādmiyat, insāniyat ; nek·khaslatī, mom·dilī.*
Humble, a. *'ājiz, nā·tsīz, gharīb, kamīn.*
Humbly, ad. *'ājizī sara.*
Humbug, s. *allam·ghallam, shkharā.*
Humid, a. *lūnd ; nam·nāk, zyam·nāk, naw-jan.*
Humidity, s. *lūnd·wālai ; zyam, nam, naw.*
Humiliation, s. *'ājizī; gharībī, nā·tsīzī ; spuk·tiyā, makh·torī.*
Humility, s. *'ājizī, gharībī, nā·tsīzī, kamīn·tob.*
Humorous, a. *toqī, washtī, khandā·bāz.*
Humour, s. *khwā, khoe, mizāj.* (matter) *ziwa, zahūb, khīrai, rīm.* (fun) *washta, toqa.* (moisture) *zyam, nam, naw.*
Humour, v.a. *nāzawul, nāz wral, khātir k.*
Hump, s. *kūb* or *kwab.* (-backed) *kūbai, chūghai.*
Hundred, s. *sal* or *sil.* (more than one-) *saw.* (one hundred) *sil.* (two, three, four, etc. hundred) *dwah-, dre-, tsalor-,* etc., *-sawa.*
Hunger, s. *lwaga, liwāl·tob.*
Hungry, a. *wagai, liwāl, naghlānd.*
Hunt, v.a. *kkhkār k.* (search) *latawul, shanal.*
Hurl, v.a. *ghurzawul, wīshtal, āchawul.*
Hurrah, in. *shābāsh ! āparīn !*
Hurricane, s. *sīla-ī, tūfān.*
Hurry, v.a. *talwār-, talwal-, jaltī-, garandai-,* etc. *k.*
Hurt, s. *khūg, zakhm, parhār ; tāwān, nuqsān, ziyān.* a. *zakhmī, parhār·jalai, jobal.* v.a. *khūgawul, jobalawul, zahīrawul ; tā-wān-, nuqsān-,* etc. *k.*
Hurtful, a. *tāwānī, ziyān·kār, nuqsānī ; muzirr, wrān·kār, stūkh.*
Husband, s. *merah, tsakkhtan, khāwand.*
Husbandman, s. *zamīndār, kikkht·gar.* (hired-) *charekār, dihqān.*
Husbandry, s. *kar, kikkht·garī, zamīndārī.* (thrift) *kormāna, khāna·darī ; sātana, bachawūna.*

Hush, in. chip! chup!
Husk, s. būr, poṭ, baṭ; sūṛī, būṭ·sūṛī.
Hut, s. jūngaṛa, kuḍalı, tsapar, manah.
Hyacinth, s. nargis, kangas. (colour) sausan.
Hyena, s. kog, sar·ṭīṭai, kaftār.
Hypochondriasis, s. khapaqān, saudā-ī.
Hypocrisy, s. makr, riyā.
Hypocrite, s. makrai, makr·jan, riyā·kār.
Hypothesis, s. qiyās, rāe, andāza, gumān.
Hysterics, s. pariyān, da pariyāno ghoṭa.

I.

I, pr. zah, khpul; mā.
Ice, s. kangal, yakh.
Idea, s. khiyāl, rāe, fikr, poh, and.
Identical, a. be·dū, hūbahū, kaṭ·maṭ, pa ṭakī.
Identity, s. ṣūrat, shān; pejandgalī; yo·wālai.
Idiom, s. iṣṭilāḥ, iṣṭilāḥī khabara, chalana.
Idiomatic, a. iṣṭilāḥī, chalanī, rawājī.
Idiot, s. gedī, kam·'aql, nā·dān, nā·poh.
Idle, a. wazgār, khālī, be·kār. (lazy) nā·rāst, sust, laṭ. (useless) 'abaṣ, be·fā-ida. (trifling) be·hūdah, wuch·puch, nā·kārah.
Idleness, s. nā·rāstī, sustī, laṭ·wālai.
Idol, s. būt, tsera.
Idolater, s. but parast, mushrik.
Idolatry, s. but parastī, shirk.
Idolize, v.a. parastī k. (admire) v.n. gro-hedal.
If, c. ki, agar. (as-) laka chī, ghūnde, ganṛa, goyā.
Ignite, v.n. baledal, swal. v.a. balawul, sedzal, or pōre k., swadzawul.
Ignoble, a. lānde·zāt, kam·aṣl, bad·aṣl, spuk, pāsū, bad·zāt.
Ignominious, a. ruswā, bad·nūm, nā·kārah, bad.
Ignominy, s. bad·namūsī, sharmindagī, rus-wā-ī, makh·torī.
Ignorance, s. nā·dānī, be·khabarī, nā·pohī, jel.
Ignorant, a. nā·dān, nā·poh, jāhil; be·khabar.
Ignorantly, ad. nā·dānista, be·khabara.
Ill, a. bad, nā·kārah, nā·sāz, nā·kkhanai, kharāb. (sick) nā·rogh, nā·joṛ, randzūr, bīmār.
Illegal, a. nā·rawā, ḥarām.
Illegitimate, a. ḥarāmī, ḥarāmūnai, ḥarām zādah.
Illiberal, a. shūm, shūm·shaghāl, bakhīl.
Illiterate, a. nā·lwustai, jāhil, ummī.
Ill-natured, a. bad·khoe, bakhīl, sūṭ·būṭ.
Illness, s. nā·joṛ·tiyā, nā·rogh·tiyā, āzār, bīmārī.
Illtimed, a. be·wakht, be·ṭāng.
Illumination, s. rokkhnā-ī, ranṛā-ī; chirāgh·dān.
Illuminate, v.a. rokkhān-, ranṛā-, etc. k., chirāgh·dān k.
Illusion, s. khām khiyāl, ghulatī, fareb.
Illustrate, v.a. kkhayal—kkhowul, tsarganda-wul, kkhkārah k., bayānawul, tamṣīl k.
Illustration, s. bayān, kkhowūna, miṣāl.
Illustrious, a. nūm·war, nāmdār, nāmar.
Im-, negative prefix. (in comp.) be-, nā-, kam-.
Image, s. but, tsera; ṣūrat, shakl.
Imaginary, a. khiyālī, wahmī, gumānī.
Imagination, s. khiyāl, qiyās, fikr, gumān, rāe.
Imagine, v.a. qiyās-, fikr-, etc. k.
Imbecile, a. kam·'aql, nā·tuwān, palwanḍ.
Imbibe, v.a. tskkhal or skal, dzbekkhal, rawdal; wuchawul.
Imbue, v.a. rangawul; khaṛob k.; ḍakawul.
Imitate, v.a. pairawī k., naql k., swāng k.
Imitator, s. pairaw; nāqil; swāngai.
Immaculate, a. be·gunāh, be·'aib, pāk ṣāf, spīn·spetsalai, nog.
Immaterial, a. be·wujūd, nābūd; khushai, nā·kār.
Immature, a. ūm, khām, kachah, umghalan, nīma·khwā, nīmgaṛai.

Immediately, ad. *os, pa de sā'at, sam da lāsa, pa ṭakī, dam dar ḥāl.*
Immemorial, a. *la yād na bāhir, da yāda ter.*
Immense, a. *be·ḥadd, be·nihāyat, be·shān ; loe, ghaṭ, star, bashpaṛ, nāpaṛ.*
Immensely, ad. *be·qiyāsa, be·shāna, be·kacha,* etc.
Immerse, v.a. *ḍūbawul, gharqawul, ghūpa-, ghoṭa-,* etc. *warkawul.*
Imminent, a. *nijdai, rātlūnai, prewatūnai.*
Immoderate, a. *be·ḥisāb, be·kach, be·andāzah ; nā·parhez·gār.*
Immodest, a. *be·sharm, be·ḥayā, be·makh.*
Immodesty, s. *be·sharmi, be·hayā·tob, be·makh·tob.*
Immolate, v.a. *qurbān-, ṣadqa-, zār-,* etc. *k.* (-oneself) v.n. *qurbān-,* etc. *ked.*
Immoral, a. *bad·kār, bad·kirdār, ḥarām·kār.*
Immortal, a. *be·marg, jāwīdān.*
Immortality, s. *baqā, jāwīdānī.*
Immortalize, v.a. *jāwīdān k., pātai k.* v.n. *pāedal, jāwīdān ked., pātai ked.*
Immoveable, a. *maẓbūṭ, qā-im, pāedūnai.*
Immunity, s. *khalāṣī, āzādī, najāt.*
Immutable, a. *be·tabdīl.*
Impair, v.a. *kamawul, spukawul, wrānawul.*
Impart, v.a. *pohawul, khabarawul ; warkawul.*
Impartial, a. *rāst·kār, 'ādil, rikkhtīnai, ṣādiq, niyāw kawūnkai, be·mrasta.*
Impassable, a. *be·lār, be·gūdar, band.*
Impatient, a. *be·ṣabr, be·zgham ; jalt, tund, tez.*
Impeach, v.a. *d'awa k., tuhmat pore k.*
Impede, v.a. *haṭālawul, kariyābawul, nkkhlawul, man'a k.*
Impediment, s. *haṭāl, kariyāb, āṛ, nkkhatai.*
Impel, v.a. *zoral, tezal, zghalawul, chalawul.*
Impend, v.n. *dzwaṛandedal, nijdai rasedal.*
Impending, a. *nijdai ; dzwaṛand.*
Impenitent, a. *nā·toba·gār, nā·pakkhemān.*
Imperative, a. *ḥukmī, farẓī ; amr.*
Imperceptible, a. *puṭ, nā·m'alūm.*
Imperfect, a. *nīmgaṛai, ūm, nīma·khwā.*
Imperial, a. *bādshāhī.* (hair on chin) *charekār.*
Imperious, a. *kibr·jan, khāntamā, khpul·sar.*
Imperishable, a. *pāedār, qā-im, lā·zawāl, pātedūnai, be·marg.*
Impertinent, a. *be·dzāe, be·adab, wīṭakai.*
Impervious, a. *klak, ṭīng ; be·lār, band.*
Impetuous, a. *tund, tez, gaṛandai, jalt.*
Impetus, s. *zor, quwat.*
Impious, a. *be·dīn, kāfir.*
Implacable, a. *be·raḥm, sakht·dil, kāṇrai·zṛah, nā·pīrzo da pakhulā, bad·dukkhman.*
Implant, v.a. *khakkhawul, njatal.*
Implement, s. *kālai, hatiyār, sāz.*
Implicate, v.a. *nkkhlawul, gaḍawul ; malgarai-, sharīk-,* etc., *k.*
Implicit, a. *kāmil, pūrah, tamām.*
Implore, v.a. *minnat-, d'uā-,* etc. *k.*
Imply, v.a. *m'anā-, dalīl-,* etc. *laral, nakkha-, ishārat-,* etc. *k.*
Import, s. *m'anā ; da pradī mulk māl.*
Import, v.a. *da pradī mulk māl khpul waṭan ta rāwṛal.*
Important, a. *drūnd, grān, ẓarūr.*
Importune, v.a. *taqāẓā k., lagiyā ghokkhtal.*
Impose, v.a. *āchawul, lagawul, kegdal.* (upon) *ghulawul, ṭagal, fareb-,* etc. *warkawul.*
Impost, s. *tāwān, sāw, bāj ; maḥṣūl, nāgha.*
Impostor, s. *ṭag, chal·bāz, bāna·khor, farebī, darghal, sādū, ḥīla·bāz.*
Imposture, s. *ṭagī, ghulat, fareb, droh.*
Impotent, a. *nā·tuwān, 'ājiz ; nā·mard.*
Impoverish, v.a. *khwār-, gharīb-,* etc. *k.*
Impracticable, a. *na·kedana, na·shwūnkai.*
Imprecate, v.a. *kkhera-, n'alat-, bad·d'uā-,* etc. *k.*
Impregnate, v.a. *ḍakawul ; blārba k.*
Impress, v.a. *ṭāpa-, chāpa-,* etc. *k.,* or *-wahal ; kkhke·manḍal.* (-on the mind) *tākīd k.*

Impression, s. *ṭāpa, c̲h̲āpa*; *nak̲k̲h̲a, dāg̲h̲*; *gumān, k̲h̲iyāl, fikr.*
Imprint, v.a. *ṭāpa-, c̲h̲īpa-*, etc. *k.*; *dāg̲h̲awul.*
Imprison, v.a. *qaid-, band-*, etc. *k.*
Improbable, a. *la 'aqla lire* or *-bāhir.*
Improper, a. *nā-munāsib, na-kk̲h̲anai, nā-sāz, nā-rawā, nā-kār, kānah.*
Improve, v.a. *joṛawul, rag̲h̲awul.* v.n. *joṛedal, rag̲h̲edal.*
Improvement, s. *kk̲h̲egaṛa, joṛ-tiya.*
Improvident, a. *be-tadbīr, kotāh-andes̲h̲.*
Imprudent, a. *be-k̲h̲abar, be-fikr.*
Impudent, a. *be-adab, gustāk̲h̲*; *be-ḥayā.*
Impulse, s. *zor, quwat, ḥarakat.*
Impulsive, a. *tund, tez, gaṛandai, talwalai.*
Impure, a. *nā-pāk, palīt, murdār.*
Impute, v.a. *lagawul, pore k.*
In, p. *danana, kk̲h̲ke, pa kk̲h̲ke.*
In-, negative prefix. (in comp.) *be-, lā-, nā-.*
Inability, s. *nā-tuwānī, lā-ts̲ārī, 'ājizī.*
Inaccessible, a. *nā-mūndanai.*
Inaccurate, a. *g̲h̲alaṭ, nā-durust.*
Inactive, a. *sust, laṭ, s̲h̲adal*; *be-kār*; *prot.*
Inadequate, a. *kam, la-ag*; *nā-qābil.*
Inadmissible, a. *nā-qabūl, band, man'ah.*
Inadvertent, a. *be-k̲h̲abar, be-fikr.*
Inanimate, a. *be-dz̲ān, be-sāh, muṛ.*
Inapplicable, a. *nā-munāsib, nā-sāz.*
Inattentive, a. *be-parwā, be-k̲h̲abar.*
Inaugurate, v.a. *kk̲h̲kenawul, wudrawul.*
Inauspicious, a. *bad-bak̲h̲t s̲h̲ūm-bak̲h̲t, asī.*
Incalculable, a. *be-s̲h̲umār, be-ḥisāb, be-kac̲h̲.*
Incantation, s. *jādū, koḍa, siḥr, dam, hūda, pāṛ, mantar, du'ā, t'awīẕ.*
Incapable, a. *nā-qābil, nā-tuwān, be-was.*
Incautious, a. *be-tadbīr, nā-k̲h̲abar-dār.*
Incendiary, s. *s̲h̲ūs̲h̲a-ī mār, or lagawūnkai, or pore kawūnkai.*
Incense, s. *'ūd.* (-dish) *majmir.*
Incense, v.a. *k̲h̲apah k., kaṛawul.*
Incentive, s. *sabab, bā'iṡ*; *lamsūn.*

Incessant, a. *lagiyā, mudām, hames̲h̲.*
Incessantly, ad. *har sā'at, sā'at pa sā'at.*
Incest, s. *mor-, k̲h̲or-, lūr-*, etc. *g̲h̲odī.*
Incident, s. *wāqi'a, ḥādiṡa, c̲h̲al, wārida.*
Incidentally, ad. *nā-gumāna, nā-gahāna.*
Incision. s. *ts̲īra, zak̲h̲m, parhār.*
Incite, v.a. *lamsawul*; *pārawul*; *agayal.*
Inclination, s. *k̲h̲wā, mīna, zṛah, s̲h̲auq.*
Incline, v.a. *k̲h̲wā ta k., mayan k, zṛah lagawul*; *ṭīṭawul.* v.n. *k̲h̲wā ta ked.*, etc.
Include, v.a. *s̲h̲āmil-, yo-dz̲āe-, dāk̲h̲il-*, etc. *k.*; *dz̲āyawul.*
Incog, ad. *pa puṭa.*
Incoherent, a. *be-joṛ, be-hūdah, be-k̲h̲ūd.*
Income, s, *āmad, ḥāṣil.*
Incommode, v.a. *taklīf warkawul.*
Incomparable, a. *be-siyāl, lā-ṡānī, be-miṡāl.*
Incompatible, a. *muk̲h̲ālif.*
Incompetent, a. *nā-qābil, nā-tuwān.*
Incomplete, a. *nīmgaṛai, nā-tamām.*
Incomprehensible, Inconceivable. a. } *be-qiyās, s̲h̲andah, la 'aqla lire* or *-bāhir.*
Inconclusive, a. *be-iṡbāt, be-dallīl*; *nā-zbād, nā-ṡābit.*
Incongruous, a. *be-joṛ, nā-sāz, be-ṭikānah, be-hūdah, bar-k̲h̲ilāf, nā-muwāfiq.*
Inconsiderate, a. *be-liḥāẕ, be-parwā, be-g̲h̲aur. be-fikr, be-tadbīr, g̲h̲āfil.*
Inconsistent, a. *be-jor*, etc. (*v.* Incongruous).
Inconsolable, a. *g̲h̲am-jan, nūl-jan, be-tasallī.*
Inconstant, a. *nā-pāedār, nā-qalār, be-wafā.*
Incontestible, a. *ṡābit, zbād, lā-dz̲awāb, qat'a-ī.*
Incontinent, a. *be-parhez, bad-laman, bad-parhez.*
Incontrovertible, a. *zbād*, etc. (*v.* Incontestible).
Inconvenience, s. *be-ārāmī, rabaṛ, taklif, harj.*
Inconvenient, a. *be-dz̲āe, nā-kārah, nā-munāsib.*

Incorporate, v.a. *gaḍawul, yo-dzāe k., laṛal.*
Incorrect, a. *nā-durust, ghalaṭ, darogh-ĵan.*
Incorrigible, a. *bad-sakht, hets da kkhah, lā-'ilāj.*
Incorruptible, a. *be-fanā, pāedār.*
Increase, v.a. *ziyātawul, wadānawul, ḍerawul.* v.n. *ziyātedal, wadānedal, ḍeredal.*
Increase, s. *ziyāt-wālai, wadānī, der-wālai.*
Incredible, a. *bē-i'tibār, shandah.*
Incrust, v.a. *lewawul.*
Incubate, v.n. *kuṛaka kkhkenāstal; pakhedal.*
Inculcate, v.a. *pohawul, pahmawul, tākīd k., kkhayal—kkhowul.*
Incumbent, a. *farẓ, lāzim, wājib, ẓarūr.*
Incur, v.n. *pīrzo-, lā-iq-,* etc. *ked.* v.a. *rāwṛal, lagawul, āchawul, ākhistal.*
Incurable, a. *lā-'ilāj, lā-dawā, lā-tsār.*
Incursion, a. *chapāo, dāṛa-dopa, hapa-dapa, tākht-tārāj, halla.*
Indebted, a. *qarẓ-dār, porawuṛai.*
Indecent, a. *pūch, chūnkai; be-ḥayā, be-nang; nā-lā-iq, nā-munāsib; be-adab, be-pardah.*
Indeed, in. *rikkhtiyā! khudāe-go! āyā! he!* ad. *haḍo, yara, kho.*
Indefatigable, a. *miḥnatī, sā'ī, kokshikshī.*
Indefinite, a. *be-ṭikānah, be-kach.*
Indemnity, s. *badal, tāwān, nāgha.* (-for blood) *diyat.* (-for abduction) *swara.*
Indenture, s. *iqrār-nāma, 'ahd-nāma.*
Independent, a. *khpul-sar, da khpul wāk khāwand; yāghī, sar-kakkh.*
Indescribable, a. *lā-bayān.*
Index, s. *nakkha, nikkhān; dallīl.* (-of a book) *fihrist.* (-finger) *kkhowūnai; mis-wāka gūta.*
India, s. *hind, hindūstān.* (language of-) *hindko.* (Mussalmān native of-) *hindkai.* (Pagan native of-) *hindū.*
Indian-corn, s. *jwār, ghaṭ jwār, maka-ī.*
Indicate, v.a. *kkhayal—kkhowul.*
Indication, s. *kkhowūna; nakkha; dallīl.*
Indifferent, a. *be-parwā, be-khabar; khushai.*
Indifferently, ad. *hase, be-parwā-ī sara.*
Indigent, a. *khwār, ḥājat-man, muḥtāj, muflis.*
Indigestion, s. *bad-haẓmī, agheṛ, aṭer.*
Indignant, a. *khapah, qahr-ĵan, qahr-nāk.*
Indignity, s. *spuk-tiyā, makh-torī, sharmin-dagī.*
Indigo, s. (-plant) *wasma.* (-dye) *nīl.* (-maker) *nīl-gar.*
Indirect, a. *kog, tsatskan, girzedalai.*
Indirectly, ad. *pa trats; pa chal sara; pa waṣīle sara.*
Indiscreet, a. *be-tadbīr, be-sha'ūr, kam-'aql.*
Indiscriminate, a. *gaḍ-waḍ, alwal.*
Indispensable, a. *ẓarūr, lāzim, wājib; farẓ.*
Indisposed, a. *nā-khwakkh, nā-rāẓ; nā-rogh, nā-joṛ.*
Indisputable, a. *lā-radd, qaṭ'a-ī, yaqīnī.*
Indistinct, a. *dund; puṭ; nā-ṣāf.*
Individual, a. *biyal, judā, mufrid, yawādzai.* s. *tan, kas, saṛai, wagaṛai, gawai.*
Individuality, s. *nātka-ī, yawādzai-wālai, yo-wālai, biyal-wālai.*
Individually, a. *biyal-biyal, yo-yo, judā-judā.*
Indolent, a. *sust, laṭ, nā-rāst, shalaṭ.*
Indubitable, a. *be-shakk, be-shubha, be-gumān.*
Induce, v.a. *lamsawul, targhīb warkawul.* (bring on) *rāwṛal, paidā k., kheĵawul, porta k.; 'amal-, pāzah-,* etc. *k.*
Indulge, v.a. *nāzawul, khāṭir k.; pālal, nmāndzal; bakkhal, mihrbāngī k.*
Indulgent, a. *mihrbān, khāṭir-dār, nāz wṛūnkai, narm, bakkhūnkai.*
Indurate, v.n. *klakedal, ṭīngedal.*
Industrious, a. *miḥnatī, kokshikshī.*
Industry, s. *miḥnat, kokshiksh, mushaqqat.*
Inebriate, v.a. *nasha warkawul, be-khūd-, be-hokkh-,* etc. *k.; mast k.*
Ineffable, a. *lā-bayān, be-bayān.*

Inefficacious, a. *be·pāzah, nā·kārah, 'abaṣ, be·tāṣīr, be·aṣr, khushai, spuk.*
Inequality, s. *lwaṛ·ĵawar·tiyā, zīg·wālai, nā·hawār·tiyā.*
Inert, a. *be·ḥarakat*; *be·pāzah*; *sust, laṭ.*
Inestimable, a. *be·bahā, be·qīmat*; *grān.*
Inevitable, a. *muqarrar, qaṭ'a-ī.*
Inexcusable, a. *be·'uẕr, be·ḥujjat, lā·dzawāb.*
Inexhaustible, a. *be·pāyān, be·ḥadd, be·nihāyat. be·and, be·ḥisāb.*
Inexorable, a. *sakht, nā·tars, kāṉrai·zṛah.*
Inexpedient, a. *be·dzāe, nā·munāṣib, nā·kkhanai, nā·sāz.*
Inexperienced, a. *nā·wāqif, nā·āmokhtah, nā·'ādat, nā·āshnā, nā·balad.*
Inexpert, a. *kam·ustāẕ, be·hunar, kachah.*
Inexplicable, a. *lā·bayān, nā·m'alūm.*
Infallible, a. *nā·khaṭā, qādir, nā·ghalaṭ.*
Infamous, a. *bad, baḍ·namūs, makh·tor.*
Infamy, s. *bad·namūsī, makh·torī, ruswā-ī.*
Infancy, s. *māṣhūm-*, or *m'aṣūm·wālai, bachai-, tandai-*, etc. *-tob.*
Infant, s. *māshūm, tandai, bachai, kachoṭai, waṛkoṭai, kamkoṭai, wṛūkai, pa-ī·rawai.*
Infantry, s. *piyādah, mlā·taṛ*; *palṭan.*
Infatuated, a. *lewanai, fareftah, khushai.*
Infatuation, s. *lewantob, fareftagī, khushī·tob.*
Infect, v.a. *bangawul, bonṟawul, gazak k., wahal, lagawul.*
Infer, v.n. *pohedal.* v.a. *ganṟal.*
Inference, s. *khulāṣa, ḥāṣil, natīja.*
Inferior, a. *kam·pāyah, kam·aṣl, kamtar, spuk, adnā*; *lāndai, kūz, lar, kkhkatanai.*
Infernal, a. *doghakkhī, jahannamī.*
Infidel, s. *kāfir, be·dīn, be·īmān, be·islām.*
Infidelity, s. *kufr, be·dīnī, be·īmānī.*
Infinite, a. *be·nihāyat, be·ḥadd, be·and, be·shān, be·pāyān, be·kach, be·shumār.*
Infirm, a. *ṭap, nā·tuwān, kamzor, ẓa'īf.*
Inflame, v.a. *balawul, swadzawul.* v.n. *baledal, sedzal, swal.*

Inflammation, s. *swai.*
Inflate, v.a. *pūkal, paṛsawul.* v.n. *paṛsedal.*
Inflect, v.a. *ṭīṭawul, kagawul, aṛawul, girzawul.*
Inflexible, a. *klak, sakht, zīg, krosand*; *khpulsar, sar·kakkh, ṭakanṟai, hoḍai.*
Inflict, v.a. *pore k., āchawul, rasawul, lagawul, warkawul, kawul, kṛal.*
Influence, s. *pāzah, 'amal, aṣı tāṣīr.*
Influenza, s. *dūmai, nuzla, zukām, sāṛa, yakhnī.* (to have-) *sāṛa-, yakhnī-*, etc. *wahal.*
Inform, v.a. *khabarawul, āgāh k.*; *pohawul, kkhayal—kkhowul.*
Information, s. *khabar*; *āgāhī.*
Informer, s. *mukhbir, tsārai.*
Infringe, v.a. *mātawul.*
Infuse, v.a. *āchawul, gaḍawul*; *lamdawul*; *damawul, dam warkawul.*
Ingenious, a. *ḥikmatī, hunar·man, pohānd.*
Ingenuous, a. *rikkhtūnai, nek, karah, sādah, spīn, rāst, sam, pāk·ṣāf.*
Inglorious, a. *spuk, halak, be·nām, be·nang.*
Ingraft, v.a. *pewand-, qalam-*, etc. *lagawul*; *kkhke·manḍal, khakkhawul, lagawul.*
Ingrate, a. *namak·ḥarām, nā·shukr·guẕār.*
Ingratiate, v.a. *lār ākhistal* or *-mūndal.*
Ingredient, s. *juz, shai*; *gaḍa.*
Ingress, s. *nanawātah, dakhl.* (-and egress) *wātah·nanawātah, rāshah·darshah.*
Inhabit, v.a. *astoga-, mīshta-*, etc. *k.* v.n. *osedal, āstedal.* (colonize) v.a. *ābādawul.*
Inhabitant, s. *osedūnkai, astogūnkai.*
Inhale, v.a. *sāh-, dam-*, etc. *pa·porta ākhistal* or *-rākāgal—rākkhkal.*
Inherent, a. *ẕātī, aṣlī, jibillī.*
Inherit, v.a. *mīrāṣ-* or *mīrāt ākhistal* or *-mūndal.* v.n. *mīrāt·khor ked.*
Inheritance, s. *mīrāṣ* or *mīrāt.*
Inheritor, s. *mīrāt khor, wāriṣ.*
Inhospitable, a. *bakhīl, shūm, be·makh.*

Inhuman, a. *nā·insān, nā·tars, be·dard.*
Inimical, a. *mukhālif, bad·niyat, dukkhman, khwā bad.*
Inimitable, a. *be·naẓīr, be·miṣāl.*
Iniquitous, a. *bad, nā·ḥaqq, be·inṣāf.*
Iniquity, s. *badī, be·inṣāfī, nā·ḥaqqī, ẓulm, gunāh, pasāt, wabāl, baza.*
Initial, a. *wṛūnbanai, awwalanai.*
Initiate, v.a. *jārī k., chalawul, rawānawul; āmokhtah k., lagawul, lwalawul; bāolī warkawul.*
Injection, s. *nanayastah; ḥuqna.*
Injudicious, a. *be·tadbīr, be·shu'ūr, nā·lā-iq, nā·kkhanai, nā·kkhāyastah.*
Injunction, s. *ḥukm, amr, kariya, tākīd.* (prohibition) *qadaghan.*
Injure, v.a. *tāwān-, ziyān-,* etc. *rasawul; āzārawul, khūgawul; wrānawul, habatah k.*
Injurious, a. *mozī, muẓirr; ziyān·kār, nuqṣānī, tāwānī; randz rasawūnkai, stūkh.*
Injury, s. *nuqṣān, ziyān, tāwān, īẕā, ẓarar.*
Injustice, s. *be·inṣāfī, nā·ḥaqqī, ẓulm.*
Ink, s. *siyāhī.* (red-) *shangrip.* (-stand) *mashwānṛa-ī.*
Inlaid, a. *jaṛāo.*
Inmate, s. *osedunkai, astogūnkai; hamsāyah, kilai·wāl.*
Inn, s. *srāe, rab...*
Innate, a. *ẕātī, aṣlī, jibillī.*
Innocent, s. *māshūm* or *m'aṣūm, be·gunāh, pāk ṣāf, spīn, nek, be·quṣūr, be·taqṣīr.*
Innovation, s. *nawai dastūr, -chalan,* etc.
Innumerable, a. *be·shumār, be·ḥisāb.*
Inoculate, v.a. *rag wahal.*
Inoffensive, a. *be·gunāh, be·quṣūr; gharīb.*
Inordinate, a. *be·andāzah, be·kach, be·ḥadd.*
Inquietude, s. *na·qalār·tiyā, be·ārām·tiyā.*
Inquire, v.a. *pukkhtedal, pukkhtana-, tapos-* or *tapakus-, saẇāl-,* etc. *k.* (-into) *laṭawul, ...*
Inquirer, s. *ṭālib, pukkhtana-, pursān-, ṭalab-,* etc. *kawūnkai.*
Inquiry, s. *tapos, pursān, tālāsh, taḥqīqāt.*
Inroad, s. *ḍūsa, dāṛa·dopa, chapāo, halla.*
Insane, a. *lewanai, saudā-ī, khushai.*
Insanity, s. *lewantob, saudā.*
Insatiable, a. *ḥirṣ·nāk, ghārai, bad·liwāl.*
Inscribe, v.a. *likal, kāgal—kkhkal.*
Inscription, s. *lik; sar·nāma.*
Insect, s. *chinjai, khazanda.*
Insensible, a. *be·hokkh, be·khūd, be·khabar, be·ḥiss; be·parwā, be·dard.*
Insert, v.a. *nanabāsal—nanayastal, kkhke·bāsal—kkhke·yastal, mandal, kkhke·mandal; gayayal; khakkhawul, njatal.* (write) *kāgal—kkhkal, likal.*
Inside, s. *danana; bāṭin; laṛmūn.*
Insidious, a. *darghal, drohai, ṭag·bāz, farebī, ḥīla·bāz.*
Insight, s. *wuqūf, shnākht, pejāndah, poh, līdah, kātah, m'arifat.*
Insignia, s. *nakkhe, 'alāme, nikkhānūna.*
Insignificant, a. *nā·tsīz, spuk, khushai.*
Insincere, a. *nā·rāst, makar, be·īmān, be·wafā, nā·khāliṣ, dwah·rangai.*
Insinuate, v.a. *nana·* or *kkhke·bāsal—yastal; ishārat k., gumān rāwṛal.*
Insipid, a. *be·khwand, balmangah* or *balmagai.*
Insist, v.a. *zoral, tākīd k.; jah k.*
Insolent, a. *be·adab, gustākh, sar·kakkh.*
Insolvent, a. *nā·dār, dīwālī.*
Inspect, v.a. *katal, līdal, goral, tamāsha-, nandāra-, mulāḥaẓa-,* etc. *k.*
Inspection, s. *katana, līdah, tamāsha,* etc.
Inspector, s. *nāẓir, dāroghah, katūnkai.*
Inspiration, s. *ilhām, ladūn, waḥī; sāh. dam, rākkhkalai sāh* or *-dam.*
Inspire, v.a. *ilhām k.; sāh ākkhistal* or *-rākāgal—rākkhkal.*
Instal, v.a. *kkhkenawul, wudrawul, muqarrar k., walāṛawul.*

Instalment, s. *qisṭ, ūgṛā-ī.*

Instance, s. *wāqi'a*; *nakkha*; *miṣāl.* (for-) *pa miṣāl.*

Instant, s. *laḥẓa, dam, drang.* a. *ḥāẓir*; *ḥāl.*

Instantly, ad. *pa ṭakī, os, pa de sā'at, sam da lāsa, dam dar ḥāl.*

Instead, ad. *pa dzūe, pa badal, pa 'iwaẓ.*

Instigate, v.a. *lamsawul, lamsūn k.*

Instigation, s. *lamsūn, targhīb.*

Instigator, s. *lamsūnai.*

Instinct, s. *shu'ūr, 'aql, hokkh, sud.*

Institute, v.a. *wudrawul, muqarrar k., taṛal. jārī k., walāṛawul.*

Instruct, v.a. *lwalawul, kkhayal—kkhowul, tarbiyat-, kkhowuna-,* etc. *k.*; *pohawul.*

Instruction, s. *kkhowuna, sabaq, t'alīm,* etc.

Instructor, s. *ākhūn, ustāẓ, mu'allim.*

Instrument, s. *kālai, hatiyār, ālat.* (agent) *waṣīla, wāsiṭa.* (cause) *bā'iṣ, 'illat, sabab.* (deed) *sanad, qibāla.*

Instrumental, a. *komakī, madad·gār.*

Insufficient, a. *kam, la-ag*; *nāqiṣ, nā·qābil.*

Insult, v.a. *spuk wayal, kanzal* or *kkhkandzal, be·'izzat-, be·makh-,* etc. *k.*

Insuperable, a. *mushkil, gṛān, na·shwūnai.*

Insurgent, s. *balwā·gar, yāghī·gar, pasātī.*

Insurrection, s. *balwā, pasāt, patna.*

Integral, a. *pūrah, amānī, ṣābat.*

Integrity, s. *rikkhtīn·tob, nekokārī, rāstī.*

Integument, s. *tsarman, postakai, poṭ*; *paṭ, khwar.*

Intellect, s. *'aql, hokkh, poha, pahm.*

Intelligence, s. *khabar*; *poh, hokkhyār·tiyā.*

Intelligent, a. *pohānd, pahm·nāk, 'aql·man, hokkhyār, khabar·dār.*

Intemperance, s. *bad·parhezī, bad·pālī*; *bad·mastī, bad·'amalī.*

Intemperate, a. *bad·parhez·gār, sharābī, nasha·khor, bad·'amal, bad·kār.*

Intend, v.a. *niyat-, qaṣd-, irāda-,* etc. *k.*

Intense, a. *ḍer, nihāyat, sakht, bad.*

Intensity, s. *ḍer·wālai, zor, ziyātī,* etc.

Intent, a. *lagiyā, mashghūl.* s. *maṭlab, niyat, qaṣd, muda'ā, murād.*

Intention, s. *niyat,* etc. (*v.* Intent).

Intentionally, ad. *pa qaṣd.*

Inter, v.a. *khakkhawul.*

Intercede, v.a. *bakkhana-, khalāṣī-,* etc. *ghokkhtal, shafā'at k.*; *gwākkh-* or *gwākkh·grandai k.*

Intercept, v.a. *nīwul, lānde k., stūnawul*; *nkkhlawul, hiṭālawul.*

Intercessor, s. *sipārish-, shafā'at-,* etc. *kawūnkai*; *gwākkh·grandai, mandz·garai.*

Interchange, s. *badal, adal·badal, len·den.*

Intercourse, s. *'ilāqa, lār, suḥbat, rāshah·darshah.*

Interdict, v.a. *qadaghan-, man'a-,* etc. *k.*

Interest, s. *kār, gharaẓ, maṭlab*; *kkhegaṛa, sūd, gaṭa, naf'a, fā-ida*; *brakha, wesh, ḥiṣṣa.*

Interested, a. *gharaẓ·man, khpul·maṭlab, gharaẓī.* (self-) *khpul·gharaẓ.*

Interesting, a. *khwand·nāk, maza·dār, dil·chasp.*

Interfere, v.a. *gharaẓ k., lās lagawul, -āchawul, -warwṛal,* or *-pa kkhke khwadzawul.*

Interim, s. *mandz, miyān, miyandz.*

Interior, a. *danananai, darūnī, bāṭinī.*

Interlace, v.a. *agayal, lānde·bānde k., gayayal.*

Interlude, s. *tamāsha, nandāra, swāng.*

Intermeddle, v.a. *lās lagawul,* etc., *dast·andāzī k., dakhl-, gharaẓ-,* etc. *k.* (*v.* Interfere).

Intermediate, a. *mandzwai.*

Interminable, *be·sar, be·and, be·ḥadd.*

Intermission, s. *nobat, wār*; *nāgha*; *furṣat.*

Intermit, v.n. *pa·nobat-, pa·wār-,* etc. *rātlal.*

Intermittent, a. *wārī.* (-fever) *wareza.*

Internal, a. *bāṭinī, darūnī, dananānai.*

Internals, s. *laṛmānah.*

Interpose, v.n. *pa·mandz rātlal—rāghlal.*

v.a. *pa·mandz kegdal*, or *kkhkegdal—kekkh-odal*, or *kkhkekkhodal*, etc.; *gwākkh-* or *gwākkh·grandī k.*

Interpret, v.a. *tarjuma k., pohawul, kkhayal-kkhowul, m'anā kkhkārah k.*

Interrogate, v.a. *pukkhtedal, sawāl·dzawāb-, tapos-*, etc. *k.*

Interrupt, v.a. *kariyābawul, hiṭālawul, band·awul, nkkhlawul, ḥarakat k.*

Interruption, s. *kariyāb, hiṭāl, harj, khalal, nkkhatai, ḥarakat.*

Interstice, s. *darz, rakhna; khūna; gruṭ.*

Interval, s. *mandz, miyān; wār.*

Intervene, v.n. *pa·mandz rātlal—rāghlal; gwākkh-* or *gwākkh·grandī k.*

Intervention, s. *pa·mandz rātlana; gwākkh.*

Interview, s. *dīdan, līdah, kātah, mulāqāt.*

Intestate, a. *be·waṣīyat.*

Intestine, s. (large-) *kulma, laṛmūn.* (small-) *larai, ūjarai.*

Intimate, a. *khamsor, gaḍ; wāqif; balad.* s. *yār, āshnāe, mal, rafīq.*

Intimate, v.a. *khabarawul; wayal.*

Intimately, ad. *pa kkhah shān sara.*

Intimation, s. *khabar; nakkha, ishārat.*

Intimidate, v.a. *yerawul* or *werawul.*

Into, p. *pa kkhke, kkhke, pa mandz kkhke.*

Intolerant, a. *be·ṣabr, be·zgham.*

Intoxicate, v.a. *be·khūd k., nasha warkawul; mast k., kaipī k.*

Intoxication, s. *nasha, kaip; be·khūdī, mastī.*

Intractable, a. *sar·kakkh, sar·zor, khpul·sar, ṭakanrai, hoḍai.*

Intrenchment, s. *sangar, bāra, morcha.*

Intrepid, a. *maṛanai, tūrzan, zṛah·war, be·bāk, dilāwar, bahādur.*

Intricate, a. *grān, mushkil; kog·wog, pech·dār; arjal·barjal, tsapolai.*

Intrigue, s. *jorikkht, sāzish, kār·sāzī; lār, 'alāqa, rāz·o·niyāz, yārāna.*

Intrinsic, a. *zātī, aṣlī.*

Introduce, v.a. *nana-* or *kkhke bāsal—yastal.* (-a person) *pekkhawul.* (a custom) *chala-wul, jārī k.* (to a place) *rāwustal.*

Introduction, s. *nanaⁱyastah; mulāqāt; de-bācha.*

Intrude, v.a. *dūsa k., nanawatal, lās laga-wul, -āchawul,* etc.

Intrust, v.a. *spāral, pāslawul, ḥawāla k.*

Intuition, s. *ilhām, ladūn; m'arifat, poh, pahm.*

Intwine, v.a. *agayal, gayayal, ngharal-nghakkhtal.*

Inundate, v.a. *hūk-, lāhū-,* etc. *k., niyūz-, nīz-,* etc. *wṛal.* (-a field) *kharob k.*

Inundation, s. *sailāb, nīz* or *niyūz, tughiyānī,* etc.

Inure, v.a. *āmokhtah-, 'ādat-,* etc. *k., rugd·awul.*

Invade, v.a. *halla-, dāṛa-, chapāo-, dūsa-,* etc. *k.* v.n. *khatal, prewatal, pre·mātedal.*

In vain, ad. *'abaṣ, be·fā·ida.*

Invalid, a. *bāṭil, 'abaṣ, nā·kārah, nāqiṣ.* s. *nā·jor, nā·rogh, randzūr, za'īf.*

Invaluable, a. *be·bahā, grān·bahā, be·qīmat.*

Invariable, a. *be·tabdīl, be·biyal·tūn, pāedār.*

Invariably, ad. *har·kala, mudāman, hamesha.*

Invasion, s. *halla, chapāo, tākht, dūsa, dāṛa.*

Invective, s. *peghor, kanzal* or *kkhkandzal kkhera, malāmat, tuhmat, tor.*

Inveigle, v.a. *ghulawul, ṭagal, damawul, dam-, fareb-,* etc. *warkawul.*

Invent, v.a. *jorawul, nawai·ḥikmat bāsal-yastal, nawai paidā k.*

Invention, s. *ḥikmat, chal.*

Inventory, s. *siyāha, daftar, fard.*

Inverse, a. *aṛawul, naskor, wājgūn, 'aks, apūṭah, chapah.*

Invert, v.a. *aṛawul, naskorawul 'aks-,* etc. *k.*

Invest, v.a. *warkawul, bakkha!; poslawul, āghūstawul; īsārawul* or *ḥiṣārawul, ger k.*

Investigate, v.a. *tapahus* or *tapos-*, *pukkhtana-*, *pursān-*, *taḥqīq-*, etc. *k.*, *pukkhtedal*, *laṭawul*, *shanal.*

Inveterate, a. *kuhand*, *pakhwānai*, *zoṛana i*; *pokh*, *klak*, *sakht.*

Invidious, a. *ḥasad·nāk*, *kīna·war*, *wiyāṛ·ĵan.*

Invigorate, v.a. *quwat warkawul*, *quwat·nāk-*, *maẓbūṭ-*, *takṛah-*, *tāzah-*, etc. *k.*

Invisible, a. *puṭ*, *ghā-ib*; *wruk.*

Invite, v.a. *sat k.*, *balal.*

Inviting, a. *dil·kakkh*, *dil·chasp*, *dil·rubā*; *maza·dār*, *khwand·nāk.* s. *sat kawuna.*

Invocation, s. *d'uā*; *d'awat*; *ghokkht.*

Invoice, s. *siyāha*, *bījak*, *chalān.*

Invoke, v.a. *d'uā k.*, *balal*, *nūm ākhistal*, *ghokkhtal.*

Involuntary, a. *be·ikhtiyār*, *be·was*, *be·wāk.*

Involve, v.a. *āchawul*, *nkkhlawul*, *nīwul.*

Inward, a. *danananai*, *darūnī*, *bāṭinī.*

Inwrought, a. *jaṛāo*; *kūṭalai.*

Irascible, a. *qahr·nāk*, *ghuṣṣa·nāk*, *tund.*

Ire, s. *ghuṣṣa*, *ghaẓab*, *qahr*, *bṛos·wālai.*

Irksome, a. *sakht*, *grān*, *drūnd*, *rabaṛ·ĵan.*

Iron, s. *ospana.* (-slag) *ospankharai.* (bar-) *kashai.* (-monger) *lohār*, *āhan·gar.*

Iron-gray, a. *nīlai.*

Irony, a. *ṭoqa*, *khandā*, *pekkha.*

Irradiate, v.n. *dzalakedal*; *rūnredal.*

Irrational, a. *be·hūdah*, *nā·poh*, *be·'aql.*

Irregular, a. *be·tartīb*, *be·ā-īn*, *be·qā'ida*; *nā·lā-iq.*

Irrelevant, a. *be·dzāe*, *be·nisbat*, *nā·kārah.*

Irreligious, a. *be·dīn*, *bilmāz*, *be·mazhab.*

Irremediable, a. *lā'ilāj*, *lā·chār*, *lā·dawā.*

Irreproachable, a. *be·gunāh*, *be·malāmat.*

Irresistible, a. *zorāwar*, *maẓbūṭ*, *be·band.*

Irresolute, a. *be·himmat*, *nā·qalār*, *nā·mard.*

Irretrievable, a. *ter*, *wruk*, *lāṛ*; *lā·'ilāj.*

Irreverent, a. *be·adab*, *be·makh.*

Irrigate, v.a. *oba-*, *watar-*, *kharob-*, *lūnd-*, etc. *k.*

Irritable, a. *khapah·nāk*, *bṛos*, *khaṛ.*

Irritate, v.a. *pārawul*, *ṭongawul*, *agayal*, *rabṛawul*, *ṭongāra k.*

Irritation, s. *khapagī*; *ṭongāra*; *pārawūna*; *dard*, *pasāt*, *swai.*

Irruption, s. *halla*, *tākht*, *ḍūsa*, *dāṛa*; *khuṭ*, *eshnā*; *dāra*, *fawāra.*

Island, s. *bela*, *jazīra.* (sandbank) *chara.*

Isolated, a. *biyal*, *yawādzai*, *judā.*

Issue, s. *anjām*, *natīja*, *ḥāṣil*; *pāzah*; *gaṭa*; *alwād*, *zawzāt*; *lāṛ*, *wātah*; *war*, *khula.*

Issue, v.n. *watal*, *bahedal*, *chaledal*, *prewatal.* (-an order) v.a. *chalawul*, *jārī k.*

It, pr. *haghah*, *dā*, *dah*, *de*, *di*, *e.*

Itch, s. *khārikkht*, *koe*, *kaha*; *pishak*, *spūnrai.* v.n. *khārikkhtedal*, *kaha-*, etc. *ked.*

Item, s. *shai*, *tsīz*, *kālai.*

Itinerate, v.n. *girzedal.* v.a. *gakkht-*, *sail-*, etc. *k.*

Itself, pr. *khpul*, *khpul dzān.*

J.

Jackal, s. *gīdaṛ*, *sūrlanḍ*, *shaghāl.*

Jackdaw, s. *qāghah.*

Jacket, s. *kurta*, *nīm·tana-ī.*

Jade, s. (horse) *tap·dangar ās.* (woman) *pūhaṛa-*, *shalata-*, etc. *-kkhadza*, *gashta-ī*, *baghara-ī.*

Jagged, a. *zīg*, *lwāṛ.*

Jail, s. *qaid khāna*, *bandī·khāna*, *zindān.*

Jailer, s. *da qaid·khāne dārogha.*

Jam, s. *zokkha*, *khog·pakhalai*, *murabba.* v.a. *bandawul*, *ṭīngawul*, *klakawul.*

January, s. *māh.*

Jar, s. *loṭkai*, *mangai*, *khum*, *maṭkai*, *batakai.* (-of leather) *daba*, *kupa-ī*, *jāba.*

Jargon, s. *wucha·pucha-*, *gaḍa·waḍa-*, *aṛa·baṛa-*, etc. *-khabara*, or *-wrāsha.*

Jasmine, s. *rāmbel·chāmbel.*
Jaundice, s. *ziyaṛai.*
Jaunt, s. *sail, gakkht.*
Javelin, s. *bala, barcha, neza, shalgai.*
Jaw, s. *jāma.* (upper-) *portana-ī jāma.* (lower-) *kkhkatana-ī jāma.* (-angle) *kaj.*
Jay, s. *shīn·tagh.*
Jealous, a. *bad·gumān, wiyaṛ·jan, sūndah.*
Jealousy, s. *bad·gumānī, wiyāṛ, rashk.*
Jeer, v.a. *khandā pore k.*
Jehovah, s. *allah, yāhū, khudāe ta'ālā.*
Jelly, s. *zokkha; māya.*
Jeopardy, s. *khatra, wera, muhimm.*
Jerk, v.a. *pṛakawul; ṭel wahal.*
Jest, s. *ṭoqa, washta, malanḍa, maskhara.*
Jester, s. *ṭoq·mār, washtai, malanḍai, maskharā·chī, pekkhe·gar.*
Jesus, s. *īsā.* (-Christ) *hazrat īsā.*
Jet, s. *dāra, fuwāra, shutraka.* (-bead) *shaba.* (-black) a. *tak·tor.*
Jew, s. *jahūd.*
Jewel, s. *gāṇra, kālai, zewar.*
Jeweller, s. *zar·gar.*
Jingle, s. *shṛang, gṛanj, krach.* v.n. *shṛangedal, gṛanjedal.*
Job, s. *kār.* (a little-) *kārgoṭai.*
Jockey, s. *chābuk·sawār.*
Jocose, a. *ṭoqī, washtī, khandā·bāz* or *·rūe.*
Jocularity, s. *washta·ṭoqa, khandā·bāzī.*
Jocund, a. *khūsh·rūe, kkhād, khūsh·hāl.*
Jog, v.a. *ṭakaṛ-, ṭel-, gasa-,* etc. *wahal.* v.n. *ṭaparedal.*
Join, v.a. *joṛawul, lagawul, pewand k., gaḍawul.* v.n. *gaḍedal, yo dzāe ked.*
Joint, s. *joṛ; band, pewand; ghūṭa.*
Jointure, s. *mahr, dahadz, dod.*
Joke, s. *ṭoqa, washta, malanḍa.*
Jollity, s. *kkhādī, khūsh·hālī.*
Jolly, a. *kkhād, kkhād·man, khwakkh; rogh·moṭ.*
Jolt, s. *ṭakaṛa, ḍaka, ṭel; tīndak, budrī.*
Jot, s. *ṭakai, pūṭai, batsarai, ṭoṭa, zarra.*
Jovial, a. *khwakkh,* etc.. (*v.* Jolly).
Journal, s. *roz·nāmcha.*
Journey, s. *safar, pand.* (a day's-) *mazal* or *manzil.*
Joy, s. *kkhādī, khūsh·hālī.* (over rival) *sakha.*
Joyful, a. *kkhād·man, khūsh·hāl.*
Joyfully, ad. *pa kkhādī sara, khūsh·hālī-, khwakkhī-,* etc. *-sara.*
Jubilee, s. *akhtar,'īd; kkhādī, mela.*
Judge, s. *hākim, qāzī, munṣif.*
Judge, v.a. *'adālat-, inṣāf-, niyāw-,* etc. *k.*; *qiyās-, fikr-,* etc. *k.*; *gaṇral.*
Judgment, s. *hukm, fatwā; 'aql, poha.* (opinion) *fikr, rāe, qiyās.* (-seat) *mahkama.* (-day) *hashr, ākhirat, qiyāmat.*
Judicature, s. *hukm, qazā.*
Judicial, a. *shara'ī.*
Judicious, a. *hokkhyār, pohānd, 'aql·man.*
Jug, s. *kūza, kūza·ṛa-ī, khumra-ī, kanja-ī.*
Juggler, s. *bāzī·gar, jādū·gar, koḍ·gar.*
Juice, s. *oba, pa-ī, ras, gūṛa-ī, rub; naw, zyam, nam.*
July, s. *pashakāl, sāwaṇr.*
Jumble, v.a. *gaḍ·waḍ k.*
Jump, v.a. *ṭop-, ṭrap-,* etc. *wahal, dangal.*
Juncture, s. *joṛ, band, pewand; wakht, tāng.*
June, s. *hāṛ.*
Junior, a. *kishar.*
Jurisdiction, s. *hukūmat, 'amaldārī, wāk.*
Jurisprudence, s. *fiqha.*
Jury, s. *jirga m'arika.* (-man) *jirgatū.*
Just, a. *'ādil, munṣif, rikkhtīnai, rāst; jukht, barābar, sam.* ad. *surup, faqaṭ.*
Justice, s. *inṣāf, 'adālat, niyāw, dād.*
Justifiable, a. *rawā, wājib.*
Justification, s. *hujjat.*
Justify, v.a. *'uzr-, hujjat-,* etc. *rāwṛal.*
Justly, ad. *pa haqqa, pa rikkhtiyā.*
Justness, s. *rikkhtīn·tob, rāstī, nekī.*

Juvenile, a. *kishar, dzwān.* s. *ĵanrai, zalmai, halak, workai.*

Juvenility, s. *ĵanṛī·tob, halak·wālai, dzwānī, zalmī·tob.*

K.

Keen, a. *terah, dam·dār*; *jalt, tez, tund.* (acid) *brekkhan.* (eager) *garm, tod, liwāl.*

Keenness, s. *terah·wālai*; *tund·wālai,* etc.

Keep, v.a. *sātal, ĵghoral, khundiyal, khundī k.*; *pālal, parwaral, nmāndzal.* (-watch) *gālal.* (observe) *manal.* (-back) *pātai k., pātawul, stūnawul.* (possess) *laral.* (-an engagement) *pūrah-, adā-,* etc. *k.*

Keep, v.n. *pātedal, pātai ked., pāedal, osedal.*

Keeper, s. *sātandoe, sātūnkai, ĵghorai, pālūnkai, khundī kawūnkai.*

Keeping, s. *sātana, pālana, ĵghorana, khundī kawūna*; *pāedana, osedana, pātedana.*

Keepsake, s. *yād·gār, yād·dāsht.*

Kernel, s. *chaka-ī, maghzai, zaṛai.*

Kettle, s. *dechka, deg, khum.* (earthen-) *kaṭwa-ī.*

Kettledrum, s. *naghāra, ḍamāma, ḍūkāṛa, ḍūmbakai, tambal.*

Key, s. *kunja-ī.* (-hole) *da jandre khula.*

Kick, v.a. *lata-, laghata-,* etc. *wahal.*

Kid, s. *warghūmai, chelai, serlai, psharlai, wuzgarai.*

Kidnap, v.a. *botlal—bīwul, bota k., takkhtawul.*

Kidney, s. *pukkhtawarga.* (-bean) *lobiyā.*

Kill, v.a. *waĵal* or *waĵlal, muṛ k., qatlawul.* (for food) *ḥallālawul.*

Killed, a. *maqtūl, waĵalai, muṛ kaṛai*; *ḥallāl kaṛai.*

Killer, a. *qātil, waĵlūnai, khūnī, muṛ-* or *marg kawūnkai.* (in comp.) *-kush.*

Killing, s. *khūn-, muṛ-, marg-, qatl-,* etc. *-kawūna, waĵlana.*

Kiln, s. *paja*; *baṭ.*

Kin, s. *ragai, khpul, khekkh, 'azīz.*

Kind, a. *mihrbān*; *makhawar.*

Kind, s. *zāt, aṣl, rang, nog, qism, shān.*

Kindle, v.a. *balawul, pūkal, swadzawul.* v.n. *baledal, swal, sedzal.*

Kindly, ad. *pa mihrbāngī sara.*

Kindness, s. *mihrbānī* or *mihrbāngī.*

Kindred, s. *khpul·walī, khekkhī.* a. *yo·shān, ragai, hum·rang, hum·jins.*

King, s. *bādshāh, shāh, sulṭān.*

Kingdom, s. *bādshāhat, sulṭanat, rāj.*

Kingfisher, s. *māhī·khwurak, babozai.*

Kinsman, s. *khpul, khekkh.* (paternal-) *plār·ganai.* (maternal-) *mor·ganai.*

Kiss, s. *kkhkul, macha, chapa-ī.* v.a. *kkhkulawul, machawul, chapa-ī-, kkhkul-,* etc. *k., koka-ī-, khula-,* etc. *-ākhistal.*

Kitchen, s. *langar, jal·nāna-ī, ngharai.*

Kite, s. *ṭapūts.* (paper-) *godā, patang.*

Kitten, s. *pishongaṛai.*

Klick, v.a. *ṭak wahal.*

Knack, s. *ḥikmat, chal, pech, kārī·garī.*

Knapsack, s. *dzola-ī, gūḍai, bana-ī, butskha.*

Knave, s. *ṭag, darghal, chaṛland, farebī, be·īmān, chal·bāz, chal·walai.*

Knavery, s. *ṭagī, ṭag·bāzī, chal·bāzī,* etc.

Knavish, a. *ṭag·bāz, be·īmān, farebī.*

Knead, v.a. *aghagal—äkkhal.* (-the limbs) *manḍal, kkhke·manḍal, chāpī k.*

Knee, s. *zangūn, ḍoga.* (-cap) *zangānah·starga.*

Kneel, v.a. *ḍoga-, zangūn-,* etc. *-lagawul.* v.n. *pa ḍogo-. zangāno-,* etc. *-kkhkenāstal.*

Knife, s. *chāṛa.* (pen-) *chaṛūka-ī, chāqū.*

Knit, v.a. *gayayal, agayal*; *ḍūr k.* (-the brows) *starge brandawul.*

Knitting, s. *ḍūr.* (-needle) *dūk.*

Knob, s. *ghūṭai, pūṭai, ghūnḍai*; *pāṛsob, māṭus, pūpaka*; *rasaula-ī, ghunḍāṛai.*

Knock, v.a. *ṭraq-, ṭap-, ṭak-,* etc. *-wahal.*

(-up against) *ṭakaṛ-, ḍaka-*, etc. *-khwuṛal.* v.n. *blosedal, lagedal, jangedal.*

Knot, s. *ghūṭa, taṛa, bandaṉr.*

Know, v.a. *m'alūmawul, peĵandal, gaṉral, zdah k.* v.n. *khabaredal, pohedal, zdah ked.*

Knowing, a. *zdah, khabar·dār, hokkhyār, pokh, wāqif.*

Knowingly, ad. *pa 'aql sara, pa khabar sara.*

Knowledge, s. *poha, 'aql, khabar, 'ilm.*

Known, a. *zdah, peĵāndah, m'alūm.*

Knuckle, s. *band, da gūte band.* (-bone) *bujal, ṭaka, arghund.*

L.

Label, s. *sar·nāma, ṭīka.*

Laboratory, s. *kār·khāna.*

Laborious, a. *miḥnatī, kokshikshī*; *mushkil, grān, sakht.*

Labour, s. *miḥnat, kokshiksh, sa'ī, mushaqqat, mazdūrī*; *rabaṛ*; *kār, kasb, pesha.* (childbirth) *langa, langedana.* (-pain) *stam.*

Labour, v.a. *miḥnat-, mazdūrī-*, etc. *k.* (be in-) v.n. *langedal.* (worry oneself) v.n. *rabṛedal.* (to strain) v.a. *stam·wahal.*

Labourer, s. *mazdūr*; *kasb·gar.*

Labyrinth, s. *kaga·waga, warṭa, mār·pech.*

Lac, s. (gum) *da pala-ī chīṛ.* (dye) *lāk.* (100,000) *lak.*

Lace, s. *jālaka-ī, jāla-ī, muqaish.*

Lacerate, v.a. *shlawul, wrarawul, chāk k.*; *mātawal, ghwutsawul.*

Laceration, s. *shledah, wraredah, chāwd*; *tsīra, parhār, zakhm.*

Lack, v.n. *muḥtāj-, ḥājat·man-*, etc. *ked.* v.a. *ghokkhtal.*

Lad, s. *halak, zaṉrai, ghunḍāyah, zalmai.*

Ladder, s. *andarpāya, pawṛa-ī, pārchang.*

Lade, v.a. *bār āchawul, legdal—lekkhal, ḍakawul.*

Ladle, s. *kaṛecha-ī, harkāra.* (small-) *kāchogha, tsontsa-ī, chamcha-ī* or *tsamtsa-ī.*

Lady, s. *bībī, merman, ṣāḥiba.* (-fly) *bībī·pāto bakhmaia-ī.*

Lag, v.n. *pātedal, ṭaparedal.*

Laity, s. *'āmmiyān.* (one of the-) *'āmmī.*

Lake, s. *loe ḍanḍ, tālāw* or *tālāb.*

Lamb, s. *wrai, ga-aḍūrai.* (wether-) *wuch·kūl.*

Lame, a. *guḍ, khūg, kaṛam.*

Lameness, s. *guḍ·wālai.*

Lament, v.a. *afsos-, gham-, wāwailā-*, etc. *k.*, *ĵaṛal, wīr-, hāe·hāe-, hāe·hūe-, ĵaṛā-*, etc. *k.*, *wainā wayal.*

Lamentation, s. *afsos, jaṛā, wīr, sānda, faryād*, etc.

Lamenter, s. *wīṛa·ĵalai, wainā wayūnkai*, etc.

Lamp, s. *chirāgh, ḍīwa.* (-stand) *ḍīwat.* (-black) *kajal, lūgai.* (-black cup) *masa.* (-wick) *bāta-ī.*

Lance, s. *neza, bala, barcha.*

Lance, v.a. *tsīral*; *tsīkhal, tetsal.*

Lancet, s. *nashtar* or *nekkhtar.*

Land, s. *mzaka* or *zmaka, zamīn.* (country-) *mulk, hewād.* (own-) *waṭan, būm.* (table-) *bāwra-ī, būṛa, steza.* (ploughed-) *sādīn.* (sown-) *shudyāra.* (bare-) *ḍāga, ṭikārkai.* (fallow-) *waḍ.* (waste-) *shāṛ.* (patch of-) *paṭai*; *pāṛa.* (irrigated-) *watar, ābī.* (unirrigated-) *lalamī.* (inundated-) *khaṛob.* (marsh-) *jaba.* (village-) *ada-ī, wanḍ.* (church-) *sīra-ī, bogarai.*

Land, v.n. *kūzedal.* v.a. *kūzawul.*

Landholder, s. *dawtarī* or *daftarī, jāgīr·dār, zamīn·dār, brakha·khor.*

Landlord, s. *dawtarī, zamīn·dār, nāyak*; *korbah, meṛah, khāwand, tsakkhtan, māl·dār.*

Landmark, s. *tsalai, pūla.*

Lane, s. *kūtsa.*

Language, s. *ĵiba, wrāsha.*

Languid, a. *ṭap, staṛai, stomān, māndah, haukah*; *sust, laṭ, shalat, kāṛai·wāṛai.*

Languish, v.n. *mṛāwedal* or *mṛāmedal, wuchedal, kamanṛedal; kaṛedal, nūledal, zahedal*; *staṛai-, stomān-, zahīr-,* etc. *ked.*

Languor, s. *sustī, stomānī, māndagī.*

Lantern, s. *fānūs.*

Lap, s. *gheg, ghūzai; laman, pitskai, dzola-ī.*

Lap, v.a. *tsaṭal.* (wrap) *nghaṛal—nghakkhtal.*

Lapidary, s. *muhr·kan.*

Lapse, v.n. *teredal, ghuzāredal, ter watal.*

Large, a. *loe, star, ghaṭ, 'azīm.*

Largeness, *loe-, star-,* etc., *-wālai.*

Largesse, s. *bakhkshiksh, bakkhana, in'ām, khairāt.*

Lark, s. *kha·aṛāra, kopla, agan.*

Larynx, s. *ḥalq, wucha·ghāṛa; stūnai.*

Lascivious, a. *mast, shokhī, shahwatī, hawas·nāk.*

Lasciviousness, s. *mastī, shahwat, naus, hawas.*

Lash, s. *bachawai, bachokai, bachakarai; karoṛa.*

Lash, v.a. *karoṛa wahal; taṛal.*

Lass, s. *jina-ī, peghla, lūr, khoraka-ī.*

Lassitude, s. *sustī, stomānī.*

Last, a. *wrustai, wrustanai, ākhir, pasīn.*

Last, v.n. *pāedal, chaledal, pātedal, osedal.*

Lasting, a. *pāedār, qā-im, mazbūṭ.*

Lastly, ad. *wrusto, ākhir.*

Latch, s. *hūl, aṛam, aṛamai.*

Latchet, s. *rog, tasma.*

Late, a. *nā·wakht, pasīn; osanai; mutawaffī.*

Lately, ad. *osan, nan wradz, da la-ago wradzo.*

Lateness, s. *nā·wakhtī; lārghah, drang.*

Latent, a. *puṭ, ghalai.*

Later, a. *nawai.*

Lather, s. *zag, kaf.*

Latitude, s. *plan·wālai, arat·wālai, sor* or *psor.*

Latitudinarian, s. *be·shar'a, āzād·ṭab'a saṛai.*

Latter, a. *wrustanai, pasanai.*

Lattice, s. *jālakai, shabaka, j'afarī.*

Laud, v.a. *stāyal, stāyana k.*, or *-wayal.*

Laugh, v.a. *khandal, khandā k.*

Laughter, s. *khandā, qah·qaha, hanṛ·hanṛ.*

Launch, v.a. *obo ta kūzanul; ghwurzawul, chalawul, āchawul, wīshtal.*

Lave, v.a. *wīndzal* or *mīndzal, wlal, lambawul.*

Lavish, a. *khartsī, isrāfī, musrif.*

Lavish, v.a. *kharts-, tāwān-, isrāf-,* etc. *k.*

Law, s. *fiqha.* (divine-) *shar'a, sharī'at.* (rule) *qā'ida, qānūn, ā-īn, rasm.* (justice) *'adālat, inṣāf, niyāw.* (right) *ḥaqq, rawā.* (Afghan-) *pukkhtūn·walī.*

Lawful, a. *rawā, ḥallāl.*

Lawsuit, s. *muqaddama, d'awa, qaẓiya.*

Lawyer, s. *qāẓī, faqīh.*

Lax, a. *sust, prānatai, spaṛdalai, arat.*

Laxative, a. *pos-, narm-,* etc. *-kawūnkai.* s. *pos·jāṛ, narm·jullāb, mūnzij.*

Lay, v.a. *gdal* or *īgdal, yakkhodal* or *īkkhodal, yakkhal* or *īkkhal, kegdal* or *kkhkegdal, kekkhodal* or *kkhkekkhodal, kekkhal* or *kkhkekkhal.* (-hold of) *ākhistal, nīwul.* (-down) *tsamlawul.* (-on) *āchawul, lagawul.* (-in) *ṭolawul, gaṭal.* (-out) *gazawul* or *ghazawul.*

Lay, s. *ghazal.*

Layer, s. *bragh, tah.* (-of bricks) *rada.*

Layman, s. *'āmmī.*

Laziness, s. *sustī, nā·rāstī, laṭ·wālai.*

Lazy, a. *sust, nā·rāst, laṭ, shaṭal* or *shalaṭ.*

Lead, s. *sīka, sīsa; mas.* (red-) *sendūr.* (white-) *sapeda.*

Lead, v.a. *rāwustal, biyāyal—bīwul, botlal—bīwul.*

Leader, s. *sardār, nāyak, sar·guroh, peshwā.*

Leaf, s. *pānṛa.* (of a book) *waraq.* (-of a door) *pala, tanba.*

League, s. *para, janba, gundi; bandanṛ,*

wāda, lafẓ, taṛa, jorikkht, qaul. (measure) *farsakh.*
Leak, v.n. *tsātsedal.*
Leaky, a. *tsātsedūnai, māt.*
Lean, a. *narai, ḍangar, khwār, lāghar.*
Lean, v.a. *takiya k., ḍaḍa lagawul.*
Leanness, s. *ḍangar·tob, narai·wālai.*
Leap, v.a. *dangal, traplal, ṭop wahal.*
Leap, s. *ṭop, dang, trap.*
Learn, v.a. *zdah k., yādawul.*
Learned, a. *zdah, yād, āmokhtah* ; *'ālim, pohānd.*
Learner, s. *shāgird, ṭālib, sabaq lwustūnai.*
Learning, s. *'ilm.*
Lease, s. *gānṛa, ijāra.*
Least, a. *kisharīn, kamtarīn, la ṭolo na la-ag* or *-wūṛ.* (at-) ad. *bāre, kho, ākhir.*
Leather, s. *tsarman.* (-dresser) *dabbāgh.* (-worker) *tsamyār, mochī.* (-strop) *rog, tasma.* (-bottle) *chāgul, ĵa-ī, batak.* (-scraper) *zarbiyāng.*
Leave, v.a. *pregdal, prekkhodal, prekkhal* ; *rukhṣat ākhistal.* v.n. *rawānedal, tlal—lāṛal.*
Leave, s. *rukhṣat, ijāzat, ḥukm, izan.*
Leaven, s. *khamīra, māya, tomna.*
Leavings, s. *jūṭa, pāte, pas·khurdah.*
Lecher, s. *kāsīr, lawanḍ, qachar, chaṭ.*
Lecture, s. *sabaq, dars.* v.a. *sabaq wayal.*
Ledge, s. *ghāṛa, morga, ĵa-ī, ḍaḍa* ; *kamar.*
Leech, s. *ĵawara.*
Leek, s. *gandana.*
Leer, v.a. *pa·trats katal* ; *pa·zarana-ī katal.*
Lees, s. *khaṭbel, matra.*
Left, a. *pātai, bāqī.* (not right) *kīnṛ, gats.* (-handed) *gatsai.* v.n. *pātai ked.*
Leg, s. (whole-) *kkhānga.* (below knee) *paṛkai, lengai.* (-of a table, etc.) *pāya, kkhpa* or *pkkha.* (-of drawers) *pāentsa.* (-of mutton, fowl, etc.) *patūn.*
Legacy, s. *mīrāt, waṣīyat, hiba.*
Legal, a. *shara'ī, rawā.*
Legate, s. *astādzai, wakīl, elchī.*
Legation, s. *elchī·garī* ; *jirga, m'arika.*
Legend, s. *rawāyat, qiṣṣa, tazkira.*
Legerdemain, s. *bāzī·garī, jādū·garī, naẓar·bandī.*
Legion, s. *ḍala, ganṛ 'ālam* ; *tuman, dasta, ulus.*
Legislate, v.a. *ḥukm-, ā-īn-, qānūn-,* etc. *chalawul.*
Legislator, s. *ḥākim, shari'yat·jārī kawūnkai.*
Legislature, s. *sarkār, 'adālat.*
Legitimate, a. *rawā, ḥallāl.*
Legume, s. *palai.*
Leisure, s. *wazgār·tiyā, furṣat.*
Lemon, s. *nībū, tursh nāranj,*
Lend, v.a. *por warkawul, qarẓ warkawul.* (a thing itself to be returned) *'āriyatī warkawul.*
Lender, s. *qarẓ-, por-,* etc. *-warkawūnai.*
Length, s. *ūgd·wālai.*
Lengthen, v.a. *ūgdawul.*
Lenient. a. *mulā-im, narm, ḥalīm.*
Lenity, s. *mulā-im·tob, narm·wālai, raḥm.*
Lent, s. *roĵa.* (Muhammadan) *ramẓān.*
Lentils, s. *moṭ, mahe* ; *chanṛa* ; *ma-ī* ; *lobiyā.* (cooked-) *paitī, rāṛa.*
Leopard, s. *pṛāng, baur, baurgai, yūz.*
Leper, s. *koṛī, bragai, pesai.*
Leprosy, s. *koṛ, brag, pes.*
Less, a. *la-ag, kam, lāndai.*
Lessen, v.a. *la-agawul, kamawul.* v.n. *la-agedal, kamedal.*
Lesson, s. *dars, sabaq* ; *pand, naṣīḥat.*
Lest, c, *mabādā, hase di na wī, kkhā-ī.*
Let, v.a. *pregdal, prekkhodal, prekkhal, prekkhawul.* (-go) *yalah-, khalāṣ-, āzād-,* etc. *k.* (hire) *karīh* or *kreha-,* etc. *warkawul.* (allow) *izan-, ḥukm-, rukhṣat-,* etc. *warkawul.*

Let, s. *āṛ, kariyāb, hiṭāl.*
Lethargy, s. *sustī, laṭ·wālai.*
Letter, s. *ḥarf*; *khaṭṭ, chīṭa-ī, rawāna.*
Levee, s. *dalbār.*
Level, a. *sam, hawār, barābar, sat.* v.a. *samawul, naṛawul, hawārawul.*
Lever, s. *aṛām, dah·marda.* (-for water) *dīngara-ī.*
Levity, s. *spuk·wālai, halak·wālai.*
Levy, v.a. *ṭolawul, yo dzāe-, jam'a-,* etc. *k.*
Lewd, a. *bad·mast, shahwat·nāk.* (-woman) *ṭashmaka-ī, shatāha.*
Lewdness, s. *mastī, shahwat.*
Lexicon, s. *lughat.*
Liable, a. *shwūnkai, pīrzo.*
Liar, s. *darogh·jan, darghal.*
Libel, s. *peghor, tor, tuhmat, bad·namūsī, ruswā-ī, malāmat.*
Liberal, s. *sakhī, bakkhūnkai, warkawūnai.*
Liberate, v.a. *āzādawul, khalāṣawul, pregdal, wurhawul, yalah k.*
Liberated, a. *yalah, āzād, khalāṣ.*
Libertine, s. *lawanḍ, chaṭ, lūtsak, qachar.*
Liberty, s. *yalah·tob, khalāṣī, āzādī*; *wāk, ikhtiyār*; *rukhṣat, ijāzat.*
Libidinous, a. *bad·mast, shahwat·nāk.*
Library, s. *kitāb·khāna.*
License, s. *izan, ḥukm, parwāna, sanad.*
Licentious, a. *bad·laman, bad·parhez·gār, bad·kār, ḥarām·kār*; *sar·kakkh.*
Lick, v.a. *tsaṭal.* (beat) *wahal, ṭakawul.*
Lid, s. *bargholai, sar·pokkh.*
Lie, s. *darogh.* v.a. *darogh wayal.*
Lie-down, v.n. *mlāstal, tsamlāstal, gazedal* or *ghazedal.* (-concealed) *ghalai kedal.*
Lieutenant, s. *nā-ib, qā-im muqām, jam'a·dār.*
Life, s. *dzān, jwāk, jwand*; *jwandūn, rozgār, zindagānī, ḥayāt.*
Lifeless, a. *be·dzān, be·sāh, muṛ.*
Lifetime, s. *'umr, jwandūn, ḥayāt.*
Lift, v.a. *porta k., khejawul, ūchatawul.*
Ligament, s. *pala, rag.* (-of the heel) *kūchai, spīna.* (-of horse's leg) *pai.*
Ligature, s. *taṛūn, taṛa, band, paṭa-ī, skoe.*
Light, s. *raṇṛā, rokkhnā-ī.* a. *rokkhān, rūṇr*; *spuk, halak.* v.a. *rūṇrawul, rokkhān k.* (-a fire) *balawul.* v.n. *rūṇredal, rokkhān ked.* (-as fire) *baledal.* (descend) *kūzedal, prewatal, nāziledal.*
Lighten, v.a. *spukawul, kamawul.* v.n. *rūṇredal, brekkhedal, dzalkedal.*
Lightness, s. *spuk·wālai.*
Lightning, s. *brekkhnā, barq.*
Like, a. *gund, miṣāl, ghūndai, rang, shān.* ad. *laka, pa shān, ghūndi, hase.* s. *pasand, khwakkh.*
Like, v.a. *khwakkh-, pasand-, qabūl-,* etc. *k.* v.n. *khwā·ta ked.*
Likelihood, s. *shān, shakl, ṣūrat, gumān.*
Likely, a *shwūnai.* ad. *kkhā-ī, ghūnde.* (most-) *aghlab, ghāliba.*
Liken, v.a. *miṣāl-, tamṣīl-,* etc. *k., barābarawul, joṛawul.*
Likeness, s. *tsera, ṣūrat, taṣwīr, miṣāl, tamṣīl.*
Likewise, ad. *hum, 'alāwa, ziyāt la de na.*
Liking, s. *mīna, shauq, khwā.*
Lily, s. *sausan.* (water-) *nīlofar.*
Limb, s. *band, andām.* (-of a tree) *kkhākh, khrand.*
Lime, s. *chūna*; *kūnai.* (-kiln) *paja.*
Limestone, s. *da chūne kāṇrai.* (nodulated-) *qurut·kāṇrai.*
Limit, s. *ḥadd, brīd, pūla, ṭikāna.* v.a. *ḥadd-,* etc. *taṛal.*
Limp, v.n. *guḍedal, ṭaparedal, ṭapal.*
Limpid, a. *spīn, pāk, ṣāf, narai.*
Line, s. *līk, līka, karkkha, khaṭṭ.* (rope) *pa-aṛai, biyāsta, rasa-ī.* (row) *qaṭār, para, tsīṛa.* (clothes-) *tsakai, paikal, saha, tanāw.* (-of a book) *jadwal.*
Lineage, s. *aṣl, nasal, mūnḍ, nasab.*
Lineament, s. *ṣūrat, khāl·o·khaṭṭ, rang, ḍaul.*

Linen, s. *khāmtā, karbās.* (-draper) *bazzāz.*
Linger, v.n. *kaṛedal, zahīredal, nūledal.* (delay) v.a. *drang-, lārghah-, dzanḍ-,* etc. *k.* v.n. *pātedal, ṭaparedal, pātai ked.*
Linguist, s. *pa jibo āmokhtah* or *-maṛanai.*
Lining, s. *astar, zerāstar.*
Link, s. *kara-ī.* (torch) *mash'al, shonṭa-ī.*
Linseed, s. *alsī, da sanr zaṛai* or *-tukhm.*
Lintel, s. *darshal, sarāna.*
Lion, s. *zmarai* or *mzarai, babar·zmarai, sher.*
Lip, s. *shūnḍa.* (-of a cup) *morga.* (hare-) *shūnḍ·pārah kanḍā.*
Liquid, a. *narai, oblan.* (melted) *wilī.*
Liquidate, v.a. *pūrah-, adā-,* etc. *k.*
Liquor, s. *oba* ; *'araq* ; *sharāb.*
Liquorice, s. *khwaga·wala.*
Lisp, v.a. *ṭataṛai-, gāngūra-, nkkhati jiba-,* etc. *wayal.*
List, v.a. *ghokkhtal* ; *āwredal* or *ārwedal.*
List, s. *siyāhī, fard, fihrist* ; *jārwja-ī.*
Listen, v.a. *āwredal, nghwatal, ghwag bāsal— yastal, -kegdal—kekkhodal, -nīwul,* etc. (spy) *ghwag tsāral.*
Listless, a. *be·dzān, be·sāh, be·dam, sust, laṭ.*
Literal, a. *lughawī* ; *aṣlī* ; *rikkhtīnai, jukht.*
Literary, a. *'ilmī* ; *kitābī.*
Literati, s. *mullāyān.*
Literature, s. *'ilm, 'ilm·o·faẓal.*
Litigate, v.a. *d'awa-, qaẓiya-,* etc. *k.*
Litigious, a. *jagṛāū, qaẓiya·kār, tākrārī.*
Litter, s. *ḍola-ī, anbāla-ī.* (camel-) *kajāwa.* (grass) *wākkhah.* (refuse) *khazala, khāshāk.*
Little, a. *la-ag, kam.* (small) *wor, wuṛūkai, pūṭai.* ad. *la-ag·kūṭī* or *lakūṭī, pitsānrai, khāsha, ẓarra.*
Littleness, s. *la-ag·wālai, wuṛūk·wālai.*
Live, v.a. *jwand-, jwāk-, rozgār-,* etc. *k., jwandūn-, 'umr-,* etc. *terawul.* v.n. *jwandai ked., osedal.*
Livelihood, s. *rozī, rozgār, rizq, guẓrān.*
Lively, a. *chālāk, chust* ; *khūsh·ṭab'a, shokhīn.*
Liver, s. *īna, dzigar.*
Livery, s. *jāma, libās, bāna.*
Livid, a. *sperah, ziyaṛ, shīn.*
Living, a. *jwandai* ; *jān·dār,* s. *rozgār, rozī, guẓrān, rizq.*
Lizard, s. *samsara, tsarmaḷ·khkai, khādama-ī, karborai.* (iguana) *ghārandūnai.*
Lo, in. *gora! wāh!*
Load, s. *bār, poṭai.* (half-) *anḍa-ī.* (for head) *panḍa, panḍūkai.*
Load, v.a. *bārawul, legdal—lekkhal* ; *ḍakawul*
Loadstone, s. *āhan·rubā.*
Loam, s. *maṭa·khāwra, maṭīna·zmaka.*
Loan, s. *qarẓ, por.* (of a thing itself to be returned) *'āriyat.*
Loath, a. *nā·rāẓ, nā·khwakkh, daregh·man.*
Loathe, v.a. *bad manal, kagal, ghandal, kraka ākhistal, chinjawul.*
Loathsome, a *kraka·nāk, kagalai, chinjan, makrūh, ghāndah.*
Loathing, s. *kraka, kagah, ghandana, chinjana.*
Local, a. *makānī, khāṣṣ.*
Lock, s. *jandra, qulf.* (-of hair) *zulf, tsūnra, tsunraka, kajak, wal.* (-plaited) *kontsa-ī, orbal.* (-of wool) *waṛa-ī.* (-of goat's hair) *ojghūna.* (-of a gun) *chaq·maq.*
Lock, v.a. *jandra lagawul* or *-band k.* (stick) v.n. *nkkhatal, jangedal.*
Locker, s. *ṣandūq, taunra-ī, kandū·ṛai.*
Locket, s. *t'awīz.*
Locomotion, s. *ḥarakat* ; *sail, girzedūn.*
Locust, s. *mlakh.*
Lodge, s. *jūngaṛa, takiya, dzāe, āstāna, kor.*
Lodge, v.n. *osedal, āstedal.* v.a. *ṭikāo-, astoga-, kilai-,* etc. *k., dzāe nīwul.* (place) *gdal,* etc.
Lodger, s. *osedūnkai, āstedūnkai, astogūnkai.*
Lodging, s. *ṭīkāo, dera, dzāe.*
Loft, s. *koṭa, bām, chat.*
Lofty, a. *ūchat, hask, dang, buland, lwaṛ*

Log, s. *garga, mūnḍ, tsaṭ.*
Logic, s. *manṭiq, da munāẓire 'ilm.*
Loins, s. *mlā, shā·laṇḍa, ḍūḍa*: (side of-) *ta-ashai.*
Loiter, v.a. *drang-, lārghah-, dzanḍ-,* etc. *k.* v.n. *ṭapal, ṭaparedal, pātedal, pātai ked.*
Loll, v.a. *takiya-, ārām-,* etc. *k., loṭ·pot k.* v.n. *tsamlāstal, rghaṛedal—rghakkhtal.* (hang out) *watalai dzwaṛandedal.*
Lonely, a. *yawādzai, tsaṛah, biyal, tanhā.*
Long, a. *ūgd.* (duration) *ḍer·pā.* (distance) *ḍer, lire* or *liri.* (-ago) ad. *lire·lārghah, larghūne.* (as long as) ad. *hombra chi, tso chi, tar haghah pore chi.*
Long, v.n. *liwāl-, ūgai-, mayan-,* etc. *ked.* v.a. *ghokkhtal.*
Longevity, s. *zoṛ·tiyā, zoṛ·wālai.*
Longing, s. *liwāl·tob*; *mīna, armān, shauq, raghbat, khwā.*
Look, s. *katal, līdal, goral, kasal, naẓar k.*
Look, s. *kātah, līdah, naẓar, nigāh.*
Looking, s. *katana, līdana.* (-glass) *āhīna.* (-for the thumb) *ārsa-ī, shast.*
Looks, s. *ṣūrat, shakl.*
Loom, s. *rach, shāna.*
Loop, s. *pulwākkha, gharwandai, ghuryāsha.*
Loose, a. *prānatai, arat, āzād, yalah, khushai, gharand*; *spaṛdalai.*
Loose, v.a. *pregdal, prekkhodal*; *khalāṣawul, āzādawul, yalah k.*; *spaṛdal, prānatal*; *arat k.*
Looseness, s. *arat·wālai.* (-of bowels) *nāstah*
Lop, v.a. *prekawul* or *prekṛal, ghūṭ-, lanḍ-,* etc. *k.*
Lord, s. (God) *khudāe, rabb.* (master) *mālik, tsakkhtan, meṛah.* (owner) *khāwand, ṣāḥib.* (spiritual-) *sayad, pīr, ḥaẓrat.* (temporal) *sardār, khān, malik.*
Lordly, a. *khāntamā, kibr·jan.*
Lordship, s. *sardārī, khānī, malikī.* (your-) *ḥaẓrat.*

Lose, v.a. *wrukawul.* (at play, etc.) *bāelal* v.n. *pa-aṛ ked.* (-in trade) *ziyān-, tāwān-* etc. *k.*
Loser, s. *pa-aṛ, bāelūnai.*
Loss, s. *ziyān, tāwān, nuqṣān, troṭa, talaf.*
Lost, a. *wruk, puṭ*; *bāelalai.*
Lot, s. *qismat, naṣīb, bakht.* (share) *brakha, wesh, wanḍ.* (die) *hisk, pucha, qur'a.*
Lottery, s. *qur'a·bāzī, sharṭī.*
Loud, a. *ūchat·āwāz, shor·nāk, tāo.*
Loudly, ad. *pa tāo sara.*
Lounger, s. *nā·rāst*; *hujrai.*
Louse, s. *spaga.* (-nit) *richa.* (crab-) *broṛa.* (cattle-) *konr, kūnai, kāna, wrādza.*
Lousy, a. *spagan.* (mean) *gandah.*
Love, v.n. *mayan-, 'āshiq-,* etc. *ked.* v.a. *mīna-, muḥabbat-, 'ishq-,* etc. *laral* or *k.*
Love, s. *mīna, muḥabbat, 'ishq*; *mayan·tob, 'ishq·bāzī, āshnā-ī, yārī.*
Lovely, a. *kkhkulai, kkhāyastah, peǰ·makhai* or *pa-ī·makhai.*
Lover, s. *yār, āshnāe, mayan, 'āshiq, m'ashūq.*
Low, a. *kūz, lāndai, kkhkatah, lar, past.* (mean) *spuk, dūn, gandah.* (-stature) *mandarai.* (-price) *wel, arzān.* (-spirited) *malūl, zahīr.* (-breed) *kam·aṣl, lāndai·ẓāt, pāsū.*
Low, v.n. *ghurchedal, ghuṛunbedal.* v.a. *naṛal, nāra-, ḍarān-,* etc. *wahal.*
Lower, a. *kkhkatanai, kūz, lar, lāndai.*
Lower, v.a. *kūzawul, kkhkatah-, lāndai-,* etc. *k.*; *ṭīṭawul.* (lessen) v.a. *spukawul, kamawul.* (as the sky) v.n. *toredal, ṭīṭedal.* (frown) v.a. *brandawul, brand katal.*
Lowland, s. *sama, maidān*; *tahana.*
Lowly, a. *gharīb, kamīn, ḥalīm.*
Lowness, s. *kūz-, kkhkatah-,* etc. *-wālai.*
Loyal, a. *khair·khwāh, wafā·dāṛ, namak·ḥallāl.*
Lucid, a. *ṣāf, spīn*; *tsargand, kkhkārah.*

Luck, s. *bakht, qismat, naṣīb.*
Lucky, a. *bakhtāwar, barakatī, nek·bakht.*
Lucrative, a. *sūd·man, fā-ida·man, naf'a·nāk.*
Lucre, s. *duniyā, daulat, māl, sūd,*
Ludicrous, a. *khandā·nāk, washtī, ṭoqī.*
Lug, v.a. *rākāgal—rākkhkal, kashāla k.*
Luggage, s. *asbāb, partal; balā·batar.*
Lukewarm, a. *taṛam.*
Lull, v.a. *lala-ī-, lalo-, ṭāṭa-ī-, ḍīng·ḍīnga-ī-,* etc. *k.; khob-, ārām-,* etc. *rāwṛal; damawul, ūdah k.; saṛawul, kamawul.*
Lumbago, s. *tsak.*
Lumber, s. *balā·batar, be·kkhai, nā·pakār.*
Luminous, a. *rokkhān, rūnr.*
Lump, s. *ghaṭai, ghūnḍūrai, peṛa, chaka-ī, chakṛa-ī.* (all of a-) *sūṭ·būṭ, aluwal.*
Lunacy, s. *lewan·tob, saudā.*
Lunatic, s. *lewanai, saudā-ī.*
Luncheon, s. *nihārai, nwaṛa-ī, da paste doḍa-ī.*
Lungs, s. *sagai, parpūs.*
Lurch, v.n. *tsangzan ked.*
Lure, v.a. *ghulawul, ṭagal; pa dalbe nīwul, pa tam'e-* or *pa tāmbe-,* etc. *nīwul.*
Lurk, v.n. *ghalai kkhkenāstal, puṭedal.* v.a. *pasūnai-, tsawai-,* etc. *nīwul.*
Lurking-place, s. *pasūnai, tsawai, puṭgana-ī.*
Luscious, a. *khog, khwand·nāk, maza·dār.*
Lust, s. *shahwat, mastī, nas, naus.*
Lustful, a. *shahwat·nāk, mast.*
Lustre, s. *ranrā, dzalak, brekkhnā.*
Lustrous, a. *rūnr, brekkh·nāk, dzalak·nāk.*
Lusty, a. *zorāwar, tuwānā, quwat·nāk, tandrust; maghzan, gagar, kaṭah, peṛ, chāgh.*
Lute, s. *shpela-ī, bindla-ī.*
Luxuriance, s. *prewānī, ziyātī, wadānī, ḍer·wālai, ābādī.*
Luxuriant, a. *prewān, ziyāt, wadān, ḍer.*
Luxurious, a. *nafs·parast, ārām·ṭalab.*
Luxury, s. *moṛ·tiyā, ārām·tiyā.*
Lynx, s. *pṛāng·pīsh, yūz.*

M.

Mace, s. *amsā, lawaṛ, ḍāng, ḍāngora-ī, gruz, koṭak.*
Macerate, v.a. *khuṛīnawul, pastawul, khushtawul, lūnd sātal.*
Machination, s. *band, taṛa, joṛikkht.*
Machine, s. *kūlai, hatiyār.*
Mad, a. *lewanai, saudā-ī, khushai.*
Madam, s. *bībī, merman.*
Madder, s. *rodang, majīt.*
Madness, s. *lewan·tob, saudā.*
Magazine, s. *zakhīra, khizāna, ganj.*
Maggot, s. *chinjai, kīkkhai.*
Magic, s. *jādū, koḍa, siḥr.*
Magician, s. *jādū·gar, koḍ·gar, siḥr·gar.*
Magistrate, s. *ḥākim, 'amal·dār.*
Magnanimity, s. *himmat, zṛah.*
Magnanimous, a. *himmat·nāk, zṛah·war.*
Magnet, s. *āhan·rubā, chumbak·kānrai.*
Magnificence, s. *raunaq, dabdaba, tamtarāq.*
Magnificent, a. *raunaq·dār.*
Magnify, v.a. *ziyātawul, ghaṭ-, loe-,* etc. *k.* (praise) *stāyal, ṣanā wayal.*
Magnitude, s. *loe-, ghaṭ-, star-,* etc. *-wālai.*
Maid, s. *jina-ī, peghla.* (bond-) *wīndza, kanīza.* (servant-) *mazdūra, chūra-ī, sahela-ī.* (bride's-) *wreyaza* or *wre-aza, wrā·bānra-ī, mūnja-ī, īnga.*
Mail, s. *zghara; chalqat, zira.* (a man in-) *zghar·yālai.*
Maim, v.a. *guḍawul, khūgawul, kaṛam k.; jobalawul, ghwutsawul, zam·zmolai k.*
Maimed, a. *guḍ, khug, jobal, ghwuts, kaṛam, zam·zmolai, zakhmī, parhār·jalai, parhār·jan, māt·guḍ, sukṛuk.*
Main, a. *wṛūnbanai, awwalanai, wṛūnbai.*
Mainly, ad. *akṣar, ziyāt, ḍer, ghāliban, aghlab.*
Maintain, v.a. *iqrār-, d'awa-,* etc. *k.; wayal.*

(defend) *jghoral, khundī k.* (support) *parwaral, pālal, sātal.*

Maintenance, s. *rozī, khwurāk, parwarish.*

Maize, s. *jwār, ghaṭ-jwār.* (ear of-) *wagai.* (ear cone of-) *shata-ī.*

Majestic, a. *shāhī, bādshāhī; loe, ghaṭ, 'azīm.*

Majesty, s. *dabdaba, raunaq, jalāl; ḥazrat; salṭanat.*

Major, a. *loe, mashar; ziyāt, akṣar.*

Make, v.a. *joṛawul, kawul, paidā k.* (-amends) *tāwān warkawul.* (-away with) *wrukawul, puṭawul; wajlal, mur kawul.* (-good) *pūrah-, adā-,* etc. *k.* (-known) *khabarawul.* (-of, or understand) *pohedal.* (-out) *tsargandawul, kkhkārah-, daryāft-,* etc. *k.* (-over) *spāral, pāslawul, gumāral.* (-sure of) *yaqīn ganṛal.* (mix) *gaḍawul.* (-up, as a quarrel, etc.) *pakhulā k., gwākkhal, gwākkh-grandī k.* (collect) *ṭolawul.* (-towards) *khwā-ta-, lorī-ta-,* etc. *tlal—lāṛal.* (-much of) *nāzawul, nmāndzal.*

Make, s. *shakl, ḍaul, ṣūrat.*

Maker, s. *joṛawūnkai.* (in comp.) *-gar, -sāz, -kār.*

Making, s. *joṛawūna, sākht.*

Malady, s. *maraẓ, āzār, bīmārī, randz, nā-joṛ-tiyā, nā-rogh-tiyā.*

Male, a. *nar, nārīnah.* (-of cattle for breeding) s. *mīndah* or *hīndah.* (stallion) *turum.*

Malediction, s. *kkhera, bad-d'uā, l'anat.*

Malefactor, s. *gunāh-gār, bad-kār.*

Malevolence, s. *khwā-badī, kīna, badī.*

Malevolent, a. *khwā-bad, kīna-war.*

Malice, s. *kīna, badī, bughẓ.*

Malignant, a. *kīna-waṛ, bad.*

Malinger, v.a. *bāna-, lamghara-ī-,* etc. *k.*

Mallet, s. *molai, ḍabalai, baghdar.* (washerman's-) *tsobāṛai.*

Maltreat, v.a. *bad-sulūk k., be-makh k., wahal.*

Mamma, s. *aba-ī, ada-ī, mor.*

Mammon, s. *daulat, duniyā, nafs.*

Man, s. *saṛai, wagaṛai, gaṛai; bashar, insān, bandah.* (wild-) *banṛ-mānū.*

Manacles, s. *da lās karī.*

Manage, v.a. *chalawul, kawul, sambālawul, tadbīr k., band taṛal.*

Manageable, a. *da kawulu, da sambālawulu,* etc. *pa qābū, gharīb; spuk, āsān.*

Management, s. *kār-sāzī, tadbīr, intiẓām.*

Manager, s. *kār-sāz, pesh-kār, dāroghah.*

Mandate, s. *ḥukm, farmān, farmā-ikkht.*

Mane, s. *wrag, yāl, okkhī, owī.*

Mange, s. *khārikkht, pam, pūn, garg, pa-akh.*

Manger, s. *ākhor.*

Mangle, v.a. *mātawul, kanḍ-kapaṛ-, ṭoṭe-ṭoṭe-, chūr-laṭ-, char-chūr-, daṛ-daṛ-,* etc. *k.*

Mango, s. *am.* (-tree) *da am wana.*

Mangy, a. *paman, pa-akhai, gargai.*

Manhood, s. *dzwānī, zalmī-tob; mardī.*

Maniac, s. *lewanai, saudā-ī.*

Manifest, a. *tsargand, kkhkārah, bartser, ẓāhir.* v.a. *tsargandawul, kkhkārah-,* etc. *k., kkhayal—kkhowul.*

Manifestly, ad. *bartseran, pa jār* or *-ẓāhir.*

Manifestation, s. *tsargand-tob, kkhkārah-wālai; iẓhār, jār.*

Manifesto, s. *ishtihār, jār, iẓhār-nāma.*

Manifold, a. *ḍer, bragh-bragh, braghan.*

Mankind, s. *sarai, wagaṛai, gaṛai, insān, bashar.*

Manliness, s. *saṛī-tob, maṛanī-tob, nārīn-tob.*

Manly, a. *maṛanai, nārīnah.*

Manner, s. *shān, ṭaur, toga, rang, yang, wajha; ḍaul. chāl-chal, ṭaraḥ.*

Mannerly, a. *sulūkī, makhawar, adabī.*

Manners, s. *chāl, ādāb, khoe-khaṣlat, makh.*

Manœuvre, s. *chal, ḥikmat; tadbīr, band; fareb, lamghaṛa-ī.*

Manor, s. *dawtar, jāgīr, mulk; wanḍ, ada-ī.*

Mansion, s. *koṭa, mena.* (storied) *mānra-ī, ḥawela-ī.*

Manslaughter, s. *marg, khūn, qatl.*

Manslayer, s. *qātil, khūnī, marg kawūnkai.*

Mantle, s. (man's-) *chogha, kosai, junga·kaṛi shaṛa-ī; lūnga-ī, shamla, shāl.* (woman's-) *tsādar, paṛūnai, pachorai, chāyal, oḍana-ī, yaklā-ī.*

Manual, a. *dastī, da lās.* s. *kitāb.* (in comp.) *-nāma.*

Manufacture, s. *ḍast·kārī, joṛikkht, sākht.*

Manufacturer, s. *joṛawūnkai, kārī·gar.*

Manufactory, s. *kār·khāna.*

Manure, s. *sara, sarā.*

Manuscript, s. *dast·khaṭṭ; qalamī kitāb.*

Many, a. *ḍer, gaṇr.* (too-) *ziyāt.* (how-) *tso, tsomra.* (so-) *hombra, daghombra.* (as many as) *hombra chi.* (-coloured) *rangā·rang.* (-times) *ḍer dzala, wār·wār.*

Map, s. *nakhkkha, naqsha,*

Mar, v.a. *wrānawul, kharāb-, habatah-,* etc. *k.*

Marble, s. *mardaka.* (-stone) *marmar.*

March, s. *kūch, safar, pand.* (month) *chetar.*

Mare, s. *āspa, mādyān.*

Margin, s. *ghāṛa, morga, tselma, tsanḍa, ĵa-ī, laman.* (-of a book) *ḥāshiya.*

Marine, a. *daryābī.*

Mark, s. *nakkha; dāgh.* v.a. *nakkha lagawul; dāghawul; nazar-, fikr-,* etc. *k.*

Marked, a. *nakkha·dār; dāghī; mashhūr.*

Market, s. *bāzār, ganj, haṭa-ī, manḍha-ī.*

Marketable, a. *bāzārī; chalanī.*

Marl, s. *maṭa·khāwra, maṭīna·zmaka.*

Marquee, s. *khaima, dera.*

Marriage, s. *wādah, nikāḥ.* (-feast) *kkhādī.* (-procession) *janj, wrā.* (-male guest) *jānjī, wrā·bānrai, mānjī.* (-female guest) *wrā·bānra-ī, wre-aza, mānja-ī.* (-gift) *belak.*

Married, a. (-man) *wādah·kaṛai.* (-woman) *wādah·shawi.* (under coverture) *maṛokkha.* v.n. *wadedal.*

Marrow, s. *māghzah, maghz.*

Marry, v.a. *wadawul, nikāḥ taṛal.* (-a husband) *tsakkhtan-, meṛah-,* etc. *k.* (-a wife) *kkhadza k.*

Marsh, s. *jaba.*

Marshy, a. *jaba·nāk, lūnd, zyam·nāk.*

Mart, s. *bāzār, ganj, haṭa-ī.*

Martial, a. *jangī, lakkhkarī.*

Martyr, s. *shahīd.*

Martyrdom, s. *shahādat.*

Marvel, v.n. *hariyānedal, hariyān* or *ḥairān ked., rabṛedal.*

Marvellous, a. *'ajab, 'ajīb, 'ajūbah, badī'a.*

Masculine, a. *nar, nūrīnah, saṛai.*

Mash, s. *oghra, atūb, daliya.* v.a. *paz wahal.*

Mask, s. *parda, tsera; libās, swāng; fareb, bāna, chal.* v.a. *parda-,* etc. *k.; puṭawul, pokkhal.*

Mason, s. *rāj, m'imār.*

Mass, s. *ghunḍa, peṛa, chakṛa-ī; dala-ī, ḍera-ī.*

Massacre, s. *qatl, qatl·'āmm.* v.a. *qatlawul.*

Massive, a. *loe, ghaṭ, star; drūnd.* (-person) *khṛīs, nāpaṛ, punḍ, gagar.*

Mast, s. *tīr, loe stan da jahāz.*

Master, s. *khāwand, tsakkhtan, meṛah, nāyak, mālik.* (-of a house) *korbah.* (tutor) *ākhūn. ustād.* (school-) *mullā, mu'allim.*

Master, v.a. *lānde k., sambālawul. barai mūndal.*

Mastery, s. *barai; ḥukūmat.*

Masticate, v.a. *ĵowul* or *ĵoyal, chīchal, kṛapawul.*

Mastiff, s. *khaḍal, ghaṭ ghartsanai·spai.*

Mat, s. *pūzai, pūhaṛ, anḍerai.*

Match, s. (contest) *bāzī, sharṭ.* (equal) *makhai, jorah, gund, siyāl; sārai, samsorai, hum·dzolai.* (gun-) *patīla, bāta-ī.* (fire-) *shonṭa-ī; shūsha-ī.* (marriage) *koĵdan.* (-maker) *rebār, dallāl, mandz·garai.*

Match. v.a. *barābarawul, joṛawul, lagawul; jangawul.* v.n. *barābaredal, joṛedal, lagedal.*

Matchless, a. *be-miṣāl, be-siyāl, be-naẓīr, lā-ṣānī.*
Mate, s. *mal, mal-garai, joṛah, yār.*
Material, a. *jismī, tan-dār* ; *ẓarūr, grān.*
Materials, s. *kālī, hatyār, asbāb, sāmān.*
Materially, ad. *ḍer, ziyāt, nihāyat.*
Maternal, a. *morunai.* (-relation) s. *mor-ganai.*
Mathematics, s. *'ilm da riyāẓī.*
Matrix, s. *qālib, sāncha.*
Matrimony, s. *wādah.* (state of-) *wādah-tūn.*
Matron, s. *mor, merman, bībī, spīn-sara.* (-of a house) *korbana.* (-under coverture) *maṛokkha.*
Matted, a. *arjal-barjal, tsapolai, nkkhatai.*
Matter, s. *jism, māda, jauhar.* (affair) *kār, khabara.* (thing) *tsīz, shai.* (pus) *ziwa* or *zawa, zahūb, rash.* (dirt) *khīra, chirk, chikhai.* (concern) *gharaẓ.*
Mattock, s. *kodāla-ī, sakkhsora, saspor, kasha-ī.*
Mattress, s. *tolā-ī, nihālī, toshak, taltak.*
Mature, a. *pokh, pūrah, kāmil.*
Maturely, ad. *pa fikr-, ghaur-*, etc. *-sara.*
Maturity, s. *pokh-wālai, kamāl.*
Maul, v.a. *wahal, ṭakawul, kūṭal, māṭawul.*
Maund, s. *man, las daṛa-ī.*
Maw, s. *jajūra.*
Mawkish, a. *balmangah* or *balmagai, be-khwand.*
Maxim, s. *matal, wayai, qānūn, masla.*
May, s. *jeṭ.*
Maze, s. *kaga-waga, pech-o-kham.*
Meadow, s. *warsho, chaman, kurūgh.*
Meagre, a. *ḍangar, narai, rangai, mahīn.*
Meal, s. *oṛah.* (fine-) *maidah.* (coarse-) *dal.* (rice-) *khamacha.* (pulse-) *rāṛa.*
Mean, a. *bakhīl, shūm* ; *spuk, dūn* ; *ıandai-zāt, kam-aṣl* ; *mandzwai, āwsaṭ.* s. *mandz.*
Mean, v.a. *m'anī-, maṭlab-*, etc. *laral* ; *qaṣd k.*

Meander, v.n. *girzeḍal, pechedal.*
Meaning, s. *m'anī, maṭlab* ; *qaṣd, mudd'ā.*
Meanness. s. *bakhīlī, shūm-wālai, spuk-tiyā.*
Means, s. *m'arifat, wasīla, wāsiṭa* ; *kabl.* (property) *panga, saga, māya* ; *māl, kharts.* (manner) *wajha, shān, rang, ṭaur.* (by no-) *hets-chare, kruṭ.* (by what-) *pa tsa shān.*
Meantime, } ad. *pa de mandz kkhke.*
Meanwhile, }
Measles, s. *sharai, sara-makha.*
Measure, v.a. *mech-, kach-*, etc. *k.* (weigh) *jokal, talal.* (divide) *weshal.*
Measure, s. *mech, kach* ; *tol, andāza, joka* ; *wesh.* (action) *kār, chal, band, tarkīb.* (grain-) *kuṛai, ogai, daṛa-ī.* (verse) *wazn.* (-in music) *tāl, tāng.* (-for land) *pa-aṛai.* (beyond-) ad. *la ḥadda ter.*
Measureless, a. *be-kach, be-andāzah, be-ḥadd, be-shān, be-qiyās.*
Meat, s. *ghwakkha.* (food) *khwurāk, ḍoḍa-ī, ghiẓa.*
Mechanic, s. *kasb-gar, pesha-war.*
Mechanism, s. *ṭarkīb, joṛikkht, sākhtagī.*
Medal, s. *ṭughma* ; *nakkha.*
Meddle, v.a. *gharaẓ k., lās lagawul, -āchawul, -war-wṛal*, etc.
Medial, a. *mandzwai, miyānah.*
Mediate, v a. *gwākkhal, gwākkh-grandī k.*
Mediation, s. *gwākh* ; *sipārish.*
Mediator, s. *gwākkh-grandai* ; *mandz-garaı.*
Medical, a. *ṭibbī.* (-man) s. *ṭabīb.*
Medicine, s. *dawā, dārū, darmān.* (science of-) *ṭibb.* (practice of-) *ṭibābat, ṭabībī.*
Mediocrity, s. *nīmgarī-tob, ausaṭ.*
Meditate, v.a. *fikr-, ghaur-, andekkhnā-*, etc. *k.*
Medium, a. *mandzwai, miyānah.* s. *wasīla, wāsiṭa, m'arifat.*
Medley, s. *gāḍera, aṛgajah, gaḍ-waḍ.*
Meek, a. *ḥalīm, gharīb, pos, narm.*
Meekness, s. *ḥalīm-tob, gharībi, pos-wālai.*
Meet, a. *pīrzo, wājib, munāsib, lā-iq.*

Meet, v.n. *pekkhedal, wrānde-, miliyā-,* etc. *ked.*; *jangedal, lagedal, yo·dzāe ked.* (find) v.a. *mūndal.*
Meeting, s. *majlis, ṭolai*; *mulāqāt, dīdan*; *jirga, jumā'at.* (-place) *borjal, ṭīkāo.*
Meetness, s. *pīrzowuna, pīrzo·wālai, lā-iq·wālai, munāsibat.*
Melancholy, a. *gham·jan, malāl*; *saudā-ī.* s. *nūl, gham*; *saudā.*
Mellow, a. *pokh, khurīn, pos*; *paṭakh.*
Melodious, a. *khush·āwāz, khūsh·bāng.*
Melody, s. *sarod, badala. tarāna.*
Melon, s. (water) *hindwāna, tarbūza.* (musk) *kharbūza*; *dastambol.* (sweet-) *khaṭakai, sarda, kand·yālai.* (wild-) *kākoṛa, kāl-kūnḍa-ī.* (bitter-) *tarkha kākoṛa.*
Melt, v.a. *wīlī k.*; *oba k.* v.n. *wīlī ked.*; *oba ked.*
Member, s. (-of the body) *andām, band.* (partner) *sharīk, brakha·khor.* (-of an assembly) *majlisī, jirgatū.* (clause) *juz, faṣl.*
Membrane, s. *parda, jāla-ī.* (-of belly) *spekkhta.* (-of the heart) *dzān·khwal.*
Memoir, s. *tazkira, tawārīkh.*
Memorable, a. *qābil-* or *lā·iq da yād.*
Memorandum, s. *yād·dāsht, yād·gārī.*
Memorial, s. *yād·gār*; *'arẓī, darkhwāst.*
Memory, s. *yād, ḥifẓ.*
Menace, v.a, *raṭal, traṭal, ḍabawul, dāṛal.*
Mend, v.a. *joṛawul, raghawul.* (-clothes) *bezal, pezal.* v.n. *joṛedal, raghedal.*
Mendicant, s. *faqīr, gadāe*; *ṭālib.*
Menial, s. *nokar, chūrai, mazdūr.*
Menses, s. *ḥaiẓ, zaṛūkī.*
Menstrual, a. *ḥaiẓī.* (-woman) *ḥaiẓ·dāra, ḥaiẓa, bilmāza.* (-cloth) *ḍerān.*
Mensuration, s. *mech, kach.*
Mental, a. *bāṭinī, qalbī.*
Mention, v.a. *yādawul*; *wayal, khabarawul.*
Mercantile, a. *da saudāgarī, tijāratī.*
Mercenary, a. *khpul·gharaẓ, duniyā·parast, zar·āshnāe.* (-soldier) *mlā·taṛ.*
Merchandise, s. *māl, jins, saudā*; *saudāgarī, banj, bipār* or *wapār, tijārat.*
Merchant, s. *saudā·gar, wapārī, banjārī*; *seṭ*; *parāchah.*
Merciful, a. *mom·dil, raḥm·dil.* (-God) *raḥīm, raḥmān, karīm.*
Merciless, a. *be·raḥm, be·dard.*
Mercury, s. *pārā, sīmāb.*
Mercy, s. *raḥm, raḥmat, khwā·khūgī.*
Merely, ad. *sirp, surup, ta-ash, khālī, faqaṭ.*
Meridian, s. *gharma, ṭakanra·gharma.*
Merit, s. *ḥaqq, qadr, yarz*; *ṣawāb.*
Meritorious, a. *wājib, lā-iq*; *ṣawābī.*
Merriment, s. *kkhādī, khūsh·ḥālī, khandā, washta·ṭoqa.*
Merry, a. *kkhād, kkhād·man, khūsh·ḥāl, khandā·rūe.*
Mesh, s. *tor, jāla-ī. shabaka.*
Mess, s. *qatagh, ngolai.* (-of herbs) *sāgīnrai.* v.a. *ḥānḍa-ī-wālī k.*; *chūka k.*
Message, s. *khabar, paighām, karya.*
Messenger, s. *astādzai, qāṣid, harkārah.*
Messmate, s. *hānḍa-ī·wāl.*
Metallic, a. *kānī.*
Metaphor, s. *miṣāl, majāz, kināyat.*
Metaphysics, s. *'ilm da maujūdāt.*
Mete, v.a. *weshal*; *mech-, kach-,* etc. *k.*
Metempsychosis, s. *tanāsukh.*
Meteor, s. *lūk, laka-ī, shughla.*
Method, s. *tartīb, shān, rang, ḍaul, ḥikmat toga, yang*; *ṭaur, ṭarīqa.*
Methodise, v.a. *tartībawul.*
Metre, s. *wazn, mech, mīzān.*
Metropolis, s. *pāe·takht, dāru·l·mulk.*
Mettle, s. *gaṛand·wālai, tund·wālai*; *maṛāna*
Mettlesome, a. *gaṛandai, tund, tez*; *maṛanai*
Mew, v.a. *miyāw k.*
Midday, s. *gharma, ṭakanra·gharma, nīma wradz.*

Middle, a. *mandzwai, miyānah*. s. *mandz* or *miyandz*. (-finger) *mandza·gūta*.
Middling, a. *nīmgaṛai, hase*.
Midge, s. *māshai, ghamāsha*. (water) *jak, jakh*.
Midnight, s. *nīma·shpa, shūma*.
Midst, a. *mandzwai, miyānah*.
Midway, s. *nīma·lār, pa lāri*.
Midwife, s. *qābila, dā-ī*.
Mien, s. *tsihra, ṣūrat*; *rang, ḍaul*; *chāl, yūn*.
Might, s. *quwat, zor, was, tuwān, bram, qudrat*.
Mighty, a. *zorāwar, maẓbūṭ, tuwānā, qawī*.
Mitigate, v.a. *kaḍa wṛal, legdal—lekkhal, kūch-, naql-*, etc. *k*.
Milch, a. *langa, pa-ī·wara*.
Mild, a. *ḥalīm, narm, pos, khog*; *emaṇ*.
Mildew, s. *chanṛāsa, chata-ī*.
Mildness, s. *ḥalīm·tob, narmī, pos·wālai*, etc.
Military, a. *jangī, lakkhkarī*.
Milk, s. *pa-ī, shaudah*. (sour-) *khaidak, praṇṛ*. (curdled-) *māstah*. (butter-) *shomle* or *shlonbe, kha-areṛai*. (whey) *tarwe*. (caudle-) *matar* or *matra, kaṛa*. (-pail) *doṇṛa-ī, lawaghūna*. (-maid) *ghobana*. (-man) *ghobah*. (-and water) *lassī*. (first-) *wargah*.
Milk, v.a. *lwashal*.
Milkless, a. *wucha, zāṛa-ī*.
Mill, s. (hand-) *mechan*. (water-) *jaranda, āsiyā*. (oil-) *gāṇṛa-ī*. (-stone) *da mechani gaṭa*.
Miller, s. *jarand·garai, muẓd·garai, āsiyā·wān*.
Millet, s. *ghokkht, gdan, kārah*.
Million, s. *las laka*.
Mimic, s. *pekkhe·gar, malanḍai, swāngai*.
Mimicry, s. *pekkha, malanda, swāng*.
Mince, v.a. *qīma-, ṭoṭe·ṭoṭe-, reze·reze-*, etc. *k., warjal*.
Mind, s. *zṛah, dil, dzān*; *'aql, poha, pahm, hokkh*; *khwā*; *gharaẓ*; *fikr, rāe*; *yād*. (presence of-) *ausān, baidārī*. (out of one's-) *ausān·tlalai*.
Mind, v.a. *yād laral, manal, fikr-*, etc. *k*.
Mindful, a. *yādawar, khabar·dār, hokkhyār*.
Mine, s. *kān*; *surang, naqab*. pr. *dzamā, khpul*.
Mine, v.a. *kān·kanal, -kanaudal*, or *-kanastal, surang wahal*. (-a house) *kanḍar mātawul* or *k*.
Miner, s. *kān·kanūnkai*; *surang wahūnkai, naqab·zan*; *kanḍar kawūnkai*.
Mingle, v.a. *gaḍawul, laṛal, ṛaqawul*.
Minister, s. (-of state) *wazīr*. (agent) *wakīl, nāẓir, nā-ib, gumāshtah, dīwān*.
Minister, v.a. *khidmat k.*; *warkawul*.
Ministry, s. *khidmat*.
Minor, a. *kashar* or *kishar*; *la-ag, kam*.
Minority, s. *kishar·tob, wuṛūk·wālai*; *la-ag, kam*.
Minstrel, s. *muṭrib, sandar·bol, sarodī, mīrāṣī, ḍum*.
Mint, s. *ṭaksāl, ẓarb·khāna*. (the plant) *n'anā, pūdīna*.
Minute, s. *laḥẓa, sā'at, dam*. (note) *yād·gār*.
Minute, a. *narai, mahīn, bārīk*; *pūṭai, pitsāṇṛai*.
Minutely, ad. *pa kkhah shān sara*.
Miracle, s. *karāmat, m'ujaza*.
Miraculous, a. *'ajab, 'ajīb, karāmatī*.
Mirage, s. *sarāb*.
Mire, s. *khaṭa, chikaṛ, chakṛaba*.
Mirror, s. *ā-īna, shīsha, hindāra*. (-for the thumb) *shasht, ārsā-ī*.
Mirth, s. *kkhādi, khūsh·ḥālī, khwakkhī, khandā*.
Miry, a. *chikṛan, khaṭolan*.
Misapply, v.a. *be·dzāe lagawul, 'abaṣ k*.
Misapprehension, s. *nā·pohī, khaṭā*.
Misbegotten, a. *ḥarāmī, pa khaṭā paidā*, or *ghalat·paidā*.

Misbehaviour, s. *bad·chāl, bad·sulūkī, nā·rāstī.*

Miscarry, v.n. *wrukedal.* (abort) v.a. *geḍa ghurzawul, ziyān-, tāwān-,* etc. *k.*

Miscellaneous, a. *biyal, judā* ; *be·tartīb, gaḍ·waḍ.*

Miscellany, s. *jung, gāḍera, aṛgaja.*

Mischief, s. *tāwān, nuqṣān, ziyān* ; *dukkh·manī, badī* ; *pasāt* ; *shar, sharārat* ; *wīta, shokhī.*

Mischievous, a. *mozī, muzirr, ziyān·kār, tawānī* ; *bad, kharāb, sharīr.* (-boy) *wītakai.*

Misconduct, s. *bad 'amalī, -kārī, -chalan,* etc.

Miscreant, s. *kāfir, bad·zāt, mardūd.*

Misdeed, s. *gunāh, quṣūr, taqṣīr, wabāl.*

Miser, s. *shūm, bakhīl, tang·dast.*

Miserable, a. *khwār, tabāh, kharāb·khastah.* (worthless) *nā·kārah, nā·tsīz, nā·kas.*

Misery, s. *khwārī, tabāhī, khasgī* or *khastagī, nā·kasī, tangsiyā, nā·chārī, muflisī.*

Misfortune, s. *āfat, balā, bad-, kam-, tor-,* etc. *-bakhtī, nāzila, muṣībat.*

Mislay, v.a. *wrukawul, be·dzāe kegdal* or *kkhkegdal.*

Mislead, v.a. *ghulawul, gumrāh k.*

Mismanage, v.a. *be·tadbīrī k., wrānawul, kharābawul.*

Miss, v.a. *khaṭā k.* v.n. *ter watal.*

Missing, a. *puṭ, wruk.*

Mission, s. *āstawuna, risālat.*

Missionary, s. *āstādzai.*

Misspell, v.a. *peza-ī-, hezgī-, hijgī-,* etc. *pa khaṭā wayal* or *-k.*

Mist, s. *laṛa, dund, gard, ghubār.*

Mistake, s. *khaṭā, būlāwa, ghalaṭ.*

Mistress, s. *merman, korbana* ; *m'ashūqa, yāra, āshnāya, 'aurata.*

Mistrust, s. *shakk, bad·gumān, wiswās.* v.a. *shakk-,* etc. *laral.*

Mistrustful, a. *shakk·man, bad·gumānī, wiswāsī, be·i'tibār, stāra·prewatai.*

Misty, a. *dund, gard·jan, ghubārī.*

Misunderstanding, s. *nā·pohī, nā·pahmī* ; *mānṛai, marawar·tiyā* ; *mīrtsī, badī.*

Mite, s. *pūṭai, batsarai, pitsāṇrai* ; *richa.*

Mitigate, v.a. *la-agawul* ; *kamawul, saṛawul.*

Mix, v.a. *gaḍawul* ; *laṛal, ṛaqawul.*

Mixed, a. *gaḍ* ; *laṛalai.*

Mixture, s. *gaḍa, gāḍera* ; *murakkab.*

Moan, s. *zwergai* or *zgerwai, bilāṇra, heng, angahār.* v.a. *zwergai-,* etc. *k.*

Moat, s. *kanda, kāha-ī, khandaq.*

Mob, s. *paṛk, ṭolai, ḍala, ghol, gaṇr.*

Mob, v.a. *ger k., īsārawul* or *ḥiṣārawul.*

Mock, v.a. *pekkhe k., khandā pore k.*

Mockery, s. *pekkha, khandā, ṭoqa.*

Mode, s. *shān, rang, toga, ṣūrat, wajha* ; *chāl, chalan, ṭaur, dastūr, rasm, ṭarīqa.*

Model, s. *naqsha, namūna* ; *nakkha, ḍaul* ; *qālib, kālbūt.* v.a. *pa nakkhe-,* etc. *joṛawul.*

Moderate, v.a. *sambālawul, kamawul.*

Moderate, a. *mandzwai, miyānah, muwāfiq.*

Moderation, s. *ṣabr, zgham, parhez.*

Modern, a. *nawai, osanai, osan.*

Modest, a. *sharm-, ḥayā-, ghairat-,* etc. *-nāk, sharm·sār* ; *nek, pāk·laman.*

Modesty, s. *sharm, ḥayā,* etc.

Modify, v.a. *ṣūrat-,* etc. *warkawul* ; *badlawul.*

Modulate, v.a. *āwāz joṛawul, sarod k., tarāna-, sandara-, zamzama-,* etc. *wayal.*

Moiety, s. *nīm, nīmai, nīmāyah.*

Moist, a. *lūnd, zyam·nāk, nam·nāk, naw·jan.*

Moisten, v.a. *lūndawul* or *lambdawul.*

Moisture, s. *lūnd·wālai, zyam, naw, nam.*

Mole, s. *potai, ghunḍa-ī, ḍera-ī, kha-aṭ* ; *damdamā.* (-of the skin) *ta-apai, khāl.*

Molest, v.a. *pārawul, rabṛawul, zoral.*

Molestation, s. *āzār, rabaṛ, ṭongāṛa, blos,* etc.

Mollify, v.a. *narmawul, pastawul, saṛawul.*

Molten, a. *wīlī, wīlī shawai.*

Moment, s. *laḥza, dam, sā'at, drang* ; *parwā, fikr, gharaẓ.*

Momentary, a. *teredūnai, nā·pāedār.*

Momentous, a. *drūnd, grān, mushkil* ; *ẓarūr, muhimm.*

Monarch, s. *bādshāh, amīr, sulṭān.*

Monarchy, s. *bādshāhī, salṭanat.*

Monday, s. *pīr, gul.*

Money, s. *rok, ṭanga, naghd* or *naqd, paisa, rūpa-ī.* (-changer) *ṣarrāf.*

Moneyed, a. *daulat·man, duniyā·dār, māl· dār, da rūpo paiso khāwand.*

Moneyless, a. *ta·aṣh lās, be·daulat, muflis.*

Mongoose, s. *nolai.*

Mongrel, a. *nīmchah, dwah·ragah.*

Monition, s. *naṣīhat, pand.*

Monitor, s. *nāṣih, pand warkawūnkai.*

Monkey, s. *bīzo, shādo.*

Monopoly, s. *khāṣṣ saudā, ijāra.*

Monotonous, a. *yo·shān, yo·wazn.*

Monsoon, s. *parshakāl.*

Monster, s. *dew, dad, rawai* ; *bawr·mānū.*

Monstrous, a. *haul·nāk, 'azīm, 'ajīb.*

Month, s. *myāsht.* (solar-, used with refer- ence to agriculture and the seasons, com- mencing at April) *wīsāk, jeṭ, hāṛ, pashakāl, bādro, asū, kātak, mangar, poh, māh, pa- gawr, chaitr.* (lunar-, used with reference to dates, festivals, etc.) *hasan husen, ṣafara, wrūnba·ī khor, dwayama khor, driyama khor, tsalorama khor, da khudāe myāsht, da sho qadr* or *da barāt myāsht, da roje myāsht, da wurūkī akhtar myāsht, khālī* or *miyāna, da loe akhtar myāsht.*

Monthly, ad. *myāsht pa myāsht, māh·wārī.*

Monument, s. *tsalai, nikkhān, nakkha.* (tomb) *maqbara, qabr, khāda.*

Mood, s. *hāl, shān* ; *rang, khoe.*

Moody, a. *khapah, malāl, sūṭ·būṭ.*

Moon, s. *spogma-ī.* (new-) *myāsht.* (-less)

worogma-ī. (-light) *spogma-ī, rabawra.* (-stroke) *bar.* (-struck) *bar·wahalai.*

Moor, s. *habshī, zangī.* (marsh) *jaba.*

Moor, v.a. *langar āchawul, lagawul, taṛal.*

Mope, v.n. *ghamedāl, nūledal* ; *malāl kedal.*

Mopish, a. *gham·jan, nūl·jan, malāl.*

Moral, a. *pāk, pākīzah, nekokār.* s. *naṣīhat, pand* ; *hāṣil, gharaẓ.*

Morality, s. *nekī, nekokārī, rikkhtīn·tob.*

Moralize, v.a. *pand wayal, naṣīhat wayal.*

Morals, s. *nek·chalan, nekokārī, sīrat.*

Morally, ad. *pa haqq, pa rikkhtiyā.*

Morass, s. *jaba, bokkhtana, taramna, yala.*

Morbid, a. *kharāb, wrān* ; *nā·joṛ, nā·rogh.*

More, a. *ziyāt, nor.* (-and more) *nor ziyāt.* (-or less) *la·ag ziyāt.*

Moreover, ad. *bal, balki, wale, nor, siwā la de na.*

Morning, s. *sahr* or *sahār.* (-star) *starga.* (to-morrow-) *ṣabā* or *ṣubha.*

Morose, a. *sūṭ·būṭ, bad·khoe, triw·makh, tursh·rūe, bakhīl.*

Morrow, s. *ṣabā, ṣubha.* (day after-) *bul· ṣabā.*

Morsel, s. *nwaṛa-ī, gola* ; *pitsānṛai, pūṭai.*

Mortal, a. *fānī, tlūnai, teredūnai.* (human) *insānī, bashārī, wagaṛai.* (deadly) *qātil, kārī, halākil.*

Mortal, s. *saṛai, wagaṛai, gawai, insān, bashar.*

Mortality, s. *ajul, marg, maut* ; *saṛī·tob, bashriyat, insāniyat.*

Mortar, s. *baghara-ī.* (cement) *kūnai, gach.*

Mortgage, v.a. *gāwra-, graw-,* etc. *k.*

Mortification, s. *gazak, skhā·wālai* ; *randẓ, da zṛah nūl, paskhāk.*

Mortify, v.n. *gazak-, skhū-,* etc. *ked., wrost· edal.* v.a. *karawul, sedzal, āzārawul.*

Mosque, s. *jumā'at, masjid.*

Moss, s. *da wano waran khwar* ; *babar wākkhah chi da wano pa poṭ bānde ṭūkegī.*

Most, a. *akṣar, ziyāt, nihāyat.*

Mostly, ad. *akṣar, ziyātī, aghlab, ghāliban.*
Mote, s. *khas, khasanṛai, khāsha.*
Moth, s. *or-pukkht, patang; da zaṛūko chinjai.*
Mother, s. *mor, aba-ī, ada-ī.* (-in-law) *khwākkha.* (grand-) *nyā, anā.* (great grand-) *warla·anā, da nyā mor.* (great great grand-) *lā·warla·anā, da nyā nyā.* (step-) *ba-an·mor, maira·mor.* (-less) *yasīr, be·mor, mor·muṛai.* (-of pearl) *sīpa-ī.*
Motion, s. *ḥarakat, khwadzedana.*
Motive, s. *sabab, bā'iṣ, maṭlab, mūjib, kabl.*
Motley, a. *brag, gag, chrag·brag, brag·yālai; gad·wad; rangīn.*
Motto, s. *'alāma, nakkha.*
Mould, s. *qālib, kālbūt, sāncha.* (mildew) *zang, chanṛāsha.* (earth) *khāwra.* (manure) *sara.*
Mould, v.a. *joṛawul, tanḍal, ṣūrat-, ḍaul-,* etc. *waṛkawul.*
Moulder, v.n. *sharhedal, wrostedal, khāwre ked.*
Mouldy, a. *zang·jan, chanṛeshan.*
Moult, v.a. *kurīz k., rajawul.* v.n. *rajedal.*
Mound, s. *ḍera·ī, ghunḍa-ī, potai, kha-aṭ, rāsha, rashaka, tall.*
Mount, v.n. *khatal.* (-upon) *sparedal.* v.a. *khejawul.* (-a jewel) *jaṛāo k.*
Mountain, s. *ghar, koh.* (-ridge) *ghākkhai, kamar.* a. *ghartsanai, kohistānī.* (-goat) s. *ghartsah.*
Mountaineer, s. *kohistānai, rohilai, ghartsanai.*
Mountainous, a. *ghartsan, kohistān.*
Mourn, v.a. *jaṛal, wīr k., wainā wayal.* v.n. *kaṛedal, nūledal, ghamedal.*
Mourner, s. *wīr·jalai, gham·khor.*
Mournful, a. *wīr·nāk, gham·nāk.*
Mourning, s. *wīr, jaṛā; gham, nūl; wainā wayana.*
Mouse, s. *magakūṛai.* (-hole) *sūṛa.*
Mouth, s. *khula.* (small-) *khulga-ī.*
Mouthful, s. *nwaṛa-i, maṛa-ī, gola.*
Move, v.a. *khwadzawul.* v.n. *khwadzedal.*
Movement, s. *ḥarakat, khwadzedana.*
Mow, v.a. *lau k., rawdal, rebal.*
Mower, s. *lau·garai.*
Much, a. *ḍer, prewān.* s. *prewānī, ḍer·wālai.* (how-) *tsomrc.* (so-) *hombra.* (so much so) *tar daghah pore.*
Mucilage, s. *chīṛ, salekkh, leṭa-ī, l'uāb.*
Mucilaginous, a. *salekkh·nāk, laha·jan, l'uāb·dār, chīṛan.*
Mucus, s. *laha, l'uāb.* (-of nose) *kaṛmeza, kanṛ, khaṛmat, gṛang.* (-of bowels) *rama, ṛap.* (-of urethra, etc) *maza-ī.*
Muck, s. *sara, ḍerān, khīrai, rash.*
Mud, s. *lāha, khaṭa, chīkaṛ.* (-for building) *paskha.*
Muddy, a. *khaṭolan, kha-aṛ, chikṛan.*
Muffle, v.a. *nghaṛal—nghakkhtal, puṭawul, pokkhal.*
Mug, s. *piyāla, kanḍoloṭai.*
Mulberry, s. *tūt.* (royal-) *shāh·tūt.* (seedless-) *be·dāna tūt.* (black-) *tor·tūt.* (white-) *spīn·tūṭ.* (grey-) *bor·tūt.*
Mulct, v.a. *tāwān-, nāgha-,* etc. *ākhistal.*
Mule, s. *khachar* or *kachar, qātar.*
Multiform, a. *rangā·rang.*
Multiplication, s. *bragh, ẓarb, joṛ.*
Multiplicity, s. *prewānī, ḍer·wālai, ziyāt·wālai.*
Multiply, v.a. *ẓarb-, bragh-,* etc. *k., ḥisāb·joṛawul.* (increase) v.a. *ziyātawul, wadānawul, ḍerawul.* v.n. *ziyātedal, wadānedal, ḍeredal.*
Multitude, s. *lakkhkar, pauz* or *fauj, ḍala, ganṛ khalq* or *-'ālam.*
Mumble, v.a. *baṛ·baṛ-, pus·pus-, gūn·gūn*, etc. *k.*
Mummy, s. *momiyāe.*
Munch, v.a. *kṛapawul, jowul* or *joyal, chīchal.*
Mundane, a. *duniyā·ī.*

Munificence, s. *sakhī-tob, sakhāwat, bakkhan-tob.*

Munificent, a. *sakhī, sakhāwatī, bakkhana kawūnkai.*

Murder, s. *marg, khūn, qatl.* (price of-) *diyat.* v.a. *khūn-*, etc. *k.*, *muṛ k.*, *waĵal* or *waĵlal.*

Murderer, s. *khūnī, qātil, marg kawūnkai.*

Murderous, a. *khūn-khwār, khūnāṛai.*

Murky, a. *tor, dund, tīrah, gard-ĵan.*

Murmur, v.a. *baṛ-baṛ-, ṭar-ṭar-*, etc. *k.* (complain) *māna-, gila-*, etc. *k.* (-as a brook) *juṛ-juṛ k.* (-as the belly) *quṛ-quṛ k.* s. (-of conversation) *gungosai, pus-pus, zwag-zwūg, kkhkālwa.*

Murrain, s. *ṭak, ṭak-sarai.*

Muscle, s. *ghwakkha, līnda-ī.*

Muscular, a. *ghwakkha-war, gagar, mazai. khṛīs.*

Muse, v.a. *fikr k.* v.n. *fikr-man ked.*

Museum, s. *'ajā-ib-khāna.*

Mushroom, s. *kha-areṛai, gūmāndū, samā-rūgh.*

Music, s. *sarod, zamzama, tarāna.*

Musical, a. *sarodī, khūsh-āwāz.*

Musician, s. *sarod-gar, muṭrib, ḍum, mīrāṣī.*

Musk, s. *mukkhk.* (-pod) *mush-kunḍa-ī.* (-rat) *mukkhkai mayak. mukkhkīn mayak.*

Musket, s. *ṭopak, bandūkh.*

Muslin, s. *malmal.*

Must, v. imp. *boya chi, zarūr* or *lāzim dai chi.* (he must do it) *boya chi wu e kawī* or *kī.* Must is also expressed by using the past participle of the verb with *boya.* Ex. (it must be done) *kaṛalai boya.* Or it is expressed by using the infinitive alone with the third person singular present tense, of the auxiliary *yam.* Ex. (we must go) *mūnga ta tlal dai.*

Mustard, s. *sharsham.* (wild-) *awrai.* (-tops) *ghandal.* (-seed) *mandaw.* (-threshed stalks) *kāmbūra.*

Muster, v.a. *shmeral, shmāral, sān nīwul.*

Musty, a. *wr ?t, skhā*; *chanreshan.*

Mutable, a. *nā pāe-dār, be-qalār.*

Mute, a. *gung, lal*; *chip, ghalai.*

Mutilate, v.a. *mātawul, prekawul, kharāb k.*; *ĵobalawul, ghwutsawul, kaṛam k.*

Mutineer, s. *yāghī-gar, pasātī.*

Mutinous, a. *yāghī, sar-kakkh.*

Mutiny, s. *yāghī-garī, balwā, pasāt.*

Mutter, v.a. *baṛ-baṛ-, ṭar-ṭar-, pus-pus-*, etc. *k.*

Mutton, s. *da ga-ade ghwakkha.* (shoulder of-) *walai.* (leg of-) *patūn.*

Mutual, a. *da dwāṛo palo* or *-lorīo* or *-khwāo*; *ṭarafain, jānibain.*

Mutually, ad. *yo bul sara, dzabla.*

Muzzle, s. *poza, ūrbūz, tambeza.* (-for the mouth) *tambūzak, tambezai, korai.* v.a. *khula bandawul, tambūzak*, etc. *taṛal* or *-lagawul.*

Myriad, s. *las zara*; *tūmān.*

Myself, pr. *zah khpul, khpul-dzān.*

Mysterious, a. *puṭ, nā-m'alūm, ghā-ib.*

Mystery, s. *ghā-ib, puṭa-khabara.*

N.

Nail, s. *mekh, mogai.* (-of finger, etc.) *nūk.*

Nail, v.a. *ṭakawul.* (pay cash) *rok warkawul.*

Naked, a. *barbanḍ* or *barmanḍ, lūts.* (stark-) *lūts-pūts, lūts-lapaṛ, lūts-laghaṛ.*

Nakedness, s. *barbanḍ-tob, laghaṛ-tob, lūts-wālai.*

Name, s. *nūm, nām.* v.a. *nūm kegdal* or *kkhkegdal.* (mention) *nūm ākhistal, yāda-wul.*

Named, a. *nūmedah, nūmāndai.*

Namely, ad. *y'ane, maṣlan, ganre.*

Namesake, s. *hum·nām, pa nāmah sharīk.*
Nap, s. *ṭūk.* (sleep) *khob, parnā, churt.*
Nap, v.a. *khob-, parnā-,* etc. *wṛal.* v.n. *khob zangedal.*
Nape, s. *tsaṭ; waja.*
Napkin, s. *rūe·māl, dast·māl.*
Narration, a. *bayān; qiṣṣa, rawāyat, naql.*
Narrator, s. *nāqil, qiṣṣa kawūnkai.*
Narrow, a. *tang.* v.a. *tangawul.* v.n. *tangedal.*
Narrowly, ad. *pa sakhtī sara; pa fikr sara.*
Narrowness, s. *tang·wālai; tangsiyā; bakhīl·tob.*
Nasty, a. *nā·kārah, makrūh, kagalai; nā·pāk, palīt, khīran, murdār.*
Nation, s. *qām, ulūs, tabār, firqa.*
National, a. *qāmī; waṭan·dost.*
Native, a. *aṣlī, ẕātī; waṭanī, mulkī, wilāyatī.* s. *waṭanī, wilāyatī, balad.* (-country) *waṭan, wilāyat.*
Nativity, s. *paidā-ikkht, zegedah.*
Natural, a. *ẕātī, ṭab'a-ī.* (-son) *ḥarāmī.*
Naturalize, v.a. *khpulawul, sharīk k.*
Naturally, ad. *pa·khpula.*
Nature, s. *khoe, khaṣlat, lokkhai, mizāj, ṭab'a, ṭabī'at.* (world) *naṛa-ī, duniyā, 'ālam.*
Naught, s. *hets.*
Naughty, a. *bad, kharāb, nā·kārah.*
Nausea, s. *mīkkh·mīkkhai, kaha, koe, bāka-ī, kraka, kūz·kātah.*
Nauseate, v.a. *chinjawul, kūz katal* or *-goral.* v.n. *chinjedal, mīkkh·mīkkh ked.*
Nauseous, a. *chinjan, kraka·nāk, bad·khwand.*
Naval, ad. *jahāzī, dariyābī.*
Navel, s. *nū* or *nūm.*
Navigate, v.a. *jahāz chalawul.*
Nay, ad. *nah, yah, āyā.*
Near, a. *nijdai.*
Nearness, s *nijdekī,*
Neat, a. *pākīzah* or *pāzīkah, sādah, spetsalai.*
Neatness, s. *pākīzagī, spetsal·tob, joṛāb.*

Necessarily, ad. *kkhā-ī, boya, khwāh·ma-khwāh.*
Necessary, a. *lāzim, ẓarūr, bāedah, wājib.* (it is-) *boya chi, lāzim dai.* s. *chār·choba.* (to go to the-) *awdas k.*
Necessitous, a. *ḥājat·man, muḥtāj, darmāndah.*
Necessity, s. *ḥājat, ẓarūrat.*
Neck, s. *mara-ī, ghāṛa, markanḍa-ī.* (nape) *ormeg.*
Necklace, s. *amel, kār, psol.* (-ring) *oga-ī.*
Necromancer, s. *siḥr·gar, koḍ·gar, jādū·gar.*
Necromancy, s. *siḥr, koḍa, jādū.*
Nectar, s. *āb da ḥayāt, da kawṣar oba.*
Need, s. *ḥājat, ghokkht, ẓarūrat.* v.a. *ḥājat-,* etc. *laral, ghokkhtal.*
Needful, a. *ḥājat·man; lāzim, ẓarūr, pa·kār.*
Needle, s. *stan.* (eye of-) *swam* or *spam.* (packing-) *sparkhai.* (knitting-) *dūk, sīmak.* (-work) *ganḍal, skoe.*
Needless, a. *'abaṣ, be·fā-ida, nā pakār, be·kkhai.*
Needy, a. *muḥtāj, ḥājat·man.*
Nefarious, a. *bad, nā·kārah, nakkhanai.*
Negative, a. *nahī, nafī.* v.a. *man'a-, nahiya-,* etc. *k.*
Neglect s. *ghaflat, be·fikrī, be·khabarī, be·parwā-ī.*
Negligent. a. *ghāfil, be·khabar, be·parwā.*
Negotiate, v.a. *sawāl·dzawāb-, m'amala-, jirga-, kār·rozgār-, khabara-,* etc. *k.*
Negotiator, s. *dallāl, rebār, mandz·garai.*
Negro, s. *ḥabshī, zangī.*
Neigh, s. *shashnrai, hanr.* v.n. *shashnredal, hanredal.*
Neighbour, s. *gāwanḍai, hamsāyah.*
Neighbourhood, s. *gāwanḍ, cham.*
Neither, c. *na yo na bul.*
Nephew, s. (sister's son) *khora-e.* (brother's son) *wrārah.* (clansman's son) *'azīz.*
Nerve, s. *pla, rag, wuja; himmat, zṛah, quwat.*

Nerveless, a. *be·himmat, be·zṛah, nā·mard.*
Nervous, a. *yer·man, harānd, yeredūnkai.*
Nest, s. *jāla, āshiyānc.*
Net, s. (fish-) *jāla.* (bird-) *jāl.* (-for hay, etc.) *trangaṛ, korai, lad, shalīta.*
Nether, a. *lar, lāndai, kūz.*
Nettle, v.a. *pārarul, ṭongawul, khapah k.* s. *jalbang.* (-rash) *laṛama.*
Never, ad. *hechare, haḍo, kets·kala, la·sara.*
Nevertheless, ad. *walekin, magar, sara la de.*
Neuter, a. *hijrai.* (-verb) *lāzimī.*
Neutral, a. *biyal, judā.*
New, a. *nawai, tāzah, osanai.* (-cloth) *kora, shaḍala, batī ḍaka.*
News, s. *khabar.* (good-) *zerai, sār.* (-paper) *akhbār.*
Next, a. *nijdai.* (the-) *bul.* (-time) *biyā.*
Nib, s. *tsūka, peza.* (beak) *makkhūka.*
Nibble, v.a. *chīchal.*
Nice, a. *khwand·nāk, maza-dār.* (accurate) *jukht, barābar, joṛ.* (fine) *narai, bārīk.* (delicate) *nāzuk.*
Nicely, ad. *pa maze sara, pa kkhah shān sara.*
Niche, s. *ṭāq, tāqcha, darai, rap.*
Nick, s. *barghanḍ, jghanḍ, kandaw.* (-of time) *ṭāng, neṭa, puk, mūda.*
Nickname, s. *laqab.*
Niece, s. (brother's daughter) *wrera.* (sister's daughter) *khordza.* (clanswoman's daughter) *khor·lanṛa.*
Niggard, a. *bakhīl, shūm, tang·dast.*
Nigh, a. *nijde, tsakha* or *khatsa.*
Night, s. *shpa.* (all-) *kara-ī·shpa.* (last-) *begāh, barāyah, begana-ī-, parūna-ī-, barana-ī-*, etc. *shpa.* (to-) *nan·shpa, mākkhām, begāh.* (dark-) *tora·shpa, torogma-ī.* (moonlight-) *spogma-ī, ranrā·shpa.* (-blind) a. *sho·kor* or *sham·kor.* (-blindness) *sham·kor·tiyā.* (-attack) *sho·khūn.* (-watching) *sho·gīrī.*
Nightingale, s. *bulbul, kastūra.*

Nightmare, s. *khapasa* or *khapaskai, rawai.*
Nimble, a. *gaṛandai, chust, chālāk, tak·lāstai, jalt, tez, zghard.*
Nine, a. *nuh.* (ninth) *nuham.* (-fold) *nuh·bragh, nuh·chand.*
Nineteen, a. *nuh·las.* (nineteenth) *nuh·lasam.*
Ninety, a. *nawe.* (ninetieth) *nawiyam.*
Nip, v.a. *shūkawul.* (pinch) *skūnḍal.* (-with cold) *sedzal, wahal.*
Nippers, s. *ambūr, nūtsai.*
Nipple, s. *tai.*
Nitre, s. *kkhora.* (nitrous) a. *kkhoran.*
No, ad. *na, yah, āyā.* (-one) *hets·tsok.*
Nobility, s. *amīr·tob, sāwū·tob, sharāfat.*
Noble, a. *aṣīl, sāwū, ashrāf; loe, ghaṭ, zbarg.* s. *amīr, arbāb, khān.*
Nobly, a. *amīr·shān.*
Nobody, s. *hets tsok, hets kas; nā·tsīz, nā·kas, lā shai.*
Nocturnal, a. *da shpe.* (-pollution) *shaiṭān khaṭā.*
Nod, v.a. *sar ṭīṭawul.* v.n. *khob zangedal.*
Node, s. *pāṛsob, stagh, ghunḍārai, margharai.*
Noise, s. *ghag, zwag, ghāw, shor, chagh, bāng*, etc. (to make a-) *ghagawul, chaghawul, zwag-*, etc. *k.* v.n. *ghagedal, chaghedal.*
Noisome, a. *kagalai, gandah, kraka·nāk, bad.*
Noisy, a. *shor·mār, ghag·mār, shor·pusht, ghāw·nāk, zwag·nāk.*
Nominal, a. *khiyālī, nāmī.*
Nominate, v.a. *muqarrar k., wudrawul, kkhkenawul; nūm ākhistal* or *-kkhayal—kkhowul.*
Nomination, s. *muqarrar kawuna, wudrawuna.*
None, a. *hets.*
Nonexistence, s. *nisht·wālai, nestī.*
Nonexistent, a. *nishtah, nest.*
Nonplus, v.a. *hariyānawul, rabṛawul lā·dzawāb-, lā·chār-, band-*, etc. *k.*

Nonsense, s. *wucha·pucha-, be·hūda-, dūza-,* etc.*-khabara, qatāra, shkhara, kitī·pītī,* etc.

Nonsuit, v.a. *bāelawul, pa-aṛ k.*

Nook, s. *gūṭ, gokkha.*

Noon, s. *gharma, ṭakaṇra·* or *ṭakanda·gharma.*

Noose, s. *pulwākkha, gharwandai, gharāsha, pakhwandai, kamand, zanda-ī.* (-of hair) *lūma, lūmaka.*

Nor, c. *na.* (nor one nor the other) *na yo na bul.*

North, s. *shamāl, quṭb, kkhai ṭaraf.* (-star) *quṭb storai.*

Northward, a. *quṭb khwā* or *-lorai* or *-dada,* etc.

Nose, s. *poza.* (-bag) *tobra.*

Nosegay, s. *gul·dasta.*

Nostril, s. *spegma, spenga.*

Not, ad. *na.* imp. *ma.* (-at all) *la sara, hado.*

Notable, a. *mashhūr, nūm·war* ; *lā-iq da yād.*

Notch, s. *barghand, jghand, wut.*

Note, s. *nakkha, 'alāmat.* (letter) *khaṭṭ, chīṭa-ī.* (bond) *hujjat, tamassuh.* (voice) *tarāna, bāng, āwāz.* (musical-) *zīr, trang, wazn.* (memo.) *yād·dāsht.* (marginal-) *hāshiya.*

Note, v.a. *qiyās-, fikr-, ghaur-,* etc. *k.* (write) *līkal, kāgal—kkhkal, darj k.* (look) *katal, goral, lidal, nazar k:*

Noted, a. *mashhūr, nūm·war, nām·dār.*

Nothing, s. *hets, hets shai* ; *nā·tsīz.*

Notice, s. *nazar, lihāz, mulāhiza* ; *khabar, iṭṭilā'a, jār.* v.a. *nazar-,* etc. *k.*

Notify, v.a. *khabarawul, jār wahal.*

Notion, s. *khiyāl, gumān, fikr, wahm.*

Notoriety, s. *zwag, shuhrat, āwāza.*

Notorious, a. *mashhūr, m'alūm, tsargand.*

Notwithstanding, c. *walekīn, magar, sara la de, har tsomra, bā·wujūd.*

Noun, s. *ism, nūm.*

Nourish, v.a. *sātal, pālal, nmāndzal, parwaral.*

Nourisher, s. *pālūnkai, sātūnkai,* etc.

Nourishing, s. *pālana, sātana.* a. *quwat·nāk.*

Nourishment, s. *parwarish, pālana* ; *khwurāk.*

Novel, a. *nawai.* s. *qiṣṣa, naql.*

November, s. *magar.*

Novice, s. *shāgird, nawai āmokhtah, kachah.*

Now, ad. *os, dā sā'at.* (-adays) *nan·wradzi.*

Nowhere, ad. *hets·charta, hets·dzāe.*

Nowise, ad. *hets·shān, hets·rang.*

Noxious, a. *ziyānī, nuqṣānī, tāwānī, mozī, muzirr.*

Nudity, s. *barband·tob, lūts·wālai.*

Nugatory, s. *'abas, nā kārah, lā hāṣil, be·fā-ida.*

Nuisance, s. *wabāl, mozī, muzirr.*

Null, a. *'abas, bāṭil, spuk, khushat.*

Numb, a. *ūdah, be·hiss.* (with cold) *qarqechan, marghechan.*

Number, s. *shumār* or *shmer, hisāb, 'adad.* v.a. *shmeral* or *shmāral, hisāb k.*

Numberless, a. *be·shumār, be·hisāb.*

Numeration, s. *shumār* or *shmer, hisāb.*

Numerous, a. *der, gaṇr, frewān, wadān.*

Nuptial, a. *nikāhī.* (-ceremony) *wādah.* (-knot) *nikāh.* (-song) *kkhādiyāna.* (-feast) *kkhādī.*

Nurse, s. *dā-ī.* v.a. *pālal, tai warkawul.*

Nurture, s. *parwarish, pālana.* v.a. *pālal, parwaral.*

Nut, s. *jawz.* (Nutmeg) *jauza.*

Nutriment, } s. *khwurāk, khwāṛah, ghizā,*
Nutrition, } *parwarish.*

Nutritious, a. *quwat·nāk, quwat bakkhūnkai.*

Nymph. s. *hūra, parī.*

O.

O (sign of vocative), *o, wo, ai, yā.* in. *āh, e, eh, he, hāe.* (in pain) *wāe, wā-ī.*

Oak, s. *balūṭ.* (-apple) *māzū.*

Oakum, s. *saṇr, paṭ.*

Oar, s. *chapa.*

Oath, s. *qasam, saugand, ḥalaf.*

Obdurate, a. *sakht, be-dard, be-raḥm; ṭakanrai, hoḍai. khpul-sar, sar-kakkh.*

Obedient, a. *farmān-wrūnkai, ḥukm-manūnkai, tābi'a-dār.*

Obeisance, s. *salām, ādāb; sijda.*

Obelisk, s. *munāra, tsalai, stan; khaza* or *khāda.*

Obese, a. *peraṛ, tsorb, ghaṭ, punḍ, lwāṛ, peṛ.*

Obey, v.a. *manal, ḥukm pa-dzāe rāwṛal, tābi'a-dārī k.*

Object, s. *shai, tsīz; gharaz̤, niyat, maṭlab.*

Object, v.a. *'uzr-, takrār-, ḥujjat-,* etc. *k.; daregh k.*

Objection, s. *'uzr, ḥujjat, takrār; daregh.*

Oblation, s. *qurbān, ṣadqa, dzār; naz̤r, niyāz.*

Obligation, s. *farz̤, sharṭ, wājib; neṭa, wāda, taṛa, bandanr, lafz̤, qaul; minnat, khāṭir-dārī.*

Oblige, v.a. *minnat-dār-, khāṭir-dār-,* etc. *k.* (force) *zoral, be-was k.*

Obliged, a. *minnat-dār, iḥsān-man.*

Obliging, a. *khāṭir-dār, makhawar, mihrbān.*

Oblique, a. *tratskan, kog, kṛīng.*

Obliterate, v.a. *wrānawul, wrukawul, wahal.*

Oblivion, s. *her-wālai, nisiyān.*

Oblivious, a. *her-man, be-fikr, nisiyān-kawūnkai.*

Oblong, a. *ūgd.*

Obloquy, s. *peghor, tuhmat, tor, malāmat.*

Obnoxious, a. *moz̤ī, muz̤irr, be-kkhai.* (liable) *shwūnkai, lāndai, maghlūb.*

Obscene, a. *pūch, palīt, murdār, pūhaṛ, nā-pāk.*

Obscure, a. *tor, tīrah; dund, kha-aṛ, gard-man, gard-jan; puṭ, nā m'alūm; kam z̤āt* or *-aṣl,* or *-nogai,* etc.

Obscurity, s. *tyāra, tor-tam, z̤ulmat.*

Obsequies, s. *fātiḥa* or *pātā, lās-nīwah, d'uā.*

Obsequious, a. *khūshāmad-gar, ḍirpalai, jig-jigiyā.*

Observance, s. *makh, adab, khidmat: 'amal; ist'imāl; dastūr, rasm, ṭarīqa.*

Observation, s. *naz̤ar, mulāḥiz̤a; līdah, kātah; khabara, wayai.*

Observe, v.a. *katal, goral, līdal, naz̤ar k.; manal; wayal, khabara k.*

Obsolete, a. *ghair ist 'imāl, -chalan, -riwāj,* etc. *mansūkh, band, bāṭil.*

Obstacle, s. *aṛ, band, nkkhatai, kariyāb.*

Obstinate, a. *sar-kakkh, khpul-sar, hoḍai, haṭai.*

Obstreperous, a. *jang-yālai, shorī, takanrai, pasātī.*

Obstruct, v.a. *haṭālawul, kariyābawul, nkkhla wul, bandawul, man'a k.*

Obstruction, s. *aṛ, band, nkkhatai.*

Obtain, v.a. *mūndal, gaṭal, biyā-mūndal.* v.n. *jārī ked.; chaledal, lagedal.*

Obtrude, v.a. *dūsa k.* v.n. *be-dzāe nanawatal, -rāghlal, -prewatal,* etc.

Obtuse, s. *pa-ats* or *p-uts.* (stupid) *pūhaṛ, kawdan.* (not pointed) *lwāṛ, ghaṭ.*

Obviate, v.a. *girzawul, man'a k., lār nīwul.*

Obvious, a. *tsargand, kkhkārah, z̤āhir, bartser.*

Occasion, s. *heṛ, plā, dzal, guz̤ār; nobat, neṭa, mūda, wakht.* (cause) *bā'iṣ, sabab.* (need) *pa-kār, z̤arūr, gharaz̤.*

Occasion, v.a. *paidā k., rāwṛal, khejawul, kawul, kṛal.*

Occasionally, ad. *kala-kala, kala-nā-kala.*

Occupation, s. *kār, kasb, mashghulā, chār.*

Occupy, v.a. *mashghūlawul, lagawul, dzāyawul; dzāe nīwul, ākhistal, lānde k.; 'amal k.*

Occur, v.n. *kedal, prewatal, nāziledal, wāqi'a ked.* (-to the mind) *yādedal.*

Occurrence, s. *wāqi'a, ḥal, ḥādiṣa, ittifāq.*

Ocean, s. *baḥr, qālī-* or *qārī dariyāb.*

Ochre, s. *ziyaṛa-khāwra.* (red-) *bagwa, sara-khāwra.*

October, s. *kātah.*

Odd, a. *'ajab, 'ajīb.* (not even) *tāk* or *ṭāq.* (-and even) *tāk·o·juft.*

Odds, s. *farq, biyal·tūn, biyal·wālai, tafāwat.* (strife) *patna, steza.* (gain) *zor, aghlab.* (-and ends) *balāe·batar.*

Ode, s. *ghazal, landa-ī, sandara, chār·bait.*

Odious, a. *makrūh, kagalai, ghāndah, kharāb, nā·khwakkh, nā·pasand, khwā·bad.*

Odium, s. *malāmat, peghor, tor, tuhmat*; *kīna, badī, khwā·badī.*

Odoriferous, a. *khūsh·bū-ī·dār, bū-ī·nāk.*

Odour, s. *bū-ī, bo* or *boe.* (sweet-) *khūsh·bū-ī* or *khūsh·boe.*

Œsophagus, s. *sara·ghāṛa, ḥalq.*

Of, p. *da.* (on account-) *dapāra da.*

Off, ad. *lire* or *liri.* (-hand) *sam da lāsa.* (to go-, come-, etc.) v.n. *lire ked.* (to go off, as a gun, etc.) v.n. *khalāṣedal, chaledal.* (well-) a. *mor.* (-and on) ad. *kkhkata·porta.*

Offal, s. *ūjarai, larai*; *murdār*; *jūṭa, pas·khurda.*

Offence, s. *gunāh, taqṣīr, wabāl.* (pique) *mānrai, marawar·tiyā*; *randz, khapagī.*

Offend, v.a. *gunāh-*, etc. *k.*, *marawar-*, etc. *k.*, *khapah-*, etc. *k.*

Offended, a. *marawar, khapah, bezār.*

Offender, s. *gunāh·gār, taqṣīrī.*

Offensive, a. *bad, nā·pasand, kharāb*; *mozī, muẓirr.*

Offer, v.a. *warkawul.* (sacrifice) *qurbān-, ṣadqa-*, etc. *k.* (devote) *nazr-, niyāz-*, etc. *gdal* or *īgdal.* (present) *nazrāna-, pekkh·kakkh-*, etc. *warkawul.* (attempt) *qaṣd-, niyat-*, etc. *k.* (propose) *wayal, pukkkhtedal.*

Offering, s. *qurbān, ṣadqa, dzār*; *nazr, niyāz.*

Office, s. *kār, khidmat*; *dzāe, 'uhda, manṣab.* (-room) *daftar·khāna.* (good-) *sulūk, mrasta.* (bad-) *bad·sulūk, badī.*

Officer, s. *sardār, 'uhda·dār, manṣab·dār.*

Official, a. *sarkārī, khidmatī.*

Officiate, v.a. *khidmat k., nā-ib·garī-, qā-im·muqāmī-*, etc. *k.*

Officious, a. *harbaṛai, 'alwalai*; *khidmatī.*

Offspring, s. *alwād, zāwzād, farzand, tūng.*

Often, ad. *wār·wār, bār·bār, ḍer·dzala.*

Ogle, v.a. *zarana-ī-, dzīr-*, etc. *k.*, *pa·zarana-ī katal, starge wahal, pa·trats katal.*

Oh, in. *āh! eh! he! hāe! wāe! wāh!*

Oil, s. *tel.* (-man) *telai.* (-press) *gānra-ī.* (-cake) *kal.* (-jar) *daba.* (hair-) *pulel* or *fulel.*

Oily, a. *ghwaṛ, tel·jan.*

Ointment, s. *malham, paha, tab.*

Old, a. *zoṛ, kuhand.* (-man) *spīn·gīrai, būḍā.* (-woman) *spīn·sara, būḍa-ī.* (-age) *zoṛ·tiyā, zoṛ·wālai.*

Olive, s. *kkhona* or *kkhawana, zaitūna.*

Omelet, s. *khāgīna.*

Omen, s. *pāl.* (good-) *akhtar.*

Ominous, a. *bad·pāl, bad·shugun.*

Omission, s. *khaṭā, quṣūr, ter·wātah.*

Omit, v.a. *terawul, herawul, pregdal.*

Omnipotent, a. *qādir, kirdigār.*

Omnipresent, a. *ḥāẓir·o·nāẓir, har dzāe.*

On, p. *pa, bānde, pre, par, da bānde, da pāsa, pre·bānde.* (in front) *wrānde, makh·kkhke.*

Once, ad. *yo dzal, -heṛ, -wār, -guzār*, etc., *yawa·plā.* (-before) *pakhwā, wrānde.* (at-) *os, pa ṭakī, pa de sā'at.* (all at-) *yak·lakhta, nātsāpa, tsaṭ·waṭ.*

One, a. *yo.* (in comp.) *yak.* (every-) *har·yo.*

Oneness, s. *yo·wālai, yaktā-ī.*

One's-self, pr. *dzān, khpul·dzān*; *nafs.*

Onerous, a. *drūnd, grān, mushkil, sakht.*

Onion, s. *piyāz.*

Only, ad. *sirp* or *surup, faqaṭ, khālī, ta-ash.* a. *yawādzai, tsaṛah, biyal.*

Onset, s. *halla, tsot, guzār, brīd.*

Onward, ad. *wrānde, makh·kkhke.*

Ooze, v.n. *tsātsedal, watal.* s. *lāha, khaṭa.* (green-) *ūbṛa-ī.* (moisture) *zyam, naw.*

Opaque, a. ***dund,*** *kha-aṛ, ganr, gūr.*

Open, a. *prānatai, wāz, arat.* (clear) *ṣāf, spīn.* (apparent) *tsargand, kkhkārah.* (-as a door) *lire* or *liri.*

Open, v.a. *prānatal, aratawul.* (undo) *spaṛdal.* (spread-) *khwarawul, ghwarawul.* (-as a flower) v.n. *khwaredal, ghwaredal.* (as a door) v.a. *lire k.*

Opening, s. *prānatana*; *spaṛakkhtana*; *khwaredana,* etc. (orifice) *khula, sūṛa.*

Openly, ad. *pa tsargand, pa jār* or *-ẓāhir.*

Openness, s. *arat·wālai*; *tsargand·tob.*

Operate, v.a. *kār-, 'amal-, pāzah-, aṣar-,* etc. *k.*

Operator, s. *kār·kawūnkai, fā'il*; *kār·guẕār.*

Opinion, s. *fikr, rāe, tadbīr, khiyāl, gumān, qiyās.*

Opiniative, a. *khpul·rāe, khpul·sar, kibr·ĵan.*

Opium, s. *apīm, afiyūn, tiriyāq.*

Opponent, s. *mudda'ī, mukhālif, ẓidd*; *dukkhman.*

Opportune, a. *munāsib, jukht, pa·dzāe, pa·wakht.*

Opportunity, s. *wakht, ṭāng, neṭa, nobat, sā'at, puk.*

Oppose, v.a. ***man'a*** *k., haṭālawul, bandawul, lār nīwul, jangawul, muqābala k.* v.n. *makhā·makh-,* etc. *ked., jangedal.*

Opposite, a. *makhā·makh, wṛāndai*; *mukhālif, aks.*

Opposition, s. *ẓidd, hoḍ*; *jang, dukkhmanī, badī.*

Oppress, v.a. *zoral, ẓulm-, jafā-,* etc. *k., āzārawul.*

Oppression, s. *ẓulm, jafā, dzaur, zorāwarī, zabardastī, zor, ziyātī.*

Oppressor, s. *ẓālim, jafā·kār, zorāwar.*

Opprobrious, a. *bad, nā·kārah, bad·namūs, ruswā-ī.*

Option, s. *wuk, ikhtiyār, khwakkh, pasand, raẓā.*

Opulent, a. ***daulat·man,*** *māl·dār,* ***duniyā·dār.***

Or, c. *yā.* (-else) *ki·na, kanra*; *ganre.*

Orach, s. *sārma.*

Oracle, s. *kalām.* (person) *zbarg.*

Oral, a. *zabānī, wayai.*

Orange, s. *nāranj.* (colour) *sūr·bor.*

Oration, s. *w'aẓ, khabara, taqrīr.*

Orator, s. *w'aẓ kawūnkai, taqrīrī, sukhan·sāz.*

Orb, s. *tsarkh.* (-of sun, etc.) *kakoṛai, ṭakai, chakla-ī*; *qurṣ.*

Orbicular, a. *ghunḍ, ghunḍ·man.*

Orbit, s. *daur, daurān.*

Orchard, s. *bāgh.*

Ordain, v.a. *muqarrar k., wudrawul, farmāyal, wayal.*

Ordeal, s. *āzmekkht, imtiḥān.*

Order, s. *tartīb, tadbīr*; *ḥukm, farmā-ikkht, farmān, amr*; *qām, ẕāt, nog, rang*; *dastūr, ṭarīqa, rasm.* (in order that) *tso chi.*

Order, v.a. *farmāyal, ḥukm k.*

Orderly, a. *ārāstah, pa tartīb, pa qā'ida.*

Ordinance, s. *ḥukm, amr*; *shar'a, qānūn*; *sunnat*; *qā'ida, ā-īn.*

Ordinary, a. *'āmm, jārī, chalanī*; *spuk, halak.*

Ordnance, s, *top, top·khāna.*

Ordure, s. *ghul, murdār, khīra.*

Ore, s. *khāwra, kānrai.* (copper-) *da tāmbe kānrai.* (iron-) *da ospane khāwra.*

Organ, s. *ālat, 'aẓū.* (musical-) *bāja.*

Organize, v.a. *joṛawul, tarkīb k., tanḍal.*

Orifice, s. *khula, sūṛa.* (small-) *swam* or *spam.*

Origin, s. *aṣl, nogai, munḍ, wekh, būnsaṭ.*

Original, a. *aṣlī, awwal, nog.*

Originally, ad. *wṛūnbe, pa aṣl, pa awwal.*

Originate, v.a. *paidā-, jārī-,* etc. *k., chalawul, bāsal—yastal, kāgal—kkhkal.*

Ornament, s. *zewar, kālai, gānra* or *gahana*; *zeb, zīnat*; *andzor, kkhewa, singār.* (-for the head) *t'awīẓ, gul, dāṛa-ī, ṭīk.* (-for the ear) *lakkhta-ī, wāla-ī.* (-for the nose) *pezwān, natka-ī, chār·gul, pīsha-ī.* (-for the neck) *amel, ūga-ī, baḍa-ī.* (-for the arm) *kara, wakkhai, kanganr, bangrai, gūjra-ī, bāhū, ma-aṭkai.* (-for the feet) *pāekara, pakhwandai, pāenzeb.* (-for the finger) *tsalai, gūṭa, anrwat, shasht, ārsā-ī.*

Ornament, v.a. *joṛawul, andzorawul, dzān-, ḍaul-,* etc. *joṛawul, kkhewa-, singār-,* etc. *k.*

Orphan, s. *yatīm, yasīr, plār·muṛai, mor·muṛai.*

Orpiment, s. *hartāl, zarnīkh.*

Orthodox, a. *momin, sunnī, īmān·dāṛ, chār·yārī; sūchah, rikkhtīnai, rāst·man.*

Oscillate, v.n. *dzwarandedal, zangedal, ra-pedal.* v.a. *ṭāl khwuṛal* or *-wahal.*

Oscillation, s. *zangedana, ṭāl, zāngo.*

Ostensible, a. *tsargand, kkhkārah, jār* or *ẓāhir.*

Ostentation, s. *lāpa, dzān kkhkārah·kawūna, dzān stāyana.*

Ostentatious, a. *lāpai, ṭatai, dzān kkhkārah kawūnkai, dzān stāyūnkai* or *-stāyana kawūnkai.*

Ostler, s. *ṭeliyā, nokar, nafar.*

Other, pr. *nor, bul.* (-wise) ad. *·nor·shān, būl·shān; ka·na, ganra, kanra.*

Otter, s. *saglāo* or *sanglāo, sīndlāo.*

Ought, v. imp. *boya chi, kkhā-ī chī.*

Ounce, s. *nīma·chīṭāka-ī.*

Our, ours, pr. *dzamūnga* or *dzamūga.*

Ourselves, pr. *mūng·* or *mūg·khpul.*

Out, ad. *bāhir, warchane* or *wardzane.* (expelled) a. *sharaṛai.* (expended) a. *pūrah, tamām.* (extinguished) a. *muṛ, soṛ.* (get out!) in. *lire sha, biyarta sha.*

Outcast, s. *sharalai, sharūnai, pradai.*

Outer, a. *bāhir; pradai, begānah, oprah.*

Outlaw, s. *farārī ghal, yāghī·gar, sharūnai.*

Outlet, s. *khula, lār; warkh; ghwagai.*

Outline, s. *nakhkkha* or *naqsha, kīl, karkkha.*

Outlive, v.n. *pāedal, pātedal, bachedal.*

Outrage, s. *zor, ẓulm, ziyātī, jafā, be·satrī.*

Outright, ad. *sam da lāsa, tsaṭ·waṭ; amānī, pūrah, pāk·ṣāf.*

Outside, s. *bāhir, malh.* (without) p. *warchane* or *wardzane.* (on the-) p. *pās, dapāsa, bānde.*

Outstrip, v.a. *pa zghākkht-* or *pa daw-,* etc. *lānde k.,* or *-wrusto preẓdal.*

Outward, a. *bāhir, bartser, oprah.*

Outwardly, ad. *bartseran, pa jār, ẓāhiran.*

Outwit, v.a. *ṭagal, ghulawul.*

Oval, a. *ūgd, ghunḍ·man,*

Oven, s. *tanūr.*

Over, p. *pās, bānde, da bānde.* (across) *pore.* (above) *da pāsa.* (more-) *ziyāt, ḍer.*

Overbalance, v.n. *dranedal, sangzan ked.*

Overbearing, a. *zabardast, zorāwar, ẓālim; kibr·jan, maghrūr, khpul·sar, khpul·rāe.*

Overcast, a. *ganr, gūr, puṭ, tor, siwrai·kaṛai.*

Overcome, v.a. *lānde k., pa-aṛ k., barai mūndal, wahal, mātawul.*

Overflow, v.n. *toyedal* or *toe ked., lāhū ked.*

Overhaul, v.a. *laṭawul, atsanral, shanal.*

Overhear, v.a. *āwredal, ghwag tsāral.*

Overleap, v.a. *pore dangal.*

Overlook, v.a. *katal, līdal, goral.* (forgive) *bakkhal, pulawul.* (pass over) v.n. *ter watal.*

Overplus, s. *ziyātī, bāqī, junga.*

Overpower, v.a. *lānde k., pa-aṛ k.*

Overrate, v.a. *ziyāt ganral* or *-shmeral.*

Overrule, v.a. *ḥukm mātawul* or *-wahal.*

Overrun, v.a. *tākht·tārāj-, lūṭ-, tālā-, wairān-,* etc. *k.* (spread) v.n. *khwaredal, ghwaredal, wīṛedal.*

Overseer, s. *peshkār, dārogha.* (of crops) *kakkhai.*

Overset, v.a. *naskorawul, aṛawul.*

Oversight, s. *khaṭā, ter·wat.*

Overt, a. *tsargand, kkhkārah, prānatai, ẓāhir.*

Overtake, v.a. *lānde k., nīwul.*

Overthrow, v.a. *mātawul, wahal, pa-aṛ-*

lānde-, etc. *k.*; *naṛawul*, *ghūrzawul*. (ruin) *pāe·māl-*, etc. *k.*, *latārawul*. (in wrestling) *parzawul*.

Overthrow, s. *māṭ*, *shikast*, *pa-aṛ*.

Overture, s. *sawāl*, *pukkhtana*, *khabara*.

Overturn, v.a. *naskorawul*, *aṛawul*, *pa-aṛ·makh k.*

Overwhelm, v.a. *ḍūbawul*, *gharqawul*.

Owe, v.n. *porawuṛai-*, *qarẓ·dār-*, etc. *ked*.

Owl, s. *gūngai*, *chagharū*.

Own, pr. *khpul*.

Own, v.a. *khpulawul*, *laral*; *manal*, *ganral*; *qabūlawul*, *iqrār k.* v.n. *qā-il ked*.

Owner, s. *khāwand*, *meṛah*, *tsakkhtan*, *mālik*.

Ox, s. *ḍangar*; *ghwāe* or *ghwayai*, *ghutskai*.

Oxymel, s. *sikanjabīn*, *turanjabīn*.

Oyster, s. *kastūra*.

P.

Pace, s. *qadam*, *yūn*, *gām*; *chāl*, *tag*, *raftār*.

Pacify, v.a. *pakhulā k.*, *saṛawul*, *rogha·joṛa-*, etc. *k.*; *tasallī-*, *dilāsa-*, etc. *warkawul*.

Pack, s. *bār*, *peṭai*, *panḍ*, *laḍ*. (half-) *anḍai*. (-ropes) *wākkhkai*, *siyala-ī*. (-sack) *malaw*, *ghundai*, *tsaṭa*. (-net) *trangaṛ*, *korai*, *laḍ*, *shalīta*. (-saddle) *kata*, *pālān*. (party) *paṛk*, *ṭolai*.

Pack, v.a. *dzāyawul*, *taṛal*, *ṭolawul*, *nghaṛal* —*nghakkhtal*.

Packet, s. *gāṭla-ī*, *panḍūkai*, *panḍa*, *geḍai*.

Packthread, s. *natsai*, *muzai*.

Pad, s. *manjala* or *manjīla*; *bālikkhtak*, *bālikkhtgoṭai*, *moṛa*.

Paddle, v.a. *chape wahal*. (in water) *lānbo k.*

Padlock, s. *jandra*, *qulf*.

Pagan, s. *but·parast*, *kāfir*, *gabr*.

Paganism, s. *but·parastī*, *kāfir·tob*.

Page, s. *ṭeliyā*, *nokar*, *jilaw·dār*; *mra-e*, *ghulām*. (-of a book) *safḥa*.

Pageant, s. *tamāsha*, *nandāra*.

Pail, s. *taghār*, *gaḍhal*, *ḍol*, *satal*, *maṭkai*. (milk-) *donra-ī*, *lawaghūna*.

Pain, s. *khūg*, *daṛd*, *zakhm*, *'azāb*, *swai*. v.a. *khūgawul*, *daṛdawul*, *zahīrawul*. v.n. *khūgedal*, *daṛdedal*, *zahīredal*, *swal*.

Painful, a. *daṛd·man*, *zakhmī*, *khūg·man*.

Pains, s. *kokshiksh*, *miḥnat*, *sa'ī*. (-of childbirth) *da langedo daṛd*.

Paint, v.a. *rangawul*, *rang lagawul*.

Painting, s. *rangawūna*; *tsera*, *taṣwīr*, *naqsha*.

Pair, s. *bragh*, *qulba*, *joṛa*.

Palace, s. *dargāh*, *bārgāh*, *daulat·khāna*.

Palatable, a. *khwand·nāk*, *maza·dār*.

Palate, s. *tālū*. (soft-) *kūmai*.

Pale, s. *sperah*, *sperchan*, *be·rang*; *ziyaṛ*, *shīn*, *spīn*; *kha-aṛ*, *īro·rang*. (stake) s. *mogai*.

Palisade, s. *keṛ*, *bāra*.

Pall, s. *tsādar*, *kapan* or *kafan*.

Palliate, v.a. *spukawul*, *kamawul*, *la-agawul*.

Pallid, a. *sperah*, *sperchan*, *ziyaṛ*, *shīn*, *kha-ar*.

Palm, s. *warghawai*, *khapar*, *lapa*. (-measure) *tsapak*. (-tree) *khajūr*.

Palpable, a. *tsargand*, *kkhkārah*, *bartser*.

Palpitate, v.n. *rapedal*, *laṛzedal*, *ḍrakedal*.

Palpitation, s. *laṛza*, *ḍradzedana*, *ḍrakedana*, *rapedana*. (-of heart) *khafqān*.

Palsied, a. *shall*, *guzan wahalai*.

Palsy, s. *guzan*.

Paltry, a. *spuk*, *khushai*, *nā·kārah*.

Pamper, v.a. *nāzawul*; *maṛawul*.

Pamphlet, s. *risāla*, *woṛ* or *wūṛ kitāb*, *juz*.

Pan, s. (metal) *tabakhai*, *dechka*, *kaṛahai*, *baṭ*. (pottery) *lokkhai*, *kaṭwa-ī*, *taba-ī*, *maṭkai*. (of wood) *kkhānak*, *kachkol*.

Panacea, s. *aksīr*.

Pancake, s. *paṛāta*, *weshala*, *kāk*, *kakoṛai*.

Pander, s. *baṛwā*, *dallāl*. v.a. *dallālī k.*

Pane, s. (-of glass) *ā-īna*.

Panegyric, s. *stāyana, ṣanā, t'arīf.*

Panegyrist, s. *stāyana-, ṣanā-*, etc. *goe* or *-wayūnkai.*

Pang, s. *tsirīka, brekkh, dard.* (death-) *dzān·kandan.*

Pangolin, s. *kishor.*

Panic, s. *tor, tara, haibat, wera, khof.* (-struck) *tor khwūṛalai, weredalai.*

Pannier, s. *kawāra, kāra, kajāwa.*

Pant, v.a. *sā pa landa ākhistal.*

Pantaloons, s. *partūg, tambān, shalwār.* (the string) *partūghākkh.* (the hem) *bada.* (the leg) *pāentsa.* (the fork) *khakkhtag.*

Panther, s. *prāng, baur, baurgai.*

Pantry, s. *ambār·khāna.*

Pap, s. (teat) *tai.* (paste) *leṭa-ī, oghra, atob.*

Papa, s. *bābā, bābū*; *plār.*

Paper, s. *kāghaz.*

Par, s. *barābar·wālai, twal, gundī.*

Parable, s. *matal, miṣāl.*

Parade, s. *dabdaba, tamtarāq.* (military) *qawā'id, sān.* (-ground) *qawā'id·gāh, maidān.*

Paradise, s. *jannat, bihikkht.*

Paradox, s. *da 'aqla lire, aṛawuli khabara.*

Paragraph, s. *juz, qiṭ'a.*

Parallel, a. *sam, barābar, sara sam.*

Paralysis, s. *guzan, shall.* (-of face) *laqwa.*

Paralytic, a. *shall, guzan·wahalai.*

Paramount, a. *mashar, ghaṭ, loe.*

Paramour, s. *yār, āshnāe, m'ashūq.*

Parapet, s. *mard·rau, kangūra*; *sangar, bāra, panāh.*

Paraphrase, s. *tarjūma, sharaḥ.*

Parasite, s. *khūshāmad·gar, ḍirpal*; *ṭufailī, lwegand, taghārai.*

Parboil, v.a. *nīm·josh k., nīma·khwā eshawul.*

Parcel, s. *gāṭla-ī, butskha, butskhaka.* (-of land) *bakhra, wesh, paṭai.*

Parch, v.a. *wrītawul, talawul, alwoyal, teyal, kaṛawul.* v.n. *wuchedal, wrītedal, kaṛedal.*

Parched, a. *wrīt, teyalai, alwoyalai*, etc. (-grain) s. *nīna, pūlah.*

Parchment, s. *raqq.*

Pardon, s. *bakkhal, m'uāf k.*

Pare, v.a. *khriyal, togal, tarāshal.* (-the nails) *nūkūna ākhistal.* (a tree) *lakkhte prekawul* or *-shūkawul.*

Parent, s. *mor, plār.*

Parentage, s. *aṣl, kor, nogai, khāndān, khūna, nasal, nasab.*

Paring, s. *tarāza, chūr.*

Parish, s. *tapa, kandai, cham, mālat, wanḍ.*

Parity, s. *barābarī, samsor·tiyā. siyālī, gundī.*

Park, s. *kkhkār·gāh.* (artillery-) *top·khāna.*

Parley, v.a. *sawāl·dzawāb-, khabare-*, etc. *k.*

Parliament, s. *da ulus jirga, da qām majlis.*

Parlour, s. *dar·dālān.*

Paroxysm, s. *ghoṭa, nobat, bārī.*

Parrot, s. *totā, totī.*

Parry, v.a. *girzawul, bachawul, daf'a-, lire-*, etc. *k., bandawul, man'a k.*

Parsimonious, a. *kam·kharts, tang·dast, bakhīl.*

Parson, s. (moslem-) *imām.* (pagan-) *bāmbanr.* (christian) *pādrī.*

Part, s. *brakha, ḥiṣṣa, wesh.* (-of debt) *ūgrā-ī, qisṭ.* (place) *dzāe, zmaka.* (piece) *ṭoṭa.* (side) *janba, para, ṭaraf.* (-of speech) *kalima.* (for the most-) *akṣar.* (own-) *khpul·dzān.* (a small-) *la-ag·shān.* (to take in ill-) *bad manal.* (to take in good-) *kkhah manal.*

Part, v.a. *biyalawul, dwah·dzāe k., judā k.* (share) *weshal.* (-with) *pregdal, prekkhodal, prekkhawul, prekkhal, tark k.* v.n. *biyaledal, dwah·dzāe-, judā-*, etc. *ked.*, *lwukkhtal.* (take leave) *rukhṣatedal.*

Partake, v.a. *brakha ākhistal.* v.n. *malgarai-, sharīk-, brakha·khor-*, etc. *ked.*

Partaker, s. *brakha·khor, sharīk*; *malgarai, mal.*

Partial, a. *ṭaraf-dār, janba-dār*; *mayan*; *nimgaṛai.*

Partiality, s. *ṭaraf-, janba-*, etc. *-dārī, mrasta, pās-wālai*; *mīna, sela*; *k͟hwā.*

Participate, v.n. *malgarai-, s͟harīk-, gaḍ-*, etc. *ked.*

Participle, s. (active-) *ismi-fā'il.* (passive-) *ismi-mafa'ūl.*

Particle, s. *ṭakai, pits͟hāṇrai, pūṭai, ẕarra, reza.*

Particular, a. *k͟hāṣṣ.* s. *k͟habara*; *tafṣīl*; *juz-o-kul.* (in-) ad. *k͟huṣūṣan, pa ṭakī.*

Partisan, s. *para-, janba-, gundī-*, etc. *-dār*; *malgarai, mal, s͟harīk*; *yār, komakī.*

Partition, s. *wes͟h, taqsīm*; *parda, dīwāl.*

Partly, ad. *la-ag-s͟hān, nīme-nīme, yo la-ag ts͟a.*

Partner, s. *mal, malgarai, s͟harīk, brak͟ha-k͟hor, ambāz.*

Partnership, s. *malgīrī, malgar-tiyā, s͟hirākat, ambāzī.*

Partridge, s. (black-) *tārū.* (grey-) *tang-zarai* or *tangẕarai.* (Greek-) *zarkah.*

Parts, s. (talents) *'aql, poha, s͟ha'ūr, dānis͟h.* (regions) *hewād, zmaka, mulk.* (districts) *tapa, pargana.* (private-) *ṣūrat, tor-wek͟hk͟h-tah, andām-nihānī, da parde dzāe.*

Parturition, s. *lang-wālai, langedana.* (delivery) *k͟halāṣī.*

Party, s. *ṭolai, paṛk.* (person) *kas, tan.* (meeting) *majlis.* (convivial-) *ṣuḥbat.* (side) *para, janba, gundī, ṭaraf.* (family-) *c͟ham, firqa, k͟hel, qām.*

Pass, v.n. *teredal, c͟haledal, tlal—lāṛal.* (-over) *pore watal.* (-by) *ter watal.*

Pass, s. (ford) *gūdar.* (ferry) *pataṇr, gūdar.* (hill-) *g͟hāk͟hk͟hai, kotal.* (defile) *tanga-ī, darra.* (road) *lār.* (permit) *parwāna.* (state) *ḥāl, nobat.* (stroke) *guẕār, dūw, wār.*

Passage, s. *lār, darak, gūdar*; *safar.*

Passenger, s. *musāfir, rāh-rau.*

Passion, s. *qahar, g͟huṣṣa.* (lust) *nafs, hawas, s͟hahwat.* (love) *mīna, 'is͟hq.* (suffering) *quwat, zg͟ham, ṣabr.* (ardour) *tāo.*

Passionate, a. *qahar-jan, g͟haẕab-nāk*, etc. *bṛos, k͟hīr, tund-, tod-, tez-*, etc. *mizāj* or *-k͟hoe.*

Passive, a. *be-ḥarakat, prot, walāṛ.* (in grammar) *mafa'ūl, majhūl.*

Passport, s. *rawāna, parwāna.*

Past, a. *ter, tilai, tlalai.* (-and forgotten) *ter-o-her.*

Paste, s. *batī, leta-ī*; *atob.* (-board) *kāntī.*

Pastern, s. *lās, kk͟hpa.* (-leathers) *pak͟h-wandai.* (-joint) *gīṭa-ī.*

Pastime, s. *tamās͟ha, loba, bāzī, mas͟hg͟hulā.*

Pastor, s. *s͟hpūn, gūjar.* (spiritual-) *imām, hādī, s͟hek͟h, pīr.*

Pastry, s. *wes͟hala, parāṭa, g͟hunzāk͟hk͟ha.*

Pasture, s. *wāk͟hk͟hah, giyāh, 'alaf, ts͟ar.* (-ground) *ts͟arā-gāh, maira, wars͟ho.* v.n. *ts͟aredal.* v.a. *ts͟arawul, piyāyal, powul.*

Pasturing, s. *ts͟ar, piyāyana, powuna.*

Pat, a. *juk͟ht, joṛ, sam, barābar, drust.* s. *ṭas, ṭaq, trak.* v.a. *lās wahal pa c͟hā bānde, dilāsa warkawul k.* (slap) *ṭas*, etc. *wahal, ṭaqawul.*

Patch, v.a. *joṛawul.* (-cloth) *bezal* or *pezal, ganḍal, ṭūkai-, k͟hak͟hk͟htagai-*, etc. *pore ganḍal.* s. *ṭūkai, marīṇra, pīna, joṛ, pewand*, etc.

Patent, s. *sanad, parwāna, farmān.*

Paternal, a. *plāranai.* (-relation) *plār-ganai.*

Path, s. *lār, wāṭ.* (bye or foot-) *ts͟aṛa lār* or *-wāṭ.*

Pathetic, a. *zṛah-swai, k͟hwā-k͟hūgai, dzigar-swai.*

Patience, s. *ṣabr, zg͟ham, sah.* (to have) v.a. *ṣabr-*, etc. *laral*, or *k.*

Patient, a. *ṣābir, zg͟ham-, ṣabr-*, etc. *-nāk.* s. *bīmār, marīẓ, nā-joṛ, randzūr, nā-rog͟h.*

Patriarch, s. *mas͟har, spīn-gīrai*; *nīkah, zbarg.*

Patrimony, s. *mīrāt, dawtar, milk.*

Patriot, s. *watan·dost.*
Patrol, s. *shab·gakkht*; *qarāwal.*
Patron, s. *murabbī, pushtī, nāyak.* (-saint) *pīr.*
Patten, s. *kanrāwa.*
Patter, v.a. (as rain) *darahār-,shirahār-*, etc. *k.*, or *-wahal.*
Pattern, s. *nakkha, namūna*; *qālib.*
Paucity, s. *kam·tiyā, tangsiyā, qīmatī, kākhtī, qātī.*
Pauper, s. *gadāe, faqīr, nā·dār, nā·kas.*
Pause, v.a. *dama k., fikr k.* v.n. *wudredal.*
Pave, v.a. *farsh·bandī k.*
Pavilion, s. *khaima.*
Paw, s. *mangul, panja, changul.*
Pawn, v.a. *graw-, gānra-*, etc. *k.*
Pay, s. *talab, tankhwāh, mawājib*; *kharts, mazdūrī, shukrāna.* (-master) *bakhshī, khizānchī.*
Pay, v.a. *talab-*, etc. *warkawul.* (discharge) *adā-, pūrah-*, etc. *k.*
Pea, s. *matar, krāk.* (chick-) *chanra.*
Peace, s. *rogha, jora, āshtī, khair, khairiyat, aman, ārām·tiyā, āsūdagī.*
Peaceable, a. *eman, gharīb, kam·sharr.*
Peaceful, a. *āsūdah, ārām, be·patna, be·pasāt.*
Peach, s. *shaftālū.*
Peacock, s. *tāūs, mor.*
Peak, s. *tsūka, peza, sar.*
Peal, s. *daz, ghurunb.*
Pear, s. *tāngū, nāk, nāshpātai.*
Pearl, s. *marghalara, marwārīd, durr.* (mother of-) *māhī·ghwag, sadaf.* (-diver) *marjīwanrah.*
Peasant, s. *zamīndar, dihqān, charekār.*
Pease, s. *chanra, mot, mahe, ma-ī* or *mayī, māsh.* (split-) *dāl.* (ground-) *rāra, gir·gira.* (-pod) *palai.* (-husks) *sūrī, būt·sūrī.* (cooked-) *paitī.*
Pebble, s. *gīta-ī, dabara, kānrota.*
Peck, v.a. *tongawul, tongāra k., makkhūka wahal.*
Peculiar, a. *khāss*; *mutrah*; *ajīb.*
Peculiarity, s. *khāssiyat, lokkhai, khoe, khaslat.*
Pecuniary, a. *naghdī* or *naqdī.*
Pedagogue, s. *ustād, mullī, ākhūn.*
Pedestal, s. *pāya, āra, asās, wekh, dunkācha, kkhpa.*
Pedigree, s. *pera-ī, pusht, asl, nasab.*
Pedlar, s. *banjārī.*
Peel, v.a. *pot-, khwar-*, etc. *bāsal—yasta* or *-kāgal—kkhkal.* v.n. *nwaredal.*
Peep, v.a. *pa·puta-, pa·zarana-ī-*, etc. *katal*
Peep, s. *put·nazar, zarana-ī, dzīr.*
Peer, s. *sārai, makhai, samsorai, siyāl, gund arbāb, sardār, khān, malik.*
Peerage, s. *kursī·nāma*; *shajara.*
Peerless, a. *be·misāl, lā·sānī, be·siyāl, nādir,* etc.
Peevish, a. *sūt·būt, būt·ūrbūz, trīkh·rūe, khapah.*
Peg, s. *mogai, mekh, sparkhai.*
Pelf, s. *tanga, taka, paisa*; *duniyā, daulat, māl.*
Pelican, s. *kotān.*
Pellet, s. *ghundoskai, pandoskai, mardaka, gola-ī.* (-of goat's, etc. dung) *pucha.*
Pellicle, s. *tsaparkai.*
Pelt, v.a. *wīshtal, lawastal, āchawul, ghur·zawul.*
Pelvis, s. *tabakhai, spokhadza.*
Pen, s. (writing-) *qalam.* (cattle-) *bānda, shpol.*
Penalty, s. *tāwān, nāgha, jarīmāna, sazā.*
Penance, s. *kafārat.*
Pencil, s. *salā-ī, sīkh, dūk.*
Pendant, a. *dzwarand, āwezānd.* s. *zundai, zunbak.*
Penetrate, v.n. *nanawatal, ore pore watal.*
Penetration, s. *nanawātah, dakhl*; **poh, 'aql.**

Penis, s. *tsūkkhai, ḍaga, ẕakar.* (virilis) *ghenr.* (child's-) *tsakkhkūṛai, cholak.*

Penitence, s. *toba, pakkhemānī, istighfār.*

Penitent, a. *toba·gār, pakkhemān.*

Penknife, s. *chāqū, chaṛūka-ī.*

Penman, s. *kātib, kkhkūnkai.*

Pennant. s. *janḍa, bairagh, nakkha.*

Penny, s. *paisa, ṭanga, ḍāng, damṛa-ī.* (-weight) *sharshā-ī, dwa rata-ī.*

Pension, s. *waẓīfa*; *jāgīr.*

Pensioner, s. *waẓīfa·khor, jāgīr·dār.*

Pensive, s. *fikr·man, andekkh·man.*

Pentateuch, s. *tauret, kitāb da ḥaẓrat mūsā.*

Penurious, a. *shūm, bakhīl, tang·dast.*

Penury, s. *tabāhī, khwārī, tangsiyā.*

People, s. *'ālam, khalq,· wagaṛī, mardum.* (tribe) *ulus, qām, khel.* v.a. *ābādawul, wadānawul.*

Pepper, s. *mrich.* (red-) *sra·mrich.* (cubeb-) *ḍanbara.*

Perambulate, v.n. *girzedal.* v.a. *gakkht k.*

Perceive, v.a. *līdal, m'alūmawul.* v.n. *pahedal, rasedal, peǰandal.*

Perception, s. *fikr, poha, hokkh, wuqūf.*

Perch, s. (-for birds) *chakas.* v.n. *kkhkenāstal.*

Perchance, ad. *gora, gunde, ganre, kkhā-ī.*

Percolate, v.a. *chanṛal, ghalbelawul.*

Percussion, s. *ṭaq, ṭakar.*

Perdition, s. *kharābī, halākī, tabāhī.*

Peremptory, a. *qaṭa'ī, pūrah, kāfī shāfī.*

Perennial, a. *pāedār, dā-im*; *yo·kālanai, kālanai.*

Perfect, a. *pūrah, tamām, kāmil*; *pāk, be·aib.*

Perfection, s. *kamāl, kāmil·tob, tamāmī, pūrah·wālai.*

Perfectly, ad. *amānī, sarāsar.*

Perfidious, a. *be·wafā, be·īmān, namak·ḥarām.*

Perfidy, s. *be·īmānī, be·wafā-ī, namak·ḥarāmī.*

Perforate, v.a. *sūṛai k., tetsal, sīkhal.*

Perform, v.a. *kawul, kṛal, pūrah-, adā-,* etc. *k., guẕāral, tamāmawul, pa dzāe rāwṛal.*

Performance, s. *kār, kṛah, kawūna, adā.*

Perfume, s. *khūshbūī, 'aṭr.* (oil-) *fulel.*

Perfumer, s. *'aṭṭār.*

Perhaps, ad. *gunde, wī ba,* etc. (*v.* Perchance.)

Peril, s. *khaṭra, wera, khof, muhimm.*

Perilous, a. *khaṭar·nāk, wera·nāk, khof·nāk.*

Period, s. *wakht, ṭāng, nobat, mūda, neṭa, mahal, wār, plā, heṛ.*

Periodical, a. *wārī, nobatī.*

Perish, v.n. *mṛal, muṛ-, halāk-, fū·fanā-,* etc. *ked.*

Perishable, a. *fānī, nā·pāedār, teredūnai.*

Perjure, v.a. *nā·ḥaqq-,* or *darogh qasam-,* or *nā·ḥaqq saugand-,* etc. *khwuṛal.*

Permanent, a. *pāedār, maẕbūṭ, qā-im, lā·zawāl.*

Permanently, ad. *pāedārī sara, tar·tala.*

Permission, s. *iẕn, ḥukm, ijāzat.*

Permit, s. *parwāna.* v.a. *rawā laral*; *ḥukm-, iẕn-,* etc. *warkawul.*

Pernicious, a. *tāwānī, nuqṣānī, ziyānī*; *moẕī, muẕirr.*

Perpendicular, a. *negh, walāṛ, lak; jig.*

Perpetrate, v.a. *kawul, kṛal.*

Perpetual, a. *dā-imī, mudāmī, jāwīdān.*

Perpetually, ad. *har·kala, tal, tar·tala, hamesha.*

Perplex, v.a. *rabṛawul, hariyānawul, sargardānawul, hak·pak-, hekkh-, huts-,* etc. *k.*

Perplexity, s. *rabaṛ, hariyānī, sargardānī,* etc

Perquisite, s. *gaṭa, shukrāna, dastūrī.*

Persecute, v.a. *āzārawul, zoral, tangawul, khūgawul, ẕulm-,* etc. *k.*

Persecution, s. *zor, ẕulm, ziyātī*; *taqāẓa.*

Persecutor, s. *ẕālim, jafā·kār, zorūnkai.*

Perseverance, s. *himmat, sa'ī, kokshiksh.*

Persevere, v.a. *himmat-,* etc. *k.* v.n. *lagiyā osedal.*

Persist, v.a. *ḥujjat-, takrār-,* etc. *k.* v.n. *lagiyā osedal, qā-im-,* etc. *osedal.*

Person, s. *sarai, wagaṛai, gawai, kas, tan.*

(self) *khpul, dzān.* (body) *ṣūrat, andām, tan.*
Personal, a. *khpul, khāṣṣ.*
Personality, s. *ṣūrat, nātka-ī, pejandgalī.*
Personally, ad. *pa khpula, pa dzān.*
Personate, v.a. *ṣūrat-, libās-, swāng-,* etc. *k.,* or *-ākhistal* or *-joṛawul.*
Perspiration, s. *khwala.*
Perspire, v.n. *khwale kcd.*
Persuade, v.a. *rāwustal, raẓā k., tasallī,* etc. *warkawul; lamsawul; ma-ilān-,* etc. *k.*
Persuasion, s. *tasallī, dilāsa; targhīb, lamsūn.*
Pert, a. *shokh, wītak, be-makh, be-adab.*
Pertinacious, a. *ḥujjatī, takrārī, hoḍai, ṭakaṇrai.*
Pertinent, a. *joṛ, munāsib, wājib, jukht, lā-iq.*
Perturbation, s. *nā-qalār-tiyā, wiswās; gram.*
Perusal, s. *lwustana; katana, mulāḥiẓa.*
Peruse, v.a. *lwustal; katal, naẓar-,* etc. *k.*
Pervade, v.n. *pheledal, khwaredal, wīṛedal.*
Perverse, a. *hoḍai, khpul-sar, ṭakaṇrai, haṭ.*
Pervert, v.a. *girzawul, aṛawul, be-lār k.*
Pest, s. *balā, wabāl, janjāl; wabā.*
Pester, v.a. *tangawul, zoral, janjālī k.*
Pestiferous, a. *moẓī, muẓirr, ziyān-kār.*
Pestilence, s. *wabā, tāwūn* or *ṭa'ūn.*
Pestle, s. *molai, pāeko, hokla-ī.*
Pet, s. *marawar-tiyā, māṇrai; mayana.*
Petition, v.a. *'arẓ-, sawāl-, darkhwāst-,* etc. *k.,* or *-laral,* or *-ghokkhtal; 'arẓī āchawul.*
Pettish, a. *khapah, māṇrī-gar, marawar.*
Petty, a. *woṛ, kachoṭai; spuk, nā-tsīz.*
Petulant, a. *shokh, be-adab; wītak, chūnkai.*
Pewter, s. *qal'a-ī, jas.*
Phalanx, s. *palṭan, ghol, ṭol, paṛk, tamba.*
Phantom, s. *wahm, khiyāl, siwrai; rawai.*
Phenomenon, s. *awtsār; 'ajab-kār* or *-chal.*
Phial, s. *kkhīkkha.*
Philanthropist, s. *khair-khwāh, insān-dost.*
Philology, s. *'ilm da ṣarf-o-naḥw.*
Philosopher, s. *ḥakīm, ṣūfī, 'ālim, failsūf.*
Philosopher's stone, s. *kīmiyā, aksīr, pāras.*
Philosophy, s. *'ilm da maujūdāt.*
Philter, s. *ṭoṭka, t'awīz, mantar.*
Phlegm, s. *balgham, khrāshkai, grolbai.*
Phlegmatic, a. *balghamī, soṛ-mizāj.*
Phlogistic, a. *khushk, wuch, tod, garm.*
Phœnix, s. *'unqāc, humāc, quqnūs.*
Phrase, s. *khabara, wayai; lughat, 'ibārat.*
Phraseology, s. *'ibārat, maḥāwara.*
Phthisis, s. *narai-randz, diqq, sill.*
Physic, s. *dawā, dārū, darmān.* (science) *ṭibb.* (practice) *ṭibābat, ṭabībī.*
Physical, a. *ẓātī, jibillī, ṭaba'ī.*
Physician, s. *ṭabīb, ḥakīm.*
Physics, s. *'ilm da maujūdāt, ḥikmat.*
Pick, v.a. (pluck) *shūkawul, laṭawul, ṭolawul.* (select) *chuṇral, aṇrawul, chīndah k., khwakkhawul.* (-up) *ākhistal, porta k.* (teeth, etc.) *ṭunbal.* (-knot, etc.) *spaṛdal, prānatal.* (-a quarrel) *gwākkhal, gwākkhedal.*
Pickaxe, s. *kodāla-ī, kaha-ī.*
Pickle, s. *āchār.*
Pickpocket, s. *gan-kap, uchakkah-ghal.*
Picture, s. *tsera, taṣwīr, nakhkkha, ṣūrat.*
Piebald, a. *ablaq, chrag-brag, brag-yālai.*
Piece, s. *ṭoṭa, reza, ṭūk.* (patch) *ṭūkai, pīna, marīṇra.* (land) *paṭai, wanḍ.* (joint) *joṛ, pewand.*
Piecemeal, a. *biyal, judā, yo-yo.* ad. *ṭoṭe-ṭoṭe, chūr-chūr, daṛ-daṛ.*
Pier, s. *pushtu, band; pāya, stan.*
Pierce, v.a. *sūṛai k., sīkhal, tetsal, zanal, tsarkh k.; ore-pore-, pore-rāpore-,* etc. *bāsal—yastal.*
Piety, s. *taqwā, zuhd, dīn-dārī, īmān-dārī.*
Pig, s. *kharbishoe, kharbishkatai, sarkūzai.* (-of iron) *sala.*
Pigeon, s. *kauntar,* or *kotar,* or *kawtar.*
Pigmy, s. *lweshtīnak, chūnai, potai.*
Pike, s. *neza, balla, barcha, shalgai.*

Pile, s. *ḍera-ī, kat, ṭop, rashaka*; *mogai.*
Pile, v.a. *ḍera-ī-, tūda-, dalai-, rāsha-*, etc. *k.*
Piles, s. *bawāsīr, manekkhī.*
Pilfer, v.a. *puṭawul, ghlā k.*
Pilgrim, s. *ḥājī, ḥajj kawūnkai, ziyārat kawūnkai.*
Pilgrimage, s. *ḥajj, ziyārat.*
Pill, s. *gola-ī, mardakai.*
Pillage, s. *lūṭ, tālān, tākht-o-tārāj, charwr.*
Pillage, v.n. *lūṭawul, lūṭal, natal, nātārawul.*
Pillar, s. *stan*; *tsalai.*
Pillory, s. *shikanja, kāt, tsarkh.*
Pillow, s. *bālikkht, takiya.* (small-) *bālikkht-goṭai.*
Pimp, s. *baṛwā, dallāl, dahūs.*
Pimple, s. *nanaka-ī, dāna.* (on face) *dzwānaka.*
Pin, s. *stan*; *salā-ī.*
Pincers, s. *ambūr.* (small) *nūtsai.*
Pinch, s. *skūnḍāra*; *pūṭai, pitsānrai, chūndai.*
Pinch, v.a. *skūnḍal* or *tskūnḍal.*
Pine, s. *nakkhtar, sanobar.* (-torch) *shonṭa-ī.*
Pine, v.n. *kaṛedal, nūledal, dzawredal, ghamedal, pakhsedal, zahīredal, zahedal.*
Pinion, s. *wazar, tsāng*; *banra, kkhāh-par.* (fetter) *dzolana, kara-ī.*
Pinion, v.a. *sūṭ-būṭ taṛal.*
Pinnacle, s. *tsūka, peza, sar*; *kangūra.*
Pioneer, s. *bel-dār.*
Pious, a. *taqwā-, īmān-, dīn-*, etc. *-dār*, or *-larūnkai, nmāndzī, nmūndz kawūnkai*, or *-guzār.*
Pipe, s. *shpela-ī, nala.* v.a. *shpela-ī ghagawul.*
Pique, s. *mānrai, marawar-tiyā, khwā-badī, zṛah-badāwai.*
Piss, v.a. *baul-, wāṛa baul-, mutiyāze-*, etc. *k.*
Pistol, s. *tamāncha.*
Pit, s. *doghal, ṭublai, jwar-ghālai.* v.a. *jangawul.*
Pitch, s. *rānazaṛah.* (degree) *ḥadd, nobat.*
Pitch, v.a. *wudrawul, walāṛawul, khejawul.* (cast) *āchawul, wīshtal, lawastal, ghurzawul.*
Pitcher, s. *loṭkai, mangai, maṭ, maṭkai.*
Pitchfork, s. *kkhākha-ī, dre-kkhākha-ī, sānga-ī.*
Pith, s. *māghzoh, zaṛai.*
Pitiful, a. *khwā-khūgai.* (paltry) *spuk.*
Pitiless, a. *be-dard, be-raḥm.*
Pittance, s. *ṭukṛa, nwaṛa-ī, rozī.*
Pity, s. *zṛah-swai, khwā-khūgī, dard, raḥm, gham*; *afsos, daregh.*
Pivot, s. *tīrak, salā-ī*; *ḍīḍa, khulborai.*
Place, s. *dzāe, zmaka, makān.* (stead) *'iwaẓ, badal.* (rank) *pāya, martaba.* (office) *'uhda.* (residence) *astoga, meshta.*
Place, v.a. *gdal* or *īgdal, yakkhodal, yakkhal, yakkhawul, kegdal* or *kkhkegdal, kekkhodal*, etc.
Placenta, a. *prewān.*
Placid, a. *khog, narm, pos* or *post.*
Plague, s. *wabā, tāwūn*; *āfat, balā*; *wabāl*; *janjāl.* v.a. *rabṛawul, āzārawul, pa balā ākhtah k.*
Plain, a. *sam, hawār, barābar, sat.* (simple) *sādah, ṣāf, spīn.* (unmixed) *torai, spor*; *karah, sūchah.* s. *maidān, sama.*
Plainly, ad. *spīn, ṣāf, rikkhtiyā.*
Plaint, s. *gila, māna, mānrai*; *faryād, wāwailā.*
Plaintiff, s. *mudda'ī, faryādī.*
Plaintive, a. *gila-man, mānrī-gar, māna kawūnkai.*
Plait, s. *tā, taha, wal, bragh*; *jūhaṛa, kṛaṭai, gundza, chīchaṛ.* v.a. *odal*; *āgayal, chunral.*
Plan, s. *tadbīr, ḥikmat, band, chal*; *nakhkkha* or *naqsha, namūna.* v.a. *joṛawul, band taṛal, chal k.*
Plane, s. *randa.* (-tree) *chinār.*
Plane, v.a. *togal, khrayal* or *khriyal, randa k.*
Planet, s. *storai.*
Plank, s. *takhta.*

Plant, s. *būṭai, ḍakai.*
Plant, v.a. *lagawul, khakkhawul; wudrawul, lakawul, wulāṛawul.*
Plantain, s. *kela.* (herb-) *isapghol* or *spaghol.*
Plantation, s. *jangai, banr.*
Plaster, s. *lew, akhāṛah, gach, khaṭa; malham, paha, tab, ẓamād.* v.a. *lewawul, akheṛal, tapal, khaṭa k.*
Plat, s. (-of ground) *paṭai, pāṛa, ḍāga.*
Plate, s. *rikeba-ī, raghai, pashqāb.* (-of iron for baking on) *tabakhai, teghna.* (earthen ditto) *taba-ī.*
Plated, a. *mulamma.*
Platform, s. *dunkācha, gaṛwanj; manah.*
Platter, s. *kkhānak, taghārai, tabakhai, tālai.*
Plaudit, s. *shāhbāshī, āparīn.*
Plausible, a. *khog-khulai, chalwalai, khula-war.*
Play, s. *loba, bāzī; nandāra, tamāsha; jūārī.*
Play, v.a. *lobe k.* (gamble) *jūārī k.* (-the fool) *malande k.* (act) *pekkhe k.* (music) *sarod-, tarāne-,* etc. *ghagawul.* (in comp.) *-kawul, -kṛal.*
Playfellow, s. *hum-dzolai.*
Playful, a. *mast, shokhīn.*
Plaything, s. *da lobe kālai.*
Plea, s. *ḥujjat, dalīl, 'uẓr, d'awa, hira-ī.*
Plead, v.a. *wayal, lal, lawdal, 'uẓr-,* etc. *k.*
Pleasant, a. *khwand-nāk, kkhah.*
Pleasantness, s. *khwand, maza, kkhādī.*
Pleasantry, s. *khandā, washta, ṭoqa.*
Please, v.a. *rāẓī-, khwakkh-, kkhād-,* etc. *k.*; *khwand warkawul.*
Pleased, a. *khwakkh, khūsh-ḥāl, kkhād, kkhād-man.*
Pleasure, s. *khwakkhī, kkhādī, khūsh-ḥālī, khwand.* (will) *raẓā, marzī.* (spiteful-) *sakha, wiyāṛ.*
Plebeian, a. *'āmm, adnā, kam-zāt.* s. *'āmmī.*
Pledge, s. *graw, gānra.* (word) *wāda, lafẓ, bandanr, taṛa.* (token) *nakkha, yād-gār.*
Pleiades, s. *perūne, jambaq storī.*
Plenary, a. *pūrah, tamām, amānī.*
Plenipotentiary, s. *kul mukhtār, wāk-dār.*
Plenitude, s. *pūrah-wālai; ḍer-wālai.*
Plentiful, a. *ḍer, ziyāt, prewān, wadān.*
Plenty, s. *ḍer-wālai, prewānī, ziyāt-wālai, ābādī, wadānī.*
Pliable, **Pliant**, a. *narm, post, mulā-im.*
Plight, s. *ḥāl, ḥālat, chal.* v.a. *graw-, gānra-,* etc. *k.*; *wāda-, neṭa-, lafẓ-,* etc. *taṛal.*
Plod, v.a. *miḥnat-, kokshiksh-,* etc. *k.* v.n. *ṭaparedal.*
Plot, s. *band, sāzish, joṛikkht.* (-of land) *paṭai, wanḍ.* (stratagem) *chal, lamghaṛa-ī.*
Plot, v.a. *joṛawul, band taṛal, sāzish-,* etc. *k.*
Plough, s. *yiwa* or *īwa, yoya, qulba.* v.a. *īwe* or *yiwe k.*
Ploughshare, s. *pāla, saspār, spāra.*
Plover, s. *ṭīṭārai.*
Pluck, v.a. *shūkawul.* (-out) *kāgal—kkhkal, bāsal—yastal.*
Plug, s. *būja, shoṛa, mūnrai, ḍīḍa, khulborai.*
Plum, s. *bera, baḍa bera, sāwū bera, makhranai.*
Plumage, s. *banre, nazar.*
Plume, s. *zunḍai.* (-head) *qarqara.*
Plume, v.a. *banre joṛawul, dzān joṛawul.*
Plummet, s. *sahūl, chāwul.*
Plump, a. *tsorb, chāgh, ghaṭ, punḍ.*
Plunder, v.n. *lūṭ-, tālā-, nātār-,* etc. *k.*, **natal.**
Plunge, v.a. *ḍūbkai-, ghoṭa-, ghūpa-,* etc. *warkawul* or *-wahal* or *-khwuṛal.*
Plural, a. *jam'a.*
Ply, s. *tā, bragh, chūnra, chīchar, gundza.*
Ply, v.a. *chalawul, lagawul, kawul, kṛal.*
Pocket, s. *jeb; kīsa, dzola-ī.*
Pock-mark, s. *ta-ap, ta-apai.*
Pod, s. *palai, ghoza.*
Poem, s. *ghazal, chār bait, sandara.*

Poet, s. *shā'ir, qaṣīda go,e, sandar go,e.*
Poetry, s. *sh'ir, bait, naẓm.*
Poignant, a. *tez, tunā, sakht.*
Point, s. *peza, tsūka, sar.* (dot) *ṭakai, dāna, nuqta.* (spot) *dāgh, tsirīka, laka.*
Point, v.a. *terah k., peza-,* etc. *joṛawul; naẓar lagawul.* (-out) *kkhayal—kkhowul.*
Pointed, a. *peza dār* or *-larūnkai.*
Poise, v.a. *talal, jokal, barābarawul.*
Poison, s. *zahr.* v.a. *zahr warkawul.*
Poisonous, a. *zahr·nāk.*
Poke, v.a. *negh wahal; laṭawul.*
Poker, s. (fire-) *or laṛūnai.* (goad) *chūka.*
Pole, s. *lakaṛa.* (barge-) *bala-ī.* (balance-) *ḍānḍa-ī.* (North-) *quṭb.* (-star) *da quṭb storai.*
Police, s. *band·o·bast, intiẓām.* (superintendent of-) *koṭwal.* (-office) *tānṛa.* (-man) *tsoka-ī dār.*
Policy, s. *intiẓām, tadbīr, ḥikmat 'amalī.*
Polish, v.a. *mugal—mukkhal, togal, ṣaiqal k.*
Polite, a. *makhawar, sulūkī, mihrbān; dalbārī.*
Politeness, s. *makh, makhawarī, sulūk.*
Politic, a. *ḥikmatī, tadbīrī.*
Political, a. *mulkī; 'amalī, tadbīrī.*
Politician, s. *tadbīrī, jirgatū.*
Politics, s. *tadbīr da mulk* or *-salṭanat,* etc.
Poll, s. *sar, koṭai.* (-tax) *jaziya.* v.a. *lanḍ-, ghūṭ-,* etc. *prekawul.*
Pollute, v.a. *nā·pāk-, palīt-, murdār-, kakaṛ-,* etc. *k.* (-oneself) *mūṭak wahal.* (-oneself in sleep) *āwdas awukkhtal, shaiṭān khaṭā k.*
Pollution, s. *nā·pākī, palītī,* etc.; *shaiṭānī khaṭā.*
Polytheism, s. *but parastī, shirk.*
Polytheist, s. *but parast, mushrik.*
Pomegranate, s. *anangai, anangūṛai, anār.* (wild-) *narsawai.*
Pommel, v.a. *wahal, ṭakawul, kūṭal.*
Pomp, s. *dabdaba, tamtarāq, sāmāna.*

Pompous, a. *khāntamā, sar hawā.*
Pond, s. *ḍanḍ, nāwar, wasta, wangara.*
Ponder, v.a. *fikr-, ghaur-,* etc. *k.*
Ponderous, a. *drūnd, grān.*
Pony, s. *ṭaṭū, yābū.*
Pool, s. *ḍanḍūkai; ḍab, kol.*
Poor, a. *khwār, gharīb, muflis, nā·kas.*
Poorly, a. *nājoṛ, nārogh, bīmār.* ad. *nīmgaṛai.*
Pop, s. *ṭas, ṭak, ḍaz, ṭar,* etc. v.a. *ṭas-,* etc. *wahal.*
Poppy, s. *koknār, khāsh khāsh.* (wild-) *redai.*
Populace, s. *ulus, 'āmmiyān, 'awām.*
Popular, a. *'āmm, jārī, chalanī, riwāj.*
Population, s. *ābādī, wadānī; 'ālam, khalq, ulus.*
Populous, a. *ābād, wadān.*
Porch, s. *manḍaw, dahlīz.*
Porcupine, s. *shkūnr.*
Pore, s. (-of the skin) *ghūna.* (to roughen or erect the-) v.n. *ghūna zīgedal.* (aperture) *sūṛa.*
Pore, v.a. *lagiyā katal* or *-goral—līdal, dzīr k.*
Porous, a. *sūṛa·war.*
Porpoise, s. *tsūtsa, sūs.*
Port, s. *bandar.* (door) *war, darwāza.* (mien) *yūn, chāl.* (aperture) *darbacha, karka-ī.*
Portable, a. *spuk, halak, da wṛalo.*
Portal, s. *darwāza, āstāna.*
Portend, v.a. *dallīl k., āgāhī k., pāl kkhayal—kkhowul.*
Portent, s. *dallīl, āgāhī, pāl* or *fāl; bad fāl, bad shugun.*
Porter, s. *ḥammāl, mazdūr.* (gate-) *darwāza·wān, ghāw·chī.*
Portico, s. *manḍaw, dahlīz, jilau khāna.*
Portion, s. *brakha, ḥiṣṣa, wesh, nanḍ, qismat.*
Portly, a. *ghaṭ, juṣṣa·war, jasīm, khṛīs, gagar, star.*

Portmanteau, s. *khurjīn, yakhdān, rakht·dān, dzola-ī, gūdai.*

Portrait, s. *tsera, taṣwīr, ṣūrat.*

Pose, v.a. *pa-aṛ k., lā dzawāb k., hariyāna-wul.*

Position, s. *shān, wajha, ḥāl, ṣūrat.*

Positive, a. *yaqīn, qaṭa'ī, be·shakk, be·shubha.* (stubborn) *khpul rāe, khpul·sar.* (real) *aṣlī, sūchah.*

Possess, v.a. *laral, darlal.*

Possession, s. *qābū, qabẓa.* (to take-) v.a. *qābū-,* etc. *k., khpulawul, ākhistal, lānde k.* (to give-) *bakkhal* or *bakhkkhaḷ, war-kawul, kkhandal.*

Possessor, s. *meṛah, tsakkhtan, mālik, khā-wand.* (in comp.) *-larūnkai, -dār, -man, -war,* etc.

Possibility, s. *imkān, kedana, shwah.*

Possible, a. *mumkin, shwūnkai, kedūnkai.* (to be-) v.a. *imkān laral, shwal.*

Possibly, ad. *gunde, kkhā-ī, bā-īda, wī ba.*

Post, s. (office) *kār, khidmat, 'uhda.* (station) *dzāe, makān.* (military-) *tsoka-ī, tānra.* (pillar) *stan, tsalai.* (mail-) *ḍāk.* (-man) *qāṣid, ḍāk·wālā.* (express-) *chapar.*

Post, v.a. (station) *wudrawul, kkhkenawul, walāṛawul.*

Posterior, a. *wrustai, wrustanai, pastanai.*

Posteriors, s. *kūnāṭī.*

Posterity, s. *alwād, zurriyāt, nasl.* (to the latest-) *naslan b'ad naslan.*

Postpone, v.a. *drang-, lārghah-, multawī-,* etc. *k., mu'aṭṭal-, barkhwāst-, nāgha-,* etc. *k.*

Postscript, s. *tatimma.*

Posture, s. *shān, wajha, ṣūrat, ṭaur.*

Pot, s. *lokkhai.* (metal-) *kaṛahai, deg, dechka, khumṛa-ī.* (earthen-) *hānḍa-ī, kaṭwa-ī, kawdīk.* (water-) *mangai, maṭkai, loṭkai.* (-lid) *bargholai, sar·pokkh.* (-herb) *sāg, sabzī, wākkhah.*

Potato, s. *ālū.*

Potent, a. *zorāwar, maẓbūṭ, quwat·nāk, tu-wānā.*

Potentate, s. *bādshāh, amīr, sardār, malik.*

Potion, s. *sharbat, nosh, tskkhāk* or *skāk.*

Potsherd, s. *kaudai, kaudarai.*

Pottage, s. *sāgīnrai, sāg, āsh.* (-of meat, etc.) *qatagh, ngolai, sālan.*

Potter, s. *kulāl, kumhār.*

Pottery, s. *kaṭwa-ī lokkhai.* (glazed-) *kāshīn.*

Pouch, s. *jeb, kīsa*; *dzola-ī, bana-ī, gūdai*; *toshdān.*

Poultice, s. *leṭa-ī, paha, tab.*

Poultry, s. *chirg, chirgūṛī.*

Pounce, v.a. *pa panjo wahal.*

Pound, s. *nīm ser.*

Pound, v.a. *ṭakawul, kūṭal, dzabal, daṛ daṛ-, chūr chūr-,* etc. *k.*

Pour, v.a. *toyawul, āchawul.* (-out) *sandzal.* (-as rain) v.n. *oredal, tsātsedal.* (-over) v.n. *toyedal* or *to-edal.*

Pout, v.a. *būṭ ūrbūz nīwul.*

Poverty, s. *khwārī, tabāhī, muplisī, iplās, tangsiyā.*

Powder, s. *oṛah, maidah, chūr.* (gun-) *dārū.* (-horn) *kkhkar.* (medicine) *paka, kapa, kharpaṭ.*

Powder, v.a. *oṛawul, maidah-, oṛah-,* etc. *k.* (dust) *bornah k.*

Power, s. *zor, quwat*; *was, ṭāqat*; *tuwān, bram.* (authority) *wāk, majāl, ikhtiyār, ḥukm.* (possession) *qābū, qabẓa.*

Powerful, a. *zorāwar, tuwānā, maẓbuṭ, zabar-dast.*

Pox, s. *bād da farang, garmī, juẕām.* (small-) *nanaka-ī.*

Practicable, a. *shwūnkai, mumkin, da kawulo.*

Practical, a. *'amalī, ist'imālī, kṛūnai.*

Practice, s. *'ādat, 'amal, yūn, dastūr, chāl chal.*

Practise, v.a. *kawul, 'ādat-,* etc. *k., mashq k.*

Praise, s. *stāyana, ṣanā, ṣifat, t'arīf.* v.a. *stāyal, stāyana-,* etc. *wayal* or *k.*

Prance, v.a. *traplal, ṭop wahal, kharmastī k., tskhe k.*

Prank, s. *kharmastī, ṭe! ṭāl, laṭah per.*

Pray, v.a. *nmūndz k.*, or *-guzāral* ; *du'a-, minnat-*, etc. *k., darkhwāst k., ghokkhtal.*

Prayer, s. *nmūndz* ; *du'ā.* (-for Lent) *tarāwe.*

Preach, v.a. *w'az k.* ; *khuṭba lwustal.*

Preamble, s. *debācha, muqadamma.*

Precarious, a. *nā-pāedār, teredūnai, zawālī.*

Precaution, s. *dūr andeshī, wṛānde katana.*

Precede, v.n. *wṛānde tlal.*

Precedent, a. *wṛāndīnai.* s. *miṣāl, nakkha.*

Preceding, a. *pakhwānai, wṛūnbanai.*

Precept, s. *matal, miṣāl* ; *ḥukm, kariya* ; *pand, naṣīḥat.*

Preceptor, s. *ākhūn, ustāẓ* ; *nāṣiḥ, pand war-kawūnkai.*

Precinct, s. *ḥadd, pūla, brīd.*

Precious, a. *qīmat-nāk, grān-bahā, matrah* ; *'azīz.*

Precipice, s. *kamar, kanda, gaṛang, tāk.*

Precipitate, a. *jalt, tez, jalt-bāz, talwār-gandai, talwalai, haṛbaṛai.*

Precipitate, v.a. *āchawul, wīshtal, ghurzawul. lawastal* ; *dangawul* ; *jaltī-, talwār-, z-ir-* or *za-ar-*, etc. *k.* v.n. *ghurzedal, prewatal, kkhkenāstal.*

Precipitation, s. *jaltī, talwār, be-ṣabrī.*

Precise, a. *jukht, drust, joṛ, pūrah.*

Precisely, ad. *jukht, joṛ, rikkhtiyā, bedū.*

Precision, s. *barābar-wālai, jukht-wālai, taḥqīq.*

Preclude, v.a. *man'a-, band-, pore jane-.* etc. *k., stanawul, shaṛal.*

Precursor, s. }
Predecessor, s. } *peshrau, wṛānde tlūnai.*

Predestination, s. *taqdīr, qaẓā.*

Predicament, s. *ḥāl* ; *nobat, chal.*

Predicate, s. *khabar, ṣifat, m'aqūl.*

Predict, v.a. *pesh khabarī-, khabar da ghāib-*, etc. *wayal, fāl nīwul, fāl katana k.*

Predominate, v.n. *ghālib-, ghalaba-, ziyāt-, ganṛ-, ḍer-*, etc. *ked.*

Preface, s. *debācha, muqadamma.*

Prefer, v.a. *khwakkhawul, ghwarah k., kkhah ganṛal, kkhāghal* ; *sar buland-, sar farāz-, sar bālā-*, etc. *k.*

Preferable, a. *ghwarah, kkhah.*

Preference, s. *khwakkh* ; *mrasta.*

Preferment, s. *sar farāzī, pāya pa porta.*

Prefix, v.a. *wṛānde-, pa makh-*, etc. *lagawul.*

Pregnant, a. *brālba* or *blārba, ḍaka, warla, shigāra, bār-dāra.* (full) *ḍak, pūrah.* (to make-) v.a. *blārba-*, etc. *k.*

Prejudice, s. *ṭarafdārī, mrasta* ; *mīna, khwā, mā-ilān* ; *bad gumānī, khwā badāwai* ; *tāwān, ziyān.*

Prejudicial, a. *tāwānī, ziyānī, nuqṣānī, bad, muẓirr.*

Prelate, s. *imām, mujtahid.*

Preliminary, a. *wṛūnbanai, awwalanai.*

Premature, a. *be-wakht, be-ṭāng* ; *nīma khwā, kachandai, nīmgaṛai.*

Premeditate, v.a. *pesh fikrī-, pesh bandī-*, etc. *k.* ; *qaṣd-, niyat-*, etc. *taṛal*, or *k.*

Premier, a. *mashar.* s. *wazīr* ; *sarghanah.*

Premium, s. *sūd, naf'a* ; *in'ām, bakhkshiksh* ; *shukrāna, muzd.*

Preparation, s. *tayārī, dzerma, tadbīr.*

Prepare, v.a. *tayārī-*, etc. *k., joṛawul, tayār-awul.*

Preponderate, v.n. *dranedal, drūnd ked., ziyātedal, ḍeredal.*

Preponderation, s. *dranāwai, ḍer-wālai*, etc.

Preposition, s. *ḥarf.*

Prepossess, v.a. *mayan-, mā-ilān-*, etc. *k.*

Prepossession, s. *mayan-tob, mīna.*

Preposterous, a. *be-hūdah, abtar, wūch pūch* ; *naskor, aṛawulai.*

Prepuce, s. *chīchaṛa, da tsūkkha-ī tsarman.*

Prerogative, s. *ḥaqq, wāk, ikhtiyār.*

Presage, s. *pāl, dalālat, āgāhī, nakkha.*

Prescience, s. *khabar da ghā-ib, ghā-ib·dānī.*

Prescribe, v.a. *wayal, farmāyal, ḥukm k., kkhayal—kkhowul.* (medically) *nuskha līkal, -kāgal—kkhkal.* (fix) *taṛal, muqarrar k.*

Presence, s. *ḥuẓūr, khidmat.* (-of mind) *baidārī, ausān, hokkhyār·tiyā.*

Present, a. *ḥāẓir, maujūd; osan, osanai.* (at-) ad. *dā sā'at, os.* s. *bakhkshiksh, nazr, pekkhkakkh, nazrāna, shukrāna.*

Present, v.a. *bakhkkhal* or *bakkhal, kkhandal, warkawul.* (show) *bartser-, kkhkārah-, ẓāhir-*, etc. *k.* (-a gun) *naẓar lagawul.* (introduce) *pekkhawul, wṛānde-, makhā makh-*, etc. *k.*

Presently, ad. *os, dastī, pa de sā'at.*

Preservation, s. *sātana, ĵghorana, khundī·tob, bachawūna.*

Preservative, a. *sātūnai, sātandoe, ĵghorai, bachawūnkai.*

Preserve, v.a. *sātal, ĵghoral, khundiyal, khundī k., bachawul.*

Preserver, s. *sātandoe, ĵghorai, khundī·kawūnkai, bachawūnkai.*

Preside, v.a. *sardārī-, mīr majlisī-, masharī·tob-*, etc. *k.*

President, s. *sardār, mashar; mīr majlis.*

Press, v.a. (squeeze) *nachoṛawul, paz wahal, nakkhtedzal.* (-down) *drabal.* (-into) *kkhke·manḍal.* (knead the limbs) *manḍal.* (urge) *zoral, tezal.* (vex) *tangawul, dabawul.* (-to the bosom) *baṛgaṛandī k.*

Press, s. (oil-) *gānṛa-ī.* (book-) *shikanja.* (a crowd) *ḍala, ganṛ 'ālam.*

Pressure, s. *zor; bār; tangsiyā, grān·tiyā.*

Presume, v.a. *ganṛal, qiyās-, khiyāl-, gumān-*, etc. *k.; dam wahal, gustākhī k.*

Presumptuous, a. *kibr·ĵan, shokh, gustākh.*

Pretend, v.a. *bāna-, chal-, ḥīla-, lamghaṛa-ī-, ṭagī-, hira-ī-*, etc. *k.*

Pretender, s. *bāna·khor, chal·bāz.* (claimant) *d'awa·dār, mudda'ī.* (boaster) *lāpai.*

Pretension, s. *d'awa; ḥujjat.*

Preternatural, a. *karāmatī, zbarg.*

Pretext, s. *bāna, chal, hira-ī, palma, 'uẓr.*

Pretty, a. *kkhāyastah, kkhkulai, peĵ·makhai* or *pa-ī·makhai.* ad. *tsə la-ag* or *la-ag tsa, niĵde.*

Prevail, v.a. *barai mūndal, lānde-, pa-aṛ-*, etc. *k.* v.n. *ziyātedal; jārī ked., chaledal.*

Prevalence, s. *zor, ziyātī, ghalba.*

Prevalent, a. *ziyāt; jārī; zorāwar, wa-aṛ; ghālib.*

Prevaricate, v.a. *palma-, hira-ī-, guzmuzai-*, etc. *k.*

Prevent, v.a. *man'a k., kariyābawul, haṭālawul, bandawul, āṛawul.*

Preventer, s. *mān'i, man'a kawūnkai.*

Prevention, s. *man'a, haṭāl, kariyāb, āṛ, band.*

Previous, a. *pakhwānai, wṛūnbanai, wṛāndīnai, awwalanai.*

Previously, ad. *pakhwā, wṛūnbe, wṛānde, qabl, awwal.*

Prey, s. *kkhkār, māta.* (booty) *lūṭ.* (beast of-) *dad, waḥsh.*

Price, s. *bai'a, baya, bahā, qīmat.* (-current) *nirkh.*

Prick, v.a, *tsekhal, sīkhal, stan-, chūka-*, etc. *wahal, sūṛai k.*

Prickle, s. *āzghai* or *āghzai, khār.*

Prickly, a. *āzghan* or *āghzan.*

Pride, s. *kibr, mastī, wiyāṛ.* (proper-) *nang, ghairat.*

Priest, s. *imām, shekh, pīr, mullā.*

Priestcraft, s. *mullā·tob.*

Priesthood, s. *imāmat, pīr khāna.*

Primarily, ad. *wṛūnbe, awwal.*

Primary, a. *wṛūnbanai, awwalanai.*

Prime, a. *awwal, aṣlī, khāṣṣ, sāwū, karah, sūchah.*

Prime, v.a. *ranjak āchawul.*

Primitive, a. *zoṛ, pakhwānai, awwalanai; aṣlī, zātī.*
Primogeniture, s. *mashar-tob, loe-wālai, loyat.*
Prince s. *shāh-zādah, malik.*
Princess, s. *shāh-zāda-ī, malika.*
Principal, a. *mashar, awwal, sardār; sar, loe, ghaṭ.* s. *panga, saga, māya, aṣl; sardār, sar, sarghanah, mashar.*
Principality, s. *ṣūba, rāj, qalam-rau.*
Principally, ad. *akṣar, awwalan, khuṣūṣan.*
Principle, s. *aṣl, awwal sabab, jauhar; bā'iṣ, jihat; mazhab, dīn; qānūn, ā-īn.*
Print, v.a. *chāp k., chāpa wahal.*
Prior, a. *wṛūnbanai, wṛāndīnai, pakhwānai, awwalanai.*
Privity, s. *awwaliyat, wṛāndīn-tob.*
Prison, s. *qaid-* or *bandī khāna, zindān.*
Prisoner, s. *qaidī, bandī, asīr; naẓar-band.*
Privacy, s. *khilwat, parda, parda-pokkhī, puṭ-wālai, yawādzī-tob, biyal-wālai.*
Private, a. *puṭ, yawādzai, tanhā, tsaṛah, biyal.*
Privately, ad. *pa puṭa, pa parde.*
Privation, s. *nisht-wālai, nābūdī.*
Privilege, s. *ḥaqq; khalāṣī, āzādī.*
Privities, s. *ṣūrat, satr, tor-wekkhtah, andām nihānī, da sharm dzāe.*
Privy, a. *khabar-dār, baidār, wāqif, āgāh.* s. *chār choba, jāe-ẓarūr.*
Prize, s. *in'ām; bāzī, shart, daw; lūṭ, gaṭa, tālā.* (-fighter) *pahlawān.*
Prize, v.a. *kkhah-, 'azīz-, grān-,* etc. *ganral.*
Probability, s. *ṣūrat, shakl; kedana.*
Probable, a. *shwūnkai, kedūnkai.*
Probably, ad. *gunde, kkhā-ī, wī ba* or *ba wī.*
Probation, s. *āzmekkht; umed-wārī.*
Probationer, s. *umed-wār.*
Probe, v.a. *sīkh-, salā-ī-,* etc. *wahal, tsekhal, sīkhal, sūghawul.*
Probity, s. *nekī, rikkhtīn-tob, rāstī.*
Problem, s. *masla, sawāl.*
Problematical. a. *shakk-man, shakk-dār.*
Proboscis, s. *khaṛtam* or *khaṛṭūm, sūnḍak.*
Proceed, v.n. *tlal—lāṛal, chaledal, rawānedal, drūmedal, teredal; watal, paidā ked.* v.a. *kawul, kṛal.*
Proceeding, s. *kār, kṛah, 'amal, mu'amala, chal.*
Proceeds, s. *gaṭa, sūd, paidā-ikkht.*
Process, s. *tarkīb, chalan, shān, ṭaur, rang; jagṛa, mu'amala, muqadamma.*
Procession, s. *swarlī; tamāsha.*
Proclaim, v.a. *munādī k., ḍamāme-, jār-,* etc. *wahal, mashhūr-, jārī-,* etc. *k.*
Procrastinate, v.a. *drangī-, dzanḍ-, lārghah-, multawī-,* etc. *k.*
Procreate, v.a. *zegawul, rāwṛal, paidā k.*
Procurable, a. *muyassar, da mūndalo, da paidā kawulo, mūndūnai.*
Procure, v.a. *mūndal, paidā k., rāwṛal, rasawul.*
Procurer, s. *dallāl, rebār.*
Prodigal, a. *khartsī, iṣrāfī, tāwān kawūnkai.*
Prodigality, s. *kharts, tāwān, iṣrāf, chakhṛaba.*
Prodigious, a. *'ajīb, 'aẓīm, loe, ghaṭ, nāpaṛ.*
Prodigy, s. *'ajab, shanda; subḥān allah.*
Produce, v.a. *rāwṛal, paidā k.*
Produce, s. *ḥāṣil, paidā-ikkht; sūd, gaṭa, naf'a.*
Productive, a. *rāwṛūnkai, paidā kawūnkai.* (-land) *ghala-kheza, ghala-būda, zorāwara, lap-tsaṭa.* (-cattle) *pa-ī-wara.* (-tree) *mewa-dāra.* (-animal) *zeganda-ī.*
Profane, v.a. *nāpāk-, palīt-, murdār-, bilmāz-,* etc. *k.*
Profane, a. *bilmāz, ḥarām, nā-rawā,* etc.
Profess, v.a. *manal, wayal, iqrār k., lal, lawdal.*
Professedly, ad. *pa tsargand, pa jār* or *ẓāhir.*
Profession, s. *iqrār, qaul; kār, kasb.*
Professor, s. *ustād, mullā, mu'allim.*

Proffer, v.a. *nazr-, nazrāna-, pekkhkakkh-*, etc. *warkawul*; *wrānde-, pekkh-*, etc. *k.*; *'uzr k.*

Proficient, a. *pokh, hokkhyār, kārī·gar, khabar·dār.*

Profile, s. *tratskan ṣūrat, tratskana tsihra.*

Profit, s. *sūd, gaṭa, kkhegaṛa, fā-ida, naf'a, būd.* v.a. *gaṭal, sūd-*, etc. *mundal.*

Profitable, a. *sūd·man, fā-ida·man.*

Profligate, a. *lawanḍ, bad·kār, chaṭ. qachar.*

Profound, a. *jawar, star*; *ghaṭ, loe*; *narai, bārīk.*

Profundity, s. *jawar·tiyā, star·wālai*; *loeyat*, etc.

Profuse, a. *tāwānī, khartsī*; *ḍer, frewān, wadān.*

Profusion, s. *tāwān, kharts*; *frewānī, wadānī*, etc.

Progenitor, s. *nīkah, plār·nīkah.*

Progeny, s. *alwād, zāwzād, farzand, nasl, tūng.*

Prognostic, s. *nakkha, 'alāmat, dalīl.*

Prognosticate, v.a. *pesh khabarī k., fāl katal.*

Progress, v.n. *tlal—lāṛal, chaledal, rawānedal.* s. *tlana, chalan, rawānagī.*

Progression, s. *chāl, tah, yūn, raftār.*

Progressive, a. *chaland, rawān.*

Prohibit, v.a. *man'a-, qadaghan- kariya-*, etc. *k.*

Project, s. *tadbīr, band, ḥikmat, tajwīz.*

Projection, s. *tsūka, peza*; *ghunḍa*; *pāṛsob.*

Prolapsus ani, s. *būṛa-ī, watana da kulme.*

Prolific, a. *zeganda-ī*; *mewa·dāra*; *tukhm·reza.*

Prolix, a. *ūgd, ṭūland* or *tūlānd.*

Prolong, v.a. *ūgdawul. ṭūl k,*; *ziyātawul.*

Prominent, a. *ūchat, khatalai*; *tsargand, kkhkārah.*

Promiscuous, a. *gaḍ waḍ, laṛalai, aṛgajah.*

Promise, s. *wāda, lafẓ, qaul, bandanṛ, oe, neta.* v a. *wāda-*, etc. *taṛal* or *k.*

Promising, a. *shwūnai, kkhah, nek bakht, kkhāyastah, joṛ.*

Promissory, a. *sharṭī, qarārī.* (-note) *tamassuk.*

Promontory, s. *khatali zmaka, peza, sar.*

Promote, v.a. *ziyātawul, khejawul*; *sar farāz-, sar buland-, pāya pa porta-*, etc. *k.*

Promotion, s. *sar farāzī, sar bulandī.*

Prompt, a. *chust, chālāk, tayār, gaṛandai.*

Prompt, v.a. *kkhayal—kkhowul*; *yād warkawul*; *lamsawul.*

Promptitude, s. *chālākī, chustī, tayārī.*

Promulgate, v.a. *munādī k., ḍamāme-, jār-*, etc. *wahal, mashhūr k.*

Prone, a. *pa-aṛ·makh*; *prot*; *ṭīṭ*; *mā-ilān, tayār.*

Prong, s. *kkhākha-ī, dwa kkhākha-ī.*

Pronoun, s. *ẓamīr.*

Pronounce, v.a. *wayal*; *ḥukm-, fatwā-*, etc. *k.*

Proof, s. *dalīl, ḥujjat, zbād* or *iṣbāt.* a. *āzmayalai, pokh, āzmūdah.*

Prop, s. *pusht, pushtībān, aṛam, aṛamkai.*

Propagate, v.a. *zegawul, paidā-, jārī-*, etc. *k.*

Propel, v.a. *zghalawul, chalawul, rawānawul*; *āchawul, wīshtal, ghurzawul.*

Propensity, s. *shauq, raghbat, khwā, mīna, mā-il.*

Proper, a. *khāṣṣ*; *rawā*; *kkhah, kkhāyastah. joṛ, wājib, munāsib, pīrzo, drust.*

Properly, ad. *aṣlan* or *pa aṣl*; *pa kkhah shān sara, pa rikkhtiyā.*

Property, s. *māl, milk*; *khoe, khaṣlat, lokkhai, khāṣṣiyat, ṣifat.*

Prophecy, s. *ghā-ib go-ī, da ghā-ib khabara.* v.a. *ghā-ib wayal, da ghā-ib khabarawul.*

Prophet, s. *paighāmbar, nabī, rasūl.*

Propitiate, v.a. *khwā saṛawul* or *-kkhah k., mihrbān k., pakhulā k.*; *kafārat-, ṣadqa-, qurbān-*, etc. *k.*

Propitious, a. *mubārak, nek, mihrbān.*

Proportion, s. *brakha, andāza, qadr, wesh.* v.a. *barābar-*, etc. *k.*, *samawul*; *weshal.*

Propose, v.a. *'arz-, sawāl-, darkhwāst-*, etc. *k.*; *tapos* or *tapahus-, pukkhtana-*, etc. *k.*

Proprietor, s. *merah, tsakkhtan khāwand, mālik, nāyak, khaṣam.*

Propriety, s. *kkhāyast·wālai, drust·wālai, nek chalan, munāsibat, lā-iqat, pīrzo·wālai.*

Prorogue, v.a. *barkhwāst-, mauqūf-, nāgha-*, etc. *k.*

Prose, s. *naṣr.* (-writer) *naṣr nawīs.*

Prosecute, v.a. *chalawul, kawul, lagiyā k.* v.n. *lagedal, mashghūledal, lagiyā osedal.* (sue) v.a. *d'awa-, faryād-*, etc. *k.*, *ghāṛa-, grewa-*, etc. *nīwul.* v.n. *pase prewatal, pase lagedal.*

Prosecutor, s. *mudda'-ī, laman-, ghāṛa-*, etc. *nīwūnkai, d'awa-*, etc. *kawūnkai.*

Proselyte, s. *murīd, m'utaqid.*

Prospect, s. *nandāra, līdah, nazar,* (likelihood) *ṣūrat.* (hope) *umed.*

Prosper, v.n. *barakatī-, bakhtawar-*, etc. *osedal* or *-ked.*; *wadānedal, ābādedal, maṛedal.*

Prosperity, s. *barakat, bakht, nek bakhtī*; *ābādī, wadānī, moṛ·tiyā.*

Prosperous, a. *barakatī, iqbāl·man, sa'ādat·man, bakhtawar*; *moṛ, ābād, wadān.*

Prostitute, s. *kachana-ī, lola-ī.*

Prostitution, s. *kachana-ī·tob, lola-ī·tob.*

Prostrate, a. *pa-aṛmakh, prot.* v.n. *pa-aṛmakh prewatal.* v.a. *sijda k.*; *naṛawul, ghuzārawul*; *parzawul.*

Prostration, s. *pa-aṛmakh·tob*; *sijda*; *kamzor·tiyā.*

Protect, v.a. *bachawul, panāh k., nanawātah manal, sātal, jghoral, khundī-, khaṣamāna-*, etc. *k.*; *pālal, nmāndzal.*

Protection, s. *panāh*; *sātana*, etc. (asylum) *nanawātah.*

Protector, s. *sātandoe, jghorai*; *pālūnkai*; *nāyak.*

Protest, v.a. *iqrār k., lal, lawdal*; *raṭal, traṭal*; *nāre-, faryād-*, etc. *k.*

Protract, v.a. *ūgdawul*; *drang-, lārghah-*, etc. *k.*

Protrude, v.n. *bāhar watal, khatal.*

Protuberance, s. *ghunḍakai, pāṛsob, pūpaka.*

Proud, a. *kibr·jan, bādī, mast, khāntamā, maghrūr.*

Prove, v.a. *ṣābit-, ṣubūt-, zbād-, rikkhtiyā-*, etc. *k.* (try) *āzmāyal, āzmekkht k.* (happen) v.n. *kedal, shwal, prewatal, khatal.*

Provender, s. *wuch wākkhah dapāra da tsārwo.*

Proverb, s. *matal, miṣāl, maṣal.*

Proverbial, a. *matalī*; *mashhūr.*

Provide, v.a. *rāwṛal, paidā k., tadbīr-, tayār-, dzerma-*, etc. *k.*, *khabar ākhistal, khabar gīrī k.*; *warkawul*; *shart taṛal.* (-against) *pesh·fikrī k.*

Provided, c. *pa shart, pa ṣūrat, pa ḥāl.*

Providence, s. *khudāe, rabb, razzāq.* (foresight) *dūr andeshī, pesh·fikrī.*

Provident, a. *dūr andesh, khabar·dār.*

Providentially, ad. *da khudāe pa ḥukm sara, da rabb pa mihrbāngī sara.*

Province, s. *ṣūba, pargana, tapa*; *kār, khidmat*; *gharaz.*

Provision, s. *tadbīr, fikr*; *dzerma, tayārī.*

Provisions, s. *khwurāk, khwāṛah, ṭa'ām, ghizā.* (-for a journey, etc.) *azūqa, tokkha, tantosh, tsawrai.* (-for an army, etc.) *rasad, zakhīra, sūrsāt.*

Provisional, a. *shartī.*

Proviso, s. *shart.*

Provocation, s. *pārawuna, ṭongāra*; *grwākkh.*

Provoke, v.a. *pārawul, zoral, āgayal, grwākkhal, khapah k.*

Prowess, s. *maṛāna, maṛanī·tob, tūrzan·tob, bahādūrī, dzwānmardī.*

Prowl, v.n. *ghalai girzedal, gakkht k.*

Proximate, a. *nijde, nizd, rātlūnai.*

Proximity, s. *nijdekī* or *nizdekī.*

Proxy, s. *badalī, 'iwaẓī ; nā-ib.*

Prudent, a. *khabardār, pokh, hokkhyār.*

Prune, v.a. *prekawul, tarāshal, shūkawul.*
(-as birds) *banre jorawul, waza-ar tsandal.*
s. *ashārai, kishta.*

Pry, v.a. *zarana-ī-, tsār-, jāsūsī-, dzīr-,* etc. *k.*

Psalm, s. *zabūr ; stāyai.*

Puberty, s. *dzwānī, bulūghat, zalmī·tob.*

Public, a. *'āmm, mashhūr; tsargand, kkhkārah.*
s. *khalq, 'āmmiyān, ilas* or *ulūs.*

Publicity, s. *shuhrat, gada.*

Publicly, a. *pa tsargand, pa jār* or *pa ẓāhir.*

Publish, v.a. *mashhūr-, ẓāhir-, gad-,* etc. *k.*

Pucker, s. *jung, gundza, chunr, kratai, chīchar.*

Puddle, s. *tsaparai, dandūkai.*

Puff, s. *pū, pūk.* (-of wind) *tsapa.* **v.a.**
pūkal, pūk wahal; parsawul, tyak k.

Pugilist, s. *mūka-ī-* or *sūk wahūnkai, musht·*
zan.

Puisne, a. *kashar, kachotai.*

Puissant, a. *zorāwar, quwat·nāk.*

Pull, v.a. *rākāgal—rākkhkal.* (-out) *kāgal—*
kkhkal, bāsal—yastal. (-along) *kashāla k.*
(-down) *narawul.* **s.** *kakkh, rākkhkah.*

Pullet, s. *chirgūrai, chūchai.*

Pulley, s. *tsarkha-ī.*

Pulp, s. *māghzah.*

Pulpit, s. *mimbar.*

Pulsate, v.n. *drazedal.* **v.a.** *tsirīke wahal.*

Pulsation, s. *draz, tsirīka.*

Pulse, s. *nabẓ, rag.* (to feel the-) *nabẓ*
katal. (pea) s. *chanra, mot, māhe, māsh,*
ma-ī or *mayī.*

Pulverize, v.a. *orawul, orah-, maidah-,* etc. *k.*

Pump, v.a. *oba pa nalo rākāgal—rākkhkal* or
-bāsal—yastal; matlab-, rāz-, etc. *bāsal—*
yastal.

Pumpkin, s. *kadū.* (-seed) *kadū zarai.*

Pun, s. *latīfa, dwa ma'nī khabara.*

Punch, v.a. *sūrai k.; sūk wahal.*

Punctual, a. *pūrah, sūchah, rikkhtīnai.*

Punctuality, s. *rikkhtīn·tob, rāstī.*

Punctually, ad. *jukht·pa nete* or *-wakht.*

Puncture, s. *sūra, tsīra.*

Pungent, a. *tez, tund.*

Punish, v.a. *sazā warkawul, wahal, tānān*
ākhistal.

Punishment, s. *sazā, 'uqūbat, siyāsat.*

Puny, a. *kachotai, kuchinai, kharmandai,*
potai, wor, khamachah, worūkai.

Pupil, s. *shāgird, murīd, chelah.* (-of eye)
torai, bātor, kasai, lema, tagh.

Puppet, s. *godā, goda-ī, nāwaka-ī, nenzaka,*
nāzaka.

Puppy, s. *kūtrai, kungarai.*

Purchase, v.a. *pa bai'e ākhistal, pīral, pīrodal.*

Purchaser, s. *pa bai'e ākhistūnkai, pīrūnkai.*

Pure, a. *pāk, ṣāf, harah, sūchah, khāliṣ,*
torai, kkhah ; pāk laman, nek, pākīzah or
pāzīkah ; pūrah.

Purely, ad. *surup, ta-ash, khālī.*

Purgative, a. *mushil, jullābī.*

Purgatory, s. *i'raf.*

Purge, s. *jullāb, jār.* **v.a.** *jullāb-,* etc. *war-*
kawul. **v.n.** *nāstah lagedal, pa dastūno*
kkhkenāstal.

Purification, s. *pākawuna.* (ceremonial)
awdas, tebūn, or *temūn,* or *tayammum,*
tahārat.

Purify, v.a. *pākawul, pāk-, pākīzah-, ṣāf,*
etc. *k., spetsal* or *spedzal.*

Purity, s. *pākī, pakīzagī, pāk-, ṣāf-,* etc.
-wālai, spetsal·tob ; rikkhtīn·tob.

Purple, a. *arghawānī, tor sūr.*

Purport, s. *ma'nī, ma'nā, matlab.*

Purpose, s. *niyat, qaṣd, irāda, murād, gharaẓ.*
(on-) ad. *pa qasd.* (to what-?) *tsa la, tsa*
dapāra, wale. (to the-) *ṣanāb, jor, jukht.*
v.a. *niyat-,* etc. *taral,* or *larul,* or *k.*

Purr, v.a. *khur wahal, khur khur k.*

Purse, s. *hamiyānī, kīsa, būtskhaka.*
Purslain, s. *warkhāṛai, khulfa* or *khurfa.*
Pursuant, a. *muwāfiq.* (-to) ad. *pa mūjib.*
Pursue, v.n. *pase zghaledal—zghākkhtal*; *pase tlal, -lagedal, -ked.*, etc.
Pursuit, s. *zghākkht, tekkhta*; *mashghūlā, kār*; *kokshiksh, tapos, talāsh.*
Purulent, a. *zawlan.*
Purvey, v.a. *khwurāk-, rasad-, sūrsāt-, zakhīra-*, etc. *ṭolawul.*
Pus, s. *zawa* or *ziwa, ra-ash, zahūb, khīrai.*
Push, v.a. *ṭel-, ḍakka-*, etc. *wahal.*
Pusillanimous, a. *nāmard, yer·man.*
Pustule, s. *nanaka-ī, dāna*; *kharai.*
Put, v.a. *gdal* or *īgdal, īkkhodal, īkkhawul, īkkhal, kkhkegdal*, etc., *lagawul.* (-away) *lire k., sharal.* (-off) *mu'aṭṭal-, drang-*, etc. *k.* (-on) *āghostal, pa dzān-*, etc. *k.* (-out) *muṛ k.* (-together) *joṛawul, yo dzāe k., ṭolawul.* (-up with) *wṛal, zghamal.*
Putrefy, v.n. *wrostedal, pūdah-, skhā-*, etc. *ked.*; *sharhedal.*
Putrid, a. *wrost, skhā, pūdah.*
Puzzle, v.a. *hariyānawul, rabrawul, hak pak k., ḥairān* or *hariyān-, sarāsīmah-*, etc. *k.* s. *pech, ghūṭai, kaga waga.*

Q.

Quack, s. *lāpai, nīmgaṛai ṭabīb, -mullā*, etc.
Quack, v.a. *qā qā k.*
Quadrilateral, a. *chār gūṭlai.*
Quadruped, s. *tsārwai, dāba, suṭūr.*
Quadruple, s. *tsalor bragh, tsalor chand.*
Quaff, v.a. *skal, tskal* or *tskkhal.*
Quagmire, s. *bokkhtana, khaṭa, palanda, taramna.*
Quail, s. *mṛaz, nwaṛaz.*
Quaint, a. *'ajīb*; *laṭīf, nāzak, bārīk.*
Quake, v.n. *laṛzedal, rapedal, pṛakedal.*

Qualification, s. *lā-iqat, qābilyat.*
Qualified, a. *lā-iq, qābil, yarzan.*
Quality, s. *khoe, khaṣlat, ṣifat, ṭab'a, lokkhai.* (rank) *martaba, pāya, darja, kor.*
Qualm, s. *bāka-ī, chāl.* (-of conscience) *gram.* (to have a-) *bāka-ī-*, etc. *k.*; *gram ked.*
Quantity, s. *qadr, andāza, wazn.*
Quarrel, v.a. *jang-, jagaṛa-, qaẓiya-*, etc. *k.*
Quarrelsome, a. *jang·yālai, jagṛāū, bādī.*
Quarry, s. (game) *kkhkār.* (stone-) *da kānro kān.*
Quart, s. *ser.*
Quarter, s. *pāo, tsalorama brakha.* (side) *khwā, lorai, tselma, rokh*; *aṛakh, tsang, dada.* (district) *palaw, cham, khel, kandai, maḥalla.* (asylum) *panāh, nanawātah, āmān, amn.* (lodging) *dzāe, astoga, borjal, ṭikāo.*
Quash, v.a. *mātawul.* (annul) *bāṭil k.*
Quaver, v.n. *trangedal*; *laṛzedal, rapedal, pṛakedal.*
Quay, s. *pushta, dunkācha.*
Queen, s. *malika.* (-at chess, etc.) *wazīr.*
Queer, a. *'ajab, 'ajīb.*
Quell, v.a. *kkhkenawul, saṛawul, mātawul, lānde-, man'a-*, etc. *k.*
Quench, v.a. *saṛawul, muṛ k.*
Query, s. *sawāl, tapos* or *tafaḥus.*
Quest, s. *talāsh, ṭalab, tagā pū.*
Question, s. *sawāl, tapos, pukkhtana*; *gumān, shakk, shubha.* v.a. *pukkhtedal, sawāl-*, etc. *k., gumān-*, etc. *laral.*
Questionable, a. *shakk·man, gumānī.*
Quibble, s. *hira-ī, palma, lamghaṛa-ī, ḥīla, chal.*
Quick, a. *za-ar* or *zir, jalt, gaṛandai, chālāk, zghard, tez, talwār·gandai.* (alive) *jwandai.* s. *ūra-ī, jwanda-ī ghwakkha.*
Quicken, v.a. *jwandai k.*; *za-ar* or *zir-*, etc. *k.*
Quickly, ad. *zir zir, pa talwār, pa gaṛandī.*

Quickness, s. *talwār, garand-wālai.*
Quicksand, s. *bokkhtana, ghal shiga.*
Quicksilver, s. *pārā, sīmāb.*
Quiet, a. *chup, ghalai; qalār, ārām.* s. *qalār-tiyā, ārām-tiyā, āsūdagī.*
Quietly, ad. *ro ro, pa qalār sara.*
Quietness, s. *ghalī-tob; ārām-tiyā; gharībī.*
Quill, s. *banra, shāh par* or *kkhāh par.*
Quilt, s. *brastan; nihālī, tolā-ī, toshak.*
Quince, s. *biha-ī* or *bī.* (-seed) *bī dāna.*
Quinsy, s. *haspa, khunāq.*
Quintessence, s. *jauhar, aṣl; khulāṣa.*
Quit, v.a. *pregdal, prekkhodal, prekkhal, tark k.*
Quite, a. *pūrah, amānī, sarāsar, tamām, wāṛah, ṭol ṭāl.* (in comp.) *tak-, ṭap-*, etc.
Quiver, s. *laṛza, paṛak.* (-for arrows) *shkhwalai, tar kakkh.*
Quiver, v.n. *laṛzedal, rapedal, paṛakedal.*
Quota, s. *brakha, wesh, ḥiṣṣa.*
Quote, v.a. *sanad rāwṛal, da bul chā khabara* (or *wayai*) *yādawul.*

R.

Rabbit, s. *khargosh, koranai soe.*
Rabble, s. *ḍala, paṛk, ganr khalq.*
Race, s. *manḍa, zghākkht.* (generation) *aṣl, nasl, ẓāt, khāndān, kor, noga.*
Rack, s. *shikanja, tsarkh, pāna, kāṭ.* v.a. *pa shikanjo-*, etc. *khejawul, 'aẓābawul.*
Radiance, s. *brekkhnā, ranrā, palwasha.*
Radiant, a. *brekkh-nāk, rūnr, dzalkan.*
Radiate, v.n. *brekkhedal, dzalkedal, rūnredal.*
Radical, a. *aṣlī, ẓātī.*
Radish, s. *mūla-ī, turp.*
Raffle, v.a. *pa hisk-, pa pucho-, pa qur'o-*, etc. *khartsawul.*
Raft, s. *jāla, beṛa.*
Rafter, s. *bensh, lakaṛa, paṭera.*
Rag, s. *chirra, paṛūkai, pārcha, purza, khartsoṛai.*
Rage, s. *qahr, ghuṣṣa, ghaẓab, tāo; saudā.*
Ragged, a. *ṭūkī ṭūkī.* (in rags) *gand* or *kind poksh.* (uneven) *zīg, lwāṛ jawar, kandai kaudarai.*
Raging, a. *ghaẓab-nāk, qahr-jan, khapah, eshānd.*
Rail, v.a. *keṛ-, bāra-, shpol-*, etc. *taṛal* or *-lagawul.* (abuse) *peghor warkawul, kanzal* or *kkhkandzal.* (blame) *malāmatawul, raṭal, traṭal.*
Raiment, s. *āghostan, zaṛūkai, nwarai, jāma, pokkhāk, libās.*
Rain, s. *bārān.* (slight-) *rangai bārān, pūna.* (heavy-) *ganr bārān, shebah.* (spring shower) *hakkhma, wasa.* (hot weather-) *parshakāl.* (-bow) *shna kāsa, sara kāsa, da būḍa-ī ṭāl.*
Rain, v.n. *oredal, tsātsedal, bārānedal.*
Raise, v.a. *pātsawul, khejawul, porta k.* (erect) *walāṛawul, wudrawul, lakawul.* (educate) *pālal, nmāndzal, parwaral.*
Raisin, s. *watska, mewa.*
Rake, s. *pāṛa, ghākkhawar, panj-gakkhai; lawanḍ, chaṭ, kāsīr, lūtsak.*
Rake, v.a. *ghākkhawar girzawul, panj-gakkhai wahal; kāsīrī-*, etc. *k.* (search) *laṭawul.* (collect) *ṭolawul.*
Rally, v.a. *ṭīngawul, sambālawul, joṛawul, maẓbūṭ k., komak rasawul.* (jeer) *khandā-, ṭoqa-*, etc. *k.*
Ram, s. *mag, ga-ad.* (fighting) *ghūch.*
Ram, v.a. *manḍal, kkhke manḍal.*
Ramble, v.n. *girzedal, sail k.*
Rambler, s. *gashtai, āwārah, lawanḍ.*
Ramify, v.n. *khwaredal, wīṛedal, pheledal.*
Rammer, s. *pāeko, ḍabalai, bargho.*
Rampant, a. *mast, shokhīn.*
Rampart, s. *kkhahr panāh, bāra, sangar.*

Rancid, a. *skhā, wrost, trīw, trīkh.*

Rancour, s. *kīna, bughz, khwā badī, 'inād.*

Random, a. *tawakkulī, qismatī.* (at-) ad. *hase.*

Range, v.a. *sail-, gakkht-*, etc. *k.* v.n. *girz-edal.* (set) *tartībawul, sambālawul.*

Rank, s. *martaba, pāya, dzāe, darja; para, ṣaff, qatār.* a. *wrost, skhā, bad·būī·dār.* v.a. *para-*, etc. *taṛal; ganṛal, shmeral.*

Rankle, v.n. *baledal, eshedal, khūyedal* or *khū-edal, swal.*

Ransack, v.a. *laṭawul, shanal; tālā-, lūt-*, etc. *k.*

Ransom, s. *būnga.*

Rant, v.a. *lāpe shāpe wahal; baq baq-, baṛ baṛ-*, etc. *k.*

Rap, v.a. *wahal, trakawul, ṭak wahal, ṭak-awul.*

Rapacious, a. *lūṭ·bāz, ghārat·gar; khūnāṛai.*

Rape, v.a. *bikr mātawul, pa zabardastī gho-wul.* (-seed) *awrai.*

Rapid, a. *gaṛandai, za-ar* or *zir, jalt, tez, tund.*

Rapidity, s. *jaltī, talwār, tundī, tezī.*

Rapine, s. *lūṭ, ghārat, tālān, tākht tārāj.*

Rapture, s. *ḍera khūsh·ḥālī, josh, eshnā.*

Rare, a. *nādir, matrah, kam paidā.* (thin) *narai.*

Rarify, v.a. *narai-, mahīn-, bārīk-*, etc. *k.*

Rarely, ad. *kamtar, la-ag.*

Rascal, s. *ḥarāmī, laṛalai, badm'āsh, char-lanḍ.*

Rash, a. *talwalai, talwār·gandai, jalt, be·tad-bīr, zir.* (-on the skin) *garmaka, laṛama, sra makha, jarmoṛa, nanaka-ī, dzwānaka.*

Rasp, v.a. *sohān-, chausār-*, etc. *wahal*, or *k.*; *sūlawul, zīgawul, zdoyal.*

Rat, s. *magak, magah, samandai.* (musk-) *mukkhkai magak.*

Rate, s. *bai'a, qīmat, nirkh; andāza, ḥisāb; shān, ṭaur.* v.a. *bai'a-*, etc. *taṛal; an-dāza-*, etc. *k., ganṛal.* (scold) *raṭal, traṭal, dāṛal.*

Rather, ad. *wṛūnbe, awwal, lā.*

Ratify, v.a. *qabūlawul, muqarrar k.*

Ratio, s. *andāza, wazn.*

Rational, a. *'aql·man, pohānd; munāsib.*

Rationality, s. *'aql, poh, pahm, sha'ūr.*

Rattle, v.a. *shṛangawul, gṛanjawul, ga-arahār k.* s. *chanṛ chanṛai, gṛanjāū.*

Ravage, v.a. *tālā-, wairān-, ūjāṛ-, kkhpo lānde-*, etc. *k., latāṛawul, natal.*

Rave, v.a. *be·khūdə khabare k., baṛ baṛ k.*

Raven, s. *kāgh.*

Ravenous, a. *liwāl, wagai, naghlānd.*

Ravine, s. *khwaṛ, kandạ, kas.*

Ravish, v.a. *bikr shlawul* or *-mātawul; pa zor ākhistal; satr ākhistal.*

Raw, a. *ūm* or *om, nīma·khwā, nīm·pokh, kachah.* (abraded) *sūdah, sūlawulai.* (-cold) *soṛ.*

Rawness, s. *om·wālai; sāṛa.*

Ray, s. *palwasha, partaw, dzalak, shughla.*

Raze, v.a. *naṛawul, kkhpo lānde-, latāṛah-*, etc. *k.*

Razor, s. *ustura, pāka-ī.* (-strap) *paṭaka.*

Reach, v.n. *rasedal, rātlal, rāghlal.* (touch) *lagedal, jangedal.* (-out) *ghazedal* or *gazedal.* (fetch) v.a. *rāwṛal.*

Reaction, s. *zor, quwat.*

Read, v.a. *lwustal, kitāb katal.*

Readiness, s. *tayārī, chālākī.*

Reading, s. *lwustūn.* (-the Qurān) *qirāt.*

Ready, a. *tayār, chālāk, ḥāẓir.*

Real, a. *rikkhtīnai, aṣlī, sūchah, karah.*

Reality, s. *rikkhtiyā, rikkhtīn·tob, ḥaqīqat.*

Realize, v.a. *mūndal, gaṭal; paidā-, ḥāẓir-*, etc. *k.*

Really, ad. *rikkhtiyā, khudāe go.*

Realm, s. *mulk, rāj, bādshāhī; hiwād.*

Reap, v.a. *lau k., rebal, rawdal; mūndal, gaṭal.*

Reaper, s. *lau·garai; gaṭūnkai.*

Rear, s. *wrūstai, shā, dumbāl.* (in the-) ad. *wrūsto, pa shā, pastana.*

Rear, v.a. *khejawul, pātsawul, walārawul.* v.n. *walāredal, pātsedal, khatal.* (-up) *negh-, lak-, jig-,* etc. *walāredal* or *-ked.* (nourish) *parwaral, pālal, nmāndzal.*

Reason, s. *'aql, poh, pahm.* (cause) *sabab, kabl, bā'is ; mūjib, wāsiṭa, jihat.* (proof) *dalīl, hujjat.* (right) *haqq. insāf.* v.a. *bahs-,* etc. *k.*

Reasonable, a. *wājib, munāsib, kkhāyastah, kkhah.*

Rebel, s. *yāghī·gar. sar·kakkh.* v.a. *yāghī· garī-, sar·kakkhī-,* etc. *k.* v.n. *yāghī-,* etc. *ked.*

Rebellious, a. *yāghī, ṭughiyān.*

Rebound, v.a. *tīndak wahal, ṭop wahal.*

Rebuke, v.a. *malāmatawul, raṭal, dāṛal ;* (-oneself) *gram k.*

Recall, v.a. *biyā balal, stūnawul* or *stanawul ; yādawul.*

Recant, v.a. *rāe badlawul.* v.n. *girzedal, jārwatal, stūnedal* or *stancdal ; munkiredal.*

Recapitulate, v.a. *biyā bayānawul.*

Recede, v.n. *wrusto ked., stanedal, haṭedal, pastana ked., jārwatal.*

Receipt, s. *rasīd, hujjat, tamassuk.*

Receive, v.a. *ākhistal ; manal.*

Recent, a. *nawai, osanai, nan wradzanai.*

Recently, ad. *os, pa zir mūde.*

Receptacle, s. *khūna, dzāe, kor, makān.*

Reception, s. *ākhistah ; manana ; istiqbāl; melmastiyā.*

Recess, s. *ṭāq, ṭāqcha, rap, dara-ī ; gūṭ, gokkha.* (suspension) *barkhwāst, wazgār· tiyā, t'aṭīl.*

Recipe, s. *nuskha.*

Reciprocal, a. *da dwāṛo paṛo, -loro, -dado,* etc., *ṭarfain, jānibain.*

Recite, v.a. *bayānawul, yādawul, naql k.*

Reckon, v.a. *shmeral, shumāral, hisābawul ; ganral.* v.n. *pohedal, pahmedal.*

Reclaim, v.a. *joṛawul, sambālawul, ābādawul, wadānawul.*

Recline, v.n. *tsamlāstal, tsamlal, mlāstal. ghazedal* or *gazedal.*

Recluse, s. *gokkha·nishīn.*

Recognisance, s. *iqrār·nāma.*

Recognition, s. *pejāndah, pejandgalī.*

Recognize, v.a. *pejandal.*

Recoil, v.a. *tīndak wahal.* v.n. *sianedal, pa biyarta jārwatal..*

Recollect, v.a. *yādawul ; zdah k.*

Recollected, s. *yād, zdah.*

Recommend, v.a. *sipārish k., spāral.*

Recompense, v.a. *tāwān-, badal-,* etc. *war· kawul.*

Reconcile, v.a. *pakhulā k., rogha joṛa k., khwā saṛawul ; manal, barābarawul.*

Record, s. *daftar, tawārīkh.* v.a. *līkal, darj k.*

Recorder, s. *qānūn·goe, sarishta·dār.*

Recount, v.a. *bayānawul.*

Recover, v.n. *raghedal, joṛedal.* v.a. *biyā· mūndal.*

Recovery, s. *raghedana, joṛedana ; biyā· mūndah.*

Recreation, s. *sail, tamāsha, loba, wazgār·tiyā.*

Recriminate, v.a. *chighawul, sara kanzal k., lagiyā sara peghorūna warkawul.*

Recruit, v.a. *hosā-,* etc. *k., dama warkawul ; pūrah-,* etc. *k., nawai nokar k.*

Rectify, v.a. *joṛawul, sam-, drust-,* etc. *k.*

Rectitude, s. *rikkhtīn·tob, nekī, rāstī, sawāb.*

Rectum, s. *chustai, kulma.*

Recumbent, a. *mlāst, prot, ghazedalai.*

Recur, v.n. *rātlal, rāghlal ; yādedal.*

Red, a. *sūr, lāl, surkh, rat.*

Redeem, v.a. *khalāsawul, āzādawul, bach· awul.*

Redress, v.a. *tāwān warkawul, dādrasī , niyāw-,* etc. *k.*

Reduce, v.a. *kamawul, lanḍawul, saṛawul*; *rāwṛal.*

Reduction, s. *kam·tiyā, la-ag·wālai*; *troṭ, zwam.*

Redundant, a. *ziyāt, ḍer.*

Reed, s. *ḍūrma, darwai, nal, shpelai, lūkha.*

Reel, s. *aṭerān, tsarkhai.* (-of thread) *aṭa* or *aṭeha.* (dance) *atanr.*

Refer, v.a. *pukkhtedal, spāral, līdal—goral, katal, lagawul, nisbat laral.* v.n. *lagedal.*

Reference, s. *nisbat, 'alāqa, ta'alluq, lār.*

Referee, s. *munṣif.*

Refine, v.a. *pāk-, ṣāf-, spīn-*, etc. *k., narai-*, etc. *k.*

Refit, v.a. *joṛawul.*

Reflect, v.a. *fikr-, ghaur-*, etc. *k.*; *siwrai-, 'aks-*, etc. *āchawul.*

Reflux, s. *jārwātah, stūnedah.*

Reform, v.a. *nawai joṛawul, ārāstah k.*

Refractory, a. *yāghī, sar·kakkh, ṭakanrai.*

Refrain, v.a. *parhez k., dzān sātal.* v.n. *ḍaḍa ked.*

Refresh, v.a. *hosā-, tāzah-*, etc. *k., dama warkawul, khwā saṛawul.*

Refreshment, s. *khwūrāk, naharai, ṭa'ām*; *ārām, dama.*

Refuge, s. *āsra, panāh*; *nanawātah, amn.*

Refugee, s. *nanawātai, panāh·gīr.*

Refulgent, a. *rūnr, rokkhān, brekkh·nāk.*

Refund, v.a. *stūnawul* or *stanawul, biyarta-, pastana-*, etc. *warkawul*; *tāwān warkawul.*

Refuse, v.a. *namanal, naqabūlawul, daregh-, ibā-*, etc. *k.*, or *-rāwṛal.*

Refute, v.a. *bāṭil-, radd-*, etc. *k.*; *gram k.*

Regain, v.a. *biyā mūndal.*

Regal, a. *bādshāhī.*

Regard, v.a. *naẓar-, nigāh-*, etc. *k., katal*; *manal*; *fikr-*, etc. *k., khabar ākhistal*; *ganral.*

Regardless, a. *be·khabar, be·parwā.*

Regent, s. *qā-im muqām, nā-ib.*

Regimen, s. *pāl, parhez, tīmār.*

Regiment, s. *palṭan.* (-of horse) *risāla.*

Region, s. *zmaka, mulk, hiwād.*

Register, s. *daftar, sijill, shajara.*

Regret, s. *afsos, daregh, armān, tartāb, stomānī, pakkhemānī.* v.a. *afsos-*, etc. *k.* v.n. *stomānedal, pakkhemān ked.*

Regular, a. *barābar, sam, hawār, drust*; *qānūnī, ā-īnī, intiẓāmī.*

Regulation, s. *ā-īn, qānūn*; *tartīb.*

Reject, v.a. *lire k., sharal*; *jārbāsal—jāryastal*; *nā·qabūl*; *nā·khwakkh-*, etc. *k.*

Reign, v.a. *bādshāhī-, rāj-, ḥukm-*, etc. *k.*

Reimburse, v.a. *warkawul, tāwān-, badal-, 'iwaẓ-*, etc. *warkawul, stūnawul, pūrah-*, etc. *k.*

Rein, s. *wāga, mlūna*; *jalab, bādgol.*

Reinstate, v.a. *pa dzāe kkhkenawul* or *-muqarrar k.*

Rejoice, v.a. *kkhādī-, khūsh·ḥālī-*, etc. *k.* v.n. *kkhādedal, khūsh·ḥāledal, kkhād·man ked.* (spitefully) v.a. *sakha-, wiyāṛ-*, etc. *k.*

Rejoin, v.a. *joṛawul, lagawul.* v.n. *gaḍedal.*

Reiterate, v.a. *dubāra-, biyā biyā-, wār wār-*, etc. *wayal.*

Relate, v.a. *bayānawul, wayal, qiṣṣa k.*; *nisbat-, 'alāqa-*, etc. *laral.* v.n. *lagedal.*

Relation, s. *bayān, qiṣṣa*; *nisbat-, 'alāqa-, khpul, khekkh, 'azīz.* (paternal-) *plār·ganai.* (maternal-) *mor·ganai*, etc.

Relationship, s. *khpul·walī, khpulawī, 'azīz·walī* or *'azīz·galwī, khekkhī*; *ragai, haḍ.*

Relative, s. *khpul, khekkh*, etc. (*v.* Relation) a. *nisbatī.*

Relax, v.a. *arat-, sust-*, etc. *k.*

Relaxation, s. *arat·wālai, sust·wālai*; *sustī*; *wazgār·tiyā.*

Release, v.a. *āzādawul, khalāṣawul, wurhawul, yalah k., pregdal, prekkhodal, prekkhal.*

Relent, v.n. *narmedal, mulā-im ked.*

Relentless, a. *be·raḥm, sang·dil, kāṉrai zrah.*
Reliance, s. *bāwar, umed, takiya, tawakkul.*
Relief, s. *madad, komak*; *ārām*; *badlī.*
Relieve, v.a. *madad-, komak-,* etc. *rasawul*; *ārām warkawul*; *badlī k.*
Religion, s. *dīn, īmān, maẕhab, kesh.*
Religious, a. *dīn·dār, īmān·dār, nmānḏzī, nmūnḏz·guẕār*; *dīnī, maẕhabī.*
Relinquish, v.a. *pregdal, prekkhodal, prekkhal, tark k.*
Relish, v.a. *khwand-, maza-,* etc. *warkawul, maza·dār-, khwand·nāk-,* etc. *k.*
Reluctance, s. *daregh, stomānī.*
Reluctant, a. *nārāẓ, stomān.*
Rely, v.a. *bāwar-, takiya-, tawakkul-,* etc. *k.*
Remain, v.n. *pātedal, pāedal, osedal, pātai ked.*
Remainder, s. *bāqī, pātai.*
Remains, s. *pas·khurda, jūṭa.* (mortal-) *muṛai.*
Remark, v.a, *naẓar-, nigāh-,* etc. *k., yādawul, wayal.*
Remarkable, a. *'ajīb, 'ajab*; *mashhūr.*
Remedy, s. *'ilāj, dawā, tsāra, darmān, tadbīr.* v.a. *'ilāj-,* etc. *k., joṛawul, raghawul.*
Remember, v.a. *yādawul, yād laral, pejandal*; *zdah k.*
Remembrance, s. *yād*; *pejāndah.*
Remind, v.a. *yād warkawul.*
Remiss, a. *sust, ghāfil, soṛ, narm.*
Remit, v.a. *bakkhal, pulawul, mu'āf k.* (send) *āstawul, legal.* (lessen) *kamawul, la-agawul.*
Remittance, s. *bakkhana*; *āstawūna*; *kamawūna.*
Remnant, a. *bāqī, pātai.*
Remonstrance, s. *'arẓī*; *takrār*; *gila.*
Remorse, s. *paskhāk* or *pakhsāk, pakkhemānī.*
Remote, a. *liri* or *lire, prat.*
Remove, v.a. *liri k., khejawul*; *kaḍa wṛal, legdal—lekkhal, kūch k.*

Remunerate, v.a. *ajr-, ujrat-, miḥnat-,* etc. *warkawul*; *tāwān-, shukrāna-,* etc. *warkawul.*
Rend, v.a. *shlawul, tsīral, tsāk k., mātawul, wrarawul.*
Render, v.a. *kawul, kṛal, rāwṛal.*
Rendezvous, s. *borjal.* v.n. *ṭoledal, yo dzāe ked.*
Renew, v.a. *biyā kawul, -rāwṛal, -ākhistai,* etc. *nawai-, tāzah-,* etc. *k.*
Rennet, s. *tomna, māya*; *siyalai.*
Renounce, v.n. *munkiredal, jārwatal.* v.a. *inkār-,* etc, *k., pregdal, prekkhodal, prekkhal.*
Renowned, a. *nāmwar, mashhūr.*
Rent, a. *shledalai, tsīralai.* s. *tsāk, tsīra, darz.* (hire) *kreha, kirāha*; *ijāra.*
Rent, v.n. *shledal* or *tsīredal*; *wraredal.*
Renunciation, s. *inkār, tark.*
Repair, v.a. *joṛawul, pewand-, marammat-,* etc. *k.*
Repartee, s. *ḥāẓir dzawābī.*
Repast, s. *naharai, nāshta, ḍoḍa-ī.*
Repay, v.a. *badal-, tāwān-,* etc. *warkawul*; *qarẓ-, por-,* etc. *khejawul*; *pūrah-, adā-,* etc. *k.*
Repeal, v.a. *bāṭil-, radd-,* etc. *k.*
Repeat, v.a. *biyā-, ḍubāra-,* etc. *wayal, bayānawul, mukarrar wayal.*
Repeatedly, ad. *biyā qa biyā, daf'atan.*
Repel, v.a. *liri k., shaṛal, raṭal, haṭālawul.*
Repent, v.a. *toba bāsal—yastal.* v.n. *stomānedal, pakkhemān ked.*
Repentance, s. *toba, stomānī, pakkhemānī.*
Repentant, a. *toba·gār, stomān, pakkhemān.*
Repine, v.n. *kaṛedal, nūledal, ghamedal.*
Replete, a. *pūrah, ḍak, moṛ.*
Reply, v.a. *dzawāb-, pāsukh-,* etc. *warkawul.*
Report, s. *khabar, āwāza*; *bāng-, ḍaz, ghag.* v.a. *khabarawul, khabar warkawul*; *bāng wayal*; *ḍaz wahal, ghagawul.*

Repose, v.n. *tsamlāstal, mlāstal, ghazedal*; *ūdah ked.* v.a. *khob-, ārām-*, etc. *k.*

Reprehensible, a. *malāmatī, nākārah.*

Represent, v.a. *'arẓ k.*; *kkhayal—kkhowul.*

Representation, s. *'arẓī*; *tsera, ṣūrat*; *tamāsha.*

Representative, s. *ṛakīl, nō-ib, qā-im muqām.*

Reprimand, v.a. *malāmai k., taqawul, ratal.*

Reprisal, s. *bota, bramta.*

Reproach, v.a. *peghor warkawul*; *gila k.*

Reprobate, s. *gumrāh, mardūd, wruk lāṛ.*

Reprove, v.a. *malāmatawul, tratal, ratal, dāṛal.*

Reptile, s. *chinjai, khazanda.*

Republic, s. *da ulas* or *ulūs jirga*; *da jirgo hukūmat.*

Repudiate, v.a. *inkār k., sharal, kkhayal.*

Repugnance, s. *kraka*; *daregh.*

Repugnant. a. *mukhālif, kagalai.*

Repulse, v.a. *mātawul, takkhtawul, haṭālawul.*

Reputable, a. *mu'atabar, i'tibārī.*

Reputation, s. *nūm, nang, abrū, i'tibār.*

Request, v.a. *darkhwāst-, 'arẓ-, sawāl-*, etc. *k., ghokkhtal, pukkhtedal.*

Require, v.a. *ghokkhtal, hājat laral.*

Requisite, a. *pakār, lāzim, ẓarūr.*

Rescue, v.a. *khalāṣawul, wurhawul, bachawul.*

Resemblance, s. *barābarī, mushābihat.*

Resembling, a. *ghondi, pa shān, pa rang.*

Resent, v.a. *bad manal.*

Resentment, s. *kīna, badī, dukkhmanī.*

Reserve, v.a. *sātal, khundiyal, khundī k.*

Reservoir, s. *ḥauẓ, baha-ī, dand, tālāw.*

Reside, v.n. *āstedal, osedal, pātedal.* v.a. *astoga-, meshta-* etc. *k.*

Resident, s. *osedūnkai, astogūnkai, āstedūnkai.*

Residue, s. *bāqī, pātai*; *tarka.*

Resign, v.a. *pregdal, prekkhodal, preḵkhal*; *tark k.*; *spāral, pāslawul*; *bakkhal.*

Resignation, s. *tark, prekkhodana*; *spārana, spārakkhtana*; *tawakkul*; *ist'ifā.*

Resin, s. *rāndzaṛah, chūrel*; *jāwla.*

Resist, v.a. *maẓbūṭī-, barābarī-, jang-*, etc. *k.* v.n. *ṭīng-, klak-, maẓbūṭ-*, etc. *wudredal*, or *ked., hatedal.*

Resolute, a. *maẓbūṭ, klak, ṭīng, zṛah-war.*

Resolution, s. *qaṣd, niyat.*

Resolve, v.a. *qaṣd k., niyat taṛal.*

Resort, v.a. *rāsha darsha k.*

Resound, v.n. *ghagedal, ghuṛunbedal.*

Resource, s. *chāra, 'ilāj*; *chal, ḥikmat.*

Respect, s. *'izzat, adab*; *nisbat, 'alāqa.* (with respect to) *pa ḥaqq kkhke.* (in many respects) *pa dero khabaro kkhke.* (in every respect) *pa hare khabare.* v.n. *grohedal*; *manal.*

Respectable, a. *mu'atabar, 'izzat-nāk.*

Respectful, a. *adab kawūnkai.*

Respective, a. *khāṣṣ*; *khpul khpul.*

Respire, v.a. *sāh ākhistal.*

Respite, s. *furṣat*; *wazgār-tiyā*; *nāgha.*

Response, s. *dzawāb, pāsukh.*

Responsibility, s. *zimma*; *tāwān.*

Responsible, a. *zimma-dār, tāwān warkawūnkai.*

Rest, s. *ārām-tiyā, qalār-tiyā*; *ārām, qalār* or *qarār, furṣat.* (pause) *wār, dama.* (sleep) *khob.* (prop) *aṛam.*

Rest, a. *tāqī, pātai*; *nor, nor tol.*

Restive, a. *sar-kakkh, sar-zor, takanṛai.*

Restless, a. *be-ārām, nā-qalār.*

Restore, v.a. *biyā pa dzāe walāṛawul, pa biyarta warkawul.*

Restrain, v.a. *sambālawul, bandawul, man'a k., īsārawul, haṭālawul.*

Result, s. *ḥāṣil*; *'amal*; *khatah*; *pāzah.*

Resume, v.a. *biyā ākhistal.*

Resurrection, s. *ākhirat, ḥashr, qiyāmat.* (day of-) *wradz da ḥashr*, etc.

Retail, v.a. *bel bel-, la-ag la-ag-*, etc. *khartsawul, lāgī k.*

Retain, v.a. *sātal, laral, khundī k.*

Retaliate, v.a. *badal-, jazā-, qiṣāṣ-*, etc. *ākhistal*; *bota-, bramta-*, etc. *k.*
Retard, v.a. *haṭālawul, kariyābawul*; *drang-, lārghah-, multawī-*, etc. *k.*
Retch, v.a. *bāka-ī-, qai-, chāl-*, etc. *k.*, *jārbāsal—jāryastal, kūz katal, zmake ta goral.*
Reticular, a. *jāl·dār, jālī.*
Retinue, s. *swarlī*; *jalab.*
Retire, v.n. *wrusto-, biyarta-*, etc. *ked.*, *haṭāledal, pastana jārwatal* or *-tlal—lāṛal pātsedal*; *puṭedal.*°
Retired, a. *puṭ, yawādzai, bel* or *biyal.*
Retirement, s. *yawādzī·tūn, bel·tūn.*
Retract, v.n. *girzedal, landedal.* v.a. *inkār-, bāṭil-*, etc. *k.*, *jārbāsal—jāryastal.*
Retreat, v.n. *takkhtedal, haṭāledal, biyarta-*, etc. *ked.* s. *tekkhta, māt.* (cover) *puṭgana-ī, psūnai, tsawai.* (asylum) *panāh, nanawātah.*
Retrench, v.a. *kamawul, la-agawul, landawul.*
Retribution, s. *sazā, siyāsat, badal, jazā.*
Retrieve, v.a. *sambālawul, biyā mūndal.*
Return, v.n. *girzedal, jārwatal, stūnedal, āwukkhtal, pastana rātlal—rāghlal.* v.a. *pa biyarta āstawul, stūnawul.*
Return, s. *jārwātah*; *badal.* (profit) *sūd, gaṭa.* (answer) *dzawāb.* (form) *ṣūrat ḥāl.*
Reveal, v.a. *tsargandawul. kkhkārah k.*, *parda porta k.*, *wayal.*
Revel, v.a. *mastī-, bad mastī k.*
Revenge, v.a. *badal-, qiṣāṣ-*, etc. *ākhistal.*
Revengeful, a. *kīna·war.*
Revenue, s. *bāj, khirāj, maḥṣūl, sāw.*
Revere, v.a. *zbarg ganral* or *-manal.* v.n. *grohedal.*
Reverence, s. *grohedana, manana*; *sat, adab*; *salām, sijda.*
Reverse, v.a. *naskorawul, aṛawul, apūṭah k.*
Reverse, a. *naskor, aṛawulai*; *apūṭah.* s. *āfat, balā, bad-* or *tor bakhtī.*

Review, v.a. *nandāra-, tamāsha-, dzer-*, etc. *k.*
Revile, v.a. *kanzal, kanzal k.*, *kkhkandzal, peghor warkawul.*
Revolution, s. *tsarkh, daur*; *balwā, pasāt.*
Revolve, v.n. *churledal, tsarkhedal, girzedal.* v.a. *fikr-, ghaur-*, etc. *k.*
Reward, s. *ujrat, miḥnat*; *bakkhana, in'ām ṣawāb, barakat.*
Rheumatism, s. *bād, wo.*
Rhinoceros, s. *gendai.*
Rhubarb, s. *rewand.* (fresh) *rawāsh.*
Rhyme, s. *radīf, nazm.*
Rib, s. *pukkhta-ī.*
Riband, s. *paṭa-ī, rekkha*; *pekawai.*
Rice, s. *wrīja.* (-in the husk) *shola.* (broken-) *khamacha.* (boiled-) *kamoda, chalāū.* (-straw) *palāla.* (-field) *shol·gara, shālī·zāra, kadhal.* (-planting) *nihālī.*
Rich, a. *māl·dār, duniyā·dār, daulat·man.*
Riches, s. *māl, duniyā, daulat.*
Rick, s. *dala-ī, ḍera-ī.*
Rid, v.a. *liri k.*, *jārū k.*, *ta-ashawul, khalāṣawul, āzādawul, wurhawul, rihā k.*
Riddle, s. *mu'amma.* (sieve) *ghalbel.*
Ride, v.n. *swaredal* or *sparedal.* v.a. *swarlī k.*
Rider, s. *swor* or *spor*; *sparlanai.*
Ridge, s. *kamar, pushta* or *pukkhta, ghākkhai.*
Ridicule, s. *khandā, ṭoqa, pekkha, malanḍa.*
Ridiculous, a. *khandā·nāk, ṭoqī, malanḍai.*
Rifle, v.a. *shūkawul, natal, lūṭawul.*
Rig, v.a. *joṛawul. tartībawul.*
Right, a. *rikkhtiyā, drust, jukht, rāst, joṛ, wājib, rawā, barābar, kkhāyastah, kkhah.* (-hand) *kkhai.* in. *jukht! joṛ! drust!* etc. s. *ḥaqq*; *wāk, ikhtiyār*; *māl, milk*; *'adl, inṣāf*; *kkhai.* v.a. *joṛawul, samawul*, etc.
Righteous, a. *nek, nekokār, rikkhtīnai, rāst·bāz, pāk, ṣawābī.*
Righteousness, s. *nekī, rāstī, rikkhtīn·tob, ṣawāb.*

Rightful, a. *haqq·dār, haqq·man.*

Rigid, a. *klak, lak, zīg, ne<u>gh</u>, sa<u>kht</u>, <u>t</u>sak, ṭīng.*

Rigidity, s. *klak·wālai, zīg·wālai,* etc.

Rigour, s. *sa<u>kh</u>ti; sāṛah, ya<u>kh</u>nī; laṛza.*

Rigorous, a. *sa<u>kh</u>t, zīg; soṛ, ya<u>kh</u>.*

Rim, s. *<u>gh</u>āṛa, morga, <u>t</u>sanda, ja-ī.* (wheel-) *kīra-ī, garda-ī; drakaṛ.*

Rind, s. *baṭ, paṭ, poṭ, <u>kh</u>war, postakai.*

Ring, s. *kara-ī.* (finger-) *<u>t</u>salai.* (nose-) *pezwān, natka-ī.* (ear-) *<u>ch</u>ala, wālai.* (neck-) *oga-ī.*

Ring, v.n. *trangedal, <u>shr</u>angedal, gṛanjedal.*

Ringdove, s. *gūgu<u>sh</u>tū, qumrī, spalama, tatawa, kur·kura-ī.*

Ringleader, s. *sarguroh, sar<u>gh</u>anah, nāyak.*

Ringlet, s. *<u>t</u>sūnṛa, <u>t</u>sunraka, zulfa, gesū.*

Ringworm, s. *pi<u>sh</u>ak, spūnrai.*

Rinse, v.a. *wīn<u>dz</u>al* or *mīn<u>dz</u>al, wlal.*

Riot, s. *balwā, pasāt, <u>kh</u>ar<u>kh</u>akkha.* (revel) *<u>kh</u>ar mastī, bad mastī, ṭel ṭāl.*

Riotous, a. *balwā·gar, pasātī, sar·ka<u>kh</u>; mast.*

Rip, v.a. *<u>t</u>sīral, <u>t</u>sāk k., <u>sh</u>lawul.*

Ripe, a. *po<u>kh</u>, <u>kh</u>urīn.*

Ripple, s. *<u>t</u>saparkai, pa<u>ch</u>a.*

Rise, v.n. *pā<u>t</u>sedal, porta ked., walāṛedal, <u>kh</u>atal.*

Rise, s. *<u>kh</u>ātah, taraqqa-ī.*

Risk, s. *<u>kh</u>aṭra, muhimm, bāk, yera.*

Rite, s. *ṭarīqa, rasm; ma<u>z</u>hab, sunnat.*

Rival, s. *du<u>kkh</u>man, raqīb.* (-wife) *ba-an.*

Rivalry, s. *du<u>kkh</u>manī, raqībī.*

River, s. *sīnd, dariyāb, nahar.*

Rivulet, s. *la<u>kkh</u>tai, aṛā<u>kh</u>, wela.*

Road, s. *lāṛ, rāh, wāṭ.*

Roam, v.n. *girzedal, rammedal, <u>kh</u>u<u>sh</u>ai girzedal.*

Roan, a. *samand.*

Roar, v.a. *nᵃra·, tanṛ·, dᵉrān·,* etc. *wahal.* v.n. *<u>gh</u>aredal, <u>gh</u>uṛunbedal.*

Roast, v.a. *wrītawul, kabābawul, talawul, teyal.*

Rob, v.a. *<u>sh</u>ūkawul, lūṭawul, natal, <u>gh</u>lā k., lāṛ wahal.*

Robber, s. *<u>gh</u>al, <u>sh</u>ūk·māṛ, lāṛ wahūnkai.*

Robbery, s. *<u>gh</u>lā.* (highway-) *<u>sh</u>ūka.*

Robe, s. *jāma, ā<u>gh</u>ostan, libās.* (-of honour) *<u>kh</u>alāt* or *<u>kh</u>il'at.*

Robust, a. *ma<u>z</u>būṭ. ta<u>kr</u>ah, mazai, gagar.*

Rock, s. *tīga, gaṭ.*

Rock, v.a. *<u>kh</u>wa<u>dz</u>awul, ṭāl wahal, jūṭa·ī warkawul, zangawul, <u>sh</u>anawul.* v.n. *zangal, zangedal, <u>kh</u>wa<u>dz</u>edal, <u>sh</u>anedal.*

Rocky, a. *kā<u>nr</u>e<u>dz</u>, sanglā<u>kh</u>, gaṭīn.*

Rod, s. *la<u>kkh</u>ta, hamsā* or *amsā.*

Rogue, s. *ṭag, ṭag·bāz, <u>ch</u>al·baz, farebī.*

Roguery, s. *ṭagī, ṭag·bāzī, <u>ch</u>al·bāzī, fareb.*

Roll, v.a. *n<u>gh</u>aṛal—n<u>gh</u>akkhtal.* (-on the ground) v.n. *r<u>gh</u>aṛedal—r<u>gh</u>akkhtal, lots poṭs ked.*

Roll, s. *n<u>gh</u>akkht; wal, pe<u>ch</u>, tāo.* (-of paper) *dasta, fard.* (list) *daftar, sijill.* (plait) *bra<u>gh</u>.*

Roller, s. *māla, mandānro.* (bandage) *paṭa-ī.*

Romance, s. *qiṣṣa; daro<u>gh</u>·jana <u>kh</u>abara.*

Romantic, s. *'ajab, 'ajīb; <u>kh</u>iyālī.*

Romp, v.a. *ṭel ṭāl·, <u>kh</u>ar mastī·, laṭah per·,* etc. k., *<u>kh</u>ajūnko·, <u>t</u>s<u>kh</u>e* or *<u>t</u>ske·,* etc. k.

Roof, s. *<u>ch</u>at, <u>t</u>sapar, bām, koṭa.* (of mouth-) *tālū.*

Rook, s. *qā<u>gh</u>ah.*

Room, s. *<u>kh</u>ūna, <u>dz</u>āe, koṭa.* (public-) *hujra.*

Roomy, a. *arat, prānatai.*

Roost, s. *<u>ch</u>akas, basera.* v.a. *basera k.*

Root, s. *we<u>kh</u>, wula, mūnḍ; ·bonsaṭ, kūnsuṭ, bunyād.*

Root up, v.a. *we<u>kh</u>·, mūnḍ·,* etc. *bāsal—yastal, -kāgal—k<u>kh</u>kal; mūnḍ·, bonsaṭ·,* etc. <u>kh</u>eja·wul.

Rooted, a. *<u>kh</u>akkh, ma<u>z</u>būṭ, njatai.*

Rope, s. *pa-aṛai, rasa-ī.* (hair-) *wākkhkai, siyala-ī.* (palm-leaf-) *būnr, biyāsta.*

Rosary, s. *tasbīḥ, tasbe.* (one bead of-) *tasba.*

Rose, s. *gul.* (wild white-) *phulwāṛai.*

Rosin, s. *ṛāndzaṛah.*

Rot, v.n. *wrostedal, sharhedal, skhā ked., bonredal.*

Rotate, v.n. *tsarkhedal, churledal, girzedal.*

Rotation, s. *tsarkh; daur.* (in-) ad. *wār pa wār sara.*

Rotten, a. *wrost, skhā, sharhedalai, bonredalai.*

Rough, a. *lwāṛ, zīg, klak; zmokht, trīkh, brekkhan.*

Round, a. *ghunḍ, ghunḍ·man.* s. *gakkht; guzār.* p. *chāpera.* (to turn-) v.n. *girzedal; churledal.*

Roundness, s. *ghunḍ·wālai.*

Rouse, v.a. *pātsawul, wīkkhawul, baidār k.*

Rout, v.a. *takkhtawul, mātawul, tār pa tārawul.* s. *tekkhta, māt, tār pa tār, shikast.*

Route, s. *lār, rāh.*

Rove, v.n. *girzedal.* v.a. *sail-, gakkht-,* etc. *k.*

Row, s. *para, kat, qaṭār, tsīṛa, ṣaff.*

Row, v.a. *chape wahal.*

Royal, a. *bādshāhī.*

Rub, v.a. *mugal—mukkhal, mālish k.*

Rubber, s. *māla, muhra.* (flesh-) *khīsa.*

Rubbish, s. *khadzala, khāshāk, waṛkhara.*

Ruby, s. *l'al, yāqūt.*

Rudder, s. *singāwanr, sukkān.*

Ruddy, a. *sūr, l'al* or *lāl.*

Rude, a. *be·adab; nā·dān; lwāṛ.*

Rudiment, s. *aṣl, wekh, mūnḍ.*

Rue, v.n. *toba·gār-, pakkhemān-, stomān-,* etc. *ked.*

Rue, s. (wild) *spelanai, spānda, sipand.*

Rueful, a. *toba·gār, stomān; gham·jan, malūl.*

Ruffian, s. *ṭag, ḥarāmī, khūnāṛai, ghal.*

Ruffle, v.a. (-the feathers) *banre tārawul.* (-the skin) *ghūne zīgawul.* (crumple) *jungawul.* (disturb) *pārawul.*

Rug, s. *ghālīcha* or *qālīcha; namad, lamtsa-ī; krāsta, kosai, shaṛa-ī.*

Rugged, a. *zīg, lwāṛ, klak; kānredz, sanglākh.*

Ruin, v.a. *wrānawul, kharābawul, ujāṛawul, latāṛawul, habatah-, abtar-, chauṛ-, ṛang-,* etc. *k.*

Ruination, s. *wrānī, kharābī.*

Ruinous, a. *wrān, wujāṛ, māt guḍ,* etc.; *tāwānī, ziyānī, nuqṣānī.*

Ruins, s. *kanḍar, kharāba.*

Rule, s. *qānūn, qā'ida, ṭarīqa, ā-īn, lār; 'amal, ḥukm, ḥukūmat.*

Ruler, s. *ḥākim, sardār, khān, amīr; misṭar, saṭar-* or *jadwal kakkh, lauḥa.*

Rumble, v.a. *juṛ juṛ-, qur qur-,* etc. *k.* v.n. *ghaṛedal, ga-aredal, ghuṛunbedal.*

Ruminate, v.a. *shkhwand wahal* or *k.; fikr k.*

Rummage, v.a. *laṭawul, shanal.*

Rumour, s. *āwāza, khabara, afwāh.*

Rump, s. *kūnāṭai, surīn; ḍuḍa* or *or ṭūṭa.*

Rumple, v.a. *jungawul, mātawul, kṛatī-,* etc. *k.*

Run, v.n. *zghaledal—zghākkhtal, drūmedal.* v.a. *manḍe wahal.* (-away) v.n. *takkhtedal.* (-on) *chaledal.* (flow) *bahedal, rawānedal.* (-after) *pase zghaledal* or *-prewatal.* (-over) *toyedal* or *to-edal.* (-out) *watal; tamāmedal.* (-down) *lāndi k.; kagal, ghandal.* (-up) *khatal.* v.a. *khejawul.* (-away with) *takkhtawul.*

Runaway, s. *takkhtedūnai.*

Rupee, s. *rupa-ī.*

Rupture, s. *māt.* (disagreement) *wrānī.* (hernia) *tsūhṛa.*

Rural, a. *dihātī, dzangalī.*

Rush, v.a. *halla-, ḍūsa-,* etc. *k.* v.n. *khatal; watal.*

Rust, s. *zang.*

Rustic, a. *dihqānī, gawār, lwār.* s. *kilī·wāl, dihqān, ghunḍāyah.*
Rustle, v.a. *shirahār-, ga-arahār-,* etc. *k.*
Rut, s. *kīla, līk, karkkha.* (heat) *mastī.*
Ruthless, a. *be·raḥm, be·dard, kānrai zṛah.*
Ruttish, s. *shahwat·nāk, mast.* (-female) *tera, sema.* (in comp.) *-ema* or *-yama.*

S.

Sable, a. *tor*; *mushkai.* (-fur) *samūr, postīn.*
Sabre, s. *shamsher, tūra, tegh.*
Sack, s. *tsaṭa, ghundai, juwāl.*
Sack, v.a. *tālā·, lūṭ-, nātār-,* etc. *k., natal.*
Sacred, a. *pāk, majīd, muqaddas.*
Sacrifice, s. *qurbān, ṣadqa, dzār.*
Sad, a. *gham·jan, dil·gīr, āzurdah, malūl.*
Saddle, s. *zīn, kātī.* (-pad) *ṭogham* or *toghal, kejam, qajarī.* (-cloth) *zīn·pokkh.* (-girth) *tātang, tāng.* (-pad) *kho·gīr.* (-bag) *khūrjīn.* (-pommel) *ngūbai, kāsh, āna.* (-straps) *kānjogha.* v.a. *zīn taṛal.*
Saddler, s. *sarrāj, zīn sāz.*
Sadness, s. *gham, nūl, dil·gīrī*; *saudā.*
Safe, a. *salāmat, amn amān, khair ṣalāh.* (-guard) *panāh, pushta.* (meat-) *tsakai.*
Saffron, s. *gūngū, kangū, z'afarān.*
Sagacious, a. *hokkhyār, pohānd, 'aql·man.*
Sagacity, s. *poh, pahm, sha'ūr.*
Sage, s. *'āqil, dānā, 'aql·man.* s. *ḥakīm, zbarg.*
Sail, s. *bādwān.*
Sailor, s. *mallāḥ, jahāzī.*
Saint, s. *walī, abdāl, zbarg, pīr.* (the saints) *auliyā, āstāna·dārān.*
Sake, p. *dapāra, wāsta*; *la kabla.*
Salacious, a. *mast, shahwat·nāk.*
Salamander, s. *samandar.*
Salary, s. *ṭalab, muwājib, tankhwāh.*
Sale, s. *plor, prolana, prowuna, kharts, bai'a.*
Saline, a. *mālgīn, kkhora·nāk, kkhoran.*
Saliva, s. *lāṛa* or *lānra, tūk, tūkai.*
Salivate, v.a. *khula rānwṛal.*
Sallow, a. *ziyaṛ*; *skānr.*
Sally, v.a. *tākht-, tsoṭ-, halla-,* etc. *k.*
Salt, s. *mālga.* (-collector) *mālgbah.* (-meat) *lāndai.* a. *mālgīn, namkīn.* (-less) *balmagai, balmangah.*
Saltpetre, s. *kkhora.*
Salubrious, a. *kkhah muwāfiq.*
Salutary, a. *sūd·man, fā-ida·man.*
Salutation, a. *d'uā, salām.*
Salute, v.a. *salām-, salāmī-,* etc. *k.*
Salvation, s. *khalāṣī, najāt, rihā-ī.*
Salve, s. *malham, paha, tab.*
Same, a. *haghah, daghah.* (in comp.) *yo-, hum-.* (the-) ad. *bedū.*
Sameness, s. *yo shānī, yoyat, barābarī.*
Sample, s. *namūna, nakkha.*
Sanctify, v.a. *pāk-,* etc. *k.*; *muqaddas ganral.*
Sanction, s. *ḥukm, izn, ijāzat.* v.a. *ḥukm-,* etc. *k.*
Sanctuary, s. *dargāh*; *panāh.*
Sand, s. *shiga, reg.* (-bank) *char.*
Sandal, s. *tsapla-ī, gāwlai.* (-wood) *chandanr.*
Sandy, a. *shiglan.*
Sane, a. *hokkhyār, hokkh·man, khabar·dār.*
Sanguinary, a. *khūnāṛai, khūn khwār.*
Sanguine, a. *sūr*; *qawī*; *umed·wār.*
Sap, s. *pa-ī, oba, gūṛa-ī, rub.*
Sap, v.a. *surang wahal*; *mūnḍ bāsal—yastal.*
Sapient, a. *'aql·man, dānā.*
Sapling, s. *khalai, buzghalai*; *nihāl*; *keṛa.*
Sarcasm, s. *tarkha khabara, l'an ṭ'an.*
Sash, s. *paṭka, lūnga-ī, mlā wastanai*; *jāl.*
Satan, s. *shaiṭān, iblīs.*
Satiate, v.a. *marawul, ḍakawul.*
Satiety, s. *moṛ·wālai, moṛ·tiyā, maṛa khwā.*
Satin, s. *aṭlas, dariyā-ī.*
Satire, s. *ṭoqa, pekkha.*
Satisfaction, s. *razā·mandī, khāṭir khwāhī.*
Satisfactory, a. *khāṭir khwāh, joṛ, ghwarah.*

Satisfy, v.a. *rāẓī-, khāṯir jam'a-*, etc. *k.*; *maṛawul, saṛawul*; *pohawul.*

Saturate, v.a. *khaṛob-, serāb-*, etc. *k.*; *khusht k.*

Saturday, s. *khālī, shamba.*

Sauce, s. *chāshnī*; *kkhorwā.*

Saucepan, s. (metal) *dechka, kaṛahai.* (pottery) *kaṭwa-ī, kodai.*

Saucy, a. *be·adab, shokhīn, wītak, chāwdīnak.*

Sausage, s. *kulma.*

Savage, a. *dzangalī, waḥshī*; *ẓālim, khūnāṛai.*

Save, v.a. *bachawul, sātal, khundī-, sarfa-*, etc. *k.*

Saving, s. *sūd, gaṭa, sarfa.* ad. *siwā, baghair.*

Saviour, s. *bachawūnkai, shafī.*

Savour, s. *khwand, maza, tsaka.*

Saw, s. *ara.* (-dust) *chūr.*

Say, v.a. *wayal, khabare k.*; *lal* or *lawdal.*

Sayer, s. *wayūnkai*; *lūnai* or *lūnkai.*

Saying, a. *wayana*; *khabara, wayai.*

Scab, s. *khīg, waṛ, khwaṛ.*

Scabbard, s. *teka, kāṭī, miyān.* (-mounting) *pāenak, mūnāl, tahnāl.*

Scaffold, s. *manā*; *garwanj*; *dunkācha.*

Scald, v.a. *swadzawul.* v.n. *swal, sedzal.* (-head) s. *ganja.*

Scaldheaded, a. *ganjai, suḍar, lenḍah.*

Scale, s. *tala.* (-cup) *pala.* (fish-) *khwar, tsaparkai.* (gradation) *kach, mech.* (skin) *khwar, poṭ.*

Scales, s. *tala, tarāzū, mīzān.* (beam) *ḍānḍa-ī.*

Scale, v.n. *khatal.* (peel) *lwaṛedal, nwaṛedal.*

Scan, v.a. (verse) *wazn k., jokal, talal.* (examine) *katal, āzmāyal, shanal, laṭawul.*

Scandal, s. *tuhmat* or *tūmat, tor, peghor, ruswā-ī.*

Scanty, a. *la-ag, kam, rangai, pitsāṇrai.*

Scar, s. *dāgh*; *ta-apai*; *ṭakai*; *nughai.*

Scarce, a. *la-ag, kam, matrah, pitsāṇrai.*

Scarcely, ad. *kamtar, pa mushkil sara, hīla.*

Scarcity, s. *kam·tiyā, tangsiyā, kākhti* or *qaḥṯī.*

Scare, v.a. *yerawul, tarhawul, bugnawul.*

Scarecrow, s. *tsera.* (bogie) *bau, bagalola-ī.*

Scarf, s. *paṭka, lūnga-ī*; *oḍana-ī, dū·paṭa.*

Scarify, v.a. *kkhkar lagawul, wīne bāsal—yastal.*

Scarlet, a. *sūr, lāl.*

Scatter, v.a. *khwarawul, tār pa tārawul,*

Scavenger, s. *jārū kakkh.* (at shrines, etc.) *mīnjawar.*

Scene, s. *nandāra, tamāsha.* (place) *dzāe.*

Scent, s. *bo, bū-e* or *bū-ī.* v.a. *bū-ī k., bū-ī ākhistal.*

Scheme, s. *tadbīr, ḥikmat, band*; *chal, lamghaṛa-ī*; *maṯlab, niyat.*

Schism, s. *khalal, pasāt, mīrtsī*; *rifẓ.*

Schismatic, a. *rāfiẓī, khārijī*; *pasātī.*

Scholar, s. *shāgird, ṯālib*; *'ālim, mullā.*

School, s. *maktab, madrasa.* (-boy) *dzaṇrai.* (-master) *ākhūn, mullā, ustād, mu'allim.* (-fellow) *hum dars, hum sabaq, hum dzolai.*

Science, s. *'ilm, ḥikmat, hunar.*

Scirrhus, s. *yaga.*

Scissors, s. *biyātī, qainchī, ghachī.*

Scoff, v.a. *kanzal-, ṭoqe-, pekkhe*, etc. *k.*

Scold, v.a. *raṭal, traṭal, dāṛal, ṭaqawul, malāmatawul, peghorawul.*

Scope, s. *niyat*; *gharaẓ*; *arat·wālai*; *dzāe.*

Scorch, v.a. *kaṛawul, alwoyal, lūghaṛan-, lūlapah-, kaskar-, sūngaṭ-, saṭkūrai-*, etc. *k.*

Score, v.a. *shmeral, shumāral, ḥisābawul*; *līkal, karkkha kāgal—kkhkal, -bāsal—yastal.* (scratch) *gargal, garawul.*

Score, s. *karkkha, khaṯṯ*; *ḥisāb*; *shil*; *sabab.*

Scorn, v.a. *spuk ganṛal.*

Scorpion, s. *laṛam.*

Scoundrel, s. *bad ẕāt, ḥarāmī.*

Scour, v.a. *mugal—mukkhal, togal, skoyal, zdoyal.*

Scourge, v.a. *karoṛa-, qamchī-, dira-*, etc. *wahal.*

Scout, s. *dzarai, tsārī, jāsūs, yalah-dār.* v.a. *tsāral, tsār-, zarana-ī-*, etc. *k.*

Scowl, v.a. *starge brandawul.*

Scramble, v.a. *lūṭ māt k.*

Scrap, s. *ṭoṭa, reza· pūṭai, pitsānrai.*

Scrape, v.a. *garawul, togal, khriyal, gargal.*

Scrapings, s. *tarāshe.* (pot-) *koyanai, koela.*

Scratch, v.a. *garawul, gargal, skoyal.*

Scream, v.a. *chigha-, nāra-, sūra-*, etc. *wahal.*

Screen, v.a. *parda-, panāh-*, etc. *k., puṭawul, pokkhal*; *bachawul.*

Screw, s. *pech, marwat.*

Scribe, s. *kātib, līkūnkai, kkhkawūnkai.*

Scrip, s. *bana-ī, gūdai, dzola-ī.*

Scripture, s. *kitāb da majīd.* (C.) *tauret, zabūr, injīl.* (H.) *shāstar.* (M.) *qurān, furqān.*

Scrofula, s. *anjīr.*

Scroll, s. *daftar, fard, ṭomār*; *nghakkhtai kāghaz.*

Scrotum, s. *khoṭa, da khoṭo pūkanra-ī.*

Scrub, v.a. *mugal—mukkhal, togal.*

Scruple, v.a. *shakk-, shubha-, gumān-*, etc. *laral.*

Scrupulous, a. *wahmī, wiswāsī, shakkī.*

Scrutinize, v.a. *āzmāyal, laṭawul, shañal, talal.*

Scrutiny, s. *āzmekkht, shanana, imtiḥān.*

Scuffle, v.a. *parzawul, ṭel wahal, sara nkkhlawul.*

Sculk, v.n. *ghalai ked., puṭedal.*

Sculptor, s. *naqqāsh, but sāz, sang tarāsh.*

Scum, s. *jakh, rag, kaf.*

Scurf, s. *pa-akh, poṭakai, khīg.*

Scurrilous, a. *jiba-war, kanzal kawūnkai.*

Sea, s. *dariyāb, qālī dariyāb, baḥr.*

Seal, s. *muhr.* (-stone) *ghamai.* (-cutter) *muhr kan.* v.a. *muhr layawul.*

Seam, s. *joṛ, skoe, ganḍal, darz.*

Sear, v.a. *dāghawul.*

Search, v.a. *laṭawul, shanal, talāsh k.*

Season, s. *wakht* or *waqt, mūda, neṭa*; *mausam* or *mosim, faṣl.*

Season, v.a. *namkīn-, maza-dār-*, etc. *k., maṣālah-*, etc. *warkawul* or *-āchawul*; *pokh-, mazbūṭ-*, etc. *k.*

Seasonable, a. *joṛ, jukht, barābar.*

Seasonably, ad. *pa wakht, pa neṭe, pa mūde.*

Seasoning, s. *maṣālah* or *masāla*; *mālga.*

Seat, s. *kursī, da nāst dzāe*; *dzāe, muqām.* v.a. *kkhkenawul* or *kenawul.*

Secede, v.n. *jārwatal, stūnedal.*

Seclude, v.a. *belawul, yawādzai-, judā-*, etc. *k.*

Seclusion, s. *tanhā-ī, bel-tūn*; *ghalī-tob.*

Second, a. *dwayam, ṣānī, bul.* s. *pal, laḥza*; *mal, yār, komakī, pushtī, madad-gār.* v.a. *madad k., pushtī-, komak-*, etc. *warkawul.*

Secondly, ad. *ṣānī-an, biyā, bul.*

Secresy, s. *parda, parda pokkhī, ghalī-tob, tara-ī, puṭ-wālai.*

Secret, a. *puṭ, pinham.* (in-) ad. *pa puṭa, pa tara-ī, pa parde.* s. *rāz, sirr, puṭa khabara.*

Secretary, s. *munshī.*

Secrete, v.a. *puṭawul, pokkhal*; *paidā k.*

Secretion, s. *rezish.*

Secretly, ad. *pa puṭa, pa parde, pa tara-ī.*

Sect, s. *firqa, mazhab, ummat*; *zāt, noga.*

Sectary, s. *rāfiẓī, khārijī.*

Section, s. *juz, faṣal, sipāra*; *para, janba, gundī.*

Secular, a. *duniyā-ī, 'āmmī.*

Secure, a. *salāmat, amn, amān*; *mazbūṭ, qā-im, ṭīng,* v.a. *sambālawul, mazbūṭ-*, etc. *k., sātal, khundī k.*

Security, s. *salāmatī, panāh, amānat.* (bail) *ẓāmin.* (bond) *ẓamānat.* (false-) *be-khabarī.*

Sedan, s. *ḍola-ī, anbāla-ī.* (camel-) *kajāwa.*

Sedate, a. *qalār, ghalai.*

Sedentary, a. *be-ḥarakat, nāst.*

Sediment, s. *khaṭbel, matar.*
Sedition, s. *yāghī-garī, balwā-tob, patna, pasāt.*
Seditious, a. *pasātī, balwā-sāz, balwā-gar, yāghī-gar, yāghī, mufsid, sar-kakkh.*
Seduce, v.a. *ghulawul, darghalawul, be-lāri k.*
Sensation, s. *darghal-tob, ghulawuna, fareb.*
See, v.a. *katal* or *kasal, goral—līdal, nazar k.* (perceive) v.n. *pohedal, rasedal.* in. *gora!*
Seed, s. *tukhm. dāna.* (-of stone fruit, melons, etc.) *zaṛai.* (progeny) *alwād, zāwzad* or *zawzāt, tūng.* (sperm) *manī, mardī.*
Seeing, s. *līdah, kātah, nazar.* a. *bīnā.* (-that) ad. *dzaka.*
Seek, v.a. *laṭawul, talāsh k.; ghokkhtal, d'uā-,* etc. *k.*
Seem, v.n. *kkhkāredal, m'alūmedal.*
Seemingly, ad. *pa kkhkārah, pa līdah, pa kātah.*
Seemly, a. *munāsib, kkhāyastah, joṛ, lā-iq.*
Seize, v.a. *nīwul, ākhistal, qabz-, giriftār-,* etc. *k.*
Seldom, ad. *kamtar, kala nā kala.*
Select, v.a. *khwakkhawul, chunral, anrawul, pasand-, qabūl-, chīndah-, ghwarah-,* etc. *k.*
Self, pr. *dzān, khpul.*
Selfish, a. *khpul gharaz, khpul maṭlab, gharazī, gharaz-man, khpul nafs.*
Sell, v.a. *khartsawul, prowul, ploral* or *prolal, pa bai'e warkawul.*
Seller, s. *khartsawūnkai, prowūnkai,* etc.
Semen, s. *mardī, manī.*
Senate, s. *jirga; majlis; dīwān.*
Senator, s. *jirgatū, majlisī.*
Send, v.a. *āstawul, legdal* or *legal.* (-for) *rābalal, balal, ghokkhtal, ṭalab k.*
Senior, a. *mashar, loe.*
Senna, s. *sana makī.*
Sensation, s. *ḥiss, dzān, sāh, sud.* (to have-) v.n. *pa dzān pohedal.* v.a. *ḥiss-,* etc. *laral*
Sense, s. *'aql, poha, pahm; m'anī; hokkh, sud, khabar.* (to have-) v.a. *'aql-,* etc. *laral.*
Senseless, a. *be-ḥiss,* etc.; *be-hūdah, be-m'anī.*
Sensible, a. *baidār, hokkhyār, khabar-dār.*
Sensitive, a. *dzān-dār, jwandai.*
Sensual, a. *nafsānī, shahwatī, mast.*
Sensuality, s. *nafs parastī; mastī; shahwat, nafs.*
Sentence, s. *ḥukm, fatwā.* (of Quran) *āyat.* v.a. *ḥukm-,* etc. *k.*
Sentiment, s. *fikr, rāe, poha.*
Sentinel, s. *pāsbān, pahra-dār, tsoka-ī-dār.*
Separate, v.a. *biyalawul* or *belawul, judā k.* v.n. *biyaledal, lwukkhtal, lwaṛedal.* a. *bel* or *biyal, judā.*
Separately, ad. *biyal biyal, judā-judā.*
Separation, s. *biyal-tūn, judā-ī, biyal-wālai.*
September, s. *asū.*
Sepulchre, s. *gor, qabr; laḥd.*
Sequel, s. *'āqibat, ākhir; khatm.*
Sequester, v.a. *biyalawul; qurq k.*
Seraglio, s. *zanāna, ḥaram srāe.*
Serene, a. *qalār, ārām; spīn, shīn, ṣāf.*
Series, s. *qaṭār; hār, laṛ; silsila.*
Serious, a. *drūnd, grān, muhimm.*
Sermon, s. *w'az; khuṭba; pand, naṣīḥat.*
Serpent, s. *mār.* (python) *kkhāh mār.* (viper) *mangor, mangarai.* (amphisbœna) *laṭka, landa-ī.*
Serpentine, a. *mār pech, walandai, kog wog, kālkūchan.*
Servant, s. *nokar, khidmat-gār, mazdūr.*
Serve, v.a. *nokarī-, khidmat-, mazdūrī-,* etc. *k.* v.n. *kedal, lagedal, chaledal.*
Serviceable, a. *pa-kār, fā-ida-man, sūd-man.*
Servile, a. *khūshāmad-gar, chāplūs, ḍirpal.*
Servility, s. *khūshāmad-garī, chāplūsī,* etc.
Sesamum, s. *kunzala.*
Session, s. *majlis, jalsa, maḥkama.*
Set, s. *joṛa; firqa; para, gundī.* a. *jaṛāo.* v.a. *gdal* or *īgdal, īkkhodal, īkkhal, kegdal* or *kkhkegdal,* etc., *lagawul, joṛawul, khejawul, kkhkenawul* or *kenawul.* v.n.

kūzedal, prewatal. (-out) *rawānedal, drūmal, drūmedal, tlal—lāṛal.*

Settle, v.a. *astoga k., dzāe nīwul, ābādawul.* (fix) *muqarrar k., wudrawul, kkhkenawul.* (arrange) *tartībawul, atsanral, samawul, barābarawul.* (compose) *saṛawul.* (-an account) *pūrah-, adā-,* etc. *k.* (-a difference) *pakhulā k., gwākkh-grandī k.* (-down) v.n. *kenāstal* or *kkhkenāstal.*

Settled, a. *qalār, ārām; nāst, prot; pūrah, adā.*

Settlement, s. *bandobast.* (colony) *ābādī.* (marriage-) *kābīn.* (-of dispute) *rogha, joṛa, faiṣal.*

Seven, a *owah.* (seventh) *owam.*

Seventeen, a. *owah-las.*

Seventy, a. *awwyā.* (seventieth) *awwyāyam.*

Sever, v.a. *prekawul, biyalawul; lwaṛawul.*

Several, a. *dzani, b'aẓi, tso, ḍer.*

Severally, ad. *yo yo, biyal biyal, judā judā.*

Severe, a. *sakht, tez, tund, klak.*

Sew, v.a. *ganḍal, skoe k.* (darn) *bezal, pezal.* (-up) *agayal.*

Sex, s. *jins, ẕāt.*

Sexton, s. *mūaẕẕin; mīnjawar* or *mujāwir.*

Shabby, a. *spuk, khwār; pūhaṛ; khushai.*

Shade, s. *sorai, siwrai.*

Shadow, s. *sorai; 'aks; panāh.*

Shaft, s. *tīr, ḍānḍa-ī, stan.* (-of a well) *koṭa.* (-of a carriage) *bāzū, gānḍa-ī.*

Shaggy, a. *babar, waṛan.*

Shagreen, s. *kīmukht.*

Shake, v.a. *khwadzawul, tsanḍal, kkhorawul, rapawul.* (-down) *drabal.* v.n. *khwadzedal, rapedal, laṛzedal, kkhoredal.*

Shallow, a. *pāyāo* or *pāyāb; nādān, nīmgaṛai.*

Sham, s. *bāna* or *bahāna, lamghaṛa-ī, chal, ṭagī.* a. *jūṭah, nāsarah, darogh-jan.* v.a. *bāna-,* etc. *k.*

Shame, s. *sharm, hayā; sharmindagī; makh, ghairat.*

Shameful, a. *ruswā, bad; sharmsār, sharmnāk; ghairat-man* or *ghairat-nāk.*

Shameless, a. *be-sharm, be-hayā, be-nang, be-makh,* etc.

Shampoo, v.a. *chāpī k., manḍal.*

Shank, s. *kkhānga; tsānga; kkhākh; lasta.*

Shape, s. *shakl, ṣūrat, ḍaul, rang.*

Share, s. *brakha, wesh, ḥiṣṣa, wanḍa.* (plough-) *pāla, saspār.*

Share, v.a. *weshal.* v.n. *sharīk ked.*

Sharer, s. *brakha-khor, sharīk.*

Sharp, a. *terah, tez.* (sour or acid) *trīw, trīkh, brekkhan.* (active) *chālāk.* (clever) *pohānd.*

Sharpen, v.a. *terah-,* etc. *k.*

Sharper, s. *ṭag, ṭag-bāz, darghal.*

Shatter, v.a. *chūr chūr-, daṛ daṛ-, ṭoṭe ṭoṭe-, reze reze-, kanḍ kapaṛ-,* etc. *k.*

Shave, v.a. *khriyal* or *khrayal; togal.*

Shaving, s. *ṭoṭkai, tarāza, tūtankai.*

Shawl, s. *shāl.* (-for waist) *abra.*

She, pr. *hagha, dā, de, da, e.*

Sheaf, s. *geḍa-ī.*

Shear, v.a. *skūstal, skūl-* or *skwal k., kaṭeyal.*

Shears, s. *biyātī, khorkhal, kāz, skūlai.*

Sheath, s. *teka, miyān; kāṭī.*

Shed, s. *chopāṛ, jūngaṛa, kaḍala, manḍaw, kūḍa-ī.*

Shed, v.n. *rejedal; to-edal* or *toyedal.* v.a. *āchawul, ghurzawul, toyawul.*

Sheep, s. *ga-aḍ, ga-aḍūrai.* (long-tailed-) *herṛai, berṛai, barra.* (-owner) *ga-aḍbah.* (-cot) *shpol, bānḍa.* (ewe-) *ga-aḍa, meg.* (ram) *mag, ga-aḍ.* (wether) *wuch-kūl.*

Sheer, a. *ṣāf, pāk.*

Sheet, s. *tsādar, dū-paṭa.*

Shelf, s. *ṭāq, ṭāqcha, darai, rap.*

Shell, s. *gūjai, sīpa-ī.* (cowrie) *kunjaka, kawḍa-ī.* (fruit) *poṭ, postakai.*

Shelter, s. *panāh, amn* or *aman; nanawātah.*

v.a. *panāh-.* etc. *warkawul*; *pokkhal, puṭawul.*

Shepherd, s. *shpūn.* (-boy) *shpankai.*

Sherbet, s. *guṛobai, sharbat.*

Shield, s. *spar, ḍāl, salaṭ.* (-handle) *dastmāya, da guda-ī laṛ.* (boss) *patrai.*

Shield, v.a. *bachawul, ĵghoral, sātal, panāh-,* etc. *k.*

Shift, s. *ḥikmat, chal, band, chāra.* (evasion) *hira-ī, lamghaṛa-ī, ḥīla, bāna.* (shirt) *ganḍolai, pepna-ī, khata, qamīṣ.*

Shift, v.a. *khwadzawul, badalawul, girzawul.* v.n. *khwadzedal, girzedal, āwukkhtal.*

Shine, v.n. *brekkhedal, dzalkedal* or *dzaledal, rūnredal, rokkhānedal.*

Shining, a. *brekkh·nāk, rokkhān, rūnr, dzalkān.*

Ship, s. *jahāz, beṛa-ī.*

Shirt, s. *qamīṣ, khata, ganḍolai, pepna-ī.*

Shiver, v.n. *rapedal, regdedal, larẓedal.* s. *larẓa.* (break) *mātawul.* (*v.* Shatter.)

Shoal, s. *ṭolai, sail, ghol, pāyāo*; *char.*

Shock, s. *ḍaka, ṭakar.*

Shocking, a *makrūh, kraka·war* or *·nāk.*

Shoe, s. *panra, pāezār, jūṭa-ī*; *mochanra, kokkha, jiṡta.* (-maker) *mochī, tsamyār.* (horse-) *na'l.* (to put on-) v.a. *pa kkhpo k., na'l k.* or *-lagawul.*

Shoot, v.a. *wīshtal, ṭopak-,* etc. *khalāṣawul* or *chalawul.* v.n. *ṭūkedal, zarghūnedal.*

Shop, s. *dūkān, haṭa-ī*; *kār·khāna.* (-keeper) *dūkān·dār, banriyā, kaṭrī.*

Shore, s. *ghāṛa.* (near-) *rā·pori ghāṛa.* (far-) *pori ghāṛa.*

Short, a. *lanḍ, kotāh.* (less) *kam, la-ag.* (size) *mandarai, khamachah.*

Shorten, v.a. *lanḍawul*; *kamawul.* v.n. *lanḍedal*; *kamedal.*

Shortly, ad. *pa lanḍa, za-ar* or *zir, pa drang sā'at.*

Shot, s. (small) *chara.* (bullet) *mardakai.* (cannon-) *gola-ī.* (stroke) *guzār.* a. *wīshtai.*

Shoulder, s. *oga.* (-blade) *walai.*

Shout, v.a. *nāra-, chigha-,* etc. *wahal, bāng wayal.*

Shove, v.a. *ṭel-, ḍaka-, ṭakar-, ṭāl-,* etc. *wahal.*

Shovel, s. (iron) *yūm* or *yīm, kara.* (wooden) *rāshbel.*

Show, s. *nandāra, tamāsha.* v.a. *kkhayal—kkhowul, kkhkārah-, bartser-,* etc. *k., tsargandawul*; *pohawul, pahmawul.*

Shower, a. *jaṛa-ī, bārān.* (spring-) *wasa.* (heavy-) *shebah.* (slight-) *pūna.* v.n. *oredal, bārānedal, tsātsedal.*

Showy, a. *raunaq·dār, kkhāyastah, ḍaulī.*

Shred, s. *rekkha, paṛūkai, reza, purza.*

Shrewd, a. *pokh, hokkhyār, chirg, kāgh.*

Shriek, v.a. *nāra-, sūra-, chigha-,* etc. *wahal.*

Shrine, s. *ziyārat, āstāna, dargāh.*

Shrink, v.n. *haṭedal*; *stanedal*; *bugnedal*; *jārwatal.* (as the belly) *wuchedal, kawt ked.*

Shrivel, v.n. *wuchedal, kawt ked., chichar ked.*

Shroud, s. *kafan, tsādar.*

Shrub, s. *būṭai, jāṛa, ḍakai.* (thorny-) *karkanra.*

Shrubbery, s. *janga-ī, jāṛ.*

Shudder, v.n. *laṛzedal, ghūne zīgedal, regdedal.* v.a. *ġagaṛodze nīwul*; *kraka ākhistal.*

Shuffle, v.a. *ṛaqawul, laṛal, gaḍ·waḍawul.* (equivocate) *janra-, hira-ī-, lamghaṛa-ī-,* etc. *k., palma wayal.* (in gait) v.n. *ṭaparedal.*

Shun, v.a. *parhez k., ḍaḍa ākhistal.* v.n. *bugnedal, takkhtedal, ḍaḍa ked.*

Shut, v.a. *bandawul, lagawul.* (as a door) *pori k.* (as the eyes) *puṭawul.* (as a book) *ṭap wahal.*

Shutter, s. *parda, takhta.* (-of a door) *tamba, palc.*

Shy, a. *yer·man, harānd*; *sharmsār.* v.n. *bugnedal.*

Sick, a. *nā·rogh, nā·joṛ, bīmār, randzūr*

(-of) *bezār, staṟai stomān.* (-of food, etc.)
sekan. (-at stomach) *mīkkh mīkkh, chinje-dalai.*

Sickle, s. *lor, lawa* or *lawāor.*

Sickly, a. *maraẕī, za'īf, nā·roĝh.*

Sickness, s. *nā·joṟ·tiyā, bīmārī, āzār, randẕ.*

Side, s. *palaw, tselma, roḵh, ḵhwā, lorai ; aṟḵh, ḍaḍa, tsang ; ĝhāṟa ; taraf, para, janba.* (-piece) *bāzū.*

Sideways, ad. *pa trats.*

Sieve, s. *ĝhalbel, parwezai ; chaj, tsap.*

Sift, v.a. *ĝhalbelawul, chaj-,* etc. *wahal ; chunral, chānrawul ; laṭawul, shanal.*

Sigh, v.a. *aswelai k.*

Sight, s. *naẕar ; līdah, kātah ; tamāsha, nandāra.*

Sign, s. *nakkha, alāma.* v.a. *dast ḵhaṭṭ k.*

Signal, s. *nakkha, ishāṟat, nikkhānī.*

Signet, s. *muhr, ĝhamai.*

Significant, a. *m'anī·dār, m'anawī.*

Signification, s. *m'anī, matlab.*

Signify, v.a. *m'anī laral.*

Silence, s. *ĝhalī·tob.* in. *chup !*

Silent, a. *ĝhalai, chip.*

Silently, ad. *ro ro, ĝhalai ĝhalai.*

Silk, s. *rekkham.* (-worm) *da rekkham chinjai.* (-cocoon) *pela, ĝhoza.*

Silken, a. *rekkhmīn.*

Silly, a. *sādah, kawdan, nādān.*

Silver, s. *spīn zar.* (-smith) *zar·gar.*

Similar, a. *barābar, ĝhondai, gund, yo shān.*

Simile, s. *matal, miṣāl, tashbīh.*

Simper, v.n. *musedal.*

Simple, a. *sādah, sarah, karah ; spor, torci.*

Simpleton, s. *pūhaṟ, kawdan, gedī ḵhar.*

Simply, ad. *sirp* or *surup, ḵhālī, ta-ash.*

Sin, s. *gunāh, wabāl, taqṣīr, ḵhaṭā, baza.*

Since, ad. *laka chi ; pas, dzaka chi.* (-when?) *kala, la kūma.*

Sincere, a. *ri⟨·kḥtīnai, rāst·bāz, karah, sādah.*

Sinew, s. *pai, pla, rag, wuja.*

Sinful, a. *gunāh·gār, taqṣīrī.*

Sing, v.a. *sarod-, sandare-,* etc. *wayal.*

Singe, v.a. *swadzawul.* v.n. *swal, sedzal.*

Singer, s. *sarodī, mutrīb, sandar·goe.*

Single, a. *yo, yawādzai, witar, tsaṟah, tāk.* (-fold) *yawastawai, yak·tā.* · (unmarried) *lawand.*

Singly, ad. *yo yo.*

Singular, a. *wāḥid ; 'ajab.*

Sinister, a. *nā·rāst, bad, kog, tratskan.*

Sink, v.a. *ḍūbawul, ĝharqawul.* v.n. *ḍūbedal, ĝharqedal.*

Sinner, s. *gunāh·gār, bad kār, taqṣīrī.*

Sip, v.a. *skal* or *tskal* or *tskkhal, chūpal, zbekkhal.* (taste) *tsaṭal, tsakal.*

Sir, s. *ṣāḥib, jī, bābū, lālā.*

Sire, s. *plār ; ḥazrat.*

Sister, s. *ḵhor.* (husband's) *ndror.* (by brother) *bābī, wrandār, wandyār.* (by husband's brother) *yor.* (wife's) *kkhīna, ḵhwakkhīna.* (foster-) *da to ḵhor.* (tribal-) *ḵhoringa.* (-hood) *ḵhoringa-ī.*

Sit, v.n. *kenāstal* or *kkhkenāstal.*

Site, s. *dzāe, zmaka.*

Sitting, s. *nāstah* or *kkhkenāstah.*

Situation, s. *dzāe ; 'uhda, darja ; ḵhidmat, kār.*

Six, a. *shpag.* (sixth) *shpāgam.*

Sixteen, a. *shpāṟas.* (sixteenth) *shpāṟasam.*

Sixty, a. *shpetah.* (sixtieth) *shpetam.* (-one) *yo shpetah.* (-two) *dwah shpetah,* etc.

Size, s. *qadr, andāza ; slekkht ; batī.*

Skein, s. *tranjai, tranjūkai, aṭa* or *aṭeha.*

Sketch, s. *naqsha* or *nakhkkha, taṣwīr.* v.a. *naqsha-,* etc. *kāgal—kkhkal,* or *-līkal,* or *-bāsal—yastal.*

Skewer, s. *sīḵh, sīḵhcha, salā-ī, sparḵhai.*

Skilful, a. *qābil, poḵh, kāṟ⟨gar, hunar·man.*

Skill, s. *huwar, kārī·garī, qābiliyat.*

Skim, v.a. *zag liri k.* or *-āḵhistal.* (-over) *naẕar pa zir terawul.*

Skin, s. *tsarman, poṭ.* v.a. *tsarman-*, etc. *liri k.*, or *-bāsal—yastal* or *-kāgal—kkhkal.*

Skip, v.a. *trapa-, ṭop-*, etc. *wahal, khajūnko-, tskhe-*, etc. *k.*

Skirmish, s. *ṭas ṭūs, dandūkār.*

Skirt, s. *laman, ĵa-ī, pītskai*; *ghāṛa, tselma.*

Skittish, a. *be·qalār, yer·man*; *mast, shokhīn.*

Skull, s. *kapara-ī, kakara-ī.*

Sky, s. *āsmān.* (clear-) *shīn āsmān.* (dark-) *ganr* or *gūr·āsmān.*

Slab, s. *takhta.* (stone-) *tīga, siyādza.*

Slack, a. *sust, arat, prānatai*; *laṭ, nā·rāst.*

Slake, v.a. *saṛawul.*

Slander, s. *tuhmat* or *tūmat, tor, peghor palma.* v.a. *tūmat-, tor-*, etc. *pori k.*, *peghor warkawul, palma wayal.*

Slanting, a. *tratskan, sar ĵawar, rewand.*

Slap, v.a. *ṭas-, tsāpeṛa-, kṛap-*, etc. *wahal.*

Slash, v.a. *ghwutsawul, tsīral*; *wahal*; *tsanḍal.*

Slattern, a. *pūhaṛ, shaṭal* or *shalaṭ, shāwlai nāwlai.*

Slaughter, s. *qatl, khūn, qatli'āmm.*

Slave, s. *mra-e, ghulām, agar* (f.) *wīndza, barda, agara.*

Slavery, s. *mra-e·tob, ghulāmī.*

Slay, v.a. *qatlawul, muṛ k., waĵal* or *waĵlal.* (-for food) *ḥallālawul.*

Slayer, s. *qātil, khūnī.*

Sleek, a. *tsorb, chāgh*; *ghwaṛ*; *ṣāf, spetsalai, spīn.*

Sleep, s. *khob.* v.a. *khob k.* v.n. *ūdah-, bīdah-*, etc. *ked.* (to put to-) v.a. *ūdah k.*, *tsamlawul.*

Sleepy, a. *khob·nāk, parnā-, khob-*, etc. *-wṛai*; *drane starge.*

Sleeve, s. *lastūnrai, āstīn.*

Slender, a. *narai, trandz, nāzak, mahīn, bārīk.*

Slice, s. *tarāza, ṭoṭkai.*

Slide, v.n. *kkhwahedal* or *kkhwa-edal, kkhakedal, laghzedal.*

Slight, a. *la-ag, kam*; *spuk, halak.* (*v.* Slender) v.a. *spuk ganral, spuk naẓar k.*

Slim, a. *narai, trandz.* (*v.* Slender).

Slime, s. *chiqaṛ, khaṭa, lāha.* (vegetable-) *ubṛa-ī.*

Slimy, a. *chiqran, kkhwai.*

Sling, s. *machoghna* or *machaloghza, trankūtsa.* (the cup of a-) *gāṭa-ī.* (cradle) *zāngo, gahwāra, amel* or *ḥamā-il.* v.a. *wīshtal.*

Slip, v.n. *kkhwahedal.* (*v.* Slide). (-away) *teredal.* (-from the memory) *heredal.* (-from sight) *puṭedal.* (-from the hand) *khalāṣedal, yalah ked.*

Slip, s. *kkhwaheduna, laghz*; *khaṭā, ter wat*; *ṭoṭa, rekkha paṭa-ī*; *qalam.*

Slipper, s. *panra, kokkha, paizār* or *pāezār, jista.*

Slippery, a. *kkhwai, laghzan, chiqran.*

Slit, v.a. *tsīral, shlawul, chawul, chāk k.* s. *tsīra, chāwd, daṛa, chāk* or *chāq.*

Sloping, a. *tratskan, rewand, sar ĵawar, sar lwaṛ.*

Slothful, v.a. *sust, laṭ, nā·rāst, kāhil, shaḍal.*

Slough, s. *chiqaṛ* or *qīchaṛ, bokkhtana*; *khwar, postakai, tsarman.*

Sloven, s. *pūhaṛ, palīt, shalaṭ* or *shaṭal.*

Slow, a. *sust, laṭ, ro, qalār.*

Slowly, ad. *ro ro, qalār qalār.*

Sluggard, a. *shaḍal, laṭ, ārām ṭalab.*

Sluice, s. *warkh, ghwagai*; *mūra-ī.*

Slur, s. *dāgh, laka*; *tor, peghor.* v.a. *dāghawul, wrānawul.*

Slut, s. *pūhaṛa, shalaṭa*; *hujra-ī, gashta-ī*; *spa-ī.*

Sly, a. *chalwalai, chal·bāẓ.*

Smack, v.a. *ṭas-, ṭaq-, tsāpeṛa-*, etc. *wahal.* (taste) *tsaka, khwand, maza.*

Small, a. *wor, la-ag, warūkai, wūṛkoṭai, pūṭai, mandarai, kachoṭai, kuchinai, kharmandai.*

Smallness, s. *la-ag-walai, wuṛūk-wālai.*

Smallpox, s. *nanaka-ī.* (scar) *ta-apai.* (chicken) *katswak.*

Smart, a. *chālāk, chust, tez, tund.* v.a. *swai k.* v.n. *swal, sedzal.*

Smear, v.a. *lewawul, tabal, ghwaṛ k.*; *akheṛal.*

Smell, s. *bū, bū-ī.* v.n. *bū-ī tlal.* v.a. *bū-ī k.*

Smile, v.n. *musedal.* v.a. *muskai k.*

Smite, v.a. *wahal.*

Smith, s. *lohār, āhan-gar.* (gold-) *zar-gar.*

Smoke, v.a. *lū-, lūgai-,* etc. *k.* (as tobacco) v.a. *skal* or *tskkhal.*

Smoky, a. *lūghaṛan.*

Smooth, a. *sam, hawār, barābar*; *narm.* v.a. *samawul, atsanral, hawārawul,* etc.

Smother, v.a. *sāh bandawul, ghāṛa-, mara-ī-,* etc. *-khapa k., sāh ḍūbawul.*

Smut, s. *pūch go-ī.* (mildew) *tor, chanrāsha.*

Snail, s. *shāpeṭai, gūjai, da kārghah paaska-ī.*

Snake, s. *mār.* (-charmer) *pāṛū.*

Snap, v.a. *chīchal*; *mātawul*; *chuṭkī k.* (-as a dog) *ghapal, dāṛal.*

Snare, s. *dām.* (different kinds) *lūma, lūmaka, lwīna, jāl, ghūnḍārai, paṛka, talaka, laṭ, kuṛka-ī, honrā.*

Snarl, v.a. *ghapal, dāṛal.*

Snatch, v.a. *pa ḥamle ākhistal, shūkawul, ghoṭa k., tsapa wahal.*

Sneak, v.n. *ghalai keḍ., puṭ girzedal.*

Sneer, v.a. *spuk naẓar k., poza-* or *ūrbūz būṭawul.*

Sneeze, v.n. *pranjedal, prachedal.* v.a. *ngai k., ngal.*

Snipe, s. *karak, ṭamṭīl.*

Sniff, v.n. *sūnredal, sūghedal.*

Snore, v.a. *kha-ar wahal, kha-arkai k.*

Snort, v.n. *prashedal, sūnredal.*

Snot, s. *kaṛbeza* or *kaṛmeza.*

Snout, s. *poza, ūrbūz, tambūza.*

Snow, s. *wāwra.* v.n. *wāwre oredal* or *-prewatal.*

Snub, v.a. *dāṛal, raṭal, ṭaqawul.*

Snuff, s. *sūnr.* (tobacco) *nās, naswār.* v.n. *sūnredal.* v.a. *naswār k.*

Snug, a. *puṭ, ghalai*; *khwakkh, moṛ.*

So, ad. *hase, dā-hase, dā rang, hase shān, laka.* (-much) *hombra, tsombra.* (-much so) *tar de ḥadda pori.* (-long as) *tso chi, hombra chi.* (-be it) *wī di, hase di wī.* (it may be-) *wi ba, hase ba wī.* (-that) *tso chi.* (-often as) *har kala chi.* (-and so) *palānkai.*

Soak, v.a. *lūndawul, khushtawal.* (-up) v.a. *wuchawul, tskhal.*

Soap, s. *ṣābūn.* v.a. *ṣābūn lagawul.*

Sob, v.a. *zgerwai* or *zwergai-, salga-ī* or *sugala-ī-, ārkhakkh-, alhang-,* etc. *k., kūk wahal, ĵaṛal, pa raṭo raṭo ĵaṛal.*

Sober, a. *parhez-gār, parhezī*; ***hokkhyār**, baidār.*

Sociable, a. *majlisī, ṣuḥbatī, **melmah-dost.***

Society, s. *ṣuḥbat, majlis*; *shirakat, malgartiyā, malgīrī, malgar-tob.*

Sod, s. *chūm, lūṭa.*

Sodden, a. *khuṛīn, post, oblan.*

Sodomite, s. *kūnī, kūnīgai.*

Sodomy, s. *kūnī-tob. bachī-bāzī, **halak-bāzī**, lawāṭat, ighlām.*

Soft, a. *pos* or *post, narm, mulā im.*

Softly, ad. *ro ro, pa qalār.*

Soil, s. *mzaka* or *zmaka, khāwra.* (country) *waṭan, wilāyat*; *mulk, hiwād.* (manure) *sara.* v.a. *palīt-, khīran-, kakaṛ-,* etc. *k.*

Sojourn, v.n. *āstedal, osedal.* v.a. *astoga, mesht-, ṭīkāo-,* etc. *k., dzāe nīwul*; *musāfiri k.*

Sojourner, s. *osedūnkai, **astogūnkai**; **musāfir**.*

Solace, s. *tasallī, ārām*; *khwakkhi*. v.a. *tasallī-*, etc. *warkawul, pokkhal*.

Solder, v.a. *qala'ī k., joṛawul*.

Soldier, s. *spāhī, lakkhkarī*. (heavy armed-) *puṭ spāhī*. (light armed-) *tsaṛah spāhī*. (irregular) *mlā taṛ, jazāelchī*.

Soldiership, s. *spāhī-garī*; *spāhī-tob*.

Soldiery, s. *lakkhkar, fauj* or *pauj, ḍal*.

Sole, a. *yawādzai, tsaṛah*; *yak-tā*. s. *khapaṛ, tala, warghawai*. (-of a shoe) *talai*.

Solely, ad. *sirp* or *surup, ta-ash, faqaṭ*.

Solemn, a. *grāh, drūnd*; *'ibrat-nāk*.

Solemnize, v.a. *manal*; *'urs-, 'īd-, 'ibādat-*, etc. *k., qā-im-, rawā-*, etc. *laral*.

Solicit, v.a. *ghokkhtan, minnat-*, etc. *k*.

Solicitation, s. *ghokkht, minnat, darkhwāst, sawāl*.

Solicitous, a. *andekkh-man, wiswāsī, fikr-man*.

Solicitude, s. *andekkhnā, wiswās, fikr, gham*.

Solid, a. *klak, ṭing, sakht, drūnd, gaṇr, pokh, khyam*.

Solidity, s. *klak-*, etc. *-wālai, dranāwai*.

Solitary, a. *yawādzai, tanhā, biyal, tsaṛah*.

Solitude, s. *tanhā-ī, biyal-tūn*; *dzangal, ba-yābān*; *gokkha, khilwat*.

Solve, v.a. *prānatal, tsargandawul*; *wīlī k*.

Solvent, a. *zar-dār, māl-dār*; *wīlī kawūnkai*.

Some, a. *la-ag, la-ag ḍer*; *dzane, tsok, kūm, tsa*.

Somebody, s. *palānkai, tsok, kūm, kas, tan*.

Somehow, ad. *yo shān sara, tsa chal sara*.

Something, s. *shai, tsīz*. a. *la-ag ḍer, pitsānrai*.

Sometimes, ad. *kala kala*.

Somewhat, a. *la-ag, kam, pitsānrai*. ad. *la-ag-kūṭī* or *lakūṭī, tsakho, la-ag shān*.

Somewhere, ad. *chare*.

Son, s. *dzoe*. (-in law) *zūm, zūmgai*. (grand-) *nwasai*. (great grand-) *kaṛwasai*. (step-, by father) *parkaṭai*. (step-, by mother) *ba-anzai*. (brother's) *wrārah*. (sister's-) *khora-e* or *khoraye*. (only-) *kashai*.

Song, s. *sandara, saroḍ, badala, ṭapa, tarāna*.

Sonnet, s. *chār bait, ghazal, lanḍa-ī, sandara*.

Soon, ad. *zir, pa zir mūde, pa la-ag sā'at kkhke*.

Sooner, ad. *wṛūnbe, awwal*.

Soot, s. *lūgai, mas, dūna*; *koyina*.

Soothe, v.a. *tasallī warkawul, khwā saṛawul, pokkhal*.

Soothsayer, s. *pāl-* or *fāl-goe*, or *-katūnkai*.

Sooty, a. *lūghaṛan*.

Sop, s. *nwaṛa-ī*. v.a. *chūka k., khushtawul*.

Sorcerer, s. *jādū-gar, koḍ-gar, siḥr-gar*.

Sorcery, s. *jādū, koḍa, siḥr*.

Sordid, a. *shūm, bakhīl, tang-dast, stagh*.

Sore, s. *parhār, zakhm*. a. *zakhmī, khūg*.

Sorrel, s. *tarūkai*.

Sorrow, s. *gham, nūl*; *randz, afsos*; *pakkhe-mānī, stomānī*; *armān, tartāb*. v.n. *gham-edal, nūledal, randzedal, pakkhemānedal, stomānedal*. v.a. *afsos-, armān-*, etc. *k*.

Sorrowful, a. *gham-jan, gham-nak, nūl-jan, dil-gīr*.

Sorry, a. *toba-gār, pakkhemān, stomān*. (vile) *nā-kārah, khushai, hets shai*.

Sort, s. *qism, rang, shān, noga*. v.a. *chunral, atsanral, tartībawul, chīndah k*.

Sot, s. *bangī, sharābī, nasha-khor*.

Soul, s. *rūḥ, nafs, dzān*. (souls) *arwāḥ*.

Sound, a. (honest) *sūchah, karah, rikkhtīnai*. (healthy) *joṛ, rogh moṭ, tandrust*. (safe) *salāmat, pūrah, ṣābit, amānī*. (right) *jukht, barābar, sam*.

Sound, s. *ghag, zwag, bāng, ḍaz*. v.a. *ghagawul, zwag k., bāng wayal, ḍaz wahal*.

Soundly, ad. *pa kkhah shān sara*.

Soundness, s. *tandrustī, salāmatī*; *ṣiḥḥat*.

Soup, s. *kkhorwā*.

Sour, a. *trīw*.

Source, s. *munḍ, wekh, aṣl, sar, bonsaṭ*.

Souse, v.a. *lūndawul, khushtawul*; *ḍūbawul*.

South, s. *suhel, kīnr-ṭaraf*.

Sovereign, s. *bādshāh, sulṭan, amīr.*

Sow, v.a. *karal, kar k.* (-for another) *bogarai k.*

Space, s. *dzāe.* (-of time) *mūda, wakht, 'arṣa.*

Spacious, a. *arat, prānatai, dzāe·war.*

Spade, s. *yūm* or *yīm, kara.*

Span, s. *lwesht, langor, anang, gadozai.*

Spar, s. *bensh, tīr, largai.* (small-) *chanra; aṛam, aṛamkai.*

Spar, v.a. *jang k., sūkūna sara wahal, lāsuna sara tsandal.*

Spare, v.a. (save) *bachawul, bakkhal, pulawul.* (forego) *pregdal, prekkhodal, prekkhal.* (give) *warkawul.*

Spare, a. (scanty) *kam, la-ag, rangai.* (slender) *narai, trandz.* (short) *land, tang.* (unoccupied) *khālī, wazgār.* (superfluous) *ziyāt, pāltū.*

Sparing, a. *kam·kharts, tang·dast.*

Spark, s. *batsarai, batsarkai, ghuṛutskai.*

Sparkle, v.n *brekkhedal, dzalkedal, rūnredal.*

Sparkling, a. *brekkh·nāk, dzalkān, rūnr.*

Sparrow, s. *chanr chanr, chughuk.*

Spasm, s. *ghoṭa, ṭāo, pech.*

Spatter, v.a. *tsiṛīke wahal; dāghawul, palītawul.*

Spavin, s. *haḍai, oba.*

Speak, v.a. *wayal, khabare k., lal.*

Spear, s. *neza, balla, barcha, shalgai.*

Special, a. *khāṣṣ.*

Specie, s. *zar, naghd* or *naqd.*

Species, s. *zāt, rang, qism, noga.*

Specific, a. *zātī, nogai,* s. *mujarrab.*

Specimen, s. *namūna, nakkha, miṣāl.*

Spec, s. *ṭakai, laka, tsiṛīka, dāgh.*

Speckled, a. *ṭak·yālai, brag·yālai.*

Spectacle, s. *tamāsha, nandāra.*

Spectacles, s. *chashme, chashmake.*

Spectator, s. *ɩ.andārchī, tamāsha·bīn.*

Spectre, s. *rawai, khapaskai; siwrai.*

Speculate, v.a. *fikr-, qiyās-, khiyāl-,* etc. *k.*

Speculative, a. *fikr·man, khiyālī, aṭkalī.*

Speculator, s. *atkal·bāz, saudāgar.*

Speech, s. *jiba, wayai, wayana, khabara, wrāsha, sukhun.*

Speechless, a. *gūng, lāl, lā dzawāb.*

Speed, s. *talwār, talwal, jaltī, garandī·tob.*

Speedily, ad. *pa talwār, pa garandī, pa jaltī.*

Speedy, a. *garandai, za-ar* or *zir, jalt, tez.*

Spell, s. *jādū, kod, mantar.*

Spell, v.a. *paiza-ī-, pakkhoya-, hijgī-,* etc. *k.*

Spend, v.a. *kharts-, ṣarf-,* etc. *k., lagawul.* (pass) *terawul.* (emit) *khalāṣawul, chalawul.* v.n. *chaledal, kamedal, teredal, khalāṣedal.*

Spendthrift, s. *khartsī, tāwānī, iṣrāfī.*

Sphere, s. *tsarkh; ghūndai.*

Spherical, a. *ghūnd, ghūnd·man.*

Spice, s. *maṣālah* or *masāla.*

Spider, s. *jolā.* (tarantula-) *ghanra.*

Spigot, s. *būja, khulborai, ḍiḍa.*

Spike, s. *wagai, khosha.* (nail) *mogai.*

Spill, v.a. *toyawul, ghurzawul, āchawul.* v.n. *toyedal* or *to-edal, prewatal, bahedal.*

Spin, v.a. *tsarkha k.; tsarkhawul, churlawul, girzawul.* v.n. *tsarkhedal, churledal, girzedal.*

Spinach, s. *pālak.*

Spindle, s. *dūk, barandai, jalak, tsarkhai, tsarkhalgai, girzandai, tsākkhaị.* (stalk) *tīla-ī, nāṛa.*

Spinning, s. *tsarkhawuna.* (-wheel) *tsarkha.*

Spire, s. *munāra.*

Spirit, s. *rūh, nafs, dzān; dam, sāh; zṛah, dil; himmat, maṛāna; nang, ghairat; khoe, mizāj; 'araq, jauhar.*

Spirited, a. *zṛah·war, maṛanai, himmat·nāk, nang·yālai, ghairat·nāk* or *ghairat·man.*

Spiritual, a. *rūhānī, bāṭinī.*

Spit, v.a. *tūkal, tū-, tūkānrai-,* etc. *ghurzawul.*

Spit, s. *sīkh, sīkhcha.*
Spite, s. *kīna, ẓidd, khwā badī, 'adāwat, 'inād, 'aks, rakha, droh, ghach.* (in spite of) *par 'aks, par khilāf.*
Spiteful, a. *kīna·war, khwā bad, 'inādī.*
Spittle, s. *tū, tūk, tūkānrai, lāṛa, lānra.*
Splash, v.a. *tsiṛīke-, charaq-,* etc. *wahal, lawastal.*
Spleen, s. *torai.* (spite) *kīna, khwā badī.*
Splendid, a. *rokkhān, dzalkān; loe, ghaṭ.*
Splendour, s. *raunaq, dabdaba, tamtarāq.*
Splice, s. *joṛ, pewand.* v.a. *joṛawul, pewand k.*
Splint, s. *tūtankai.* (-in horses) *hadai.* (surgical) *takhta, kalokkhta, kalola. skanḍa.*
Splinter, s. *ṭoṭkai, daṛa, kak, tarāza.*
Split, v.n. *chāwdal, shledal.* v.a. *chawul, shlawul.* (peas, grain, etc.) *dal k., dalawul.*
Spoil, v.a. *wrānawul, kharābawul, habatah-, 'abaṣ-, rang-, abtar-,* etc. *k.* (plunder) *lūṭawul, shūkawul, natal, tālā-,* etc. *k.* s. *lūṭ, tālā, shūka, ghārat, gaṭa.*
Spontaneously, ad. *pakhpula.*
Spoon, s. *chamcha-ī* or *tsamtsa-ī* or *tsontsa-ī, kāchogha.* (large) *kaṛecha-ī, harkāra.*
Sport, s. *loba; khandā, ṭoqa washta; kkhkār.* v.a. *lobe k.; khandā-,* etc. *k.; kkhkār k.*
Sportsman, s. *kkhkārī.*
Spot, s. *ṭakai, laka; dāgh, 'aib, tsiṛīka; dzāe.*
Spotted, a. *chrag brag, gaḍ, ṭak·yālai, brag·yālai.*
Spout, s. *tsūkkhka, tsakkhkūṛai.* (of water, etc.) *dāra, fawāra; charaq.* v.n. *pa dāro-,* etc. *watal* or *-bahedal.* v.a. *dāra-,* etc. *wahal.*
Sprain, s. *wal, tāo, pech.* v.a. *wal-,* etc. *khwuṛal.*
Sprawl, v.n. *rghaṛedal—rghakkhtal, lots pots ked.*
Spread, v.a. *khwarawul, wīṛawul, phelawul.* v.n. *khwaredal, wīṛedal, pheledal.*
Sprig, s. *lakkhta, kkhākhcha.*
Sprightly, a. *chust, chālāk; kkhād, kkhād·man; mast, shokhīn.*
Spring, s. (season) *sparlai, būhār.* (source) *chīna, chashma.* (leap) *ṭop, trapa, dang. ghurzang.* (elasticity) *dam.* (instrument) *kamāncha.* (bound) *tīndak, khachūnai.*
Spring, v.a. (leap) *ṭop-,* etc. *wahal, dangal, traplal.* (bound) *tīndak-,* etc. *wahal.* (germinate) v.n. *ṭūkedal, zarghūnedal.* (issue) v.n. *khatal, watal, jārī ked.*
Sprinkle, v.a. *charqāo k., tsātsawul, tsiṛīkawul.* (-from mouth) *pūg wahal.*
Sprout, s. *khalai, buzghalai, ghandal, tegh.* v.n. *ṭūkedal, zarghūnedal, ghundzedal.*
Spruce, a. *ḍaulī, joṛābī, spīn spetsalai, kṛah wṛah, kkhāyastah, pāk ṣāf.*
Spruceness, s. *joṛāb, kkhāyast, kkhāyast·wālai.*
Spur, s. *mamrez* or *mahmeza.* (cock's-) *khāro.* v.a. *tezal, pūnḍa-* or *pūnḍa-ī-, mamrez-,* etc. *wahal.*
Spurious, a. *jūṭah, nā·sarah, nā·karah.*
Sputter, s. *tsir, sakkhā, dzaz.* v.a. *tsir-,* etc *wahal.*
Spy, s. *tsārī, jāsūs, zarai, mukhbir.* v.a *tsāral, tsār-, zarana-ī-, jāsūsī-,* etc. *k.*
Squabble, v.a. *jagṛa-, qaẓiya-, steza,* etc. *k.*
Squalid, a. *palīt, gandah, khīran, murdār.*
Squall, s. (wind) *sīla-ī, jakaṛ, jam jakaṛ* (cry) *chigha, ĵaṛā.* v.a. *chighawul, ĵaṛal*
Squander, v.a. *iṣrāf-, talaf-,* etc. *k., wrukawul.*
Square, a. *chār gūṭlai, chār kunjai, murabb'ah.*
Squash, v.a. *chīt pīt k., paz wahal.*
Squeamish, a. *mekkh mekkh.*
Squeeze, v.a. *nichoṛawul.* (-out) *nakkhtedzal.* (press) *manḍal.* (flatten) *chīt k.*
Squint, v.a. *pa kago-, pa kṛingo-, pa chapako-,* etc. *stargo katal.*
Squirrel, s. *bilūngaṛai, gidaṛai, bilawṛai.*

Squirt, s. *pichkāra-ī.* v.a. *pichkāra-ī wahal.* (-from the mouth) *pūg wahal; mazmaza k.*
Stab, v.a. *pa chāṛe-*, etc. *negh wahal, sūk wahal.*
Stable, a. *pāedār, qā-im, mazbūṭ.* s. *ṭabela.*
Stack, s. *dala-ī, ṭap, ḍera-ī.*
Staff, s. *lakaṛa; amsā; ḍānḍa-ī.* (shepherd's) *aṛamkai, konṭai.* (stem) *chaṛ.*
Stage, s. *mazal* or *manzil.* (degree) *darja.* (platform) *manā; dunkācha; gaṛwanj.*
Stagger, v.n. *rapedal, laṛzedal; gaḍ waḍ tlal, ṭaparedal; hak pak ked., hariyānedal.*
Stagnant, a. *band, walāṛ.* (-water) *ḍab.*
Stain, s. *dāgh, laka, tsiṛīka.*
Stair, s. *pārchang, pawṛa-ī, andarpāya.*
Stake, s. (peg) *mogai.* (post) *dār, sūla-ī.* (at play) *daw, shart.*
Stale, a. *zoṛ, begānai, baranai.*
Stalk, s. *nāṛa, tila-ī; mūnḍ, ḍakai.*
Stall, s. *dzāe, khūna; ākhor.*
Stallion, s. *sānr, turum.*
Stammer, v.n. *tartaredal.* v.a. *guzmuzai k.*
Stammerer, s. *tartarai, chāṛā, tatai.*
Stamp, s. *chāp; muhr; manḍa; rang.* v.a. *chāp wahal; muhr lagawul; manḍal, manḍa wahal.*
Stampede, s. *ghwa-e-manḍ.*
Stand, v.n. *wudredal, walāṛedal, pātsedal.* (-fast) *tam ked.* (-at bay) *haṭedal, jah-* or *jig ked.* (erect) *neghedal, lak ked.*
Standard, s. *nakkha, nikkhān, togh, janḍa, bairaq* or *bairagh.*
Standing, a. *walāṛ, negh; lak; jig; pāedār.*
Staple, s. *saudā.* (lock-) *hūl, aṛam.* (hook) *kunḍa.*
Star, s. *storai.* (planet) *starga.*
Starch, s. *batī.* v.a. *batī ḍakawul.*
Stare, v.a. *ghaṭ katal.*
Starling, s. *sarkhaka.*
Start, v.n. *rawānedal, tlal—lāṛal, drūmedal, drūmal.* (fear) *bugnedal, tarhedal.*
Startle, v.a. *bugnawul, tarhawul, yerawul.*
Starve, v.n. *da lwuge mṛal* or (v.a.) *-muṛ k.*
State, v.a. *bayānawul, wayal, lal, lawdal.*
State, s. *ḥāl, ḥālat; shān, shauqat; rāj, mulk.*
Statement, s. *ṣūrat ḥāl, bayān, wayai; ḥisāb.*
Station, s. *dzāe; mazal; darja, martaba.* v.a. *wudrawul, kkhkenawul, walāṛawul.*
Statue, s. *but, tsera.*
Stature, s. *qadd, qāmat.* (tall) *dang.* (short) *mandarai.*
Statute, s. *qānūn, qā'ida, ā-īn.*
Stay, v.n. *osedal, pātedal, pātai-, tam-*, etc. *ked., āstedal.* (prevent) *man'a k., haṭālawul, kariyābawul.*
Stead, s. *dzāe, badal, 'iwaz.*
Steadfast, Steady, a. } *mazbūṭ, qā-im, pāedār, qalār.*
Steal, v.a. *ghlā k., puṭawul.* (-upon) *chapāo k.* (-away) v.n. *puṭedal.*
Stealth, s. *ghalī·tob, puṭ·wālai; ghlā.* (by-) *ghalai ghalai, puṭ puṭ.*
Steam, s. *bukhār, brās.*
Steep, a, *ūchat, hask; jawar; lwaṛ, kamar.*
Steep, v.a. *khushtawul, lūndawul.*
Steer, s. *skhwandar, skhwandarkai.*
Steer, v.a. *chalawul, kkhayal—kkhowul.*
Stem, s. *kkhākh, khaṛand, ṭanga, ḍanḍara, mūnḍ.* (of grasses, etc.) *nal, nāṛa.*
Stem, v.a. *bandawul, man'a k., haṭālawul.*
Stench, s. *bad·bū-ī, skhā·bū-ī, soṛ·bū·ī.*
Step, s. *qadam, gām; chāl, yūn; pāya, darja.*
Sterile, a. *shanḍ.* (as land) *kkhora·nāk.*
Stern, a. *trīkh, sakht, klak.* s. *shā, wrusta.*
Stew, s. *pulāo, qorma, dam pukht.*
Steward, s. *dīwān, kārdār.*
Stick, s. *largai, hamsā; lawaṛ, ḍāng, koṭak.*
Stick, v.n. *nkkhatal, nkkhledal, chaspedal, lagedal.* (pierce) v.a. *sīkhal, tetsal.* (-into) *nṣatal, kkhke·manḍal, khakkhawul, kkhke·bāsal—kkhke·yastal.*

Stickle, v.a. *takrār-, ḥujjat-,* etc. *k.*

Stiff, a. *ṭing, klak; lak, neg̱ẖ; zīg, lwāṛ; ṯsak.*

Stifle, v.a. *sāh bandawul.*

Stigma, s. *tor, tuhmat, pegẖor; dāg̱ẖ, laka.*

Stigmatize, v.a. *tor-, tuhmat-,* etc., *pori kawul, pegẖor warkawul.*

Still, a. *g̱ẖalai, cẖup; walāṛ, qalār; band, be·ḥarakat.* (water) *dab.* ad. *tar osa, os hum, lā.* s. *k̲ẖum.*

Stimulate, v.a. *zoral, tezal; wīkkẖawul, pāṯs-awul, baidār k.; lamsawul.*

Sting, s. *nekkẖ; las̲ẖa.* v.a. *nekkẖ wahal.*

Stingy, a. *s̲ẖūm, bak̲ẖīl, tang·dast, sak̲ẖt.*

Stink, v.n. *bad-, sk̲ẖā-, soṛ-,* etc. *bū-ī tlal.*

Stipulate, v.a. *wāda-, bandanṛ-, neṭa-,* etc. *k.,* or *-taṛal.*

Stir, v.a. *k̲ẖwadzedal, kkẖoredal.* v.a. *laṛal, ṛaqawul, k̲ẖwadzawul, kkẖorawul.*

Stirrup, s. *rikāb.* (-leather) *dawāl, tasma.*

Stitch, s. *skoe.* v.a. *gandal, skoe k., skoyal, agayal.*

Stock, s. *ṯsaṭ.* (tree) *mūnḍ, g̱ẖaṛand.* (-for legs) *kāṭ.* (source) *aṣl, noga.* (gun-) *kundāg̱ẖ.* (store) *panga, saga, māya.*

Stocking, s. *jorāba, moza.* (leather-) *māsa-ī.*

Stocks, s. *kāṭ.* (torture-) *pāna, kunda.* (to put in the-) *pa kāṭ k̲ẖejawul, pāna ṭakawul.*

Stomach, s. *geda, k̲ẖeṭa; ūjrai.* (crop) *jajūra.*

Stone, s. *kānrai, gaṭ, tīga, giṭai,* (-of the bladder) *gīṭa-ī.* (grave-) *k̲ẖāda* or *k̲ẖaza.* (ring-) *g̱ẖamai.* (-of fruit) *haḍ.* v.a. *pa kānro-, pa gaṭo-,* etc. *wīs̲ẖtal* or *-muṛ k., sangsār k.*

Stony, a. *kānredz, sanglāk̲ẖ, tarāṛah.*

Stool, s. *pera-ī, moṛa.* (purge) *dast, nāstah.*

Stoop, v.n. *ṭītedal.* v.a. *sar ṭīṭawul.*

Stop, v.a. *pātawul, pātai k., man'a k., band-awul, īsārawul; wudrawul, walārawul; hiṭālawul, kariyābawul; nkkẖlawul.* v.n. *pātedal, pātai ked., osedal; bandedal;*

īsāredal; wudredal, walāredal; nkkẖledal, nkkẖatal.

Stopper, s. *būja, s̲ẖoṛa; mūnrai; k̲ẖulborai, dīda.*

Store, s. *ambār, ganj, ḍerai; saga, panga, māya.* (-house) *koṭa, ambār k̲ẖāna, k̲ẖazāna.* v.a. *ṭolawul, jam'a k., yo dzāe k.*

Stores, s. *zak̲ẖīra, sūrsat, rasad; tokkẖa, ṯsawrai; asbāb, sāmān; hatiyāṛ, kālī.*

Stork, s. *ḍing.*

Storm, s. *sīla-ī, tūpān* or *ṭūfān.* v.a. *halla-, hamla-,* etc. *k.* (-by night) *sho·k̲ẖūn k.*

Story, s. *qiṣṣa, naql.* (stage) *mazal, mahal.*

Stout, a. *mazbūṭ, g̱ẖaṭ, kaṭah; gagar, k̲ẖrīs, nāpaṛ; lwāṛ, punḍ, ṭanḍ.*

Stow, v.a. *dzāyawul, kkẖke·mandal, kkẖke-gdal, kkẖekkẖodal, ʾkẖekkẖal.*

Straddle, v.n. *cẖinge kkẖpe tlal—lāṛal.*

Straggle, v.n. *k̲ẖor k̲ẖor-,* or *k̲ẖwarai k̲ẖwarai-, tār pa tār-,* etc. *girzedal.*

Straight, a. *sam, neg̱ẖ, sat.*

Straightway, ad. *sam da lāsa.*

Strain, v.a. *g̱ẖalbelawul, cẖānrawul.* (labour) *stam wahal.* (endeavour) *ḥadd k.*

Strainer, s. *cẖānra, g̱ẖalbel, parwezai.*

Strait, s. *tanga-ī; tangsiyā, tangī, sak̲ẖtī.*

Strange, a. *pradai, begānah; 'ajab.*

Stranger, s. *nā·ās̲ẖnāe, nā·balad, pradai.*

Strangle, v.a. *mara-ī-, g̱ẖāṛa-,* etc. *k̲ẖapa k.*

Strap, s. *tasma, rog.* (-of churning staff) *barangai.* (shoulder-) *paṭa.*

Stratagem, s. *cẖal, hīla, fareb, lamg̱ẖaṛa-ī.*

Stratum, s. *brag̱ẖ, tā.*

Straw, s. *k̲ẖas, k̲ẖasanrai, kāna-ī.* (Maize-) *ṭānṭa.* (Rice-) *palāla.* (Mustard-) *kām-būra.* (Pulse-) *kaṭī.* (broken-) *būs* or *būsī.*

Stray, v.n. *wrukedal, gumrāh-, be·lār-, k̲ẖaṯā-,* etc. *ked., k̲ẖus̲ẖai girzedal.*

Streak, s. *kīl, līka, karkkẖa.* (-of light) *par-taw, palwas̲ẖa.*

Stream, s. *dāra, sailāb, chala, chalānda.* v.n. *bahedal, chaledal, jārī ked.*
Street, s. *lār, kūtsa.*
Strength, s. *zor, quwat, bram, tuwān, ṭāqat.*
Strengthen, v.a. *zor-*, etc. *warkawul, mazbūt-, klak-*, etc. *k.*
Strenuous, a. *sargcrm, mazbūt, klak.*
Stress, s. *zor, quwat; dranāwai, bār.*
Stretch, v.a. *rākāgal—rākkhkal, ūgdawul.* (-out) *ghazawul.* v.n. *ūgdedal; ghazedal.*
Strew, v.a. *khwarawul, rejawul* or *rejdawul, satrai watrai-, tār pa tār-, khwarai-*, etc. *k.*
Strict, a. *sakht, klak, ṭīng, tang; jukht, joṛ.*
Strictly, ad. *pa rikkhtiyā.*
Stride, s. *tūlānd.* v.n. *va tūlānd tlal—lāṛal.*
Strife, s. *patna, steza, mīrtsī, jagṛa, 'adāwat.*
Strike, v.a. *wahal, jangawul.*
String, s. *mazai.* (tie) *tanra-ī.* (-of beads) *laṛ, hār.* (-of cattle) *qaṭār.* v.a. *pewdal.*
Stringy, a. *rekkha-dāṛ.*
Strip, s. *paṭa-ī, pāra, tarāza, rikkhkai, paṛūkai.*
Strip, v.a. *barbandawul; shūkawul.*
Stripe, s. *karkkha.* (blow) *guzār.* (whip) *karoṛa.*
Stripling, s. *halak, janrai; zalmai, ghundāyah.*
Strive, v.a. *mihnat-, kokshiksh-*, etc. *k.*; *zidd-, qaṣd-*, etc. *k.*
Stroke, s. *guzār.* (at play) *daw.* v.a. *-lās wahal* or *-girzawul*, etc.
Stroll, v.n. *girzedal.* v.a. *sail-, gakkht-*, etc. *k.*
Strong, a. *mazbūt, klak, mazai, zorāwar.*
Structure, s. *tarkīb, joṛawūna; shakl, ṣūrat.*
Struggle, v.a. *parzawul; jang k.; mihnat k.*
Strumpet, s. *gashta-ī, baghara-ī, hujra-ī, kāsīra, kūtsa gashta, kachana-ī, lola-ī.*
Strut, v n. *pa ḍaul tlal—lāṛal*, or *-girzedal.*
Stubble, s. *drūza, kharīz, nāṛ, ṭānṭa.*
Stubborn, a. *ṭakanrai, khpul-sar, hoḍ, jah, sar-kakkh, khpul-rāe.*
Stud, s. *ghūṭa-ī, gul-mekh.* (-of horses) *galla.*
Student, s. *shāgird, ṭālib da 'ilm.*
Study, v.a. *fikr k.; zdah k.*
Stuff, s. *tsīz, shai; asbāb, sāmān, kālai; rakht, zaṛūkai, ṭūkai; be-hūda-, khusha-ī-, pūcha-, ḍūza-*, etc. *khabara.*
Stuff, v.a. *manḍal, kkhke-manḍal.*
Stumble, v.a. *ṭīndak-, ṭakar-, budrī-, kangas-, skandarī-*, etc. *khwuṛal.*
Stump, s. *mūnḍ, kharanḍ, tsaṭ.* (-of a tooth) *daṛa, wekh.*
Stun, v.a. *parghazī-, gans-, dap-, sar-kawdan-, be-hokkh-*, etc. *k.*
Stupid, a. *kawdan, palwanḍ, gedī khar, nā-poh, kam 'aql.*
Stupefy, v.a. *be-hokkh-, be-khūd-*, etc. *k.*
Sturdy, a. *mazai, mazbūṭ, gagar, nāpaṛ, ghaṭ, khṛīs.*
Stutter, v.n. *tartaredal.*
Sty, s. (in the eyelid) *gholawunkai.*
Style, s. *inshā, 'ibārat; nūm, laqab.* v.a. *wayal, balal* or *bolal, nūm ākhistal* or *-warkawul, -lagawul.*
Subdue, v.a. *lāndi k., qābū k., wahal.*
Subject, s. *r'ayat, tābi'a-dār; khabara, maṭlab, mazmūn.* (in grammar) *fā'il.* v.a. *lāndi k., r'ayat-*, etc. *k.*
Sublime, a. *ūchat, buland; ghaṭ, loe.*
Submissive, a. *tābi'a-dār, farmān wrūnkai.*
Submit, v.a. *farmān wṛal, hukm manal, tābi'a-dārī k.; pekkhawul, wṛāndi gdal* or *-kkhkegdal*, etc.
Subordinate, a. *kashar; kkhkatanai, lāndīnai.*
Suborn, v.a. *pa mok-* or *pa baḍe gaṭal* or *-mūndal, -paidā k.*, etc. *baḍa-*, etc. *warkawul.*
Subscribe, v.a. *manal, qabūlawul, nūm līkal, dast khaṭṭ k.*
Subscription, s. *manana, dast khaṭṭ; bakkhana, bakhkshiksh.*

Subsequent, a. *wrustai, wrustanai, pasanai, akhīr.*
Subsequently, ad. *wrusto, pas, ākhir.*
Subservient, a. *madad-gār, komakī, madad-,* etc. *warkawūnkai.*
Subside, v.n. *kamedal, la-agedal*; *kkhkenāstal, prewatal.*
Subsidy, s. *pekkh-kakkh, khirāj, n'al-bandī.*
Subsist, v.n. *pāedal, osedal, pātedal, pātai ked.* v.a. *rozgār-, guzrān-,* etc. *k.*; *pālal, nmāndzal.*
Subsistence, s. *rozī, rozgār, guzrān, ĵwand, ĵwandūn.*
Substance, s. *shai, tsīz*; *māl, duniyā, daulat*; *sar, aṣl*; *khulāṣa, jauhar*; *māya, saga.*
Substantial, a. *pāedār, mazbūṭ*; *maujūd, aṣlī*; *māl-dār, daulat-man.*
Substantiate, v.a. *rikkhtiyā-, rikkhtīnai-, ṣābit-, zbād-,* etc. *k.*
Substantive, s. *shai, nūm*; *aṣl.*
Substitute, s. *badal, 'iwazī.*
Subterfuge, s. *ḥira-ī, bāna, lamgharạ-ī, palma.*
Subtile, a. *narai, bārīk, mahīn.*
Subtle, a. *hokkhyār, pokh*; *chal-bāz, ḥīla-bāz.*
Subtract, v.a. *ākhistal, prekawul, bāsal—yastal.*
Subvert, v.a. *wrānawul, naskorawul, naṛawul.*
Succeed, v.a. (follow) *pairawī k.* v.n. *pase lagedal, pase rātlal—rāghlal.* (prosper) v.a. *was chalawul, bakht mūndal, kār gaṭal.* (conquer) v.a. *pa-aṛ k., barai mūndal.* v.n. *wa-aṛ ked., was chaledal.*
Success, s. *wa-aṛāna, barai, bakht, barakat, gaṭa.*
Successful, a. *wa-aṛ, barakatī, bakhtāwar.*
Succession, s. *wār, dzāe nīwah.*
Successive, a. *wārī, pa wār rātlūnai.*
Successively, ad. *wār pa wār, pala pase.*
Successor, s. *pairaw, qā-im muqām.*
Succour, s. *mrasta, madad, komak.*
Succulent, a. *obĵan, pa obo ḍak, serāb.*
Succumb, v.n. *la brama prewatal, lāndi ked.*
Such, p. *hase, dā-hase, done.* (-a one) *palānkai, tsok.*
Suck, v.a. *chūpal, zbekkhal.* (-the breast) *rawdal.*
Suckle, v.a. *tai warkawul.*
Suckling, s. *tai rawdūnkai, tandai* or *tankai.*
Suction, s. *chūpana*; *rākkhkana.*
Sudden, a. *nāgahān, nā-gumān, tsaṭ waṭ.*
Suddenly, ad. *nāgāh, nātsāpa, nā-gumāna.*
Sudorific, a. *khwale rāwṛūnkai, da khwalo dawā.*
Sue, v.a. *d'awa-, muqaddama-,* etc. *k.*; *ghokkhtal, minnat k.*
Suffer, v.a. *zghamal, wṛal, khwuṛal, rākāgal—rākkhkal.* v.n. *zghamedal, petsal, sahal, sahedal.* (allow) *pregdal, prekkhodal, prekkhal*; *ijāzat-, izn-, ḥukm-, rukhṣat-,* etc. *warkawul.*
Sufferer, a. *khūg-man, dard-man, randzūr.* (in comp.) *-khor, -kakkh, -man,* etc.
Suffering, a. *khūg*; *zgham-nāk, ṣabr-nāk.*
Sufficient, a. *bas, kāfī, ḍer*; *lā-iq, qābil.*
Suffocate, v.a. *sāh-, dam-,* etc. *bandawul.*
Sugar, s. *shakara, tarī, nabāt.* (raw-) *gūṛa.* (-candy) *qand.* (-cane) *ganna, ponḍa, khū.*
Suggest, v.a. *ishārat-, 'arz-, kkhowuna-,* etc. *k., wayal.*
Suit, v.a. *joṛawul, barābarawul, samawul, lagawul, dzāe laral, pīrzowul.* v.n. *barābaredal, lagedal, pīrzo ked., pa-kār rātlal—rāghlal.*
Suit, s. (-of clothes) *joṛa.* (-of cards) *rang.* (law-) *d'awa, muqaddama, jagṛa.* (petition) *'arz, sawāl.* (retinue) *swarlī, jalab.* (wish) *ghokkht, darkhwāst.*
Suitable, a. *joṛ, barābar, munāsib, wājib, pīrz-, kkhāyastah, kkhah, yarzan.*
Suitor, s. *mudd'aī*; *ṭalab-gār.*
Sulky, a. *marawar, mānṛī-gar, khapah.*
Sulphur, s. *gogaṛ, gogird.*

Sultry, a. *dūp, garm.*
Sum, s. *ṭol ṭāl, jam'a, mablagh, kull.* v.a. *ḥisāb k.*
Summary, s. *mujmal, khulāṣa.* a. *lanḍ.*
Summer, s. *oṛai, dubai, tābistān.* (-house) *chopāṛ.*
Summit, s. *sar, peza, tsūka.*
Summon, v.a. *balal, rābalal, ṭalab k.*
Summons, s. *ṭalab nāma*; *bālah, balana.*
Sumptuous, a. *grān qīmat, be-bahā*; *shāh kharts.*
Sun, s. *nwar* or *nmar.* (-beam) *partaw.* (-shine) *pitāo, gharma.* (-rise) *nwar khātah.* (-set) *nwar prewātah.* (-dial) *da sirrī tsalai.* (-flower) *gul da nwar parast.*
Sunday, s. *itwār, yak shamba.*
Sundry, a. *aṛgajah, balāe batar, dzane, b'aẓe, biyal.*
Superabundant, a. *ḍer, ziyāt, frewān.*
Superb, a. *'aẓīm, be bahā, be siyāl, lā ṣānī.*
Supercilious, a. *kibr-jan, maghrūr, khāntamā.*
Superficial, a. *nīmgaṛai, kachah*; *bāhir, wardzane.*
Superficies, s. *makh, zmaka, maidān, zamīn.*
Superintendent, s. *nāẓir, kār kawūnkai, dāroghah, sardār, mīr majlis.*
Superior, a. *mashar*; *ghwarah*; *loe, ghaṭ, star*; *bar, pāsanai, portanai.*
Supernatural, a. *la 'aqla bāhir, khilāf la 'ādata.*
Superscription, s. *sar-nāma.*
Supersede, v.a. *bāṭil k., lāndi k.*
Superstition, s. *wahm, bāṭil īmān.*
Supine, a. *sat, stūnī-stagh.* (careless) *be parwā, sust*; *laṭ, nā-rāst.*
Supper, s. *da māskhutan ḍoḍa-ī*; *shūma.*
Supplant, v.a. *shaṛal, pa-chal sara be dzāyawul.*
Supple, a. *narm, mulā-im, pos* or *post.*
Suppliant, a. *riyāz-man, minnat-dār.*
Supplication, s. *minnat, du'ā.*
Supply, v.a. *warkawul, rasawul, rāwṛal, paidā k.*
Support, v.a. *wṛal, zghamal, petsal.* (nourish) *pālal, nmāndzal.* (keep) *sātal, jghoral, khundī k.* (assist) *pushtī-, komak-, āṛ-, mrasta-,* etc. *k.*
Support, s. *āṛ, pushta*; *komak, mrasta*; *parwarish.*
Supporter, s. *pushtībān, takiya*; *pālūnkai, sātūnkai, sātandoe, jghorai.*
Suppose, v.a. *ganṛal, angeral, qiyās-, fikr-, khiyāl-,* etc. *k.* v.n. *pohedal.*
Suppress, v.a. *kkhkenawul, lāndi k., man'a k., mātawul, bandawul.* (conceal) *puṭawul.*
Suppurate, v.n. *zawlan ked., khūyedal, pakhedal.*
Supreme, a. *ṣadar*; *kull mukhtār, loe, ghaṭ.*
Sure, a. *yaqīn, rikkhtīnai, wāq'ī*; *maẓbūṭ, pokh.*
Surely, ad. *rikkhtiyā, yara, be shakka.*
Surety, s. *ẓāmin.* (the thing) *ẓamānat.*
Surface, s. *makh, zmaka, maidān, zamīn.*
Surfeit, s. *agheṛ, ateṛ, sekan.* v.a. *agheṛal, ateṛal, be prate-, be-khrate-,* etc. *khwuṛal.* v.n. *sekan ked.*
Surge, v.n. *ghurzedal.* v.a. *chape wahal.*
Surgeon, s. *jarrāḥ, ṭabīb.*
Surly, a. *bakhīl, trīkh-* or *tursh rūe, sūṭ būṭ.*
Surname, s. *da qām-, da khel-, da khāndān-,* etc. *nūm* or *nāma*; *laqab, nūm.*
Surplus, s. *pātai, ziyātī, bāqī.*
Surprise, v.a. *hariyānawul, rabṛawul*; *chapāo k.* v.n. *be-khabar rasedal, nātsāpa prewatal.*
Surrender, v.a. *pāslawul, spāral.*
Surround, v.a. *īsārawul, gerawul.*
Survey, v.a. *mech-, kach-,* etc. *k.*; *katal, kasal, goral—līdal, naẓar-,* etc. *k.*
Survive, v.n. *pāedal, jwandai pātai ked.*
Suspect, v.a. *shakk-, shubha-, gumān-,* etc. *laral.*

Suspend, v.a. *dzwarandawul, āwezānd k.* (-from office) *mu'attal-, man'a-, band-,* etc. *k.*

Suspense, s. *shakk, shubha, wiswās, andekkhnā.*

Suspicion, s. *gumān, shubha, shakk; tuhmat, tor, peghor, sigāl.*

Sustain, v.a. *wṛal, zghamal, petsal, khwuṛal, kāgal—kkhkal.* (aid) *madad-, pushtī-, komak-,* etc. *warkawul.* (keep) *sātal, ĵghoral, khundī k.* (cherish) *pālal, nmāndzal.*

Sustenance, s. *rozī, khwuṛāk, parwarish.*

Swagger, v.a. *ḍūze-, lāpe-, lāpe shāpe-,* etc. *wahal.*

Swallow, s. *totakarai.* (swift) *totakai.* (sand martin) *totakarkai.*

Swallow, v.a. *nghaṛdal, terawul.*

Swallow-wort, s. *spalma-ī.*

Swamp, s. *jaba.*

Swan, s. *qāz.*

Swarm, s. *ṭol, paṛk, lakkhkar, ganṛa gūnṛa.* (-of bees) *ghubār.* (-of locusts) *lakkhkar.*

Swarthy, a. *skāṇr; ghanum rang.*

Swathe, v.a. *nghaṛal — nghakkhtal, paṭa-ī taṛal.* (a babe) *seznī taṛal, blegdal.*

Sway, v.a. *ḥukm chalawul, ḥukūmat k.* (bias) *mā-il-, mā-ilān-,* etc. *k., rāwustal.*

Swear, v.a. *qasam-, saugand-,* etc. *khwuṛal.* (-falsely) *darogh-, nāḥaqq-,* etc. *qasam khwuṛal.*

Sweat, v.n. *khwale ked.*

Sweep, v.a. *jārū k.*

Sweeper, s. *jārū·kakkh, shāhī khel, muṣallī, chūrai.* (-of a mosque, etc.) *mīnjawar.*

Sweepings, s. *khāshāk, khadzala, kharshan, warkhaṛa.*

Sweet, a. *khog, shīrīn, khwand·nāk.*

Sweetheart, s. *yār, yāra; mayan, mayana; 'āshiq, 'āshiqa; m'ashūq, m'ashūqa; āshnāe, āshnāya.*

Sweetish, a. *khog·nāk, khog·loṛai.*

Sweetmeat, s. *qanāt, mityā-ī, shīrīnī.* (varieties) *amrasa, ghunzākkhai, dzalobai, rewṛa-ī, laṭū, batāsa, ḥalwā, pāpar,* etc. etc. (-seller) *ḥalwā-ī.*

Sweetness, s. *khog·wālai, khog·loṛ.*

Swell, v.n. *paṛsedal, punḍedal, tyak ked.*

Swelling, s. *pāṛsob.*

Swift, a. *gaṛandai, jalt, tez, zir.*

Swim, v.a. *lānbo wahal* or *k.* v.n. *pa lānbo tlal—lāṛal, rawānedal, chaledal.*

Swimmer, s. *lānbo·zan.*

Swindler, s. *darghal, ṭag, sādū.*

Swing, s. *ṭāl, gahwāral.* (cradle) *zāngo.* (whirligig) *banṛe·chagh.* v.a. *ṭāl wahal, zangawul.* v.n. *zangal, zangedal.*

Switch, s. *lakkhta, keṛa.*

Swivel, s. *zambūrak, shāhīn.*

Swoon, s. *parghaz.* v.n. *parghazī prewatal.*

Swoop, v.a. *pa chape-, pa ghoṭe-, pa guzār-,* etc. *wahal* or *-nīwul.*

Sword, s. *tūra, tegh.* (-spear) *sela.* (-knot) *zunḍai, kīlak.*

Swordsman, s. *tūrzan, tūra·bāz.*

Sycophant, s. *khūshāmad·gar, ḍirpal.*

Sylvan, a. *dzangalī, dashtī.* s. (satyr) *banṛ mānū.*

Symbol, s. *nakkha, nikkhān, 'alāmat.*

Sympathy, s. *khwā·khūgī, zṛah swai.*

Symptom, s. *nakkha,* etc. (*v.* Symbol).

Synod, s. *jirga-* or *majlis da shekhāno* or *-da imāmāno* or *-da mullāyāno.*

Syntax, s. *naḥw.*

Syringe, s. *pichkāra-ī, ḥuqna.*

Syrup, s. *gūṛa-ī, qiwām, zokkha, rub.*

System, s. *qānūn, ā-īn, qā'ida, ṭarīqa.*

T

Table, s. *mez, takhta; naqsha.* (-cloth) *dastar·khwān.* (-cover) *chāndanī.*

Tablet, s. *lauḥ, takhta.*
Tacit, a. *ghalai, chup.*
Tactics, s. *da jang ḥikmat.*
Tail, s. *lama, laka-ī.* (-bone) *laka lamai.* (-less) *landai.* (fat tailed) a. *lamarar.*
Tailor, s. *darzī, khaiyāṭ.*
Taint, v.a. *bonrawul, wrost-, skhā-,* etc. *k.*
Take, v.a. *ākhistal, nīwul, lāndi k.* (-in) *dzāyawul.* (suppose) *ganral.* (effect) *pāzah k.* (carry) *yosal, wṛal.* (lead) *botlal—bīwul.* (-off) *bāsal—yastal.* (-out) *kāgal—kkhkal.* (-care of) *sātal, jghoral, khundī k.* (-down) *kūzawul.* (-care) *pahm k.*
Talc, s. *abraq, da shige gul, zarbarakh.*
Tale, s. *qiṣṣa, naql, rawāyat.* (-bearer) *chughl·khor, mawās.*
Talent, s. *'aql, sha'ūr, poh, hunar.*
Talk, v.a. *wayal, khabare k.* s. *wayana, khabara; wrāsha, wayai; gangosai.*
Tall, a. *ūchat, hask, dang, lwaṛ.*
Tallow, s. *ghwaṛ, spīna, mū.*
Talon, s. *nūk, mangul, changul, panja.*
Tambourine, s. *tambal, ḍūmbakai, ḍūmkai.*
Tame, a. *āmokhtah, el, koranai.* v.a. *āmokhtah k., elawul.*
Tamper, v.a. *lās lagawul, lamsawul, lamsūn k.*
Tan, v.a. *dabbāghī k., tsarman joṛawul* or *-pakha k.* (-by the sun) v.n. *swal, sedzal.*
Tank, s. *ḍanḍ, ḥauẓ, tālāo, nāwar.*
Tanner, s. *dabbāgh, tsamyār.*
Tantalize, v.a. *pa umed nā umed k.*
Tap, v.a. *ṭak-, trak-,* etc. *wahal.* (pierce) *tsīkhal, sūṛai k.*
Tape, s. *paṭa-ī; niwāṛ.*
Taper, s. *bāta-ī, patīla.* a. *gāo dum, trandz.*
Tar, s. *rāndzaṛah, chūṛel.*
Tardy, a. *sust, laṭ, drangai.*
Tardiness, s. *sust·wālai, drang, dzanḍ.*
Target, s. *mūkha, nakkha, kuhāṛa; ḍāl, spar.*
Tarnish, v.a. *khīran-, kakaṛ-, murdār-,* etc. *k.*
Tarry, v.n. *osedal, pātedal; walāṛedal, wudredal; lārghah-, dzanḍ-, drang-,* etc. *k.*
Task, s. *kār, mashghūlā; dars, sabaq; miḥnat.*
Tassel, s. *zunḍai, zunbak.*
Taste, s. *khwand, maza, tsaka; tsakindan.* v.a. *khwand-,* etc. *-wahal, ākhistal,* or *-k., tsakal.*
Tattle, v.a. *bak bak-, baṛ baṛ-, ṭar ṭar-,* etc. *k.*
Taunt, v.a. *pekkhe-, ṭoqe-, khandā-,* etc. *pore k.*
Tawny, a. *skānr, ghanum rang.*
Tax, v.a. *bāj-, khirāj-, sāw-, maḥṣūl-,* etc. *lagawul* or *-taṛal.* (cattle-) s. *sargalla, goshī.* (land-) *kulang, sarghala, sar·sabzī.* (house-) *lūgī·tāwān, khāna·shumārī.* (poll-) *jaziya.*
Tea, s. *chāe.* (-cup) *piyāla.*
Teach, v.a. *kkhayal—kkhowul, pohawul; lwalawul, tarbiyat-, t'alīm-,* etc. *k., āmokhtah-, 'ādat-, zdah-,* etc. *k.*
Teacher, s. *ākhūn, ustād, mu'allim.*
Tear, v.a. *shlawul, tsīral, wrarawul, chāk k.* v.n. *shledal, tsīredal, wraredal.* (-out) *kāgal—kkhkal, bāsal—yastal.*
Tear, s. *okkha.* (-ful) a. *okkhan.*
Tease, v.a. *pārawul, tangawul, ṭongawul.*
Tedious, a. *drūnd, grān, sakht.*
Teem, v.n. *ganr ked., ḍeredal, wadānedal.*
Tell, v.a. *wayal, khabarawul; bayānawul; kkhayal—kkhowul.* (-tales) *chughlī k.*
Temerity, s. *be·adabī; be·tadbīrī; be·bākī.*
Temper, s. *khoe, khaṣlat, lokkhai, mizāj, ṭab'iyat.* (-of metals) *āb, dam.*
Temperate, a. *barābar, joṛ, muwāfiq; parhez·gār; m'utadil, na tod na soṛ.*
Tempest, s. *sīla-ī, tūpān* or *ṭūfān.*
Temple, s. *'ibādat·gāh, masjid, jumā'at.* (-of Mecca) *qibla, k'aba.* (-of Jerusalem) *bait ul muqaddas.* (-of the head) *lweganda, ṭek.*
Temporal, a. *duniyā-ī, fānī, jahānī.*
Temporary, a. *teredūnai, la-ag wradzanai.*

Temporize, v.a. *drang-, lārghah-, multawī-,* etc. *k.*

Tempt, v.a. *ghulawul, darghalawul, lamsawul, targhīb-,* etc. *warkawul.*

Ten, a. *las.* (tenth) a. *lasam.* (-fold) *las bragh*; *las pa yo.* (-times) *las hera, las dzala.*

Tenable, a. *klak, ṭīng, maḥkam, mazbūṭ.*

Tenacious, a. *klak, ṭīng, sakht; bokkht, slekkhtnāk*; *shūm, bakhīl*; *khpul rāe.*

Tenant, s. *hamsāyah, faqīr, ijāra-dār, āsāmī.*

Tend, v.a. *sātal, jghoral*; *khabar ākhistal, khidmat k.* (-flocks) *shpanī k.* v.n. *girzedal, mā-il-, ma-ilān-,* etc. *ked.*

Tendency, s. *mā-il-, khwā*; *gharaẓ*; *maṭlab, mudd'ā.*

Tender, a. *nāzak, narm, mulā-im, post.*

Tendon, s. *pala, rag, wuja.* (-of horse's leg) *pai.* (-of the heel) *spīna, kūchai.*

Tendril, s. *zela, bela.*

Tenesmus. s. *kānga, tāo, pech.*

Tenet, s. *masla*; *bāwar, īmān*; *ṭarīqa.*

Tenor, s. *m'anī*; *yūn, chalan.* (in music) *dzīr.*

Tense, a. *rākkhkalai, klak, ṭīng.*

Tent, s. *ḍera, tambū, khaima.* (nomad's) *kigda-ī.* (-in surgery) *bāta-ī.* (-rope) *māndara, mazai.*

Tenth, a. *lasam.* (-part) s. *lasama brakha.*

Tepid, a. *taṛam, nīm garm.*

Term, s. *khabara, wayai, lafẓ.* (time) *neṭa, mūda.* (stipulation) *sharṭ, taṛa, wāda, bandanr.* (limit) *ḥadd.* (phrase) *'ibārat.* (good terms) *rogha joṛa, pakhulā.*

Termagant, s. *jiba-wara, jang-yāla-ī.*

Terminate, v.n. *tamāmedal, pūrah ked., anjāmedal.* v.a. *tamāmawul,* etc.

Terrace, s. *dunkācha.* (-of a house) *chat, bām.*

Terrible, a. *haul-nāk, khof-nāk.*

Terrify, v.a. *yerawul, tarhawul.*

Territory, s. *mulk, zmaka, hiwād.*

Terror, s. *yera* or *wera, tor, khof.* (-struck) *tor khwuṛalai.*

Test, v.a. *āzmāyal* or *āzmoyal, āzmekkht k.*

Testament, s. (Old) *tauret.* (New) *injīl,* (will) *waṣiyat nāma.*

Testicle, s. *and, haga-ī, khoṭa.*

Testify, v.a. *shāhidī-, gawāhī-,*etc. *lal* or *lawdal,* or *-warkawul.*

Testimonial, s. *rāẓī-nāma*; *gawāhī-nāma.*

Testimony, s. *gawāhī, shāhidī.*

Tether, v.a. *taṛal.* s. *shkal* or *shkel, wandar.*

Text, s. *matan, aṣl.* (of Qurān) *āyat.*

Texture, s. *tarkīb, joṛawuna, sākht.*

Than, ad. *la—na.*

Thank, v.a. *shukr k., -bāsal—yastal, -guzāral. -pa dzāe rāwṛal,* etc.

Thankful, a. *shukr guzār.*

That, pr. *haghah, e, kūm, dā.* c. *tso chi, dapāra da.*

Thatch, s. *tsapar, chat.*

Thaw, v.n. *oba ked.*; *wilī ked.*

The, art. *haghah, daghah, dā.*

Theft, s. *ghlā.*

Theme, s. *masawda* or *musawadda*; *manshā.*

Then, ad. *hāla, pas*; *tro, bāre*; *nor, biyā.*

Thence, ad. *dzaka, la haghe na.* (-forth) *pas, pas la haghe na.*

Theology, s. *fiqha.*

Theory, s. *'ilm, qiyās, khiyāl.*

There, ad. *halta, hore, horta, hagha khwā.*

Thereabout, ad. *la-ag ḍer* or *la-ag ziyāt, nijde, takhmīnan.*

Therefore, ad. *pas, dzaka, tro.*

Thick, a. *ghaṭ, ṭīng, lwāṛ*; *ganr, tat, ṭal* (-as the voice) *bog, ḍaḍ.*

Thicket, s. *jangai, jāṛ, jāmbṛa, karkanr.*

Thief, s. *ghal, uchakah, chakah ghal.*

Thigh, s. *wrūn, patūn, kkhānga.*

Thimble, s. *gūtma.*

Thin, a. *narai, mahīn, bārīk, trandz, nāzak.* (lean) *ḍangar, khwār.* (scanty) *rangai.*

Thing, s. *shai, tsīz, kālai.*

Think, v.a. *fikr-, qiyās-, khiyāl-*, etc. *k.*; *gumān-, andekkhnā-*, etc. *k.*; *ghaur-, parwā-*, etc. *k.*; *ganral, angeral.* v.n. *pohedal.*

Third, a. *driyam* or *dre-am.* (-part) s. *driyama brakha.*

Thirst, v.n. *tagai ked.* s. *tanda, tagai·wālai.*

Thirsty, a. *tagai.*

Thirteen, a. *diyārlas.*

Thirty, a. *dersh.* (thirtieth) *dersham.* (thirty-one) *yo dersh.* (-two) *dwah dersh*, etc.

This, pr. *dā, daghah, dah, de, hāyah.* (-very one) *bedū, pa ṭakī.*

Thistle, s. *āzghakai, kārīza.*

Thither, ad. *halta, hore, horta, warhīsta, hagha khwā.*

Thong, s. *tasma, rog.*

Thorax, s. *taṭar, gargas, gogal, sīna.*

Thorn, s. *āzghai* or *āghzai, khār.* (-bush) *ghana, karkanra.* (-apple) *dātūra.* (-apple seed) *tora dāna.* (thorns) *ghane.*

Thorny, a. *āzghan* or *āghzan, khār·dār*

Thorough, a. *pūrah, pokh, bashpaṛ, amānī.*

Thou, pr. *tah, tā, de, di.*

Though, c. *agarchi, siwā la de na.* (as-) *laka chi.*

Thought, s. *fikr, qiyās, khiyāl*; *ghaur, khabar, parwā*; *gumān, sigāl*; *andekkhnā.*

Thoughtful, a. *fikr·man, andekkh·man.*

Thoughtless, a. *be·fikr, be·parwā, be·khabar.*

Thousand, a. *zar.* (two-) *dwah zara*, etc.

Thraldom, s. *qaid, band, nkkhatai.*

Thrash, v.a. *wahal, ṭakawul, kūṭal,* (-corn) *ghobal k.*

Thrashing-floor, s. *khirman, dirmand.*

Thread, s. *spanrsai, tār, mazai.* v.a. *pewdal, peyal.*

Threaten, v.a. *ḍabawul, ḍabka k.*

Three, a. *dre* or *dri.* (-fold) *dre bragh*; *dre pa yo.*

Threshold, s. *āstān, dargāh*; *dahlīz.*

Thrice, ad. *dre heṛa, -dzala, -plā, -guzāra*, etc.

Thrifty, a. *kam kharts, kam tāwān kawūnkai, bachāū, kifāyat kawūnkai.*

Thrive, v.n. *wadānedal, ābādedal, maṛedal.*

Throat, s. *mara-ī, markanḍai, ghara-ī.* (fauces) *ghāṛa, ḥalq.*

Throb, v.a. *tsiṛīka wahal.* v.n. *ḍrazedal.*

Throne, s. *takht, masnad, gadda-ī.*

Throng, s. *ṭol, paṛk, ḍala, ganra gūnra.*

Through, p. *pore, pa mandz kkhke.* (-and through) *pore ore, ore rāpore.* (by means of) *pa m'arifat, la kabla.*

Throughout, ad. *amānī, sarāsar.*

Throw, v.a. *wīshtal, āchawul, ghurzawul, lawastal.* (-up) *jārbāsal—jāryastal*; *pregdal, prekkhodal, prekkhal, tark k.*

Thrust, v.a. *negh wahal*; *ṭel-, ḍaka-, sūk-*, etc. *wahal.* (-into) *manḍal, kkhke·manḍal*; *nana-*, or *kkhke·bāsal—nana-*, or *kkhke·yastal.*

Thumb, s. *ghaṭa-gūta.*

Thump, v.a. *ḍab-, ṭak-, sūk-, gasa-*, etc. *wahal.*

Thunder, s. *tālanda, tanrā.* (-bolt) *tandar, ṭaka.* v.n. *ghuṛunbedal, ghaṛedal.*

Thursday, s. *pānshamba, da ziyārat wradz.*

Thus, ad. *hase, dā·hase, hase shān, dā shān, dā rang.* (-much) *done, hombra, daghombra.*

Thwart, v.a. *wār khaṭā k., wrānawul, aṛawul, 'aks-, ẓidd-*, etc. *k.*

Thyself, pr. *tah khpul.*

Tick, s. (sound) *ṭak, ṭas.* (louse) *kūnai, kana, konr, wrādza.*

Ticket, s. *chīṭa-ī*; *sar·nāma.*

Tickle, s. *takha.* v.a. *takhawul, takhnawul.* v.n. *takhedal, takhnedal.*

Tidings, s. *khabar.* (good-) *zera, zerai.* (the bearer of good-) *zera·garai.*

Tidy, a. *ḍaulī, spīn spetsalai.*

Tie, s. *taṛūn, tanra-ī, wandanai.* v.a. *taṛal, lagawul.*

Tiffin, s. *nāshta, nahārai.*

Tiger, s. *zmarai* or *mzarai.*

Tight, a. *tang, chust, rākkhkalai, klak.*

Tighten, v.a. *tangawul, klakawul, rākāgal—rākkhkal.*

Till, p. *tar haghah pore.* (when?) *tar kala pore.* (-now) *tar osa pore.*

Till, v.a. *kar-, īwe-,* or *yawe-,* etc. *k., zmaka aṛawul.*

Tillage, s. *kar, īwe,* or *yiwe,* or *yawe.*

Timber, s. *largai*; *bensh.*

Time, s. *wakht* or *waqt.* (season) *neṭa, mūda, nobat, ṭāng.* (age) *'umr, kāl*; *zamāna, daur.* (turn) *wār, heṛ, plā, dzal, guzār.* (leisure) *wazgār·tiyā, furṣat.* (-in music) *tāl, wazn.* (at all times) *har wakht, har kala.*

Timid, a. *yer·man, harānd, wiswāsī, yere-dūnkai.*

Tin, s. *qal'aī.* (-man) *qal'aī·gar.*

Tinder, s. *khū, khpah, baḍagāl.*

Tinge, s. *rang.* v.a. *rangawul.*

Tingle, v.n. *shṛangedal.* (tickle) *takhnedal.* (with pain) *swal, brekkhedal.*

Tiny, a. *woṛ, woṛkoṭai, pūṭai, kharmandai.*

Tip, s. *sar, peza, tsūka, nūka.*

Tire, v.n. *staṛai-, stomān-, haukah-, māndah-,* etc. *ked.* v.a. *staṛai-,* etc. *k.*

Tiresome, a. *drūnd, grān, rabaṛ·nāk.*

Tithe, s. *'ushr.* (-to servants) *chūngai.*

Titillate, v.n. *takhnedal, koe-, kaha-,* etc. *ked.*

Titillation, s. *takhai, koe, kaha, megī megī.*

Tittle, s. *nūm, nāma, laqab, khitāb.* (right) *ḥaqq.*

Titter, s. *muskai.* v.n. *musedal.*

Tittle, s. *zarra, khas, pitsānrai, pūṭai, ṭakai.*

Tittle-tattle, s. *gap shap, bak bak, lāp shāp, zwag pak.*

To, p. *ta.* (-day) *nan.* (-morrow) *sabā* or *ṣabāḥ.* (-night) *nan begā, mākkhām.* (-morrow night) *sabā begā.* (-me) *rā ta.* (-thee) *dar ta.* (-him, etc.) *war ta.*

Toad, s. *chīndakh.* (-stool) *kha-areṛai, gū-māndū.*

Toast, v.a. *wrītawul, alwoyal, teyal, talawul.*

Tobacco, s. *tambākū.* (-pipe) *chilam.*

Toe, s. *da kkhpe* or *pkkhe gūta.*

Together, ad. *yo dzāe, dzabla, sara.*

Toil, v.a. *miḥnat-, kokshiksh-, tagāpū-,* etc. *k.*

Toilette, s. *kkhewa, singār.*

Token, s. *nakkha, nikkhān, 'alāmat.*

Tolerate, v.a. *wṛal, zghamal*; *rawā ganral, pregdal, prekkhodal, prekkhal.*

Toll, s. *maḥṣūl, chūngai, tāwān.*

Tomb, s. *qabr, gor, maqbara.* (the niche) *laḥd.* (the tablet) *khaza* or *khāda.*

Tone, s. *zwag, ghag, āwāz, bāng.* (elasticity) *dam.*

Tongs, s. *ambūr.*

Tongue, s. *jiba.*

Tonsil, s. *da jibe laṛ, haḍ.*

Too, ad. *hum, lā.* (-much) *ḍer, ziyāt.*

Tool, s. *kālai, hatiyār, ālat.*

Tooth, s. *ghākkh.* (molar-) *dāṛa, da jāme ghākkh.* (decayed-) *chinjo khwuṛalai ghākkh.* (-pick) *ghākkh ṭanbūnai* or *sūṛa-yūnkai* or *skoyūnkai, khilāl.* (-brush) *miswāk.* (-ache) *ghākkh khūgai, da ghākkh dard.* (-less) *kaṛshap, kanḍās.*

Top, s. *sar, tsūka, peza.* (on-) *dapāsa, da-bāndi, pa porta.* (toy) *tsarkhandūkai, chalkha-ī, churlanda-ī, lāḍū, bahna.*

Topic, s. *mazmūn, manshā, mudd'ā.*

Topknot, s. *tsanra-ī.*

Topsyturvy, a. *naskor, aṛawulai, pa-aṛ·makh.*

Torch, s. *shūsha-ī*; *mashāl.* (-of pine wood) *shonṭa-ī.*

Torment, s. *'azāb, āzār.* v.a. *'azābawul, āzārawul, khūgawul, kaṛawul.*

Torpid, a. *sust, laṭ*. (-with cold) *marghechan, qarqechan*.

Torrent, s. *dāra, sailāb, nīz* or *niyūz, chalānda*.

Tortoise, s. *shamshata-ī, kashap*.

Torture, s. *'azāb*. (instruments of-) *shikanja, pāna, kāṭ, tsarkh*. v.a. *'azābawul; pāna warkawul, pa shikanjo-, pa kāṭ-, pa tsarkh-*, etc. *khejawul*.

Toss, v.a. *ghurzawul, āchawul, lawastal*. v.n. *ghurzedal*. (-money) v.a. *shīr khaṭ k*.

Total, a. *ṭol, amānī, pūrah, tamām, wāṛah*. s. *ṭol ṭāl, jam'a*.

Totally, ad. *amānī, sarāsar*. (in comp.) *tak-, ṭap-*, etc.

Totter, v.n. *ṭaparedal*.

Touch, v.a. *lās lagawul* or *-warwṛal; masa-, lams-*, etc. *k*. v.n. *lagedal, jangedal, blodal, blosedal*.

Touchy, a. *tod-*, or *tund mizāj*.

Tough, a. *klak, sakht, ṭīng*.

Tour, s. *daur, safar, gakkht; sail*.

Tow, s. *sanṛ, da sanṛo paṭ*.

Towards, p. *khwā ta, lorī ta, makh ta, ḍaḍe ta, palaw ta*, etc. (-me) *rāhīsta*. (-thee) *dar hīsta*. (-him, her, it, them) *war hīsta*.

Towel, s. *dast·māl, rūmāl*.

Tower, s. *bruj* or *burj*.

Town, s. *kkhahr, kilai, dih*.

Townsman, s. *kkhahr·wāl, kilī·wāl, da kkhahr-, da kilī-*, etc. *saṛai*.

Toy, s. *da lobe kālai*. v.a. *lobe k.; nāz k*.

Trace, s. *nakkha, darak, belga*. v.a. *belga bāsal—yastal; nakhkkha* or *naqsha kāgal —kkhkal* or *līkal*.

Track, s. *pal, manḍ, darak; lār, rakkh*. v.a. *pal-*, etc. *goral—līdal-, -mūndal, -laṭawul*, etc.

Tract, s. *maidān, zmaka; mulk, hiwād*. (treatise) *risāla, nāma*.

Tractable, a. *narm, gharīb, mulā-im*.

Trade, s. *saudāgarī, warkṛah rākṛah, lāgī, saudā; kasb, kār*. v.a. *saudāgarī-*, etc. *k*.

Trader, s. *saudāgar, wapārī, banjārī, parānchah*. (travelling-) *rawānī, lohānī*.

Tradesman, s. *kasb·gar, pesha·war*.

Tradition, s. *ḥadīs, khabara, naql, wayai*.

Traditional, a. } *wayali* or *rāghlali khabara*,
Traditionary, } *da peṛc pa peṛo khabara*.

Traduce, v.a. *tor-, tuhmat-*, etc. *pore k., peghor warkawul, bad·nāmawul, kagal, ghandal*.

Traffic, v.a. (*v*. Trade.)

Tragical, a. *gham·nāk, haibat·nāk, haul·nāk*.

Trail, v.a. *rākāgal—rākkhkal, kashāla k*.

Train, v.a. *āmokhtah k.; bāolī warkawul; kkhayal—kkhowul, lwalawul; pālal*.

Train, s. (escort) *swarlī, jalab*. (-of a dress) *laman*. (series) *qaṭār*.

Trait, s. *'ādat; nakkha; karkkha*.

Traitor, s. *namak ḥarām, ṭag, darghal*.

Trammel, s. *jāl, lūma, dām; paikaṛa*.

Trample, v.a. *latāṛawul, kkhpo lāndi-, pāemāl-, ghwa-emanḍ-*, etc. *k., ghobalawul*.

Trance, s. *parghaz, da periyāno ghoṭa, be·khūdī*.

Tranquil, a. *qalār, walāṛ, ārām*.

Tranquilize, v.a. *ārāmawul, qalārawul, saṛawul, walāṛawul*.

Transact, v.a. *mu'āmala-, kār-, rozgār-*, etc. *k., chalawul, lagawul, jārī k., rawānawul*.

Transaction, s. *kār, rozgār, m'uāmala, khabara*.

Transfer, v.a. *wṛal, rasawul; spāral, pāslawul*.

Transfix, v.a. *ore pore tetsal* or *-sīkhal, pewdal*.

Transgress, v.a. *mātawul; khaṭā k*.

Transient, a. *teredūnai, nā·pāedār, fānī*.

Translate, v.a. *tarjuma k., naql k*.

Transmit, v.a. *āstawul, legal, rasawul*.

Transparent, a. *ṣāf, shaffāf; bārīk*.

Transpire, v.n. *tsargandedal, kkhkārah ked., watal, khatal, m'alūmedal.*

Transport, v.a. *wral, yosal; botlal—bīwul; legdal—lekkhal; jalā-watan k.*

Transpose, v.a. *arawul, badlawul, gaḍwaḍ-awul.*

Transverse, a. *tratskan, kog.*

Trap, s. *dām.* (net-) *jāl, drwah gaza.* (noose-) *lūma, lūmaka, ghundārai.* (springe) *laṭ, talaka, qurqa-ī.* (catch-) *park, honrā.* (ambush) *psūnai, tsarai, puṭgana-ī.* v.a. *nīwul, nkkhlawul.*

Trappings, s. *kālī, asbāb.* (armour) *drasta, wasla.* (horse-) *bargastawān.*

Trash, s. *balāe batar, khadzala, khāshāk.*

Travel, v.a. *safar-, sail-, musāfirī-,* etc. *k.*

Traveller, s. *musāfir.*

Tray, s. *khwān, khwāncha, sīnī.*

Treacherous, a. *be-īmān, be-wafā, darghal-bāz.*

Treachery, s. *be-īmānī, darghal-tob.*

Treacle, s. *gūṛa, awlū, kak; tiriyāq.*

Tread, v.a. *kkhpa-* or *pkkha-, qadam-,* etc. *gdal,* or *-īgdal,* or *-kkhkegdal.* (-upon) *latāṛah-, laṭ paṭ-, kkhpo lāndi-,* etc. *k.* (as birds) v.n. *khatal.* (-corn) v.a. *ghobal k.* (after one) *pala pase tlal.*

Treason, s. *namak ḥarāmī, pasāt, darghal-bāzī, ghadr,*

Treasure, s. *khazāna, ganj, daulat.*

Treasurer, s. *khazānchī.*

Treasury, s. *khazāna, tūng; makhzan.*

Treat, v.a. (parley) *sawāl dzawāb-, khabara-,* etc. *k.* (use) *sulūk-, mu'āmala-,* etc. *k.* (guest) *ẓiyāfat-, melmastiyā-, sat-,* etc. *k.* (-well) *kkhah sulūk k.* (-badly) *bad sulūk k.* (-a disease) *chāra-, 'ilāj-,* etc. *k* (manage) *joṛawul, chalawul.* (mention) *yādawul, bayānawul.*

Treaty, s. *'ahad, qaul-qarār, taṛa, bandanr.*

Treble, a. *dre bragh, dre chand.* (in music) *dzīr* or *zīl.*

Tree, s. *wana, drakhta.* (small-) *ḍakai.* (Mulberry-) *tūt.* (Sissoo-) *shewa.* (Acacia modesta) *palosa.* (Acacia Arabica) *kīkaṛ.* (Pine-) *nakkhtar.* (Cedar-) *diyār.* (Plane-) *chinār.* (Melia sempervirens) *shanḍa-ī, bukāyanra.* (Seris-) *srīkh.* (Willow-) *wala.* (Olive-) *kkhona.* (Tamarisk-) *ghaz.* (Bauhinia variegata) *koliyāṛ,* etc. etc.

Tremble, v.n. *rapedal, regdedal, laṛzedal.*

Tremendous, a. *haibat-nāk; bashpaṛ, loe.*

Tremor, s. *laṛza, gagaṛodza.*

Trembling, s. *rapedūn, laṛzedana.*

Trench, s. *kanda, kaha-ī.*

Trencher, s. *kkhānak, pīna, taghār.*

Trepidation, s. *laṛza, rapedana, gagaṛodza.*

Trespass, s. *gunāh, wabāl, taqṣīr, khaṭā.*

Trial, s. *āzmekkht, imtiḥān.*

Triangle, s. *dre gokkha, muṣallaṣ.*

Tribe, s. *qām* or *qaum, firqa, tabār, khel.*

Tribulation, s. *gham, randz, mīrtsī, paskhāk, āfat, balā.*

Tribunal, s. *maḥkam, 'adālat.*

Tribute, s. *pekkh-kakkh, khirāj, bāj, 'ushr.*

Trice, s. *pal, laḥẓa.*

Trick, s. *fareb, lamghaṛa-ī, ghulat, ṭagī, chal.* (habit) *'ādat, khoe.* v.a. *ṭagal, ghulawul.*

Trickle, v.n. *tsātsedal.*

Triennial, a. *dre kālanai.*

Trifle, s. *khasanrai, nā-tsīz, lā shai, hets.*

Trifle, v.a. *lobe k., 'abaṣ k., jakh wahal.*

Trifling, a. *spuk, khushai, be-hūdah, pūch.*

Trim, v.a. *joṛawul, atsanral, drust k.*

Trinity, s. *taṣlīṣ, ṣalāṣa.*

Trinket, s. *kālai, zewar, gānra.*

Trip, v.a. *tīndak-, ṭakar-, budrī-, kangas-, skandarī-,* etc. *khwuṛal.*

Tripe, s. *ūjarai, kulma.*

Triple, a. *dre bragh, dre chand, dre ṭarafah.*

Tripod, s. *dre pāya, darbala-ī.*

Trite, a. *zoṛ, pakhwānai, mashhūr.*

Triturate, v.a. oṛawul, oṛah-, maidah-, etc. k. dalawul, dzabal.

Trivial, a. spuk, khushai, adnā.

Triumph, v.a. barai mūndal, or -gaṭal. (joy over enemy) wiyāṛ-, sakha-, etc. k.

Troop, s. paṛk, ghol, galla, tanba, ṭol, ṭolgai. (-of horse) risāla.

Trooper, s. bār-gīr, turk sawār.

Trophy, s. ghanīmat, lūṭ, shūka, yzṭa.

Trot, v.a. pa ḍugland-, pa dachko-, etc. tlal.

Trouble, s. rabaṛ, miḥnat, diqq-dārī, randz, āzār, dzaur. v.a. rabṛawul, āzārawul, diqq k.

Troublesome, a. rabṛūnai, rabaṛ-nāk, diqq-dār, janjālī.

Trough, s. pūl, nāwa, tarnāo.

Trowel, s. karanḍa-ī.

Trowsers, s. paṛtūg, shalwār, tambān. (-band) paṛtūghākkh. (-hem) baḍa. (-fork) khakkh-tag. (-leg) pāentsa.

Truant, a. gashtai, khushai, hujrai.

Truce, s. m'arika, rogha joṛa, ṣulḥa.

Trudge, v.n. ṭaparedal, ro ro tlal.

True, a. rikkhtiyā, rikkhtīnai, sūchah, karah, rāst, pokh, pūrah.

Truly, ad. pa rikkhtiyā ; yara.

Trumpet, s. tūrai, būq.

Trunk, s. (box) ṣandūq, taunra-ī. (tree) mūnd, tanga, garga. (body) ṣūrat, tan. (snout) khartam, sūnḍak.

Trust, s. bāwar, i'tibār, sā-wīsā, khal ; umed, takiya, āsra, tawakkul ; amānat, ḥawāla ; por, qarẓ, nasiyah.

Trust, v.a. bāwar-, etc. k. or laral ; amānat-, etc. gdal or īgdal, spāral, pāslawul ; por-, etc. warkawul.

Trustee, s. ẕimma-dār, amānat-dār.

Trusty, a. i'tibārī, īmān-dār, wafā-dār.

Truth, s. rikkhtiyā, rāstī.

Try, v.a. āzmāyal or āzmoyal, āzmekkht k., s'aī-, kokshiksh-, etc. k., was chalawul ; 'adālat k.

Tub, s. taghār, ḍol, satal, gaḍhal.

Tube, s. shpela-ī, nala, tsūkkhka.

Tuesday, s. naha, sih shamba.

Tuft, s. zunḍa-ī, ghūncha. (-of hair) tsaṛa-ī or tsanra-ī ; parcham or parkham. (bird's) chār khwalak. (-of grass, etc.) kalokkhta.

Tug, v.a. rākāgal—rākkhkal.

Tuition, s. tarbiyat, t'alīm ; parwarish.

Tumble, v.n. prewatal, lwedal, (roll on the ground) rghaṛedal—rghakkhtal, lots pots k. v.a. bāzī-garī-, naṭ-bāzī-, etc. k.

Tumour, s. pāṛsob, ghumba, ghunḍārai, stagh.

Tumult, s. balwā, ghulghula, zwag-zūg, shor, shor-shaghab.

Tune, s. sarod, tarāna, badala, wazn.

Turban, s. pagṛa-ī, paṭkai, dastār, manḍos. (end of-) shaklai, shamla.

Turbid, a. kha-aṛ, lāha-jan, khaṭolai.

Turbulence, s. pasāt, shor.

Turbulent, a. pasātī, shor-nāk.

Turf, s. chūm, lūṭa, kulūkh.

Turmeric, s. korkamān.

Turn, s. tsarkh, daur. (twist) tāo, wal, pech, marwat. (time) wār, guẕār ; heṛ, plā, dzal. (walk) sail, gakkht. (bend) kag-lech, ḥālkūch.

Turn, v.n. girzedal, tsarkhedal, churledal, āwukkhtal, badledal. (-back) jārwatal, stūnedal, or stanedal, pastanah ked. (become) kedal, shwal. v.a. girzawul, tsarkhawul, churlawul. (-back) stūnawul. (-over) aṛawul. (-out) shaṛal. (-from) shā k., pregdal.

Turnip, s. ṭepaṛ, shalgham.

Turpentine, s. rāndzaṛah.

Turret, s. buj ; kangūra.

Tutor, s. ākhūn, ustād, mu'allim.

Twang, s. ṭang, trang. v.n. ṭangedal, trangedal.

Tweezers, s. nūtsai.

Twelve, a. *dwah·las.* (twelfth) *dwah·lasam.* (-month) *kāl, dwah·las myāshti.*
Twenty, a. *shil.* (twentieth) *shilam.* (-one) *yo·wīsht.* (-two) *dwah·wīsht*, etc.
Twice, ad. *dwah hera, -guzāra, -dzala, -wāra*, etc.
Twig, s. *lakkhta.*
Twilight, s. *shafaq*; *sapede.*
Twins, s. *jora, bragh.* (one of-) *braghūnai.*
Twine, s. *mazai, tār.*
Twine, v.a. *pech-, tāo-, wal-*, etc. *khwural.*
Twinkle, s. (of time) *pal, lahza.* (-of a star) *palwasha.* v.n. *dzalkedal* or *dzaledal.*
Twirl, v.a. *churlawul, tsarkhawul, tsandal* or *tsandawul.*
Twist, s. *pech, wal, tāo, marwat.* v.a. *pech-*, etc. *warkawul.* (fold) *nghakkhtal.* (bend) *ṭīṭawul, krīngawul.*
Twitter, v.a. *chanr chanr-*, etc. *k.*
Two, a. *dwah, dwe.*
Type, s. *nakkha, 'alāmat, noga, misāl.*
Tyrannize, v.a. *jabr-, zulm-*, etc. *k.*
Tyranny, s. *zulm, zor, ziyātī, zabardastī, jafā.*
Tyrant, s. *zālim, jābir, jafā·kār.*
Tyro, s. *shāgird, mubtadī, nawai āmokhtah.*

U.

Udder, s. *ghulāndza.*
Ugly, a. *bad·ṣūrat, bad·shakal, mushād.*
Ulcer, s. *nāsūr*; *yaga.*
Ultimate, a. *ākhir, wrustanai, pasīn.*
Ultimately, ad. *ākhir, wrusto, pas.*
Umbrage, s. *sorai* or *siwrai, gūr, ganr, chatr.* (offence) *marawar·tiyā, mānrai*; *mīrtsī.*
Umbrella, s. *chatra-ī.*
Umpire, s. *mandz·garai, munṣif.*
Un-, neg. prefix. (in comp.) *be-, nā-, lā-*, etc.
Unable, a. *nā·tuwān, nā·qābil.*
Unanimous, a. *yo zrah, yo jihat, yo ittipāq, pa yawe khule* or *-jibe.*
Unavailing, a. *'abaṣ, be·fā,ida, nā·pakār.*
Unawares, ad. *nātsāpa, nāgāh, yak lakhta.*
Unbecoming, a. *nā·lā-iq, nā·munāsib, nakkhanai, nā·kkhandah.*
Unbelief, s. *kufr, be·īmānī, kāfir·tob.*
Unbeliever, s. *kāfir, be·dīn, be·īmān.*
Unbosom, v.a. *prānatal, wayal, parda lirī-*, or *porta k., tsargandawul.*
Unbroken, a. *amānī, pūrah, salāmat.*
Unbutton, v.a. *tanra-ī-, palwākkha-, ghūṭa-ī-, gharāsha-*, etc. *prānatal* or *spardal.*
Unceremonious, a. *khamsor, be·takalluf.*
Uncertain, a. *nā·m'alūm, be·ṭikānā.*
Unchaste, a. *bad laman, shatāh, nā·pāk.*
Uncircumcised, a. *nā·solat* or *nā·sunnat, shopā.*
Uncivil, a. *be·adab, be·makh, lwār, dzaban.*
Uncivilized, a. *lwār, pūhar, shār.*
Uncle, s. (paternal) *trah, kākā, ākā.* (maternal) *māmā, nūe.*
Unclean, a. *palīt, nā·pāk, khīran, murdār.*
Unclouded, a. *shīn, ṣāf.*
Uncomfortable, a. *be·ārām, nā·khwakkh.*
Uncommon, a. *nādir, matrah, kamtar.*
Unconcerned, a. *be·parwā, be·khabar, be·gham, be·fikr.*
Uncouth, a. *lwār, pūhar, shār, dzaban.*
Uncover, v.a. *barbandawul, bargholai-, sar·pokkh-*, etc. *liri k.* (the head) *sar tor k.* (the face) *be·satr-, be·parde-*, etc. *k.* (a roof) *spardal.*
Unction, s. *mālish, mukkhana.*
Unctuous, a. *ghwar.*
Uncultivated, a. *ghair ābād, shār, wujār, wairān.*
Undecided, a. *wiswāsī, andekkh·man*; *nā·tamām, nīmgarai, nīma·khwā.*
Undefiled, a. *pāk, pākīzah, ṣāf.*
Undeniable, a. *lā·radd, qaṭ'a-ī.*

Under, ad. and p. *lāndi, dalāndi, kkhkata, kkhkiya.* (-part) s. *talai, lāndi khwā.* (-most) a. *lāndīnai, kkhatanai.*
Undergo, v.a. *wṛal, zghamal, khwuṛal.*
Underhand, ad. *pa puṭa, pa tara-ī, pa parde.*
Undermine, v.a. *surang wahal; naṛawul; wekh-, mūnḍ-,* etc. *wahal* or *khejawul.*
Underneath, ad. *dalāndi, kkhkata, kkhkiya.*
Underrate, v.a. *lāndi-, spuk-, nā·tsīz-,* etc. *ganṛal, ghandal, kagal.*
Understand, v.a. *pohedal, pahmedal, rasedal.*
Understanding, s. *poha, pahm, 'aql; joṛikkht, maṣlaḥat.*
Undertake, v.a. *ākhistal, porta k., khejawul, kawul, chalawul, lās lagawul.*
Undertaking, s. *kār, mu'āmala.*
Undervalue, v.a. *spuk-, kam-, nā·tsīz-,* etc. *ganṛal.*
Underwood, s. *jangai, dzangal, jāṛ, karkanṛ.*
Undivided, a. *pūrah, tamām, amānī.*
Undo, v.a. *spaṛdal, prānatal, khwarawul.*
Undone, a. *spaṛdalai* or *spaṛai; wrān, kharāb.*
Undoubted, a. *yaqīn, be·shakk aw shubha.*
Undress, v.a. *jāme-,* etc. *bāsal—yastal.*
Undulate, v.n. *laharedal, ghurzedal.*
Uneasy, a. *be·ārām, nā·qalār; andekkh·man, wiswāsī.*
Unemployed, a. *kariyāb, khushai, be·kār, aṭāl, wazgār.*
Uneven, a. *lwaṛ jawar, kandai kawdarai, kkhkata porta, nā·hawār.*
Unexampled, a. *be·siyāl, lā·ṣānī, be·miṣāl.*
Unexpected, a. *nā·gahān, nā·gumān.*
Unexpectedly, ad. *nā·tsāpa, nāgāh.*
Unfair, a. *nā·rāst, nā·ṣāf.*
Unfaithful, a. *be·īmān, be·wafā.*
Unfeeling, a. *be·dard, kānṛai zṛah, be·raḥm.*
Unfit, a. *nā·lā-iq, nā·qābil.*
Unfold, v.a. *prānatal, spaṛdal, tsargandawul, kkhkārah k* v.n. *khwaredal, ghwaredal, ṭūkedal.*

Unforeseen, a. *nā·m'alūm, nā·līdah.*
Unfortified, a. *be·panāh, khushai.*
Unfortunate, a. *kam·bakht, bad·naṣīb, lā·chār, stāra prewatai.*
Unfounded, a. *bāṭil, be·hūdah.*
Unfruitful, a. *shanḍ, be·mewa, nā·mewa·dār.*
Unfurnished, a. *khushai, be·sāz, be da kālo.*
Ungird, v.a. *mlā prānatal.*
Ungodly, a. *be·dīn, nā·khudā·tars.*
Ungovernable, a. *sar·zor, sar·kakkh, yāghī.*
Ungrateful, a. *namak ḥarām, nā·shukr·guzār, nā·ḥaqq·shinās.*
Unguarded, a. *be·khabar, ghāfil.*
Unhappy, a. *khapah, malūl, dil·tang, nā·khwakkh, nā·kkhād.*
Unhealthy, a. *nā·joṛ; nā·muwāfiq.*
Unheard, a. *nā·āwredah.*
Unholy, a. *ḥarām, nā·pāk, bilmāz, nā·rawā.*
Uniform, a. *barābar, sam, hawār, yo·shān.* s. *jāma, joṛa, libās.*
Unimaginable, a. *be·qiyās.*
Uninhabited, a. *ghair·ābād, wairān, wujāṛ.*
Union, s. *joṛ, pewastūn, taṛūn; rogha, joṛa, ittipāq; joṛikkht, malgar·tiyā.*
Unit, s. *yo.* (Unity) s. *yo·wālai, yak·tā-ī.*
Unite, v.a. *joṛawul, lagawul, pewand k.*
United, a. *pewastah; yo zṛah, yo jihat.*
Unitedly, ad. *pa ittipāq sara.*
Universal, a. *kullī, amānī, muṭlaq.*
Universally, ad. *bil·kull, sarāsar, tamāmī.*
Universe, s. *duniyā, jahān, naṛa-ī.*
Unjust, a. *be·inṣāf; nā·ḥaqq.*
Unknowingly, ad. *pa nā·dānī sara, nā·pohī sara, be·khabarī sara.*
Unlawful, a. *ḥarām, nā rawā, nā·ḥaqq.*
Unlearned, a. *jāhil, nā·lwustai, ammī.*
Unless, ad. *magar* or *mangar, ganṛa* or *kanṛa* or *ka na.*
Unload, v.a. *bār·kūzawul, ta-ashawul.*
Unlucky, a. *kam·bakht, be·naṣīb, shūm·bakht, bad·bakht, stāra prewatai.*

Unmarried, a. *lawand, nā·wādah karai.* (f.) *peghla, nā·wādah·shiwi.*
Unmeaning, a. *a. be·m'anī, be·hūdah.*
Unmoved, a. *pāedār, qā-im, mazbūt, ting.*
Unoccupied, a. *khālī, khushai; wazgār.*
Unpack, v.a. *prānatal, spardal, ghwarawul.*
Unprotected, a. *khushai, be·panāh, be·wasīla.*
Unravel, v.a. *prānatal, spardal, ghwarawul, khwarawul, wīrawul.*
Unreasonable, a. *be·dzāyah, nā·munāsib.*
Unripe, a. *om, nīma·khwā, nīm·pukhtah, nīmgarai, kachah, khām.*
Unrivalled, a. *be·siyāl, lā·sānī, be·misāl.*
Unroll, v.a. *prānatal, spardal, ghwarawul, khwarawul, wīrawul.* v.n. *ghwaredal, wīredal, khwaredal.*
Unruly, a. *sar·zor, sar·kakkh.*
Unsafe, a. *khatr·nāk, be·amn.*
Unsatisfied, a. *nā·rāz, nā·khwakkh.*
Unsatisfactory, a. *nā·sāz, nā·pīrzo.*
Unseasonable, a. *be·dzāe, be·tāng, be·khratai, be·wakht.*
Unseen, a. *put, ghā-ib, nā·līdah.*
Unserviceable, a. *nā·pakār, nākārah.*
Unsheltered, a. *khushai, be·panāh.*
Unshod, a. *abl, kkhpa·* or *pkkha·abla.*
Unsuccessful, a. *pa-ar, bāelūnkai.*
Untamed, a. *dzangalī, wahshī; lwār, dzaban.*
Untidy, a. *shadal, pūhar, shārlai·wārlai.*
Untie, v.a. *prānatal, spardal.*
Until, ad. *tar—pore, tso chi.* (-when?) *tar kala pore.* (-now) *tar osa pore.*
Untimely, a. *be·tāng, be·wakht, be·khratai.*
Unto, p. *ta, la, lara, wa—ta,* etc. (-me) *rā ta, rā lara, lā la, lā lara, mā ta,* etc. (-thee) *dar ta, da la, dar lara, tā ta, wa tā ta, tā wa tā,* etc. (-him, her, it, them) *war ta, wa la, war lara, haghah ta, hagho ta,* or *-la,* or *-lara.*
Untold, a. *be·hisāb, be·shumār; nā·wayalai, nā·guftah.*

Untoward, a. *nā·kārah; arawulai; bad.*
Untrue, a. *darogh·jan, jūtah, nā·rāst.*
Untruth, s. *darogh, kizb, nā·rāstī.*
Untwist, v.a. *spardal, prānatal, khwurawul.*
Unusual, a. *kam·ist'imāl, kam·chalan, shāzz.*
Unveil, v.a. *be·satr-, be·parde-,* etc. *k., bar-bandawul.*
Unwary, a. *be·khabar, ghāfil.*
Unwearied, a. *tāzah, nā·starai, hosā.*
Unwell, a. *nā·jor, nā·rogh.*
Unwieldy, a. *loe, ghat, star, drūnd.*
Unwilling, a. *nā·rāz, daregh·man.*
Unworthy, a. *nā·lā-iq, nā·pīrzo.*
Up, p. *bāndi, porta, pās.* (-on) *pa-, par-, pri-,* etc. *bāndi.* (-to) *-ta, -la, -lara, -pore.* (-and down) *lar bar, kūz pās, kkhkata porta, lāndi bāndi, lwar jawar.*
Upbraid, v.a. *malāmatawul, peghorawul, taqawul, ratal, tratal, dāral.*
Uphold, v.a. *sambālawul, khejawul, porta nīwul, pushtī-, komak-,* etc. *warkawul.*
Uplift, v.a. *khejawul, porta ākhistal* or *k.*
Upon, ad. *bāndi, dapāsa, dabāndi, pa·bāndi, pri·bāndi.*
Upper, a. *bar, pāsanai, portanai.*
Upright, a. *walār, negh, jig, lak; rikkhtīnai, rāst·man, nek.*
Uprightness, s. *walār·tiyā, negh·wālai,* etc.; *nekī, rikkhtīn·tob, rāstī.*
Uproar, s. *balwā, ghāl·o·ghūl, shor·shaghab.*
Upset, v.a. *naskorawul, arawul, narawul, āchawul, ghurzawul; toyawul, sandzal.* v.n. *naskoredal, naredal, lwedal, prewatal; toedal.*
Upshot, s. *anjām, gata. hāsil.*
Upside-down, a. *naskor, arawulai.*
Upwards, ad. *pās, porta, bar; ziyāt.*
Urbanity, s. *makhawarī, nek sulūkī.*
Urge, v.a. *zoral, tezal, chalawul, rawānawul; tākīd-, taqāza-,* etc. *k.; lamsawul.*
Urgent, a. *zarūr, tang, sakht.*

Urine, s. *baul, mitiyāza, peshāb.*

Usage, s. *sulūk.* (custom) *rasm, dastūr.* (habit) *'ādat, chalan.* (rule) *ā-īn, qā'ida.*

Use, s. *kār, fā-ida*; *'amal, ist'imāl.*

Use, v.a. *pa·kār rāwṛal, lagawul, chalawul*; *'amal-*, etc. *k.*; *sulūk-*, etc. *k.*

Useful, a. *fā-ida·man, sūd·man, pa·kār.*

Useless, a. *nā·kārah, 'abaṣ, khushai, be·fā-ida.*

Usual, a. *ist'imālī, jārī, chalanī.* (as-) *pa·dastūr.*

Usually, ad. *akṣar, aghlab.*

Usurer, s. *sūd·khor, ribā·khor.*

Usurp, v.a. *shūkawul, nā·ḥaqq ākhistal, pa·zor-, pa·zabardastī-*, etc. *-lāndi k., -dzān ta ākhistal.*

Usurpation, s. *shūka, pa·zor-*, etc. *ākhistana.*

Usury, s. *sūd, ribā.*

Utmost, a. *nihāyat, ḥadd.*

Utter, a. *nihāyat, bashpaṛ, amānī.*

Utter, v.a. *wayal, lal, lawdal*; *chalawul, jārī k.*

Utterly, ad. *sarāsar, amānī, tamāmī.*

Uvula, s. *kūmai, laṛ.*

Uxorious, a. *kkhadza·dost* or *·parast.*

V.

Vacant, a. *ta-ash, khālī, khushai.*

Vacate, v.a. *ta-ashawul, khālī-*, etc. *k.*

Vacation, s. *t'aṭīl, farāghat, wazgār·tiyā, furṣat.*

Vagabond, s. *lawanḍ, lūtsak, chaṭ, kūtsa·gard, hujrai, awārah, qachar.*

Vagary, s. *khiyāl, wahm.*

Vague, a. *nā·m'alūm, khushai.*

Vain, a. *'abaṣ, bāṭil, be·fā-ida*; *wiyāṛ·jan, bādī, khpul·rāe, khāntamā, bād·hawā.*

Vainly, ad. *'abaṣ, be·fā-ida.*

Valiant, a. *maṛanai, tūrzan, zṛah·war, bātor. dilāwar, bahādur, zmarai.*

Valid, a. *maẓbūṭ, maḥkam, qā-im*; *joṛ, drust, rikkhtīnai, zbād.*

Valley, s. *dara, sama, maidān.*

Valour, s. *maṛāna, tūrzan·tob, zṛah·war·tob, maṛanī·tob, zmarī·tob, bahādurī.*

Valuable, a. *qīmat·nāk, grān bahā.*

Value, v.a. *bai'a-, qīmat-*, etc. *taṛal* or *-lagawul* or *k.*; *qadr-, 'izzat-*, etc. *pejandal, ganṛal.*

Valve, s. *ghwagai, warkha*; *war, tamba, pala.*

Van, s. *pesh·khaima*; *harāwul, qarāwul.*

Vanish, v.n. *puṭedal, lwukkhtal—lwuṛedal, wrukedal*; *ālwatal*; *wuchedal.*

Vanity, s. *wiyāṛ, dam, lāpa shāpa*; *be·hūdagī, spuk·tiyā*; *khpul·sarī, bād hawā-ī.*

Vanquish, v.a. *pa-aṛ-, māt-, lar-, lāndi-*, etc. *k., barai mūndal.*

Vapid, a. *be·khwand, balmagai, balmangah.*

Vapour, s. *bukhār, bṛās*; *laṛa*; *lūgai*; ***ghubār.***

Variable, a. *nā·qalār, nā·pāedār, nīma khwā.*

Variance, s. *dukkhmanī, mīrtsī, kharkhakkha*; *patna, pasāt, 'aks*; *gwākkh*; *ẓidd.*

Variation, s. *biyal·wālai, farq.*

Variegated, a. *rangā·rang, brag·yālai.*

Variety, s. *rang pa rang, raqam pa raqam*, etc.

Various, a. *biyal·biyal, rangā·rang, shānā·shān, judā·judā, dzane.*

Varnish, v.a. *rangawul, rang lagawul, batī ḍakawul. lāk-, slekkh-*, etc. *lagawul.*

Vary, v.n. *badledal, āwukkhtal, girzedal, biyaledal.* v.a. *badlawul, āwukkhtal*, etc.

Vassal, s. *humsāyah, faqīr, r'aīyat.*

Vast, a. *loe, ghaṭ, star, 'aẓīm.*

Vastly, ad. *nihāyata, be·shāna.*

Vat, s. *ḥauẓ.*

Vault, s. *gunbata, qubba.* (cellar) *tah khāna.* (cave) *smats, ghār.* (tomb) *qabar, laḥad.*

Vault, v.a. *ghurzang-, tīndak-, ṭop-, khachūnai-*, etc. *wahal, dangal*; *gunbata-*, etc. *joṛawul.*

Vegetable, s. *wākkhah, dakai, būṭai.* (greens) *sāg, sabzī.*
Vegetate, v.n. *ṭūkedal, zarghūnedal.*
Vehement, a. *sakht, tod, tund, tez.*
Vehicle, s. *gāḍa-ī*; *swarlī* or *sparlī.* (means) *m'arifat, wasīla, wāsiṭa.* (in medicine) *badragha* or *badraga.*
Veil, v.a. *parda-, maizar-, oḍana-ī-, bolqa* or *burq'a-*, etc. *pa·sarawul, satr pokkhal* or *k.*, *puṭawul, pokkhal.*
Vein, s. *rag, nas.* (jugular) *kkhāh rag.*
Velocity, s. *gaṛand·wālai, za-ar·* or *zir·tiyā, jaltiyā.*
Velvet, s. *bakhmal, makhmal.*
Venal, a. *zar dost, zar parast.*
Vend, v.a. *khartsawul, ploral* or *prolal, prowul.*
Venerable, a. *zbarg, loe.*
Venerate, v.a. *manal, zbarg ganṛal.* v.n. *grohedal.*
Venery, s. *gho, ghowuna, kor·wālai. 'imā'a, sūḥbat.* (chase) *kkhkār.*
Venesection, s. *rag wahana.*
Venetian, s. *kaṛka-ī.*
Vengeance, s. *badal, qiṣāṣ*; *qahr, qiyāmat, balāe.* (to take-) v.a. *badal-*, etc. *ākhistal.* (with-) *pa qahr.*
Venial, a. *da bakkhalo, da pulanvulo*; *rawā.*
Venom, s. *zahr.*
Venomous, a. *zahr·nāk, zahr·dār.*
Vent, s. *sūṛa, khula, lār, war.* (-of a chimney) *dūd·* or *lū·kakkh.* (-of a canal) *warkh, ghwagai.* (to give-) v.a. *khalāṣawul, pregdal, prekkhodal, prekkhal.*
Ventilator, s. *bād·kakkh, bād·rau.*
Venture, s, *khaṭra.* (chance) *daw.* (fate) *naṣīb.* (at a-) *pa tawakkul.* v.a. *himmat-, qaṣd-*, etc. *k.*; *daw k.*
Venturesome, a. *himmatī, himmat·nāk, bakht·bāz.*
Venus, s. (star) *gūp, da melmana starga, zuhra.*

Veracity, s. *rikkhtīn·tob, rāstī, ḥaqq.*
Verb, s. *f'il.* (active-) *f'il i mut'addī.* (passive-) *f'il i majhūl.* (neuter-) *f'il i lāzimī.*
Verbal, a. *zabānī, wayalai.* (-noun, active participle) *ism i fā'il.* (-gerund) *ism i maṣdar.* (present participle) *ḥāṣil bil maṣdar.*
Verbatim, ad. *khabara pa khabare, ḥarf pa ḥarf, ṭakai pa ṭakī, ḥarfan ḥarfan.*
Verdant, a. *shīn, zarghūn, tar o tāzah.*
Verdict, s. *ḥukm, fatwā, faiṣal.*
Verdigris, s. *zangār.*
Verdure, s. *shīn·wālai, shīn wākkhah, sabzī.*
Verge, s. *ghāṛa, morga, tsanḍa, laman, ja-ī.*
Verge, v.n. *girzedal, ma·ilān ked.*, *rasedal, lagedal, jārwatal, āwukkhtal.*
Verify, v.a. *rikkhtīnai-, zbād-, taḥqīq-*, etc. *k.*
Verily, ad. *rikkhtiyā, yara.*
Verity, s. *rikkhtiyā, rikkhtīn·tob, rāstī.*
Vermicelli, s. *māeche.*
Vermin, s. *mozī dzanāwar, chinjī·minjī, khazande·mazande, mlakh·magak*, etc.
Vernacular, s. *mulkī, waṭanī, wilāyatī*; *da waṭan wrāsha* or *-jiba.*
Verse, s. *naẓm, sh'ir, bait.* (-of Quran) *āyat.*
Version, s. *naql, tarjuma.*
Vertigo, s. *girzedana da sar, akar, pa stargo tyāra, sar churlai* or *-girzai.*
Very, ad. *der, ziyāt.* (this-) *bedū, pa ṭakī.*
Vesicle, s. *tanṛāka.*
Vespers, s. *nmākkhām.*
Vessel, s. *lokkhai, kaṭwa-ī.* (blood-) *rag.* (boat) *beṛa-ī, jahāz.*
Vestibule, s. *manḍaw, dahlīz.*
Vestige, s. *nakkha, pal, ṭakai.*
Vesture, s. *aghostan, nwarai, pokkhāk, jāma.*
Vetch, s. *chanṛa, moṭ, kṛāk.*
Veteran. a. *zoṛ, pokh, pūrah.*
Vex, v.a. *pārawul, ṭongawul, rabṛawul, kaṛawul.*
Vexation, s. *ṭongāṛa, rabaṛ, khapagī, diqqat.*

Vexatious, a. *rabaṛ·nāk, khūg·nāk, janjālī, āzār rasawūnkai.*

Vial, s. *kkhikkha.*

Vibrate, v.n. *rapedal, regdedal, prakedal; zangal, zangedal, kkhoredal.*

Vice, s. *badī, 'aib, sharārat.* (instrument) *zambūr.*

Viceroy, s. *qā-im muqām, nā-ib; nāzim, nawwāb.*

Vicinity, s. *nijdekī, gāwand.*

Vicious, a. *bad, nākārah, bakhīl, 'aib·nāk.*

Vicissitude, s. *wār, nobat, wakht, tāng.*

Victim, s. *qurbān, jār or dzār, ṣadqa.*

Victor, s. *bar, wa-aṛ, ghālib, pa-aṛ kawūnkai.*

Victorious, a. *wa-aṛ, bar, barai mūndūnkai, or -mūndalai, or -gaṭalai.*

Victory, s. *bardi, wa-aṛāna.*

Victuals, s. *khwurāk, khwāṛah, qūt, ṭa'ām, ghizā.*

Vie, v.a. *barābarī k., was chalawul, ḥadd k.*

View, s. *nazar, nandāra, tamāsha, līdah, kātah, dzīr, mulāḥiza; niyat, maṭlab, gharaz.* v.a. *goral, līdal, katal, kasal, nazar-, etc. k.* (to have in-) v.a. *niyat-, etc. laral.* (to consider) v.a. *ganral.*

Vigil, s. *sho·gīrī, tsoka-ī.*

Vigilance, s. *baidārī, khabar·dārī, hokkhyār-tiyā.*

Vigilant, a. *baidār, khabar·dār, hokkhyār, wikkh.*

Vigorous, a. *zorāwar, quwat·nāk, tawānā, qawī.*

Vigour, s. *zor, quwat, barm or bram, tuwān, tāqat, tāo.*

Vile, a. *bad, kharāb, nā·kārah, dūn, khwār, spuk, palīt, murdār.*

Vilify, v.a. *tor-, tuhmat-, etc. pore k., peghor warkawul, kanzal or kkhkandzal, ghandal, kagal, bad nāmawul, ruswā k.*

Village, s. *kḷlai, dih.*

Villager, s. *kilī·wāl, da kilī saṛai.*

Villain, s. *bad·m'ash, bad·zāt, ḥarāmī. chulur, charḷand.* (farm servant) *dihqān, charekār.*

Villanous, a. *bad, nā·kārah, ḥarām·kār.*

Villany, s. *sharārat, pasāt, bad·zātī, ṭagī, namak·ḥarāmī.*

Vindicate, v.a. *ṣābitawul, pūrah-, zbād-, rikkhtiyā-, qā-im-, etc. k.; 'uzr rāwṛal.*

Vindication, s. *iṣbāt, zbād; 'uzr.*

Vindictive, a. *kīna·war.*

Vine, s. *tāk, kwar.* (-yard) *raz.*

Vinegar, s. *sirka.*

Violate, v.a. *mātawul; wrānawul.*

Violence, s. *zor, zulm, jabar, zabardastī, jafā; sakhtī, tūndī; qahr, ghazab.*

Violent, a. *sakht, tund, tez; qahr·nāk, ghazab·nāk.*

Violin, s. *rabāb, sārinda, ghachaka.*

Viper, s. *mangor, mangarai.*

Virgin, s. *peghla, ja-an, jūna-ī, jina-ī, bākira.*

Virility, s. *mardī, quwat da bāh.*

Virtually, ad. *pa wāq'ī, pa aṣl, pa rikkhtiyā.*

Virtue, s. *nekī, nekokārī, ṣawāb.* (quality) *lokkhai, ṣifat, khoe, khaṣlat, khāṣṣiyat.*

Virtuous, a. *nek, nekokār, ṣawābī, pāk, pāk·laman, nek·khoe, ·khaṣlat, ·bakht, etc.*

Virulent, a. *sakht, tund, tez, jābir, qātil.*

Visage, s. *makh, tsihra, rūe, gūna, bashra, ṣūrat.*

Viscid, a. *barwai, bokkht, slekkht·nāk, chaspān.*

Visible, a. *kkhkārah, tsargand, bartser, awtsār, zāhir.*

Vision, s. *nazar, līdah, kātah.* (dream) *khob, khiyāl.*

Visionary, s. *khiyālī, wahmī.*

Visit, v.a. *līdah-, kātah-, dīdan-, mulāqāt-, etc. k.* (a shrine) *ziyārat k.*

Vital, a. *jwandai; da marg aw jwāk.*

Vitality, s. *dzān, jwandūn, jwāk.*

Vitals, s. *laṛmānah, dzigar, īna.*

Vitiate, v.a. *spukawul, habatah k., wrānawul, kharābawul, tabāh k.*

Vitriol, s. *totā*. (blue-) *nīla·totā*. (green-) *shna·*, or *sabza·totā*.

Vituperation, s. *malāmat, peghor, tor, tuhmat, kanzal*, or *kkhkandzal*.

Vivacious, a. *kkhād, khūsh·ḥāl, khandā·rūe*.

Vivid, a. *rūnr, rokkhān, brekkh·nāk*; *ĵwandai*.

Vocabulary, s. *lughat, da kalimo kitāb*.

Vocation, s. *kār, kasb, pesha*.

Vocative, s. *nidā, bāng, ghag*.

Vociferate, v.a. *bāng wayal, nāra-, chigha-, sūra-*, etc. *wahal, chighawul*.

Vogue, s. *chāl, chalan, dastūr*. (in-) *rawā*.

Voice, s. *āwāz, bāng, zwag, ghag*. (active-) *sīgha i m'arūf*. (passive-) *sīgha i majhūl*.

Void, a. *ta-ash, khālī, khushai*; *'abaṣ, bāṭil*.

Void, v.a. *jārbāsal—jāryastal, ghurzawul*. (-at stool) *ghul k., kharal*.

Volition, s. *wāk, ikhtiyār, ghokkht*.

Volley, s. *shilak, bāṛ, dandūkār*.

Voluble, a. *ĵiba·war*; *chālāk*.

Volume, s. *kitāb, jild*; *qadr, andāza*.

Voluntarily, ad. *pa khpulā*.

Voluntary, a. *khpul·wāk, khpul·ikhtiyār*.

Voluptuary, s. *geḍa·parast, shahwat·parast*.

Voluptuous, a. *geḍa-* or *kheta-, shahwat-, nafs-*, etc. *parast*.

Vomit, v.a. *jārbāsal—jāryastal, qai-, bāka-ī-, chāl-*, etc. *k., kūz katal, zmake ta katal, -goral*, etc.

Voracious, a. *liwāl, wagai*.

Vortex, s. *ghurzai, gharq·āb, gird·āb*.

Votary, s. *ghulām, mra-e*; *ḥājat·man, niyāz·man*; *parastār, manūnkai*.

Vote, s. *lafẓ, qaul, khabara, wayai*. v.a. *khwakkhawul, qabūlawul, pasandawul*.

Vouch, v.a. *gawāhī-, shāhidī-*, etc. *warkawul*, or *-lal*, or *-lawdal*; *dalīl-, ḥujjat-*, etc. *-warkawul*; *wayal*.

Voucher, s. *ḥujjat, dalīl, sanad*; *gawāh, shāhid*.

Vouchsafe, v.a. *bakkhal, warkawul, mihrbāngī k*.

Vow, s. *neṭa, wāda, sharṭ, qaul, lafẓ*; *nazr, niyāz*. v.a. *neṭa-*, etc. *k.* or *-taṛal*; *nazr-*, etc. *warkawul, -warwṛal*.

Vulgar, a. *'āmm*. (mean) *spuk, nā·kārah*. (the-) *'āmmiyān, 'awāmm*.

Vulture, s. *ganjai, gargas*.

Vulva, s. *kus*.

W.

Wabble, v.n. *khwadzedal, zangedal*.

Wad. s. *būja, ḍīḍa, shoṛa*; *manjīla*.

Waddle, v.n. *arate-* or *chīnge kkhpe tlal—lāṛal*.

Wade, v.n. *pa obo kkhke girzedal*.

Wafer, s. *ṭika-ī, chaka-ī, tsaparkai*.

Waft, v.a. *rasawul, ālwūzawul, āstawul*.

Wag, s. *pekkhe·gar, ṭoq·mār, malanḍai, maskharāchī, washtai*.

Wag, v.a. *khwadzawul, tsanḍal, rapawul*.

Wage, v.a. *kawul, kṛal, chalawul, ākhistal*.

Wager, v.a. *sharṭ taṛal, daw k*.

Wages, s. *ṭalab, tankhwāh, miḥnat, kharts, muzd, mazdūrī*; *muwājib*.

Wagon, s. *gāḍa-ī, 'arāba*.

Wagtail, s. *māmūlaka, shīn·topa-ī, ziyaṛānaka*.

Wail, s. *wīr, wainā, wāwailā, ĵaṛā, sānda*.

Wailing, a. *wīra·ĵalai, ĵaṛānd*.

Waist, s. *mlā, lanḍa*.

Wait, v.n. *osedal, pātedal, pātai ked., wudredal*; *ḥāẓir osedal*. (-upon) v.a. *khidmat k*.

Waiter, s. *khidmat·gār*.

Waive, v.a. *pregdal*, etc. *tark k*.

Wake, v.n. *wīkkhedal, pātsedal, baidār ked*. v.a. *wīkkhawul, pātsawul, baidār k*.

Wakeful, a. *wīkkh, baidār, khabar·dār*.

Walk, v.n. *tlal—lāṛal, drūmal* or *drūmedal, chaledal, girzedal, pa kkhpo tlal.*

Walk, s. *sail, gakkht*; *chāl, yūn*; *lār.*

Wall, s. *dīwāl.* (side wall of a house) *chana.* (-eyed) a. *chaghar.* (to build a-) v.a. *dīwāl wahal* or *-khejawul.*

Wallet, s. *bana-ī, gūḍai, dzola-ī, chamta.*

Wallow, v.n. *rgharedal—rghakkhtal, lots-pots ked.*

Walnut, s. *akoṛ, ūghz.* (soft-) *chaghza-ī.* (hard-) *maṭāk.*

Wan, a. *ṭap, ziyaṛ, sperah.*

Wand, s. *amsā, lakkhta.*

Wander, v.n. *khushai-, dar ba dar-*, etc. *girzedal, rammedal*; *be-lār-, gumrāh-*, etc. *ked.*

Wane, v.n. *kamedal, zahedal, la-ag-, zawāl-*, etc. *ked., prewatal.*

Want, s. *ghokkht, ḥājat, darkhwāst.* (penury) *tangsiyā, khwārī.* (deficiency) *troṭa, waṭa.*

Want, v.a. *ghokkhtal, ḥājat laral*; *pukkhtedal. sawāl-, darkhwāst-*, etc. *k.*

Wanting, a. *kam, nāqiṣ, nīmgaṛai, ḥājat-man.*

Wanton, a. *mast, shokh, shahwat-nāk, bad-laman, shatāh, lashmakai, be-ḥayā.*

War, s. *jang, jadal*; *patna, kharkhakkha.* (civil-) *khāna-jangī.* (religious-) *ghazā, jihād.*

Warble, v.a. *chanr-chanr-, chighāra-, bul-ghāk-*, etc. *k.*

Ward, v.a. *sātal, ĵghoral, khundī k.* (-off) *raf'a-daf'a k., bachawul.*

Ward, s. *kandai, mālat, maḥalla, cham.*

Ware, s. *māl, jins, saudā, asbāb, shai, tsīz.* (-house) *kār-khāna, māl-khāna, ambār.* (hard-) *da ospane kālī.* (crockery-) *kaṭwī lokkhī.*

Warily, ad. *pa hokkhyār-tiyā-, pa baidārī-, pa pahm-, pa khabar-dārī-*, etc. *-sara.*

Warlike, a. *jangī.*

Warm, a. *tod, garm.* (luke-) *taṛam.*

Warmth, s, *tod-wālai, todūkha, garmī.*

Warning, s. *khabar, āgāhī.* (example) *'ibrat.* (to give-) v.a. *khabar-*, etc. *k.*; *'ibrat war-kawul.* (to take-) v.a. *'ibrat ākhistal.*

Warp, v.a. *pech-, tāo-*, etc. *warkawul.* v.n. *kagedal.*

Warp, s. *pūda, tār*; *tanasta, kanrai.*

Warrant, s. *parwāna, sanad, barāt, ḥukm-nāma.*

Warrant, v.a. *wayal*; *wāk-, ikhtiyār-*, etc. *warkawul*; *rawā-, rikkhtiyā-, sūchah-*, etc. *ganral* or *k.*; *pushtī-, madad-*, etc. *war-kawul.*

Warrantable, a. *rawā, lāzim, shara'ī.*

Warranted, a. *sharṭī, qarārī.*

Warrior, s. *ghāzī, jangī, mujāhid.*

Wart, s. *zakha.*

Wary, a. *hokkhyār, pokh, chirg, kāgh, gharand.*

Wash, v.a. *wīndzal* or *mīndzal, wlal.* (-one-self) *lambal, ghusl k.* (-for prayers) *awdas-, waẓū-*, etc. *k.*

Washerman, s. *dobī.* (-woman) *dobanra.* (-of the dead) *ghāsil.* (-his boiler) *khūm.* (-mallet) *tsobāṛai.*

Wasp, s. *ḍanḍāra, ḍanbara, sra macha-ī, ghālboza.*

Waste, v.a. *'abaṣ kharts k., iṣrāf-, tāwān-, talaf-*, etc. *k., wrukawul.* v.n. *wuchedal, kaṛedal, zahedal.*

Waste, a. *wairān, wujāṛ, kharāb, shāṛ.* s. *maira, shāṛa*; *tāwān, iṣrāf, talaf.*

Wasteful, a. *muṣrif, iṣrāfī, talaf kawūnkai.*

Watch, v.a. *tsoka-ī-, pahra-, pāswānī-*, etc. *k.*; *sho-gīrī-, baidārī-*, etc. *k., kashak gālal, ĵghoral.*

Watch, s. *gaṛa-ī, sā'at.* (-maker) *gaṛa-ī-*, etc. *-sāz* or *-joṛawūnkai.* (-house) *tānra.* (-tower) *bruj.* (-man) *pāswān, tsoka-ī-dār, pahra-dār.* (-man over fields, cattle, etc.) *kakkhai.* (-word) *nakkha, lafẓ.*

Watchful, a. *khabar·dār, baidār, hokkhyār.*

Water, s. *oba, āb.* (-carrier) *mashkī, saqāo.* (-bag) *mashk, ja-ī; palānra.* (-course) *khwar, kanda, kas, shela.* (-closet) *chār·choba.* (-cresses) *tartezak, halam.* (-fall) *dāra, tsādar.* (-fowl) *hīla-ī.* (-lily) *nīlofar.* (-man) *mahanrah, mānrgai.* (-melon) *hind-wāna, tarbūza.* (-mill) *ĵaranda, āsiyā.* (-pot) *loṭkai, mangai.*

Watery, a. *ob·lan, ob·ĵan, abī; lūnd khūsht, zyam·nāk.*

Wattle, s. (hedge) *keṛ.* (bird's-) *jajūra, ghuṭ·yālai.*

Wattle, v.a. *agayal, gayayal* or *gayawul.*

Wave, s. *chapa, mauj, lahar.*

Wave, v.n. *zangal* or *zangedal; laharedal.* v.a. *tsandal, kkhorawul, hanawul.*

Waver, v.n. *rapedal, tsrapedal; wṛāndi wrusto-, be·qalār-, be·ārām-,* etc. *ked.*

Wavering, a. *nā·qalār.*

Wax, s. *mūm.* (-cloth) *mūm·jāma.* (sealing-) *lāk.*

Way, s. *lār; ṭaur, shān, toga, rang; ṭarīqa, dastūr, chalan.*

Waylay, v.a. *lār nīwul, psūnai k.*

Wayward, a. *sar·kakkh, khpul·sar; wītak, shokh.*

We, pr. *mūng, mūg, mū.*

Weak, a. *nā·tuwān, kam·zor, 'ājiz, ẓa'īf, zahīr, kam·quwat, kam·ṭāqat, māndah.* (low) *spuk, khwār, nā·tsīz.* (as tea, etc.) *narai, mahīn.*

Weakness, s. *kamzor·tiyā, na·tuwānī, 'ājizī.*

Wealth, s. *duniyā, daulat, māl, zar.*

Wealthy, a. *duniyā·dār, daulat·man, zar·dār, tuwān·gar.*

Wean, v.a. *la to na ghūṭ k.*

Weanling, s. *zāṛai, ghūṭkai, būhārai.*

Weapon, s. *wasla, drasta, hatiyār, kālai.*

Wear, v.a. *āghostal, pa dzān k.,* or *-āchawul.* (rub) v.n. *sūledal.* (waste) *zaṛedal.* (last) *chaledal, teredal, pāedal.*

Wearisome, a. *drūnd, grān, staṛai kawūnkai.*

Weary, a. *staṛai, stomān, haukah.*

Weather, s. *āsmān, bād, hawā, mosam, wradz.* (-cock) *bād numāe* or *-kkhowūnkai.*

Weave, v.a. *ūdal* or *odal.*

Weaver, s. *jolāh, dahor.* (-loom) *shāna, rach.* (-beam) *paleṭanr* or *paṭelanr.* (shuttle) *mākū.* (-brush) *māla.* (-paste) *batī.* (-yarn) *tanasta.* (-yarn beam) *hata.* (-web) *būda* or *pūda.* (-reeds) *nala, dūrma.* (-spindle) *garzanai.* (-reel) *nicha.*

Web, s. *tanasta, kanrai, būda.* (spider's-) *jāla-ī.*

Wed, v.a. *wadawul, wādah k., nikāḥ taṛal.* v.n. (applied to the woman) *wadedal, wādah ked.*

Wedding, s. *wādah, nikāḥ.* (-party) m. *janj.* f. *wrā.* (-guest) m. *jānjī, mānjī, wrā·bānrai.* f. *wre-aza* or *wreyaza, wrā·bānra-ī, mānja-ī.*

Wedge, s. *pāna, shpetai.*

Wednesday, s. *chār shamba.*

Weed, s. *wākkhah.* v.a. *lalūn-, goḍ-,* etc. *k.*

Weeding, s. *lalūn, goḍ, pūjī.* (-hoe) *rambai.*

Week, s. *hafta.*

Weekly, ad. *hafta pa hafte.*

Weep, v.a. *ĵaṛal, okkhe toyawul.* (mourn) *wīr-, wāwailā-,* etc. *k., wainā wayal.*

Weeper, s. *wīra·ĵalai, wainā wayūnkai; ĵaṛānd.*

Weeping, s. *ĵaṛā; wīr, wāwailā.*

Weevil, s. *gūnr, buza.*

Weigh, v.a. *talal, tol k., jokal.*

Weight, s. *tol, jok; wazn, andāza; dranāwai, drūnd·wālai; bār.* Bazar weights (two lbs.) *ser,* (oke = 7 sers) *ogai.* (quarter oke) *kuṛhai.* (4 sers) *daṛa-ī.* (10 daṛa-ī or maund) *man.* (8 maunds) *kharwār.* (¼ ser) *pāo.* (½ ser) *dwah·pāwa.* (¾ ser) *dre pāwa.* (1¼ ser) *pīndzah pāwa.* (1½ ser) *yo·nīm ser.* (1¾ ser) *pāo kam dwah sera.*

(2 sers) *dwah sera.* (2¼ sers) *pāo bāndi-* or *pāo dapāsa—dwah sera.* (2½ sers) *dwah-nīm sera*, etc. (2 oz.) *chīṭāka-ī.* (1 oz.) *nīma chīṭāka-ī.* (½ oz.) *sharshā-ī.* (¼ oz.) *nīma sharshā-ī.* (2 drs.) *paisa.* Jeweller's weights. *rata-ī* = 1·8 gr.; *māsa* = 8 *rata-ī*; *misqāl* = 4 *māsa* + 3½ *rata-ī*; *tola* = 12½ *māsa* or 180 grs.

Weighty, a. *drūnd, grān.*

Welcome, a. *mubārak, kkhah, khwakkh, khair.* s. *mubārakī, du'ā da khair, rogh-baṛ, bara-gaṛa, bar-gaṛandī.* in. *har-kala har-kala! pa khaira-* or *pa khair sara rāghlai ye! khairāt di rāwuṛ!* v.a. *joṛ tāzah sara k., mubārakī warkawul.* (to be-) v.n. *pa khaira-*, or *pa khair sara rāghlal.*

Welfare, s. *khairiyat, tandrust-wālai, kkhegaṛa, bihbūdī, bihtarī*; *wadān-wālai, ābād-wālai.*

Well, s. *kūhai, chāh.* (-with lever) *ḍingara-ī, yak-langa.* (-with steps) *baha-ī.* (-with wheels) *arhaṭ.*

Well, a. *kkhah, joṛ, rogh*; *nek, khwakkh, mubārak.* ad. *kkhah, pa kkhah shān sara.* (very-) *ḍer kkhah.* (-done!) *ākh* or *ākhkkh, ākhkkhai.* (-then) *biyā, nor.* (as-) *hum.* (as well as) *laka chi.* (-nigh) *nijde.* (-born) a. *sāwū, aṣīl.* (-wisher) *khair-khwāh, du'ā-goe.*

Wen, s. *baura-ī, kala-ī, rasaula-ī, ghumba.*

Wench, s. *wīndza, mazdūra, khidmat-gāra, suhela-ī*; *ja-an, jina-ī, peghla, kkhadza*; *kachana-ī, lola-ī.*

West, s. *nwar prewātah, qibla, maghrab.* (-ward) *nwar prewātah khwā.*

Wet, a. *lūnd, khusht, naw-jan, nam-nāk.*

Wether, s. *wuch-kūl.*

Wetness, s. *lūnd-wālai, khusht-wālai*; *nau, zyam.*

Wetnurse, s. *dā-ī.*

What, pr. *kūm, tsok, tsa.* (-else?) *nor tsa.* (-then?) *biyā.*

Whatever, pr. *har kūm, har tsok*, etc.; *kūm chi, har chi.*

Wheat, s. *ghanum.*

Wheedle, v.a. *ghulawul, darghalawul, dam warkawul.* (coax) *jigī-, hāṛe-, jāna-*, etc. *k.*

Wheel, s. *tsarkh.* (-spoke) *tīrai, palai, shpeshtai.*

Wheel, v.n. *girzedal, churledal, tsarkhedal.*

Wheeze, v.a. *sāh pa ūchata ākhistal, sāh shranganwul.*

Whelp, s. *bachai, kūtrai.*

When, ad. *kala, kūm wakht.*

Whenever, ad. *har kala chi, har-*, or *kūm wakht chi.*

Where, ad. *charta, kūm dzāe, kūma khwā.* (no-) *hets charta, hets dzāe.*

Whereas, ad. *dzaka chi, la de na, balki, wale.*

Whereat, ad. *pas, biyā, nor, pa de.*

Wherefore, ad. *pas, dzaka, la kabla.*

Wherever, ad. *har charta chi, har-*, or *kūm dzāe chi.*

Whet, v.a. *terah-, tez-*, etc. *k.*

Whether, c. *ki, yā, khwāh.*

Whetstone, s. *psān, belho* or *belāo, barjo, tsarkh.*

Whey, s. *tarwe, lassī*; *mājūban* or *mā ul joban.*

Which, pr. *kūm, kūm yo.*

While, s. *wakht* or *waqt, mūda.*

Whilst, ad. *tso chi, hombra chi, tar haghah pore chi.*

Whim, s. *wahm, khiyāl.*

Whine, v.a. *prang-, rangaṭ-, kūk-*, etc. *wahal.*

Whip, s. *karoṛa, dura, tāziyāna, qamchīna.* v.a. *karoṛa-*, etc. *wahal* or *-lagawul.*

Whirl, v.a. *girzawul, churlawul, tsarkhawul.* v.n. *girzedal, churledal, tsarkhedal.*

Whirligig, s. *baṛen-chagh, jalandarai, churla-ī, bāmbūra.*

Whirlpool, s. *ghurzai, gird·āb, gharq·āb.*
Whirlwind, s. *borbūka-ī.*
Whiskers, s. *kāna-ī.*
Whisper, v.a. *pus pus k., ro ro pa ghwag kkhke wayal.*
Whistle, v.a. *shpela-ī wahal* or *-ghagawul.*
Whit, s. *ṭakai, khasanrai, pūṭai, pitsānrai, zarra.*
White, a. *spīn, saped* or *safed.*
White-ant, s. *oenah.*
Whiteness, s. *spīn·wālai.*
Whither, ad. *charta, kūma khwā.*
Whitlow, s. *kharai, shīnai.*
Whizz, s. *sagh.* v.a. *sagh k.*
Who, pr. *tsok, kum.* (-ever) *har tsok chi.*
Whole, a. *pūrah, amānī, tamām; drust, salāmat.* s. *ṭol, wāṛah.* (-sale) *ṭālah.*
Wholesome, a. *kkhah, ghwarah, joṛ, muwāfiq.*
Wholly, ad. *amānī, sarāsar, bil·kull, muṭlaq.*
Whore, s. *kachana-ī, lola-ī, kāsīra, shatāha.*
Whoremonger, s. *kāsīr, zinā·kār.*
Why, ad. *wale? tsa la?*
Wick, s. *bātai, patīla.*
Wicked, a. *bad, bad·kār, gunāh·gār, sharīr.*
Wickedness, s. *badī, bad·kārī, sharārat, gunāh.*
Wicket, s. *kaṛka-ī, tambaṛa-ī.*
Wide, a. *plan, arat, psorawar* or *sarah·war.* (-open) *chīng, wīt.* (-as a door) *liri.*
Widen, v.a. *planawul, aratawul; chīngawul, wītawul.*
Widow, s. *kūnda.* (-hood) *kūnḍ·tūn.*
Widower, s. *kūnd.*
Width, s. *plan·wālai, arat·wālai, psor, sor.*
Wield, v.a. *chalawul, girzawul.*
Wife, s. *kkhadza, artīna, merman, kor, ṭabar.* (cotemporary-) *ba-an.* (under coverture) *maṛokkha.* (brother's-) *wrandār* or *wandyār, bābī.* (son's-) *ngor.* (husband's brother's-) *yor.*
Wild, a. *dzangalī, wahshī, dashtī, ṣaḥrānai; khiyālī, wahmī; be·tartīb, nā·parhez·gār; be·qaid, sar·kakkh.* s. *dzangal, maira, ṣaḥrā.* (-beast) *dad, waḥsh.*
Wilderness, s. *dzangal, dakkht, ṣaḥrā, maira.*
Wile, s. *bāna, chal, lamghaṛa-ī, ḥīla, fareb.*
Wilful, a. *khpul·sar, khpul·rāe, sar·kakkh.*
Wilfully, ad. *pa qaṣd.*
Will, s. *marẓī, raẓā; wāk, ikhtiyār; khwakkhī, kāl·khwāhī; was, ḥukm.* (testament) *waṣiyat·nāma.* (good-) *nek·khwāhī, khair·khwāhī, nek·sigālī.* (bad-) *bad·khwāhī, bad·sigālī.*
Will, v.a. *ghokkhtal, khwakkhawul; farmāyal.*
Willing, a. *rāẓī, raẓā·man, khwakkh.* (God-) *da khudāe pa ḥukm sara, inshā allahu ta'ālā.*
Willingly, ad. *pa khwakkhī sara, pa dwāṛo stargo.*
Wily, a. *chal·bāz, farebī, bāna·khor, ḥīla·bāz.*
Win, v.a, *gaṭal, mūndal, wṛal, pa-aṛ k.* v.n. *ghālib-, wa-aṛ-,* etc. *ked.* (-a battle) *barai mūndal.* (-over) *rāwustal, grohedah k.*
Wind, s. *bād, wo, hawā.* (breath) *sāh, dam.* (to take-) v.a. *dama k.,* or *-nīwul, sāh ākhistal.* (hot-) s. *lū, paro, tod bād.* (cold-) *sūla-ī, soṛ bād.*
Wind, v.a. *tsarkhawul.* (envelope) *nghaṛal—nghakkhtal.* (twist) *tāwawul, tāo-, pech-, wal-,* etc. *warkawul; tāo-, kālkūch-,* etc. *khwuṛal.* v.n. *girzedal, kagedal.*
Winding, a. *pech·dār, wahlandai, kog·wog.* s. *tāo, pech, kalkūchaka, kag·lech.* (-sheet) *kafan, tsādar.*
Window, s. *darbacha* or *darīcha, kaṛka-ī.*
Windpipe, s. *wucha ghāṛa, ḥalq.*
Windy, s. *bādī, hawā·dār.*
Wine, s. *sharāb.* (-bibber) *sharāb·khor.*
Wing, s. *wazar, tsānga, banṛa; bāzū.*
Wink, s. *chashmak, ghamza.* v.a. *zegma-* or *zezma-, starga-,* etc. *wahal.* (blink) *dzambal, brandawul.* (-at faults) *starge puṭawul.* (hint) *ishāra k.*

Winner, s. *gaṭūnkai, wa-aṛ, pa-aṛ kawūnkai.*
Winning, s. *gaṭana, wa-aṛāna.*
Winnow, v.a. *chaj-, tsap-,* etc. *k.* or *-wahal, ālwūzawul.*
Winter, s. *ĵamai* or *ĵimai, sāṛa.*
Wipe, v.a. *masha k., pāk-, ṣāf-,* etc. *k., mugal—mukkhal. jārū k.*
Wire, s. *tār.* (-drawer) *jandra, tār·kakkh, rākkhko.* (to draw-) v.a. *tār kāgal—kkhkal.*
Wisdom, s. *'aql, poha, pahm, sha'ūr, wuqūf.*
Wise, a. *'aql·man, pohānd, dānā, hokkhyār, 'āqil.* s. *shān, rang, ṭaur, toga.*
Wisely, ad. *pa 'aql-,* etc. *-sara.*
Wish, s. *ghokkht, ārzū, mudd'ā, hanḍa, shauq.* v.a. *ghokkhtal, ārzū-,* etc. *laral.*
Wishful, a. *ārzū·man, rāghib, liwāl.*
Wisp, s. *kalokkhta.*
Wit, s. *zīrakī.*
Witch, s. *jādū·gara, koḍ-, siḥr-,* etc. *-gara.* (-craft) *jādū-,* etc. *-garī.*
With, p. *sara, khatsa* or *tsakha.*
Withal, ad. *sara la de, ziyāt la de na.*
Withdraw, v.a. *stanawul, pa biyarta ākhistal.* v.n. *jārwatal, stanedal, biyarta ked.*
Wither, v.n. *mṛāmedal* or *mṛāwedal, wuchedal, kamanṛedal, pezai-, maṛghechan-,* etc. *ked.*
Withers, s. *mandaw, wulai.*
Withhold, v.a. *stanawul; ghundī k.*
Within, p. *danana, pa kkhke.*
Without, p. *bāhir, warchani* or *wardzani.* (not possessed of) *be-, lā-, nā-, ghair-,* etc.
Withstand, v.a. *āṛ-, man'a-,* etc. *k.* v.n. *wudredal, teredal, pāedal, ṭīng ked., walāṛedal.*
Witness, s. *gawāh, shāhid; gawāhī, shāhidī; gawāhī-,* etc. *-lūnai* or *-lūnkai,* or *-warkawūnkai.* v.a. *katal, goral—lidal.* (to give-) v.a. *gawāhī-,* etc. *lal* or *-lawdal,* or *-warkawul.* (to be-) v.n. *gawāh-,* etc. *ked.*

Wittol, s. *dahūs, bagharai.*
Witty, a. *zīrak, tez·pahm.*
Wits, s. *'aql, hokkh, ausān.* (out of his-) *ausān·tlalai.*
Wizard, s. *jādū·gar, bāzī-, koḍ-, siḥr-,* etc. *-gar.*
Woe, s. *gham, randz; afsos, daregh.*
Woeful, a. *gham·ĵan, gham·nāk, andekkh·man.*
Wolf, s. *sharmakkh, lewah.*
Woman, s. *kkhadza, artīna, arwata, 'aurata, zanāna.* (lying in-) *langa, zarghāla, tsalwekkhta-ī.*
Womb, s. *riḥam, ganṛanai.*
Wonder, v.a. *'ajab k.* v.n. *hariyānedal.*
Wonder, s. *hariyānī* or *ḥairānī.* (-struck) *hak·pak, hak·hariyān.*
Wonderful, a. *'ajab, 'ajīb, badī'ah.*
Wont (to be), v. imp. Is expressed by the continuative past tense of verbs Ex. *rātah ba* or *ba rātah,* he used to come or was wont to come.
Wont, s. *'ādat, dastūr.*
Wood, s. *largai.* (forest) *banṛ.* (grove) *jangai.* (fire-) *bālanṛ, khāshāk.*
Wool, s. *waṛa-ī, pashm.*
Woollen, a. *waṛīnah, pashmīnah.*
Woolly, a. *waṛan, babar.*
Word, s. *khabara, wayai, lafẓ, wayana.* (news) *khabar.* (-of honour) *qaul.* (in a-) *gharaẓ.*
Work, s. *kār, kasb; khidmat, miḥnat; shughl, mashghūlā.* (effect) *pāzah, 'amal.*
Work, v.a. *kār-,* etc. *k., kawul, kral.*
Workman, s. *kār kawūnkai, kasb·gar, kārī·gar.*
Workmanship, s. *kārī·garī.*
World, s. *auniyā, jahān, naṛa-ī, 'ālam.*
Worldly, a. *duniyā-ī; duniyā parast.*
Worm, s. *chinjai, khazanda.* (Guinea-) *nārū.* (Tape-) *kadū zaṛai.* (intestinal) *wagha.* (Ascarides) *kīkkha.* (-of a still) *marwat.*

Wormwood, s. *tarkha, mastiyāra.*

Worn, a. *zoṛ; be·dzān, be·ḥāl.* (frayed) *sūdah, sūledalai.* (exhausted) *ṭap, staṛai.*

Worry, v.a. *pārawul, ṭongawul, kaṛawul, zoral.*

Worse, a. *nor bad.* (-than he) *la haghah na bad.*

Worship, s. *'ibādat, sijda.* (title) *ḥaẓrat.* v.a. *parastī-, 'ibādat-,* etc. *k.*

Worsted, a. *pa-aṛ, māt, bāelalai.* s. *ojghūnai, waṛa-ī; natsa-ī* or *antsa-ī, wākkhkai.* (ball of-) *spandakh.*

Worth, s. *bai'a, bahā, qīmat; qadr; kkhegaṛa.* v.n. *arzedal.*

Worthless, a. *be·fā-ida, nā·kārah, 'abaṣ, khushai, nā·tsīz, habatah, hets da kkhah.*

Worthy, a. *kkhāyastah, kkhah, lā-iq, wājib, yarzan, pīrzo.*

Wound, s. *parhār, zakhm.* v.a. *jobalawul, ghwutsawul, zakhmī k.*

Wounded, a. *parhār·jalai, jobal, ghwuts, zakhmī, zam·zmolai.* v.n. *jobaledal, ghwuts-,* etc. *ked.*

Wrangle, v.a. *jagṛa-, qaẓiya-, steza-,* etc. *k.*

Wrangler, s. *jagṛāū, jang·yālai, qaẓiya·kār, ḥujjatī, takrārī.*

Wrap, v.a. *nghaṛal—nghakkhtal.*

Wrapper, s. *lifāfa.*

Wrath, s. *qahr, ghaẓab, bros·wālai.*

Wrathful, a. *qahr·jan, ghaẓab·nāk, bros, khīr.*

Wreak, v.a. *āchawul, ghurzawul, khalāṣawul, chalawul, mātawul, lagawul.*

Wreath, s. *tāo, wal, pech; hār, laṛ.*

Wreck, s. *tālān, tabāhī, kharābī, halākat.*

Wrench, v.a. *tāo-, pech-,* etc. *warkawul; kāgal—kkhkal, bāsal—yastal; shūkawul.*

Wrest, v.a. See preceding word.

Wrestle, v.a. *parzawul k.*

Wrestler, s. *pahalwān, parzawul kawūnkai.*

Wretch, s. *kam·bakht, bad·naṣīb, khāna kharāb.*

Wretched, a. ***khwār, tabāh, be·kas, lā·chār.***

Wretchedness, s. ***khwārī, tabāhī, tor·bakhtī.***

Wright, s. *darūzgar, tarkānr.* (in comp.) ***-gar.***

Wring, v.a. *tāwawul; nichoṛawul.*

Wrinkle, s. *chīchaṛ, jūhaṛa, gundza.*

Wrist, s. *maṛwand, band.*

Write, v.a. *līkal, kāgal—kkhkal.*

Writer, s. *kātib, līkūnkai, kkhkūnkai.*

Writing, s. *līkal, kkhkal, khaṭṭ.*

Writhe, v.n. *pechedal, lamghaṛa-ī ked.*

Wrong, a. ***nā·rawā, nā·ḥaqq, nā·kkhanai, be·inṣāf; ghalaṭ, khaṭā, bad.*** s. ***ẓulm, zabardastī, jafā, nā·ḥaqqī, nuqṣān, nā·rawā-ī, ẓarar.*** (right or-) ***ḥaqq nā·ḥaqq.***

Wry, a. *krīng, kog, tsoṛ.*

Y.

Yard, s. *gholai, anganr, hadera; gaz.*

Yarn, s. *spanrsai, mazai.*

Yawn, v.a. *aswelai k., argamai k.*

Yea, ad. *ho, āre.*

Year, s. *kāl.* (this-) *sag-* or *saganai kāl,* or *sakh-* or *sakhanai kāl.* (next-) *rātlūnai-* or *makhai kāl.* (last-) *paṛos-,* or *paṛosag-,* or *paṛosganai kāl.* (-before last) *waṛam kāl.* (three years ago) *lā waṛam kāl.* (-by year) *kāl pa kāl.* (every-) *har kāl.* (whole-) *kāl·o·dīn, wāṛah kāl, kāl·o·sar.* (-old, in comp.) *-kālah, -kālanai.*

Yearn, v.n. *kaṛedal, nūledal, liwāl ked., pechedal, pakhsedal.*

Yeast, s. *khamīra, tomna, māya.*

Yell, v.a. *chigha-, sūra-, nāra-,* etc. *wahal.*

Yellow, a. *ziyaṛ.*

Yelp, v.a. *ghapal.*

Yes, ad. *ho, āre; āyā!*

Yester, ad. *parūnai, begānai.* (-day) *parūn, parūna-ī wradz.* (day before-) *waṛama wradz.* (two days before-) *lā waṛama wradz.* (-night) *begāh, begāna-ī-* or *parūna-ī-shpa.* (night before-) *warama shpa.*

Yet, c. *wale, walekin, lekin, magar.* (beside) *'alāwa, siwā, lā.* (still) *os hum, tar osa.* (again) *biyā.*

Yield, v.a. *rāwṛal, warkawul, paidā k.* (consign) *spāral, pāslawul.* (consent) *manal, qabūlawul.* (give way) v.n. *kamedal.*

Yoke, s. *jugh, ṭauq.* (fastening rope) *sarbānḍa.* (-peg) *jaghūnḍai.* (couple) *qulba, joṛa, juft.*

Yonder, ad. *halta, hori* or *hūri, hūrita, horta.*

You, pr. *tāsū, mo.*

Young, a. *dzwān.* s. *bachai.*

Youngster, s. *halak, janrai, zalmai.*

Youth, s. *dzwān, zalmai, ghunḍāyah*; *dzwānī, zalmī-tob.*

Z.

Zeal, s. *garmī, shauq, ghairat, tapāk.*

Zealot, s. *zāhid, shekh, ghairat-man.*

Zealous, a. *garm, tund, tez.*

Zephyr, s. *bād da ṣabā, nasīm*; *narai wo* or *-bād.*

Zest, s. *khwand, maza.*

Zigzag, s. *kaga waga, kṛīng pṛīng.*

Zinc, s. *jas, jasta.*

PART - II

PUSHTO–ENGLISH

A

DICTIONARY;

PUKKHTO OR PUKSHTO AND ENGLISH.

ABBREVIATIONS.

a. adjective; ad. adverb; c. conjunction; in. interjection; pl. plural; s.m. substantive masculine; s.f. substantive feminine; v.a. verb active; v.n. verb neuter; p. preposition; pr. pronoun; part. particle; Irr. irregular; Def. defective.

A. Arabic; P. Persian; S. Sanskrit; H. Hindī; T. Turkī.

N.B. The letters څ *dz* and ځ, ج *j*, څ *ts* and چ *ch*, ج *j* and ز *z*, or ږ, ژ, ق *q* and ک *k* are sometimes used the one for the other. The long vowels ا *ā*, و *o* or *ū*, and ي *e* or *ī* are often replaced by their corresponding short vowels َ *a*, ُ *u*, and ِ *i*. The letter م *m* preceding ب *b* in a word is often changed to ن *n*.

The letter ږ ژ has the sound of *z* in *azure* amongst the Western Afghans, and of *j* in *just* amongst the Eastern Afghans. ږ *g* has the same sound as ږ ژ amongst the Western tribes, and the sound of گ *g*, for which it is often changed, amongst the Eastern tribes. ښ has the sound of *kkh* amongst the Eastern Afghans, and of *ksh* amongst the Western Afghans, by whom it is often changed to ش *sh*.

ابل

alif, The first letter of the Pukkhto alphabet; is often interchanged with the short vowel *zabar*, especially in the vocative case; is sometimes added as the initial letter to words commencing with و or ي, as in اورور *oror* for ورور *wror*, ايواځي *īwādzai* for يواځي *yawādzai*.

آب *āb*, s.m. Water; lustre; reputation, honour. P.

ابا *abā*, in. Father! A. *ibā*, s.f. Denial, refusal. A.

آباد *ābād*, a. Cultivated, peopled, prosperous. P.

آبادي *ābādī*, s.f. Cultivation, prosperity. P.

اباسين *abāsīn*, s.m. The father of rivers. The Indus. Also written *abāsīnd*.

ابتدا *ibtidā*, s.f. Beginning, commencement. A.

ابد *abad*, s.m. Eternity. A. *abadan*, a. Eternal.

ابدال *abdāl*, s.m. A saint. A.

ابدالي *abdālī*, s.m. Name of an Afghan clan in the country between Kandahar and Herat. *abdālai*, s.m. A man of the tribe.

آبرو *ābrū*, s.m. Honour, reputation, name, renown. P. *abrū*, s.m. The eyebrow. P.

ابره *abra*, s.f. The outer cloth of a garment; a sash for the waist. P.

آبريښم *ābrekkham* or *ābreksham*, s.m. New silk, floss silk. P. (*ābresham*).

ابل *abl*, a. Barefooted, unshod; powerless, weak. S. (*abal*). *kkhpa-abla*, a. Barefooted, unshod.

ابله *ablah*, a. Foolish, silly, stupid. A.
ابئي *aba-ī*, s.f. A mother.
آپرين *āparīn*, in. Bravo! well done! P. (*āfarīn*).
اپريدي *aprīdī*, s.m. Name of a tribe of Pathans in the Kohat hills. Also written *afrīdī*.
اپس دنډئي *apas-ḍanḍa-ī*, s.f. Name of a game; tip-cat; bat and ball.
اپلت *aplat*, a. Obscene, dirty, filthy.
اپوټه *apūṭah*, a. Inverted, reversed, inside-out. H.
اترنګ *atrang*, s.m. Name of a plant, used in dyeing and medicine (*asclepias echinata*). H.
آتش *ātash*, s.m. Fire (in comp. only). P.
اتفاق *ittifāq*, s.m. Agreement, concord. A.
اتفاقي *ittifāqī*, a. Accidental. A.
اتم *atam*, a. The eighth.
اتنړ or اتڼ *atanṛ*, s.m. A kind of dance, a jig, a reel, round dance.
اتوار *itwār*, s.m. Sunday. S.
اتوب *atob*, s.m. Gruel, pap.
اته *atah*, a. Eight. *atah-las*, a. Eighteen.
اتيا *atiyā*, a. Eighty. *atiyāyam*, a. Eightieth.
اټال *aṭāl*, a. Idle, unemployed, out of work.
اټکل *aṭkal*, s.m. Conjecture, guess. H.
اټه *aṭa*, s.f. A ball, reel, or skein of thread. H. (*aṭṭī*).
اټيران *aṭerān*, s.m. A reel for thread. H.
اټيرل *aṭeral*, v.n. To be dyspeptic.
اټيرنه *aṭerana*, s.f. Indigestion, dyspepsia.
اټيه *aṭiya*, } s.f. See اټه.
اټيهه *aṭeha*, }
اثبات *iṣbāt*, s.m. Confirmation, proof. A.
اثر *aṣr*, s.m. Effect, mark, sign. A.
اجاره *ijāra*, s.f. Farm, hire, rent. A.
اجازت *ijāzat*, s.m. Leave, permission, order. A.
اجر *ajar*, } s.m. Hire, wages, reward. A.
اجرت *ujrat*, }
اجل *ajal*, s.m. Fate, death. A.
اڅڼرل *atsanṛal*, v.a. To arrange, harmonize, level, smooth.

اچت *uchat*, a. Elevated, high, lofty. s. (*unchā*).
اچرلي *ucharlai*, s.m. The forehead, brow.
آچو *āchū*, s.f. A raspberry; the bush and fruit.
آچول *āchawul*, v.a. To cast, throw, fling.
آخ *ākh*, in. Ah! Good! Well! How good! A.
اخاړه *akhāṛah*, s.m. Plaster; daubing, plastering.
اخبار *akhbār*, s.m. Intelligence, news; a newspaper (pl. of خبر A.).
اختر *akhtar*, s.m. A star; good omen, good fortune; a festival. *loe-akhtar*, the great festival; name of a month corresponding with *zī-hijja*. *wṛūkai-akhtar*, the little festival, or the month corresponding with *shawāl*. P.
آخته *ākhtah*, a. Castrated; involved, caught, entangled, trammeled. P.
اختيار *ikhtiyār*, s.m. Authority, power; option, choice. A.
آخر *ākhir*, s.m. Conclusion, end. ad. At last, finally. A.
آخرت *ākhirat*, s.m. Futurity. A.
آخستل *ākhistal*, v.a. To accept, take; appropriate, seize, capture. A. (*akhaz*)?
آخښ *ākhkkh* or *ākhksh*, in. Alas! Heigho! See آخ.
اخګر *akhgar*, s.m. Live coal, hot ember. P.
اخلاص *ikhlāṣ*, s.m. Sincerity, kindness, affection. A.
آخون *ākhūn*, s.m. A tutor, teacher, master. Also written *ākhūnd*. P.
اخيړل *akheṛal*, v.a. To daub, plaster, smear.
ادا *adā*, s.f. Payment, performance. A.
ادب *adab*, s.m. Courtesy, politeness, respect. A.
ادنا *adnī*, a. Inferior, mean, small. A.
ادوبدو *adūbadū*, a. Distended, tumefied, blown, swelled.
ادينه *adīna*, s.f. Friday; Sabbath. P.

ادئ *ada-ī*, s.f. Fields, plots of land round a village. Mother.

اذان *azān*, s.m. Call to prayer. A.

اذن *izn*, s.m. Leave, permission, order. A.

اذوقه *azūqa*, s.f. Food, provisions, victuals. A.

اراخ *arākh*, s.m. A brook, rivulet, water-course.

اراده *irāda*, s.f. Design, desire, wish. A.

آراسته *ārāstah*, a. Adorned, arranged, composed. P.

آرام *ārām*, s.m. Comfort, ease, rest. P.

ارباب *arbāb*, s.m. A noble, chief, lord (pl. of رب A.).

اربوز *urbūz*, s.m. The snout, muzzle.

ارت *arat*, a. Loose, open, wide. *aratawul*, v.a. To loosen.

ارتاو *artāw*, s.m. See پرتاب.

ارتل *aratal*, v.a. To break wind; widen.

آرته *ārta* or ښپه آرته *kkhpa-ārta*, s.f. Name of a wedding ceremony; the first visit of a lover at the house of his affianced, on the third day after betrothal; he takes some present for his affianced bride and is in return regaled with sherbet and cakes. After this ceremony, but not before, he can visit at the bride's house whenever convenient. S. (*ārtā*). *kkhpa-ārtūn*, s.m. Courtship.

ارتينه *artīna*, s.f. A woman, wife; female. A. (*'aurat*).

ارجل برجل *arjal-barjal*, a. Entangled, noosed, trapped.

آرخښ *ārkhakkh*, s.m. A gasp, gurgle.

اردو *urdū*, s.m. A camp, cantonment. T.

ارز *arz*, s.m. Price, alue. P.

ارزان *arzān*, a. Cheap, inexpensive. P.

آرزو *ārzū*, s.m. Desire, want, wish. P.

ارزيدل *arzedal*, v n. To be worth, fetch.

اروړمي *argamai*, s.m. A belch, eructation.

ارړي *argai*, s.m. See preceding. P. (*ārogh*).

آرسئ *ārsa-ī*, s.f. A small mirror worn on the thumb by women. H.

ارغند *arghund*, s.m. A knuckle bone.

ارګ *arg*, s.m. A citadel, palace. P.

ارګجه *argajah*, a. Mixed, miscellaneous. H.

ارمان *armān*, s.m. Regret, sorrow; desire, wish. in. Woe! Alas!

اروته *arwata*, s.f. A woman, wife, female. A. (*'aurat*).

آرويدل *ārwedal*, v.a. To hear, listen.

آره *āra*, s.f. A base, foundation. *ara*, s.f. A saw. P.

ارهټ *arhat*, s.m. An irrigation well worked by wheels. H.

ارهر *arhar*, s.m. Name of a pulse, "pigeon pea" (*Cytisus cajan*). H.

ارهنډ *arhanḍ*, s.m. The castor oil tree (*Ricinus communis*). S.

آري *āre*, ad. Yea, yes, verily, aye. P.

آړ *āṛ*, s.m. Difficulty, obstruction; a screen, shelter; a fetter, bond. H.

اړامکي *aṛāmkai*, s.m. A shepherd's crook.

اړخ *aṛkh*, s.m. Armpit; flank, side.

اړم *aṛam*, s.m. A buttress, prop, support.

اړمي *aṛamai*, s.m. A small prop, a bar; the bar of a door.

اړنګ بړنګ *aṛang-baṛang*, a. Confused, entangled.

اړول *aṛawul*, v.a. To overturn, upset, invert, turn over.

اړيړئ *aṛeṛa-ī*, s.f. A stop, catch, bolt; the small cross-bars to which the waterpots of an irrigation wheel are fastened.

اړيکي *aṛekai*, s.m. The bar or bolt of a door or window; a small prop or support; hindrance, obstacle.

آزاد *āzād*, a. Free, liberated, loose. P.

آزار *āzār*, s.m. Affliction, distress. P. *izār*, s.m. Trowsers, drawers. P.

آزرده *āzurdah*, a. Sad, sorrowful, grieved. P.

ازغن *azghan*, a. Thorny, prickly.

ازغي *azghai*, s.m. A thorn, prickle.

آزمايښت *āzmāyikkht* or آزميښت *āzmekkht*, s.m. Proof, trial, test. P. (*āzmā-īsh*).

آزمايل *āzmāyal* or آزمويل *āzmoyal*, v.a. To examine, proof, test, try. P. (*āzmūdan*).

اريل *agayal*, v.a. To wattle, net; stitch, sew; to provoke, urge, incite, instigate.

آس *ās*, s.m. A horse. P. (*asp*).

اسامي *asāmī*, s.m. A tenant, client; defendant. A.

آسان *āsān*, a. Easy, facile. P.

اسباب *asbāb*, s.m. Chattels, goods (pl. of سبب A.).

اسپغول *ispag͟hol*, s.m. Name of a herb (*Plantago ispaghula*). The seeds are used in medicine. P.

اسپند *ispand*, s.m. Name of a plant; the Syrian rue (*Peganum harmala*). The seeds are used in medicine, and the dried herb as incense to drive away evil spirits. P.

آسپه *āspa*, s.f. A mare. *aspa*, s.f. Quinsy; scurvy.

استاځي *astād͟zai*, s.m. A messenger, delegate, apostle.

استاذ *ustāẕ*, s,m. A master, teacher. P. (*ustād*).

آستان *āstān*, s.m. A threshold; shrine of a saint; family, house. P.

استر *astar*, s.m. The lining of a dress. P.

استره *astura*, s.f. A razor. P.

استوژه *astoǰa*, } s.f. Abode, dwelling, residence.
استوګه *astoga*, } Also *astogana*.

استوګونکي *astogūnkai*, s.m. Resident, dweller.

استيفا *istīfā*, s.f. Renouncing; resignation. A.

آستين *āstīn*, s.m. A sleeve. P.

آستول *āstawul*, v.a. To send, transmit, despatch, depute. P. (*firistādan*).

آستيدل *āstedal*, v.n. To abide, dwell, reside. P. (*istādan*). See *osedal*.

اسراف *isrāf*, s.m. Extravagance, prodigality, waste. A. (*iṣrāf*).

آسره *āsra*, s.f. Hope, refuge, trust, reliance. S. (*āsrā*).

اسلام *islām*, s.m. The Muhammadan religion. A.

آسمان *āsmān*, s.m. The sky, heaven. P.

اسو *asū*, s.m. Name of the sixth Hindu month. September-October. S. (*āsin*)

آسوده *āsūdah*, a. Contented, tranquil, quiet. P.

اسويلي *aswelai*, s.m. A gape, sigh, yawn.

اسي *asī*, a. Unfortunate, unlucky. *asa-ī*, s.f. Hoar-frost.

آسيا *āsiyā*, s.f. A water-mill. P.

اسير *asīr*, s.m. A captive, prisoner. P.

اشارت *is͟hārat*, s.m. A hint, nod, sign, wink. A.

اشاري *as͟hārai*, s.m. A dried apricot.

اشر *as͟harr*, a. Abusive, wicked, vicious, obscene. A.

اشتوکه *as͟htoka*, s.f. Concord, peace. P. (*ās͟htī*).

اشتها *is͟htihā*, s.f. Appetite, desire. A.

آشناي *ās͟hnāe*, s.m. A friend, lover. P. (*ās͟hnā*). *ās͟hnā-ī*, s.f. Friendship, intimacy.

آښل *āk͟khal*, v.a. To knead or mix dough. Def. in pres. ten. See آغږل.

آښلي *āk͟khalai*, s.m. Dough. a. Kneaded.

اصل *aṣl*, s.m. Lineage, origin, source; capital. A.

اصلي *aṣlī*, a. Genuine, original. A.

اصيل *aṣīl*, a. Noble, well bred. A.

اطلاع *iṭṭilā'* s.f. Notice, information. A.

اعتبار *i'tibār*, s.m. Credit, trust, reliance. A.

اعجوبه *a'jūbah*, s.m. A miracle, prodigy, wonder. A.

اغ دغ *ag͟h-dug͟h*, s.m. Fraud, deceit, imposture.

اغر *ag͟har*, s.m. Fixing the arrow on the bowstring preparatory to shooting.

آغزکي *āg͟hzakai*, s.m. Name of a thorny plant.

آغزن *āg͟hzan*, a. Thorny, prickly.

آغزي *āg͟hzai*, s.m. A thorn, prickle.

آغږل *āg͟hagal*, v.a. To knead or mix dough. Def. in past ten. See آښل. P. (*āg͟his͟htan*).

اغلب *ag͟hlab*, ad. Most likely, most probably. A.

آغله *āg͟halah*, a. Mixed, kneaded; good, pleasing.

آغوستل *āg͟hūstal*, v.a. To dress, put on clothes, attire. P. (*āg͟hastan, āg͟handan*).

آغوستن *āg͟hostan*, s.m. Apparel, dress, raiment, clothing.

آغوستول *āg͟hostawul*, v.a. To attire, clothe, dress.

اغيړل *ag͟heṛal*, v.a. s. (*ajīran*). See اتيړل.

آفت *āfat*, s.m. Calamity, misfortune. A.

افسوس *afsos*, s.m. Grief, sorrow, regret. in. Alas! pity! ah! P.

افغان *afg͟hān*, s.m. An Afg͟hān.

افيم *afīm*, s.m. Opium. A. (*afiyūn*).

اقبال *iqbāl*, s.m. Good fortune, prestige, good auspices. A.

اقرار *iqrār*, s.m. Argument, assurance, confession. A.

اقليم *iqlīm*, s.m. Country, climate, region. A.

اکا *akā*, s.m. A paternal uncle.

اکثر *akṣar*, a. Most. ad. Mostly, generally. A.

اکر *akar*, s.m. Giddiness, vertigo.

اکوبکو *akū-bakū*, s.m. Name of a bird; name of a game; it is played with cakes of moist clay of a globular shape, hollowed out, and made to explode by being dashed on a hard surface with the opening downwards.

اکوړ *akoṛ*, s.m. A walnut; the tree.

اکوړي *akoṛai*, s.m. A kind of leather, tanned red.

آگاه *āgāh*, a. Apprized, aware, informed. P.

اگر *agar*, s.m. A captive, slave, bondsman. P. c. If. P.

اگرچه *agarc͟hi*, c. Although, though. P.

اگرمي *agramai*, s.m. See اروېمي.

اگن *agan*, s.m. Name of a bird; the skylark. H.

اگئي *aga-ī*, s.f. An egg.

آل *āl*, s.m. Children, progeny. A.

الاج *alāj*, s.m. A carder or comber of cotton. A. (*ḥallāj*).

الاجي *alājī*, s.f. A comb for clearing cotton of its seeds.

الاستي *alāstī*, a. Absent, invisible.

البته *albatta*, ad. Certainly, undoubtedly, of course. A.

الجه *ulja*, s.f. Booty, plunder.

السي *alsī*, s.f. Linseed. H.

الفت *ulfat*, s.m. Familiarity, friendship, intimacy, kindness. A.

آلفته *āluftah*, a. Vexed, troubled, distressed. P.

القصه *alqiṣṣa*, ad. In fine, in short. A.

الله *allah*, s.m. God. in. Good God! My God! Oh God! A. *allah-bās͟h*, s.m. Greeting, shaking hands.

آلو *ālū*, s.m. A kind of plum; a plum. P.

الوان *alwān*, s.m. A kind of cotton cloth dyed red; coloured cloth. A.

آلوتل *ālwatal*, v.n. To fly, float in the air.

الوچه *alūc͟ha*, s.f. A kind of plum. P.

آلوده *ālūdah*, a. Soiled, stained, spattered. P.

آلوزول *ālwuzawul*, v.a. To make fly; to sift or winnow corn, etc., by throwing it up in the air against the wind.

الوس *ulūs*, s.m. A clan, people, tribe. T.

الول *aluwal*, a. All of a heap, by the run, all in a lump.

الوويل *alwoyal*, v.a. To parch, roast, scorch, burn.

الوي *alawai*, a. Parched, roasted, scorched, burnt.

الهنگ *alhang*, s.m. Crying, sobbing, blubbering.

امام *imām*, s.m. The chief priest of a mosque; the large bead of a rosary. A.

امان *amān*, s.m. Protection, quarter, safety. A.

امانت *amānat*, s.m. Deposit, trust. A.

اماني *amānī*, a. All, entire, whole. ad. Entirely, wholly. s.f. Deposit, security, trust. A.

امبار *ambār*, s.m. A heap, a store of grain, etc. P.

امبوړ *ambūṛ*, s.m. Forceps, pincers, pliers. P.

آمدني *āmadanī*, s.f. Income, revenue; import. P.

آمدرفت *āmad-raft*, s.m. Coming and going, intercourse, thoroughfare. P.

امر *amr*, s.m. Command, order; affair, business. A.

امرسه *amrasa*, s.f A kind of sweetmeat.

امسا *amsā*, s.f. A staff, stick. A. (*'aṣā*).

امكان *imkān*, s.m. Possibility. A.

امل *amal*, s.m. Intoxication; habitude.

املي *amalī*, s.m. A man addicted to intoxicating drugs.

املوك *amlūk*, s.m. Name of a tree that bears an edible fruit (*Diospyros sp.*).

امن *aman*, s.m. Safety, security, asylum. A.

آموخته *āmokhtah*, a. Learned, taught; experienced, habituated, accustomed. P.

اميد *umed*, s.m. Expectation, hope; pregnancy. P.

امير *amīr*, s.m. A noble, grandee, ruler. A.

اميل *amel*, s.m. An ornament for the neck; a necklace of charms, etc. A. (*ḥimā-il*).

آمين *āmīn*, ad. Amen, so be it. A. *amīn*, s.m. A guardian, umpire, trustee. a. Constant, faithful, trusty. A.

انا *anā*, s.f. A grandmother, paternal or maternal. *warla-anā*, s.f. A great grandmother.

انار *anār*, s.m. A pomegranate. P.

انبالي *anbāla-ī*, s.f. A howdah; a sedan or litter for women, carried on a pole by men. A. (*'amārī*).

انجام *anjām*, s.m. Accomplishment, end. P.

انجير *anjīr*, s.m. Scrofula; diseased glands in the neck.

انڅئي *antsa-ī*, s.f. Cord, string, twine. H. (*āns*).

انډ *and*, s.m. An age, cycle of five hundred years; idea, thought, fancy; testicle, egg. S.

اندازه *andāza*, s.f. Measure, quantity; guess. P.

اندرپايه *andarpāya*, s.f. A ladder, steps, stairs.

اندركه *andarka*, s.f. A coat, doublet. S. (*angarkhā*).

اندرور *andror*, s.f. A husband's sister. See ندرور.

آنده *inda*, s.f. A sip, gulp, mouthful.

انديښ *andekkh* or *andeksh*, s.m. Meditating, cogitating, thinking. P. (*andesh*).

انديښنه *andekkhna*, s.f. Anxiety, care, thought, dread. Also *andekkhnā*.

انډوخړ *andokhar*, s.m. Name of a game; baste the bear. Called also *swara-ḍabala-ī*, The basters riding on the backs of other boys round the bear.

انډي *andai*, s.m. A bundle, package.

انډيري *anderai*, s.m. A mat made of palm leaves.

انذور *anzor* or انځور *andzor*, s.m. Ornament, decoration, embellishment.

انسان *insān*, s.m. Man, mankind. A.

انسټ *ansit*, s.m. Name of a plant.

انصاف *inṣāf*, s.m. Equity, justice. A.

انعام *in'ām*, s.m. A favour, gift, present. A.

انكار *inkār*, s.m. Denial, negation. A.

انګازه *angāza*, s.f. Echo, resonance, reverberation.

انګبين *angabīn*, s.m. Honey; the comb. P.

انګړ *angar*, s.m. A house, mansion.

انګڼر *anganr*, s.m. An area, court, yard. S. (*āngan*).

انګولا *angolā*, s.f. The howl of a wild animal.

انګه *inga*, s.f. A bride's maid or attendant for the first few days after marriage. *anga*, s.f. A frock, coat. S. (*angā*).

انګئي *anga-ī*, s.f. Name of a game; prisoners' bars.

انګيټئي *angeta-ī*, s.f. A chafing dish. H. (*angethī*).

انګيرل *angeral*, v.a. To fancy, imagine, suppose, think. P. (*ingārdan*).

اننګ *anang*, s.m. A pomegranate; the space between the thumb and fore-finger; a short span.

اننګوړي *anangūrai*, s.m. A small pomegranate.

اننګي *anangai*, s.m. The cheek.

آنه *āna*, s.f. The pommel of a saddle.

انئي *ana-ī*, s.f. A woman's name; Annie.

انړل *anṟal*, v.a. To grind, powder, triturate.

انړول *anṟawul*, v.a. To choose, gather, pick, select, separate, sort.

انوټ *anwaṭ*, s.m. A ring for the thumb or great toe. H.

او *aw*, c. And, also. *ao*, ad. Aye, yes. *o*, in. Oh! Halloa! Hie!

اوار *awār*, s.m. Booty, plunder, spoil; injustice, delay, tyranny. P.

آواره *āwārah*, a. Dissolute, vagabond; spiritless, mean.

آواز *āwāz*, s.m. Voice, sound, report. P.

آوازه *āwāza*, s.f. Rumour, report, fame, celebrity.

اوبال *obāl*, s.m. A crime, fault, sin. A.

اوبړئي *obṛa-ī*, s.f. The green vegetation in ponds, etc. Confervæ; duckweed.

اوبنړه *obanṟa*, s.f. The caul; the membrane enveloping the fœtus.

اوبه *oba*, s.f. Water, liquid, fluid. P. (*āb*). A splint in the leg of a horse, etc. *oblan*, a. Watery, sodden.

اوپره *ūprah*, a. Foreign, strange.

اوپتر *awtar*, a. Ruined, spoiled; dissolute, wanton, deranged. A. (*abtar*).

اوجاړ *ūjāṛ*, a. Desert, waste, desolated, ruined. S.

اوجري *ūjrai*, s.m. An entrail, gut; tripe. H. (*ūjh*).

اوڅار *awtsār*, a. Clear, evident, manifest. s.m. symptom, sign, evidence, mark. H. (*ūjāl*).

اوچت *ūchat*, a. High, lofty, raised, elevated. S. (*ūnchā*).

اودرول *ūdarawul*, v.a. To fix, set up, pitch (as a tent); to halt, stop, stay (as a boat, cattle, etc.); to make stand.

اودریدل *ūdaredal*, v.n. To abide, halt, stop, stay, stand up, stand still.

اودس *awdas*, s.m. Washing the hands, a form of ablution before prayers; purification. P. (*āb-dast*).

اودل *ūdal*, v.a. To weave, braid, net. P. (*āwīdan*).

اوده *ūdah*, a. Asleep, sleeping. *ūda*, s.f. A charm, blowing, breathing upon by way of charm; mesmerism. (The power is supposed to be acquired by direct commission from above, or by inheritance). Also written *hūda*. A. (*'uhda*).

اوډنئي *oḍana-ī*, s.f. A woman's veil or mantle. S. (*oṛhnā*).

اور *or*, s.m. Fire. S. (*āg*).

اوراوره‌کي *or-orahkai*, s.m. Name of a plant; the wild onion or leek; it is used as a condiment.

اوربوشه *orbūsha*, s.f. A barley corn. *orbūshe*, pl. Barley.

اوربوشينه *orbūshīna*, s.f. Barley-meal, barley-bread.

اوربل *orbal*, s.m. A curl, ringlet, or lock of hair on the forehead.

اورپښت *orpukkht*, s.m. A moth.

اورلړوني *or-laṛūnai*, s.m. A fire-poker.

اورمیږ *ormeg*, s.m. The neck, throat.

اورنړي *oranṟai*, s.m. A swaddling-cloth, a baby's winding sheet. S. (*oṛhnī*).

آورول *āwrawul*, v.a. To cause to hear.

اوره *orah*, s.m. A cloud, the clouds. P. (*abr*).

اوره‌کي *orahkai*, s.m. A firefly, glow-worm.

آوري *āwrai*, s.m. Mustard seed; name of a herb; wild mustard.

اورئي *ora-ī*, s.f. The gums; quick of the nails.

اوريځ *oryadz*,
اوريځه *oryadza*, } s.f. A cloud.

آوریدل *āwredal*, v.a. To hear, listen, P. (*āwrīdan*).

اوریدل *oredal*, v.n. To rain, drizzle. P. (*bārīdan*).

اوډ *oṛ*, s.m. A weaver's tool; the web through which the woof passes.

اول *awwal*, a. First, foremost. A.

اولاد *awlād*, s.m. Progeny, issue, children. A. Also written *alwād*.

اولو *awlū*, s.m. Treacle, molasses.

اوله *olah*, s.m. A flock of lambs kept separate from their mothers.

اوم *om* or *ūm*, a. Crude, raw, uncooked, unripe, immature. P. (*k͟hām*). *awam*, a. The seventh.

اومه *omah*, s.m. Name of a plant. It is used in tanning, and is added to snuff to increase its pungency.

اونګئ *ūnga-ī*, s.f. The moon.

اوني *ūnai*, s.m. A babbler, chatterer.

اووم *owam*, a. The seventh.

اووه *owah*, a. Seven.

اووي *owī*, s.m. A cock's comb; a horse's mane.

اوه *awah*, a. Seven. *awa*, s.f. A pimple, pustule, vesicle.

اوي *oe*, s.m. Consent, promise, pledge.

اويا *awiyā*, a. Seventy.

اويزاند *awezānd*, a. Hanging, pendant, suspended. P. (*āwez*).

اوينه *oenah*, s.m. The white ant.

اهاړ *ahāṛ*, s.m. Name of the third Hindu month. June-July.

اي *ai*, in. Oh! Halloa! sign of the vocative case. P.

آيا *āyā*, in. No! Is it! Really! How odd! P. ad. No, not at all, never.

ايړي *eṛrai*, s.m. The long-tailed sheep. S. (*bheṛī*).

ايره *īra*, s.f. Ash. *īre*, pl. Ashes.

ايړي *eṛai*, s.m. See ايړړي.

ايسار *īsār*, a. Hindered, stopped, surrounded. s.m. A castle, fort; embarrassment; perplexity. A. (*ḥiṣār*).

ايستل *estal*, v.a. To draw out, extract, expel. Also *yastal*. Def. in. pres. ten. See باسل.

اوړنبي *oṛunbe*, ad. Firstly, first, formerly, previously. Also written *wṛūnbe*. *oṛunbanai* or *wṛunbanai*, a. Former, previous.

اوړنئ *oṛana-ī*, s.f. See اوډنئ.

اوړول *oṛawul*, v.a. To powder, grind, pulverize.

اوړه *oṛah*, s.m. Flour, meal, powder.

اوړي *oṛai*, s.m. Summer.

اوږغونه *oǰg͟hūna*, s.f. A goat's hair. *oǰg͟hune*, pl. Goat's hair.

اوږد *ūgd*, a. Long, extended.

اوږمکئ *ugmaka-ī*, s.f. The moon; moonlight.

اوږه *ūga*, s.f. Garlic. *oga*, s.f. The shoulder.

اوږي *ogai*, s.m. A measure of grain, etc. equal to 14lbs. *oga-ī*, s.f. An ornament for the neck; a necklet or collar of silver or gold.

اوس *os*, ad. Now, at this time.

اوسپنخړي *ospank͟haṛai*, s.m. Iron slag or dross.

اوسپنه *ospana*, s.f. Iron.

اوسط *awsaṭ*, a. Medium, mean, middling. A.

اوسن *osan*, a. Existing, present.

اوسني *osanai*, a. Modern, late, recent.

اوسي *osai*, s.m. A deer, gazelle.

اوسيدل *osedal*, v.n. To abide, exist, remain, dwell, reside, stay. See *āstedal*.

اوښ *ūk͟kh*, s.m. A camel. P. (*ūs͟htur*).

اوښبه *ūk͟kh͟hbah* or *ūks͟hbah*, s.m. A camel-man, an owner of camels.

آوښتل *āwuk͟kh͟htal*, v.a. To change, turn, alter. P. (*bāz-gas͟htan*).

اوښه *ok͟kha*, s.f. A tear. P. (*as͟hk*).

اوښي *awk͟khai*, s.m. A brother-in-law; wife's brother; sister's husband. A. (*ak͟h*, brother). *ok͟khī*, s.m. The mane of a horse.

اوغان *awg͟hān*, s.m. An Afghan.

اوغز *ūg͟hz*, s.m. A walnut.

اوګره *ogra*, s.f. Porridge, pap, gruel. P. (*og͟hrā*).

اوګرائي *ūgṛā-ī*, s.f. A portion, part, instalment; a debt paid at different times. H.

ایشنه *eshana*, s.f. Agitation, ferment, ebullition, effervescence. P. (*josh*).

ایشول *eshawul* v.a. To boil, heat, make boil. P. (*joshandan*).

ایشیدل *eshedal*, v.n. To boil, bubble, effervesce. P. (*joshīdan*).

ایښل *ekkhal* or *īkkhal*, v.a. To lay, put, place, set. Also *yakkhal*. Def. in pres. ten. See ږدل. P. (*nishāndan*).

ایښودل *ekkhodal*, or *īkkhodal*, } v.a. See ایښل.
ایښول *ekkhawul*, or *īkkhawul*, }

ایل *el* or *īl*, a. Domestic, tame, not wild.

ایله *elah*, a. Free, liberated. P. (*yalah*).

ایمان *īmān*, s.m. Faith, religious belief. A.

ایمن *eman*, a. Calm, gentle, patient.

ایمنه *emna*, s.f. A woman's name.

اینځر *īndzar*, s.m. A fig; the tree. P. (*anjīr*).

آئین *ā-īn*, s.m. Law, rule, regulation. P.

آئینه *ā-īna*, s.f. A mirror, looking-glass; the liver, the gall bladder.

اینه *īna*, s.f. The gall bladder, the liver, lungs and heart, the vitals.

ایوه *īwa*, s.f. A plough, ploughing.

ب

ب *be*. The second letter of the Pukkhto alphabet. It is often changed for و in words adopted from the Persian and Sanscrit.

بَ *ba* or به *ba*, part. The sign of the future and continuative past tenses of verbs.

با *bā*, p. With, by. Only used in comp. with words from the Persian. P.

باب *bāb*, s.m. Account, business, matter; chapter or section of a book; door, gate. A.

بابا *bābā*, in. Father! Sire! A term of affection and respect used towards old men, and by children to a grandfather. T.

بابت *bābat*, s.m. Affair, business; item, article; account, on account of. A.

بابړ *bābaṛ*, s.m. Name of an Afghan clan.

بابکو *bābako*, in. Dear child! A term of affectionate address to a child.

بابو *bābū*, in. Father! Sire! A term of affection or esteem used towards a father or old man.

بابي *bābī*, s.f. A brother's wife, sister-in-law. in. Mother! Granny dear! s.m. Name of an Afghan clan.

باتور *bātūr*, s.m. An eagle; brave, valiant (corrupt: of P. *bahādur*). *bātor*, s.m. The pupil of the eye.

باتئ *bāta-ī*, s.f. A wick, match, candle, spile; bougie, a tent for a wound. S. (*battī*).

باټ *bāṭ*, s.m. A hone, grindstone.

باټینګنړ *bāṭīnganṛ*, s.m. The egg-plant (*solanum longum*). P. (*baingan*).

باج *bāj*, s.m. Tax, toll, impost, duty. P.

باجره *bājra*, s.f. Indian corn, spiked millet (*Holcus spicatus*). P. (*bājrā*).

باجه *bājah*, s.m. Wife's sister's husband, brother-in-law.

باد *bād*, s.m. Air, wind; rheumatism. P.

بادام *bādām*, s.m. An almond. P.

بادخور *bād·khor*, s.m. A disease of horses; œdema. Name of a kind of hawk. P.

بادخورک *bād·khorak*, s.m. The sparrow-hawk. P.

بادرنګ *bādrang*, s.m. A cucumber. P.

بادرو *bādro*, s.m. Name of the fifth Hindu month. August-September. S. (*bhādon*). *bādraw*, s.m. An air-hole, ventilator. Also *bād·khāna*. P.

بادشاه *bādshāh*, s.m. Monarch, sovereign, king. P.

بادکښ *bād·kakkh*, s.m. A ventilator, chimney. P. (*bād·kash*).

بادګوله *bād·gola*, s.f. Colic, flatulent colic. P.

بادوان *bād·wān*, s.m. A sail, wing; a shade or screen for a lamp. P.

بادهوا *bād·hawā*, s.f. A paper kite. P.

بادي *bādī*, a. Flatulent, windy ; haughty, proud.
بادګول *bāḍgol*, s.m. A leading string, rein, head rope of a horse. H. (*bāgḍor*).
بار *bār*. s.m. A burden, load ; time, occasion, turn, place. P.
باران *bārān*, s.m. Rain ; a shower, downpour. P.
بارخو *bārkho*, s.f. The cheek, side of the face.
بارک *bārak*, s.m. A man's name, Barak. *bārakzī*, s.m. The clan Barak. *bārakzai*, s.m. A man of the clan Barak. *bārakza-ī*, s.f. A woman of the clan Barak. The late Amir Dost Muhammad Khan was the head of this now famous clan.
بارکښ *bār-kakkh*, s.m. A rope, cord, etc. for tying up baggage ; a beast of burthen. a. burthen-bearing ; meek, humble. P. (*bār-kash*).
باره *bāra*, s.f. A rampart, fortification, enclosure, ditch, entrenchment, fence. P.
باریک *bārīk*, a. Fine, narrow, slender, subtile. P.
باري *bāre*, ad. Once ; at length ; then.
باړ *bāṛ*, s.m. A volley of musketry. An iron dish for roasting grain. S.
باړه *bāṛa*, s.f. An enclosure, sheepfold. S. (*bāṛā*).
باز *bāz*, s.f. A female falcon. P. See جرّه
بازار *bāzār*, s.m. A market, mart. P.
بازو *bāzū*, s.m. The arm ; side of a bedstead ; fold of a door ; the flank, side of anything. P.
بازوبند *bāzū-band*, s.m. An ornament for the arm. P.
بازي *bāzī*, s.f. Cheat, trick, deception, stratagem ; play, sport, game. P.
بازیګر *bāzī-gar*, s.m. A tumbler, rope-dancer, juggler ; cheat, impostor.
باس *bās*, s.m. A privy, necessary ; odour, smell. S.

باسل *bāsal*, v.a. To extract, draw out, pull out. Def. in past tense. See ایستل.
باښه *bākkha*, s.f. A sparrow-hawk. P. (*bāsha*).
باښین *bākkhīn*, s.m. A sparrow-hawk. P. (*bāshīn*).
باطل *bāṯil*, a. Futile, useless, vain. A
باطن *bāṯin*, a. Concealed, internal. A
باعث *bā'is*, s.m. Account, cause, reason. A.
باغ *bāgh*, s.m. A garden, grove, orchard. P.
باغوان *bāghwān*, s.m. A gardener.
باقي *bāqī*, s.m. Arrears, balance, remnant ; existing, remaining. A.
باک *bāk*, s.m. Anxiety, dread, fear. P.
باکي *bāka-ī*, s.f. Nausea, sickness. H. (*ūbkā-ī*).
باګو *bāgū*, or / باګولي *bāgola-ī*, s.f. } A bogy, goblin, ghost.
بالښت *bālikkht*, s.m. A bolster, pillow. P. (*bālish*). *bālikkht-goṭai*, s.m. A cushion.
بالښتک *bālikkhtak*, s.m. A cushion, pad.
بالغ *bāligh*, a. Adult, mature, full-grown. A.
بالڼ *bālanr*, s.m. Fuel, fire-wood.
بالین *bālīn*, s.m. A bolster, pillow, cushion, pad. P.
بام *bām*, s.m. The roof of a house. P.
بامبڼ *bāmbanr*, s.m. A Brahmin. S. (*bāmhan*).
بامبڼه *bāmbanra*, s.f. A blaze, conflagration. A Brahmin woman.
بامبیلکي *bāmbī-lakai*, s.m. A kind of butterfly.
باندِ *bāndi*, / باندي *bānde*, } p. Above, atop, on, upon.
باڼډه *bānḍa*, s.f. A cattle or sheep-pen ; a hamlet. S. (*bāṛā*).
باڼ *bānr*, s.m. Cordage made of palm-leaves.
باڼه *bānra*, s.f. The eyelash.
بانکیا *bānkiyā*, s.m. A fop, beau. H. (*bānkā*).
بانګ *bāng*, s.m. A call, cry, shout. P.
بانګیدل *bāngedal*, v.n. To low, bleat, bellow.
بانه *bāna*, s.f. An excuse, pretence, sham, pretext. P. (*bahāna*).
باور *bāwar*, s.m. Belief, faith, credit, trust. P.

باوسير *bāwsīr*, s.m. Hemorrhoids, piles. A. (*bawāsīr*).

باولي *bāolī*, s.f. The drag on which hawks, dogs, etc. are trained and taught to hunt. A well, with steps to the water. H. *bāolī-warkawul*, v.a. To initiate, train, teach.

باهر *bāhar*, ad. Outside, without, beyond, foreign. S.

باهو *bāhū*, s.m. An ornament for the arm.

بائيده *bā-īdah*, a. Fit, proper, necessary, suitable. ad. Necessarily, of necessity, it behoves.

بائيكر *bā-īkar*, s.m. Name of a shrub (*Adhatoda vasica*). H. (*bākar*).

بائيلل *bā-elal*, v.a. To fail, forfeit, lose. P. (*bākhtan*).

ببر *babar*, a. Hairy, shaggy. P.

ببوزي *babozai*, s.m. A fan made of palm leaves, a fan. Name of a bird, the kingfisher.

ببئي *baba-ī*, s.f. Name of a bird. An affectionate term for "mother."

بت *but*, s.m. An image, idol, figure, form, model. One of the walls that supports the cross-beam of a Persian wheel.

بتان *batān*, s.m. See پتان.

بتر *batar*, a. Worse, very bad. P. (*badtar*).

بتك *batak*, s.m. A water cruse, in the shape of a double convex disc, made of leather or pottery.

بتكي *batakai*, s.m. Dimin. of preceding.

بته *bata*, s.f. A heron, crane.

بتي *batī*, s.f. Glue, paste, starch, size.

بټ *baṭ*, s.m. A furnace, kiln; an iron pot or dish for roasting grain; bark, rind, husk; prosperity, good luck.

بټه *baṭa*, s.f. Husked or pounded barley.

بجز *bajuz*, p. Except, besides, save, without. P.

بجل *bujal*, s.m. Ankle-joint, knuckle-bone. P.

بڅخه *butskha*, s.f. A clothes-bag, bundle of clothes. T. (*buqcha*).

بڅخكي *butskhaka-ī*, s.f. A reticule, small bag for collyrium, needles, etc.

بڅري *batsarai*, بڅركي *batsarkai*, s.m. A spark, scintillation.

بچاو *bachāo*, s.m. Escape, protection, shelter, H. *bachawul*, v.a. To save, shelter, etc.

بچري *bachrai*, s.m. An ass's colt, young donkey.

بچكري *bachakarai*, s.m. The lash of a whip; end of a sling.

بچو *bachū*, in. Dear babe! Baby dear! Baby! A term of affectionate address to a child.

بچونګړي *bachūngaṛai*, s.m. A babe, infant, a very young animal.

بچوي *bachawai*, s.m. The lash of a whip; end of a sling; a band or ribbon for fastening women's hair; a tassel of braided cords attached to the back hair of women.

بچي *bachai*, s.m. A babe, infant, child, young one. P. (*bacha*).

بحث *bahs*, s.m. Argument, discussion, controversy. A.

بحر *bahr*, s.m. The ocean, sea. A.

بخت *bakht*, s.m. Fate, fortune, luck. P.

بخره *bakhra*, s.f. Lot, portion, share. P.

بخښ *bakhksh*, s.m. Lot, share, portion; bestowing, giving; forgiveness. P. (*bakhsh*).

بخښښ *bakhkshiksh*, s.m. Donation, gift, grant. P. (*bakhshish*).

بخښل *bakhkkhal* or *bakhkshal*, v.a. See ببښل. P. (*bakhshīdan*).

بخښنه *bakhkkhana*, s.f. Pardon, forgiveness, forgiving; giving, bestowing.

بخملئي *bakhmala-ī*, s.f. Name of an insect of a scarlet colour, the scarlet lady; called also *bībī-pāto*. (From A. *makhmal*).

بخيل *bakhīl*, s.m. A miser, niggard. a. Vicious, ill-tempered, spiteful, stingy. A.

بخيلي *ba<u>kh</u>īlī*, s.f. Avarice, stinginess; obstinacy, vice, ill-temper, spite.

بد *bad*, a. Bad, evil, vicious. P.

بدر *badar*, s.m. The silky cotton tree (*Bombax heptaphyllum*). *badar·kand*, or *badar·kā<u>n</u>rai*, s.m. The gum resin of the tree: used in medicine. The silky cotton is used as a stuffing for pillows.

بدرگه *badraga*, s.f. A convoy, escort, guide. A. (*badraqa*).

بدرئي *badra-ī*, s.f. A woman's name. *budrī*, s.f. A stumble, trip; loss, injury, damage.

بدعا *bad'uā*, s.f. A curse, malediction. P. (*bad d'uā*).

بدل *badal*, s.m. Exchange; revenge, retaliation. A. *badalawul*, v.a. To exchange, etc.

بدلمن *bad·laman*, a. Wanton, dissolute, unchaste.

بدله *badala*, s.f. Melody, music, tune.

بدن *badan*, s.m. The body. A.

بدي *badī*, s.f. Enmity, evil, mischief.

بڈائي *baḍā-ī*, s.f. Dignity, rank; magnitude, greatness. S. (*baṛā-ī*).

بڈگال *baḍagāl*, s.m. The silky down on the flower spike of the bullrush. H. (*baṛā gālā*). See لوخه.

بڈه *baḍa*, s.f. A bribe, douceur; the upper hem of a pair of trousers, through which passes the fastening band.

بر *bar*, a. High, upper, top; victorious, successful. s.m. A stroke of the moon, moonblast. *bar wahalai*, a. Moon-struck.

برابر *barābar*, a. Abreast, equal, even, level, alike, smooth, straight.

برايه *barāya*, ad. Last night, yesternight.

برباد *barbād*, a. Ruined, wasted, thrown away. P.

بربره *burbura*, s.f. A bubble. P. (*bulbulā*).

بربست *barbast*, s.m. Chattels, effects, goods. P.

بربنډ *barbanḍ*, a. Bare, naked, uncovered. P. (*barahna*).

برپا *barpā*, a. Raised, set on foot, commenced. P.

برج *bruj*, s.m. A turret, tower, bastion. P. (*burj*).

برجو *barjo*, s.f. A hone, whetstone. Also *barjo kā<u>n</u>rai*.

برڅير *bar<u>ts</u>er*, a. Clear, manifest, evident, visible.

برڅيرن *bar<u>ts</u>eran*, ad. Apparently, manifestly, visibly, clearly.

برخه *bra<u>kh</u>a*, s.f. See بخره.

برړه *baraṛa*, s.f. Name of a shrub (*Periploca aphylla*).

برطرف *bartaraf*, a. Apart, aside, dismissed, turned off, discharged. A.

برغ *bra<u>gh</u>*, s.m. A fold, layer, plait; duplication, multiplication, fold.

برغټ *bar<u>gh</u>uṭ*, s.m. A wild cat.

برغنډ *bar<u>gh</u>anḍ*, s.m. A notch, dent, nick.

برغو *bar<u>gh</u>o*, s.m. The cleaning rod of a gun.

برغوټي *bar<u>gh</u>oṭa-ī*, s.f. A disease of the parotid gland, mumps.

برغوږ *bar<u>gh</u>wag*, s.m. An ear-drop, pendant, or ring.

برغولي *bar<u>gh</u>olai*, s.m. A dish-cover, lid.

برغوني *bra<u>gh</u>ūnai*, s.m. A twin, one of twins.

برکت *barakat*, s.m. Blessing, prosperity, fortune. A.

برکتي *barakatī*, a. Blessed, fortunate, prosperous.

برګ *brag*, a. Spotted, speckled, streaked. s.m. A leper.

برګړندي *bargaṛandai*, s.m. Embracing, hugging, cuddling.

برګستوان *bargastawān*, s.m. Mail armour for a horse; sword proof trappings. P. (*bargastān*).

برګويټ *bargweṭ*, s.m. A man's name. One of the great ancestors of <u>Kh</u>aṭak clan.

برګه *barga*, s.f. A beam, rafter. H. (*bargā*).

برګي *bragai*, s.m. Leprosy; a leper.

برم *bram,* s.m. Force, power, strength; guard, protection. P. (*barm*).

برمته *baramta,* s.f. Reprisal, seizing the property or persons of an offending tribe or family in retaliation for injuries done, and as pledges or hostages for restitution or settlement.

برمنډ *barmanḍ,* a. See بربنډ.

برمه *barma,* s.f. An auger, gimlet, centre-bit or borer, worked with a bow and string. H. (*barmā*).

برند *brand,* a. Frowning, scowling, staring. P. (*barham*).

برندول *brandawul,* v.a. To frown, scowl.

برندي *barandai,* s.m. A spindle for twisting thread. A teetotum, spun by two strings pulled in opposite directions.

برني *baranai,* a. Stale, old, yesterday's.

بروړه *baroṛa,* s.f. A wood-louse; crab-louse; name of a venomous insect. Nettlerash, hives. *broṛah,* s.m. Mixed meal of pulses and cereals. See رارړه.

برونړۍ *barwanṛa-ī,* s.f. The socket in which the pivot of an irrigation wheel works.

بروي *barwai,* a. Viscid, glutinous, sticky, starchy.

بره *barrah,* s.m. A kid, lamb, sheep. P.

بره‌ګړه *bara-gaṛa,* s.f. Embrace, hug.

برهم *barham,* a. Confused, disconcerted, vexed. P.

بري *barai,* s.m. Victory, success, triumph.

بريت *bret,* s.m. The mustache. P. (*burut*). *brīt,* s.m. Boundary, limit, separation. P. (*burīd*).

بريږن *bregan,* s.m. The bleat of a goat or sheep.

بريښ *brekkh,* s.m. Piercing, lancing, pricking or stabbing pain; a throb, spasm, cramp, stitch; a cutting pain. P. (*burrish*).

بريښنا *brekkhnā,* s.f. brilliancy, lustre, splendour; lightning.

بريښيدل *brekkhedal,* v.n. To glitter, shine; lighten. A. (*baraq*).

بړاس *bṛās,* s.m. Heat, steam, vapour.

بړانده *baṛānḍa,* s.f. A conflagation, blaze.

بړبړ *baṛbaṛ,* ad. Often, repeatedly, frequently. P. (*bārbār*).

بړبړي *baṛbaṛai,* s.m. A prattler, gabbler, chatterbox.

بړبوکۍ *baṛbūka-ī,* s.f. A dust devil, whirlwind.

بړستن *bṛastan,* s.f. Coverlet, quilt, counterpane.

بړني *baṛanai,* s.m. Name of a tree.

بړوا *baṛwā,* s.m. A pimp. H. (*bhaṛwā*).

بړوټ *bṛūṭ,* s.m. Name of a grass (*Cyperus verticillatus*).

بړوس *bṛūs,* a. Angry, furious, savage, enraged. *bṛūs-wālai,* s.m. Anger, rage, wrath.

بړينڅغ *baṛenchagh,* s.m. A whirligig; a cross bar balanced on the top of an upright post, on which as a pivot it is made to revolve by the riders, who sit in chairs attached to the ends of the cross bar.

بز *buz,* s.m. A he-goat. P.

بزاز *bazāz,* s.m. Cloth-merchant, draper, mercer. P.

بزغاله *buzghālah,* s.m. A kid. P.

بزغلي *buzghalai,* s.m. A bud, sprout, young shoot.

بزه *baza,* s.f. Sin, crime. P. Name of a shrub. See بائيکر. *bza,* s.f. A she-goat; a curlew. P.

بژه *bjah,* a. Chopped, minced, cut up.

بس *bas,* a. Enough, plenty, sufficient.

بساط *bisāt,* s.m. A display, show, or spread of things, as furniture, merchandize, etc. bedding, sheeting, flooring. A.

بسمه *basma,* s.f. Indigo. S.

بسمل *bismil,* a. Sacrificed. *bismil kawul,* v.a. To sacrifice.

بسم الله *bismillah,* In the name of God. *bismillah kawul,* v.a. To commence, begin.

بسيا *basiyā,* a. Cultivated, peopled, inhabited. S

بشپړ *bashpar*, a. Complete, entire, perfect.

بشر *bashar*, s.m. Man, mankind. A.

بشره *bashra*, s.f. Face, visage, countenance.

بشري *basharī*, a. Human, of man.

بشکه *bushka*, s.f. Name of a plant, used as a pot-herb; goosefoot (*Chenopodium album*).

بشنج *bashanj*, s.m. Character, reputation, name.

بښل *bakkhal*, v.a. To give, pardon, forgive, excuse. See بخښل

بښنه *bakkhana*, s.f. A gift, pardon, forgiveness.

بط *bat*, s.m. A duck. A.

بعد *b'ad*, ad. After, subsequently. A.

بعيد *b'aīd*, a. Far, remote. A.

بغارګ *bghārg*, a. Double, duplex, two-fold.

بغاره *baghāra*, s.f. A scream, shriek.

بغبغو *baghbagho*, s.m. The rice bird (*Ardea torra*).

بغدر *baghdar*, s.m. Hammer, mallet. S. (*mugdar*).

بغرږ *bagharg*, s.m. Rebound, recoil, return. Double, duplex.

بغرګه *bgharga*, s.f. A breach, gap; a deep wound. P. (*bughāra*).

بغري *bagharai*, s.m. A pimp; term of abuse. *baghara-ī*, s.f. A mortar; *vulva*; a term of abuse. P. (*ghubāra*).

بغض *bughz*, s.m. Hatred, malice, rancour, spite. A.

بغل *baghal*, s.m. The armpit, side; embrace. P.

بغير *baghair*, ad. Besides, except, without. A.

بقا *baqā*, s.f. Eternity, perpetuity. A.

بقال *baqāl*, s.m. A corn chandler, grocer, A.

بک *bak*, s.m. Jabber, gabble, prattle, talk. S.

بک بکي *bak-bakai*, s.m. A gabbler, prattler, chatterbox.

بکاره *bakārah*, s.m. Courier, messenger. H. (*bakārā*).

بکاول *bakāwul*, s.m. A cook, victualler. P.

بکاينړ *bakāyanr*, s.m. Name of a tree (*Melia sempervirens*). H. (*bukāyan*).

بکري *bakra-ī*, s.f. A flint, quartz.

بګلولي *bagalola-ī*, s.f. A bogy, goblin, scarecrow, hag.

بګلي *baglai*, s.m. A crane, heron; the rice bird. H. (*baglā*).

بګنيدل *bugnedal*, v.n. To shy, start, fear. *bugnawul*, v.a. To frighten, scare, start.

بګوړه *bagora*, s.f. A kind of cheese; dry curds; the Persian *qurūt*.

بګوه *bagwa*, s.f. Red ochre, red clay.

بل *bul*, a. Another, other, different. *bal*, a. Burnt, fired, ignited, kindled, lighted.

بلا *balā*, s.f. Affliction, calamity, misfortune.

بلابتر *balā-batar*, s.m. Lumber, trash, rubbish.

بلاربه *blārba*, a. Pregnant, with young.

بلاربيدل *blārbedal*, v.n. To conceive, become pregnant. *blārbawul*, v.a. To make pregnant.

بلاغند *balāghund*, s.m. Name of a tree and its fruit (*Ægle marmelos*).

بلانړه *bilānrah*, s.m. A moan, groan, wail.

بلاوه *bulāwa*, s.f. Mistake, error. H. (*bhūl*).

بلبل *bulbul*, s.m. A nightingale; a shrike. A kind of dance, a reel. P.

بلد *balad*, s.m. A guide, resident. a. Acquainted, familiar. P.

بلغاک *bulghāk*, s.m. The twitter of birds.

بلغم *balgham*, s.m. Phlegm, mucus. P.

بلکه *balki*, ad. But, nay, rather. A.

بلګه *balga*, s.f. A clue, trace, track, etc. of stolen goods.

بلل *balal*, v.a. To call, summon, convoke. H. (*bulānā*).

بلماز *bilmāz*, a. Prayerless, profane, unholy, impure, corrupt. P. (*be-namāz*).

بلمګي *bilmagai*, } a. Saltless, tasteless, without flavour. (Corrupt: of *be-mālga*).
بلمنګي *bilmangai*, }

بلند *buland*, a. High, lofty, tall. P.

بلندي *bulandai*, s.m. An eminence, height, elevation.

بلو *balaw*, s.m. A hone, razor-strop, whetstone.

بلوا *balwā*, s.f. Mutiny, riot, tumult. A.

بلوڅ *balots*, s.m. A Baloch; the tribe.

بلودل *blodal*, v.a. To chafe, fret, abrade, graze, rub, touch; to vex, annoy, worry. P. (*burīdan.*)

بلور *bilaur*, s.m. Crystal, glass. P.

بلوس *blos*, s.m. A rub, graze, touch; annoyance, vexation.

بلوسيدل *blosedal*, v.a. See بلودل.

بلوغت *bulūghat*, s.m. Puberty, adolescence, youth. A.

بلول *balawul*, v.a. To burn, kindle, set alight, fire, ignite.

بلونګړي *bilūngaṛai*, s.m. A squirrel.

بله *bala*, s.f. A javelin, dart, pike. H. (*ballā*).

بلۍ *bala-ī*, s.f. The edge of a roof, eaves; door-bolt, boat-hook, barge-pole. H. (*ballī*).

بليدل *baledal*, v.n. To burn, blaze, take fire, ignite. H. (*balnā.*)

بليږدل *blegdal*, v.a. To swaddle, swathe.

بم *bam*, s.m. A bass, deep, or hollow sound. A.

بمبره *bambara*, s.f. A wasp, hornet.

بُن *ba-an*, s.f. A cotemporary or rival wife; each of a man's several wives is *ba-an* to the other. The children by one wife are *ba-anzī* to those by the others. See بُنزي.

بنا *binā*, s.f. Preparation; foundation, building, edifice. A.

بنات *banāt*, s.m. Broad-cloth, woollen cloth. H.

بنبل *banbal*, s.m. The beard of grasses, etc.

بنبوله *banbola*, s.f. A wicker box coated with clay for the storing of grain.

بنج *banj*, s.m. The horse chestnut tree, the fruit. *banaj*, s.m. Trade, merchandise. S.

بنجاري *banjārī*, s.m. A trader, peddler, grain merchant. S. (*banjārā*).

بنجخ *banjakh*, s.m. Name of a plant, the seed of which contains cowitch.

بنجۍ *banja-ī*, s.f. The Cassia tree.

بند *band*, s.m. A band, fastening, knot, tie; a joint, knuckle; arrest, captivity, imprisonment; artifice, dodge, trick. P.

بندر *bandar*, s.m. An emporium, sea port. P.

بندلۍ *bindla-ī*, s.f. A flute, fife, whistle.

بندڼ *bandanr*, s.m. Promise, covenant. S. (*bandhan*).

بندوخ *bandūkh*, s.m. A gun, matchlock. T. (*bandūq*).

بندوبست *bandobast*, s.m. Arrangement, management, settlement. P.

بنده *bandah*, s.m. A servant, slave, bondsman; a creature. P.

بندي *bandī*, s.m. A captive, prisoner. S. *banda-ī*, s.f. An ornament for the neck; an ornamental shoulder sling worn by women. S.

بُنزي *ba-anzai*, s.m. Step-son; son of the husband by another wife. (See پرکټي). *ba-anza-ī*, s.f. Step-daughter; a former or other wife's daughter.

بنګ *bang*, s.m. The hemp plant (*Cannabis Indicus*). H. (*bhang*).

بنګي *bangī*, s.m. One addicted to the use of bang, or any other intoxicating drug; a drunkard.

بنګښ *bangakkh*, s.m. Name of a Pathan tribe located about Kohat.

بنګول *bangawul*, v.a. To taint, corrupt, pollute.

بنۍ *bana-ī*, s.f. A wallet or bag made of an entire kid's skin; bellows made of a pair of such skins attached to one nozzle.

بنياد *bunyād*, s.m. Base, origin, foundation. A.

بنړ *banr*, s.m. A wood, forest. S. (*ban*).

بنړمانو *banr-mānū*, s.m. A wild man, man of the woods. S. (*ban-manukh*).

بورجل *borjal*, s.f. An abode, home, house, resort; a place of resort, assignment, or meeting. A. (*marja'*).

بورګي *baurgai*, s.m. A panther, small leopard.

بورنه *bornah*, s.m. Dredging, flour, meal, etc. used to sprinkle upon meat, dough, etc. Also بورنړه.

بوره *būra*, s.f. A woman who has lost her child by death.

بوري *baura-ī*, s.f. A bunion, corn.

بوړه *bauṛa*, s.f. An elevated plateau, table-land, or flat bit of land on a hill side.

بوړي *būṛai*, s.m. The cog of a Persian wheel. a. Chipped, cracked (as a cup); clipped, slit, split (as the nose or ears). *būṛa-ī*, s.f. Name of a disease (*prolapsus ani*).

بوزه *boza*, s.f. Fermented liquor, beer. P.

بوزينه *bozīna*, s.f. Leather of a red colour, prepared from goat skins. P.

بوږ *bog*, a. Hoarse, rough, husky voice. s.m. A sore throat, aphonia, loss of voice.

بوس *būs*, s.m. Chaff, chopped straw. H. (*bhūs*).

بوساړه *būsāṛa*, s.f. A stack of būs.

بوستان *bostān*, s.m. A flower-garden. P.

بوښت *bokkht*, a. Sticky, adhesive. s.m. A quicksand, bog, quagmire.

بوښتنه *bokkhtana*, s.f. A bog, quicksand.

بوغ *būgh*, s.m. A wooden bowl or cup.

بوق *būq*, A bugle, clarion. A.

بوکه *boka*, s.f. A water-bucket. H.

بوکي *bokī*, s.m. Name of an Afghan clan.

بوګري *bogarai*, s.m. Church land, glebe; land given to priests and holy men free of rent; ploughing and sowing, free of cost, for priests, etc. or for one another.

بول *baul*, s.f. Urine. A. *waṛa-baul kawul*, v.a. To make water, urinate. *loya-baul kawul*, v.a. To go to stool, ease oneself.

بولاق *bolāq*, s.m. An ornament for the nose. H.

بنړه *banṛa*, s.f. A quill, large feather; a feather.

بنړکه *banṛaka*, s.f. A feather, small feather.

بنړئ *banṛa-ī*, s.f. Name of a tree; mistletoe. *banṛai*, a. Red-haired, rufus; shock-headed.

بنړيه *banṛiyah*, s.m. A Hindu shopkeeper. S. (*banniyā*).

بنفشه *binafsha*, s.f. A violet, the plant. P.

بو *bū* or *bo*, s.m. Odour, scent, smell. P. *baw*, s.m. A goblin, scare-crow.

بوتکي *būtkī*, s.f. Name of a gold coin; Belgian ducat.

بوتلل *botlal*, v.a. To carry away, conduct, lead, convey. Only applied to animate objects. See بيول.

بوته *bota*, s.f. Carrying away, leading off, etc. See برمته.

بوتي *botai*, s.m. A young camel. P.

بوټ *būt*, a. Surly, cross, sullen, ill-tempered. Also *sūṭ-būṭ*.

بوټسوړي *būṭsūṛī*, s.m. Chaff, bran, husks, shell, etc.

بوټي *būṭai*, s.m. A plant, herb, bush, shrub. *būṭī*, pl. Drugs, vegetable medicines; flowers embroidered, painted, or carved. H. (*būṭā*).

بوجه *būja*, s.f. A bung, cork, stopper, plug.

بوڅکۍ *būtska-ī*, s.f. The lobe of the ear.

بود *būd*, s.m. Existence, being; profit, gain.

بوده *būda*, s.f. (In weaving) the woof of the web. P.

بوډاګي *būḍāgai*, s.m. A decrepid old man. H. (*būṛhā*).

بور *baur*, s.m. A panther, leopard. *bor*, s.m. A dent, chip, flaw, fracture. a. grey, brown; a grey horse. H. (*bhūrā*). *būr*, s.m. Husk, skin, chaff; the linear leaves of the pine, tamarisk, and similar trees. A father who has lost a child by death.

بورا *baurā*, s.m. A large black bee. S. (*bhaunṛā*).

بولقه **bolqa**, s.f. A sheet or mantle with eyelets to see through : it is a woman's outdoor dress, and covers the whole body from head to foot : it is only used by women living in cities or large towns. A. (*burqa'*).

بوم **būm**, s.m. A country ; an owl ; a native or home-bred person ; a guide. a. Acquainted, familiar, habituated. P.

بومیا **būmiyā**, s.m. A conductor, guide, resident.

بونسټ **bonsaṭ**, s.m. Foundation, origin, root ; name of a plant.

بونگه **būnga**, s.f. Black-mail, ransom.

بونر **būnr**, s.m. A disease of the nose, ozœna ; one afflicted with the disease. Cordage made of palm leaves, and used for netting of beds, etc. H. (*bān*). **bonr**, s.m. A buzz, hum (as of a bee or fly).

بونریدل **bonredal**, v.n. To buzz, hum ; putrefy, rot, become fly-blown, tainted, etc. **bonrawul**, v.a. To taint, fly-blow, pollute, etc.

بوهار **būhār**, s.m. Spring. P. (*bahār*).

بوهاري **būhārai**, s.m. A weanling, an animal newly weaned from its mother.

بویه **boyah**, a. Necessary, proper, indispensable. ad. Necessarily, properly, fitly.

به **ba**, A particle used as the sign of the future and continuative past tenses. Also written بـ.

بها **bahā**, s.f. Cost, price, value. A.

بهادر **bahādur**, s.m. A champion, hero. a. Courageous, brave. P.

بهادري **bahādurī**, s.f. Bravery, courage. **bahādurai**, s.m. A little hero, a coward.

بهانر **bihānr**, s.m. A colt, young horse.

بهانیه **bahāniyah**, a. Costly, expensive, valuable, precious.

بهبود **bihbūd**, a. Advantageous, profitable. P.

بهبودي **bihbūdī**, s.f. Advantage, profit, gain, good. A large knife, dagger.

بهتان **buhtān**, s.m. Calumny, defamation ; lying. A.

بهتر **bihtar**, a. Better, preferable, well. P.

بهتري **bihtarī**, s.f. Advantage, welfare.

بهره **bahra**, s.f. Lot, share ; gain, profit. P.

بهشت **bihikkht**, s.m. Heaven, paradise. P. (*bihisht*).

بهگنر **bhaganr**, s.m. A fly, gadfly.

بهم **baham**, ad. Together, one with another. P.

بهنه **bahna**, s.f. A top, whip-top. P.

بهي **baha-ī**, s.f. A masonry tank or reservoir, with steps leading down to the water. **bihī**, s.f. A quince, the tree. P.

بهیدل **bahedal**, v.n. To float, flow, stream, pass, rush, gush. s. (*bahnā*).

بي **be**, p. Without, void of. Used in composition as a privative particle, and equivalent to the English prefixes *in-*, *im-*, *ir-*, *un-*, etc., and the affix *-less*. Ex. *be-hokkh*, insensible ; *be-ṣabr*, impatient ; *be-adab*, irreverent ; *be-wafā*, unfaithful ; *be-shakk*, doubtless, etc. P.

بیا **biyā**, ad. Again, afresh, once more. P. (*bāz*).

بیابان **bayābān**, s.m. A desert, waste, wilderness. P.

بیاتي **biyātī**, s.m. Scissors, shears, clippers.

بیاسته **biyāsta**, s.f. Cable, cord, rope ; the rope of a Persian wheel, to which the water-pots are fastened.

بیاموندل **biyāmūndal**, v.a. To acquire, gain, get, find, recover, regain, obtain.

بیان **bayān**, s.m. Explanation, recital, relation. P.

بیانول **bayānawul**, v.a. To explain, recite, relate, tell, say, describe.

بیایل **biyāyal**, v.a. Def. in past ten. See بیول.

بیبي **bībī**, s.f. A lady, married woman. H. *bebe*, in. Sister dear ! (to an elder sister).

بیرتي **be-partai** or *be-pratai*, a. Gormandizing, surfeiting ; gluttonous, greedy.

بيت *bait*, s.m. A couplet, verse; house, temple. A. *bet*, s.m. A cane, rattan. S.

بيټ *baiṭ*, s.m. The name of one of the three sons of Kais. He is also called بټن *baṭan*, and the tribe descended from him بټني *baṭanī*. See كيس.

بيخ *bekh*, s.m. A root; origin, foundation. P.

بيخرتي *be-khratai*, a. Excessive, much, very much; unseasonable, inopportune, out of time; unbounded, without limit.

بيد *bed*, s.m. A willow tree. P.

بيدار *baidār*, a. Awake, vigilant, alert, watchful; conscious, sensible. P. (*bedār*).

بيداري *baidārī*, s.f. Wakefulness, sleeplessness; vigilance, alertness, watching. P.

بيدو *bedū*, ad. Identical, the same, exactly.

بيده *beda*, s.f. The coil or twist into which lucerne, vetches, etc. are rolled, preparatory to storing for winter use. *bīdah*, a. Asleep, sleeping.

بيديا *bediyā*, s.f. A desert, wilderness. A. (*bādiyā*).

بيرته *biyarta*, ad. Back, back again, return; aside, apart, away.

بيرغ *bairagh*, s.m. Banner, standard. A. (*bairaq*).

بيرنړ *beranr*, s.m. A kind of grass.

بيره *bera*, s.f. Name of a thorny bush (*zizyphus jujuba*); the berry. S. (*ber*). A fetter, manacle. H.

بيړه *beṛa*, s.f. A float, raft. S. (*beṛā*).

بيړئ *beṛa-ī*, s.f. A boat, barge.

بيزل *bezal*, v.a. To darn, hem, baste.

بيزار *bezār*, a. Annoyed, vexed; disgusted, sick of. P.

بيزو *bīzo*, s.m. A monkey.

بيساک *baisāk*, s.m. Name of the first Hindu month. April-May. S. (*baisākh*).

بيستئ *biyasta-ī*, s.f. Coarse cloth, canvass, baize.

بيسر *bīsar*, s.m. A small nose-ring, worn as an ornament by women. H.

بيش *besh*, a. More; superior (in comp. only). P.

بيشه *besha*, s.f. A forest, wood. P.

بيعه *bai'a*, s.f. Barter, exchange. trade. A. (*bai'*).

بيعانه *bai'āna*, s.f. Deposit, security, earnest-money.

بيک *biyak*, s.m. Harpoon, five-pronged fork.

بيگا *begā*, s.f. See بيگاه.

بيگار *begār* or *bīgār*, s.m. A pressed labourer (with or without pay). H.

بيگاري *bīgārī*, s.f. Forced labour. s.m. A pressed labourer. H.

بيگانه *begānah*, a. Foreign, strange, unknown. P.

بيگانگي *begānagī*, s.f. Strangeness, being foreign, not of the same house, not domestic. P.

بيگاني *begānai*, a. Last preceding, last past, preceding, stale, last night's, yesterday's.

بيگاه *begāh*, s.m. The evening. Also بيگا *begā*.

بيل *biyal* or *bel*, a. Apart, distinct, separate. H. (*byorā*). *bel*, s.m. Name of a tree and its fruit (*Ægle marmelos*); a creeper, climbing plant.

بيلاو *belāw*, s.m. A hone, razor strop.

بيلتون *biyaltūn*, s.m. Absence, separation; difference, distinction.

بيلچه *belcha*, s.f. A mattock, hoe. P.

بيلک *belak*, s.m. A wedding-gift from bridegroom to the bride; an enemy, rival, guardian; an arrow tip. P.

بيلگه *belga*, s.f. See بلگه.

بيله *bela*, s.f. An island, delta, sandbank.

بيم *bīm*, s.m. Awe, fear, dread. P.

بيمار *bīmār*, a. Sick, ill. s.m. A sick man. P.

بيماري *bīmārī*, s.f. Disease, sickness. P.

بينا *bīnā*, a. Seeing, having sight. P.

بيند *bend*, s.m. See بيده *beda*.

بينش **bensh**, s.m. A beam, rafter.
بيوره **bewrah**, a. Clear, manifest, simple, plain.
بيول **bīwul**, v.t. To conduct, lead, take along, convey. Applied only to animate objects. See بوتلل. P. (*bi-bur*)?
بيوه **bewa**, s.f. A widow. P.
بيه **baia**, s.f. Price, value. A. (*bai'*).
بيهودگي **behūdagī**, s.f. Absurdity, nonsense, folly.
بيهوده **behūdah**, a. Absurd, idle, foolish, frivolous. P.

پ

پ **pe**, The third letter of the Pukkhto alphabet. It is frequently used for ف. Ex. آپرين *āparīn* for آفرين *āfarīn*, etc.
پَ **pa**, p. By, with, for; in, into, within; above, on, upon. Also written په. P. (*bā*).
پا **pā**, s.m. The foot, leg. Used in comp. only. Ex. *pā-band*, s.m. A hobble, fetter. a. Bound, clogged, fettered, tethered. P.
پاپړه **pāpra**, s.f. The herb fumatory (*Fumaria officinalis*). H. (*phāphrī*).
پاتو **pāto**, s.f. Name of a scarlet insect. See بخملي.
پاتي **pātai**, a. Left, remaining; abiding, staying.
پاتيدل **pātedal**, v.n. To remain, survive, be left. Also *pātai-kedal*.
پاټي **pāṭa-ī**, s.f. The cup or pan of a sling or pellet bow.
پاڅول **pātsawul**, v.a. To arouse, awaken, stir up; raise, set up, elevate.
پاڅيدل **pātsedal**, v.n. To arise, rise, get up, sit up.
پاداش **pādāsh**, s.m. Revenge, requital, retaliation. P.
پادشاه **pādshāh**, s.m. Sovereign, king, emperor. P.
پادشاهي **pādshāhī**, s.f. Royal, regal; empire, kingdom. P.
پارا **pārā**, s.f. Mercury, quicksilver. S.
پارچنګ **pārchang**, s.m. A ladder, steps, stairs.
پارچه **pārcha**, s.f. A bit, fragment, scrap, shred; the water trough of an irrigation well. P.
پارو **pārū**, s.m. A kind of rake.
پارول **pārawul**, v.a. To annoy, vex, disturb, irritate, excite, stir up.
پاره **pāra**, s.f. A bit, scrap, slip, shred. P.
پاړبنج **pāṛbanj**, s.m. Name of a tree, horse chesnut.
پاړو **pāṛū**, s.m. A snake charmer. *pāṛū-k.*, v.a. To charm.
پاړه **pāṛa**, s.f. A patch of unploughed land in a field; unfinished work, incomplete action; a kind of rake.
پاړي **pāṛai**, s.m. The hog deer (*cervus porcinus*). H. (*pāṛhā*).
پازه **pāzah**, s.m. Action, effect, operation, result.
پازيکه **pāzīkah**, a. See پاکيزه
پاس **pās**, p. Above, aloft, on, upon. s.m. Attention, observation, watch. P. An ointment made of oil and lime, and used as a remedy for mangy camels.
پاسخ **pāsukh**, s.m. Answer, reply. P.
پاسلول **pāslawul**, v.a. To entrust, commit, recommend.
پاسنګ **pāsang**, s.m. Balance, weight. P.
پاسني **pāsanai**, a. Upper, higher, high, superior.
پاسو **pāsū**, a. Ill-bred, vulgar, low, mean.
پاسوان **pāswān**, s.m. A shepherd, watchman, guard, sentinel. P. (*pāsbān*).
پاسواني **pāswānī**, s.f. Guarding, watching, keeping; protection; occupation of a shepherd.

پاشنه *pā<u>sh</u>na*, s.f. The heel of a door; the socket in which it revolves; the heel. P. (*pā<u>sh</u>nā*).

پاښ *pā<u>kkh</u>*, s.m. Name of a mountain near the Kā₅I<u>gh</u>ar hill in the Ta<u>kh</u>ti-Sulaimān range. It is described as the spot first colonized by the Pu<u>kkh</u>tūn nation on their arrival from the West.

پاغنده *pā<u>gh</u>unda*, s.f. A ball or roll of carded cotton ready for spinning. P.

پاک *pāk*, a. Clean, pure; holy, innocent. P.

پاکلمن *pāk-laman*, a. Chaste, modest; holy, pure. P. (*pāk-dāman*).

پاکول *pākawul*, v.a. To cleanse, purify, wash.

پاکي *pākī*, s.f. Cleanliness, purity; cleaning, purifying; chastity, innocence; a razor. P.

پاکيزه *pākīzah*, a. Chaste, clean, pure, holy. P.

پال *pāl*, s.m. Abstinence, diet, regimen; augury, omen, presage. A. (*fāl*).

پالان *pālān*, s.m. A pack saddle. P.

پالک *pālak*, s.m. Garden spinach. H.

پالل *pālal*, v.a. To cherish, rear, educate, protect. S. (*pālnā*).

پالنګ *pālang*, s.m. A bedstead, bed. S. (*palang*).

پالوده *pālūda*, s.f. A kind of vermicelli. P. (*fālūda*). A kind of wild plum.

پاله *pāla*, s.f. A ploughshare. S. (*phāl*).

پالهنګ *pālhang*, s.m. A tether; a log tied to the neck of an ox, etc. to prevent its straying. P.

پاليز *pālez*, s.m. A melon field. P. (*fālez*).

پانشنبه *pān<u>sh</u>amba*, s.f. Friday. P. (*panj-<u>sh</u>amba*).

پانه *pāna*, s.f. A wedge for splitting wood; thumbscrew, mode of torture. H. (*phanī*).

پانړ *pā<u>nr</u>*, s.m. A cliff, precipice, steep bank.

پانړه *pā<u>nr</u>a*, s.f. A leaf, leaf of a tree or book. S. (*pannā*).

پاو *pāo*, s.m. A fourth, quarter. S.

پائي *pā-ī*, s.f. A halter, leading string; pins used by weavers in weaving. H. *pāe*, s.m. The foot. P.

پاياب *pāyāb*,
پاياو *pāyāo*, } a. Fordable, within depth. P.

پايابه *pāyāba*, s.f. A float, a buoy.

پائيدل *pa-edal*, v.n. To endure, last, remain, tarry, survive. P. (*pā-īdan*).

پائيکو *pa-eko*, s.f. A crusher, pounder, thresher, flail, roller.

پائيله *pā-ela*, s.f. An anklet with bells; an ornament for the feet.

پائيمال *pā-emāl*, a. Trampled, ruined, crushed.

پاينده *pāyandah*, a. Constant, durable, lasting.

پائينڅه *pā-en<u>ts</u>a*, s.f. The leg of a pair of drawers. P. (*pā-en<u>ch</u>a*).

پائينک *pā-enak*, s.m. The mounting at the end of a sword scabbard.

پايه *pāya*, s.f. A step; dignity, rank; foundation. P.

پپئي *pupa-ī*, s.f. A kiss on the cheek.

پت *pat*, s.m. Character, reputation, honour. S.

پتاو *pitāo*, s.m. Sunshine, sun's rays. P. (*partau*).

پتري *patrai*, s.m. A clamp, metal binding; the boss of a shield. H. (*pattar*).

پتنګ *patang*, s.m. A moth; paper kite. S.

پتنه *patna*, s.f. Anarchy, civil war, strife; sedition, rebellion. P. (*fitna*).

پتنړ *pata<u>nr</u>*, s.m. The stand of a spinning wheel; a ferry, passage across a river. H. (*pātan*).

پتون *patūn*, s.m. The thigh, shank.

پته *pata*, s.f. A card, ticket.

پتيره *patīra*, s.f. Unleavened bread.

پټ *paṭ*, s.m. Delirium, madness; bark of a tree. *puṭ*, a. Concealed, secret, hidden, covered.

پټ پټانړي *puṭ-puṭā<u>nr</u>ai*, s.m. Name of a game; hide and seek.

پتخ *paṭakh*, a. Hard, tough; decayed, worn. s.m. A razor strop.

پتکه *paṭka*, s.f. A girdle, sash, waist-cloth. S. (*paṭkā*.)

پتکي *paṭkai*, s.m. A small turban. *paṭakī*, ad. Immediately, instantly, on the spot; the same, very same, identical.

پتگني *puṭgana-ī*, s.f. Ambuscade, ambush, lair, cover.

پتو *paṭū*, s.m. A kind of woollen cloth. S.

پتوار *paṭwār*, s.m. Bailiff, land steward, village accountant. H.

پتوسکي *paṭūskai*, a. A little, very little, some, few.

پتول *puṭawul*, v.a. To conceal, cover, hide, veil.

پته *paṭa*, s.f. A shoulder belt, sword belt.

پتي *paṭai*, s.m. A field, patch of cultivated land. *paṭa-ī*, s.f. The alphabet; writing tablet; bandage, plaister.

پتيدل *puṭedal*, v.n. To abscond, hide.

پتيره *paṭera*, s.f. A beam, rafter, large timber.

پتيلنړ *paṭelanṛ*, s.m. See پليتنړ. H. (*paṭelā*).

پجه *paja*, s.f. A furnace, kiln. H. (*pajāwā*).

پڅ *pa-aṯs* or *p-uṯs*, a. Blunt, dull, obtuse.

پڅاڼړي *piṯsāṉṛai*, a. Small, little, few, some.

پڅکه *piṯska*, s.f. Corner, end, nib, point.

پڅيدل *pa-aṯsedal* or *p-uṯsedal*, v.n. To become blunt, obtuse, dull.

پچنه *pac͟hana*, s.f. A scratch, prick, prod, cut; a scarifier, cupping instrument.

پچني *pac͟hanai*, a. Scarified, cupped, pricked.

پچواړي *pac͟hwāṛa-ī*, s.f. Heel ropes for a horse. H.

پچه *puc͟ha*, s.f. Orbicular dung (as of camels, deer, etc); a lot or share of land; a ripple or catspaw on the surface of water.

پخ *pa-akh* or *p-ukh*, s.m. Scurf, dandriff, scab, scale. *pak͟h*, s.m. A hiss, spit (as of a cat, etc.). *pak͟h-wahal*, v.a. To hiss, spit (as a cat).

پخپله *pak͟hpula*, ad. Spontaneously, voluntarily, of own accord.

پخته *puk͟htah*, a. Baked, cooked, dressed, ripe; shrewd, expert, knowing; firm, solid, strong. P.

پخساک *pak͟hsāk*, s.m. Distress, grief, sorrow, solicitude. P. (*pak͟hs͟hā*).

پخسول *pak͟hsawul*, v.a. To distress, annoy, trouble, worry.

پخسه *pak͟hsa*, s.f. Stiff clay or mud, used to build walls; mire, mud, slush.

پخسيدل *pak͟hsedal*, v.n. To desire, fret, pine, yearn, long.

پخلا *pak͟hulā*, a. Appeased, conciliated, pacified, reconciled, on speaking terms.

پخلي *pak͟halai*, a. Cooked, prepared, dressed; cooking, dressing, preparing (food); firm, solid, sound; experience, maturity, ripeness. *puk͟halai*, s.m. the hooping cough.

پخوا *pak͟hwā*, a. Former, previous, prior. ad. Before, ere now, previously.

پخواني *pak͟hwānai*, a. Ancient, former, preceding.

پخول *pak͟hawul*, v.a. To cook, dress, prepare.

پخوندي *pak͟hwandai*, s.m. A button hole, loop; an ornament for the feet, anklet.

پخه *pa-ak͟ha* or *p-uk͟ha*, s.f. Chaff, husk, skin; leafy covering of the ear of Indian corn.

پخي *pa-ak͟hai* or *p-uk͟hai*, a. Scabby, scurfy.

پخيدل *pak͟hedal*, v.n. To ripen, mature; boil; suppurate.

پخيل *pak͟hiyal*, s.m. Perspiring, sweating.

پدود *padod*, ad. As if, just as, like, similarly. P.

پديد *padīd*, a. Clear, evident, manifest. P.

پډه *paḍa*, s.f. A species of willow.

پر *par*, s.m. A feather, quill; wing; the flat board of a water or other wheel. S. *pur*, a. Complete, full, loaded (in comp. only). P. *parr*, s.m. The whirr of a snipe, quail, etc. taking wing. H. (*phurr*). *pri*, p. On, upon, atop (in comp.). See پري

پراټه *parāṭa*, s.f. A kind of bread made in thin layers of pastry. H. (*parāṭhā*).

پراچه *parāchah*, s.m. A pedlar, hawker, travelling merchant; mule driver; descendant of a Hindu converted to Islam.

پراچګي *parāchaga-ī*, s.f. A female of the preceding.

پراګنده *parāgandah*, a. Dispersed, scattered. P.

پرانتل *prānatal*, v.a. To loose, open, undo, untie. P. (*farākhtan, farāzīdan*).

پرت *prat*, a. Absurd, fruitless, idle, vain; distant, far, remote.

پرتاب *partāb*, s.m. Bowshot, gunshot, range of an arrow, etc. P.

پرتل *partal*, s.m. Baggage for a journey, baggage of an army. H. Name of a game, marbles.

پرتوړ *partūg*, s.m. See پرتوګ

پرتوغاښ *partūghākkh*, s.m. The band or string for tying the *partūg*.

پرتوګ *partūg*, s.m. Loose trowsers, drawers.

پرچتي *parchaṭa-ī*, s.f. Thatch or coping of a mud wall, eaves. H. (*parchhatī*).

پرخم *parkham*, s.m. A tassel, tuft; the tuft at the end of a cow's tail. P. (*parcham*).

پُرخه *pa-arkha*, s.f. Dew, hoar frost. *parkha*, s.f. A boulder, rock.

پرداخت *pardākht*, s.m. Attention, service, care. P.

پرداز *pardāz*, s.m. Finishing, performing (in comp.). P.

پرده *parda*, s.f. A veil, curtain, screen; secrecy, privacy. P.

پردي *pradai*, a. Foreign, strange. H. (*pardes*).

پرزو *pirzo*, a. Becoming, fit, proper, suitable; inclined, partial, longing. P. (*pazīr*).

پرزول *parzawul*, v.a. To overthrow, floor; struggle, wrestle.

پرزوه *pirzawa*, s.f. Desire, wish, bent, fancy.

پرزيدل *parzedal*, v.n. To be floored, thrown, upset, prostrated, etc. in wrestling.

پرسان *pursān*, s.m. Asking, enquiry. P.

پرست *parast*, s.m. Adorer, worshipper (in comp.). P.

پرستي *parastī*, s.f. Worship, devotion, adoration. P.

پرسش *pursish*, s.m. Inquiry, interrogation. P.

پرش *prash*, s.m. A snort, sniff; sneeze.

پرشکال *parshakāl*, s.m. The hot weather rains; rainy season; name of the fourth Hindu month. July-August. S. (*barshakāl*).

پرغز *parghaz*, s.m. Convulsion, fainting fit, hysterics.

پرغزي *parghazī*, a. Stunned, faint, senseless, convulsed.

پرکار *purkār*, a. Coarse, thick, fat; well made. P.

پرکټي *parkaṭai*, s.m. A step-son: wife's son by a former husband.

پرکي *parkai*, s.m. A butterfly.

پرګار *pargār*, s.m. A pair of compasses. P.

پرګنه *pargana*, s.f. A district, province, shire. P.

پرنا *parnā*, s.f. A doze, nap; nodding, sleeping. *parnā-wṛal*, v.a. To doze, nap, nod, sleep.

پرناله *parnāla*, s.f. A gutter, drain, scupper. H.

پرنج *pranj*, پرنجي *pranjai*, s.m. A sneeze.

پرنجيدل *pranjedal*, v.n. To sneeze.

پرنړ *pranr*, s.m. Curdled, sour, or turned milk. a. Clotted, curdled (as blood, etc.).

پرو *paro*, s.m. A hot wind. S. (*purwā*).

پروا *parwā*, s.f. Anxiety, care, concern; dread, fear; wish, desire. P.

پروانه *parwāna*, s.f. An order, license, pass, warrant. P.

پروت *prot*, a. Prostrate, fallen, lying down.

پرور *parwar*, a. Cherisher, protector (in comp. only). P.

پروردګار *parwardagār*, s.m. The nourisher, God. P.

پروردہ *parwardah*, a. Cherished, nourished, bred. s.m. Dependent, protegé. P.

پرورش *parwarish*, s.m. Maintenance, support, patronage; cherishing, nourishing. P.

پرورل *parwaral*, v.a. To cherish, foster, feed, support. P. (*parwardan*).

پروړ *proṛ*, s.m. Chaff; husk of Indian corn.

پروړه *proṛa*, s.f. Chaff; husk of rice, millet, etc.

پروسکال *paroskāl*, ad. Last year.

پروسکني *parosganai*, a. Last year's, of last season.

پرولل *prolal*, | v.a. To barter, exchange, sell,
پرووُل *prowul*, | trade. P. (*farokhtan*).

پرون *parūn*, ad. Yesterday.

پروني *parūnai*, a. Yesterday's, last, last past, yester.

پرويزي *parwezaī*, s.m. A sieve. P. (*parwezan*).

پره *para*, s.f. The plate, or board of a water, or spinning wheel; a row, rank, line, file; faction, party, set. H. (*parā*).

پرهار *parhār*, | s.m. A cut, laceration, wound.
پرهر *parhar*, | H. (*prahār*).

پرهرژلي *parhar-ʒalai*, a. Wounded, cut.

پرهيز *parhez*, s.m. Abstinence, continence; sobriety, regimen. P.

پرهيزګار *parhezgār*, a. Abstemious, continent, sober, frugal. P.

پرهيزګاري *parhezgārī*, s.f. Abstinence, sobriety.

پري *pre*, p. On, upon, above, atop. *parī*, s.f. A fairy. P.

پريباسل *prebāsal*, v.a. To cast upon, fling, throw, discharge upon. Def. See پرييستل

پريدل *predal*, | v.a. To abandon, desert,
پريږدل *pregdal*, | give up; cease, desist, leave off; relinquish, let go, set free. Def. See پريښول. P. (*farohīdan*).

پريشان *pareshān*, a. Confused, perplexed. P.

پريشاني *pareshānī*, s.f. Perplexity, confusion. P.

پريښودل *prekkhodal*, | v.a. To abandon, desert;
پريښول *prekkhawul*, | let go, etc. See پريږدل P. (*faroshāndan*).

پريکول *prekawul*, v.a. To cut, sever, divide, lop off.

پريو *paryo*, s.m. A follower, pursuer. P. (*pairau*).

پريوان *prewān*, s.m. The after-birth, placenta. H. (*puren*). a. Copious, abundant, much. P. (*farāwān*.)

پريواني *prewānī*, s.f. Abundance, plenty.

پريوتل *prewatal*, v.n. To drop, fall down, tumble; to alight, fall upon, come upon. P. (*faro uftan*).

پريوتي *prewatai*, a. Fallen, s.m. Name of a plant.

پريوستل *prewastal*, | v.a. To cast, throw, fling,
پرييستل *preyastal*, | etc. upon. Def. See پريباسل.

پرييښل *preyakkhal*, v.a. See پريښودل.

پړ *paṛ*, s.m. A gaming house, where dice are played. H. (*phaṛ*). *pa-aṛ* or *p-ūṛ*, a. Beaten, conquered, overcome; losing, unsuccessful. *p-uṛ* or *pa-aṛ-kawul*, v.a. To conquer, subdue, overcome. *pa-aṛ* or *p-uṛ-kedal*, v.n. To lose, be beaten, overcome, subdued.

پړانګ *pṛāng*, s.m. A leopard, panther. P. (*palang*).

پړانګ پيش *pṛāng-pīsh*, s.m. A wild cat, lynx.

پړانه وړانه *pa-aṛāna wa-aṛāna*, s.f. Loss and gain; betting, gambling, wagering.

پړپوس *paṛpūs*, s.m. The lungs. H. (*phephṛā*).

پړسوب *paṛsob*, s.m. Tumour, swelling, inflation.

پړسول *paṛsawul*, v.a. To dilate, distend, expand. H. (*pasārnā*).

پړسيدل *paṛsedal*, v.n. To swell, tumefy, dilate.

پړق *paṛaq*, s.m. A razor strop.

پرک *paṛak*, s.m. Agitation, flutter. H. (*phaṛak*). *paṛk*, s.m. A crowd, mob, bevy, herd.

پرکول *paṛakawul*, v.a. To agitate, shake, stir.

پرکه *paṛka*, s.f. A kind of bird trap, gin.

پرکي *paṛkai*, s.m. The leg below the knee, the calf.

پرکيدل *paṛakedal*, v.n. To flutter, quiver, hover.

پُرمخ *pa-aṛma<u>kh</u>*, a. Prone, face-downwards, upset.

پرنک *pṛang*, s.m. A cry, whimper, whine.

پروکي *paṛūkai*, s.m. A riband, shred, strip, tatter.

پروني *paṛūnai*, s.m. A woman's mantle, or veil.

پُره *pa-aṛa*, s.f. Defeat, failure, loss at play.

پري *puṛai*, s.m. A cable, rope, cord.

پرين *pṛīn*, s.m. Diaphragm, hypogastrium.

پس *pas*, ad. After, behind; then, next, therefore, at length. P. *pa-as*, s.m. Flatus, wind from the bowels. *pus·pus*, s.m. Whispering H. (*phus*).

پسات *pasāt*, s.m. Mutiny, rebellion, sedition; depravity, iniquity, mischief. A. (*fasād*).

پساتي *pasātī*, a. Mischievous, quarrelsome, seditious.

پسان *psān*, s.m. A grindstone, whetstone. S. (*sān*).

پست *past*, a. Low, below; abject, mean. P.

پستنه *pastana*, ad. After, behind, back, in rear; since, subsequently.

پستو *pastu*, s.m. An inner room, cell.

پستوني *pastawunai*, s.m. Name of a tree (*Grewia Asiatica*).

پسخاک *pas<u>kh</u>āk*, s.m. See پخساک P.

پسخه *pas<u>kh</u>a*, s.f. Stiff mud or clay, used to build walls.

پسرلي *psarlai*, s.m. The spring.

پُسکي *pa-aska-ī*, s.f. Flatus, wind from the bowels. *pa-aska-ī·ā<u>ch</u>awul*, v.a. To break wind.

پسند *pasand*, s.m. Approbation, choice. a. chosen, approved. P.

پسندول *pasandawul*, v.a. To choose, approve.

پسنديدل *pasandedal*, v.n. To be chosen, approved. P. (*pasandīdan*).

پسور *psor*, a. Broad, wide.

پسول *psol*, s.m. A necklace of coins; ornament.

پسولول *psolawul*, v.a. To adorn, decorate, ornament.

پسوني *pasūnai*, s.m. Ambush, cover, lair.

پسه *psah*, s.m. Goats, sheep; goat species

پسينه *pasīnah*, a. Late, last, late sown crops. P.

پُش *pa-a<u>sh</u>*, s.m. A wheeze, sound of air forced from a bag; a blacksmith. *pa<u>sh</u>·pa<u>sh</u>*, in. Call to a cat, puss! puss!

پشت *pu<u>sh</u>t*, s.m. Ancestry; a generation of progenitors; the back; a ridge; a prop, support, help; an assistant; reservoir of a canal. P.

پشته *pu<u>sh</u>ta*, s.f. A buttress, prop, support. in. A word used to drive away a cat—away puss!

پشتي *pu<u>sh</u>tī*, s.f. A prop, buttress, support; aid, succour, help. P. *pi<u>sh</u>tai*, s.m. A terrier dog.

پشرلي *p<u>sh</u>arlai*, s.m. A yearling kid.

پشقاب *pa<u>sh</u>qāb*, s.m. A salver, tray, platter.

پشک *pi<u>sh</u>ak*, s.m. A disease of the skin; ringworm; the bald-headed vulture.

پشکالي *pa<u>sh</u>kālai*, s.m. Hay, dry fodder.

پشم *pa<u>sh</u>m*, s.m. Wool, down, fur, hair. P.

پشمي *pa<u>sh</u>mī*, a. Woolly, downy.

پشمينه *pa<u>sh</u>mīnah*, a. Woollen. *pa<u>sh</u>mīna*, s.f. A kind of woollen cloth. P.

پشو *pi<u>sh</u>o*, s.m. and f. A cat.

پشوخت *pi<u>sh</u>o<u>kh</u>uṭ*, s.m. Tonquin bean; the

seed of a climbing plant, the seed pod of which is covered with cowhage; the bean is used as a charm against evil eye, etc.

پشه *pasha*, s.f. A musquito, gnat. in. A word used to drive away a cat. P.

پښ *pakkh*, s.m. See پاښ.

پښت *pukkht*, s.m. Ancestry, lineage; back, ridge; a mountain range. P. (*pusht*).

پښتنه *pukkhtana*, s.f. Enquiry, investigation, interrogation, questioning. An Afghan or Pathan woman, a female Pukkhtūn.

پښتو *pukkhto*, s.f. The Afghan language.

پښتورگه *pukkhtawarga*, s.f. A kidney.

پښتون *pukkhtūn*, s.m. An Afghan, a Pathan; one whose language is the Pukkhto. *bar-pukkhtūn*, s.m. An upper or highland Afghan. *lar-pukkhtūn*, s.m. A lower or lowland Afghan.

پښتونخوا *pukkhtūn-khwā*, s.f. Afghanistan, the country of the Afghans, or Pathans.

پښتونوالي *pukkhtūnwālai*, / پښتونولي *pukkhtūnwalī*, s.m. The Afghan constitution, Pukkhtūn code, the manners and customs of the Pathans.

پښته *pukkhta*, s.f. A small hill. P. (*pushta*).

پښتي *pukkhta-ī*, s.f. A rib, the ribs. *pukkhtī*, s.f. Enquiry, investigation, questioning.

پښتيدل *pukkhtedal*, v.a. To ask, question, interrogate, enquire. S. (*pūchhnā*).

پښويه *pakkhwaya*, or *pakkhoya*, s.f. Orthography, spelling, naming or forming words.

پښه *pksha* or *pkkha*, s.f. The foot.

پښيمان *pakkhemān*, a. Penitent, repentant, sorry. P. (*pashemān*).

پښيماني *pakkhemānī*, s.f. Penitence, regret, sorrow.

پقير *paqīr*, s.m. A beggar, mendicant; hermit, recluse. A. (*faqīr*).

پک *puk*, s.m. Chance, opportunity, turn, time.

پکار *pakār*, a. Effective, useful, serviceable. Also په کار.

پکل *pakal*, v.a. To chuck, or jerk anything into the mouth from the palm of the hand. H. (*phānknā*). s.m. A railing, fence, screen, lattice of reeds, etc.

پکو *pako*, a. Bothered, confused, amazed.

پکه *paka*, s.f. A palm full, enough to fill the palm for a chuck into the mouth. H. (*phankā*). *paka-wahal*, v.a. To chuck into the mouth (as grain, etc.).

پگړي *pagṛa-ī*, s.f. A turband. H. (*pagṛī*).

پگڼر *paganr*, s.m. Name of the eleventh Hindu month. February-March. S. (*phāgan*).

پل *pal*, s.m. A mill stone; potter's wheel; footprint, trace; wheel, truck-wheel; one side of a pair of scales. P. (*pallā*). *pul*, s.m. A bridge, ridge, bank, embankment. P. *pul*, a. Let off, excused, acquitted, absolved.

پلا *plā*, s.f. Period, turn, time, round.

پلار *plār*, s.m. A father. P. (*padar*).

پلارگني *plārganai*, s.m. Paternal relation; father's family, connexions, household, etc.

پلاله *palāla*, s.f. Rice straw, straw of millet, corn, etc. (unbroken). S. (*parāl*). P. (*pulāl*).

پلانړه *palānra*, s.f. A pack-saddle. P. (*pālān*). Mule load of water; water skins.

پلاو *pulāo*, s.m. A kind of dish made of rice, meat, fruits, spices, etc. cooked together. P.

پلټن *palṭan*, s.f. A battalion, regiment, peloton. H.

پلټل *palaṭal*, v.a. To return, turn back, retreat; to overturn; turn, wind. H. (*palaṭnā*).

پلغت *palaghat*, ad. Quickly. P.

پلک *palak*, s.m. The eyelid; an instant, moment; a wink. P. *pa-alk*, s.m. A sledge hammer; a ploughshare.

پلکه *palka*, s.f. The blade of a sword.

پلمه *palma*, s.f. Calumny, slander; deception, falsehood, prevarication. P.

پلن *plan*, a. Broad, wide, spacious. P. (*pahan*).

پلندر *plandar*, s.m. Step-father: father to wife's children by a former husband. P. (*padandar*).

پلنده *palanda*, s.f. A bog, quagmire.

پلنول *planawul*, v.a. To widen, make broad.

پلو *palau*, s.m. Border, hem, skirt of a dress; side, direction, quarter; margin, edge, verge. P. (*pahlū*). H. (*pallā*).

پلواښه *pulwākkha*, s.f. Button-hole, loop, noose, slip-knot, lasso.

پلور *plor*, s.m. Buying and selling, trade.

پلورل *ploral*, v.a. To sell, vend. See پرولل.

پلوسه *palosa*, s.f. Name of a tree (*Acacia modesta*).

پلوشه *palwasha*, s.f. A ray of light, glitter of a star, radiance of the moon; light, glitter.

پلول *pulawul*, v.a. To acquit, absolve, excuse.

پلوند *palwand*, a. Foolish, stupid.

پله *pala*, s.f. Nerve, sinew, tendon; direction, quarter, side.

پلي *palai*, s.m. A pod, legume. S. (*phalī*). *pala-ī*, s.f. The spoke of a wheel. Name of a tree (*Butea frondosa*). S. (*palās*). *palai*, a. Afoot, on foot.

پليت *palīt*, a. Defiled, polluted, unclean. P. (*palīd*).

پليته *palīta*, s.f. A wick, match, torch. P. (*falīta*).

پليتي *palītī*, s.f. Impurity, pollution.

پليټنړ *paleṭanṛ*, s.m. A weaver's beam. See پټيلنړ.

پلينه *plenah*, پليون *plewan*, s.m. Name of a tree (*Salvadora Persica*), the root of which is used as a tooth-brush. S. (*pīlū*).

پم *pam*, s.m. Mange, itch.

پماني *pamānai*, s.m. Name of a tree (*Vitex negundo*).

پمبه *pumba*, s.f. The cotton plant. P.

پمبېڅو *pumbechū*, s.f. A cotton pod; the withered stalks of the plant.

پمن *paman*, a. Mangy, scabby.

پنا، پناه *panā*, s.f. Refuge, shelter, protection, aid. P.

پنبه *punba*, s.f. See پمبه.

پنځوس *pandzos*, a. Fifty.

پنځه *pindzah*, a. Five. P. (*panj*). *pindzah-binā*, s.f. The five foundations (of religion), viz. The belief, prayer, fasting, pilgrimage, and alms.

پنجره *pinjra*, s.f. A cage; lattice. S. (*pinjrā*).

پنجکي *panjakai*, s.m. The cross bar between the strings of a pellet-bow; a latch, catch, stop.

پنجه *panja*, s.f. A claw, hand, paw. P.

پند *pand*, s.m. Advice, counsel. P. Distance, journey. S. (*pend*).

پندانه *pundāna*, s.f. Cotton seed.

پندوک *pandūk*, s.m. A bud, blossom.

پنده *punda*, s.f. The heel.

پندئ *punda-ī*, s.f. The iron top of a spear; a disease of the fetlock, the grease.

پنډ *pand*, s.m. A package, bundle, load for the head. *pund*, s.m. A steel for striking fire from a flint. *pund-bakra-ī*, flint and steel. *pund*, s.m. A band, herd, flock; tumour, bump, swelling; *vulva*. a. Corpulent, fat, stout. P.

پنډاوچرګ *pandāw-chirg*, s.m. A game cock; fowl of a large breed with big bones and few feathers.

پنډغالي *pand-ghālai*, s.m. A common or open space outside a village on which the cattle are collected on going to and returning from pasture.

پندوس *pandos*, s.m., پندوسکي *pandoskai*, A ball, a play ball, a cricket ball.

پنډوکي *pandūkai*, s.m. A bundle, parcel, package.

پندولي *pandolī*, s.f. A portion or share of a cotton crop allotted to the women who pick it, by way of perquisite or hire for their labour. *pandol·gara*, s.f. A woman who picks the cotton crop.

پنده *panda*, s.f. A small load, bundle.

پندئي *panda-ī*, s.f. The calf of the leg. H. (*pindlī*). *punda-ī*, s.f. The heel; iron tip of a spear.

پنديدل *pundedal*, v.n. To swell, expand, distend, tumefy. P. (*pundīdan*).

پنګه *panga*, s.f. Capital, reserve, stock. S. (*punjī*)).

پنهم *pinham*, a. Concealed, hidden, secret. P. (*pinhān*).

پني *panai*, s.m. Name of a scented grass (*Andropogon muricatum*). *pannī*, s.m. Name of a Pathan tribe.

پنير *panīr*, s.m. Cheese. P.

پنيرک *panīrak*, s.m. Name of a potherb (*Malva parviflora*). The seeds and root are used in medicine.

پنړه *panṛa*, s.f. A shoe, slipper. S. (*panhī*).

پو *pū*, a. Light, smooth, slight. s.m. Enquiry, search; a puff, blast, blow, breath. P.

پوپکه *pūpaka*, s.f. A bump, swelling, tumour.

پوتي *pūtai*, s.m. A heap, mound, lump, mass.

پوټ *poṭ*, s.m. Bark, rind, shell, crust, skin. P. (*post*).

پوټسوړي *poṭ·sūṛī*, s.m. Bran, chaff, husk.

پوټکي *poṭakai*, s.m. Scurf, dandriff, scab.

پوټوسکي *poṭūskai*, a. Diminutive, wee, tiny, small. s.m. An atom, jot, tittle, bit.

پوټي *pūṭai*, a. Small, puny, wee, tiny. s.m. A bit, pinch, crumb, little bit; a dwarf, pigmy.

پوجي *pūjī*, s.f. Weeding, thinning, pruning.

پوڅکئي *potsaka-ī*, s.f. A mushroom, fungus. *pūtsaka-ī*, s.f. The lobe of the ear.

پوڅه *potsa*, s.f. Curds, cream-cheese, dry curds.

پوڅئي *pūtsa-ī*, s.f. The lobe of the ear.

پوچ *pūch*, a. Obscene, absurd, useless, foolish. P.

پوچګوئي *pūch·goī*, s.f. Obscenity, nonsense, rigmarole. *pūch·goe*, s.m. A talker of nonsense, smut, bosh, etc.

پوخ *pokh*, a. Ripe, mature; cooked, dressed; firm, strong; expert, shrewd, knowing.

پوخلي *pukhalai*, s.m. Hooping-cough; croup.

پوده *pūda*, s.f. Cloth in the loom; the warp or web. P. (*pud*). *pūdah*, a. Crumbling, decayed, rotten, mildewed. P.

پور *por*, s.m. A loan, advance; debt. *pori*, ad. To, up to; till, whilst; over, across, beyond; at, upon; as far as, near, close to. H. (*par*). See پوري.

پورتني *portanai*, a. Upper, superior, upmost.

پورته *porta*, ad. Above, atop, on, upon, over, up. a. More, greater, superior. *porta·kawul*, v.a. To raise, erect, lift, exalt. *porta·kedal*, v.n. To ascend, arise, rise.

پوروړي *porawuṛai*, s.m. A debtor; creditor; avenger.

پوره *pūrah*, a. Complete, entire, full, perfect. S. (*pūrā*).

پوري *pore*, ad. To, up to; as far as, near, close to; upon, at; till, whilst; over, across, beyond. H. (*par*). *pore·ore* or *pore·rā·pore*, Through and through, in and out, right through, from end to end, etc. *pore·kawul*, v.a. To apply, attach, fix, shut, set, place, etc.

پوريژني *pore·ǰcnai*, a. Ejected, expelled, cast out. Also پوري جني *pore·janai*.

پوړ *poṛ*, a. Half cooked (as food), half ripe (as fruit), half grown, or near puberty (as an animal). *pauṛ*, s.m. Cord, cable, rope, hobble, tether.

پوړه *poṛa*, s.f. A rake, shovel for removing stable litter. s. (*phāorī*).

پوړۍ *pauṛa-ī*, s.f. A ladder. H. (*pauṛī*).

پوزه *poza*, s.f. The nose, snout. P.

پوزي *pūzai*, s.m. A small mat made of palm leaves.

پوږ *pūg*, s.m. A blow, puff, squirt, a bellows. *pūg-wahal*, v.a. To puff, blow (as on fire); to squirt, sprinkle from the mouth (as water on cloth, etc.).

پوس *pos*, } a. Soft, supple, pliant, ductile,
پوست *post*, } elastic, tender, tractable.

پوست *post*, s.m. Bark, crust, hide, shell, skin, etc.; poppy-head or capsule. P. *post-bāsal* or *kāgal*, v.a. To flay, skin, peel, bark, shell, etc.

پوستکي *postakai*, s.m. Crust, scab, bark, rind; an untanned hide.

پوستي *postī*, s.m. A drunkard, sot; one addicted to the use of the intoxicating liquor prepared from the fresh poppy-head. P.

پوستين *postīn*, s.m. A fur coat; sheep-skin coat. P.

پوسلل *poslal*, v.a. To attire, clothe, dress.

پوش *posh*, in. Look out! Clear the way! Stand by! Have a care! H. (*poesh*) or for *poh sha* (imperative). *posh* (in comp.), covering, wearing. P.

پوښ *pokkh*, s.m. Apparel, clothing, dress. P. (*posh*).

پوښاک *pokkhāk*, s.m. Clothes, garments. P. (*poshāk*).

پوښښ *pokkhikkh*, s.m. Covering, dress, vestment. P. (*poshish*).

پوښل *pokkhal*, v.a. To clothe, cover, dress, hide, screen; to cheer, console, sympathize, etc. P. (*poshīdan*).

پوغله *poghla*, s.f. Dung of young animals, of kids and lambs before it becomes orbicular.

پوک *pūk*, s.m. A puff, blow, squirt, etc. from the mouth. H. (*phūnk*).

پوکل *pūkal*, v.a. } To blow puff, breathe on,
پوکول *pūkawul*, } inflate; to squirt from the mouth.

پوکنړۍ *pukanṛa-ī*, s.f. A bladder, the urinary bladder. H. (*phuknā*).

پوکي *pūkai*, s.m. A puff, blow, whiff.

پول *pūl*, s.m. An aqueduct; gutter, trough. P. *pūl*, s.m. A film over the eye, albugo. S. (*phūlī*).

پولاد *polād*, s.m. Fine steel. P. (*fūlād*).

پولک *pūlak*, s.m. A clamp, bit, or wedge to fix the share to the plough.

پوله *pūla*, s.f. A ridge, bank, hedge; limit, boundary, or division line or mark. *pūlah*, s.m. Parched grain. S.

پولۍ *pūla-ī*, s.f. A vesicle, blister, bleb. H. (*pholā*).

پون *pūn*, s.m. The mange.

پونه *pūna*, s.f. Drizzle, mist, small rain. H. (*phūnhī*).

پونړۍ *pūnṛa-ī*, s.f. A ball or roll of cotton prepared for spinning. H. (*pūnī*).

پوول *powul*, v.a. To graze; lead cattle to pasture. Def. in pres. ten. See پيايل.

پوه *poh*, a. Clever, intelligent, knowing, wise.

پوهاند *pohānd*, a. Clever, intelligent, learned, wise.

پوهړ *pūhaṛ*, a. Careless, untidy, slovenly, dirty; foolish, stupid, sottish. H. (*phūhar*). *pohuṛ*, s.m. A large mat made of palm leaves. H.

پوهول *pohawul*, v.a. To acquaint, inform, explain, etc.

پوهه *poha*, s.f. Judgment, intellect, understanding. P. (*fahm*).

پوهيدل *pohedal*, v.n. To understand, appreciate, perceive, know. P. (*fahmīdan*).

پويه *poya*, s.f. A canter, gallop. P.

په *pa*, P. See بَ.

په *pah*, } in. Pooh! pooh! bosh! fudge!
پها *phā*, }

پهار *pahār*, s.m. A measure of time; about three hours. S. (*pahar*).

پهره *pahra*, s.f. A watch, vigil; tour of watch; guard, sentinel. S. (*pahrā*).

پهلواړي *phulwāṛai*, s.m. A white rose; strips of clean straw, used by women to plait with the back hair (as an ornament).

پهلوان *pahlawān*, s.m. An athlete, champion, wrestler, hero, gladiator. P.

پهلواني *pahlwānī*, s.f. Heroism, athletics, wrestling.

پهم *pahm*, s.m. Intellect, mind, reason, sense, P. (*fahm*).

پهمول *pahmawul*, v.a. To acquaint, inform, etc. P. (*fahmāndan*).

پهميدل *pahmedal*, v.n. To understand, perceive, know. P. (*fahmīdan*).

پهورته *pahorta*, ad. See پورته.

پهه *paha*, s.f. A poultice, ointment, plaister.

پئ *pa-ī*, s.f. Milk; the sap of trees. S. (*pai*). *pai*, s.m. The foot; a sinew; tendon of the leg; footing, basis; track, trace; a ford. P. *pai·oba*, fordable, within depth. *pai·kawul*, v.a. To hamstring; cut a tree close to the roots. *pai·wṛal*, v.a. To know, follow, catch at the meaning, etc. *pai*, ad. After, behind, following. *pai·ā·pai*, In succession, one after another. P.

پياڅه *piyātsa*, s.m. Bread made from millet or rye.

پياخله *piyākhla*, s.f. Collar, cuff, wristband. Exhaling, perspiring, sweating.

پيادة *piyādah*, s.m. A footman; foot soldier. a. On foot, afoot. P.

پيارمه *piyāṛma*, s.f. A brace for tightening the netting of a bedstead; the crupper of a saddle; the strap of a spinning wheel, etc.

پياز *piyāz*, s.m. An onion. P.

پيازکي *piyāzakai*, s.m. Wild onion; squill.

پيازه *piyāza*, s.f. Abortion; aborting, miscarrying; clearing, dividing, splitting.

پياله *piyāla*, s.f. A cup, goblet; fire-pan of a gun. P.

پياوي *payāwai*, s.m. A float, buoy, angler's float.

پيايل *piyāyal*, v.a. To graze or pasture cattle, to tend flocks. See پوول.

پيپنئ *pepna-ī*, s.f. A chemise, shift, shirt.

پيتي *paitī*, s.f. Cooked peas or pulse.

پيټ *peṭ*, s.m. } A bundle, load, package,
پيټي *peṭai*, } burden; tumbril, box, parcel. H. (*peṭī*).

پيټي مو *peṭī·mo*, in. Fie on thee! A curse on you! The devil seize thee! H. (*phiṭī·munh*).

پيجمخي *pejmakhai*, a. Handsome; beardless, smooth-faced; light or fair complexioned.

پيڅل *petsal*, v.a. To bear, endure, suffer, undergo. P. (*pechīdan*).

پيچ *pech*, s.m. A coil, twist; screw; complication, deceit, difficulty. P.

پيچش *pechish*, s.m. Contortion, twist, gripes. P.

پيچک *pechak*, s.m. A skein or hank of thread; a reel. P.

پيچومه *pechūma*, s.f. Zigzag; elevation, rise.

پيچيدل *pechedal*, v.n. To wind, twist, writhe, coil, etc. P. (*pechīdan*).

پيخاړه *paikhāṛa*, s.f. See پوغله.

پيخال *paikhāl*, s.m. Dung of birds. P.

پيخل *paikhal*, s.m. See پخيل.

پيدا *paidā*, a. Born, created, produced. P.

پير *pīr*, s.m. A saint; spiritual guide; descendant of a saint; old man; Monday. P. *per*, s.m. Bend, curve, turn, wind, twist. H. (*pher*).

پيرامن *pairāman*, s.m. Circumference. ad. Around, about, roundabout. P.

پیراهن *pairāhan*, s.m. A frock, long shirt. P.
پیړړ *peraṛ*, a. Corpulent, fat, bulky, large.
پیرزو *pīrzo*, a. See پرزو.
پیرل *pīral*, v.a. See پیرودل.
پیروان *perwān*, s.m. See پریوان.
پیروي *pairawai*, s.m. Cream; a suckling.
پیرودل *pīrodal*, v.a. To buy, purchase. P. (*farokhtan*).
پیروني *perone*, s.f. The Pleiades.
پیري *pere*, s.m. A demon, evil spirit, one of the genii; a devil. *periyān*, pl. (*met.*) Hysterics.
پیریاني *periyānai*, s.m. A demoniac, one possessed with a devil. *periyāna-ī*, s.f. A hysterical woman.
پیړ *peṛ*, a. Fat, obese, gross; coarse, thick; bulky.
پیړزه *peṛza*, s.f. A mound, hillock, detached hill.
پیړه *peṛa*, s.f. A lump of dough; a kind of sweetmeat. S. (*peṛā*).
پیړۍ *peṛa-ī*, s.f. A chair, settle, ottoman; a generation of ancestors. S. (*pīṛhī*).
پیزار *paizār*, s.m. A shoe, slipper, sandal. P.
پیزل *pezal*, v.a. To darn, repair, mend, stitch.
پیزنه *pezna*, s.f. A sieve. P.
پیزوان *pezwān*, s.m. A nose-ring. An ornament worn in the nose by women.
پیزواني *pezwānai*, s.m. A bullock with its nose bored for a ring or bridle.
پیزه *peza*, s.f. Apex, tip, summit, top, peak.
پیزي *pezai*, a. Faded, decayed, withered. *peza-ī*, s.f. Spelling, forming syllables, joining letters. The name of a woman.
پیژاندہ *pejāndah*, a. Recognized, known, familiar. s.m. Recognition, remembrance.
پیژندګلي *pejandgalī*, s.f. Acquaintance, knowledge, recognition, familiarity.
پیژندل *pejandal*, v.a. To distinguish, recognize, know, recollect. H. (*pahchānnā*).

پیس *pes*, s.m. Leprosy; a leper. P.
پیسانړي *pīsānṛai*, s.m. A little, bit, fraction, atom, pinch, jot, etc.
پیسه *paisa*, s.f. Name of a copper coin. H. (*paisā*).
پیسي *pesai*, a. Leprous. s.m. A leper.
پیش *pesh*, a. Before, in front. The vowel point ـُ *u*. P.
پیشاب *peshāb*, s.m. Urine. P.
پیشتر *peshtar*, ad. Before, formerly. P.
پیشکار *peshkār*, s.m. An agent, deputy, manager. P.
پیشګي *peshagī*, s.m. Advance of money or wages, etc. P.
پیشلمي *peshlamai*, } s.m. The meal before
پیشمني *peshmanai*, } sunrise during the month Ramazān; an early breakfast.
پیشوا *peshwā*, s.m. A guide, leader. P.
پیشواز *peshwāz*, s.m. A gown; an open frock worn by dancing women. P.
پیشه *pesha*, s.f. Calling, trade, profession; habit, custom. P.
پیشه ور *pesha-war*, s.m. A mechanic, artificer.
پیشۍ *pīsha-ī*, s.f. A caterpillar; a small nose-ring worn as an ornament by women; a leather bag or wallet.
پیښ *pekkh*, a. Before, in front, advanced. P. (*pesh*).
پیښاور *pekkhāwar*, s.m. Name of a city and province: Peshāwar.
پیښکښ *pekkh-kakkh*, s.m. Offering, present, tribute. P. (*pesh-kash*).
پیښول *pekkhawul*, v.a. To bring forward, introduce, bring together, cause to meet.
پیښه *pekkha*, s.f. Mockery, ridicule, caricature. H. (*pekhnā*). *pekkhe-kawul*, v.a. To make faces, ridicule, ape, mock.
پیښیدل *pekkhedal*, v.n. To happen, occur, befall; to meet, encounter. P. (*peshīdan*).
پیښین *pekkhīn*, a. Ancient, prior, former. s.m. Noon, afternoon. P. (*peshīn*).

پيغام *paig͟hām*, s.m. A message. P.

پيغامبر *paig͟hāmbar*, s.m. A messenger, prophet. P.

پيغله *peg͟hla*, s.f. A damsel, maid, virgin.

پيغور *peg͟hor*, s.m. Reproach, abuse, raillery; calumny, slander. P. (*peg͟hāra*). *peg͟hor-warkawul*, v.a. To reproach, rail at, abuse; calumniate, slander.

پيک *paik*, s.m. A messenger, porter, runner. P.

پيکار *paikār*, s.m. Contest, battle, war. P. A pedlar.

پيکان *paikān*, s.m. The head of an arrow. P.

پيکر *paikar*, s.m. Countenance, face, form; likeness, portrait. P.

پيکړه *paikaṛa*, s.f. An anklet, ornament for the ankle; fetter, hobble.

پيکل *pekal*, s.m. A clothes-line, rope to hang clothes upon.

پيکوي *pekawai*, s.m. See پيبوي.

پيل *pīl*, s.m. An elephant. P.

پيله *pela*, s.f. Silkworm's cocoon; silkworm. P.

پيمان *paimān*, s.m. Promise, oath, contract. P.

پيمانه *paimāna*, s.f. A goblet; a dry measure. P.

پيمائش *paimā-ī͟sh*, s.m. Measure, limit. P.

پيمخي *paimak͟hai*, a. See پڅمخي. Also پي مخي *pa-ī-mak͟hai*.

پينځه *pīnd͟zah*, a. Five.

پينڅه *paint͟sa*, s.f. The leg of a pair of trousers. P. (*pāench͟a*).

پينل *pīnal*, v.a. To chuck into the mouth from the hand.

پينه *pīna*, s.f. A trencher, wooden bowl, kneading trough.

پيودل *pewdal*, v.a. To thread, file, string, spit. H. (*pironā*).

پيودلي *pewdalai*, a. Filed, strung, threaded.

پيوره *paiwara*, a. Milky, milk-giving, milch, full of milk. Also پي وره *pa-ī-wara*.

پيوست *pewast* or *paiwast*, s.m. Connection, junction; relationship, friendship. P.

پيوستون *pewastūn*, s.m. Adhesion, connection, attachment; contiguity, proximity, relationship.

پيوسته *pewastah*, a. Connected, joined, attached. P.

پيوند *pewand*, s.m. A joint, patch, fastening; bud, graft. P.

پيبوي *peyawai*, s.m. A band for the hair; the bunch of braids plaited with the hair of young women and allowed to hang down the back.

ت

ت *te*, The fourth letter of the Pukk͟hto alphabet.

تَ *ta*, or ته *tah*, pr. The second personal pronoun, thou. part. The sign of the dative case, to, unto. It always follows its noun.

تا *tā*, ad. As far as, to, till, whilst, so that. P. s.f. A fold, sheet, layer, plait. P. (*tah*). pr. The inflected form of the second personal pronoun in the oblique cases singular, thee, by thee, thou.

تاب *tāb*, s.m. Heat, fury, rage; endurance, suffering; power, strength; coil, twist; light, splendour. P.

تابدان *tābdān*, s.m. A sky-light, lattice. P.

تابژن *tābjan*, a. Glittering, shining. P. (*tābān*). Also written تابجن *tābjan*.

تابستان *tābistān*, s.m. The hot weather, summer. P.

تابع *tābi'*, s.m. A dependant, subject. A.

تابعدار *tābi'dār*, a. Obedient, submissive, subject. s.m. A subject; follower, dependant.

تابعداري *tābi'dārī*, s.f. Obedience, allegiance, fidelity.

تابوت *tābūt*, s.m. A coffin, bier. *tābūt-i-sakīna*, s.f. The ark of the covenant given to Adam from heaven. A.

تابين *tābīn*, s.m. A subject, follower, dependent.

تابه *tāba*, s.f. A frying-pan. P.

تاثير *tāsīr*, s.m. Effect, operation, impression. A.

تاج *tāj*, s.m. A crown, diadem; crest of a bird. P.

تاجر *tājir*, s.m. A merchant, trader. A.

تاجك *tājik*, s.m. A cultivator, peasant; mechanic. The name of a tribe; they are settled about the large cities of Afghanistan, and form the bulk of the population on the western borders of the country; their language is the Persian, and they are supposed to be descendants of the ancient Persians.

تاخت *tākht*, s.m. A gallop, run; foray, raid; attack, invasion; plunder, ravage. P.

تاخير *tākhīr*, s.m. Delay, procrastination. A.

تار *tār*, s.m. Wire; cord, thread. P. *tār-tār* or *tār-patār*, a. Confused, dispersed, scattered.

تاراج *tārāj*, s.m. Plunder, spoil, booty. P.

تارك *tārik*, s.m. Leaving, forsaking; a deserter. A.

تارو *tārū*, s.m. A black partridge; a drone, humble bee; a kind of wasp without a sting. A kind of saddle cloth.

تاروگي *tārūgai*, s.m. A kind of butterfly.

تارول *tārawul*, v.a. To scatter, disperse.

تاريخ *tārīkh*, s.m. Era, date; annals, history. A.

تاريك *tārīk*, a. Dark, obscure. P.

تاريكي *tārīkī*, s.f. Darkness, obscurity. P.

تاړ *tāṛ*, s.m. Plunder, spoil; a gang of robbers.

تاړه *tāṛah*, a. Spoiled, ruined, sacked.

تاړي *tāṛī*, s.m. Clapping the hands to express approbation, or in time to music. H. (*tārī*).

تازه *tāzah*, a. Fresh, new; green, verdant; young, robust; happy, pleased. P.

تازي *tāzi*, s.m. A greyhound; an Arab horse; a hunting dog, hound. P.

تازيانه *tāziyāna*, s.f. A whip, scourge, birch. P.

تاس *tās*, s.m. A goblet or cup of brass; a platter or tray of copper. P. Cards; a game at cards. H.

تاسو *tāsū*, pr. Plural form of the second personal pronoun: ye, you. Also written تاسُ *tāsu*.

تاغه *tāghah*, s.m. Name of a tree, the wood of which is used to make charms against the evil eye; the white poplar (*Populus albus*). H. (*tāgh*).

تافته *tāfta*, s.f. A kind of silk, taffeta; a colour of horses, cream colour. P.

تاك *tāk*, s.m. A vine. P. A precipice, cliff; mountain side. a. Odd, single, unique. A. (*tāq*).

تاكيد *tākīd*, s.m. Emphasis, injunction; confirmation. A. *tākīd-kawul*, v.a. To enjoin, insist, urge, press.

تاكيدي *tākīdī*, a. Emphatic, decided, confirmed.

تال *tāl*, s.m. Clapping the hands to music; chime. S.

تالاب *tālāb*,
تالاو *tālāo*, } s.m. A pond, tank, reservoir. P.

تالاش *tālāsh*, s.m. Investigation, inquiry, search. P. (*talāsh*). Name of a valley between Bajawar and Swat.

تالنده *tālanda*, s.f. Thunder.

تالو *tālū*, s.m. The palate; a disease of the palate in cattle. S.

تاله *tāla*, s.f. Booty, spoil, pillage, plunder, ruin; a kind of fine spring grass.

تالي *tālai*, s.m. A metal platter or tray. S. (*thālī*).

تامبه *tāmba*,
تانبه *tānba*, } s.f. Copper. S. (*tāmbā*).

تامّل *tā-ammul*, s.m. Hesitation, meditation. A.

تان *tān*, s.m. A note in music, tone, tune. S.

تاندوله *tāndola*, s.f. Name of a potherb.

تانده *tāndah*, a. Fresh, green, verdant.

تانسته *tānasta*, s.f. The warp or threads stretched lengthwise on the loom. P.

تانگ *tāng*, s.m. A band, brace, saddle-girth. P. (*tang*),

تانړه *tāṉra*, s.f. A guard, picket; police station. S. (*thānā*).

تاو *tāo*, s.m. See تاب.

تاوان *tāwān*, s.m. Amends, recompense; retaliation; debt, fine, mulct. P. Used in opposition to *qiṣāṣ*, which means actual revenge,—blood for blood,—injury for injury, etc. *tāwān-ākhistal*, v.a. To fine, mulct; take the responsibility. *tāwān-kedal*, v.n. To suffer loss, injury, etc. *tāwān-warkawul*, v.a. To make amends, compensate, pay a fine. *tāwān-kawul*, v.a. To expend, incur, etc.

تاواني *tāwānī*, a. Injurious, incurring loss, noxious.

تاوس *tāos*, s.m. A peacock. A. (*ṭāūs*).

تاوون *tāwūn*, s.m. The plague. A. (*ṭā'ūn*).

تاووني *tāwūnai*, s.m. A man afflicted with the plague.

تاويتک *tāwītak*, s.m. An ornamental charm worn on the bosom by women.

تب *tab*, s.m. A poultice, epithem.

تباخ *tabākh*, s.m. A charger, plate, dish. A. (*ṭabāq*).

تبار *tabār*, s.m. Race, family, tribe, people. P.

تباه *tabāh*, a. Ruined, spoiled; abject, wretched. P.

تباهي *tabāhī*, s.f. Ruin, wreck; depravity, wretchedness.

تبخي *tabakhai*, s.m. An iron platter for baking cakes on. A. (*ṭabāq*). The pelvis.

تبديل *tabdīl*, s.m. Alteration, change. A.

تبر *tabar*, s.m. An axe, hatchet, cleaver. P. *tabar-zīn*, s.m. A horseman's battle-axe.

تبرّک *tabarruk*, s.m. Blessing, benediction. A.

تبره *tabaṛa*, s.f. A slate, slab of stone.

تبسم *tabassum*, s.m. A smile, simper. A.

تبق *tabaq*, } s.m. A disease of cattle, the
تبخ *tabakh*, } glanders.

تبه *taba*, s.f. Fever; heat, fervour. P. S. (*tap*).

تبئي *taba-ī*, s.f. A flat dish of pottery for baking cakes on.

تپ *tap*, s.m. A mole, freckle; scar or pit of small-pox. *tap-tap*, in. A call to encourage dogs to go into a hole.

تپاس *tapās*, s.m. Labour, toil, search, enquiry. S.

تپاک *tapāk*, s.m. Esteem, regard, affection, love. S.

تپړا *tapṛā*, s.f. A potter's tool; a wooden tapper or mallet; tapping. H. (*thāpī*).

تپک *tapak*, s.m. The roll or sound of a drum. A sledge hammer. P.

تپل *tapal*, v.a. To dab, stick against; daub, smear; heap, mass, pile. H. (*thāpnā*).

تپنړئي *tapaṉra-ī*, s.f. See تپړا.

تپور *tapor*, s.m. An ornamental breast-band worn by young women; a stomacher.

تپوس *tapos*, s.m. Enquiry, search. A. (*tafaḥuṣ*).

تپه *tapa*, s.f. A district, parish; a clan, tribe. H.

تپي *tapai*, a. Freckled, pitted, scarred, spotted. s.m. A mole, freckle, scar, pit of small-pox.

تت *tat*, a. Close, compact, dense, thick. H. (*ṭhaṭh*).

تتړي *tataṛai*, a. Lisping, stammering. s.m. A lisper, stammerer.

تتمه *tatimma*, s.f. Appendix, supplement. A.

تتوه *tatawa*, s.f. A ring-dove.

تجارت *tajārat*, s.m. Commerce, trade. A.

تجربه *tajriba*, s.f. Experiment, proof, trial, test. A.

تجويز *tajwīz*, s.m. Contrivance, plan, scheme;

enquiry, consideration ; determination, judgment. A.

تیچ *tich*, s.m. The scabbard of a sword, sheath of a dagger.

تحریر *taḥrīr*, s.m. Writing correctly ; written ; dated. A.

تحصیل *taḥsīl*, s.m. Acquisition, acquirement; profit, gain ; collection ; collectorate. A.

تحفه *tuḥfah*, a. Curious, rare, choice, excellent. A.

تحقیق *taḥqīq*, a. Authentic, verified, ascertained. ad. Indeed, really, truly. s.m. Precision, exactness. A.

تحقیقات *taḥqīqāt*, s.m. Inquiry, investigation. A.

تحمل *tahammul*, s.m. Endurance, forbearance. A.

تخت *takht*, s.m. A throne. P.

تخته *takhta*, s.f. A board, plank ; sheet or paper ; bench, form ; bier. *takhta-bandī*, s.f. Boarding, planking, wainscot. *takhta-pokkh*, s.m. A stage, platform, flooring. *takhta-nard*, s.m. Backgammon. P.

تخرگ *takharg*, or *tkharg*, s.m. The armpit.

تخرگی *takhargai*, s.m. The fillet or patch in the armpit of a dress.

تخفیف *takhfīf*, s.m. Abatement, mitigation, relief. A.

تخم *tukhm*, s.m. Seed, sperm ; an egg ; a testicle. P.

تخمخ *takhmakh*, in. Fie ! shame !

تخمه *tukhma*, s.f. Origin, principle. P. Indigestion. A.

تخمینا *takhmīnan*, ad. About, nearly, by guess. A.

تخنول *takhnawul*, ۔تخول *takhawul*, v.a. To tickle. P. (*tākht*, assault, etc.).

تخنیدل *takhnedal*, ۔تخیدل *takhedal*, v.n. To tickle, titillate.

تخه *takha*, s.f. ۔تخی *takhai*, s.m. } **Tickling, titillation.**

تدارک *tadāruk*, s.m. Chastisement, retaliation ; medy, precaution ; provision, preparation. A.

تدبیر *tadbīr*, s.m. Advice, counsel, deliberation ; contrivance, management, policy ; arrangement, order. A.

تدریج *tadrīj*, s.m. Gradation, scale. A.

تذکره *tazkira*, s.f. Biography, memoir. A.

تر *tar*, a. Damp, moist. P. ad. As far as, to, until, up to, etc. It is generally followed by the adverb *pore* or *pori*. Ex. *tar-osa-pore*, until now. *tar-kala-pore*, till when ? *tar-kūma-pore*, as long as, etc. *tri*, p. See تری.

ترات *trāt*, s.m. A whip, goad.

تراته *trāta*, s.f. Piping, or edging of a dress.

تراره *tarāra*, s.f. Gravel, shingle.

ترازو *tarāzū*, s.m. A balance, scale. P.

ترازه *tarāza*, s.f. A slice, shaving, bit. P. (*tarāsha*).

تراش *tarāsh*, s.m. Cutting, clipping ; cut, form, shape ; (in comp.) -cutter, -carver. P.

تراغ *tarāgh*, s.m. A coil, plait, twist.

تراک *tarāk*, s.m. A crack, fissure ; slit, rent, tear. A. Also تراق *trāq*.

ترانه *tarāna*, s.f. Melody, music, song ; symphony, tune. P. *tarāne-wayal*, v.a. To sing.

تراوی *tarāwe*, s.f. A prayer comprising twenty genuflexions, performed at bedtime every night during the month of Ramaẓān.

ترب *turb*, s.m. A radish. P.

تربت *turbat*, s.m. A tomb, sepulchre. A.

تربور *tarbūr*, s.m. A cousin : father's brother's son.

تربوزه *tarbūza*, s.f. A water melon. P.

تربیت *tarbiyat*, s.m. Education, instruction, tuition. A.

ترپ *trap*, s.m. A leap, bound, jump ; hop, skip.

ترپلل *traplal*, v.a. To jump, vault, bound, etc.

ترپه *trapa*, s.f. See ترپ.

ترپي *trapai*, s.m. A footfall, sound of steps.

ترتاب *tartāb*, s.m. Remorse, sorrow, regret.

ترتړي *tartaṛai*, s.m. See تتړي.

ترتله *tartala*, ad. Always, ever, continually.

ترتيب *tartīb*, s.m. Arrangement, disposition, order, method. A.

ترتيزک *tartezak*, s.m. Water-cress. P. (*tezak*).

ترټل *traṭal*, v.a. To scold, reprimand, taunt; drive away, repel. See رټل *raṭal*.

ترجمه *tarjuma*, s.f. Translation, interpretation. A.

ترجمان *tarjumān*, s.m. An interpreter. A.

ترڅ *tra<u>ts</u>*, a. Slanting, sloping, aside, wry, crooked. H. (*tir<u>ch</u>hā*).

ترخ *tra<u>kh</u>*, s.m. The armpit.

ترخان *tar<u>kh</u>ān*, s.m. Free, exempted from taxation; name of a tribe of Turks; wormwood.

ترخه *tar<u>kh</u>a*, s.f. The herb wormwood, absinth (*Artemisia Judaica*).

ترخۍ *tar<u>kh</u>a-ī*, s.f. Name of a plant, wild camomile (*Anthemis nobilis*).

تردد *taraddud*, s.m. Hesitation, suspense. A.

ترس *tars*, s.m. Fear, dread, terror. P.

ترسا *tarsā*, s.m. A heretic, infidel, idolator, pagan. P.

ترسان *tarsān*, ترسناک *tarsnāk*, } a. Timid, fearful, cowardly. P.

ترسري *tarsarai*, ترسيري *tarserai*, } s.m. A headstall, halter for a horse; a freckle, spot in the skin.

ترش *tur<u>sh</u>*, a. Acid, sour; austere, crabbed, cross. P.

ترشي *tur<u>sh</u>ī*, s.f. Acidity, sourness; acids; ill-temper, austerity. P.

ترښځ *tar<u>kkh</u>a<u>dz</u>*, ترښځه *tar<u>kkh</u>a<u>dz</u>a*, } s.f. An adze; a band, fillet, or strip of cloth let into the side of a dress.

ترغيب *tar<u>gh</u>īb*, s.m. Incitement, instigation. A.

ترقي *taraqqī*, s.f. A rise, elevation, ascent; promotion, advancement; increase; proficiency. A.

ترک *turk*, s.m. A Turk; a soldier; a robber; (in poetry) a handsome youth. P. *tark*, s.m. Desertion, forsaking. A. *trak*, s.m. A crack, cleft, split; sand-crack, a disease of the hoof in cattle; a crack, the sound of splitting, bursting, tearing, etc.

ترکاڼړ *tarkā<u>nr</u>*, s.m. A carpenter,

ترکښ *tarka<u>kkh</u>*, s.m. A quiver. P. (*tarka<u>sh</u>*).

ترکلاڼړي *tarkalā<u>nr</u>ī*, s.m. Name of a Pathan tribe settled in Bajawur,

ترکه *tarka*, s.f. Legacy, bequest; effects or estate of a deceased person. A.

ترکيب *tarkīb*, s.m. Composition, mixture; make, form. A.

ترګمۍ *tarugma-ī*, s.f. A dark, moonless night; obscurity, darkness.

ترله *tarla*, s.f. A cousin: father's brother's daughter.

ترم *turum*, s.m. A stallion, kept only for covering. P.

ترمنه *taramna*, s.f. A bog, quagmire, quicksand.

ترمي ترمي *tarmai-tarmai*, a. Dispersed, scattered, dispelled.

ترناو *tarnāo*, s.m. An aqueduct, trough, gutter.

ترنځ *tran<u>dz</u>*, a. Slim, compressed, slight, spare. P. (*taranj*).

ترنج *turanj*, s.m. A citron, lime, lemon. *taranj*, s.m. Name of several plants of the orders *Euphorbia* and *Asclepias*, containing milky sap. *tranj*, s.m. A skein or roll of thread.

ترنجوکي *tranjūkai*, ترنجي *tranjai*, } s.m. Small skein of thread.

ترنکوڅه *trankū<u>ts</u>a*, s.f. A sling.

ترنګ *trang*, s.m. Twang, jar, vibration, sound.

ترنګبين *tarangabīn*, } s.m. Manna produced
ترنجبين *taranjabīn*, } from the camel's thorn (*Hedysarum alhagi*). Oxymel, honey and limejuice. S. P.

ترنګړ *trangaṛ*, s.m. A net for carrying grass, etc.

ترو *tro*, ad. Consequently, therefore, then, for that; at length, afterwards, at that time.

تروټ *troṭ*, s.m. Damage, injury; loss, deficiency.

تروټه *troṭa*, s.f. Detriment, discount.

ترور *tror*, s.f. Aunt: father's or mother's sister.

تروړئ *trora-ī*, s.f. A fox.

تروکه *tarūka*, s.f. Sorrel (*Rumex vesicarius*). Wood-sorrel (*Oxalis corniculata*).

تروه *tarwa*, a. See تريو.

تروي *tarwai*, s.m. Name of a purgative plant (*Ipomœa turpethum*). H. (*teorī*). *tarwe*, s.f. (pl. of *tarwa*) Sour milk, whey, curds and whey.

تره *trah*, s.m. Uncle: father's or mother's brother. *tara*, s.f. Greens, vegetables, potherbs. P. A kind of cucumber (*Cucumis acutangulus*). H. (*tura-ī*). Alarm, dread, fear.

ترهاو *tirhāo*, s.m. The third part of an oke. See اوري.

ترهر *tarhar*, a. Timid, fearful, nervous. s.m. Fear, alarm, dismay. Also ترهور *tarhūr*.

ترهول *tarhawul*, v.a. To alarm, frighten, start, etc. (as game).

ترهيدل *tarhedal*, v.n. To start, fear, shy, etc. (as animals). P. (*tarīdan*).

تري *tarī*, s.f. Moisture; water in opposition to land; moist or brown sugar. ad. By water. P. *tarai*, s.m. An aqueduct or canal on the side of a hill. *turai*, s.m. A kind of cucumber (*Cucumis utilissimus*). *tara-ī*, ad. Clandestinely, confidentially, secretly. *tura-ī*, s.f. A bugle. H. (*turhī*).

تري *tre*, p. From, by, than, with.

ترياک *tariyāk*, s.m. Opium. A. (*tiriyāq*).

تريز *tarīz*, s.m. A patch, piece sewed on to a dress or garment. P.

تريج *tarīj*, a. Strong, violent, rough. A.

تريخ *trīkh*, a. Bitter, nauseous; sour, austere, cross, ill-tempered. *f.* *tarkha*.

تريخي *trīkhai*, s.m. Bitterness; gall, bile; the gall-bladder; anger, malice, ill-feeling.

تريو *trīw*, a. Acid, sharp, sour; austere, crabbed, morose, cross. *f.* *tarwa*.

تريه *tariyah*, in. A shepherd's call to drive sheep, etc.

تراق *ṭrāq*, s.m. A knock, rap, tap. H. (*taṛākā*).

ترړاقي *taṛāqa-ī*, s.f. A loin clout; a cord tied round the waist, and used as a fastening for the clout covering the privates. H. (*taṛāgī*).

ترپ *ṭrap*, s.m. Haste, hurry; flutter; leap. H. (*taṛap*).

ترپول *ṭrapawul*, v.a. To agitate, disturb, flurry. H. (*taṛpānā*).

ترپيدل *ṭrapedal*, v.n. To flutter, palpitate, writhe. H. (*taṛapnā*).

ترق *ṭraq*, s.m. A pat, tap, rap, knock, slap.

ترل *taṛal*, v.a. To tie, fasten, bind, lash. P. (*tār*, thread, cord).

ترم *taṛam*, a. Lukewarm, tepid.

ترون *taṛūn*, s.m. Binding, fastening, lashing; agreement, bargain, compact, treaty.

ترنه *taṛana*, } s.f. See preceding.
تره *taṛa*, }

تري *taṛai*, s.m, Lisping; a lisper.

تزن *tuzan*, a. Base, cowardly.

تږي *tagai*, a. Thirsty. P. (*tishna*).

تسبه *tasba*, s.f. The bead of a rosary. A. (*tasbīḥ*). *tasbe*, p. A rosary, chaplet of beads.

تسخیر *taskhīr*, s.m. Capture, subjection. A.

تسکین *taskīn*, s.m. Comfort, consolation. A.

تسلی *tasallī*, s.m. Comfort, solace, consolation. A.

تسلیم *taslīm*, s.m. Resignation, obedience; obeisance, salutation; health, safety. A.

تسمه *tasma*, s.f. A thong, leather strap. H.

تش *ta-ash*, a. Empty, void, hollow. ad. Only, merely, simply. P. (*tihī*).

تشبیه *tashbīh*, s.m. Comparison, simile. A.

تشت *tasht*, s.m. A basin used to wash the hands over. P. A platter, salver, tray.

تشخانه *tashkhāna*, s.f. The fire pan of a gun. P. (*ātash·khāna*).

تشخیص *tashkhīṣ*, s.m. Ascertaining, distinguishing; valuation, assessment. A.

تشویش *tashwīsh*, s.m. Anxiety, disquietude. A.

تشی *ta-ashai*, s.m. The flank, side, hypochondrium.

تپتن *takkhtan*, s.m. See کپتن.

تپتول *takkhtawul*,) v.a. To put to flight, run
تپول *takkhawul*,) away with, carry off, elope with, etc. P. (*tākhtāndan*).

تپتدل *takkhtedal*,) v.n. To flee, decamp,
تپل *takkhal*,) retire, retreat, run away. P. (*tākhtan*).

تصدیق *taṣdīq*, s.m. Attestation, verification. A.

تصرف *taṣarruf*, s.m. Disposal, use; expenditure, extravagance. A.

تصنیف *taṣnīf*, s.m. Composition, authorship. A.

تصویر *taṣnīr*, s.m. Image, picture, portrait. A.

تعجب *t'ajjub*, s.m. Wonder, surprise, astonishment. A.

تعریف *t'arīf*, s.m. Explaining, praising. A.

تعطیل *ta'ṭīl*, s.m. Vacation; neglecting, abandoning. A.

تعظیم *t'aẓīm*, s.m. Honour, reverence, respect. A.

تعلق *t'alluq*, s.m. Relation, connection; dependence; correspondence, commerce. A.

تعلیم *t'alīm*, s.m. Teaching, tuition. A.

تعویذ *t'awīz*, s.m. An amulet, charm. A.

تغار *taghār*, s.m. A bread-tray; a bucket, pail. P.

تغارک *taghārak*, s.m. Dropsy; a small pail. P.

تغاری *taghārai*, s.m. A bread-basket; an earthenware dish or platter; a small bucket or pail. A. a. A glutton.

تغمه *taghma*, s.f. A mark, weal, welt; a medal. A.

تغیر *taghīr*, s.m.)
تغیری *taghīrī*, s.f.) Change, alteration. A.
تغیر *taghaiyur*, s.m.)

تف *taf*, s.m. Vapour, steam. P. *tuf*, s.m. Saliva. P.

تفاوت *tafāwat*, s.m. Difference, distinction: distance. A.

تفرقه *tafriqa*, s.f.)
تفریق *tafrīq*, s.m.) Division, separation. A.

تفسیر *tafsīr*, s.m. Commentary, explanation. A.

تفصیل *tafṣīl*, s.m. Detail, explanation, separation. A.

تفنگ *tufang*, s.m. A musket. P.

تقاضا *taqāẓā*, s.f. Exacting, dunning; importunity. A.

تقدیر *taqdīr*, s.m. Destiny, fate, lot. A.

تقریر *taqrīr*, s.m. Detail, relation, recital. A.

تقسیم *taqsīm*, s.m. Dividing, division, distribution. A.

تقصیر *taqṣīr*, s.m. Crime, error, fault. A.

تقلید *taqlīd*, s.m. Imitation; forging; copying; believing without enquiry. A.

تقوا *taqwā*, s.f. Piety, the fear of God. A.

تک *tak*, ad. Altogether, wholly, utterly; only used with respect to colour. Ex. *tak·tor·sarai*, a jet-black man. *taka·spīna kkhadza*, a snow-white woman.

تکبیر *takbīr*, s.m. Repeating the creed, or saying "God is great" (*allahu·akbar*). A.

تکرار *takrār*, s.m. Altercation, contention, dispute. A.

تکراري *takrārī*, s.m. A wrangler, caviller. a. Disputing, importuning, wrangling. A.

تکړه *takṛah*, a. Active, vigorous, strong, robust, healthy. *takaṛa*, s.f. A pebble; boulder.

تکل *takal*, s.m. Attempt, effort, endeavour. See کتل.

تکلاستي *taklāstai*, a. Agile, nimble, smart, active, alert.

تکليف *taklīf*, s.m. Ceremony; difficulty, inconvenience, trouble, ailment, distress, annoyance. A.

تکمه *tukma*, s.f. A button loop; the sac or tubercle of piles. P.

تکيه *takiya*, s.f. A bolster, pillow; a faqīr's stand or hut. *takiya-kalām*, s.m. An expletive, cant phrase. P.

تګ *tag*, s.m. Departure; toiling, running about.

تګاپو *tagāpū*, s.m. Bustle, toil, labour, search. P.

تل *tal*, ad. Always, ever, perpetually. *til*, s.m. Sesamum, the seed. S. *tal*, s.m. The base, bottom, foot, sole. S. (*talā*). *tall*, s.m. A hillock, mound, heap. A.

تلاش *talāsh*, s.m. Enquiry, study, search. P.

تلب *talab*, s.m. Salary, wages, hire, pay. A. (*ṯalab*).

تلتک *taltak*, s.m. Coverlet, counterpane; mattress.

تلخ *talkh*, a. Acrid, bitter, rancid. P.

تلخان *talkhān*, s.m. Meal of parched grain, made into a paste for food on a journey. P.

تلف *talaf*, s.m. Destruction, loss, ruin; prodigality, waste. A.

تلکه *talaka*, s.f. A kind of snare for catching birds, a springe.

تلل *tlal*, v.n. To go, depart, set out, leave. H. (*chalnā*). See لاړل *lāṛal*. *talal*, v.a. To balance, weigh. H. (*tolnā*).

تلوار *talwār*, s.m. Haste, speed, quickness.

تلوسه *talwasa*, s.f. Commotion, distraction. P. (*talwāsa*).

تلول *talwal*, s.m. Dispatch, haste, speed, quickness. *talawul*, v.a. To fry, grill, broil.

تلولی *talwalai*, a. Precipitate, rash, hasty, quick. *talawalai*, a. Broiled, fried, grilled.

تله *tlah*, s.m. Exit, exodus, departure, setting out. *tala*, s.f. Balance, scale; the sole of the foot.

تلی *talai*, s.m. The sole of a shoe; under surface of a thing; sole of the foot: palm of the hand. S. (*talī*). *tilai*, s.m. Form, figure, shape. *tila-ī*, s.f. The shaft of an arrow, stalks of corn, reeds, grasses, etc.; a straw, straw. H. (*tīl*).

تم *tam*, s.m. Continuance, permanence, rest. a. Staying, abiding, tarrying.

تماچه *tamācha*, s.f. A pistol; a blow, cuff, slap. A. (*ṯamāncha*).

تماشا *tamāshā*, / تماشه *tamāsha*, s.f. A show, sight, spectacle, amusement, entertainment. A.

تماکو *tamākū*, / تمباکو *tambākū*, s.m. Tobacco.

تمام *tamām*, a. Complete, entire, perfect. A.

تمامي *tamāmī*, s.f. Completion, end; perfection.

تمبل *tambal*, s.m. A kettle-drum, tambourine. A. (*ṯabal*).

تمبو *tambū*, s.m. A tent. H.

تمبوزک *tambūzak*, s.m. A muzzle; a muzzle of spikes fastened on the nose of a calf to prevent its sucking.

تمبوزي *tambūzai*, s.m. The muzzle, snout; bridge of the nose.

تمبه *tamba*, s.f. The leaf of a door; prop of a door; a group, party, herd.

تمبګۍ *tambaga-ī*, s.f. The leaf of a window or shutter.

تمبيزه *tambeza,* s.f. }
تمبيزي *tambezai,* s.m. } The muzzle, snout.

تمتراق *tamtarāq,* s.m. Grandeur, magnificence, pomp. A. (*tamtarāq*).

تمسک *tamassuk,* s.m. Note of hand, bond, receipt. A.

تمن *tuman,* s.m. A crowd, troop, party; brotherhood, connection; a score, twenty. P.

تموز *tamūz,* s.m. Heat, warmth; name of a month, July. P.

تمه *tama,* s.f. Avarice, avidity; covetousness, greediness. A. (*tama'*).

تميز *tamīz,* s.m. Discretion, sense, judgment. A.

تن *tan,* s.m. Body, person; individual. P.

تنا *tanā,* s.f. Thunder.

تناو *tanāo,* s.m. A cord, rope; strap.

تنبيه *tanbīh,* s.m. Admonition, advice, correction. A.

تنتنا *tantanā,* s.f. Fame, sound, rumour; dignity, pomp. A. (*tantanā*).

تنخواه *tankhwāh,* s.m. Salary, wages, pay. P.

تند *tund,* a. Active, fast, quick; hot, spirited, rash; acrid, pungent. P.

تندار *tandār,* s.f. Uncle's wife. See تندور.

تندر *tandar,* s.m. Thunder; a thunder-bolt; eclipse. P.

تندور *tandor,* s.f. Paternal aunt, father's brother's wife. *tandūr,* s.m. An oven. P.

تندوره *tandūra,* s.f. A cascade, waterfall.

تندوړي *tindoṛai,* s.m. The cartilage of the nose.

تندوي *tandwai,* s.m. Cartilage, gristle.

تنده *tanda,* s.f. Thirst.

تندي *tundī,* a. Acrimony; impetuosity, fierceness. P. *tandai,* s.m. An infant, babe, suckling; sprout, shoot, young plant; the forehead; the crown of the head, vertex.

تنديار *tandyāra,* s.f. Father's brother's wife. See تندار.

تنډل *tanḍal,* v.a. To make, form, mend, repair.

تنذري *tanzarai,* }
تنزري *tanzarai,* } s.m. A grey partridge.

تنکي *tankai,* s.m. A babe, suckling; sprout, shoot, young plant. a. Young, tender, unripe.

تنگ *tang,* a. Confined, narrow, tight; scarce, wanting, barren; distressed, in want; dejected, sad. P. *tung,* s.m. An ewer, vase, long-necked jar. P.

تنگسه *tangsa,* }
تنگسيا *tangsiyā,* } s.f. Distress, poverty; scarcity, want; narrowness, tightness.

تنگه *tanga,* s.f. The stock or stem of a tree; body or centre width of a garment; name of a coin equal to one-third of a rupee. H.

تنگي *tangai,* s.m. A defile, gorge, hill pass. *tangī,* s.f. Distress, poverty, want; avarice, parsimony, stinginess; narrowness, tightness. P.

تنور *tanūr,* s.m. A furnace; oven. P.

تنومند *tanomand,* a. Corpulent, robust. P.

تنها *tanhā,* a. Alone, solitary; single; apart. ad. Merely, only, singly. P.

تنهائي *tanhā-ī,* s.f. Solitude, loneliness, privacy. P.

تنړا *tanṛā,* s.f. Thunder; roar of a wild animal.

تنړاکه *tanṛāka,* s.f. A bleb, vesicle, blister.

تنړکار *tanṛakār,* s.m. Borax. P. (*tinkār*).

تنړئي *tanṛa-ī,* s.f. Button loop; strings of a dress; cord, pack thread, etc. used to tie bundles.

تو *tū,* s.m. Spittle, saliva. H. (*thūk*). *tū-tū,* in. Call to a dog. H.

توا *tawā,* s.f. A frying pan. P.

تواريخ *tawārīkh,* s.m. Annals, dates; history. A.

توان *tuwān,* s.m. Force, power, strength. P.

توانا *tuwānā,* a. Able, powerful, strong. P.

توانگر *tuwāngar,* a. Rich, wealthy; powerful, able. P.

توانګري *turvāngarī*, s.f. Opulence, wealth; ability, power. P.

توانيدل *turānedal*, v.n. To be able. P. (*turānīdan*).

توب *tob*, A particle affixed to nouns and adjectives to denote state, pursuit, or quality. Ex. *tang*, a. Tight. *tang-tob*, s.m. Tightness. *spāhī*, s.m. Soldier. *spāhī-tob*, s.m. soldiering, profession of a soldier. *saṛī*, s.m. Men. *saṛī-tob*, s.m. The state of men, humanity. A. (*tab'a*). See تيا.

توبره *tobra*, s.f. A nose bag (for a horse); saddle bag; a beggar's wallet. H. (*tobṛā*).

توبري *tobrai*, s.m. The head of an arrow, dart, etc.

توبه *toba*, s.f. Contrition, penitence, remorse. in. Fie! shame! A.

توبه ګار *toba-gār*, a. Penitent, contrite. A.

توپ *top*, s.m. A cannon, gun. T.

توپان *tūpān*, s.m. A hurricane, storm; deluge. A. (*tufān*).

توپک *topak*, s.m. A matchlock, musket. T.

توپنګچه *tūpangcha*, s.f. A pistol. P. (*tufangcha*).

توت *tūt*, s.m. The mulberry, tree and fruit. A.

توتا *totā*, s.m. } A parrot; the cock or hammer
توتي *totī*, s.f. } of a gun. H.

توتکي *totakai*, s.m. A swift, swallow.

توتکرکي *totakarkai*, s.m. A sand martin, swallow.

توتکري *totakarai*, s.m. A swift, swallow.

توتنکي *totankai*, s.m. A chip, filing, shaving, fragment. H. (*tūtan*).

توتيا *totiyā*, or نيله توتيا *nīla-totiyā*, s.f. Blue vitriol, sulphate of copper. S.

توجه *tawajja*, s.f. Attention, regard; favour. A.

توخي *tokhī*, s.m. Name of a section of the Ghilzai tribe.

تود *tod*, a. Hot, warm. P. (*tūnd*). H. (*tāt*).

تودوخه *todūkha*, s.f. Sultriness, heat, warmth.

تور *tor*, a. Black, dark. P. (*tār*). s.m. Fright, panic; slander, calumny; a net, snare. *tor-pore-kawul*, v.a. To calumniate, blacken, slander.

تورغړي *torgharai*, s.m. The arm above the elbow.

تورلمي *torlamai*, s.m. A badger.

توره *tūra*, s.f. A sword. *tora*, s.f. A copper coin, equal to half an anna.

توره آنه *tora-āna*, s.f. Name of a black coloured bird with a forked tail; the king-crow or tyrant fly-catcher. Called also *ḍāng-luka-ī*, club tail.

توره غاړه *tora-ghāra*, s.f. Hooping cough.

توري *torai*, s.m. The spleen; pupil of the eye. a. Simple, plain, pure, unmixed. *tora-ī*, s.f. A kind of cucumber (*cucumis acutangulus*). H. (*torī*).

توريت *tauret*, s.m. The Pentateuch, Old Testament. A. (*torāt*).

تورل *toṛal*, v.a. To plane, shave; polish, smooth.

توسن *tausan*, s.m. A war horse; high spirited horse. P.

توسند *tosand*, a. Dry, parched, withered. H. (*tūsā*).

توشدان *toshdān*, s.m. A pouch, cartridge-box. P.

توشک *toshak*, s.m. A mattress, quilt. P.

توښه *tokkha*, s.f. Necessaries, provisions, supplies for a journey. P. (*tosha*).

توغ *togh*, s.m. A banner, ensign, standard. P.

توغل *toghal*, } s.m. A saddle cloth of felt.
توغم *togham*, }

توقه *tūqa*, s.f. A blunt arrow; a small hill. P. (*tukka*).

توک *tūk*, s.m. Spittle. H. (*thūk*).

توکل *tūkal*, v.a. To spit. *tawakkul*, s.m. Faith, hope, reliance, trust in God. A.

توګه *toga*, s.f. Manner, method, way, mode.

تول *tol*, s.m. Gravity, weight. s. *tūl*, s.m. A crop or field ready for reaping. *twal*, a. Equal, even, same weight, six of one and half a dozen of the other.

تولاند *tūlānd*, s.m. A stride, long step; gait of a bird.

تولائي *tolā-ī*, s.f. A mattress, quilted bed.

توله *tola*, s.f. Name of a weight equal to 180 grs. (troy). s. (*tolā*).

تومان *tomān*, s.m. A sum equal to twenty rupees; a myriad; 10,000. P. See تمن.

تومت *tomat*, s.m. See تهمت.

تومنه *tomna*, } s.f. Rennet; ferment, yeast;
تومه *toma*, } essence, origin.

تونبيا *tonbiyā*, s.f. Carded cotton; thread made from carded cotton. H. (*tūmiyā*).

تونګ *tawang*, s.m. A band-box; a reed-basket for the clothes of women. *tuwang*, s.m. Magazine, store, treasury. P. *tūng*, s.f. A maiden, damsel, girl.

تونګي *tawangai*, s.m. A band-box; a small basket made of reeds, and used by women to keep jewelry, ornaments, clothes, etc. in.

تونړئ *taunra-ī*, s.f. A clothes chest, locker, safe.

توهړ *tohar*, s.m. Cactus, prickly pear. H. (*thūhar*).

توي *toe*, a. Spilt, shed, overflowed, upset (as water from a bowl).

تويول *toyawul*, v.a. To pour out, upset, spill, shed.

تويېدل *toyedal*, v.n. To overflow, flow out, be spilt.

ته *tah*, a. Going, walking, proceeding. pr. The second personal pronoun, thou. *ta*, s.f. Fold, layer, plait; the bottom, under surface. P. *ta-khāna*, s.f. A cellar, vault. P. *tih*, a. Void, empty. P.

تهان *thān*, s.m. A piece, length of cloth; manger, stall for cattle. H.

تهمت *tuhmat*, s.m. Calumny, slander, suspicion, false accusation. A.

تهنال *tahnāl*, s.m. The mounting at the end of a scabbard. P.

تهنه *tahana*, s.f. A hollow, dip in the ground.

تي *tai*, s.m. A teat, nipple.

تيا *tiyā*, A particle added to adjectives in forming nouns denoting possession of their quality. Ex. *ārām*, a. Easy. *ārāmtiyā*, s.f. Easiness. *khamsor*, a. Familiar. *khamsortiyā*, s.f. Familiarity. *grān*, a. Dear. *grāntiyā*, s.f. Dearness.

تيار *tayār* or *taiyār*, a. Ready, complete, prepared, finished.

تياره *tyāra*, s.f. Darkness, gloom, obscurity (pl. of *tor*, black).

تياري *tayārī*, s.f. Readiness; preparation. P.

تيبون *taibūn*, s.m. See تيمم.

تيښل *tetsal*, v.a. To perforate, pierce; to cram, stuff. H. (*tīsnā*).

تېر *ter*, a. Lapsed, passed, gone by. *tīr*, s.m. An arrow; beam, ridge-pole. P.

تيرک *tīrak*, s.m. The iron axle on which the stone of a mill revolves; an axle.

تېرول *terawul*, v.a. To give the male to the female; to cause to pass.

تېره *terah*, a. Acute, keen, sharp. *tera*, a. Ready for the male, in heat. *tīrah*, a. Dark, obscure. P.

تېري *terai*, s.m. Excess; passing, lapsing; excellence, superiority.

تېرېدل *teredal*, v.n. To pass, lapse, go by.

تېز *tez*, a. Acute, sharp, keen. P. *tīz*, s.m. Wind from the bowels, flatus. *tīz-āchawul*, v.a. To break wind.

تېزل *tezal*, v.a. To hasten, urge, press.

تېزندئ *tezanda-ī*, s.f. A slip knot; hangman's noose, halter, rope.

تيږه *tīga*, s.f. A boulder, rock; pebble, stone, slab.

تيشه *tesha*, s.f. A carpenter's adze. P.

تیبنته *tekkhta*, s.f. Defeat, flight, retreat.

تیغ *tegh*, s.m. A scimitar, sword. P. A sprout, shoot, blade of grass.

تیغنه *teghna*, s.f. An iron plate for baking on.

تیک *tyak*, a. Distended, inflated, expanded.

تیکه *teka*, s.f.
تیکي *tekai*, s.m. } A scabbard, sheath.

تیل *tel*, s.m. Oil. S.

تیلي *telī*, s.m. An oilman. (f.) (*telanṛa*).

تیمم *tayammum*, s.m. The ceremonial purification before prayers, with dust or sand, when water is not at hand. A.

تینبوزک *tīnbūzak*, s.m. The muzzle, snout,

تینبوزي *tīnbūzai*, s.m. A muzzle.

تیندک *tīndak*, s.m. A trip, stumble; ricochet, bound.

تییل *teyal*, v.a. To broil, fry, grill, roast.

تییني *teyanai*, s.m. A broil, grill, fry.

ټ

ټ *ṭa*, The fifth letter of the Pukkhto alphabet. It corresponds with the Sanskrit ट, represented by ٹ in the Hindūstānī, and exactly resembles it in sound.

ټاپ *ṭāp*, s.m. An impression; stamp, die, seal. H. (*thāp*).

ټاپو *ṭāpū*, s.m. An island. H.

ټاپوړه *ṭāpoṛa*, s.f. A crutch, a stilt; washerman's board or plank.

ټاپه *ṭāpa*, s.f. A stamp, die, seal, print. H. (*thāpa*).

ټاټ *ṭāṭ*, s.m. Canvas, sackcloth. H. Conceit, vanity, swagger. H. (*ṭhāṭh*).

ټاټوب *ṭāṭob*, s.m. Calmness, composure, rest, repose.

ټاټوکه *ṭāṭūka*, s.f. Name of an edible ground nut.

ټاټئ *ṭāṭa-ī*, s.f. Lullaby, rocking, swinging. *ṭāṭī*, s.m. A dandy, fop, beau.

ټاس *ṭās*, s.m. An explosion, pop, snap. bang.

ټاق *ṭāq*, s.m. A bang, explosion, discharge.

ټاقر *ṭāqar*, s.m. A decrepid old man. S. (*ṭhākur*).

ټاک *ṭāk*, s.m. The fruit of the bael tree (*Ægle marmelos*). A bang, rap, knock.

ټاکو *ṭākū*, s.m. A robber, highwayman, pirate. H. (*ḍākū*). Name of a disease in buffaloes.

ټال *ṭāl*, s.m. A swing; the branch of a tree. H. (*ṭhāl*).

ټاله *ṭāla*, s.f. Wholesale, by the lump (pl. of *ṭol*).

ټانټه *ṭānṭa*, s.f. Stalk of Indian corn. H. (*ḍānṭhī*).

ټانګ *ṭāng*, s.m. A period, season, time, term.

ټانګو *ṭāngū*, s.m.
ټانګئ *ṭānga-ī*, s.f. } Name of a tree and its fruit; a kind of pear tree.

ټبر *ṭabar*, s.f. A wife. s.m. Family, household. H.

ټبړ *ṭabaṛ*, s.m. Family, household.

ټبکي *ṭubkai*,
ټبلي *ṭublai*, } s.m. A pit, hole, cavity.

ټبي *ṭabai*, s.m. A flat stone, slate, slab of pottery, etc. used to bake cakes upon.

ټپ *ṭap*, a. Weak, haggard, worn, exhausted. s.m. A slap, hit, whack, rap; smack, thud, concussion. ad. Altogether, entirely, totally; used with adjectives to denote intensity. Ex. *ṭap-ṛūnd-saṛai*, s.m. A perfectly blind man. *ṭapa-kanṛa-kkhadza*, s.f. A completely deaf woman.

ټپټپاڼړي *taptapānṛai*, s.m. Name of a game played by children.

ټپریدل *ṭaparedal*, v.n. To totter, plod, stagger, creep, etc. (as an old man). P. (*tapīdan*).

ټپړ *ṭapaṛ*,
ټپڼړ *ṭapanṛ*, } s.m. Canvas, sackcloth. H.

ټپل *ṭapal*, v.n. See ټپریدل.

تپوڅ *ṭapūts*, s.m. A kite (*Milvus sp.*).

تپي *ṭapai*, s.m. A spot, blotch, or patch of colour on the hide of an animal.

تپيدل *ṭapedal*, v.n. See تپل.

تت *ṭat*, s.m. Conceit, vanity.

تتي *ṭatai*, s.m. A fop, beau, coxcomb; braggart.

تتر *ṭaṭar*, s.m. The breast, chest, thorax. Vertex, poll. H. (*ṭaṭrī*).

تتو *ṭaṭū*, s.m. A pony. H. Bridge of a fiddle.

تتوګي *ṭaṭūgai*, s.m. A small pony.

تتۍ *ṭaṭa-ī*, s.f. A matted screen; privy. H. (*ṭaṭī*).

تچ *ṭach*, s.m. See تاس.

تخ *ṭukh*, s.m. See توخ.

تر *ṭar*, s.m. Flatus, explosion of wind from behind; bosh, fudge, humbug.

ترتر *ṭarṭar*, s.m, Gabble, chatter, jabber.

ترق *ṭraq*, } s.m. See تق.
ترک *ṭrak*, }

تري *ṭarai*, s.m. Gabbler, chatterbox, prattler.

تريدل *ṭaredal*, v.n. To break wind; to gabble, jabber.

تز *ṭaz*, } s.m. A pop, puff; flatus. H. (*ṭhas*).
تس *ṭas*, } A slap, cuff, whack.

تستوس *ṭasṭūs*, s.m. Cracking, popping; discharge of firearms (as in a skirmish).

تسمس *ṭasmas*, a. Apathetic, dull, lazy.

تغ *ṭagh*, s.m. The pupil of the eye; the blue jay (*Coracias Bengalensis*). A creak, croak, grating sound.

تغر *ṭaghar*, s.m. A woollen carpet; felt; felt saddle cloth; old rag, clout, etc.

تغن *ṭaghan*, s.m. A coward, poltroon.

تغول *ṭaghawul*, v.a. To jar, grate, set on edge (as the teeth or nails).

تق *ṭaq*, s.m. A blow, rap, knock, whack, thump, etc. *ṭaq·kawul*, v.a. To bump, clash. *ṭaq·wahal*, v.a. To hit, strike, knock (as a nail, etc.).

تقول *ṭaqawul*, v.a. To censure, scold, reprove; to beat, batter, baste.

تک *ṭak*, s.m. Murrain, disease of cattle; a bang, slam; blow, thump, rap; a footfall, sound of feet.

تکا *ṭakā*, s.f. A footfall, sound of footsteps; explosion, sound of firearms.

تکارکي *ṭikārkai*, s.m. A plot of clear, hard, and level ground.

تکانه *ṭikāna*, s.f. Abode, lodging, residence, dwelling; boundary, limit, extent. H. (*ṭhikānā*).

تکاو *ṭikāo*, s.m. See تکانه.

تکتکانړي *ṭakṭakāṉrai*, s.m. Name of a game played by children; the clapper of a mill; a woodpecker.

تکر *ṭakar*, s.m. A jolt, push, shove. H.

تکړ *ṭukṛ*, s.m. A bit, morsel, piece. H. (*ṭukrā*).

تکسري *ṭaksarai*, a. Mangy; a term of abuse. s.m. Murrain.

تککه *ṭakaka*, s.f. A cross bar of wood placed above the blade of a spade for the foot to rest upon.

تکلاستي *ṭaklāstai*, a. Active, nimble, smart, handy.

تکنده‌غرمه *ṭakanda·gharma*, } s.f. Noon; mid-
تکنړه‌غرمه *ṭakaṉra·gharma*, } day; heat of noon or midday.

تکنړي *ṭakaṉrai*, a. Obstinate, stubborn, restive.

تکور *ṭakor*, s.m. Fomentation, poultice. H.

تکول *ṭakawul*, v.a. To beat, bruise, hammer.

تکه *ṭaka*, s.f. Animosity, jealousy, hatred; thunderbolt; knuckle-bone. *ṭakah*, s.m. A species of ibex, or mountain goat.

تکي *ṭakai*, s.m. A dot, spot, spec; mark, streak; a bullock, horse, etc. with a spot on the forehead; appointed time or place; an atom, drop, molecule. *ṭika-ī*,. s.f. A biscuit; wafer. H. (*tikiyā*); an orb, disk (as of the sun, etc.); a mark or butt for arrows; a loud laugh, guffaw. *pa·ṭakī*, ad. On the spot, at once, this minute.

تګ *ṭag*, s.m. A cheat, impostor; assassin, robber. H. (*ṭhag*).

تګي *ṭagī*, s.f. Cheating, deceiving, robbery, theft.

تل *ṭal*, a. Close, dense, thick; full, replete, satiated. s.m. Division of a town or village; cluster of houses; a field, bed of flowers; closeness, denseness.

تم *ṭam*, s.m. Bark of a dog, growl of a wild beast.

تمتيل *ṭamṭīl*, s.m. A sandpiper, snippet.

تمک *ṭimak*, s.m. The crosspole of a tent.

تنبل *ṭunbal*, v.a. To clean, pick (as the teeth); pluck, pick out (as thorns, etc.).

تند *ṭanḍ*, a. Corpulent, fat, stout.

تنګ *ṭang*, s.m. A creak, jar, twang, jingle. H. (*ṭankā*).

تنګ تونګ *ṭang·ṭūng*, s.m. Ding-dong, chime, notes of musical instruments.

تنګول *ṭangawul*, v.a. To jingle, clank, sound.

تنګه *ṭanga*, s.f. Name of a copper coin. H. (*ṭakā*). Money, wealth.

تنګيدل *ṭangedal*, v.n. To creak, jar, grate, twang.

توپ *ṭop*, s.m. A bound, jump, leap. H. (*ṭap*). A heap, pile, stack; excess, surplus.

توپک *ṭopak*, s.m. A musket, matchlock.

توپل *ṭopal*, s.m. The vertex, crown of the head.

توپۍ *ṭopa-ī*, s.f. A cap, hat, helmet; bowl or cup of a pipe. H. (*ṭopī*).

توته *ṭoṭa*, s.f. A bit, chip, fragment. A beggar's cup or tray. *ṭūṭa*, s.f. The hip, haunch. H. (*pūṭhā*).

توخ *ṭūkh*, s.m. Saliva, spittle.

توخه *ṭūkha*, s.f. } Cough, expectoration.
توخی *ṭūkhai*, s.m. }

توخلي *ṭūkhalai*, s.m. Hooping cough; croup. *ṭūkhala-ī*, s.f. Cap, head covering, bonnet.

توخيدل *ṭūkhedal*, v.n. To cough, expectorate, spit.

توغ *ṭūgh*, a. Bent, bowed, stooping.

توقا *ṭoqā*, s.m. A grasshopper.

توقمار *ṭoqmār*, s.m. A buffoon, jester, clown.

توقه *ṭoqa*, s.f. Jest, joke, pleasantry, ridicule. A. (*ẓuḥka*).

توقي *ṭoqī*, s.m. A jester, buffoon, clown.

توک *ṭok*, a. Closely woven (as cloth). *ṭūk*, s.m. An atom, bit, particle. H.

توکيا *ṭokiyā*, s.f. A cleaver, bill-hook.

توکيدل *ṭūkedal*, v.n. To bud, grow, germinate, sprout. S. (*ṭūknā*).

توکرۍ *ṭokra-ī*, s.f. A basket. H. (*ṭokrī*).

توکي *ṭūkai*, s.m. A piece of cloth, length of cloth; piece, patch, repair. H.

تول *ṭol*, a. All, the whole, total. s.m. A party, flock, gang, drove.

تولټال *ṭolṭāl*, a. All, the whole, sum total.

تولګي *ṭolgai*, s.m. A party, small herd or flock.

تولول *ṭolawul*, v.a. To collect, gather, bring together.

تولي *ṭolai*, s.m. An assembly, party, company.

توليدل *ṭoledal*, v.n. To assemble, congregate, flock, herd or crowd together.

تونګ *ṭong*, s.m. Irritation, provocation.

تونګاره *ṭongāra*, s.f. Insult, abuse, provocation, pecking. H. (*ṭungār*).

تيپر *ṭīpar*, s.m. A turnip.

تيت *ṭīṭ*, a. Bent, curved, crooked, bowed. *ṭīṭawul*, v.a. To bend, bow. *ṭīṭedal*, v.n. To be bent, bowed, inclined.

تيتاري *ṭīṭārai*, s.m. A plover, pewit, lapwing. H. (*ṭaṭīrī*).

تيتال *ṭīṭāl*, s.m. Cheat, imposture, fraud; evasion. P. (*ṭīṭāl*).

تيغ *ṭegh*, s.m. A belch, eructation.

خنبيدل *dzanbedal*, v.n. To shake, totter, quiver; move, wag, writhe. P. (*junbīdan*).

خنډ *dzanḍ*, s.m. Delay, procrastination.

خنګل *dzangal*, s.m. A wood; wilderness. S. (*jangal*).

خنړي *dzanṛai*, s.m. A boy, youth, school-boy.

خني *dzane*, or *dzine*, pr. The indefinite pronoun; any, some, certain, few. Also خنِ *dzani* or *dzini*.

خوان *dzwān*, s.m. An adult, young man. a. Adolescent, youthful. S. (*jawān*).

خواني *dzwānī*, s.f. Youth, adolescence.

خواني مرګ *dzwānī-marg*, s.m. A form of curse; early or untimely death. P. (*jawānā-marg*).

خور *dzaur*, s.m. Oppression, violence; trouble, pain; grief, sorrow. A. (*jaur*).

خوړند *dzwaṛand*, a. Hanging, pendant.

خوز *dzoz*, s.m. Name of a plant, the camel's thorn (*Hedysarum alhagī*). P. (*jāj*).

خوزجانه *dzoz-khāna*, s.f. A hut made of camel's thorn, and used as a cool retreat in the hot weather.

خولنه *dzolana*, s.f. A chain, fetter. P. (*zawlānah*).

خولي *dzola-ī*, s.f. Havresack, bag, wallet. H. (*jholī*).

خوم *dzūm*, s.m. A son-in-law. S. (*jamāī*).

خومګي *dzūmgai*, s.m. A young son-in-law.

خوي *dzoe*, s.m. A son. P. (*zāe*).

خي *dzai*, s.m. Child, son, descendant. See زي

خير *dzīr*, s.m. Contemplation, regard; look, survey, glance; a shrill sound, the highest note in music. P. (*jīl*). A kind of soft leather.

خيرمه *dzerma*, s.f. See زيرمه.

خيزمه *dzezma*, s.f. The eyelid.

خيل *dzel*, s.m. Ignorance, stupidity; obstinacy, perversity. A. (*jahl*). A line or string of buckets, etc. H. (*jel*).

ج

ج *jīm*, The eighth letter of the Pukkhto alphabet. It is sometimes substituted for the letters ز, ژ, and ش.

جابر *jābir*, s.m. A despot, oppressor, tyrant. A.

جابه *jāba*, s.f. A leathern jar or pot with a spout, used by grocers to pour out oil, etc. H. (*jhābā*).

جادو *jādū*, s.m. Magic, conjuring. P.

جادوګر *jādū-gar*, s.m. A conjuror, juggler, magician.

جادوګري *jādū-garī*, s.f. Conjuring, sorcery, magic.

جاډئي *jāḍa-ī*, s.f. A worn out old camel; a hag.

جار *jār*, s.m. Announcement, proclamation, notice. A. (*iẓhār*); a sacrifice, oblation, victim, offering. Evident, manifest. A. (*ẓāhir*).

جارباسل *jārbāsal*, v.a. To divert, turn aside, turn back; to vomit, spew. Def. See جاريستل.

جارچي *jārchī*, s.m. A crier, herald.

جارو *jārū*, s.m. A besom, broom, brush. H. (*jhāṛū*).

جاروتل *jārwatal*, v.n. To go back, return, revert.

جارول *jārawul*, v.a. To arrange or collect together the threads of the warp preparatory to weaving; to brush, sweep. H. (*jhāṛnā*).

جاري *jārī*, a. Current, flowing, proceeding. A.

جاريستل *jāryastal*, v.a. To vomit, spew; return, turn back. Def. See جارباسل.

جاړ *jāṛ*, s.m. Brambles, bushes, underwood; a brake, thicket; a purge, stool. H. (*jhāṛ*).

جاړه *jāṛa*, s.f. A bramble, bush, thorny bush.

جاسوس *jāsūs*, s.m. A detective, spy, emissary. A.

جاسوسي *jāsūsī*, s.f. Spying, duty of a detective.

تيک *ṭek*, s.m. The temple, side of the head.

تيک *ṭīk*, s.m. }
تيکه *ṭīka*, s.f. } An ornament for the forehead; a wafer of silver or gilt paper worn on the forehead. H. (*ṭīkā*).

تيکاو *ṭīkāo*, s.m. Abode, lodging, residence. H. (*ṭhikānā*).

تيل *ṭel*, s.m. A jostle, snove, push. H. (*ṭhel*).

تيل تال *ṭel-ṭāl*, s.m. Jostling; romping; dalliance.

تينچي *ṭainchī*, s.m. A fop, beau, coxcomb, puppy.

تينګ *ṭīng*, a. Close, compact, thick; coagulated, curdled; stiff, firm; tight, strong.

ث

ث *ṣe*, The fourth letter of the Arabic alphabet, and the sixth of the Pukkhto. It is only found in words adopted from the Arabic. It is sometimes pronounced *th* as in the English *think*.

ثابت *ṣābit*, a. Proved, confirmed, established; firm, durable, stable. A.

ثاني *ṣānī*, a. Second, the second. A.

ثبوت *ṣabūt*, s.m. Conviction, proof; firmness, stability. A.

ثنا *ṣanā*, s.f. Applause, praise, eulogium. A.

ثواب *ṣawāb*, s.m. A virtuous action; future reward of virtue. A.

څ

څ *dze*, or *dzīm*, The seventh letter of the Pukkhto alphabet. It is a soft form of ج, and is used instead of that letter in some words derived from the Persian and Hindī. It is also sometimes substituted for ز and س

څار *dzār*, s.m. An offering, sacrifice, victim.

څاله *dzāla*, s.f. A spider's web; bird's nest. S. (*jālā*).

څان *dzān*, s.m. Soul, life; mind, spirit; self; the privates; a lover, loved one. a. Beloved, dear. P. (*jān*).

څاندار *dzāndār*, s.m. Having life, an animal.

څانکندن *dzān-kandan*, s.m. Agony of death, the death-struggle. P. (*jān-kandan*).

څاي *dzāe*, s.m. Place, site, situation, station. P. (*jāe*). *dzāe-laral*, v.a. To fit, suit, become. *dzāe-nīwul*, v.a. To take up place or position, locate oneself; inhabit, colonize; take effect.

څبله *dzabla*, ad. Together, in company, one with another. *dzabla-bānde*, Fold on fold, etc.

څز *dzaz*, s.m. A fizz, hiss, sputter.

څکه *dzaka*, ad. Because, hence, consequently, therefore, on this account. P. (*zirāki*).

څګر *dzigar*, s.m. The liver; heart, vitals; courage, mind, pluck. P. (*jigar*).

څل *dzal*, ad. Once, one time. *yo-dzal*, once. *dwah-dzala*, twice. *dre-dzala*, thrice. *las-dzala*, ten times, etc. *dzul*, s.m. Body clothes for a horse, or for cattle. H. (*jhul*).

څلوبي *dzaloba-ī*, s.f. A kind of sweetmeat. H. (*jalebī*).

څله *dzala*, s.f. Perplexity, distraction, hesitation.

څلکيدل *dzalkedal*, }
څليدل *dzaledal*, } v.n. To glitter, shine, sparkle, lighten. H. (*jhalak*).

څما *dzamā*, The genitive case singular of the first personal pronoun زه *zah*: Mine, of me.

څمل *dzamal*, v.a. To blink, wink (as in sunlight).

څموږ *dzamūg*, }
څمونګ *dzamūng*, } The genitive plural of the first personal pronoun: Ours, of us.

څناور *dzanāwar*, s.m. An animal. P. (*jānwar*).

څنبل *dzanbal*, v.a. See څمل.

څنبول *dzanbawul*, v.a. To wag, shake; wink.

جاكي *jākai*, a. Curdled, coagulated, clotted (as blood).

جاگير *jāgīr*, s.m. Land held in fief, a pension in land, land granted by government as a reward for military service, etc. P.

جال *jāl*, s.m. A net, sash. S. a. Counterfeit, forged. A. (*j'al*).

جاله *jāla*, s.f. A raft of timber or inflated hides; a bird's nest.

جالئ *jāla-ī*, s.f. A cobweb; the green vegetation in pools and watercourses; duckweed. S. (*jālā*).

جام *jām*, s.m. A bowl, cup, goblet. P.

جامبړه *jāmbṛa*, s.f. A coppice, brake, thicket.

جامه *jāma*, s.f. Garment, dress, robe; the jaw, the upper or lower jaw bone. P.

جان *jān*, s.m. See ځان.

جانب *jānib*, s.m. Part, side. ad. Towards. A.

جانجي *jānjī*, s.m. A bridegroom's wedding guest or attendant.

جانور *jānwar*, s.m. See ځناور.

جاوجئ *jāwja-ī*, s.f. The hem, skirt, border, edging, etc. of a dress.

جاوله *jāwla*, s.f. Bees' wax, fresh resin, gluten of wheat, milky sap of plants, etc.

جاويد *jāwīd*, s.m.
جاويدان *jāwīdān*, } Endless, eternal. P.

جاويداني *jāwīdānī*, s.f. Eternity, immortality.

جاه *jāh*, s.m. Dignity, pomp, rank. P.

جاهل *jāhil*, a. Ignorant, barbarous, brutal. s.m. Fool, blockhead, ignoramus. A.

جاهلي *jāhilī*, s.f. Ignorance, stupidity.

جاي *jāe*, s.m. See ځاي.

جائداد *jā-edād*, s.m. Assets, effects, property. An assignment of land for the maintenance of troops. P.

جبر *jabr*, s.m. Force, oppression, violence. A.

جبه *jaba*, s.f. A bog, mere, marsh. H. (*jhābar*). *juba*, s.f. A frock, shirt; coat of mail. A.

جبين *jabīn*, s.m. The forehead. P.

جت *jat*, s.m. Name of a tribe located in the western parts of Afghanistan; they are largely engaged in trade.

جټ *jaṭ*, s.m. Name of a clan of Rajpūts, settled in the Panjāb; they are entirely occupied in agriculture.

جثه *jus̤s̤a*, s.f. Body, figure. A.

ججوره *jajūra*, s.f. The crop of a bird, maw, the first stomach of ruminants; double chin, dewlap. H. (*jhojh*).

ججوئ *jajū-ī*, s.f. Name of a plant, Anemone.

جخ *jak͟h*, s.m. Froth, foam. H. (*jhāg*). A midge, water-fly.

جخت *juk͟ht*, a. Accurate, even, exact. P. (*juft*).

جد *jadd*, s.m. An ancestor, grandfather. A.

جدا *judā*, s.f. Apart, separate, distinct, different. P.

جدل *jadal*, s.f. Altercation, battle, strife. A.

جدول *jadwal*, s.m. Lines drawn on the sides of a page: marginal lines in a book. A.

جديد *jadīd*, a. Fresh, new. A.

جذام *juẕām*, s.m. Leprosy. A.

جذب *jaẕb*, s.m. Absorption; imbibing, absorbing. A.

جذبه *jaẕba*, s.f. Fury, passion, rage. A.

جر *jar*, s.m. A gutter, drain; crack, fissure, cleft, etc. in the ground. P.

جراح *jarrāḥ*, s.m. A surgeon. A.

جرس *jaras*, s.m. A bell. A.

جركانړي *jur·kāṉrai*, s m. To boot, surplus, over and above, into the bargain, profit, gain.

جرگتو *jirgatū*, s.m. Member of a Jirga.

جرگه *jirga*, s.f. An assembly, council, meeting, etc. of the heads of a village community, or the representatives of a clan, for consultation and deliberation on matters affecting the interests of the people they represent; a consultation.

جرم *jurm* or *jirm*, s.m. Crime, fault, sin. A.

جرمانه *jurmāna*, s.f. A fine, penalty.

جرموړه *jarmoṛa*, s.f. Name of an eruption of the skin; hives, nettlerash.

جرندګري *jaranḍ·garai*, s.m. A miller.

جرنده *jaranda*, s.f. A mill for grinding corn, whether worked by cattle or water.

جرندئ *jaranda-ī*, s.f. A door bolt.

جره *jurrah*, s.m. A male falcon. A. See باز.

جريب *jarīb*, s.m. A measure of land equal to four kanāl. See کنال.

جريده *jarīdah*, a. Alone, solitary, unattended, unencumbered, travelling post-haste. A.

جړ *jaṛ*, s.m. Bubbling, oozing, trickling with a murmur (as water from a spring head). H. (*jhir·jhir*).

جړانګو *jaṛāngū*, s.m. Name of a tree (*Cassia fistula*).

جړاو *jaṛāo*, a. Jewelled. S.

جړجوړي *juṛ·jūṛai*, a. Trickling, murmuring, bubbling.

جړنګ *juṛang*, s.m. A creeping plant (as melons, etc).

جړئ *jaṛa-ī*, s.f. Continued rain, shower, wet weather. H. (*jhaṛī*). The root of a herb used as a remedy for snake bites. S. (*jaṛī*).

جز *juz*, s.m. A part, portion, section; division of a book containing eight leaves. A.
juz, p. Besides, except. P.

جزا *jazā*, s.f. Retaliation, requital, return; compensation, reward. A.

جزائل *jazā-el*, s.m. A rifle; long gun; swivel, wall piece, camel-gun. A.

جزايلچي *jazā-elchī*, s.m. A sharpshooter, marksman, rifleman.

جزبز *jizbiz*, s.m. A game played with knuckle bones. P.

جزبندي *juzbandī*, s.f. Binding of a book.

جزدان *juzdān*, s.m. Book-cover, bag for books.

جزيره *jazīra*, s.f. An island. A.

جزيه *jaziya*, s.f. A poll tax, capitation tax, levied by the Afghans on their subjects of another race and creed. A.

جس *jas*, s.m. Pewter. H. (*jast*).

جست *jast*, s.m. A bound, jump, leap, spring. P.

جست وجوي *just·o·jūe*, s.m. Enquiry, investigation, search. P.

جسته *jista*, s.f. A kind of boot with high narrow heels. P.

جسر *jasr*, s.m. A large, strong camel. A.
jisr, s.m. A bridge. A.

جسم *jism*, s.m. The body, living body. A.

جسه *jussa*, s.f. The human body. See جثه.

جشي *jashai*, s.m. Name of a prickly plant: the prickle of some kinds of grass.

جغ *jugh*, s.m. Yoke of a plough; yoke for oxen; a pair of oxen, S. (*jug*).

جغاغه *jaghāgha*, s.f. Name of a herb, caper spurge.

جغندر *jughandar*, s m. Beetroot. P. (*chuqandar*).

جفا *jafā*, s.f. Oppression, violence, injustice. P.

جفاکار *jafākār*, s.m. A tyrant, oppressor.

جفاکاري *jafākārī*, s.f. Tyranny, oppression.

جفت *juft*, s.m. A couple, match, pair. P.

جفتک *juftak*, s.f. A kick with both hind legs.

جق جق *jaq·jaq*, s.m. Cackle of fowls; chatter, gabble.

جک *jak*, s.m. See جغ.

جکړ *jakaṛ*, s.m. Gust of wind, wind and rain, drift of wind. H. (*jhakkar*).

جګړه *jagaṛa*, s.f. Altercation, strife, contention, wrangling. H. (*jhagṛa*).

جګناتئ *jagnāta-ī*, s.f. A kind of fine cloth, muslin.

جل *jal*, s.m. A hedge of thorns round a house. A skylark. *j-il* or *ja-al*, s.f. A damsel, maid, virgin.

جلا *jilā*, s.f. Exile, separation. A. *jilā-waṭan*, s.m. Banishment, exile, emigration.

جلاب *julāb*, s.m. Cathartic, purge. A.

جلات *jallāt*, s.m. An executioner. A. (*jallād*).

جلاجل *jalājil*, s.m. A small bell: strings of them are fastened on the necks of cattle and the ankles of women.

جلار *jalār*, s.m. An irrigation wheel worked on the bank of a stream.

جلال *jalāl*, s.m. Majesty, splendour, glory, dignity, grandeur, state. A.

جلب *jalab*, s.m. A rein; attendance, retinue, escort. A. (*jilaw*).

جلبنګ *jalbang*, s.m. The stinging nettle (*Urtica interrupta*).

جلت *jalt*, a. Quick, active, brisk, fast; hasty, rash. P. (*jald*).

جلته *jalata*, s.f. A hamper, tall wicker basket.

جلتيا *jaltiyā*, s.f. Haste, speed, hurry, etc.

جلد *jald*, a. See جلت. *jild*, s.m. A book, volume, edition. A.

جلک *jalak*, s.m. A spindle, spinning reel.

جلنانۍ *jalnāna-ī*, s.f. A kitchen, cook-house. P.

جلندرۍ *jalandara-ī*, s.f. A whirligig.

جلوه *jilwa*, s.f. Adornment, splendour; nuptial meeting or feast; blandishment, coquetry. A.

جلۍ *jala-ī*, s.f. A scream, shriek.

جم *jam*, s.m. A cluster, group; clan, tribe; faction, party, society.

جماعت *jamā'at*, s.m. Assembly, congregation, crowd; mosque, house of prayer, meeting house. A.

جمال *jamāl*, s.m. Beauty, elegance. A.

جمالګوټه *jamālgoṭa*, s.f. A purgative nut, seed of *Croton tiglium*. A.

جمدر *jamdar*, s.m. Darnel, tares, wild oats. P.

جمعه *jama'a*, s.f. Assembly, congregation; sum total, amount, whole; plural number. A. (*jama'*). *juma'a*, s.f. Friday. A.

جمله *jumla*, s.f. Aggregate, whole, sum total. A.

جن *j-in* or *ja-an*, s.f. A damsel, maid. See جل. *jinn*, s.m. A demon, devil, one of the genii. A.

جناب *janāb*, s.m. Excellency, highness, majesty; dignity, power; margin, side; threshold. A.

جنازه *janāza*, s.f. A funeral. A.

جنبان *junbān*, a. Moving, stirring, shaking. P.

جنبش *junbish*, s.m. Agitation, movement. P.

جنبق *junbaq*, a. Close, clustered, massed.

جنبه *janba*, s.f. Party, faction, clan. A. (*jānib*).

جنت *jannat*, s.m. Paradise. A.

جنج *janj*, s.m. Bridegroom's party in a marriage procession or feast: party of men who accompany the bridegroom to fetch the bride home.

جنجال *janjāl*, s.m. Difficulty, bother, trouble; contention, strife, wrangling. S.

جنجړ *janjanr*, s.m. Name of a kind of vetch.

جندره *jandra*, s.f. A padlock, instrument for drawing wire.

جنډه *janḍa*, s.f. Banner, ensign, standard, flag. H. (*jhanḍā*).

جنس *jins*, s.m. Genus, kind, species; gender; merchandise, goods, etc. A.

جنګ *jang*, s.m. Battle, combat, fight, war. P. *jung*, a. Collected, gathered, crumpled. s.m. A young camel. A collection, miscellany, assembly, gathering.

جنګه *junga*, s.f. Excess, surplus, boot, profit.

جنګي *jangī*, a. Warlike, brave. *jangai*, s.m. A grove, plantation, coppice. *jungai*, a. Collected, gathered (as cloth). s.m. A young camel.

جنوب *junūb*, s.m. The South. A.

جنون *junūn*, s.m. A madman, maniac; insanity, madness. A.

جني *jina-ī*, s.f. A girl, daughter (not arrived at puberty); a virgin; a spinster.

جو *jcu*, s.m. Barley. P.

جواب *jawāb*, s.m. Answer, reply; dismissal. A.

جوار *jwār*, s.m. Maize, Indian corn (*Zea mays*). H. (*joār*). *narī-jwār*, s.m. Indian millet (*Holcus sorghum*).

جوارگر *jūār-gar*, s.m. A gambler, gamester.

جواري *jūārī*, s.m. A gambler, gamester. H. s.f. Gambling, gaming. *jwārī*, s.m. See جوار.

جوال *jowāl*, s.m. A sack, bag. P.

جوانوان *janwāwān*, s.m. A kind of mustard or rape; the seeds yield an acrid oil, used as a cattle medicine, etc.

جواهر *jawāhir*, s.m. A gem, jewel. A.

جوبه *joba*, s.f. Emporium, market, mart. P.

جوټه *jūṭa*, s.f. Leavings, refuse (as of food, etc.); base, false (as coins, gems, etc.). S. (*jhūṭhā*). *joṭah*, s.m. A buffalo calf.

جوټي *jūṭa-ī*, s.f. Nodding, rocking (as in sleep); swaying, vibrating, swinging.

جودر *jawdar*, s.m. See جمدر.

جور *jaur*, s.m. See ځور.

جوړ *joṛ*, a. Healthy, strong, vigorous; prepared, arranged; right, correct. P. ad. Exactly, precisely, well.

جوړاب *joṛāb*, s.m. Beauty, elegance, grace.

جوړښت *joṛikkht*, s.m. Alliance, confederation, union; combination, junction.

جوړه *joṛa*, s.f. A couple, set, pair; suit of clothes. H. (*joṛā*). Peace, amity, concord, truce.

جوز *jauz*, s.m. A nut, kernel. A.

جوزه *jauza*, s.f. A nutmeg.

جوس *jawas*, s.m. Area, courtyard.

جوش *josh*, s.m. Effervescence, ebullition; heat, rage; passion, lust. P.

جوکل *jokal*, v.a. To weigh, measure. H. (*jokhnā*).

جولا *jolā*, s.m. A weaver; spider. P. (*julāh*).

جولان *jaulān*, s.m. Moving, wandering; capering, springing, lunging. P.

جولانگري *jaulāngarī*, s.m. Cantering, galloping; exercising, lunging (a horse).

جوله *jola*, s.f. See جهوله.

جولي *jola-ī*, s.f. See ځولي.

جونګړه *jūngaṛa*, s.f. A hut, hovel, cabin, shed; hamlet. H. (*jhompṛā*).

جوني *jūna-ī*, s.f. See جني.

جووه *jowa*, s.f. A gutter, drain, water channel (for irrigating a field, etc.). P. (*jūe*).

جوهر *jauhar*, s.m. A jewel, gem; essence, matter; virtue, work; the water or wavy marks on some kinds of steel.

جوهړه *jūhaṛa*, s.f. A crease, pucker, wrinkle, furrow. H. (*jhūrī*).

جه *jah*, a. Stubborn, refractory (as an animal); at bay, resisting. *ja-ja*, in. Words used to drive cattle.

جهاد *jihād*, s.m. Crescentade, war with infidels. A.

جهاز *jahāz*, s.m. A ship. P.

جهان *jahān*, s.m. The world, universe; people. P.

جهت *jihat*, s.m. Account, cause, reason; side, surface; form, manner, mode. A.

جهر *jihr*, s.m. A kind of dance performed by men.

جهل *jahl*, s.m. Ignorance, stupidity. A.

جهم جکړ *jham-jakaṛ*, s.m. Wind and rain in gusts, drifts of wind and rain. H

جهوله *jahola*, s.f. Name of a disease; chlorosis, anœmia, splenitis.

جي *jai*, s.m. A leather bag for water.

جيب *jeb*, s.m. A pocket. S.

جيټ *jet*, s.m. Name of the second Hindu month, May-June; name of a tree, Egyptian Sesbania.

جينکۍ *jīnaka-ī*, s.f. A little girl, female child.

څ

څ *tse*, The ninth letter of the Pukkhto alphabet. It is a softened form of چ for which it is substituted in many words adopted from the Persian and Hindī. It is sometimes used instead of س and ش.

څاپېړه *tsāpeṛa*, s.f. A slap, blow, cuff. S. (*chapeṭā*).

څاڅکي *tsātskai*, s.m. A drop, minim, sprinkle.

څادر *tsādar*, s.m. A sheet, veil, mantle. H. (*chādar*).

څار *tsār*, s.m. Spying, scouting.

څارل *tsāral*, v.a. To spy, scout.

څاروي *tsārwai*, s.m. Cattle; a quadruped, beast, grazing animal. P. (*chārwā*).

څاره *tsāra*, s.f. Aid, help; cure, remedy. P. (*chāra*).

څاري *tsārī*, s.m. A scout, spy.

څاښت *tsākkht*, s.m. Forenoon, midtime between sunrise and noon; a meal taken at that time, breakfast. P. (*chāsht*).

څاښتي *tsākkhtī*. s.f. Breakfast, forenoon meal.

څاښکه *tsākkhaka*, s.f. A starling.

څاښي *tsākkhai*, s.m. Spinning rod, spindle.

څاک *tsāk*, s.m. Fissure, rent, slit; opening of a pocket; skirt or corner of a dress. P. (*chāk*).

څانګ *tsāng*, s.m. } څانګه *tsānga*, s.f. } Wing of a bird; branch of a tree; pang, sharp pain.

څپ *tsap*, s.m. A winnowing tray made of reeds; winnowing. *tsap-wahal*, v.a. To winnow.

څپر *tsapar*, s.m. A thatch, thatched roof. H. (*chhappar*). A wooden frame used as a crusher to separate grain from husk.

څپرکي *tsaparkai*, s.m. A film, flake, pellicle, scale; thin sheet of water (as after rain).

څپري *tsaparai*, s.m. A puddle, pool. H. (*chhaprī*).

څپړ *tsapaṛ*, s.f. Pad of a camel's or elephant's foot; sound of soft footsteps. H. (*chhap*).

څپک *tsapak*, s.m. A hand's breadth, hand, palm. H. (*chappā*). A flake, pellicle, scale.

څپلاک *tsaplāk*, a. Crushed, squashed, pressed, squeezed. H. (*chhapākā*).

څپلۍ *tsapla-ī*, s.f. A sandal (of leather or grass. H. (*chappal*).

څپوټکي *tsapūṭkai*, s.m. An old cloth, kerchief, or duster tied over the head by women when grinding corn, sweeping the house, etc. H. (*chapoṭī*).

څپولي *tsapolai*, a. Entangled, knotted, matted (as the hair). H. (*chipatā*).

څپه *tsapah*, a. Inverted, upside down. *tsapa*, s.f. A wave, billow; blast, gust, puff, etc. of wind. H. (*chhappā*).

څپياکه *tsapiyāka*, s.f. A cow-dung cake (flat and dry), used as fuel.

څپېړه *tsapeṛah*, a. Grey, ash-coloured; pale. in. Coward! dastard! term of abuse. *tsapeṛa*, s.f. A slap with the open hand.

څپېدل *tsapedal*, v.n. To flutter, hover, flap the wings.

څټ *tsaṭ*, s.m. Nape, back of the neck.

څټک *tsaṭak*, s.m. A sledge hammer.

څټکي *tsaṭakai*, s.m. A small sledge hammer.

څټل *tsaṭal*, v.a. To lick, lap. H. (*chāṭnā*). *tsaṭal*, v.n. To be accumulated, collected, massed. s.m. Heap, mass; wholesale, by the lump. P. (*chastan*).

څټوټ *tsaṭwaṭ*, s.m. Apoplexy, sudden death.

ad. All at once, suddenly, instanter. H. (c͟hat·pat).

څتېه tsata, s.f. A sack; a sackful. H. (c͟hat).

څڅوبي tsatsobai, s.m. The coping or eaves of a roof or wall; a leaking or dropping of water.

څڅول tsatsawul, v.a. To pour by drops, drop, distil.

څڅېدل tsatsedal, v.n. To leak, trickle, drop, distil. P. (s͟hās͟hīdan).

څخو tsak͟ho, a. Some, few, somewhat, more or less. ad. Slightly, in some degree, somewhat.

څخه tsak͟hah, p. About, near, with, beside. ad. Together, altogether. P. (c͟hak͟h).

څخېدل tsk͟hedal, v.n. To crawl, creep, go on all fours (as a child). P. (c͟hak͟hīdan).

څخيکول tsk͟he·kawul, v.a. To hop, skip.

څر tsar, s.m. Food, forage, pasture. S. (c͟har).

څرپ tsrap, s.m. A flutter, flap; whirr.

څرپول tsrapawul, v.a. To flutter, flap the wings.

څرپېدل tsrapedal, v.n. To flounder, flap about (as a fish in shallow water).

څرخ tsark͟h, s.m. A wheel; grindstone; revolution, turn, spin; chance, fortune; the heavens; a kind of falcon; a stab, puncture, prick. P. (c͟hark͟h).

څرخه tsark͟ha, s.f. A reel; spinning wheel. P. (c͟hark͟ha).

څرخندوکي tsark͟handūkai, s.m. A teetotum, a boy's tōp.

څرخول tsark͟hawul, v.a. To spin, reel, twirl, turn.

څرخېدل tsark͟hedal, v.n. To revolve, spin, etc.

څرګند tsargand, a. Clear, evident, apparent, manifest, plain.

څرل tsaral, v.n. See څرېدل.

څرمن tsarman, s.f. Hide, skin; leather. P. (c͟harm).

څرمه tsarma, s.f. See څيلمه.

څروټکه tsarwatka, s.f. An ember, burning coal, live ashes.

څرول tsarawul, v.a. To graze, pasture cattle. P. (c͟harāndan or c͟harānīdan).

څرېدل tsaredal, v.n. To graze, browse, crop. P. (c͟harīdan).

څريکه tsirīka, s.f. A prick, throb, lancing or shooting pain (as of a boil, etc.). P. (c͟hark͟h). A spot, splash, stain (as of mud, etc.).

څړه tsaṛah, a. Alone, solitary; unmarried, single; light, unencumbered; simple, S. (c͟hhaṛā). tsaṛa·lār, s.f. A footpath, bye road, track, etc. only practicable for one man at a time.

څړئ tsaṛa-ī, s.f. A top knot, tuft or lock of hair on the crown of a shaven head.

څږي tsagai, s.m. The lungs, a lung.

څښاک tskkhāk or tsakshāk, s.m. Beverage, drink, liquor. k͟hwurāk·o·tskkhāk, s.m. Aliment, food, victuals, meat and drink.

څښتن tsakkhtan, s.m. Owner, proprietor, lord, master, husband.

څښکو tsakkhkū, s.f. Name of a plant (*Cassia absus*): the seeds are used as a remedy in ophthalmia. P. (c͟hāksū or c͟hāks͟hū).

څښکوړي tsakkhkūṛai, s.m. A small pipe, tube, nozzle, spout, etc.; child's penis.

څښل tskkhal, tsakkhal, or tsakshal, v.a. To drink, absorb, imbibe. P. (c͟has͟hīdan or c͟hakānīdan).

څک tsak, a. Stiff, unpliant, rigid. s.m. Lumbago. H. (c͟hik).

څکل tsakal, v.a. To taste. S. (c͟hakhnā) or P. (c͟has͟hīdan).

څکنتون tsakintūn, } s.m. Flavour, taste,
څکندن tsakindan, } savour.

څکول tskawul, v.a. To cause to drink water (as cattle); to draw, lengthen, stretch.

څکوندل tskūndal, v.a. To pinch, tweak; squeeze, wring. P. (c͟hakāndan).

څکه *tsaka*, s.f. Flavour, taste, relish; a precipice, cliff. *tsaka* or *tska*, ad. Then, therefore, thus.

څکي *tsakai*, s.m. A basket or safe suspended from the roof, to preserve the contents from cats, insects, etc. s. (*chhīkā*).

څکيدل *tskedal*, v.n. See څخيدل.

څلور *tsalor*, a. Four. P. (*chahār*).

څلورم *tsaloram*, a. Fourth.

څلويښت *tsalwekkht* or *tsalwekskht*, a. Forty. P. (*chahār-bīst*).

څلويښتي *tsalwekkhtī*, s.f. The forty days of purification after childbirth; the fortieth day after the death of a person, when the relatives visit the grave, and feed the poor, etc.

څله *tsala*, ad. Why? wherefore? what for? P. (*charā*).

څلي *tsalai*, s.m. A ring for the finger or toe. H. (*chhallā*); a pile or heap of stones on the grave of a martyr (generally somebody murdered on the way side); a pillar of mud or masonry, as a boundary mark; a mound or platform from which to watch a field; a butt or mark for arrows; a temporary platform or shed.

څليښ *tsalekkh*, }
څليښت *tsalekkht*, } s.m. Glue. P. (*saresh*).

څليښناک *tsalekkhnāk*, a. Adhesive, glutinous, cohesive, clammy, viscous.

څم *tsam*, a. Flat, smooth, level, even.

څمڅي *tsamtsa-ī*, s.f. A spoon, ladle. P. (*chamcha*).

څملاستل *tsamlāstal*, }
څملل *tsamlal*, } v.n. To lie down, recline, repose, lie flat.

څملول *tsamlawul*, v.a. To put to bed, put to rest.

څنډل *tsandal*, v.a. To agitate, shake, dust (as clothes), wave (as a sword). H. (*chhānṭnā*).

څنډه *tsanda*, s.f. Brim, margin, edge; fringe, rim, verge, side.

څنګ *tsang*, s.m. The side, flank. *tsang-pa-tsang*, ad. Abreast, side by side.

څنګزن *tsangzan*, a. Top-heavy, tilted, lurched over.

څنګل *tsangal*, }
څنګله *tsangala*, } s.f. The elbow; elbow joint; the forearm, cubit.

څنګه *tsanga*, ad. How? In what manner?

څو *tso*, a. Any, some, somewhat. P. (*chand*). ad. Till, until. P. (*chūn*). How many? how much? P. (*chand*).

څوارلس *tswārlas*, a. Fourteen.

څوباړي *tsobāṛai*, s.m. A flat piece of wood used to beat clothes in the process of washing. P. (*chobah*).

څوټ *tsoṭ*, s.m. Attack, onset, foray, sortie; a blow, contusion, hurt. s. (*choṭ*).

څوڅ *tsūts*, s.m. A porpoise. s. (*sūs*).

څورب *tsorb*, a. Fat, corpulent, stout. P. (*charb*).

څورلي *tswarlai*, s.m. A chisel; a burglar's instrument for digging through a mud wall.

څوړ *tsoṛ*, a. Crooked, wry, crumpled; emaciated, thin, withered (as a child badly nourished).

څوړي *tsoṛai*, s.m. A bullock, etc. with crumpled horns,

څوښۍ *tsūkkha-ī*, s.f. The penis of a boy; a nozzle, spout. P. (*choshak*).

څوک *tsok*, pr. Who? Which? Some, certain. Used only with reference to human beings.

څوکه *tsūka*, s.f. Apex, peak, tip, point, beak.

څوکۍ *tsoka-ī*, s.f. A guard, watch; place or station of a guard; tour of watching. H. (*chaukī*).

څول *tswal*, a. Tattered, torn, rent, worm-eaten. *tswal-tswal*, a. In rags, in tatters, in shreds.

خومبره tsombra,
خومره tsomra,
خونبره tsonbra, } ad. How much?

خونڅئي tsontsa-ī, s.f. See خمڅئي.

خونړکه tsūnraka,
خونړه tsunra, } s.f. The tuft or curl of hair left on the crown or temples of a shaven head. H. (chondā).

خوني tsone, ad. How much?

څوهره tsūhra, s.f. Hernia, rupture. H. (chūhrā).

څوي tsawai, s.m. Ambush, cover, ambuscade.

څه tsah, pr. What, any, some: what? P. (chi).

څهره tsihra, s.f. Face, countenance, visage. H. (chihrā).

څيخل tsekhal, v.a. To probe, prick, stab; cram, stuff. P. (sīkh, a probe).

څير tser, a. Like, similar, resembling.

څيره tsera, s.f. Picture, portrait, image, idol; effigy, scarecrow, grimace. P. (chehr).

څيريدل tsīredal, v.n. See شليدل.

څيړه tsīṛa, s.f. A line, file, row; party, knot, troop.

څيز tsīz, s.m. A thing, item, article, object. P. (chīz).

څيلمه tselma, s.f. Border, margin, edge, side.

چ

چ che, or chīm, is the tenth letter of the Pukkhto alphabet. It is sounded like the ch in chair.

چابک chābuk, a. Active, quick, alert. s.m. A whip. P.

چابکي chābukī, s.f. Activity, dispatch, celerity.

چاپ chāp, s.m. Impression, stamp, print; a seal; an edition; flint lock (of a gun, etc.). H. (chāmp). a. Printed, stamped. H. (chhāp).

چاپلوس chālpūs, s.m. A flatterer, wheedler, toady. P. (chālpos).

چاپلوسي chāplūsī, s.f. Flattery, toadyism.

چاپه chāpa, s.f. A stamp, die, seal; a bundle of thorns of the ber bush, after the leaves have been shaken off. H. (chāp).

چاپي chāpī, s.f. Shampooing, pressing or squeezing the limbs. H. (chāmpī).

چاپير chāper, ad. All round, roundabout, around, on all sides. H. (chaupher).

چار chār, a. Four. P. s.m. Affair, business; remedy, cure. P.

چارخولک chār-khwalak, s.m. A cock's comb, wattle.

چاره chāra, s.f. Cure, help, remedy. P.

چاړا chāṛā, a. Stammering, stuttering; dumb, mute.

چاړه chāṛa, s.f. A long knife. H. (chhurā).

چاغ chāgh, a. Healthy, plump, vigorous; fat, stout, corpulent. P. (chāq).

چاک chāk, s.m. A fissure, rent, slit, chāk-kawul, v.a. To rend, split open, disembowel. Also چاق.

چاکر chākar, s.m. Servant, help, retainer. P.

چاکري chākarī, s.f. Attendance, service. P.

چاکو chākū,
چاقو chāqū, } s.m. A penknife. P.

چاګل chāgul, s.m. A leather bottle for water. P. (chaghal).

چال chāl, s.m. Gait, motion, pace; bound, spring; custom, habit; manner, way; artifice, deceit, trick. S. Vomiting, spewing. H. (chhāl). chāl-kawul, v.a. To vomit, spew.

چالاک chālāk, a. Active, clever; dexterous, expert. P.

چالاکي chālākī, s.f. Activity, dexterity. P.

چاڼ chānr, a. Filtered, sifted, strained. H. (chhānā).

چاڼه chānra, s.f. Thatch, roofing of reeds,

twigs, etc. as a flooring for the earth of the roof. H. (*chhān*).

چانړي *chāṛrī*, s.m. A dung-beetle.

چاود *chāwd*, a. Cracked, split. s.m. A fissure, rent.

چاودل *chāwdal*, v.n. To crack, split.

چاودينک *chāwdīnak*, a. Bold, pert, saucy (as a child).

چاول *chāwul*, s.m. A plummet. H. (*sāhūl*).

چاه *chāh*, s.m. A well. P.

چايل *chāyal*, s.m. A mantle, veil of chintz.

چپ *chap*, a. The left hand, left side. P. *chip*, or *chup*, a. Silent. in. Silence! Hush! H.

چپاو *chapāo*, s.m. A foray, raid, surprise.

چپاول *chapāwul*, s.m. An advance guard of cavalry.

چپړدخ *chapaṛdakh*, s.m. A game played by boys: ducks and drakes, pitch and toss.

چپړوس *chapṛūs*, a. See چاپلوس.

چپک *chapak*, a. Squint-eyed, squinting, askew. *chapake-starge*, Squinting eyes.

چپن *chapan*, s.m. A coat, frock. H. (*chapkan*).

چپه *chapah*, a. Inverted. P. *chapa*, s.f. A billow, wave; blast, puff, gust of wind; swoop of a hawk; height or crisis of a disease; an oar, paddle. H. See څپه.

چپي *chapa-ī*, s.f. A kiss. H. (*pachchī*).

چت *chit*, a. Flattened, pressed, crushed, squashed, H. *chat*, s.m. Ceiling, roof. H. (*chhat*).

چتر *chatr*, s.m. Scar of a wound, bald spot on the head. H. (*chittī*).

چتري *chatrai*, a. Scarred, bald. s.m. Awning, canopy; umbrella. S. (*chhattar*).

چتي *chita-ī*, s.f. A titmouse. H. (*chiṭṭī*).

چټ *chaṭ*, a. Bald-faced, beardless. s.m. A rake, debauchee, profligate, vagabond; thief, robber. P. (*chattah*).

چټ پټ *chaṭ-paṭ*, ad. Hastily, quickly. H.

چټاکي *chiṭāka-ī*, s.f. Name of a weight equal to two ounces (Avoirdupois). H. (*chhaṭānk*).

چټکه *chiṭka*, s.f. A kind of red cotton cloth.

چټي *chaṭī*, s.f. Debauchery, profligacy.

چج *chaj*, s.m. A tray for winnowing corn, etc. P. (*chach*).

چجک *chajak*, s.m. The trigger of a gun.

چجه *chaja*, s.f. The poles projecting from the roof of a house; the side ribs of an ox, etc.; the crest or hood of a snake; stakes driven into the ground for catching fish. H. (*chhujā*).

چخړبه *chakhṛaba*, s.f. Mud, slime, ground saturated with rain.

چخړه *chikhṛa*, s.f. See چخي.

چخن *chikhan*, a. Rheumy, mattery; filthy, dirty. P. (*chirk*).

چخه *chikha*, in. Away! Begone! Get out! P. (*chakhe*).

چخي *chikhai*, s.m. Mucus, rheum, matter from the nose or eyes, etc.

چر *char*, s.m. Chirp, twitter of a bird; chatter, prattle of children. A sand bank, mud deposited by a flood. H. *chur*, s.m. A gutter, furrow made by running water. *chari*, ad. See چري.

چراغ *chirāgh*, s.m. A light, lamp. P. Illumination.

چرب *charb*, a. See څورب.

چربي *charbī*, s.f. Fat, tallow, suet. P.

چرت *churt*, s.m. A doze, nap; nodding. H.

چرته *charta*, ad. Where; anywhere; ever.

چرچري *char-chara-ī*, s.f. A cracker, squib, firework.

چرخ *charkh*, s.m. See څرخ.

چرړه *chirṛa*, s.f. A rag, shred, tatter. H. (*chithṛā*).

چرس *chars*, s.m. A resinous product obtained from the flowers of the Indian hemp, and used as an intoxicating drug. H. (*charras*).

چرسي *charsī*, s.m. One addicted to the use of chars.

چرغ *chargh*, s.m. Name of a kind of hawk (*Falco sacer*). P. (*charkh*).

چرک *chirk*, s.m. Dirt, filth; pus, matter. P.

چرکين *chirkīn*, a. Dirty, filthy; purulent, mattery. P.

چرگ *chirg*, s.m. A cock. a. Clever, shrewd, canny. Dappled, pied, spotted, mottled.

چرگ بانگ *chirg·bāng*, s.m. Cock-crow, day-break. Also *chir·bāng*, or *char·bāng*.

چرگ برگ *chrag·brag*, a. Piebald, spotted, streaked.

چرگک *chirgak*, s.m. The hoopoe. Also called *mullā·chargak*.

چرگوړي *chirgūṛai*, s.m. A chicken, pullet.

چرگي *chargai*, s.m. An animal with a white face, or with a spot on the forehead. S. (*charkā*).

چرلندۍ *churlanda-ī*, s.f. A humming-top.

چرلنډ *churlanḍ*, s.m. A blackguard, knave, rascal.

چرلول *churlawul*, v.a. To spin, turn, make revolve.

چرلۍ *churla-ī*, s.f. A whirligig: a child's game in which walnuts are made to spin.

چرليدل *churledal*, v.n. To spin, revolve, whirl.

چرمباز *charambāz*, s.m. The outside bullock of two or more treading corn.

چرمينه *charmīna*, s.f. Rope made of strips of raw hide. P.

چرې *chare*, ad. Ever, at any time: anywhere; where. *chare·chcre*, ad. Occasionally, sometimes, at times.

چريکار *charekār*, s.m. A farm servant, ploughman. The hair above the chin, imperial.

چړ *chaṛ*, s.m. A sandbank or deposit left by a flood, bar in a river; a cascade, waterfall; a foot soldier's pike or staff; the bread of charity collected from house to house for the poor. *chuṛ*, s.m. The heel of a door, the peg on which it revolves.

چړچه *chaṛcha*, s.f. Dissipation, luxury, excess.

چړق *chaṛaq*, s.m. A waterspout: sound of water splashing on the ground, splash, smash, crash.

چړقاو *chaṛqāo*, s.m. Sprinkling. H. (*chhirkāo*).

چړوکۍ *chaṛūka-ī*, s.f. A small knife, penknife.

چړي *chaṛī*, s.m. A collector of the bread of charity.

چسپ *chasp*, s.m. Cohesion, viscidity, stickiness. P.

چسپان *chaspān*, a. Adhesive, sticky, viscous.

چسپول *chaspawul*, v.a. To cement, glue, stick.

چسپيدل *chaspedal*, v.n. To adhere, cleave to, stick. P. (*chaspīdan*).

چست *chust*, a. Active, quick; narrow, straight; tight, close fitting (as a dress). P.

چستي *chustī*, s.f. Agility, activity, fleetness. P. *chustai*, s.m. Gut, tripe; rectum. P. (*chustā*).

چشم *chashm*, s.m. The eye. P. (In comp. only).

چشمک *chashmak*, s.m. A wink, winking. P.

چشمکه *chashmaka*, s.f. An eye-glass. *chashmake*, pl. A pair of spectacles.

چشمه *chashma*, s.f. A spring, fountain; eye-glass. P.

چشي *chishai*, s.m. Name of a plant, the seed of which sticks to the fleece of sheep, etc., burdock.

چغ *chagh* or *chigh*, s.m. Altercation, dispute; clamour, noise; shout, yell, scream. *chigh·chigh*, s.m. The cackle of fowls. *chagh·chugh*, s.m. Clamour, noise, tumult.

چغار *chughār*, s.m. Noise or song of birds; sound of a musical instrument.

چغاره *chighāra*, s.f. Clamour, outcry, noise.
چغر *chaghar*, s.m. A wall-eyed horse. P.
چغرو *chagharū*, s.m. An owl.
چغول *chaghawul*, v.a. To make a row, disturbance, noise.
چغيدل *chaghedal*, v.n. To dispute, haggle, wrangle.
چغزئ *chaghza-ī*, s.f. A kind of soft walnut. *chaghzī*, s.m. Whizz of an arrow passing through the air; crackling of wood when split.
چغک *chughuk*, s.m. A sparrow. P.
چغل *chughal*, s.m. Tell-tale, backbiter, sneak. P.
چغلي *chughlī*, s.f. Backbiting, tale-telling. P.
چغي *chughai*, s.m. A blinkard; seeing with the eyes half closed.
چف *chuf*, s.m. A breath, puff, blow (as of a charmer).
چقمق *chaqmaq*, s.m. The flint lock of a gun. T.
چقه *chuqa*, s... The cackle of fowls when angry; pecking, picking up grain, etc.
چک *chak*, s.m. A circular frame of wood or masonry, used as a foundation for wells; a disk. *chik*, s.m. Ropes used to yoke bullocks to a Persian wheel, traces.
چکچکه *chakchaka*, s.f. Clapping the hands by way of applause.
چکړ *chikar*, s.m. Mire, mud, slosh. H. (*chīkaṛ*).
چکس *chakas*, s.m. A perch, roost for birds (hawks particularly). H.
چکله *chikla*, s.f. A drop, dash, sprinkling, thimbleful.
چکلئ *chakla-ī*, s.f. The cog-wheel of a Persian irrigation wheel; a whirligig.
چکمه *chakma*, s.f. A stocking; boot. H.
چکوري *chikorai*, s.m. A newly-born calf.
چکه *chakā*, s.f. The palm, the hand; coagulated milk, curds. H. (*chakkā*). *chakah*, a. Practised, expert (as a thief). H. (*uchakkā*).
چکئ *chaka-ī*, s.f. Wafer, disk; biscuit, cake; lump, mass, clot; tail of the dumbah sheep.
چل *chal*, s.m. Artifice, deception, subterfuge, trick. S.
چلان *chalān*, s.m. Invoice, remittance, advice of despatch. S.
چلاو *chalāo*, s.m. Boiled rice. P.
چلباز *chalbāz*, s.m. A cheat, impostor, rogue.
چل چل *chal-chal*, s.m. Bustle, hurry, stir. S.
چل چلا *chal-chalā*, s.f. Bustle, stir, preparation of setting out on a journey. S.
چلر *chulur*, s.m. Blackguard, vagabond, rogue.
چلغوزي *chalghozai*, s.m. The pistachio nut; kernels of the pine seed. P.
چلقت *chalqat*, s.m. A thick padded coat for soldiers, a coat of mail.
چلکه *chalaka*, s.f. A wave, ripple, undulation.
چلم *chilam*, s.m. A tobacco bowl, smoking apparatus. H.
چلن *chalan*, s.m. Behaviour, custom, habit; currency. a. Current. S.
چلول *chalawul*, v.a. To start, set agoing; fire, shoot. H. (*chalānā*).
چله *chala*, s.f. A deluge, flood, stream, torrent. An ear-ring. H. (*chhaṛā*).
چلئ *chala-ī*, s.f. An ear of corn.
چليدل *chaledal*, v.n. To move, proceed, go, elapse, pass (as coin, etc.); flow; blow; stand, avail, succeed; walk, etc. H. (*chalnā*).
چم *cham*, s.m. See جم.
چمتاره *chamtāra*, s.f. A violin. H. (*chautārā*).
چم وخم *cham-o-kham*, s.m. A graceful gait, strut, waddle. P.
چمن *chaman*, s.m. A meadow, lawn, grass-plot. P.
چميار *chamyār*, s.m. A currier, tanner. P.
چنار *chinār*, s.m. Name of a tree, the plane tree (*Platanus orientalis*). P.

چنبیل chanbél, s.m. The jasmine. H.

چنجي chinjai, s.m. An insect, worm. H. (chunna). chinjawul, v.a. To disgust,

چنجیدل chinjedal, v.n. To be disgusted, nauseated, feel squeamish.

چند chand, a. Few, some, various, several; (in comp.) -times, -fold. ad. How many? How much? P.

چندنړ chandanṛ, s.m. Sandal wood. S.

چندنړهار chandanṛ-hār, s.m. A kind of necklace made of sandal-wood beads. S.

چنډال chanḍāl, s.m. An abject, low, mean, or worthless fellow. S.

چنډاول chanḍāwal, s.m. A rear guard of cavalry; the rear guard of an army; name of the Kazilbash troopers of Kabul. P.

چنغله changhala, s.f. A betrothed girl, bride elect.

چنغول changhol, s.m. A betrothed youth.

چنګ chang, s.m. A guitar, harp; a claw, the expanded hand. P.

چنګاښ changākkh, s.m. A crab, cray-fish. P. (changār).

چنګال changāl, } s.m. Claw, talon of bird,
چنګل changul, } the hand; the fingers. P.
changal, s.m. A measure of land equal to fifteen jarīb.

چنه chana, s.f. The short side of a house; mud wall of a house; side of a room. Barter, bargaining, haggling.

چنړاسه chanṛāsa, } s.f. Mildew, mould.
چنړاشه chanṛāsha, }

چنړچنړ chanṛ-chanṛ, } s.m. A sparrow,
چنړچنړک chanṛ-chanṛak, } cock-sparrow.

چنړکاو chanṛkāw, s.m. Sprinkling. H. (chhiṛkāo).

چنړل chunṛal, v.a. To crease, fold, plait; to select, sift, separate, pick. H. (chunnā).

چنړه chanṛa, s.f. Chick pea, vetch (Cicer arietinum). H. (channā). chunṛa, s.f. A fold, crease, pucker.

چوپاړ chopāṛ, } s.m. A summer-house,
چوپال chopāl, } arbour, temporary shed. S. (chaupāṛ).

چوپل chūpal, v.a. To suck, chew (as mangoes, sugar-cane, etc.). S. (chuhnā).

چوتي chotai, s.m. A clout or cloth worn between the legs to conceal the privates; ropes used in fastening a camel's load.

چوټي choṭī, s.m. A peak, mountain top; top-knot or crown-tuft (left on a shaven head). a. Dishevelled, unplaited, loose (as hair). H.

چوچي chuchai, s.m. A chicken, pullet. P.

چور chūr, a. Broken, bruised, shattered. S. s.m. Bit, atom, scrap; powder, filings, sawdust; sack, ruin, plunder. S.

چورنګ chaurang, s.m. Cutting off the four legs of an animal at one blow. S.

چوري chūrai, s.m. A menial servant, sweeper. H. (chūhṛā). chaura-ī, s.f. A fly flapper, generally made of horse-hair or the tail of the Tibet ox. H. (chaunṛī).

چوړ chawṛ, a. Desolate, deserted, ruined. H. chūṛ, s.m. The heel or pivot on which a door revolves.

چوړه chūṛa, s.f. A bangle, bracelet. S. (chūṛā).

چوړیل chūṛel, s.m. Tar, pitch.

چوز chūz, s.m. A young or first year's hawk. P.

چوسار chausār, s.m. A file, rasp. H.

چوغي chūghai, a. Bowbacked, bent (from age or debility).

چوک chūk, s.m. Abatement, diminution, mitigation (as of anger, etc.); damage, loss, waste; error, miss, fault. H. chauk, s.m. A market, courtyard. H. chok, a. Seated, or squatted on all fours (as a camel, etc.).

چوکه chūka, s.f. A goad, prod, prick. H. (chonkā). A sharp, pricking, or stinging pain; dipping, moistening, sopping (as bread in milk, etc. at meals.)

چوکي *chauka-ī*, s.f. A chair, stool; guard, watch; guard-house, station. H. (*chaukī*).

چوکيدار *chaukīdār*, s.m. Guard, watchman. H.

چول *chawul*, v.a. To split, rend, cleave asunder. *chol*, s.m. An arid tract, desert, waste. P. (*chūl*).

چولک *cholak*, s.m. Penis of a boy till circumcised. P.

چوم *chūm* or *chom*, s.m. A turf; clod of earth.

چونکي *chūnkai*, a. Indecent, obscene, shameless; impudent, bold, saucy.

چونگي *chūngai*, s.m. Duty, fee, tax, toll. H. (*chūngī*).

چونه *chūna*, s.f. Lime, mortar. S. (*chūnā*).

چوني *chūnai*, s.m. A dwarf, elf, pigmy; glazing on pottery, china; a gem, jewel, spark or bead.

چه *chi*, c. That, which; as, whereas; so, so that; whether, because. P.

چيتر *chetar*, s.m. Name of the twelfth Hindu month, March-April. S. (*chait*).

چيټۍ *chīṭa-ī*, s.f. A letter, note. H. (*chiṭṭhī*).

چيچړ *chīchaṛ*, s.m. A fold, crease, furrow, pucker, wrinkle.

چيچل *chīchal*, v.a. To bite, masticate, gnaw.

چيخل *chīkhal*, v.a. To goad, poke, punch.

چيرته *cherta*, ad. Where? See چرته.

چيره *chīra*, s.f. A turban with narrow twisted folds; maidenhead. S.

چيړ *chīṛ*, s.m. Gum, mucilage.

چيغه *chīgha*, s.f. A shout, scream, yell; clamour, noise, uproar. P. (*chīkh*).

چيلو *chīlū*, s.m. Name of a potherb.

چيلي *chelai* or *chīlai*, s.m. A kid, young goat. H. (*chherī*).

چيندخ *chīndakh*, s.m. A frog; bull frog.

چينګ *chīng*, a. Gaping, open, wide; straddled.

چينه *chīna*, s.f. A spring, fountain.

ح

ح *he* or *ḥā*, is the eleventh letter of the Pukkhto alphabet, and the sixth of the Arabic. It is only found in words adopted from the Arabic. It is sometimes replaced by ه, than which letter it has a different sound, being pronounced in the throat, and strongly aspirated.

حاجت *ḥājat*, s.m. Want, necessity, need. A.

حاجتمن *ḥājatman*, / حاجتمند *ḥājatmand*, a. Needy, indigent. P.

حاجي *ḥājī*, s.m. A pilgrim to Mecca: one who has made the pilgrimage to Mecca. A.

حاصل *ḥāṣil*, s.m. Produce, profit, result; corn, crops; duty, revenue; acquiring, collecting. A. *ḥāṣil-laral*, v.a. To produce, yield, give.

حاصلول *ḥāṣilawul*, v.a. To collect, acquire, gain.

حاصليدل *ḥāṣiledal*, v.n. To accrue, result, be gathered.

حاضر *ḥāẓir*, a. Present, ready, willing. A.

حاطه *ḥāṭa*, s.f. Enclosure, premises. A.

حافظ *ḥāfiẓ*, s.m. A blind man who has learnt the Quran by heart. Name of a Persian poet.

حاکم *ḥākim*, s.m. Commander, judge, master, ruler, governor. A.

حال *ḥāl*, s.m. Case, condition, state; affair, business, matter; now, present time. A.

حالت *ḥālat*, s.m. Case, condition, state.

حالي *ḥālī*, a. Modern, new, existent.

حامله *ḥāmila*, a. Pregnant, with young. A.

حبس *ḥabs*, s.m. Retention, imprisonment; prison; a prisoner. A.

حبشي *ḥabshī*, s.m. A Caffre, negro. A.

حبيب *ḥabīb*, s.m. A lover, friend. a. Beloved, dear. A.

حج *ḥaj*, s.m. Pilgrimage to Mecca. A.

حجاب *ḥijāb*, s.m. Bashfulness, modesty; curtain, veil. A.

حجام *ḥajjām*, s.m. A barber; cupper, phlebotomist. A.

حجامت *ḥajjāmat*, s.m. Shaving, cupping.

حجت *ḥujjat*, s.m. Argument, proof, reason; dispute, altercation. A.

حجتي *ḥujjatī*, a. Litigious, argumentative, quarrelsome. s.m. Wrangler, caviller, arguer.

حجره *ḥujra*, s.f. A cell, chamber, closet. A. A public room or house in each quarter of a village, for the use of travellers and visitors, hostelry. A vestry, ward.

حدّ *ḥadd*, s.m. Boundary, limit; extent, extremity, degree; impediment; definition; starting post. A.

حديث *ḥadīs̤*, s.m. A tradition; the traditions and sayings of Muḥammad. A.

حذر *ḥaz̤r*, s.m. Caution, prudence, fear. A.

حرارت *ḥarārat*, s.m. Fervour, heat, warmth. A.

حراست *ḥirāsat*, s.m. Care, watching, guarding. A.

حرام *ḥarām*, a. Forbidden, unlawful, wrong; sacred. A.

حرامي *ḥarāmī*, s.m. A bastard; robber, cheat; rogue, rascal. A.

حرص *ḥirṣ*, s.m. Greediness, ambition, avarice. A.

حرصناك *ḥirṣnāk*, a. Greedy, ambitious, covetous.

حرف *ḥarf*, s.m. A letter, particle, word. A.

حركت *ḥarkat*, s.m. A short vowel. *ḥarakat*, s.m. Action, gesture, movement; impediment, obstacle, hindrance, prevention. A.

حرم *ḥaram*, a. Forbidden, sacred. s.m. The temple at Mecca; a sanctuary. *ḥarama*, s.f. A seraglio; concubine, wife. A.

حرمت *ḥurmat*, s.m. Chastity, honour; dignity, esteem, reverence. A.

حريان *ḥariyān*, a. See حيران.

حريف *ḥarīf*, s.m. A rival, enemy; partner, associate, friend. a. Clever, cunning; pleasant, agreeable. A.

حساب *ḥisāb*, s.m. Accounts; calculation, reckoning, account. A.

حسد *ḥasad*, s.m. Envy, jealousy, malice; emulation, ambition. A.

حسرت *ḥasrat*, s.m. Grief, sorrow, regret; desire, longing, yearning. A.

حسن *ḥasan*, a. Beautiful, good; a man's name. *ḥusn*, s.m. Beauty, elegance; goodness. A.

حسن حسين *ḥasan-ḥusen*, s.m. Name of a month, the Muḥarram.

حشر *ḥas͟hr*, s.m. A concourse, meeting; resurrection of the dead. A.

حشمت *ḥas͟hmat*, s.m. Dignity, pomp, state; train, retinue. A.

حصار *ḥiṣṣār*, s.m. Citadel, fortress. A. Enclosure, fence; besieging, surrounding.

حصه *ḥiṣṣa*, s.f. Division, part; lot, portion, share. A.

حضرت *ḥaẓrat*, s.m. Dignity, presence; highness, majesty, reverence, etc. (title of respect). A.

حضور *ḥuẓūr*, s.m. Appearance, attendance, presence; your worship, etc. A.

حفاظت *ḥifāẓat*, s.m. Care, custody; keeping, protection. A.

حق *ḥaqq*, s.m. Truth, right; equity, justice; portion, lot; the Deity. A. *ḥuq*, s.m. The sound of retching, vomiting.

حقا *ḥaqqā*, in. By God! Really! True! Indeed! A.

حقنه *ḥuqna*, s.f. A clyster; syringe. A.

حقير *ḥaqīr*, a. Contemptible, vile; lean, thin. A.

حقيقت *ḥaqīqat*, s.m. Truth; sincerity; explanation, narration, account. A.

حقيقي *ḥaqīqī*, a. Accurate, certain, real, true; own; just. A.

حكاك *ḥukāk*, s.m. A lapidary. A.

حكايت *ḥikāyat* ,s.m. History, story, tale; narration. A.

حكم *ḥukm*, s.m. Command, decree, order, sentence; permission. A.

حكمت *ḥikmat*, s.m. Knowledge, wisdom; art, skill, cleverness; mystery, principle. A.

حكمتي *ḥikmatī*, a. Artful, clever, wise, skilful.

حكومت *ḥukūmat*, s.m. Authority, dominion, government, sovereignty. A.

حكيم *ḥakīm*, s.m. A doctor, physician; philosopher, sage. A.

حلال *ḥalāl*, a. Lawful, legal, right; clean, pure. A.

حلف *ḥalaf*, s.m. An oath. A.

حلق *ḥalq*, s.m. The throat, windpipe. A.

حلقه *ḥalqa*, s.f. A circle, ring; knocker for a door; a fraternity, society. A.

حلوا *ḥalwā*, s.f. A kind of sweetmeat made of flour, butter and sugar. A.

حلواي *ḥalwā-ī*, s.m. A confectioner.

حليم *ḥalīm*, a. Affable, gentle, tractable, mild. A.

حماقت *ḥimāqat*, s.m. Folly, ignorance, stupidity. A.

حمال *ḥammāl*, s.m. A porter, carrier. A.

حمام *ḥammām*, s.m. A Turkish bath, vapour bath. A.

حمايت *ḥimāyat*, s.m. Countenance, protection, support, defence, help, assistance. A.

حمايتي *ḥimāyatī*, s.m. Protector, patron, deliverer.

حمل *ḥaml*, s.m. A burden, load; pregnancy. A.

حمله *ḥamla*, s.f. Assault, attack, onset, charge. A.

حنا *ḥinnā*, s.f. See نكريزي.

حنظل *ḥanẓal*, s.m. See مرغوني.

حواله *ḥawāla*, s.f. Care, charge, custody, trust. A.

حور *ḥūr*, s.m. A boy of Paradise. A.

حوره *ḥūra*, s.f. A virgin of Paradise; black-eyed nymph. A.

حوصله *ḥauṣila*, s.f. Ambition, spirit, mettle; crop, maw, stomach. A.

حوض *ḥauẓ*, s.m. A cistern, tank, reservoir, vat. A.

حويلي *ḥawelai*, s.m. A dwelling, habitation, house; tenement, premises. A. Also *ḥawela-ī*, s.f.

حيا *ḥayā*, s.f. Bashfulness, modesty, shame. A.

حيات *ḥayāt*, s.m. Life. A.

حيران *ḥairān*, a. Astonished, amazed; perplexed, confounded. A.

حيراني *ḥairānī*, s.f. Amazement, confusion; perplexity, perturbation. A.

حيض *ḥaiẓ*, s.m. Menses, catamenia. A.

حيضه *ḥaiẓa*, s.f. A menstruous woman.

حيف *ḥaif*, s.m. Iniquity, oppression. a. Futile, useless. in. Alas! Ah! A.

حيله *ḥīla*, s.f. Artifice, pretence, deceit, trick. A.

حين *ḥīn*, s.m. Time, interval. A.

حيوان *ḥaiwān*, s.m. An animal, brute. A.

حيوانتوب *ḥaiwān-tob*, s.m. Brutality, savageness.

خ

خ *khe* is the twelfth letter of the Pukkhto alphabet, and the seventh of the Arabic. It is a guttural letter, and pronounced like the *ch* in the Scotch *loch*.

خاتم *khātim*, s.m. A seal; finger ring. A.

خاتمه *khātima*, s.f. Conclusion, end, finis. A.

خاته *khātah*, s.m. Ascent, rise; rising, ascending.

خادمه *khādama*, } s.f. Name of a kind of
خادمئ *khādama-ī*, } lizard with a bristly back.

خاده *khāda*, s.f. A grave-stone, tombstone; a pole or wooden tabletat the head of a grave.

خار *khār*, s.m. A thorn, bramble, prickle, thistle; a spike; the spur of a cock. P.

خارج *khārij*, a. Excluded, outcast, expelled. A.

خارجي *khārijī*, s.m. Name of a heretical sect amongst Moslems.

خاربښت *khārikkht*, s.m. Itch, mange. P. (*khārisht*).

خارو *khāro*, s.f. A cock's comb, wattle. P. (*khār*).

خاشاک *khāshāk*, s.m. Rubbish, litter, refuse. P. Firewood, fuel. P.

خاش خاش *khāsh-khāsh*, s.m. Poppy seed. P.

خارک *khārak*, s.m. See ښارک.

خازه *khāza*, s.f. See خاده.

خاشه *khāsha*, s.f. A straw, splinter, bit, chip, etc.; name of a disease of the eye; mote in the eye.

خاشه کښ *khāsha-kakkh*, s.m. One who extracts motes from the eye; curer of the khāsha.

خاص *khāṣṣ*, a. Excellent, noble, pure; special, private, particular; peculiar, single, sole. A.

خاصه *khāṣṣa*, s.f. A kind of bread; a kind of muslin.

خاصيت *khāṣṣiyat*, s.m. Attribute, quality, temper, disposition, nature, property. A.

خاطر *khāṭir*, s.m. Heart, soul; inclination, propensity; account, sake; will, choice. A.

خاک *khāk*, s.m. Ashes, earth, dust. P.

خاکستر *khākistar*, s.f. Ashes. P.

خاکه *khāka*, s.f. Broken rice, etc. unfit for use; a fragment, particle of gems, etc.

خاګينه *khāgīna*, s.f. Omelet, dish of fried eggs. P.

خال *khāl*, s.m. A black spot, or mole on the skin; an artificial spot for ornament on the face, breasts, etc.

خالص *khāliṣ*, a. Genuine, pure, simple. A.

خالصه *khāliṣa*, s.f. Fallow land.

خالي *khālī*, a. Empty, vacant; unmixed, pure; mere, only; idle, unemployed. s.f. Saturday; the eleventh Afghan month corresponding with *zī-qa'da*. P.

خام *khām*, s.m. The horn end of a bow. A. See اوم.

خامتا *khāmtā*, s.f. A kind of coarse cotton cloth.

خاموش *khāmosh*, a. Mute, silent, still. P.

خان *khān*, s.m. A lord, prince; a title used by all Afghans and Pathans. T.

خانتما *khāntamā*, a. Proud, arrogant, vain.

خانه *khāna*, s.f. House, room, place. P.

خاندان *khāndān*, s.m. Family, household.

خانواده *khānawāda*, s.f. Family, house, tribe.

خانومان *khānomān*, s.m. Household (as house, family, servants, cattle, furniture, goods, chattels, fixings, etc.).

خاوره *khāwra*, s.f. Dust, earth, clay.

خاورين *khāwrīn*, a. Clayey, earthy, dusty.

خاوند *khāwand*, s.m. Master, owner, husband. lord, proprietor. P.

خايه *khāya*, s.f. Testicle. P.

خبث *khubs*, s.m. Envy, malice. A.

خبر *khabar*, s.m. Advice, intelligence, news, report, rumour. A.

خبردار *khabar-dār*, a. Careful, cautious; aware, informed. A.

خبرګير *khabar-gīr*, s.m. A spy, informer; patron, protector.

خبرلوڅ *khabar-lots*, a. Eloquent, talkative.

خبرول *khabarawul*, v.a. To report, inform.

خبره *khabara*, s.f. Language, speech; affair, matter, thing.

خبريدل *khabaredal*, v.n. To be aware, acquainted, informed, etc.

خبيث *khabīs*, a. Impure, malignant, wicked. s.m. An evil spirit. A.

خپر *khapar*, s.f. Palm of the hand; sole of the foot.

خپسکي *khapaskai*, s.m. } The nightmare. A.
خپسه *khapasa*, s.f. } (*kābūs*).

خپل *khpul*, pr. Self, own. P. (*khūd*). *pa-khpul*, or *pa-khpula*, ad. Spontaneously, of own accord. P. (*bā-khūd*).

خپل سر *khpul-sar*, a. Obstinate, self-opinionated.

خپلوالي *khpul-wālai*, s.m. Connection, relationship.

خپلول *khpulawul*, v.a. To adopt, appropriate, make one's own; win over, bias, sway, predispose.

خپلوي *khpulawī*, s.f. Connection, relationship, family, kindred, friendship.

خپليدل *khpuledal*, v.n. To be related, connected; to be biassed, influenced.

خپور *khpor*, a. Blown, blossomed, expanded (as a flower): dispersed, loose, scattered.

خپه *khapah*, a. Angry, offended, displeased, vexed. *khapa*, s.f. Suffocation, strangulation. P. (*khafa*). *khpah*, s.m. Tinder, touchwood.

خپگان *khapagān*, s.m. } Anger, rage, vexa-
خپگي *khapagī*, s.f. } tion.

خپي *khapī*, s.f. See کپي.

ختر *khatar*, s.m. See خطر.

ختل *khatal*, v.n. To ascend, mount, rise; issue. P. (*khāstan*, *khez-*).

ختم *khatm*, s.m. Conclusion, end; seal. a. Done, completed. A.

ختنه *khatna*, s.f. Circumcision. A. *khatana*, s.f. Rising, mounting, ascending.

خته *khata*, s.f. A shirt, shift.

خټ *khaṭ*, s.m. A hillock, knoll, mound; a low hill; bank of clouds. *kha-aṭ* or *khaṭ*, a. Muddy, turbid, miry. *khuṭ*, s.m. Effervescence, boiling, bubbling.

خټکيدل *khuṭkedal*, v.n. To bubble, boil, effervesce; to boil with rage, etc. H. (*khaṭaknā*).

خټبيل *khaṭbel* or *kha-aṭbel*, s.m. Dregs, lees, sediment, dross, precipitate.

خټک *khaṭak*, s.m. A kind of black beetle. An unripe water melon used to make pickles. Name of a Pathan tribe settled in the low hills on the south of the Kabul river, between Peshawar and Attak.

خټکي *khaṭakai*, s.m. A kind of melon of a green colour (peculiar to Afghanistan). *khuṭkai*, s.m. Ebullition, effervescence.

خټوله *khaṭola* or *kha-atola*, a. Muddy, turbid (as water).

خټه *khaṭa* or *kha-aṭa*, s.f. Mire, mud, slush, slime. *khuṭa*, s.f. Clay, marl.

خجل *khijjil*, a. Bashful, modest. A. (*khajal*).

خجونکو *khajūnko*, a. Capering, frisky, prancing; rebounding, skipping (as a ball or stone over the surface of water).

خڅوزه *khatsoza*, s.f. A bit, fragment, chip, shred.

خڅه *khatsa*, p. See خڅه.

خچر *khachar*, s.m. A mule. H. (*khachchar*).

خچن *khachan*, a. Dirty, rheumy. See چخن.

خچه *khacha*, s.f. The little finger; a bound, ricochet, rebound.

خداي *khudāe*, s.m. God, The Deity. P. (*khudā*). *khudā-ī*, s.f. Divinity, Godhead. P.

خدايا *khudāyā*, in. Oh God! P.

خدمت *khidmat*, s.m. Attendance, duty, service. A.

خدمتي *khidmatī*, a. Attentive, diligent, heedful.

خدمتگار *khidmat-gār*, s.m. A servant, attendant.

خدنگ *khadang*, s.m. Name of a tree, from the wood of which bows are made. A poplar tree. P.

خدل *khaḍal*, s.m. A large dog in good condition; a mastiff. a. Stout, burly, muscular.

خر *khar*, s.m. An ass, donkey. P. *kha-ar*, s m. A snore. A.

خراب *kharāb*, a. Bad, depraved; spoiled, ruined; deserted, waste; abandoned, lost. A.

خرابي *kharābī*, s.f. Evil, mischief; destruction, ruin; waste.

خراج *khirāj*, s.m. Duty, revenue, rent, tax. A.

خراړه *kharāṛa*, s.f. Name of a bird; the sand grouse; a kind of sky-lark.

خراسان *khurāsān*, s.m. Name of a country. Afghanistan.

خراشکي *kharāshkai*, s.m. Phlegm, expectorated mucus, sputum. P. (*kharāsh*).

خربشوي *kharbishoe*, s.m. A boar, hog, pig.

خربوزه *kharbūza*, s.f. A musk melon. P.

خرپټ *kharpaṭ*, s.m. A powder; a palmful to chuck into the mouth.

خرپوڅه *kharpotsa*, s.f. Crawling on all fours (as a child).

خرټ *kharaṭ*, a. Fat, stout, plump.

خرټه *kharaṭah*, s.m. Cheat, hypocrite, knave.

خرجدال *kharjadāl*, s.m. See خردجال.

خرجګجګلي *kharjagjagalai*, s.m. Name of a game played by boys.

خرجين *khurjīn*, s.m. A bag, wallet, reticule. P.

خرڅ *kharts*, s.m. Expense, outlay; expenditure, means; price, fee, duty. A. (*kharch*).

خرڅوړي *khartsoṛai*, s.m. A rag, shred, tatter.

خرڅي *khartsī*, a. Extravagant, prodigal, lavish.

خرچ *khrach*, s.m. A crack, creak, crash, split; sound of splitting wood.

خرخاري *kharkhārai*, s.m. Ass's play, foolishness, nonsense; romping, boistering.

خرخښه *kharkhakkha*, s.f. Noise, tumult, discord, wrangling; a crowd, mob. P (*kharkhasha*).

خرد *khurd*, a. Little, small. P.

خردجال *khardajāl*, s.m. Antichrist.

خردګ *khardag*, s.m. Name of a plant (*Salvia pumila*).

خرس *khirs*, s.m. A bear. P.

خرسند *khursand*, a. Contented, pleased, satisfied. P.

خرشن *kharshan*, s.m. Horse dung.

خرطوم *khartūm*, s.m. Proboscis of an elephant; dewlap of bulls, etc. A.

خرغينړي *khar·ghenrai*, s.m. A toadstool, mushroom.

خرفه *khurfa*, s.f. Purslain. A.

خرقه *khirqa*, s.f. A patched garment, a kind of dress (worn by dervishes). A.

خرُکي *kha-arkai*, s.m. A snore, purr.

خرګي *khargai*, s.m. A young ass. *kha-argai*, s.m. A kind of grasshopper.

خرّم *khurram*, a. Cheerful, merry, joyful. P.

خرمن *khirman*, s.m. Harvest. P. Threshing-floor.

خرمندي *kharmandai*, a. Tiny, small, wee, little.

خرمه *khurma*, s.f. A date (fruit and tree). P. (*khurmā*).

خرنار *kharnār*, s.m. Name of a plant, mullein (*Verbascum thapsus*).

خروار *kharwār*, s.m. An ass-load. P.

خروسک *kharosak*, s.m. A disease of the throat, quinsy.

خروش *kharosh*, s.m. Bustle, stir, tumult, noise. P.

خري *kharai*, s.m. A whitlow.

خريد *kharīd*, s.m. Purchase. P.

خريدار *kharīdār*, s.m. A purchaser. P.

خريړي *khareṛai*, s.m. Curds and whey; junket. *kha-areṛai*, s.m. A kind of edible mushroom.

خريز *khirīz*, s.m. Cotton stalks or stubble.

خريطه *kharīṭa*, s.f. Bag, packet, purse; letter bag, mail. P.

خريل *khrayal*, v.a. To shave. P. (*kharāshīdan*).

خر *kha-ar*, a. Muddy, turbid; cloudy, obscure; drab, dust-coloured. *khuṛ*, s.m. Sound of vomiting or retching, hawking. *khaṛ*, s.m. A ravine, dry water course. See خوړ.

خرانگه *khrānga*, s.f. Bough or stem of a tree.

خرپ *khrap*, s.m. A crunch, crush, squash, smash.

خرتم *khartam*, s.m. See خرطوم.

خرس *khras*, s.m. Blow, clash, crash, slam.

خرل *kharal*, v.a. To dung, ease one's self, stool.

خرمت *kha-armat*, s.m. Snot, snivel, mucus of nose.

خرمور *kha-armor*, s.m. A kind of bustard, obārah.

خرند *kharand*, s.m. Stump of a tree, stubble.

خروب *kharob*, a. Watered, saturated, irrigated (as a field).

خريس *khrīs*, a. Big, burly, great; stupid, heavy, dull. s.m. A lout, lubber.

خرين *khurīn*, a. Soft, sodden (as victuals), ripe, rotten (as fruit), festered (as a sore).

خزان *khizān*, s.m. Autumn. P.

خزانه *khizāna*, s.f. Treasury, store; magazine, granary; chamber of a gun.

خزله *khazala*, s.f. Litter, refuse, sweepings, etc.

خزنده *khazanda*, s.f. A reptile, insect, creeping thing. P.

خږ *khug*, a. Bruised, hurt, injured, pained. s.m. A bruise, cut, injury, wound; ailment, malady, disease. *khag*, s.m. Death rattle, gurgle in the throat.

خس *khass*, s.m. Litter, straw, dry grass, twigs, etc. P.

خسا *khsā*, a. See سخا.

خسمانه *khasmāna*, s.f. Protection, support; custody, ownership; housewifery, domestic economy. A. (*khaṣmāna*).

خسنړي *khasanrai*, s.m. A straw, mote, dry twig, etc.

خسي *khasī*, a. Castrated, gelt. s.m. A gelding, any castrated animal. A. (*khuṣṣī*). *khsai*, s.m. See سخي.

خسيل *khasīl*, s.m. Green corn used as fodder.

خشاک *khashāk*, s.m. Refuse, litter, rubbish; dry twigs, leaves, etc. P.

خشاوزه *khashāwza*, s.f. Orris root; root of the Iris or sweet flag. See سخاوره.

خشت *khisht* or *khusht*, a. Damp, humid, moist, wet; drenched, dripping, reeking. *khusht-pusht*, a. Drenched to the skin, wet through, etc.

خشک *khushk*, a. Dry, arid, withered. P.

خشکه *khushka*, s.f. Plain boiled rice. P.

خشکي *khushkī*, s.f. Dryness, aridity; drought, dearth; dry land, travelling by land. P.

خشنود *khushnūd*, a. Contented, pleased. P.

خشي *khushai*, a. Crazy, demented, flighty; open, defenceless; unguarded, unprotected; without friends, etc. P. (*khushk* or *khush*).

خښ *khakkh*, a. Buried, interred, embedded.

خښتگ *khakkhtag*, } s.m. A piece of cloth
خښتگي *khakkhtagai*, } sewn into the fork of a pair of drawers or armpit of a coat. P. (*khash*, armpit).

خښته *khakkhta*, s.f. A brick. P. (*khisht*)

خښي *khakkhī*, s.m. Name applied to the Yusufzai tribe of Afghans. *khakkhai*, s.m. A male of the tribe. *khakkha-ī*, s.f. A female of the tribe.

خصلت *khaṣlat*, s.m. Nature, disposition; quality, virtue; custom, habit. A.

خصم *khaṣam*, s.m. A husband. A.

خصوصا *khuṣūṣan*, ad. Especially, particularly. A.

خضر *khiẓr*, s.m. The prophet Elias. A.

خط *khaṭṭ*, s.m. Epistle, letter, note; writing; a line, lineament; down on the face, youthful beard. A.

خطا *khaṭā*, s.f. Error, fault, crime; mistake, miss. A.

خطاب *khiṭāb*, s.m. Address, title. A.

خطبه *khuṭba*, s.f. A sermon preached on Fridays in Muḥammadan places of worship for the welfare and prosperity of the reigning sovereign. A.

خطر *khaṭar*, s.m. } Danger, fear, hazard, risk.
خطره *khaṭra*, s.f. } A.

خطرناک *khaṭar-nāk*, a. Dangerous, hazardous.

خطيب *khaṭīb*, s.m. A preacher. A.

خفقان *khafaqān*, s.m. Palpitation of the heart, breast-pang; vexation. A.

خگلن *khuglan*, s.m. Embers, hot ashes, hot cinders.

خل *khal*, s.m. Faith, hope, trust, belief.

خلات *khilāt*, s.m. A dress of honour, reward, present. A. (*khil'at*).

خلاص *khalāṣ*, a. Free, liberated; discharged, done. A.

خلاصه *khulāṣa*, s.f. Conclusion, inference, moral; abstract, summary. A.

خلاصي *khalāṣī*, s.f. Deliverance, freedom, release.

خلاف *khilāf*, s.m. Contradiction, opposition. a. Contrary, false. A.

خلاملا *khalā-malā*, a. Candid, frank, sincere.

خلبوري *khulborai*, s.m. A bung, cork, plug, spigot.

خلته *khalta*, s.f. A hamper (used by hill men). P. (*khalīta*). See جلته.

خلش *khalish*, s.m. Interruption, hindrance; doubt, solicitude; suspicion. P.

خلط *khalṭ*, s.m. Confusion, mixture. *khilṭ*, s.m. One of the four humours of the human body. A.

خلق *khalq*, s.m. Creation, universe; mankind, people, the world. A. *khulq*, s.m. Nature, disposition, civility, politeness. A.

خلقت *khalqat*, s.m. Creation, people, the world. A.

خلقه *khalqa*, s.f. A coat, frock, gown. A.

خلل *khalal*, s.m. Defect, injury; interruption; prejudice. A.

خلوت *khilwat*, s.m. Privacy, retirement; closet, private chamber; private conference. A.

خله *khula*, s.f. The mouth; orifice, entrance.

خلي *khalai*, s.m. Bud, shoot, sprout. S. (*kalī*).

خم *kham*, s.m. A coil, twist; curl, ringlet. *khum*, s.m. An alembic, still, retort; jar, vase; boiler. P.

خمار *khumār*, a. Drunken, intoxicated; intoxicating, languishing (as the eyes). s.m. Headache, sickness after a debauch. P.

خمبه *khamba*, s.f. A kind of corn bin made of wattles, and plastered over with clay.

خمټ *khamaṭ*, a. Plump, chubby (as a baby).

خمچه *khamachah*, a. Little, short, small. *khamacha-guṭa*, s.f. The little finger. *khamache-pukkhta-ī*, s.f. The short ribs.

خمچي *khamache*, s.f. Coarsely ground millet or rice, broken rice; millet bread. H. (*kamāch*).

خمرئ *khumra-ī*, s.f. A drinking flask or cup; a small drum carried by beggars,; a small mat of palm leaves used to pray upon. A.

خمسور *khamsor*, a. Familiar, free, unceremonious.

خمزري *khumazarai*, s.m. See شاپيانگه.

خمن *khaman*, a. Bent, curved, crooked. P. (*kham*).

خمير *khamīr*, a. Fermented, leavened. A.

خميره *khamīra*, s.f. Dough, leaven, yeast, ferment.

خنجاړه *khanjāṛa*, s.f. A kind of millet grain.

خنجر *khanjar*, s.m. A dagger. A.

خنجک *khinjak*, s.m. The mastic tree and fruit (*Pista Cabulica*).

خند *khand*, s.m. Name of a boy's game played with knuckle bones; marbles.

خندا *khandā*, s.f. A laugh; laughter. P. (*khandah*).

خندق *khandaq*, s.m. A ditch, moat, fosse. A.

خندل *khandal*, v.a. To laugh at, scoff, ridicule.

خندول *khandawul*, v.a. To cause to laugh.

خنده *khandah*, s.m. A pointer dog. Also *khandai*.

خندي *khundī*, a. Preserved, protected, kept; arranged, settled. *khundī-kawul*, v.a. To keep, preserve, take care of.

خنديدل *khandedal*, v.n. To giggle, laugh, titter. P. (*khandīdan*).

خنديل *khundiyal*, v.a. To keep, guard, protect, etc.

خنډ *khanḍ*, s.m. Stump of a tree.

خنډن *khanḍan*, s.m. Zedoary (*Curcuma zerunbet*).

خنک *khunuk*, a. Cold, cool, chilly; temperate. P.

خنکي *khunukī*, s.f. Coldness, chilliness. P.

خو *khū*, s.m. Tinder, touchwood; a kind of sugar cane. H. *kho*, ad. Certainly, surely; then, at least.

خوا *khwā*, s.f. Margin, side, direction, quarter; nature, temperament; constitution, health; desire, wish.

خوار *khwār*, a. Poor, wretched; abject, mean; lean, thin; friendless, ruined. P.

خواري *khwārī*, s.f. Poverty, beggary, ruin; distress, etc.

خواړه *khwāṛah* s.m. Food, victuals.

خواست *khwāst*, s.m. Desire, wish; want, request. P.

خواښه *khwākkha*, s.f. Mother-in-law. P. (*khwāsh*).

خواله *khwāla*, s.f. Disclosing, revealing. *khwāla-wayal*, v.a. To disclose, reveal.

خوان *khwān*, s.m. } A tray, salver, platter.
خوانچه *khwāncha*, s.f. } P. A small tray.
dastar-khwān, s.m. A table cloth, table-cover. P.

خواهش *khwāhish*, s.m. Desire, inclination, wish. P.

خوب *khob*, s.m. Sleep, slumber; a dream. P. (*khwāb*). *khūb*, a. Good, excellent; amiable, pleasant; fair, beautiful. P.

خوبي *khūbī*, s.f. Excellence, beauty, goodness, etc. P.

خوټه *khoṭa*, s.f. A testicle.

خوځول *khwadzawul*, v.a. To move, shift, remove, shake, agitate, wag.

خوځيدل *khwadzedal*, v.n. To move, shake, wag, stir.

خود *khūd*, pr. Self (in comp. only). P. *khod*, ad. See خو.

خودله *khūdala*, s.f. Bulrush, reed; the flower spike and down: the down is used as tinder.

خور *khor*, s.f. A sister. pl. *khwainde*. P. (*khwāhar*). *khor*, a. Open, expanded, blown (as a flower); dispersed, scattered; loose, dishevelled. *khwa-ar*, s.m. Scurf, scab, crust; bark, peel, rind, husk.

خوراک *khwurāk*, s.m. Food, victuals, diet, eatables. P.

خوراکي *khwurākī*, a. Edible, eatable, esculent.

خورځه *khordza*, s.f. Sister's daughter, niece.

خورجين *khūrjīn*, } s.m. Portmanteau, carpet-
خورجي *khūrjai*, } bag; a wallet, reticule. P.

خورجينه *khūrjīna*, s.f. A travelling-cap with flaps to cover the ears.

خورخلع *khorkhal*, s.m. } Shears for shearing
خورخول *khorkhwal*, } sheep.

خورلنړه *khor·lanṛa*, s.f. A sister's daughter (used by a clan or tribe to designate the daughter of any member after marriage).

خورمه *khorma*, s.f. Incipient beard, down on the face.

خورنده *khwurindah*, a. Gluttonous, gormandizer. P.

خوروول *khwarawul*, v.a. To open, expand, loose, dishevel, spread out, disperse, scatter. *khūrawul*, v.a. To feed, supply with food.

خورئ *khaura-ī*, s.f. Alum. *khawrai*, s.m. See خاوره.

خوريدل *khwaredal*, v.n. To expand; blossom, blow; to disperse, spread, scatter.

خورينګه *khorīnga*, s.f. Adopted sister, female friend.

خورينګي *khorīngai*, s.m. Sisterly love, friendship among women.

خورئ *khora-e*, s.m. Sister's son, nephew.

خوړ *khwaṛ*, s.m. A ravine, watercourse, dry bed of a river.

خوړل *khwuṛal*, v.a. To eat, feed; bite. P. (*khurdan*).

خوړول *khūṛawul* or *khwuṛawul*, v.a. To feed, victual, supply with food.

خوړه *khwaṛa*, s.f. Donation, gratuity, subscription; sandy bed of a ravine or dry watercourse.

خوږ *khog*, a. Sweet. *khūg*, a. See خ. P. (*khūsh*).

خوږلوري *khog·lorai*, a. Sweetish, pleasant.

خوږه وله *khwaga·wala*, s.f. Liquorice root.

خوش *khūsh*, a. Agreeable, pleasant. P.

خشوي *khashoe*, s.m. See غشوي.

خوشه *khosha*, s.f. An ear of corn, bunch of grapes, spike of flowers, etc. P.

خوښ *khwakkh*, a. Delighted, pleased; pleasant, agreeable; charming, attractive. P. (*khūsh*).

خوښي *khwakkhī*, s.f. Will, pleasure, choice; delight, joy, gladness. P. (*khūshī*).

خوښينه *khwakkhīna*, s.f. See ښينه.

خوف *khof*, s.m. Fear, fright, alarm. A. (*khauf*).

خوګ *khūg*, s.m. A pig, hog. P. (*khūk*).

خول *khol*, s.m. A helmet, steel cap; case, sheath. H.

خوله *khwula*, s.f. A divorced wife who is taken back and received by the husband.

خولي *khwale*, s.f. (sing. obsolete) Perspiration, sweat. P. (*khwae*).

خولئ *khola-ī*, s.f. A cap, skull-cap,

خون *khūn*, s.m. Murder, manslaughter; blood. P.

خوني *khūnī*, s.m. A murderer.

خوناق *khonāq*, s.m. A disease of the throat quinsy. A. (*khunāq*).

خوند *khwand*, s.m. Flavour, taste; pleasure delight.

خوندناک *khwand·nāk*, a. Agreeable, pleasant.

خونه *khūna*, s.f. Chamber, room; court, hall, house; family, tribe. P. (*khāna*). *khawana*, s.f. Olive tree.

خوي *khoe*, s.m. Temper, disposition, nature; custom, habit, manner. P. (*kho*).

خويد *khwīd* or *khīd*, s.m. Green corn (used as fodder). P.

خوئيدل *khwa-edal*, v.n. To slip, slide, fall.

خيابان *khayābān*, s.m. An avenue; flower bed. P.

خيار *khiyār*, s.m. Choice, selection, trial. A.

خياط *khiyāṭ*, s.m. A tailor. A.

خيال *khiyāl*, s.m. Fancy, idea, thought; opinion, suspicion; delusion, vision. A.

خيانت *khiyānat*, s.m. Embezzlement, robbery of entrusted property; perfidy, treachery. A.

خيټه *kheṭa*, s.f. See ګيډه.

خيدک *khaidak*, s.m. Sour milk.

خير *khīr*, a. Enraged, angry; sorry, vexed. P. (*khīra*). *khair*, a. Good, well. s.m. Happiness, welfare; health, goodness; alms, charity. A.

خيرات *khairāt*, s.m. Alms, charity. A.

خيره *khīra*, s.f. Dirt, filth, pollution, ordure.

خيرن *khīran*, } a. Dirty, soiled, filthy, polluted.
خيري *khīrai*, }

خيز *khez*, s.m. Bounding, leaping, rising. P.

خيژول *khežawul*, v.a. To lift, elevate, raise, erect. P. (*khezāndan*).

خيږ *khīg*, s.m. The scab of a sore. S. (*khāj*).

خيښ *khekkh*, s.m. A kinsman, relation; wife's relations. P. (*khwesh*).

خيښي *khekkhī*, s.f. Relationship by marriage.

خيک *khīk*, s.m. A large inflated hide (used to cross rivers upon).

خيل *khel*, s.m. A clan, tribe; division of a clan, family. A.

خيل‌خانه *khel-khāna*, s.f. Clan, kindred.

خيم *khyam*, a. Coagulated, solidified, hardened (as the chest, milk, etc.). A. (*qiyām*).

خيمه *khaima*, s.f. A tent, marquee. A.

د *dāl* is the thirteeenth letter of the Pukkhto alphabet; it has a soft dental sound, and is often changed to ل in words derived from the Persian and Sanskrit.

د *da*, A particle, the sign of the Genitive case; it always precedes the word it governs, and is not affected by gender or number. It is sometimes used as the sign of the Ablative case instead of the particle له. Ex. دَکلي نه *da kilī na*, for له کلي نه *la kilī na*, from the village.

دِ *di*, pr. 1. A form of the Genitive and Instrumental cases singular of the second personal pronoun ته *tah*, thou. Also written دي *de*. 2. A form of the Oblique cases singular of the proximate third personal pronoun دي *de*, he, she, it. 3. The sign of the third person in both numbers of the Imperative Mood.

دا *dā*, pr. One of the proximate demonstrative pronouns; this; that.

داب *dāb*, s.m. The large wooden axle of a Persian wheel; custom, manner; condition, situation. A.

دابه *dāba*, s.f. A quadruped, beast, brute; cattle. A.

داتکي *dātkai*, s.m. A plant used in dyeing (*Grislea tomentosa*). H. (*dhārī*).

داتوره *dātūra*, s.f. The thorn apple (*Datura fastuosa*). H. (*dhatūrā*).

داج *dāj*, s.m. Darkness, obscurity. A marriage portion: all that a wife takes with her to her husband. A. (*dahez*).

داخل *dākhil*, a. Entered, arrived. s.m. Arriving, entering. A.

داد *dād*, s.m. Equity, justice, law; revenge; (in comp.) given, bestowed. P.

دادا *dādā*, in. A term of affectionate address to a father or elder brother. Dear father! dear brother! H.

دار *dār*, s.m. Gallows, gibbet, stake. P. Dwelling, mansion. A. Master, owner, possessor, etc. (in comp.). P. A current, jet, spirt, stream. S. (*dhār*).

دارو *dārū*, s.m. Medicine, physic; gunpowder. H.

داروغه *dāroghah*, s.m. Overseer, superintendent, manager. P.

داره *dāra*, s.f. A stream, jet, spirt; cascade. S. (*dhār*).

داريال *dāryāl*, s.m. A tambourine.

دالړ *dāṛ*, s.m. A band, company, gang (of

robbers). s. (*ḍāṛ*). A jaw tooth, grinder, molar. s. (*ḍāṛh*).

دارل *dāṛal*, v.a. To bite, lacerate, tear with the teeth (as a dog, etc.). To scold, reprove, snap at.

داره *dāṛa*, s.f. A foray, raid, surprise; cattle lifting; band, gang (of robbers); molar tooth.

داستان *dāstān*, s.m. A fable, story, tale. P.

داښت *dākkht*, s.m. A potter's furnace or oven. Durability, strength, endurance. P. (*dāsht*).

داغ *dāgh*, s.m. A spot, stain, blemish, mark; scar, cicatrix; brand, cautery. P.

داغي *dāghī*, a. Spotted, stained; scarred; cauterized; branded; blemished. P.

دال *dāl*, s.m. Pulse, lentils, vetches. S. a. Expressive, significant, typical (in comp.) A.

دالان *dālān*, s.m. Anteroom, hall, vestibule. P.

دام *dām*, s.m. A net, snare, trap. P.

دامن *dāman*, s.m. Border, skirt (of a garment, etc.); base or foot of a mountain. P.

دانا *dānā*, a. Learned, wise. s.m. A wise man. P.

داناي *dānā-ī*, s.f. Wisdom, knowledge. P.

دانست *dānist*, s.m. Knowledge, opinion. P.

دانش *dānish*, s.m. Intelligence, learning, science. P.

دانګ *dāng*, s.m. Name of a small coin; the sixth part of a دينار (*dīnār*).

دانه *dāna*, s.f. A berry; corn; grain, seed; pimple, boil; speck, granule. P. *dāna-dār*, a. Granular. *tora-dāna*, s.f. A boil, black head, furuncle; name of a black seed used in medicine.

داو *dāw*, s.m. Ambuscade, ambush; opportunity, power; time, turn, stroke (at play); stake, wager; cast or throw at dice, etc. P. H.

داي *dā-ī*, s.f. Nurse, midwife. P.

دائره *dā-ira*, s.f. A circle, orbit, ring; emblems, lines, symbols (used as amulets and charms). A.

دائم *dā-im*, a. Always, continual, perpetual. A.

دباره *dubāra*, ad. Again, second time. P.

دباغ *dabbāgh*, s.m. Currier, tanner. A.

دباغي *dabbāghī*, s.f. Business of a tanner.

دباندِ *dabāndi*, } ad. Outside, upon, on top,
دباندې *dabānde*, } above, over.

دباو *dabāw*, s.m. Authority, power, strength; subjection, pressure. H.

دبدبه *dabdaba*, s.m. Dignity, pomp, state. A.

دبلي *dablai*, s.m. A box, casket. H. (*ḍibbī*).

دبه *daba*, s.f. A jar or flagon made of untanned hide, and used to hold oil, butter, etc. H. (*ḍabbā*).

دبي *dabī*, s.f. Fruit ripened in straw or leaves, etc.

دپ *dap*, a. Deafened, stunned, stupefied.

دپارَ *dapāra*, } p. For, for the sake of, on
دپاره *dapāra*, } account of.

دپټه *dupaṭṭa*, s.f. A sheet of two breadths, used as a mantle or shawl. H.

دجاج *dujāj*, s.m. Domestic fowl. A.

دختر *dukhtar*, s.f. Daughter, girl, virgin. P.

دخل *dakhl*, s.m. Access, entrance; intrusion, interference; produce, profit, advantage. A.

دخمه *dakhma*, s.f. Ambush, lair, cover.

دد *dad*, s.m. A beast of prey, rapacious animal. P.

در *dar*, s.m. A door. P. *durr*, s.m. A pearl. A. *dar*, A particle used as a pronominal dative prefix of the second person with verbs and adverbs, without change for gender or number. Ex. *dar dzam* (I come to thee), *dar bāndi* (upon thee), etc.

دراز *darāz*, a. Extended, long. P.

درامد *darāmad*, s.m. Entrance. P.

درانی *durānī*, s.m. Name applied collectively to the western tribes of Afghans. P.

درائي *darā-ī*, s.f. A kind of red silk cloth. P.

درب *drab*, s.m. A bang, crash; roll, rumble. Name of a grass (*Agrostis linearis*). H. (*dūb*).

دربار *darbār*, s.m. A court, audience hall; levee. P.

درباري *darbārī*, a. Courtly. s.m. A courtier. P.

دربچه *darbacha*, s.f. See دريچه.

دربل *drabal*, v.a. To shake, press down (as flour, etc.). *drabal*, v.n. To subside, settle, sink, fall in, break down (as a roof, etc.); to crash, crumble.

دربلئ *darbala-ī*, s.f. A tripod.

دربي *drabai*, s.m. A bang, crash, crumble, roll, rumble.

درپري *draparai*, s.m. Nettlerash, hives.

درج *darj*, s.m. A place for writing; written; a volume. A.

درجه *darja*, s.f. Degree, rank; step, stair. A.

درخته *drakhta*, s.f. A tree, shrub. P. (*darakht*).

درخواست *darkhwāst*, s.m. Appeal, demand; entreaty, request; desire, wish; proposal. P.

درد *dard*, s.m. Pain, ache, affliction; compassion, pity, sympathy. P. *durd*, s.m. Dregs, sediment. P.

دردمن *dardman*, a. Pained, afflicted, distressed. P.

درز *darz*, s.m. A crack, split, flaw; seam, suture; a rag, slip, strip, shred, etc. (of cloth). P.

درزي *darzī*, s.m. A tailor. P.

درس *dars*, s.m. A lesson, reading; lecture. A.

درست *drast*, a. All, whole, entire; fit, proper; just, true. ad. Entirely, wholly. P. (*durust*).

درسته *darasta*, s.f. Arms, armour, weapons.

درشت *durusht*, a. Rough, hard, harsh, stiff, rigid; fierce, surly, morose, stern. P.

درشتي *durushtī*, s.f. Asperity, roughness, severity, sternness, fierceness. P.

درشل *darshal*, s.f. The frame of a door.

درغل *darghal*, a. False, base (as coin, etc.). s.m. Cheat, liar, hypocrite. Depravity, treachery, vice.

درغلول *darghalawul*, v.a. To cheat, deceive, mislead. H. (*warghalānā*).

درغول *darghol*, s.m. A gap, vent, sluice (as in a canal) to carry off the water of floods, etc.

درك *darak*, s.m. Mark, sign, trace; abode, place; entrance, passage; commencement; knowledge, understanding. A.

درکړ *drakaṛ*, s.f. Main spoke of a wheel; rim or felloe of a wheel.

درگاه *dargāh*, s.m. Court, palace; threshold; throne (divine); a shrine, sanctuary, mosque. P.

درگه *darga*, s.f. A copse, brake, thicket.

درلل *darlal*, v.a. } To have, own, possess, maintain, keep, retain.
درلول *darlawul*, } See لرل.

درم *diram*, s.m. Money, specie; name of a coin; name of a weight. P. See درهم.

درمان *darmān*, s.m. Drug, medicine, remedy. P.

درماندہ *darmāndah*, a. Distressed, destitute. P.

درماندگي *darmāndagī*, s.f. Adversity, distress; poverty, penury, misery. P.

درمند *dirmand*, s.m. A threshing floor; garner; harvest heap. P. (*khirman*).

درميان *darmiyān*, a. Between, amidst, among. P.

درناوي *daranāwai*, s.m. Heaviness, solidity, weight; steadiness, constancy; courtesy, politeness, respect (to a superior).

درنده *darindah*, a. Rapacious, savage, fierce. P.

درنگ *drang*, s.m. Delay, procrastination, hesitation. P. (*dirang*).

درو *diraw*, s.m. Reaping, mowing, harvesting. P.

دروازه *darwāza*, s.f. Gate, entrance, door. P.

دروان *darwān*, s.m. A gate-keeper, porter. P.

درود *darūd*, s.m. Benediction, blessing. P.

دروزگر *darūz·gar*, s.m. A carpenter. P. (*darūd·gar*).

دروزه *drūza*, s.m. Stubble; shavings; chaff.

دروړ *darwag*, } s.m. A cut, slit, or mark
درغوړ *darghwag*, } in the ears of cattle (for recognition).

دروغ *darogh*, s.m. A lie, falsehood, untruth. P.

دروغجن *daroghjan*, } a. False, lying. s.m.
دروغژن *daroghĵan*, } A liar.

درومل *drūmal*, v.n. To go, depart, set out, run, start.

درون *darūn*, ad. In, within. P.

دروند *drūnd*, a. Heavy, weighty, ponderous.

دروه *droh*, s.m. Artifice, deceit, evasion, fraud; stratagem, feint (in war); hatred, malice, spite. S.

دروي *darwai*, s.m. Name of a reed from which mats are made (*Arundo karka*).

درويزگر *darwez·gar*, s.m. A beggar, mendicant.

درويزه *darweza*, s.f. Beggary, mendicancy. P. (*daryūza*).

درويشت *darwīsht*, a. Twenty-three.

دره *dura*, s.f. A birch, scourge, cat of three tails. A. *dara*, s.f. A glen, valley; defile, gorge, hill pass. P.

درهم *dirham*, s.m. A drachm; name of a coin equal to the twentieth of a *dīnār*. A.

درهيسته *dar·hīsta*, ad. Towards or near thee or you.

درِ *dri*, } a. Three. S. (*tirī*).
دري *dre*, }

دري *dara-ī*, s.f. A carpet. H. (*darī*).

درياب *daryāb*, s.m. River, sea, ocean. P. (*daryā*).

دريابي *daryābī*, a. Aquatic, of the sea.

دريافت *daryāft*, s.m. Enquiry, investigation; discovery, comprehension, understanding. P.

دريچه *darīcha*, s.f. A window, ventilator; air hole in a wall. P.

دريدل *daredal*, v.n. See ودريدل.

دريښاخي *dre·kkhākhai*, s.m. A three-pronged pitchfork used to winnow corn.

دريغ *dregh*, s.m. Disinclination, repugnance; sigh, sorrow. P. (*daregh*).

دريغه *dregha*, s.m. Alas! Heigh ho! P. (*dareghā*).

دريه *darya*, s.f. See داريال.

دړزيدل *drazedal*, } v.n. To flutter, palpitate,
دړکيدل *drakedal*, } bound, quiver. H. (*dharaknā*).

دړه *dare*, s.f. A chip, splinter, fragment. H. *dare·dare*, a. Shattered, in atoms, bits, etc. *dara*, s.f. A stone or weight fixed to the lighter scale of a balance to equalize both sides. H. (*dharā*). A ridge or bank of earth, high land, crest of a hill.

دړي *dara-ī*, s.f. A dry measure equal to four *ser* or eight pounds. H. (*dharī*). A frontlet, ornament worn on the forehead by women. *darai*, s.m. A shelf, cupboard.

دزد *duzd*, s.m. A robber, thief. P.

دست *dast*, s.m. Purge, stool. Cubit, hand. P.

دستار *dastār*, s.m. A turband. P.

دستک *dastak*, s.m. Account book; passport, pass; summons, warrant. P.

دستکي *dastakai*, s.m. A small rafter placed over the large beams in a roof.

دستگله *dastgala*, s.f. A glove, mitten; gauntlet.

دنبل *dunbal*, s.m. A boil, bubo. P.

دنبه *dunba*, / دمبه *dumba*, s.f. The fat-tailed sheep. P.

دند *dund*, s.m. Haze, mist, smoke; obscurity, darkness, gloom.

دندارو *dandārū*, s.m. A boil, carbuncle.

دندانه *dandāna*, s.f. Tooth of a saw or comb; a cascade, waterfall. P.

دندوکار *dandūkār*, s.m. Noise of thunder, roar of artillery, tumult; haze, smoke, etc.

دنکاچه *dunkācha*, s.f. See دوکانچه.

دنگ *dang*, a. Tall, high (in stature). s.m. A tall man; a jump, leap, vault, bound.

دنگل *dangal*, v.a. To jump, leap, bound.

دنگول *dangawul*, v.a. To make jump, leap, etc. (as a horse over a fence); to throw one off a wall, horse, etc.

دننه *danana*, p. In, within, inside. P. (*andarūn*).

دنیا *duniyā*, s.f. The world; people; wealth. A.

دو *dwa* or *do*, a. Two (in comp.). P. *daw*, s.m. See داو. *dau*, s.m. A run, race. *dau-kawul*, v.a. To run. P. (*daw*).

دوا *dawā*, s.f. Medicine, remedy; amulet, charm. A.

دوات *dawāt*, s.m. An inkstand. A.

دواړه *dwāṛah*, a. Both. Corr. of *dwah-wāṛah*.

دوبي *dūbai*, s.m. Summer, hot weather. *dobī*, s.m. A dyer, washerman. H. (*dhobī*).

دوپ *dūp*, s.m. Sunshine, glare, haze. S. (*dhūp*).

دوتر *dawtar*, s.m. Estate, hereditary, possession in land, fief. P. (*daftar*).

دود *dod*, s.m. Custom, fashion, way; dowry, property given with a bride; entertainment of a guest. a. Similar, like. ad. Likewise, similarly. *dūd*, s.m. Vapour, smoke. P.

دور *dūr*, a. Far, distant, remote. P. *davr*, s.m. Revolution, circular motion; age, cycle, period; time, turn. A.

دوران *daurān*, s.m. Time, age, cycle; vicissitude, fortune; turn, period, revolution. A.

دورمه *dūrma*, s.f. See دروي. H. (*durmā*). Pens for writing the oriental character are made from the reed stalk.

دوړه *dūṛa*, s.f. Dust, dry earth. S. (*dhūr*).

دوزخ *dozakh*, s.m. Hell. P.

دوزخي *dozakhī*, a. Infernal, hellish.

دوزه *dūza*, s.f. Bosh, folly, nonsense.

دوزي *dūzai*, s.m. A blockhead, booby, fool, simpleton, twaddler.

دوست *dost*, s.m. A friend; lover. P.

دوسه *dūsa*, s.f. A rush, forcible entry. H. (*dhasā*). *dusa-kawul*, v.a. To invade, rush into, force through, etc.

دوش *dosh*, s.m. The shoulder, back. ad. Last night. P.

دوشاله *doshāla*, s.f. A mantle or plaid made of two breadths of cloth sewn together. P.

دوشخانه *doshkhāna*, s.f. A vessel in which skins are placed preparatory to tanning. P.

دوشرل *dosharal*, s.m. A two-year-old goat, etc.

دوشنبه *doshanba*, s.f. Monday. P.

دوغ *dogh*, s.m. Butter-milk. P.

دوغبش *doghakkh*, s.m. See دوزخ.

دوک *dwak*, a. A two-year-old (colt, sheep, etc.). H. (*dok*). *dūk*, s.m. A bodkin, knitting pin; spindle. P.

دوکان *dūkān*, s.m. A shop, workshop. P.

دوکانچه *dūkāncha*, s.f. A platform, terrace; form, bench, settle (before a door or shop); seat or raised earth round a tree, etc.

دوکړه *dūkṛa*, s.f. A kind of kettle-drum.

دوگانه *dogānah*, a. Double, twofold; a prayer with two genuflexions. P.

دولت *daulat*, s.m. Riches, wealth; fortune, property; empire, state; cause, effect, means. A.

دستمايه *dastmāya*, s.f. The handle strap of a shield.

دستمبول *dastambol*, s.m. A musk melon.

دستور *dastūr*, s.m. Custom, fashion, usage; mode, manner, regulation. A clyster, enema. P.

دسته *dasta*, s.f. A handle; pestle; quire of paper; nosegay; bundle of 24 arrows; a bundle, handful; skein of thread or silk; division, brigade, etc. of an army. P.

دستي *dastī*, a. Manual, of the hand. ad. Quickly, immediately, sharply.

دسخط *daskhaṭ*, s.m. Signature. P. (*dast-khaṭṭ*).

دښت *dakkht*, s.m. Desert, wild, waste. P. (*dasht*).

دښمن *dukkhman*, s.m. An enemy, foe. P. (*dushman*).

دښمني *dukkhmanī*, } s.f. Enmity, hostility,
دښني *dukkhnī*, } hatred.

دعا *du'ā*, s.f. Benediction, blessing; prayer; imprecation, invocation. A.

دعوت *da'wat*, s.m. Convocation, invitation; entertainment, feast. A.

دعوه *da'wa*, s.f. Claim, plaint; accusation, action at law. A.

دغا *daghā*, s.f. Deceit, imposture, treachery. P.

دغدغه *daghdagha*, s.f. Alarm, call to arms; tumult. A.

دغمه *daghma*, s.f. A welt, weal, mark of a stripe.

دغه *daghah*, pr. The proximate demonstrative pronoun, this, these. A. (*dikhah* or *dak*).

دف *daf*, s.m. A tambourine. P.

دفتر *daftar*, s.m. Record, register, roll; archives; a book; land, estate, registered share of land. P.

دفعه *daf'a*, s.f. Averting, repelling; time, turn; moment. A. (*dafa'*).

دفن *dafan*, s.m. Burial; funeral. A.

دق *diqq*, s.m. Trouble, vexation; hectic fever. A.

دقيقه *daqīqa*, s.f. A minute, moment; anything minute or subtle; a trifle, unimportant matter. A.

دل *dal*, s.m. Bruised or coarsely ground grain, grits. S. (*daliyā*). *dil*, s.m. The heart, soul; courage. P.

دلازاک *dalāzāk*, s.m. Name of a tribe who formerly held the Peshawar valley, whence they were ejected by the Afghans.

دلال *dallāl*, s.m. A broker, agent, salesman; a pimp, go-between; horse dealer. A.

دلاور *dilāwar*, a. Brave, gallant, courageous. P.

دلاوري *dilāwarī*, s.f. Bravery, courage. P.

دلبار *dalbār*, s.m. See دربار.

دلبه *dalba*, s.f. A lure for hawks. A. (*ṭalaba*).

دلته *dalta*, ad. Here, hither. P. (*dar īn jā*).

دلدل *daldal*, s.m. A quagmire, quicksand. H.

دلوه *dalwa*, s.f. A bucket water-pail. A.

دلي *dala-ī*, s.f. A corn stack or rick. *dale*, ad. See دلته.

دليل *dalīl*, s.m. Demonstration, proof; director, guide. A.

دم *dam*, s.m. Breath, life; ambition, pride; moment, minute; edge of a sword; stewing over a slow fire. P. *dum*, s.m. Tail, end, extremity. P.

دماغ *dimāgh*, s.m. The brain. A.

دمامه *damāma*, s.f. A kettle-drum. P.

دمبال *dumbāl*, ad. After, behind, in rear. P.

دمباله *dumbāla*, s.f. A rear guard. P.

دمچي *dumchī*, s.f. A crupper. P.

دمدمه *damdama*, s.f. A mound, bastion, redoubt. A.

دمړي *damṛa-ī*, s.f. The eighth part of a paisa. H.

دمه *dama*, s.f. Breath, respiration; rest, repose, ease; asthma; a pair of bellows. P.

دولتئ *dolata-ī*, s.f. A kick with both hind legs.

دومي *dūmai*, s.m. } Cold, catarrh, influenza.
دومه *dūma*, s.f. }

دون *dūn*, a. Abject, base, ignoble, mean, vile. A.

دوند *dūnd*, s.m. See دند. H. (*dhundh*).

دونه *dūna*, s.f. A bonfire. H. (*dhūnī*).

دوني *dūne* or *dūnī*, ad. This much, to this extent.

دونړئ *donra-ī* or *daunra-ī*, s.f. A milk pail. H. (*dohnī*).

دوه *dwah*, a. Two.

دوهئ *dūha-ī*, s.f. Fire-place, chimney. H. (*dūhiyā*).

دوي *doe*, s.m. Custom, fashion, usage. *dwī*, pr. plural of دي *dai*, or *de*, this.

ده *dah*, pr. This. See دي. *dih*, s.m. A village. P. *dah*, in. A word used to drive or urge a horse.

دهات *dihāt*, s.m. The country. P.

دهان *dahān*, s.m. The mouth; orifice, aperture. P.

دهانه *dahāna*, s.f. Bridle bit, mouth piece. P.

دهځ *dahadz*, s.m. Dowry, marriage portion, the property the wife carries with her to her husband. A. (*dahez*).

دهړه *dahṛa*, s.f. A jaw tooth, grinder, tusk.

دهشت *dahshat*, s.m. Alarm, fear, dread, terror. A.

دهقان *dihqān*, s.m. Peasant, villager; ploughman, farm servant. P.

دهليدل *dahaledal*, v.n. To fear, quake, tremble. H. (*dahalna*).

دهمرده *dahmardah*, a. Bold, brave, strong. *dahmarda*, s.f. A lever.

دهور *dahor*, s.m. A weaver.

دهوس *dahūs*, s.m. Cuckold, term of abuse. A. (*daiyūs*).

دهه *daha*, s.f. The first ten days of Muḥarram; models of the tombs of Hasan and Husen carried about in procession during that time. P. (*dahā*).

دي *dai* or *de*, pr. This. Also written ده *dah*, دَ *da*, and د *di*. A. (*de* or *dī*).

ديار *diyār*, s.m. The cedar tree (*Cedrus deodara*).

ديارلس *diyārlas*, a. Thirteen.

ديانت *diyānat*, s.m. Honesty, probity; piety, virtue. A.

ديبا *debā*, s.f. Brocade. P.

ديباجه *debāja*, } s.f. Exordium, introduction, preface. A.
ديباچه *dībācha*, }

ديت *diyat*, s.m. Law of retaliation; price of blood, fine paid for murder, wounding, etc. A.

ديچکه *dechka*, s.f. A cauldron, stewpan, cooking pot. P. (*degcha*).

ديد *dīd*, s.m. Sight, show, spectacle. P.

ديدار *dīdār*, } s.m. Interview, sight, seeing. P.
ديدن *dīdan*, }

ديده *dīdah*, a. Seen, observed. *dīda*, s.f. The eye. P.

ديرش *dersh*, a. Thirty.

ديره *dera*, s.f. A dwelling, tent. H. (*derā*).

ديگ *deg*, s.m. A cauldron, boiler. P.

ديگچه *degcha*, s.f. Stewpan, saucepan. P.

دين *dīn*, s.m. Religion, faith. A.

دينار *dīnār*, s.m. Name of a coin, a ducat. The tenth part of a pice. A.

ديني *dīnī*, a. Religious; spiritual. A.

ديو *deo*, s.m. A demon, devil. P.

ديوال *dīwāl*, s.m. A wall. P. (*dīwār*).

ديوان *dīwān*, s.m. Divan, tribunal; steward, custodian; a book of poems, the rhymes of which end successively with every letter of the alphabet. P.

ديوانه *dīwānah*, a. Mad. See ليوني.

د

د *ḍāl* or *ḍe* is the fourteenth letter of the Pukkhto alphabet. It is similar in sound to the Sanskrit ड, and corresponds to the ڈ *ḍa* of the Hindūstānī.

داد *ḍāḍ*, s.m. Comfort, consolation.

داده *ḍāḍa*, s.f. An unripe ear of corn; the ear of Indian corn roasted for food.

دار *ḍār*, s.m. Anxiety, fear; fright, terror. H. (*ḍar*).

داره *ḍāra*, s.f. Arbour, shed, hut of branches, etc.

داګ *ḍāg*, s.m. } Clear, dry and level ground;
داګه *ḍāga*, s.f. } a patch of hard and bare ground.

دال *ḍāl*, s.m. A shield, buckler. H. (*ḍhāl*).

داندت *ḍānḍat*, s.m. A cotton carder's bow.

داندۍ *ḍānḍa-ī*, s.f. The beam of a balance; a pair of scales. H. (*ḍanḍī*). A blaze, conflagration.

دانګ *ḍāng*, s.m. A club, bludgeon, stick. H. Name of a copper coin, a penny.

دانګ لکۍ *ḍāng-laka-ī*, s.f. See توره آنه.

دانګورۍ *ḍāngora-ī*, s.f. A small club, baton.

دانګۍ *ḍānga-ī*, s.f. See تانګو.

دب *ḍab*, s.m. A slap, blow, thump. H. (*dhap*). An eddy, whirlpool; backwater, still water. Power, authority, strength. H. Fashion, shape; breeding, manners; mode, way. H. (*ḍhab*).

دبدبنی *ḍabḍabanai*, a. Anxious, irresolute, wavering.

دبدوب *ḍabḍūb*, a. Apathetic, paralyzed, senseless.

دبره *ḍabara*, s.f. A pebble, stone, boulder.

دبلۍ *ḍabala-ī*, s.f. A mallet, pestle.

دبول *ḍabawul*, v.a. To beat, thrash, pommel.

دتی *ḍaṭai*, s.m. A brag, boaster, bully; term of abuse.

دچکه *ḍachka*, s.f. A trot; amble; jolt.

دد *ḍaḍ*, a. Empty, vacant, void; deep, bass, hoarse (sound).

ددوزه *ḍaḍūza*, s.f. Haze, smoke; flame and smoke.

دده *ḍaḍa*, s.f. The flank, side; edge, border; direction.

دران *ḍarān*, s.m. A bellow, low, bray (as of ox, ass, etc.).

درپل *ḍirpal*, s.m. A flatterer, parasite, toady.

درپلي *ḍirpalī*, s.f. Flattery, toadyism.

دره *ḍara*, s.f. Chip, splinter, fragment, shred, bit.

دز *ḍaz*, s.m. Bang, burst, explosion, report. A braggart, bully, blusterer.

دزدوز *ḍaz-ḍūz*, s.m. Report of firearms; a skirmish.

دغره *ḍaghara*, } s.f. Butting, shoving, pushing;
دقره *ḍaqara*, } a butt, shove, push. H. (*ṭakkar*).

دک *ḍak*, a. Full, replete.

دکال *ḍukāl*, s.m. Dearth, famine, scarcity. H.

دکه *ḍaka*, s.f. A thrust, jolt, shove, push. H. (*dhakkā*). A clutch, grab, pounce, swoop. a. Pregnant, with young; full.

دکي *ḍakai* or *ḍikai*, s.m. A sapling, young tree; a dry stump or stalk; a twig, switch, stick, dry bush.

دګلاند *ḍuglānd*, s.m. Amble, jog, trot; ambling horse.

دګه *ḍaga*, s.f. The penis.

دګي *ḍagai*, s.m. A thin, lean, bony ox or horse, a rosinante. H. (*ḍaggā*).

دل *ḍal*, s.m. A kind of rake; cantonment, camp.

دله *ḍala*, s.f. Assembly, crowd, mob. S. (*dal*).

دم *ḍum*, s.m. Name of a tribe or caste of musicians and dancers. H. (*ḍom*).

دمامه *ḍamāma*, s.m. A drum; drumming. *ḍamāme-wahal*, v.a. To drum.

ډمډوم *ḍamḍūm*, s.m. Rattle, roll, sound of a drum.

ډنبره *ḍanbara*, s.f. Hornet, wasp. Name of a tree with thorny stems and dotted leaves; the black berries are used as pepper, and sticks are made from the branches.

ډنډ *ḍanḍ*, s.m. A pool, pond, tank.

ډنډاره *ḍanḍāra*, s.f. A hornet, wasp; a stem, stalk, sprout (of herbs); stalk of leaves.

ډنډوکي *ḍanḍūkai*, s.m. A puddle, pool, tank.

ډنګ *ḍang*, s.m. Melody, tune, modulation. H.

ډنګر *ḍangar*, a. Thin, lean, scraggy. s.m. Cattle; a bullock, buffalo. H. (*ḍāngar*).

ډنګرۍ *ḍingara-ī*, ډنګلۍ *ḍingala-ī*, s.f. A machine for drawing water from wells (by means of a lever pole, which is supported on a post, and has a bucket slung at one end and a weight fixed at the other). H. (*ḍhenklī*).

ډو *ḍaw*, s.m. Flatus, emission of wind from behind.

ډوب *ḍūb*, a. Drowned, immersed, sunk. H.

ډوډه *ḍūḍa* or *ḍiwḍa*, s.f. The hip, haunch; hip joint.

ډوډۍ *ḍoḍa-ī*, s.f. Bread; food. S. (*roṭī*).

ډور *ḍūr*, s.m. Knitting. *ḍūr-kawul*, v.a. To knit. H. (*ḍor*).

ډوزک *ḍūzak*, s.m. A brag, bully.

ډوزه *ḍūza*, s.f. Chatter, prattle, nonsense; boasting, bragging, bluster, swagger.

ډوغ *ḍūgh*, s.m. Expectoration, hawking, clearing the throat of phlegm.

ډوغل *ḍoghal*, s.m. A cavity, hole, pit.

ډول *ḍaul*, s.m. Manner, mode; dress, fashion. H. *ḍol*, s.m. A large drum; the cog-wheel of a Persian irrigation wheel; hopper, rim of a hand- or other mill. H. (*ḍhol*).

ډولکي *ḍolkai*, s.m. A small drum.

ډوله *ḍola*, s.f. A small bowl or basin; a cup, jar.

ډولۍ *ḍola-ī*, s.f. A sedan chair or litter (carried by two men). H.

ډومبک *ḍūmbak*, s.m. The rattle or roll of a drum.

ډومبکي *ḍūmbakai*, s.m. A kettle-drum, tambourine, gong, small drum.

ډيډه *ḍīḍa*, s.f. A bung, plug, stopper; the piece of wood let into the hole of the lower stone of a handmill (to hold the iron pivot on which the upper one turns). *ḍeḍa*, s.f. A kind of ear-ring. H.

ډير *ḍer*, a. Abundant, plenty, enough; many, much. H. (*ḍher*). *ḍer-wālai*, s.m. Abundance, plenty.

ډيران *ḍerān*, s.m. A dunghill; a cloth worn by women during the menses.

ډيره *ḍera*, s.f. A camp, tent, temporary lodging. H. (*ḍerā*).

ډيرۍ *ḍera-ī*, s.f. A hillock, mound, heap, pile. H. (*ḍherī*). *ḍerai*, s.m. A crowd, mob, multitude.

ډيل *ḍīl*, s.m. Dress, mode, fashion; form, manner, shape; body, bulk, size. H. *ḍīl-ḍaul*, s.m. Appearance, dress, costume, fashion.

ډينګ *ḍīng*, s.m. A crane, stork (*Ardea sp.*).

ډينګ ډينګي *ḍīng-ḍīngai*, s.m. Ding-dong, lullaby, song, chime, nursery rhyme.

ډيوالي *ḍīwālai*, s.m. A bankrupt. H. (*dewāliyā*).

ډيوټ *ḍīwaṭ*, s.m. A candlestick, lamp-stand. S.

ډيود *ḍīwad*, s.m. A kind of perfumed candle used at weddings; a lamp-stand.

ډيوه *ḍīwa*, s.f. A lamp. S. (*dīwā*).

ذ

ذ *zāl* is the fifteenth letter of the Pukkhto alphabet, and the ninth of the Arabic. It is only found in words adopted from the latter language.

ذات *z̤āt*, s.m. Essence, nature, soul; body, person, substance; breed, caste, race. A.

ذبحه *z̤abḥa*, s.f. Sacrifice, slaughter. A.

ذخيره *z̤ak͟hīra*, s.f. Store, treasure; provisions, victuals. A.

ذره *z̤arra*, s.f. An atom, bit, jot, particle, little. A.

ذكر *z̤akar*, s.m. Membrum virile. A. *z̤ikr*, s.m. Memory, recital, mention, relation. A.

ذلت *z̤illat*, s.m. Baseness, vileness, meanness. A.

ذليل *z̤alīl*, a. Abject, base, mean. A.

ذم *z̤am*, s.m. Blame, reproach. A.

ذمه *z̤imma*, s.f. Charge, trust; duty, responsibility, obligation. A.

ذوق *z̤auq*, s.m. Taste; delight, joy, pleasure. A.

ذهن *z̤ihn*, s.m. Acumen, mind, sagacity, genius. A.

ذهين *z̤ahīn*, a. Acute, sagacious, witty. A.

ر

ر *re* is the sixteenth letter of the Puk͟hk͟hto alphabet; it has a soft, but clear and distinct, sound as the *r* in the word *rain*.

را *rā*, A particle used with verbs and adverbs as a pronominal dative prefix for the first person; me, us, to me, to us. Ex. *rākawul*, to give me; *rāt͟sak͟ha*, with me, etc.

راب *rāb*, s.m. Syrup. H.

رابري *rābrī*, s.f. Caudle, gruel, pap. H.

رابطه *rābiṭa*, s.f. Bond, connection, link. A.

رابيا *rābiyā*, s.f. A pair of leather sacks or bags for carrying water upon bullocks, camels, etc.

راپور *rāpori*, راپوري *rāpore*, ad. On this side, here, hitherward, near me, us, etc.; up to me, or us.

راتګ *rātag*, s.m. Arrival, coming.

راتلل *rātlal*, v.n. To arrive, come. See راغلل.

راج *rāj*, s.m. Government, kingdom, reign, sway. S. A mason, builder, bricklayer. P.

راجا *rājā*, s.m. A title of Hindu potentates; king, prince, duke. S.

راحت *rāḥat*, s.m. Ease, quiet, repose, tranquility. A.

راړه *rāṛa*, s.f. See بروړه.

راز *rāz*, s.m. A secret, mystery. P.

رازدار *rāz-dār*, a. Trusty, faithful. s.m. A confidant.

رازق *rāziq*, s.m. The Deity; provider of daily wants. A.

راس *rās*, s.m. A bridle, leading-string, reins. H. Head; head of cattle. A.

راست *rāst*, a. Right, just, true; straight, level; right, right hand. P.

راستي *rāstī*, s.f. Fidelity, justice, loyalty. ad. Truly, indeed, really. P.

راشبيل *rās͟hbel*, s.m. A wooden shovel (used to winnow corn).

راشتلي *rās͟htalai*, s.m. Refuse grain left on the ground after removal of the corn from the threshing floor.

راشكي *rās͟hakai*, s.m. A heap, lump, small mound.

راشه *rās͟ha*, s.f. A heap of grain, provisions, supplies; eminence, hillock, mound. *rās͟ha-dars͟ha*, s.f. Visiting, acquaintance, intercourse.

راښكو *rāk͟hk͟hko*, s.m. A wire drawer; puller, drawer, strainer.

راضي *rāẓī*, a. Agreed, content, willing, satisfied. A.

راغ *rāg͟h*, s.m. A meadow, lawn; villa, summer-house; hill-side, declivity. P.

راغلل *rāg͟hlal*, v.n. To arrive, come. See راتلل.

راغه *rāg͟hah*, s.m. Mountain skirt, hill side.

رافضي *rāfiẓī*, s.m. A heretic. A.
راقي *rāqī*, s.f. Cornelian, red agate.
راكس *rākis*, s.m. The centre one of a bevy of oxen treading out corn. *rākas*, s.m. Demon, devil. S.
راكول *rākawul*, v.a. To give me, or us.
راګ *rāg*, s.m. Music, song, tune. S.
رامزدګي *rāmzadagī*, s.f. A crowbar, lever; roller.
راموسي *rāmūsai*, s.m. The musk deer.
رانجونوني *rānjūnūnai*, s.m. A box or case for rānjah.
رانجه *rānjah*, s.m. Powdered antimony (applied to the edges of the eyelids as an ornament, and as a protection from excessive glare), collyrium.
رانده *rānḍah*, a. Driven out, rejected, expelled. P.
رانيول *rānīwul*, v.a. To capture, seize, take.
راوړل *rāwṛal*, v.a. To bear, bring, carry, fetch, etc. (only applied to inanimate objects). To bear, produce, bring forth, yield (as young fruit, etc.). P. (*āwurdan*).
راوستل *rāwustal*, v.a. To lead, conduct, bring, fetch, etc. (only applied to animate objects). P. (*firistādan*).
راه *rāh*, s.m. Road, way; manner. (in comp.). P.
راهيت *rāhīṭ*, s.m. Head man of a village.
راهيسته *rāhīsta*, ad. Here, hither, this way, near me, etc.
راي *rāe*, s.m. Opinion, thought; counsel. P.
رب *rabb*, s.m. The Deity. A. *rub*, s.m. Juice, syrup. P.
ربا *ribā*, s.f. Usury. A. *ribā·khor*, s.m. An usurer.
رباب *rabāb*, s.m. A rebeck, violin. P.
رباط *rabāṭ*, s.m. Hostelry, inn, caravansary. A.
ربړ *rabaṛ*, s.m. Bother, trouble, toil, labour. H.
ربړول *rabṛawul*, v.a. To bother, worry, fatigue, drive about.
ربړيدل *rabṛedal*, v.n. To labour, toil, trudge about, fatigue oneself, etc.
ربنړه *rabanṛa*, s.f. Moonlight.
رپ *rap*, s.m. A shelf, cupboard. P. (*raf*).
رپک *rapak*, s.m. A small shelf, bracket.
رپيدل *rapedal*, v.n. To flutter, palpitate, quake, quiver, tremble, writhe, etc.
رت *rat*, A particle used with adjectives to denote intensity (mostly of colour). Ex. *rat·tor*, a. Jet black. *rat·shīn*, a. Bright green.
رتي *rata-ī*, s.f. Name of a seed used as a weight (*Abrus precatorius*). S. (*rattī*).
رُت *ra-at*, s.m. A gush of tears, violent crying. a. Ample, capacious; loose, open, expanded.
رټل *raṭal*, v.a. To reject, turn away, repel (as a visitor). To abuse, scold, taunt, reprove. H. (*raṭnā*).
رجوع *rujū'*, s.f. Turning towards, return; bent, bias. A.
رچ *rach*, s.m. A weaver's loom. H. (*rāchh*). *ruch*, s.m. Avidity, desire, pleasure (in eating). S. An ox that wounds itself by crossing the feet in walking.
رحلت *riḥlat*, s.m. Departure; death. A.
رحم *raḥm*, s.m. Compassion, kindness, mercy, pity. A. *riḥam*, s.m. The womb. A.
رحمان *raḥmān*, s.m. The Deity. a. Merciful. A.
رحمت *raḥmat*, s.m. Compassion, mercy, pity. A.
رخت *rakht*, s.m. Apparel, furniture, goods, implements; a plough; tanned leather. P.
رخسار *rukhsār*, s.m. The cheek, face. P.
رخصت *rukhṣat*, s.m. Discharge, leave, permission. A.
رخنه *rakhna*, s.f. A cleft, fissure; hole, notch, fracture, flaw. P. See نخره.
رخه *rakha*, s.f. Hatred, malice, spite.

رد *radd*, s.m. Refutation, rejection; rejoinder. A.

رده *radda*, s.f. A layer, series, row; layer of bricks in a wall; work of a day (mason's). H. (*raddā*).

رديف *radīf*, s.m. Following in regular succession (as the letters of the alphabet), the rhyming word of a poem, a man riding behind another on the same horse, etc. A.

رډ *raḍ*, a. Ajar, open, wide open; amazed, confounded, petrified, stunned.

رړۍ *raṛa-ī*, s.f. Seed of a tree (*Melia sempervircns*).

رز *raz*, s.m. A vineyard. P.

رزق *rizq*, s.m. See روزي.

رژيدل *rajedal*, v.n. To cast off, moult, shed (as hair, horns, feathers, leaves, etc.); to be dispersed, shed, dropped, scattered. P. (*rekhtan, rez-*).

رس *ras*, s.m. Extract, juice, sap. S. Arriving (in comp. only). P.

رساله *risāla*, s.f. Mission; book; essay, letter; troop of horse. A.

رساليندي *rasālīndai*, s.m. An archer, bowman.

رسد *rasad*, s.m. Grain, provision, stores; supplies collected for an army. P.

رسم *rasam*, s.m. Custom, law; model, plan. A.

رسوا *ruswā*, a. Disgraced, dishonoured. P.

رسواي *ruswā-ī*, s.f. Ignominy, disgrace, dishonour.

رسول *rasul*, s.m. A messenger, apostle; the prophet Muḥammad. A. *rasawul*, v.a. To send to, to convey to, conduct or lead to, etc.; make arrive. P. (*rasāndan*).

رسولۍ *rasawla-ī*, s.f. Bunion, corn, gall, wen; a cancer, diseased gland.

رسۍ *rasa-ī*, s.f. A cord, rope, string. S. (*rassī*).

رسيد *rasīd*, s.m. Arrival; acknowledgement, receipt. P.

رسيدل *rasedal*, v.n. To arrive, attain, reach, come up to, etc. P. (*rasīdan*).

رشته *rishta*, s.f. Line, series; connexion, relation. *rishta-dār*, s.m. Relation, kinsman. P.

رشک *rashk*, s.m. Envy, jealousy; malice, spite. P.

رشکي *rashakai*, s.m. A small mound, tumulus; heap, pile.

رشوت *rishwat*, s.m. A bribe. A.

رښتيا *rikkhtiyā*, a. True. s.f. Truth, veracity, reality. P. (*rāstī*).

رښتينتوب *rikkhtīn-tob*, s.m. Truthfulness, honesty, probity, righteousness.

رښتيني *rikkhtīnai*, } a. True, truthful, veracious; honest, upright, righteous.
رښتوني *rikkhtūnai*, }

رښکۍ *rikkhka-ī*, s.f. A band, fillet, ribbon, shred, slip, strip, fibre. P. (*resha*).

رضا *raẓā*, s.f. Assent, consent; pleasure, will. A.

رطوبت *ruṭūbat*, s.m. Humidity, wetness. A.

رعايت *ri'āyat*, s.m. Attention, favour; protection, kindness; indulgence, remission; honour, respect. A.

رعيت *ra'yat*, s.m. A subject, tenant. A.

رغبت *raghbat*, s.m. Avidity, desire, wish; pleasure; affection, esteem. A.

رغړول *rghaṛawul*, v.a. To trundle, roll (as a hoop, etc.). P. (*ghaltānīdan*).

رغړيدل *rghaṛedal*, v.n. To roll, wallow, tumble, toss (as an animal on the ground); to roll, trundle (as a stone down a slope). Def. in past ten. P. (*ghaltīdan*).

رغښتل *rghakkhtal*, v.n. See preceding word.

رغي *raghai*, s.m. A bowl, deep plate (as a soup plate); a deep and flat basket (in opposition to a shallow one).

رفتار *raftār*, s.m. Going, motion; gait, pace. P.

رفعه *raf'a*, s.f. Removing, repelling. A. *raf'a-daf'a*, s.f. Deciding, settling, finishing. A.

رفو **rafū**, s.m. Darning, mending clothes; a darn. A.

رفيق **rafīq**, s.m. Associate, comrade, friend. A.

رقص **raqṣ**, s.m. A dance, dancing. A.

رقعه **ruq'a**, s.f. A letter, note; bit, patch, piece. A.

رقم *raqam*, s.m. A royal edict; kind, sort; mode, method; mark, sign. A.

رقيب *raqīb*, s.m. Rival, enemy. A.

ركاب *rikāb*, s.m. Stirrup; escort, train. A. A platter, salver, tray. P.

ركابي *rikābī*, s.f. A plate, dish. P.

ركات *rakāt*, s.m. A genuflexion, prostration (in prayer). A. (*rak'at*).

ركښ *rakkkh*, s.m. Furrow, groove (as of a rifle); line, rut, track, scratch. P. (*rakh*).

ركن *rukn*, s.m. A pillar, prop, support. A.

ركوع *rukū'*, s.f. Bowing the head or body (in prayer). A.

ركيب *rikeb*, s.m. A stirrup iron. P. (*rakīb*).

ركيبي *rikebī*, s.f. See ركابي.

رګ *rag*, s.m. A vein; tendon; nerve. P. *rag-wahal*, v.a. To inoculate; to bleed, let blood.

رګړي *rigaṛai*, a. A child stinted in milk.

رګي *ragai*, s.m. Consanguinity, blood-relation; congenital or hereditary trait.

رمباړه *rambāṛa*, s.f. A bellow, low (as of oxen).

رمبكي *rambakai*, s.m. The bellow of a bull.

رمبه *ramba*, s.f. A borer, centre-bit, auger. H. (*barmā*).

رمبي *rambai*, s.m. A hoe, instrument for weeding; a cobbler's knife for cutting leather. H. (*ramba*).

رمز **ramaz**, s.m. A hint, nod, sign, wink. A.

رموز **ramūz**, s.m. Enigma, riddle. A.

رمول *ramawul*, v.a. To frighten, scare, terrify; to conduct or lead cattle (out to graze). H. (*ramnā*).

رمه *ra-ama*, s.f. Mucus; muco-purulent matter from the bowels; any mucous discharge; dysentery. Also *r-ima*, and mostly used in the plural as *ra-ame* or *r-ime*. P. (*rīm*). *ramma*, s.f. A herd, drove, or flock (of cattle, sheep, etc.). P.

رمي *ra-amai* or *r-imai*, s.m. Dysentery, bowel complaint.

رميدل *ramedal*, v.n. To be alarmed, terrified; to flock, herd together. P. (*ramīdan*).

رنځ *randz*, s.m. Affliction, grief, pain; disgust, offence, vexation. P. (*ranj*).

رنځور *randzūr*, a. Afflicted, sick, pained; distressed, grieved; offended, vexed. P. (*ranjūr*).

رنځول *randzawul*, v.a. To afflict, pain, vex, etc.

رنځيدل *randzedal*, v.n. To fret, grieve, be hurt, pained, distressed. P. (*ranjīdan*).

رنجروړمه *ranjaṛūma*, s.f. A collyrium box, case for powdered antimony. See رانجه.

رنجك *ranjak*, s.m. Priming powder. H.

رند *rind*, s m. Debauchee, blackguard, rake. P.

رندار *rundār*, s.f. See ورندار.

رنده *randa*, s.f. A plane; carpenter's tool. P.

رنګ *rang*, s.m. Colour; paint; kind, sort; manner, method, way. P.

رنګټ *rangaṭ*, s.m. Crying, blubbering, weeping. H. (*rohaṭ*).

رنګړ *ringaṛ*, a. } Beaten down, laid low,
رنګړي *ringaṛai*, } levelled (as crops by wind and rain).

رنګي *rangai*, a. Scanty, thin (as hair, crops, rain, etc.).

رنګين *rangīn*, a. Coloured, painted; variegated, etc. P.

رڼا *ranṛā*, s.f. Light, daylight, brilliancy, lustre, etc.

رو *ro*, a. Easy, slow, soft, quiet. *ro-ro*, ad. Gently, slowly. *rū*, s.m. Face, surface. P.

روا *rawā*, a. Allowable, lawful, right, current, proper, etc. P. *rwā*, s.f. See ورا.

رواج *rawāj*, s.m. Custom, usage, fashion. a. Customary, current, fashionable, saleable. A.

رواش *rawāsh*, s.m. Rhubarb; blanched leaf-stalk of the plant. P.

روان *rawān*, a. Current, flowing, moving, going. P. *ruwān*, a. See وران.

روانه *rawānah*, a. Despatched, departed. P. *rawāna*, s.f. A pass, passport. P.

رواني *rawānī*, s.m. Course, proceeding. P. *ruwānī*, s.f. See وراني.

روايت *riwāyat*, s.m. Fable, fiction, tale; history. A.

روبرو *rūbarū*, ad. Face to face, in front, opposite. P.

روپئي *rūpa-ī*, s.f. Name of a silver coin, rupee. S. (*rupiyā*).

روځ *rwadz*, s.f. A day, day, daytime. P. (*roz*).

روح *rūh*, s.m. Soul, spirit. A.

روخ *rokh* or *rūkh*, a. Fit, proper, ready; side, direction. P. (*rukh*).

روخي *rokhai*, s.m. Part, side (as of opponents).

رود *rod*, s.m. A river, stream. P.

رودل *rawdal*, v.a. To suck (as a child the breast). To mow, reap, cut (as corn, etc.).

رودنګ *rodang*, s.m. Madder (*Rubia tinctoria*). P.

روز *roz*, s.m. Day, daytime. (in comp). P.

روزګار *rozgār*, s.m. Employment, service; time, world. P.

روزمره *rozmarra*, ad. Always, daily, continually. P.

روزي *rozī*, s.f. Daily food, sustenance. P.

روژتي *rojatai*, s.m. A faster, keeper of Lent.

روژه *roja*, s.f. Fast, Lent. P. (*roza*).

روږد *rūgd*, a. Habituated, accustomed; affluent, comfortable. A. (*raghd*).

روست *rost*, a. Decayed, carious, corrupt, rotten; fetid, putrid, stinking. Also وروست.

روستو *rūsto* or *rwusto*, ad. See ورستو.

روښان *rokkhān*, a. Bright, light, luminous; clear, manifest, conspicuous; glittering, radiant, refulgent. P. (*roshān*).

روښن *rokkhan*, a. Bright, light, shining. P. (*roshan*).

روښنائي *rokkhnā-ī*, s.f. Brightness, light. P. (*roshnā-ī*).

روضه *rauza*, s.f. Mausoleum, tomb, garden. A.

روغ *rogh*, a. Hale, healthy, sound, vigorous, well.

روغبړ *roghbaṛ*, s.m. Shaking hands, asking after health; embracing.

روغن *roghan*, s.m. Grease, fat, tallow. P.

روغه *rogha*, s.f. Amity, peace; harmony, intercourse, friendship.

روک *rok*, s.m. Cash, ready money. S.

روګ *rog*, s.m. A strap, thong of a sandal, strap of a churning stick, etc.

روګه *rwuga*, s.f. See وروږه.

رومال *rūmāl*, s.m. A handkerchief; towel, napkin. P.

رون *rūn*, s.m. The thigh. H. (*rān*).

رونق *raunaq*, s.m. Beauty, elegance; order, symmetry; ornament, splendour. A.

رونړ *rūnṛ*, a. Bright, lustrous, radiant, shining.

روه *roh*, s.m. Name of an extensive tract occupied by the Eastern highlands of Afghanistan, between Kandahar on the west and the Indus on the east, Badakhshan on the north and Sind on the south.

روهلي *rohilai*, s.m. A Rohilla, native of Roh, so called by the people of Hindūstān; a highlander.

روي *rawai* or *riwai*, s.m. A ghost, goblin, demon; nightmare. *rūe*, s.m. Face, countenance, surface; cause, reason, sake. P.

رويت *rūyat*, s.m. Appearance, shape, etc. A.

رُويدل *rū-edal*, v.n. To cavil, dispute, wrangle.

رهته *rahata*, s.f. Content, ease, tranquility. A. (*rāḥat*).

رهټ *rahaṭ*, s.m. A wheel for drawing water, an irrigation wheel. H.

رهيل *rahel*, s.m. Reading desk, support for a book. P. (*raḥl*).

ري *rai*, s.m. Price current, rate, tariff.

ريا *riyā*, s.f. Dissimulation, evasion, hypocrisy. A. *rayā*, s.f. Braying of an ass.

رياست *riyāsat*, s.m. Command, dominion. A.

رياضت *riyāẓat*, s.m. Temperance, continence. A.

رياکار *riyā·kār*, s.m. A hypocrite. A.

ريبار *rebār*, s.m. A go-between, match-maker (between lovers or betrothed couples).

ريباري *rebārī*, s.f. Match-making, etc.

ريبدون *rebdūn*, s.m. Name of a tree (*Tecoma undulata*).

ريبل *rebal*, v.a. To mow, reap, cut (as corn, etc.).

ريچه *rīcha*, s.f. Young louse, nit, egg of a louse; a particle, jot, tittle. *rīche·rīche*, p. Atoms, particles, bits, etc.

ريخ *rīkh*, s.m. Dung of birds; loose stool, watery excrement of man or animals (as in diarrhœa). P.

ريخان *rīkhān*, a. Loose in the bowels, affected with diarrhœa, purged.

ريخي *rīkhai*, s.m. Dysentery, diarrhœa (in cattle). Tear, rent, slit (in clothes); a hole in a reservoir to let out the water.

ريدوان *redwān*, s.m. See ريبدون.

ريدي *redai*, s.m. Wild poppy; ragged robin; wild tulip.

ريزه *reza*, s.f. A bit, chip, filing, scrap, shred, etc. P.

ريږدول *regdawul*, v.a. To agitate, shake, move, etc.

ريږديدل *regdedal*, v.n. To flutter, shake, quiver vibrate.

رئيس *ra-īs*, s.m. A chief, prince, lord. A.

ريش *rīsh*, s.m. The beard (in comp.). P.

ريشل *reshal*, v.a. To spin, twist. P. (*resha*, fibre).

ريښم *rekkham*, s.m. Silk. P. (*resham*).

ريښمين *rekkhmīn*, a. Silken, silky. P. (*reshmīn*).

ريښه *rekkha*, s.f. A fibre, shred, thread, yarn, strip, etc. P. (*resha*).

ريګ *reg*, s.m. Sand (in comp.). P.

ريم *rīm*, s.m. Matter, pus, rheum; dregs, dross. P.

ريمن *rīman*, a. Purulent, mattery, filthy, etc.

رينه *rīna*, s.f. A cobbler's awl. Also *nīra*.

ريودل *riyawdal*, v.a. To raise, elevate, lift.

ريوړئ *rewṛa-ī*, s.f. A kind of sweetmeat. H. (*rewṛī*).

ريوند *rewand*, a. Sloping, slanting.

ړ

ړ *ṛe* or *ṛa* is the seventeenth letter of the Pukkhto alphabet. It has the same sound as the Sanskrit ड़ *ṛa*, or the Hindūstānī ڑ *ṛa*, with which it corresponds.

ړانځړه *ṛāndzaṛah*, s.m. Pitch, tar; crude turpentine.

ړپ *ṛap*, s.m. Mucus, slimy discharge from the bowels (as in dysentery).

ړپول *ṛapawul*, v.a. To agitate, shake.

ړپيدل *ṛapedal*, v.n. To palpitate, writhe, quiver, tremble, wag, wave, move, etc.

ړت *ṛat*, a. Red, reddish. S. (*rat*). *ṛat·ghwāye*, s.m. A red bull. *ṛata·gīra*, s.f. A red beard.

ړقول *ṛaqawul*, v.a. To mix, mingle, stir up; to jostle, shove, shake; punch, thump.

ړنبي *ṛunbai*, a. See وړنبي.

ړندول *ṛandawul*, v.a. To blind, deprive of sight.

رنديدل ṛandedal, v.n. To grow blind, become blind.

رنگ ṛang, a. Broken up, destroyed, spoiled, razed; desolate, ruined, deserted.

رواندې ṛwānde, p. See وړاندي.

روند ṛūnd, a. Blind, sightless; dark, obscure.

ري ṛī, in. A word used in driving cattle. ṛai, m. and ṛa-ī, f. A particle affixed to nouns as a sign of diminution. Ex. <u>kh</u>as, s.m. A dry stick or straw. <u>kh</u>asaṛai, s.m. A straw, splinter (such as gets blown into the eye). kūza, s.f. A water jar or gugglet. kūza·ṛa-ī, s.f. A small gugglet.

ز

ز ze is the eighteenth letter of the Pu<u>kkh</u>to alphabet, and eleventh of the Arabic. It has no corresponding letter in the Sanskrit. It is often used instead of the letters غ and ج, and sometimes also for ژ and ړ.

زاد zād, s.m. Food, provisions. A. a. Born (in comp.). P.

زار zār, a. Afflicted, lamenting. s.m. Lament, groan, complaint. P. See څار dzār.

زاري zārī, s.f. Crying, lamenting, groaning. P.

زاړي zāṛai, s.m. A weanling, young of cattle, etc. after being weaned. a. Late, former; old, worn out. zāṛa-ī, s.f. A woman, cow, etc. whose milk has run dry; an animal out of milk.

زامن zāman, s.m. pl. of څوي <u>dz</u>oe.

زانگو zāngo, s.f. A cradle, rocking chair, swing; rocking, swinging.

زانو zānū, s.m. The knee. P.

زانړه zā<u>nr</u>a, s.f. A crane, the Coolan (*Ardea courlan*).

زاهد zāhid, s.m. Hermit, monk, recluse. a. Religious, devout. A.

زاي zāe, s.m. See څوي <u>dz</u>oe.

زباد zbād, a. Proved, tested, tried, verified. A. (iṣbāt).

زبان zabān, s.m. Dialect language, speech; tongue. P.

زبر zabar, a. Above, superior; the vowel mark ـَـ a. A.

زبردست zabar·dast, a. Oppressive, powerful, violent. P.

زبرگ zburg, s.m. Ancestor, elder; saint. a. Venerable, saintlike, reverend; great, large. P. (buzurg).

زبرگي zburgī, s.f. Eminence, greatness, superiority, etc.

زبون zabūn, a. Bad, evil, wicked; faulty, unlucky. P.

زبيښل zbe<u>kkh</u>al, v.a. To suck, inhale, imbibe; to crumble, squash with the fingers (as bread, etc.).

زحمت zaḥmat, s.m. Affliction, trouble, pain. A.

زخم za<u>kh</u>m, s.m. A cut, wound, injury, sore, pain. A.

زخمي za<u>kh</u>mī, a. Wounded, hurt, pained, injured.

زخه za<u>kh</u>a, s.f. A wart; excrescence on the bark of a tree. P.

زخيره za<u>kh</u>īra, s.f. See ذخيره.

زد zad, s.m. A blow, striking (in comp). P.

زدايت zdāyat, s.m. Descent, family, race.

زدويل zdoyal, v.a. To grate, pare, rub, wear away; polish, scour, etc. P. (zidāyīdan).

زده zdah, a. Acquired, known, learned; remembered, recognized. P. (āzmūdah). zadah, a. Struck, beaten (in comp.); decayed, withered (as wood, etc.). P.

زر zar, s.m. Gold, money, riches. P. spīn·zar, s.m. Silver. srah·zar, s.m. Gold, pure gold. a. A thousand. P. (hazār). za-ar or z-ir, ad. Quickly, speedily, sharply. P. (zūd)

زراعت *zarā'at*, s.m. Agriculture, husbandry; crops, cultivation. A.

زربرخ *zarbarakh*, s.m. Talc, mica. A. (*abraq*).

زربیانګ *zarbiyāng*, s.m. Name of a currier's tool; a wooden scraper or muller for cleaning leather.

زردالو *zardālū*, s.m. An apricot. P.

زردکه *zardaka*, s.f. A carrot; name of a bird, yellow-hammer. P. (*zardak*).

زرغاله *zarghāla*, s.f. A lying-in or puerperal woman; the forty days after childbirth, puerperal state.

زرغون *zarghūn*, a. Green, verdant; sprouted, grown, germinated, fresh, new.

زرکه *zarka*, s.f. Red-legged partridge, chikor.

زرګر *zar·gar*, s.m. A goldsmith. P.

زرګیر *zar·gīr*, s.m. A thumbstall of leather (worn by archers, etc.).

زرني *zaranai*, s.m. A spy, scout, detective. *zarana-ī*, s.f. Peeping, spying; scouting, watching.

زرنیخ *zarnīkh*, s.m. Arsenic. P.

زرنړه *zaranra*, s.f. Mud, slime, ooze (as at bottom of pools, etc.). *zaranrah*, s.m. See رانځره.

زري *zarai*, s.m. A spy, scout; the sight (at the muzzle) of a gun. *zarī*, a. Golden, worked or woven with gold. P. *zare·zare*, a. Shattered, broken to atoms, etc. See ذره.

زرین *zarīn*, a. Golden. P.

زروکي *zarūkai*, s.m. A dress, garment; apparel, clothes; old rags, old clothes, etc.

زړه *zrah*, s.m. Heart, mind, soul; courage, spirit; the heart. P. (*zahra*).

زړی *zarai*, } s.m. A flat seed (as of melons,
زنړی *zanrai*, } etc.) in opposition to round ones (called tukhm).

زرګي *ziggai*, s.m. See شیشکي.

زښت *zikkht*, a. Ugly, deformed; stern, severe. P. (*zisht*).

زعفران *z'afarān*, s.m. Saffron. A.

زغ *zagh*, s.m. See ژغ.

زغاښتل *zghākkhtal*, v.n. To run, flee. Def. in. pres. ten. See زغلیدل.

زغرد *zghard*, a. Fast, quick. ad. Quickly, fleetly.

زغره *zghara*, s.f. Chain armour, mail. P. (*zira*).

زغلول *zghalawul*, v.a. To drive, put to flight, make run, urge (as a horse).

زغلیدل *zghaledal*, v.n. To run, flee. See زغاښتل. P. (*gurekhtan*).

زغمل *zghamal*, v.a. To bear, endure, undergo, sustain, suffer.

زغن *zaghan*, s.m. A kite. P.

زقوم *zaqūm*, s.m. Name of a plant, Indian cactus; it is said to form the diet of those condemned to hell. A.

زک *zik*, s.m. An inflated hide for crossing over rivers.

زکات }
زکاة } *zakāt*, s.m. Alms distributed according to the rules laid down in the Qurān. A.
زکوت }

زکام *zukām*, s.m. Catarrh, influenza, cold. A.

زکه *zaka*, c. See څکه. P. (*zirā ki*).

زکي *zakī*, a. Pious, continent. A.

زګ *zag*, s.m. Foam, froth, scum. H. (*jhāg*).

زګیروي *zgerwai*, s.m. A groan, moan, wail, whine.

زلزله *zalzala*, s.f. An earthquake. A.

زلفه *zulfa*, s.f. A curl, ringlet, lock of hair. P. (*zulf*).

زلفي *zulfa-ī*, s.f. A sword knot, tassel; door chain, staple, hook. P.

زلل *zalal*, s.m. Injury, loss, deficiency; blundering, erring; falling, stumbling. P.

زلمي *zalmai*, s.m. A youth, young man. A. (*talmīz*).

زلو *zallū*, s.m. A leech. P.

زلیچه *zalīcha*, s.f. A rug, woollen carpet. P. (*qālīcha*).

زم *zam*, s.m. Hurt, injury, wound. P. (*zakhm*). *zam·zmolai*, a. Halt, helpless, crippled, maimed. Also *zam·zambolai*.
زمانه *zamāna*, s.f. Age, time; fortune; the world; the heavens. A. *zamāna·sāz*, s.m. A time server. P.
زمبور *zambūr*, s.m. See امبور.
زمرد *zumurrud*, s.m. An emerald. P.
زمري *zmarai*, s.m. A tiger. Name of a plant, Dwarf palm (*Chamærops Richiana*).
زمزم *zamzam*, s.m. Hagar's well at Mecca. A.
زمزمه *zamzama*, s.f. A concert; singing. A.
زمستان *zamistān*, s.m. Winter. P.
زمکه *zmaka*, s.f. Land, ground, earth, soil; the earth.
زموخ *zmokh*, a. } Astringent, binding, dry,
زموخت *zmokht*, } rough (to the taste). P. (*zamukht*).
زمول *zmol*, a. } Helpless, crippled, maimed,
زمبول *zambol*, } wounded, unable to move from wounds.
زمولي *zmolai*, a. } Carried by the hands and
زمبولي *zambolai*, } legs (as a wounded man). See زم. (For *zam·bīwulai*).
زمي *zma-ī*, s.f. Name of a plant that is burnt for the potash it yields (*Suæda fruticosa*).
زمين *zamīn*, s.m. The earth; ground, soil. land. P.
زميندار *zamīn·dār*, s.m. A farmer; peasant. P.
زميداري *zamīn·dārī*, s.f. Agriculture, husbandry; an estate, farm.
زن *zan*, s.f. A woman, wife. P.
زنا *zinā*, s.m. Adultery, fornication. P.
زناکار *zinā·kār*, s.m. An adulterer, fornicator.
زنانه *zanāna*, s.f. A woman, female; wife; the women's apartments. a. Feminine. P.
زنبق *zanbaq*, s.m. The tuberose (*Polianthes tuberosa*). Flowers embroidered on a dress. P.

زنبک *zunbuk*, s.m. Tassel, knot, rosette, flower.
زنبه *zunba*, s.f. Down or hair on the body.
زنځير *zandzīr*, s.m. A chain. P. (*zanjīr*).
زندان *zindān*, s.m. A prison, jail. P.
زندگاني *zindagānī*, } s.f. Existence, life; liv-
زندگي *zindagī*, } ing, livelihood. P.
زنده *zindah*, a. Alive, living. P.
زندۍ *zunda-ī*, s.f. A halter, hangman's rope.
زنډي *zundai*, s.m. A tassel, pendent. H. (*jhund*).
زنزه *zanza*, s.f. A centipede.
زنکۍ *zanka-ī*, s.f. Cummin seed.
زنګ *zang*, s.m. Mould, rust. P. (*zangār*). Cymbal, bell (for the feet of dancing women). Name of a country, Zanguebar.
زنګل *zangal*, v.n. To hang, swing, wave, sway, etc. s.m. A forest, wood; wilderness. S. (*jangal*).
زنګول *zangawul*, v.a. To rock, swing, wave, etc.
زنګوله *zangūla*, s.f. A small bell, cymbal. P.
زنګون *zangūn*, s.m. The knee. P. (*zānū*). *zangānah·starga*, s.f. The knee cap, knee pan.
زنګي *zangī*, s.m. An African, negro. P.
زنګيدل *zangedal*, v.n. To hang, swing, wave, vibrate.
زنل *zanal*, v.a. To imbed, insert, implant; strike, thrust, hit; stab, prick, impale. P. (*zadan, zan-*).
زنه *zana*, s.f. The chin; pit of the chin. P. (*zanakh*).
زنړغوزه *zanrghoza*, s.f. A pine cone, fir cone; pine tree; seed of the edible pine. P. (*chalghoza*).
زنړي *zanrai*, s.m. A flat seed (as of melons, etc.). A boy under the age of puberty; a school-boy.
زوال *zawāl*, s.m. Decline, wane, setting. A.

زوانكه *zawānaka*, s.f. Acne, pimples on the face of youths.

زود *zūd*, ad. Quick, quickly. P.

زودي *zūdī*, s.f. Alacrity, haste, quickness.

زور *zor*, s.m. Force, power, strength; effort, violence, vigour; weight. P. *zaur*, s.m. Anxiety, grief, sorrow, pain, trouble. A. (*jaur*). *zwar*, s.m. The vowel-point zabar.

زوراور *zorawar*, a. Powerful, violent, strong. P.

زورل *zoral*, v.a. To vex, irritate; compel, force, coerce; to digest.

زوړ *zoṛ*, a. Aged, ancient, old, worn out. P. (*zāl*).

زوزات *zauzāt*, } s.m. Children, issue, progeny, offspring. P. (*zah·wa·zād*).
زوزاد *zauzād*,

زوږ *zwag*, s.m. Clamour, din, noise, sound.

زوښه *zūkkha*, s.f, A syrup or jelly prepared from ber or jujube berries.

زوغال *zūghāl*, s.m. Charcoal. P. (*zughāl*).

زولن *zawlan* or *ziwlan*, a. Purulent, suppurating, mattery.

زوم *zum*, s.m. A son-in-law. S. (*jamā-ī*). *zwam*, a. Deficient, less, little; deducted, subtracted. ad. Rarely, seldom.

زومگي *zūmgai*, s.m. A son-in-law. S. (*jamā-ī*).

زومنه *zwamna*, s.f. Deficiency, loss.

زوول *zowul*, v.a. To bear, bring forth (as young). P. (*zādan*).

زوولي *zowulai*, a. Born, brought forth.

زوه *ziwa* or *zawa*, s.f. Matter, pus, ichor.

زوي *zoe*, s.m. A son.

زويرگي *zwergai*, s.m. See زگيروي.

زه *zah*, pr. I, the first person.

زهر *zahar*, s.m. Poison. P.

زهره *zahra*, s.f. Bile; the gall bladder; courage, heart, pluck. P.

زهگير *zahgīr*, s.m. The catch or notch at the end of a bow (to hold the bow-string).

زهوب *zahūb*, s.m. Matter, discharge (of a sore), pus.

زهي *zahe*, in. Bravo! Well done! Lo! P.

زهيدل *zahedal*, v.n. To decrease, waste, grow thin.

زهير *zahīr*, a. Reduced, weakened, thin (from sickness); melancholy, sad. A.

زي *zai*, s.m. Son, child, descendant (in comp.). P. Added to Afghan surnames it denotes the clan or tribe. Ex. *Yūsufzai*, s.m. A man of clan Yusuf. *Yūsufza-ī*, s.f. A Yusufzai woman. *Yūsufzī*, s.m. pl. The Yusufzais.

زيات *ziyāt*, a. Excessive, surplus, too much; more. A. (*ziyād*).

زياتي *ziyātī*, a. Excessive, great, more. (*ziyādatī*).

زيارت *ziyārat*, s.m. A shrine; tomb of a saint; visiting a shrine. A.

زيان *ziyān*, s.m. Damage, deficiency, loss; miscarriage, abortion. P.

زيانكار *ziyān·kār*, } a. Injurious, pernicious, noxious. P.
زياني *ziyānī*,

زيب *zeb*, s.m. Beauty, elegance, ornament. P.

زيتونه *zaitūna*, s.f. The olive tree. A. (*zaitūn*).

زير *zer*, a. Below, under. The vowel point ـِ *i*. P.

زيراستر *zerāstar*, s.m. The lining of a dress. P.

زيرك *zīrak*, a. Acute, sagacious, penetrating, witty. P.

زيركي *zīrakī*, s.f. Acumen, discernment, wit. P.

زيرمه *zerma*, s.f. Arrangement, preparation, disposal, setting in order.

زيري *zerai*, s.m. Glad tidings, good news.

زيريگر *zerai·gar*, } s.m. Bearer of glad tidings.
زيريگري *zerai·garai*,

زيړ *ziyaṛ*, a. Yellow. P. (*zard*). s.m. Brass.

زيړانكه *ziyaṛānaka*, s.f. The yellow wagtail.

زيړگله *ziyaṛgula*, s.f. Name of a herb (*Calendula officinalis*).

زيړي *ziyaṛai*, s.m. Jaundice, icterus; yellowness.

زير *zīr*, a. Hard, rough, harsh, rigid, stiff; stern, austere, severe. P. (*zisht*).

زيږول *zegawul*, v.a. To beget, procreate, produce.

زيږيدل *zegedal*, v.n. To be born, begotten, brought forth. P. (*zā-īdan*).

زيست *zīst*, s.m. Existence, life; employment. P.

زيله *zela*, s.f. A creeping plant; creeper, tendril.

زيم *zyam*, s.m. Humidity, moisture, dampness.

زيمناك *zyam-nāk*, a. Damp, humid, moist.

زين *zīn*, s.m. A saddle. P.

زينت *zīnat*, s.m. Beauty, elegance; dress, ornament. A.

زينه *zīna*, s.f. A ladder, steps. P.

زيور *zewar*, s.m. Jewels, ornaments. P.

ژ

ژ *ĵe* is the nineteenth letter of the Pukkhto alphabet, and the fourteenth of the Persian, from which it is adopted. It has the sound of *s* in the word *pleasure*. By the Eastern Afghans it is sometimes used for ج or ږ, and by the Western tribes for ز.

ژامه *ĵāma*, s.f. The jaw, jaw-bone. P.

ژانه *ĵāna*, s.f. Adulation, flattery; coaxing.

ژاوله *ĵāwla*, s.f. Resin, pitch, wax, gum.

ژبه *ĵiba*, s.f. The tongue; language, speech; dialect. S. (*jībh*).

ژبونکي *ĵabūnkai*, s.m. Collar, cuff, frill etc. (of a garment).

ژر *ĵ-ir* or *ĵa-ar*, ad. Quickly, speedily. See زر *zir*.

ژرنده *ĵaranda*, s.f. A water mill. See جرنده.

ژړا *ĵaṛā*, s.f. Crying, sobbing, weeping. P. (*giriya*).

ژړل *ĵaṛal*, v.n. To weep, cry, sob, wail.

ژغند *ĵghand*, s.m. A notch, nick, dent.

ژغ *ĵagh*, s.m. See جغ.

ژغورل *ĵghoral*, v.a. To keep, preserve, protect, guard, defend, nourish, support.

ژغوري *ĵghorai*, s.m. Protector, guardian, etc.

ژغونډي *jaghūndai*, s.m. The peg in a yoke (to prevent its slipping from the ox's neck).

ژلۍ *ĵala-ī*, s.f. Hail. P. (*jāla*).

ژمی *ĵimai*, s.m. Winter, cold weather.

ژنړی *ĵanṛai*, s.m. Catgut, bow-string, fiddle-string. A boy, lad, school boy.

ژواك *ĵwāk*, s.m. Life, existence, being.

ژوبل *ĵobal*, a. Bruised, wounded, hurt.

ژور *ĵawar*, a. Deep, depressed, sunk.

ژورغالي *ĵawar-ghālai*, s.m. A pit or trench dug round the root of a tree (for water); a small pit made to hold a plant or sapling.

ژوره *ĵawara*, s.f. A leech.

ژوژ *ĵwaĵ*, s.m. See زوږ.

ژوند *ĵwand*, s.m. }
ژوندون *ĵwandūn*, } Being, life, existence.

ژوندي *ĵwandai*, a. Alive, living. P. (*zinda*).

ژوول *ĵowul*, }
ژويل *ĵoyal*, } v.a. To chew, masticate; chew the cud. P. (*ĵāwīdan*).

ژۍ *ĵa-ī*, s.f. Catgut, string of a bow or violin, etc. A water bag made of hide.

ږ

ږ *gе* is the twentieth letter of the Pukkhto alphabet, and peculiar to the Afghan language. By the Western tribes it is sounded like ژ, with which it is often interchanged. By the Eastern tribes it is pronounced as گ, for which it is generally changed. In words introduced from Persian or Sanskrit, where this letter replaces چ, it has the sound of that letter or of *z* in *azure*.

ږدل *gdal*, v.a. To fix, place, put, set, lay. Def. in past ten. See کیښول. P. (*hīdan*).

ږدن *gdan*, s.m. A kind of millet. H. (*kodon*).

ږغ *gagh*, s.m. Noise, sound; accent, voice.

ږغورل *gghoral*, v.a. See ژغورل.

ږلئ *gala-ī*, s.f. Hail. See ژلئ.

ږمنځ *gamandz*, ږمنز *gamanz*, } s.f. A comb, hair comb.

ږو *go*, ad. A word used in comp. to denote oath or affirmation. Ex. *khudāe-go*, in. By God!

ږوند *gwand*, s.m. See ژوند.

ږوږ *gwag*, s.m. Noise, clamour, din, etc.

ږوي *gawai*, s.m. A being, creature, person. See وګړي.

ږيره *gīra*, s.f. The beard. P. (*rīsh*).

ږيري *gīrai*, a. Bearded, having a beard. *spīn-gīrai*, s.m. A white beard, grey beard, old man, elder. *rat-gīrai*, s.m. A red beard, one who dyes the beard with *nakrīza* (henna).

س

س *sīn* is the twenty-first letter of the Pukkhto alphabet, and the twelfth of the Arabic. It has the same sound as the English *s* in the word *song*, and in Pukkhto is sometimes, though wrongly, changed for the letters خ and چ.

سا *sā*, s.f. Breath, life, respiration, vital spark. S. (*sāns*).

سابق *sābiq*, a. Former, preceding. A.

سابون *sābūn*, s.m. Soap. A.

سابو *sābū*, s.m. Name of a grass from which mats are made (*Panicum Colonum*).

سابه *sābah*, s.m. Name of a grass (see preceding). Vegetables, greens.

ساپټ *sāpaṭ*, ad. Completely, entirely, wholly.

ساتل *sātal*, v.a. To keep, preserve; defend, protect, shelter; nourish, support.

ساتندوي *sātandoe*, ساتونکي *sātūnkai*, } s.m. Guardian, keeper, protector, etc.

ساتول *sātūl*, s.m. A chopper, cleaver; bill-hook.

ساحر *sāḥir*, s.m. Magician, juggler, conjurer. A.

ساخت *sākht*, s.m. Make, construction; fabrication, pretence. P. A kind of leather, morocco leather.

ساختګي *sākhtagī*, s.f. Fabrication, pretence, sham.

ساخه *sākha*, s.f. A grating sound; calamity; judgment day. A. (*ṣākhat*).

ساد *sād*, a. Honest, good, trustworthy. S. (*sādh*).

سادو *sādū*, s.m. Impostor, knave, cheat.

ساده *sādah*, a. Plain, simple, unadorned; artless, candid, sincere; beardless; white. P.

سادين *sādīn*, s.m. Newly ploughed land, land prepared for sowing.

سار *sār*, s.m. Good news, glad tidings.

سارمه *sārma*, s.f. Name of a potherb.

سارنده *sārinda*, سارنګئ *sāringa-ī*, } s.f. A violin, guitar.

ساروان *sārwān*, s.m. A camel driver. P. (*sārbān*).

ساري *sārai*, a. Equal, par. s.m. A match, compeer, peer. P. (*sār*).

ساړه *sāṛa*, s.f. Cold weather; cold, frigidity.

ساز *sāz*, s.m. Accoutrements; apparatus, furniture; a musical instrument. P.

سازش *sāzish*, s.m. Confederacy, combination; plot, conspiracy. P.

سازنده *sāzindah*, s.m. Maker, peformer. P.

ساعت *sā'at*, s.m. A minute, moment, hour. A.

ساعي *sā'ī*, s.m. Enthusiasm, zeal. a. Eager, earnest, zealous. A.

ساغر *sā<u>gh</u>ar*, s.m. A bowl, goblet. P.

ساغري *sā<u>gh</u>arī*, s.m. The space between the tail and *anus* of a horse; a kind of leather, shagreen. P.

ساکن *sākin*, a. Quiet, tranquil, at rest. s.m. Resident, inhabitant. A.

ساګ *sāg*, s.m. Greens, potherbs, vegetables. S.

ساګينړي *sāgīnṛai*, s.m. A dish of rice and greens.

سالن *sālan*, s.m. Mixed or spiced food; flesh, fish, etc. eaten with rice or bread. H.

سالو *sālū*, s.m. A kind of red cloth of cotton. S.

ساله *sālah*, a. Aged (in comp. only); added to numeral adjectives denotes age or years. Ex. *<u>ch</u>ār-sālah*, a. Four years old. P.

ساليانه *sāliyānah*, a. Annual, yearly. P.

سامان *sāmān*, s.m. Apparatus, furniture, tools; arms, accoutrements. P.

سامانه *sāmāna*, s.f. Parade, pomp, state.

سامع *sāmi'*, s.m. A hearer. A.

سان *sān*, s.m. Muster, review of an army; calico; a grindstone, whetstone. P.

سانده *sānda*, s.f. Lament, wail.

ساندا *sānḍā*, s.m. Name of a kind of lizard with a thick tail. H.

سانګه *sānga*, s.f. A travelling party; a spear. S. A lament, wail; a bough, branch.

سانګئ *sānga-ī*, s.f. A pitchfork.

سانړ *sā<u>nr</u>*, s.m. A stallion, bull. S.

ساو *sāw*, s.m. Tax, tribute. *sāū*, a. Noble, well bred. P. (*<u>sh</u>āhū*).

ساونړ *sāwa<u>nr</u>*, s.m. Name of the fourth Hindu month, July-August. S. (*sāwan*).

ساه *sāh*, s.m. Breath, vital spark, life. S. (*sāns*).

ساه‌لنډي *sāh-lanḍai*, a. Asthmatic. *sāh-lanḍī*, s.m Asthma, dyspnœa, shortness of breath.

ساه‌ويسا *sāh-wīsā*, s.f. Belief, faith, trust, hope.

سايل *sāyil*, s.m. Asker, petitioner. A.

سايه *sāya*, s.f. Shade, shadow; apparition, spectre; shelter, protection; awning, canopy. P.

سب *sibb*, s.m. Reproach, reviling. A.

سبا *sabā*, s.m. Dawn, morning; morrow. A. (*ṣabāḥ*).

سبب *sabab*, s.m. Cause, motive, reason; means, instrument; affinity, connexion, relationship. A.

سبحان *subḥān*, s.m. Praising (God); the Deity. A. *subḥān-allah*, in. Good God! Oh God! A.

سبزه *sabza*, s.f. Herbage, verdure; incipient beard, bloom. *sabzah*, a. Grey, iron grey; sallow. P.

سبزي *sabzī*, s.f. Greens, vegetables. P.

سبق *sabaq*, s.m. A lecture, lesson, reading. A.

سبک *subuk*, a. See سپک.

سبوس *sabūs*, s.m. Bran, chaff. P.

سپارش *sipāri<u>sh</u>*, s.m. Recommendation, intercession. P. (*sifāri<u>sh</u>*).

سپارل *spāral*, v.a. To commit, consign, give in charge, intrust; recommend, etc. P. (*sipārīdan* or *sipurdan*).

سپاره *sipāra*, s.f. Name of a chapter in the Qurān (for *sīpāra*, thirty sections). P. *spāra*, s.f. An iron ploughshare.

سپاه *sipāh*, s.m. An army; a soldier. P.

سپاهي *spāhī*, s.m. A soldier. P.

سپر *spar*, s.m. A shield, buckler. P. (*sipar*).

سپرخي *spar<u>kh</u>ai*, s.m. A packing needle, skewer, pin.

سپرد *sipurd*, s.m. Care, charge, keeping, trust. P.

سپرغه *spa<u>gh</u>ra*, s.f. A well. (Raverty).

سپرلني *sparlanai*, s.m. Cavalier, horseman, rider.

سپرلي *sparlai*, s.m. The spring. *sparlī*, s.f. Riding, horse riding, equitation.

سپره *sapara*, s.f. Name of the second month of the Muḥammadan calendar. A. (*ṣafar*).

supra, s.f. The anus; a napkin, tablecloth. P. (*sufra*).

سپړل *sparal*, سپړدل *spardal*, v.a. To undo, unclose, unfold, unravel, open out, etc.

سپږن *spagan*, a. Lousy, full of vermin, filthy.

سپږه *spaga*, s.f. A louse. P. (*sapash*).

سپک *spuk*, a. Light, flimsy; cheap; mean, trifling. P. (*subuk*).

سپلم *spalam*, s.m. See سپېرلم.

سپلمه *spalama*, s.f. A ring-dove.

سپلمئ *spalma-ī*, s.f. Name of a plant (*Calotropis procera, Asclepias gigantea*), the mudar plant.

سپم *spam*, s.m. The eye of a needle; aperture, orifice, perforation. A. (*famm*).

سپند *sipand*, s.m. See سپېلني.

سپندخ *spandakh*, s.m. A large ball of worsted or cotton; a stuffed calf placed near a cow deprived of her own (to make her give milk).

سپڼسي *spanrsai*, s.m. Cord, thread, twine, string.

سپوخځ *spokhadz*, سپوخځه *spokhadza*, s.f. Hypogastrium, belly below the navel, pubes, pelvis.

سپور *spor*, a. Dry, plain, unmixed, stale (as food). *spora-doda-ī*, s.f. Dry bread. *spor*, a. Riding, mounted, seated upon. s.m. A horseman, cavalier. P. (*sawār*).

سپوږمئ *spogma-ī*, s.f. Moon, moonlight.

سپوڼري *spūnrai*, s.m. Ringworm, porrigo.

سپه *sipah*, s.m. See سپاه.

سپهر *sipahr*, s.m. Celestial sphere, sky; fortune, time; the world. P. *sipahar*, s.m. Afternoon, the third watch. P.

سپي *spai*, s.m. A dog, hound.

سپیازه *spiyāza*, s.f. Abortion, miscarrying, dropping the young prematurely (applied to brutes only). a. Raw, unripe; useless, foolish.

سپېټه *sapeta*, ad. Never, positively, not a bit.

سپېځل *spedzal* or *spetsal*, v.a. To clean, clear, purify.

سپېځلي *spetsalai*, a. Spotless, clean, neat, spick-span.

سپېد *saped*, a. White. P. (*safed*).

سپېدار *spedār*, s.m. The white poplar tree. P. (*safedār*).

سپېده *sapeda*, s.f. White lead; dawn, daybreak. P. (*safeda*).

سپېدي *sapedī*, s.f. Whiteness; dawn. P. (*safedī*).

سپېرکئ *sperka-ī*, s.f. Lovage (the plant and seed). (*Ligusticum ajowan*).

سپېرلم *sperlam*, s.m. The grey-tailed fox; any quadruped (cattle) with a grey or white tail.

سپېره *sperah*, a. Grey, ashy, hoary; pale, colourless, ghastly.

سپېره کي *sperah-kai*, a. Pale, ashy, ghastly; coward.

سپېږمه *spegma*, s.f. The nostril.

سپېښته *spekhta*, s.f. Membrane covering the stomach or heart; peritoneum, pericardium.

سپېلني *spelanai*, s.m. Name of a plant, Syrian rue (*Peganum harmala*).

سپیمه *spiyama*, s.f. A bitch in heat seeking the dog.

سپین *spīn*, a. White, pure, fair, spotless.

سپینګه *spenga*, s.f. See سپېږمه.

سپینه *spīna*, s.f. The tendon of the heel (*tendo Achillis*). Fat, suet, tallow.

ست *sat*, s.m. Invitation (to dinner), hospitality; civility, politeness. a. Flat, level; supine, straight on the back. H. (*chit*).

ستا *stā*, The genitive case singular of the second personal pronoun تۀ *tah*; of thee, thine.

ستار *sitār*, s.m. A guitar (of three strings), violin. P.

ستاره *stāra*, s.f. A star; a kind of firework. P. (*sitāra*). *stāra-prewatal*, v.n. To be unlucky, to have one's star in the descendant.

ستاسُ *stāsu*, ستاسو *stāso*, } pl. of ستا. Yours, of you.

ستانه *stāna*, s.f. A threshold; house, family, race (of saints particularly). P. (*āstāna*).

ستايل *stāyal*, v.a. To laud, praise, glorify, extol. P. (*sitūdan*).

ستر *satr*, s.m. Veiling, covering, concealing; privates. A. *star*, a. Big, bulky, great, huge, strapping, etc.; deep, profound (as a well). P. (*saturg*).

سترغلي *starghalai*, s.m. The orbit; eyeball.

سترگه *starga*, s.f. The eye; a planet. (Diminutive of P. *sitāra*).

ستره *satra*, s.f. A curtain, mantle, veil.

ستري *satrai*, s.m. A cut crop as it lies on the field; pile of corn sheaves; heap, pile, mass. H. (*sathrāw*). *satrai-watrai*, a. Scattered, lying about (as leaves on the ground).

ستړي *staṛai*, a. Fatigued, weary, tired, fagged. P. (*siturdah*).

ستغ *stagh*, s.m. A bot, worm in the skin of cattle; a boil or abscess produced by the worm. a. Astringent, binding, rough to the taste; mean, sordid, avaricious.

ستل *satal*, s.m. A copper pail or bucket, cauldron. P.

ستم *sitam*, s.m. Oppression, violence, tyranny. P. *stam*, s.m. Forcing, straining; labour, travail. *stam-wahal*, v.a. To force, strain (as at stool, etc.).

ستن *stan*, s.f. A needle, pin; pillar, post. P. (*sitūn*).

ستنه *stana*, s.f. Return, retreat; retrenchment.

ستنول *stanawul*, v.a. To send back, return; to take back, retrench.

ستنيدل *stanedal*, v.n. To return, go back, retire.

ستوان *satwān*, s.m. Peasemeal, meal of parched corn, pulse, etc. S. (*sattū*).

ستوخ *stokh*, ستوغ *stogh*, } a. Straight, difficult; bad, hateful. P. (*satakh*).

ستور *sutūr*, s.m. Cattle, beast of burden. P.

ستوري *storai*, s.m. A star. P. (*sitāra*).

ستوگه *stoga*, s.f. See استوگه.

ستومان *stomān*, a. Disgusted, vexed; repentant, sorry; fatigued, tired, fagged, weary.

ستون *stūn*, a. Returned, sent back; retrenched, withdrawn.

ستونول *stūnawul*, v.a. To send back, call back, recall; withdraw, retrench, subtract.

ستونيدل *stūnedal*, v.n. To return, come back; retire, etc.

ستوني *stūnai*, s.m. The larynx, *pomum Adami*.

ستوني ستغ *stūnī-stagh*, a. Supine; flat on the back.

ستيزه *steza*, s.f. Argument, controversy, dispute; quarrel, battle, conflict. P. (*siteza*). *sateza*, s.f. Table-land, flat ground on a hill side.

سټ *saṭ*, s.m. A cutler's block, a block of wood for fixing an anvil; a log, stump, root of a tree. An assault, sudden attack. The nape, back of the neck.

سټکوري *saṭkūrai*, a. Burnt, scorched, parched; dried up, withered, shrivelled; frost-bitten.

سجده *sijda*, s.f. Bowing the head and touch- the ground with the forehead, prostration, adoration. A.

سجل *sijjil*, s.m. Bond, deed, register; decree of a judge; seal of a judge. The recording angel. A.

سچ *such*, a. Pure genuine, real; candid, honest. S. Also سچه *suchah*.

سحار *sahār*, سحر *sahr*, } s.m. Dawn, daybreak; morning, forenoon; morrow, to-morrow. A.

سحر *sihr*, s.m. Sorcery, magic, jugglery. A.
سحرگر *sihr·gar*, s.m. Magician, conjurer, sorcerer.
سخ *sakh*, in. Excellent! Good! ad. The present year.
سخا *sakhā*, s.f. } Munificence, generosity, liberality. A.
سخاوت *sakhāwat*, s.m. }
سخا *skhā*, a. Putrid, rotten, stinking. H. (*ubsā*).
سخاوره *skhāwaga*, s.f. Name of a medicinal root (*Kæmpferia galanga*); orris root, root of the Iris (*Iris Persica*).
سخت *sakht*, a. Hard, strong; difficult, troublesome; obdurate, violent; austere, stingy; cruel, harsh; painful, rigid, severe. P.
سختي *sakhtī*, s.f. Difficulty, trouble; violence, cruelty; austerity, severity, etc. P.
سخر *skhar*, s.m. A father-in-law. P. (*khusar*). *sakhar*, s.m. A rock, boulder, stone.
سخره *sakhara*, s.f. A rock, boulder, stone.
سخن *sukhun*, s.m. Word, speech; affair, matter. P.
سخوښتن *skhwakkhtan*, s.m. Cinders, hot ashes.
سخوند *skhwand*, s.m. The cud. *skhwand·wahal*, v.a. To chew the cud.
سخوندر *skhwandar*, s.m. A young bullock, steer.
سخه *sakha*, s.f. Joy, delight, gladness, etc. (at the misfortune of another), crowing over an enemy.
سخي *sakhī*, a. Munificent, generous, liberal. A. *skhai*, s.m. A calf, yearling calf.
سد *sud*, s.m. Consciousness, intelligence; sensation, sense; memory. S. (*sudh*). *sadd*, s.m. A barrier, wall. A.
سر *sar*, s.m. The head; point, apex, summit, top. P. *sirr*, s.m. A mystery, secret. A.
سراب *sarāb*, s.m. Mirage, glare, vapour resembling water at a distance (seen on desert plains). A. Mica, talc. A.
سراج *sarrāj*, s.m. A saddler. A.
سراسر *sarāsar*, a. All, the whole. ad. Wholly, entirely. P.
سراسري *sarāsarī*, a. Brief, short, concise. P.
سراسيمه *sarāsīmah*, a. Amazed, confounded. P.
سراغ *surāgh*, s.m. Enquiry, search; mark, trace. P.
سرانه *sarāna*, s.f. The upper bar of a doorway or frame.
سرانجام *sarānjām*, s.m. Apparatus, utensils, materials; chattels, furniture, goods; ingredients, requisites; conclusion, accomplishment, end. P.
سرانداز *sarāndāz*, s.m. The head piece of a bed; a carpet spread at the head of a room. P.
سراي *srāe*, s.m. A caravansary, hospice, inn, hostelry; house. P. (*sarāe*).
سربانده *sarbānda*, s.f. A patch of land, or portion of a field left unploughed or uncut. A rope used to fix the yoke of a plough.
سربانډه *sarbānḍa*, s.f. Rope made of slips of raw hide; a rope for fastening the yoke of a plough.
سربسته *sarbasta*, s.f. A cloth tied round the head by women when occupied with household duties, etc. P.
سرپ *surup*, s.m. Lead. P. (*surb*). *sirp* or *srup*, ad. Simply, purely, altogether, out and out, merely, etc. P. (*ṣirf*).
سرپوښ *sarpokkh*, s.m. A cover, lid. P. (*sarposh*).
سرچشمه *sarchashma*, s.f. A fountain, spring. P.
سرحد *sarhadd*. s.m. Boundary, frontier, limit. P.
سرخ *surkh*, a. Red (in comp.). P. *surkh·bād*, s.m. Name of a disease, erysipelas. P.
سرخچه *surkhcha*, s.f. A red apricot. P.
سرخکه *sarkhaka*, s.f. A starling; a kind of Mina (*Graculus roseus*).

سرخي *surkhī*, s.f. Blight in corn, mildew; jaundice; brick dust; redness. P. *surkha-ī*, s.f. A frill or fillet of cloth sewn on to the legs of women's trousers.

سرد *sard*, a. Cold (in comp.). P.

سردار *sardār*, s.m. Chief, principal, head. P.

سررشته *sar·rishta*, s.f. Affinity, connection; office, employment; cord, rope. P.

سرژه *sarja*, s.f. A species of mountain deer.

سرسام *sarsām*, s.m, Delirium, frenzy. P.

سرسايه *sarsāya*, s.f. Alms distributed on the conclusion of the Ramazān fast. A veil given by the father to a bride on the last day of the marriage festivities. P.

سرسري *sarsarī*, a. Easy, facile. P.

سرشاهي *sarshāhī*, s.f. Name of a weight equal to half an ounce.

سرشت *sarisht*, s.m. Intellect, nature; temperament, disposition; complexion. P.

سرغنه *sarghanah*, s.m. A chief, head man. P.

سرغوند *sarghūnḍ*, s.m. A glandular tumour of the neck.

سرفه *sarfa*, s.f. Advantage, gain, profit; frugal, sparing in expense; deficiency, default; forbearance. A. (*sarf*). *surfa*, s.f. A cough. P.

سركار *sarkār*, s.m. Government, court; province, district; superintendent. P.

سركښ *sarkakkh*, a. Obstinate, rebellious, disobedient, perverse, etc. P. (*sarkash*).

سركښي *sarkakkhī*, s.f. Obstinacy, rebellion, etc.

سركنډه *sarkunḍa*, s.f. A cropped, cut, or trimmed head of hair; the hair cut short.

سركنډي *sarkunḍai*, s.m. A man or boy with the hair trimmed or cut short.

سركوزي *sarkūzai*, s.m. A pig, hog, swine.

سركول *sarkol*, s.m. A mill-dam weir.

سركه *sirka*, s.f. Vinegar. P.

سركئ *sirka-ī*, s.f. Name of a scarlet insect, the scarlet fly.

سرگردان *sargardān*, a. Bothered, confused, perplexed; wandering, at a loss, etc. P.

سرگرداني *sargardānī*, s.f. Perplexity, trouble, worry.

سرگړي *sargaṛai*, s.m. Name of a grass (*Apluda aristata*).

سرگشته *sargashtah*, a. Amazed, astonished; giddy, flighty, wandering. P.

سرگله *sargala*, s.f. A grazing tax, tax on cattle. P.

سرگين *sargīn*, s.m. Cow-dung. P.

سرما *sarmā*, s.f. Winter. P.

سرماتي *sarmātai*, s.m. Coping, eaves of a wall.

سرمال *sarmāl*, s.m. A rope used to fasten together the two halves of a bullock or camel load.

سرمايه *sarmāya*, s.f. Capital, stock, store. P.

سرمه *surma*, s.f. P. See رانجه.

سرنا *sarnā*, } s.f. A clarion, flageolet. P.
سرنائ *sarnā-ī*, }

سرناچي *surnāchī*, s.m. A flageolet player.

سرنامه *sarnāma*, s.f. Superscription, address, title. P.

سرنگ *surang*, s.m. A mine, tunnel, subterranean passage. S.

سرنگي *surangai*, s.m. A burrow, little tunnel, etc. Diminutive of preceding word.

سرواښ *sarwākkh*, s.m. A rope made of hair, and used to fasten cattle; a tether.

سروټكه *sarwaṭka*, s.f. See سكروټه.

سرود *sarod*, s.m. A song; music, melody. P.

سرودگر *sarod·gar*, } s.m. A singer, musician. P.
سرودي *sarodī*, }

سرور *sarwar*, s.m. A chief, leader. P.

سروزنه *sarwazana*, s.f. The hem in trousers, through which the waistband passes; a frill or fillet of cloth added to a pair of trousers.

سروه *sarwa*, s.f. The cypress tree. P. (*sarw*).

سره *sara*, s.f. Manure, offal, dung. *sara*, ad. With, along with, together, in company.

سره‌ور *sarah-war*, a. Ample, broad, wide. See سور.

سريخ *srīkh*, s.m. Name of a tree (*Mimosa seris*). S. (*siris*).

سريښ *sarekkh*, s.m. See سلېښ.

سرين *surīn*, s.m. The buttock. P.

سړبنړ *saṛbanṛ*, s.m. Name of the eldest son of Kais (the great ancestor of the Afghans). His tribe. *saṛbanṛai*, s.m. A male of the tribe.

سړپ *sṛap*, s.m. The sound of splashing water; squash, smash, dash, etc. H. (*suṛap*).

سړه *saṛah*, a. Done, finished; free, liberated; alone, solitary; genuine, pure.

سړه‌بنړ *saṛah-banṛ*, s.m. See سړبنړ.

سړه‌لړي *saṛa-lire*, } s.f. Fever and ague.
سړه‌لوي *saṛa-lawe*, }

سړي *saṛai*, s.m. A man, human being. *saṛī-tob*, s.m. Human nature, humanity.

سزا *sazā*, s.f. Correction, punishment, retribution. P.

سزاوار *sazāwār*, a. Deserving, fit, worthy; suitable, proper. P.

سزاول *sazāwal*, s.m. Bailiff, tax-gatherer.

سږ *sag*, ad. } This year, the current year.
سږكال *sag-kāl*, }

سږمه *sagma*, s.f. The nostril.

سږني *saganai*, a. This year's, of the present year.

سږي *sagai*, s.m. The lung. P. (*shush*).

سسپار *saspār*, s.m. A plough-share.

سسپور *saspor*, s.m. A mattock, hoe.

سست *sust*, a. Indolent, lazy, negligent; feeble, slow, languid; loose, relaxed. P.

سستي *sustī*, s.f. Idleness, laziness, etc. P.

سښا *sakkha*, s.f. Fizz, sputter, etc. (as of roasting meat).

سښسوره *sakkhsora*, s.f. See سسپور.

سطح *saṭaḥ*, s.m. A surface, flat surface. A.

سعادت *sa'ādat*, s.m. Felicity, happiness, good fortune. A.

سعيه *sa'ya*, s.f. Endeavour, effort, purpose. A. (*sa'ī*).

سغ *sagh*, s.m. See شغ.

سفر *safar*, s.m. A journey, voyage. A.

سفوف *safūf*, s.m. A powder. A.

سقاو *saqqāw*, s.m. A water carrier. A.

سک *sak*, a. Stiff. rigid. s.m. Lumbago, rheumatism. H. (*chik*).

سکاروي *skārwai*, s.m. Pleurisy; rheumatism, sciatica.

سکالوه *skālwah*, s.m. Conversation, discourse, talk, hum, buzz, murmur (of conversation).

سکانړ *skānṛ*, a. Dark complexioned, ruddy, healthy, fresh, or agreeable complexion. s.m. A horse of a light bay colour.

سکروټه *skarwaṭa*, s.f. Embers, live coal.

سکړک *sukṛuk*, a. Numbed, chilled, paralyzed with cold. *sukṛak*, s.m. Bread made of Indian corn or maize meal.

سکستل *skustal*, v.a. To shear, clip (as sheep, etc).

سکښتل *skakkhtal*, v.a. To cut, shape, design, cut out (as clothes). To clip, shear.

سکل *skal*, v.a. See څښل.

سکنجبين *sikanjabīn*, s.m. Oxymel; a drink made of lime-juice, honey and water. P.

سکندري *skandara-ī*, s.f. A stumble, trip.

سکور *skor*, s.m. Charcoal.

سکول *skwal*, s.m. Shearing. clipping. *skwal-kawul*, v.a. To shear, clip.

سکونت *sukūnat*, s.m. Habitation, residence; quiet, rest, tranquility. A.

سکونډاره *skūnḍāṛa*, s.f. A pinch; pinching.

سکونډل *skūnḍal*, v.a. To pinch, tweak.

سکوي *skoe*, s.m. A stitch; sewing. Anxiety,

solicitude. *skoe-kawul*, v.a. To stitch, hem, sew.

سکویل *skoyal*, v.a. To rub, scrape, scratch (as the skin).

سکه *sika*, s.f. Lead; coin, impression, stamp; sterling, current. A. P. *sakah*, a. Related (of the same parents), full, own. S. (*saga*). *ska*, ad. Because, therefore, then; as if, as it were.

سگ *sag*, s.m. A dog. P. *sag*, ad. See سر.

سگال *sigāl*, s.m. Suspicion. thought; calumny. P.

سگل *sugul*, s.f. A kind of buskin made of untanned leather, and worn by mountaineers as a protection for the legs from the snow.

سگلاو *sagalāw*, s.m. An otter. P. (*sagulāb*).

سگلئي *sagala-ī*, s.f. See سلگئي.

سگه *saga*, s.f. Capital, stock, store.

سل *sal* or *sil*, a. A hundred, one hundred, centum. P. (*ṣad*). *sill*, s.m. Consumption, phthisis, hectic fever. A.

سلاره *silāra*, s.f. A kind of striped cloth.

سلام *salām*, s.m. Salutation; peace, safety. A.

سلامت *salāmat*, s.m. Health, recovery; safety, salvation. A.

سلائي *salā-ī*, s.f. A bodkin, pin, skewer, pencil, etc. S. The upright pillar of a Persian wheel; a steel bodkin for applying antimony to the eyelids, etc.

سلټ *salaṭ*, s.m. A shield, buckler.

سلسله *silsila*, s.f. Chain, series, succession; descent, lineage. A.

سلطان *sulṭān*, s.m. Emperor, sovereign, king. A.

سلطاني *sulṭānī*, a. Princely, royal. A.

سلطنت *sulṭanat*, s.m. Empire, sovereignty. A.

سلگئي *salga-ī*, s.f. A sob, sigh, hiccough, sobbing cry.

سلوک *sulūk*, s.m. Behaviour, conduct, manner; intercourse, treatment, usage; attention, civility. A.

سله *sala*, s.f. A pig or mass of iron. H. (*sarī*).

سلي *salai*, s.m. An iron ring for the finger (worn as a charm against all kinds of calamities).

سليخ *salekh*, / سليښ *salekkh*, s.m. Glue; birdlime; adhesiveness, cohesion, viscidity. P. (*saresh*).

سليقه *salīqa*, s.f. Disposition, nature; address, dexterity, method, etc. A.

سم *sum*, s.m. A hoof, whole hoof (as of a horse, etc.). *sam*, a. Even, flat, level, plane, straight. *samm*, s.m. Poison, venom. A. *sam*, s.m. An arrow. A. (*sahm*).

سماع *simā'*, s.f. Hearing, listening; a song, singing. A.

سمبالول *sambālawul*, v.a. To control, manage, moderate; to prop, support; protect, preserve; arrange, settle, put in order, etc. S. (*sambhālnā*).

سمت *simt*, s.m. Path, road, way; direction, quarter. A.

سمڅ *smats*, s.f. A cavern, cave. P. (*sumuj*).

سم دلاسه *sam da lāsa*, ad. Straight from the hand, out of hand, forthwith, etc.

سمساره *samsāra*, s.f. A kind of lizard, iguana.

سمست *samist*, s.f. See سمڅ.

سمسور *samsor*, a. / سمسوري *samsorai*, Come out, ripened, matured (as corn when in ear). s.m. A peer, equal, match, compeer.

سمن *saman*, s.m. Jasmine, lily of the valley. P.

سمند *samand*, a. Dun-coloured (horse). P.

سمندر *samandar*, s.m. A salamander. P.

سمندي *samandai*, s.m. A rat of a dun colour.

سمور *sumūr*, s.m. A marten, sable; sable skin. P.

سمه *sama*, s.f. A plateau, plain. Name of the Yūsufzai plain.

سن *san*, s.m. Age, year. A.

سنار *sunār,* s.m. A goldsmith. S.
سنبل *sunbul,* s.m. Hyacinth. P. Maidenhair fern.
سنت *sunnat,* s.m. Circumcision; the traditions of Muḥammad; ordinance. A.
سنځل *sandzal,* v.a. To empty, bale, pour out. P. (*sanjīdan*).
سنج *sanj* (in comp.). A weigher. P. *sunj,* a. Empty, void, desolate, waste, deserted.
سنجاب *sanjāb,* s.m. Ermine. P.
سند *sannad,* s.m. Certificate, deed, diploma, document, grant, etc. A. *sind,* s.m. A river. The name of a country. S. (*sindh*).
سندان *sandān,* s.m. An anvil. P.
سندره *sandara,* s.f. A song; melody, song.
سنډا *sanḍā,* a. Burly, powerful, strong, stout. S.
سنډاسي *sanḍāsī,* s.m. A Hindu ascetic, devotee. S. (*sunyāsī*).
سنډه *sanḍah,* s.m. A bull buffalo. S. (*sānḍ*).
سنکيا *sankiyā,* s.f. Arsenic. S. (*sankhiyā*).
سنګ *sang,* s.m. A stone (in comp.). P.
سنګار *singār,* s.m. Decoration, dress, ornament, toilet. S.
سنګاونړ *singāwanr,* s.m. A rudder, helm; barge pole, boat hook. A. (*sukkān*).
سنګر *sangar,* s.m. Barricade, stockade. S.
سنګزن *sangzan,* a. Lop-sided, top-heavy, lurched over, over-balanced.
سنګلاخ *sanglākh,* a. Stony, rocky; difficult, arduous. P.
سنګين *sangīn,* a. Heavy, weighty; solid, hard; important, serious, difficult; stony. s.m. A bayonet. P.
سنه مکي *sanah-makī,* s.m. Senna leaves (*Cassia lanceolata*). Name of a stone, serpentine, porphyry. H.
سني *sunnī,* s.m. An orthodox Muḥammadan; one who believes in the equality of the four successors of Muḥammad. a. Catholic, orthodox, true. A. *sunnī-tob,* s.m. Orthodoxy.

سنړ *sanr,* The hemp plant (*Crotalaria juncea*); hemp. S. (*san*).
سو *sau,* a. A hundred. Only used with reference to more than one hundred. Ex. *sal* or *sil,* One hundred. *Dre-sawa,* Three hundred. S.
سوا *siwā,* p. Except, besides, without. A.
سوال *sawāl,* s.m. Question, interrogation, proposition. A.
سوانګ *swāng,* s.m. Disguise, imitation, sham. S.
سوانګي *swāngai,* s.m. An actor, imitator.
سوټبوټ *sūṭ-būṭ,* a. Cross, surly, ill-natured; withered, dry; pure, simple; disagreeable, ugly; pinioned, tightened; all of a heap, by the run, etc.
سوټه *sūṭa,* s.f. Dung of cattle (as found on pastures), scybala. A. (*sudda*).
سوځول *swadzawul,* v.a. To burn, set on fire. P. (*sokhtāndan, sozān-*).
سوچه *sūchah,* a. Genuine, pure, prime, real. S.
سوخته *sokhtah,* a. Burnt (in comp.). P.
سود *sūd,* s.m. Gain, advantage; interest, profit. P.
سودا *saudā,* s.f. Commerce, trade, marketing, etc. P. Hypochondriasis, melancholy, madness; desire, love, ambition. A.
سوداګر *saudāgar,* s.m. A merchant, trader. P.
سودائي *saudā-ī,* a. Mad, melancholy, insane. A.
سوده *sūdah,* a. Abraded, frayed, rubbed, galled. P. Genuine, pure, simple; artless. S. (*sūdhā*). *sūda,* s.f. A stoppage, obstruction (of the bowels). A. (*sudda*). *sawda,* s.f. A basket, hamper; a wicker frame used as a dish cover, meat safe, etc.
سوډر *soḍar,* s.m. A boar, wild boar. S. (*sūkar*). a. Bald, barepated.
سور *sor,* s.m. Breadth, expanse, width. H. (*chauṛ*). *sor,* a. Riding, mounted. s.m. A cavalier, horseman. P. (*sawār*). *sūr,*

a. Red. f. *sra.* P. (*surkh*). *sūr*, s.m. Name of a tribe of Afghans.

سوراغزي *sūr·āghzai*, s.m. Name of a plant with red thorns (*Catha edulis*).

سورپلي *sūr·palai*, s.m. Name of a plant, the seed pod of which is covered with red prickles; cowitch (*Mucuna pruriens*); a kind of stinging nettle; a kind of grass with barbed spikes in the beard.

سورت *sūrat*, s.m. A chapter (of the Qurān). A.

سورسات *sūrsāt*, s.m. Provisions, stores, supplies, etc. (collected for a king, or an army on the march). P.

سورلکي *sūr·lakai*, s.m. Name of a bird with a red tail; stonechat, wheatear.

سورلنډ *sūrland*, s.m. A jackal.

سورلي *swarlī*, s.f. Riding; cavalcade, suite. P. (*sawārī*). *swarlui*, s.m. A chisel; burglar's tool, jemmy, pick.

سورمل *sūrmal*, s.m. Name of a grass with barbed spikes in the beard (*Apluda aristata*).

سورميږي *sūr·megai*, s.m. The red ant.

سوره *swara*, s.f. A daughter or slave girl given as the price of murder or blood, or in exchange for a wife or girl eloped with or abducted.

سوري *sūrai*, s.m. Aperture, orifice, hole, passage. P. (*sūrākh*). *sorai* or *siwrai*, s.m. Shadow, shade. *sūre*, s.f. (pl. of *sūra*, obsolete). A bawl, bellow, shout, scream.

سوريته *sūryata*, s.f. A female slave or bondwoman who has borne a child to her master; a concubine.

سوړ *soṛ*, a. Cold, frigid, frosty. P. (*sard*).

سوړبوئي *soṛ·bū-ī*, s.f. Stink, fœtor, stench.

سوړه *sūṛa*, s.f. A burrow, hole; aperture, orifice. P. (*sūrākh*).

سوړي *sūṛai*, s.m. A fissure, crack, cleft.

سوز *soz* (in comp.). Burning. P.

سوزاک *sozāk*, s.m. Gonorrhœa. P.

سوزش *sozish*, s.m. Burning, heat, fervour; inflammation; vexation.

سوزن *sozan*, s.m. A needle; pricker, pin. P.

سوزني *sozanī*, s.f. A quilt, counterpane, coverlet. P.

سوزه *sūza*, s.f. A fillet, patch, etc. in a dress; an adze.

سوسر *sūsar*, s.m. A porpoise. S. (*sūs*).

سوسن *sausan* or *sosan*, s.m. Name of a plant, the Chinese Iris, Daurian Lily; a purple or violet colour. A.

سوغ *sogh*, s.m. A sniff, snort, snuff; sound of blowing the nose. S. (*sūngh*). *sūgh*, s.m. A pinch of snuff, or anything taken between the finger and thumb.

سوغات *saughāt*, s.m. A curiosity, rarity, present. P.

سوغالي *soghālai*, s.m. A hare's form.

سوغن *sūghan*, a. Sniffling, snorting, snuffing. s.m. A sniveller.

سوغول *sūgharwul*, v.a. To prod, poke, thrust.

سوغيدل *sūghedal*, v.n. To be pierced, stabbed, etc.

سوک *sūk*, s.m. The fist; a blow, cuff (with the fist); the stump of a tree.

سوکړ *sūkaṛ*, s.m. A tall, gaunt, thin, etc. man; a thin wiry beard.

سوکړک *sūkṛuk*, s.m. Bread made of Indian corn or maize.

سوکړه *sokṛah*, a. Dry, parched, withered. S. (*sūkhā*).

سوګند *saugand*, s.m. An oath. P.

سول *swal*, v.n. To burn, catch fire, ignite. Pr. *swadzī*. P. (*sokhtan, soz-*).

سولاغ *sūlāgh*, s.m. A hole, aperture, etc. P. (*sūrākh*).

سولاغه *sūlāgha*, s.f. A water bucket; a strainer, colander.

سولول *sūlawul*, v.a. To rub, file, rasp, grate, abrade.

سولي *sūla-ī*, s.f. A gibbet, stake; a pole, juggler's pole. s. (*sūlī*).

سوليدل *sūledal*, v.n. To fray, chafe, fret, abrade, etc.

سوم *swam*, s.m. See سپم.

سونبه *sūnba*, s.m. A socket; heel of an arrow, axe, lance, etc.; a blacksmith's punch; a sponge staff, ramrod. H. (*sumbā*).

سوندر *swandar*, s.m. See سخوندر.

سونده *sūnda*, s.f. Jealousy, suspicion.

سوند *sūnḍ*, s.m. Dry ginger. s. (*sonṭh*). See شوند.

سوندك *sūnḍak*, s.m. The trunk or proboscis of an elephant. s. (*sūnḍ*).

سونگټ *sūngaṭ*, a. Burnt, scorched; withered.

سونگي *ṣongai*, s.m. A pigmy, dwarf.

سونړ *sūnṟ*, s.m. See سوغ.

سونړول *sūnṟawul*, v.a. To blow the nose, snuff, snort.

سونړيدل *sūnṟedal*, v.n. To sniff, snuff, smell, etc.

سوور *swor*, a. Riding, mounted. s.m. A cavalier, horseman. P. (*sawār*).

سووه *sowa*, s.f. Name of a plant, sweet fennel (*Anethum sowa*). s. (*soā*).

سوه *swa*, s.f. A cloven hoof (as of oxen, sheep, etc.).

سوهاگن *sohāgan*, s.f. A favourite wife. s. See مروبنه.

سوهان *sohān*, s.m. A file, rasp. P.

سوي *sawai*, a. Consumed, burnt. *swai*, s.m. Burning, ardour; pain; compassion, pity.

سويشل *sweshal*, v.a. To milk. See لوشل.

سويه *soya*, s.f. } A hare. s. (*sasā*).
سوئي *so-e*, s.m. }

سه *sih*, a. Three (in comp.). P.

سهل *sahl*, a. Easy, facile, ad. Easily. A.

sahal, v.n. To bear, endure, suffer. s. (*sahnā*).

سهم *sahm*, s.f. Dread, awe, terror, fear. P.

سهوه *sahwa*, s.f. Mistake, error. A. (*sahw*).

سهه *saha*, s.f. Breath, life; respiration. Clothes line, clothes horse.

سهيدل *sahedal*, v.n. To endure, suffer. See سهل.

سهيل *suhel*, s.m. The star Canopus; the south. A.

سهيلي *sahelī*, s.f. A lady's maid, housemaid; a concubine, handmaid. s.

سياځه *siyādza*, s.f. A slab for grinding spices on; a cobbler's lapstone.

سياست *siyāsat*, s.m. Government; punishment. A.

سيال *siyāl*, s.m. An equal, peer; clansman, kin; like, resembling.

سيالي *siyālī*, s.f. Equality, purity, resemblance.

سياه *siyāh*, a. Black (in comp.). P.

سياهه *siyāha*, s.f. Muster, catalogue, register, etc.

سياهي *siyāhī*, s.f. Ink; blackness; register, list. P.

سيب *seb*, s.m. An apple. P.

سيپۍ *sīpa-ī*, s.f. A shell. H. (*sīpī*).

سيټ *seṭ*, s.m. A banker, merchant. s. (*seṭh*).

سيځل *sedzal*, v.n. To burn, catch fire. See سول *swal*.

سيخ *sīkh*, s.m. A skewer, spit, ramrod. P.

سيخچه *sīkhcha*, s.f. A small skewer, etc.; a prong or bayonet fixed to a matchlock. P.

سيد *sayad*, s.m. A prince, lord; a descendant of Husain, the grandson of Muḥammad. A.

سير *sair*, s.m. Excursion, jaunt, picnic, recreation, walk. A. *ser*, s.m. Name of a weight equal to two pounds. H. *ser*, a. Satiated, full, replete, etc. (in comp.). P.

سيراب *serāb*, a. P. See خړوب.

سیرت *sīrat*, s.m. Manners, morals, conduct. A.

سیرلي *serlai*, s.m. A yearling kid.

سیرۍ *sera-ī*, s.f. Rent free land given to men of the religious classes, glebe; an estate, pension in land, fief.

سیزل *sezal*, } v.n. To burn, consume, kindle,
سیځل *sedzal*, } catch fire. P. (*sokhtan, soz-*).

سیسه *sīsa*, s.f. Lead. S. (*sīsā*).

سیکړه *saikṛa*, s.f. A hundred; a centum. S.

سیکل *sekal*, v.a. To foment, toast, warm. H. (*senknā*).

سیکن *sekan*, s,m. Aversion, antipathy, disgust; dislike, loathing (of food, etc.).

سیل *sail*, s.m. Walking, rambling; flowing, current; flood; flock of birds; shoal of fishes. A.

سیلاب *sailāb*, s.m. A current, torrent, flood; deluge, inundation. a. Abounding in water. P.

سیله *sela*, s.f. Partiality, friendship, affection. A. A javelin, pike; rapier, long sword. S.

سیلي *siyalai*, s.m. Rennet; the prepared stomach of a kid or lamb filled with coagulated milk. *siyala-ī*, s.f. Rope made of goat's hair, etc. *sīla-ī*, s.f. A slap, blow with the open hands. P. (*selī*). A dust storm, whirlwind; hurricane, tempest.

سیم *sīm*, s.m. Silver. P. Wire of any kind.

سیماب *sīmāb*, s.m. Quicksilver, mercury. P.

سیمرغ *sīmurgh*, s.m. A fabulous bird, griffin. P.

سیمک *sīmak*, s.m. A weaver's bodkin; knitting needle. P.

سیمه *sema*, s.f. A mare or ass in heat (seeking the male). *sīma*, s.f. Path, way, road; quarter, side, part.

سیمیا *sīmiyā*, s.f. Vermicelli. H. (*senwiyā*).

سیند *sīnd*, s.m. A river, sea. S. (*sindh*).

سینګار *singār*, s.m. See سنګار.

سینه *sīna*, s.f. Bosom, breast. P.

سیني *sīnī*, s.m. A tray, salver. P.

سیو *sew*, s.m. An apple. P.

سیوري *sewrai*, s.m. Shadow, shade.

ش

ش *shīn*, is the twenty-second letter of the Pukkhto alphabet. It has the sound of *sh* in English, and in Persian words introduced into Pukkhto is often changed to ښ.

شا *shā*, s.f. The back; the shoulders. P. (*shāna*).

شاباز *shābāz*, s.m. The bass string of a musical instrument; a royal falcon. P.

شاباش *shābāsh*, in. Bravo! well done! P.

شاپیانګه *shāpiyānga*, s.f. Name of a plant (*Withiana coagulans*).

شاپیټي *shāpeṭai*, s.m. A small shell found in hill streams, and on mountain sides; a snail (*Achatina acicula*).

شاتر *shātar*, s.m. A groom, running footman.

شاتینګه *shā-tīnga*, s.f. The gizzard (of a fowl, etc.).

شادو *shādo*, s.m. A monkey.

شاربل *shārbal*, v.a. To churn, stir about, etc. P. (*shor dādan* or *shorīdan*).

شاړ *shāṛ*, a. Rude, unmannered, boorish. Idle, out of work, unemployed; fallow, waste, uncultivated. s.m. A boor, bumpkin, clown, clodhopper.

شاش *shāsh*, s.m. Urine. P.

شاعر *shā'ir*, s.m. A poet. A.

شاګرد *shāgird*, s.m. An apprentice, pupil, disciple. P.

شال *shāl*, s.m. A shawl. S.

شالي *shāla-ī*, s.f. Rice plant, rice crop. S. (*shālī*).

شامت *shāmat*, s.m. Adversity, bad fortune. A.

شامل *shāmil*, a. Blended, comprised, united;

included, contained. ad. Together, along with. A.

شامي *shāma-ī*, s.f. A sepulchre, tomb, vault for dead bodies.

شاميانه *shāmiyāna*, s.f. Awning, canopy. P.

شان *shān*, s.m. Affair, business; condition, degree; dignity, state; constitution, nature. a. Like, resembling; used as an adjunct of similitude. Ex. *tor·shān*, a. Blackish; *spin·shān*, a. Whitish. ad. Like, as, similar, etc. P. (*sān*).

شانه *shāna*, s.f. A weaver's comb. P.

شاول *shāwul*, s.m. A plummet, plumb-line. H. (*sāhūl*). P. (*shāqul*).

شاولي واولي *shāwlai·wāwlai*, a. Careless, untidy; foolish, indiscreet; loose, dishevelled.

شاه *shāh*, s.m. A king; a title assumed by men of the *pīr* class. P.

شاهتره *shāhtara*, s.f. Name of a herb, common fumitory (*Fumaria officinalis.*). P.

شاهد *shāhid*, s.m. A witness. A.

شاهده *shāhida*, s.f. A sweetheart, mistress. P.

شاهدي *shāhidī*, s.f. Evidence, testimony. A.

شاهزاده *shāh·zādah*, s.m. A prince, king's son. P.

شاهزادئي *shāh·zāda-ī*, s.f. A princess. P.

شاهي *shāhī*, a. Kingly, royal. s.f. Sovereignty, reign. P.

شاهين *shāhīn*, s.m. A kind of falcon. P.

شايان *shāyān*, a. Legal, worthy, suitable. P.

شايد *shāyad*, ad. Perhaps, possibly, perchance. P.

شب *shab*, s.m. Night (in comp.). P.

شب بو *shab·bo*, s.m. The tuberose lily (*Polianthes tuberosa*). P.

شبکه *shabaka*, s.f. A lattice, latticed window; a net, reticulated veil. P.

شبنم *shab·nam*, s.m. Dew; hoar frost. P.

شبه *shiba*, s.f. Agate, coral; a bead. P.

شبهه *shubha*, s.f. Uncertainty, doubt; suspicion; hesitation. A.

شپاړس *shpāṛas*, a. Sixteen.

شپږ *shpag*, a. Six. P. (*shash*).

شپشتي *shpishtai*, s.m. The spoke of a wheel.

شپنغوده *shpan·ghoda*, s.f. Name of a bird, the shepherd's deceiver, lapwing, pewit.

شپنکي *shpankai*, s.m. A shepherd-boy.

شپني *shpanī*, s.f. Shepherd life, tending sheep.

شپول *shpol*, s.m. A sheep cot, sheep pen, or fold; a thorn hedge; halo round the moon.

شپون *shpūn*, s.m. A shepherd. P. (*shubān*).

شپه *shpa*, s.f. Night. P. (*shab*).

شپيته *shpetah*, a. Sixty.

شپيتي *shpetai*, s.m. A wedge to cleave wood with.

شپيشتي *shpeshtai*, s.m. A wedge; a kind of clover. P. (*supust*).

شپيشتري *shpeshtarai*, s.m. A kind of trefoil or vetch (*Medicago denticulata*).

شپيلئي *shpela-ī*, s.f. A tube, pipe, barrel of a gun; fife, flute, whistle; hollow reed; blowpipe. *shpelai*, s.m. Whistling, a whistle. *shpelai ghagawul*, v.a. To whistle.

شتاب *shitāb*, s.m. Haste, quickness, speed. a. Hasty, quick, rash. P.

شتاه *shatāh*, a. Artful, cunning; immodest, lewd. A.

شتاهه *shatāha*, s.f. A lewd, wanton, etc. woman.

شترلړ *shuturlaṛ*, s.m. The bar or beam that prevents the ropes of a Persian wheel (on which are fastened the water pots) from coming in contact with each other.

شترکه *shuturaka*, s.f. A cascade; spurt, jet, gush (of water).

شتري *shuturī*, s.f. Name of a kind of cloth made of camel's hair. P.

شته *shta*, A form of the third person singular and plural, present tense of the auxiliary verb يم *yam*, I am; there is, there are. P. (*hast*).

شتي *shata-ī*, s.f. A barbed arrow; the spike or ear of maize after the grain has been removed; the green mould on old walls; the green scum on stagnant pools.

شتل *shaṭal*, a. Lazy, indolent. See شدل.

شجاع *shujā'*, a. Brave, bold, courageous. A.

شجاعت *shujā'at*, s.m. Bravery, courage. A.

شجره *shajara*, s.f. List of saints; genealogical table. A.

شخرلي *shatsurlai*, s.m. A chisel.

شخ *shakh*, a. Hard, rough, tough, rigid, stiff. P.

شخره *shkhaṛa*, s.f. Gibberish, nonsense, twaddle, trash; crowd, mob, multitude.

شخوده *shakhūdah*, a. Clawed, scratched. P.

شخول *shkhwal*, s.m. Din, tumult, noise; rumble, murmur, rustle.

شخولي *shkhwalai*, s.m. A quiver for arrows.

شخوند *shkhwand*, s.m. The cud. *shkhwand-wahana*, s.f. Chewing the cud, ruminating. *shkhwand-wahunkai*, s.m. A ruminant, an animal that chews the cud. See سخوندر *skhwandar*.

شدت *shiddat*, s.m. Force, violence, vehemence. A.

شدني *shudanī*, a. Possible, practicable, probable. P.

شدياره *shudyāra*, s.f. Land ploughed and made ready for sowing. P. (*shudkār*).

شديد *shadīd*, a. Difficult; acute, intense; vehement, violent. A.

شدل *shaḍal*, a. Indolent, lazy, slow; unbleached or unwashed cloth.

شر *sharr*, s.m. Villany, wickedness, depravity, evil. A. *shir*, s.m. Pitter-patter, sound of falling rain; the whizz of an arrow passing through the air.

شراب *sharāb*, s.m. Wine, spirits. A.

شرارت *sharārat*, s.m. Depravity, villany, wickedness. A.

شراکت *shirākat*, s.m. Partnership, fellowship. A.

شربت *sharbat*, s.m. Sherbet, beverage, drink. P.

شرحه *sharḥa*, s.f. Commentary, explanation; allowance, pay, rate. A.

شرشاي *sharshā-ī*, s.f. See سرشاهي.

شرط *sharṭ*, s.m. Agreement, bargain; stipulation, condition; bet, wager; mark, sign. A.

شرطي *sharṭī*, a. Conditional; a bargainer, better. A.

شرعه *shar'a*, s.f. Muḥammadan law; equity, law. A.

شرعي *shar'a-ī*, a. According to law, legal. A.

شرغشي *sharghashai*, s.m. Name of a reed from the stalks of which stools, baskets, etc. are made (*Saccharum sara*, and *S. spontaneum*).

شرغه *sharghah*, a. A horse with a white forehead, or with white eyes.

شرك *shirk*, s.m. Infidelity, paganism; company, society, partnership. A.

شركت *shirkat*, s.m. Partnership. A.

شرم *sharm*, s.m. Bashfulness, modesty, shame. P.

شرمښ *sharmakkh*, s.m. A wolf.

شرمناك *sharm-nāk*, a. Bashful, modest, unassuming. P.

شرمنده *sharmindah*, a. Ashamed, disgraced, shamed. P.

شرمندگي *sharmindagī*, s.f. Disgrace, shame. P.

شرمول *sharmawul*, v.a. To disgrace, shame, dishonor; to rape, ravish.

شرميدل *sharmedal*, v.n. To blush, be modest, be abashed, ashamed, etc.

شروع *shurū'*, s.f. Beginning, commencement. A.

شري *sharai*, s.m. The measles; a rash on the body of infants; tooth-rash. A. (*ṣharā*).

شرير *sharīr*, a. Wicked, depraved, vicious. A.

شريعت *sharī'at*, s.m. Muḥammadan law; equity, justice, law. A.

شريف *sharīf*, a. Noble, eminent. A.

شريفه *sharīfa*, s.f. The eave of a roof; projecting ledge of a wall.

شريک *sharīk*, s.m. Accomplice, ally; comrade, partner. A.

شړته *sharata*, s.f. See شړهته.

شړشم *sharsham*, s.m. Mustard (the plant and seed). P. (*sarshaf*). S. (*sarson*).

شړل *sharal*, v.a. To eject, depose, turn out, drive away. A. (*shārid*).

شړنګ *shrang*, s.m. A jingle, clink, chink; chime, ring, echo,

شړنګول *shranganwul*, v.a. To jingle, ring, etc.

شړنګيدل *shrangedal*, v.n. To chime, jingle, ring, tinkle, etc. P. (*charangīdan*).

شړونکي *sharūnkai*, } a. Deposed, expelled,
شړوني *sharūnai*, } ejected.

شړهته *sharhata*, s.f. A barleycorn, grain of barley; a particle, bit, small quantity.

شړهيدل *sharhedal*, v.n. To crumble, decay, decompose, rot, become sodden, etc. H. (*sarnā*).

شړئ *shara-ī*, s.f. A blanket. A. (*sh'ar*).

شست *shast*, s.m. The space between the thumb and forefinger; a thumbstall (used by archers); aim, sight (as of a gun or arrow). P.

شستئ *shasta-ī*, s.f. Name of a plant (*Chrysanthemum Indicum*).

ششت *shasht*, s.m. A mirror attached to a ring, and worn on the thumb by women.

ششني *shashanai*, } s.m. The neigh of a
ششڼي *shashanrai*, } horse.

ششڼيدل *shashanredal*, v.n. To neigh.

شعر *shi'r*, s.m. Poetry, verse. A.

شعله *shu'la*, s.f. A blaze, flame. A.

شعور *shu'ūr*, s.m. Intellect, reason, knowledge. A.

شغ *shagh*, s.m. Whizz, whirr (as of a bullet or bird passing through the air), etc.

شغال *shaghāl*, s.m. A jackal. P.

شغرب مغرب *shaghrib-maghrib*, s.m. East and west. A. (*mashriq-maghrib*).

شغل *shughl*, s.m. Employment, occupation. A.

شغله *shughla*, s.f. See شعله.

شفا *shifā*, s.f. Cure, recovery; remedy. A.

شفاعت *shafā'at*, s.m. Entreaty, intercession, recommendation. A.

شفتالو *shaftālū*, s.m. A peach. P.

شفق *shafaq*, s.m. Twilight, dusk. A.

شفقت *shafaqat*, s.m. Clemency, compassion, kindness, mercy. A.

شک *shakk*, s.m. Doubt, suspicion; hesitation, uncertainty. A.

شکار *shkār*, s.m. Alkali, potash.

شکال *shkāl*, s.m. Hobbles for the fore feet of a horse. See شکيل.

شکايت *shikāyat*, s.m. Complaint, accusation. A.

شکر *shukr*, s.m. Gratitude, thanks. A.

شکرانه *shukrāna*, s.f. Gratitude, thanks; premium, fee, payment for service done. P.

شکره *shakara*, s.f. Sugar. P. (*shakar*).

شکري *shikrai*, s.m. A kind of falcon or hawk. P. (*shikrah*). *shkarai*, s.m. A flat basket of a circular shape. H. (*sikhar*).

شکست *shikast*, a. Broken, fractured; dispersed, worsted, beaten. P.

شکل *shakl*, s.m. Appearance, figure, form, etc. A.

شکلي *shaklai*, s.m. The end or tail of a turband.

شکم *shikam*, s.m. The belly (in comp.). P.

شکمن *shakk-man*, a. Doubtful, dubious, suspicious.

شکنجه *shikandza*, s.f. A press, vice; bookbinder's press; stocks for the legs; rack, pillory; torture. P. (*shikanja*).

شکور *shkor*, }
شکير *shker*, } s.m. A flat basket. H. (*sikhar*).

شکونړ *shkūnr*, s.m. A porcupine.

شکيل *shkel*, s.m. P. (*shikīl* or *shigil*). See شکال.

شګاره *shigāra*, s.f. A pregnant woman or animal.

شګري *shigrai*, s.m. A priming horn, powder horn.

شګلن *shiglan*, a. Sandy, gravelly.

شګوفه *shigūfa*, s.f. A bud, blossom. P.

شګه *shiga*, s.f. Sand, gravel.

شل *shall*, a. Paralyzed, palsied. P. *shal*, s.m. A pike, javelin, spear. P. *shil*, a. Twenty, a score.

شلانده *shlānda*, s.f. A toad, frog.

شلټ *shalaṭ*, a. See شتل.

شلخي *shalkhai*, s.m. Name of a pot-herb; common dock (*Rumex acutus*).

شلغم *shalgham*, s.m. A turnip. P.

شلک *shilik*, s.m. A discharge, salvo, round, volley, salute, boom of a gun. A. (*shalakh*).

شلم *shilam*, a. Twentieth.

شلوار *shalwār*, s.m. Trowsers, pants. P.

شلول *shlawul*, v.a. To tear, rend, split, break, burst. H. (*chīrānā*).

شلوم *shlom*, s.m. }
شلونبي *shlonbe*, s.f. } See شوملي.

شليته *shalīta*, s.f. A large sack or net for baggage, etc. (when loaded on cattle). P.

شليدل *shledal*, v.n. To burst, tear, split, break, etc. H. (*chīrnā*).

شمار *shumār*, s.m. Counting, reckoning. P.

شمارل *shmāral*, v.a. To count. See شميرل.

شمال *shamāl*, s.m. The North; North wind. A.

شمځي *shamdza-ī*, s.f. Spine, back-bone.

شمشتي *shamshata-ī*, s.f. A tortoise.

شمشير *shamsher*, s.m. A sword. P.

شمعه *sham'a*, s.f. A candle, lamp. A.

شمکلي *shamkalai*, s.m. The unwoven end of a web or warp (used as a duster, etc.).

شمکور *shamkor*, a. Night-blind, nyctalopic. s.m. One who is subject to night-blindness. P. (*shab-kor*).

شمکوري *shamkorī*, s.f. Night-blindness, nyctalopia.

شمکي *shamkai*, s.m. Name of a plant used in medicine; vervain.

شمله *shamla*, s.f. The end of a turband; a shawl or sash for the waist.

شموخه *shamūkha*, s.f. Name of a grass and its seed (*Panicum frumentaceum*). P. (*shāmākh*).

شمه *shama*, s.m. An atom, jot, particle; odour, perfume. A.

شميرل *shmeral*, v.a. To count, compute, reckon. P. (*shumārīdan*).

شناخت *shnākht*, s.m. Acquaintance, recognition, knowledge. P. (*shinākht*).

شناز *shināz*, s.m. An inflated hide, used to cross rivers upon. P. (*shinā*, swimming).

شنبه *shanbah*, s.m. Saturday. P.

شنده *shandah*, a. Desperate, inconceivable, incredible, impossible.

شنډ *shanḍ*, a. Barren, sterile, unproductive, unfruitful. H. (*sanḍhar*).

شنډي *shanda-ī*, s.f. Name of a tree (*Melia sempervirens*); evergreen bead-tree.

شنګرپ *shingrip*, s.m. Cinnabar, vermillion. P. (*shangarf*).

شنګړي *shingra-ī*, s.f. Tower, keep, hornwork of a fort; a mould for casting pottery, etc.

شنل *shanal*, v.a. To explore, look, search, try, sound, etc. P. (*shāndan*, to comb).

شنوا *shinwā*, a. Hearing. P. (*shinudan*).

شنه *shna*, Feminine of شين, which see.

شني *shnai*, s.m. Name of a tree and its fruit (*Pistacia Kabulica*), the mastic tree.

شنيدل *shanedal*, v.n. To flutter, writhe, quiver, wriggle, shake, etc.

شو *sho* or *shaw*, s.m. See شب.

شو پا *shopā*, a. Uncircumcised; term of abuse.

شوپرک *sho·parak*, s.m. A bat. P. (*shab·para*).

شوتل *shotal*, s.m. Name of a trefoil (*Trifolium repens*). P. (*shaftal*). Name of a potherb (*Malva parviflora*), marsh mallow.

شوخ *shokh*, a. Cheerful, humorous; playful, mischievous; insolent, pert; wanton, saucy. P.

شوخون *sho·khūn*, s.m. A night attack, surprise. P. (*shab·khūn*).

شوخي *shokhī*, s.f. Fun, mischief, frolic; coquetry, lewdness, wantonness. P.

شودده *shaudah*, s.m. Milk.

شور *shor*, s.m. Cry, noise, riot. P.

شوړه *shoṛa*, s.f. The beard of grasses; a wisp of grass or straw used as a plug or bung.

شوشک *shūshk*, s.m. The curve of an arch.

شوشي *shūsha-ī*, s.f. A firebrand, torch. P. (*shūzha*).

شوق *shauq*, s.m. Desire, inclination; fondness, love; gaiety, cheerfulness; curiosity. A.

شوقدر *sho·qadar*, s.m. Name of a festival on the 14th of the month *sh'abān* (*shabi·barāt*). P. (*shab·qadr*).

شوک *shūk*, a. Plucked, robbed, stripped, etc. *shūk·pūk*, a. Plucked bare, bare as a bone.

شوکاڼري *shokāṇrai*, s.m. A flat stone used to bake cakes upon; soapstone, firestone, (used for the vent hole of a furnace, etc.).

شوکت *shaukat*, s.m. Dignity, pomp, state. A.

شوکور *sho·kor*, a. See شمکور.

شوکول *shūkawul*, v.a. To pluck, pick, cull; to rob, strip, tear off, etc. P. (*shūkhūdan*).

شوکه *shūka*, s.f. Plundering, robbing, stripping (as passengers on the roads). The beak of a bird.

شوګه *shūga*, s.f. A kind of rice.

شوګير *sho·gīr*, a. Watching by night, vigilant; a night watch, vigil. P. (*shab·gīr*).

شوګيري *sho·gīrī*, s.f. Watching at night, awake all night, etc.

شول *shwal*, v.n. To be, become, exist. P. (*shudan*).

شولخ *sholakh*, s.m. The skin of the tongue.

شولګره *sholgara*, s.f. A rice field, a rice swamp.

شوله *shola*, s.f. The rice plant. P. (*shālī*). *shūla*, s.f. The colic. S. (*sūl*).

شوم *shūm*, a. Miserly, stingy; unfortunate, vile; hungry, faint. A.

شوملي *shomle*, s.f. (pl. of *shomla*, obsolete). Butter milk, curds, and whey.

شومه *shūma*, s.f. The watch between midnight and daylight; food taken at that hour; food given to the friends of a deceased person on the night of the funeral. P.

شومي *shūmī*, s.f. Hunger, faintness; stingyness, niggardliness; misfortune, etc. A.

شونټي *shonṭa-ī*, s.f. A pine torch, slips of resinous pine wood used as torches, matches, etc.

شونډ *shūnḍ*, s.m. The lip. S. (*honṭh*).

شونډپاره *shūnḍ·pāra*, s.f. Hare lip.

شونډک *shūnḍak*, s.m. The proboscis of an elephant.

شونډه *shūnḍa*, s.f. The lip.

شوه *shawa*, s.f. Name of a tree, the sisoo (*Dalbergia sisoo*).

شوي *shoe*, s.m. Coarse cotton cloth.

شها *shahā*, s.f. A mistress, sweetheart. A.

شهاب *shihāb*, s.m. A meteor, falling star. A. *shahāb*, s.m. Milk and water. A.

شهتير *shahtīr*, s.m. A rafter, beam. P.

شهد *shahd*, s.m. Honey. P.

شهده *shuhdah*, s.m. A blackguard, debauchee, rake, libertine, profligate. H. (*shuhdā*).

شهرت *shuhrat*, s.m. Fame, renown; divulging, celebrating, publishing. A.

شهلا *shahlā*, a. Hazel-eyed. A.

شهند *shahand*, s.m. A kind of falcon.

شهوت *shahwat*, s.m. Lust, concupiscence. A.

شهوتناک *shahwat-nāk*, } a. Lascivious, lewd,
شهوتي *shahwatī*, } lustful; lust exciting. A.

شهيد *shahīd*, s.m. A martyr, witness. a. Killed. A.

شهين *shahīn*, s.m. A kind of falcon; a camel gun, a wall piece, carronade. P. The beam of a balance.

شي *shai*, s.m. An article, item, thing. A.

شهيبره *shebara*, s.f. A continued fever.

شيبه *shebah*, s.m. A downpour, heavy shower (of rain).

شيخ *shekh*, s.m. A chief, prelate; venerable old man; a title given to converts to Islam. A.

شيدا *shaidā*, a. Love mad; in love. P.

شير *sher*, s.m. A lion, tiger. P. *shīr*, s.m. Milk (in comp.). P.

شيرازه *shīrāza*, s.f. The stitching at the back of a book; the curtain or wall of a fort. P.

شيرخشت *shīr-khisht*, s.m. A kind of manna. P.

شيرخط *shīr-khaṭ*, s.m. Heads and tails, pitch and toss, tossing money for play. (*shīr*, head; *khaṭ*, tail).

شيره *shīra*, s.f. Batter, pap. P.

شيرين *shīrīn*, a. Sweet; affable, gentle, pleasant, etc. (in comp.). P.

شيشک *shīshk*, s.m. Name of a plant (*Lithospermum arvense*).

شيشکي *shīshkai*, s.m. A hedgehog. P. (*chizak*).

شيشه *shīsha*, s.f. A mirror, looking glass. P.

شيطان *shaitān*, s.m. The devil, Satan. A.

شيطاني *shaiṭānī*, s.f. Devilry, wickedness.

شيعه *shī'ah*, s.m. A follower of the sect of 'Ali; a heretic, infidel; sectarian. A.

شيله *shela*, s.f. A ravine, gully, watercourse; dry bed of a river.

شين *shīn*, a. Green, verdant; fresh, clear; blue, azure (as the sky). f. *shna*.

شيني *shīnai*, s.m. A whitlow; a tick, dog-louse.

شيوه *shewa*, s.f. Declivity, slope, slant. P. (*sheba*). Business, profession, trade; custom, habit; toilet, decoration; coquetry.

ښ

ښ *kkhīn* or *kshīn*, called also *kheshīn*, is the twenty-third letter of the Pukkhto alphabet. It is a combined form of خ and ش and corresponds in sound with the Hindi ख or ष. By the Yusufzais and Eastern Afghans generally, it is pronounced as *kkh*, and by the Khaṭaks and Western tribes as *ksh*. It is very often substituted for ش in words introduced from the Persian.

ښاپيرک *kkhāperak*, s.m. A bat. P. (*shab-parak*).

ښاپيري *kkhāperai*, s.m. A fairy; the king of the fairies. P. (*shāh-parī*).

ښاخ *kkhākh*, s.m. Branch or bough of a tree; the branch or arm of a river, etc. P. (*shākh*).

ښاخئ *kkhākha-ī*, s.f. A pitchfork, prong.

ښاد *kkhād*, a. Delighted, happy, pleased, gay, etc. P. (*shād*).

ښادان *kkhādān*, } a. Joyous, happy, gay.
ښادمن *kkhād-man*, }

ښادي *kkhādī*, s.f. Delight, joy, happiness, pleasure, etc. P. (*shādī*).

ښاديانه *kkhādiyāna*, s.f. Festivity, music, song; rejoicing. P. (*shādiyāna*).

ښارک *kkhārak*, s.m. The piece of wood (in the mouth of the upper millstone) through which the iron axle of a hand-mill passes; a piece of wood in the mouth of a churning jar or bottle for the passage of the churn stick.

ښرګ *kkhārag*, s.m. The jugular vein. P. (*shāh rag*).

ښاروني *kkhārūna-ī*, s.f. A starling.

ښاغل *kkhāghal*, v.a. To gratify, please, content; to choose, like, prefer.

ښامار *kkhāmār*, s.m. King of serpents, a dragon. P. (*shāh·mār*).

ښانک *kkhānak*, s.m. A kneading dish, trencher, a wooden platter. P. (*shānak*).

ښانګه *kkhānga*, s.f. The lower limb, thigh and leg, inferior extremity.

ښانګه‌ور *kkhānga·war*, a. Long-legged, spindle-shanked.

ښايست *kkhāyast*, s.m. Beauty, comeliness, elegance, grace; worthiness, propriety, fitness. Also *kkhāyast·wālai*.

ښايسته *kkhāyastah*, a. Handsome, beautiful, comely; worthy, fit, proper; well, good. P. (*shā-īstah*).

ښائي *kkhā-ī*, ad. May be, perhaps, possibly, probably. P. (*shāyad*).

ښپه *kkhpa*, s.f. The foot.

ښتري *kkhatrī*, s.m. A Hindu trader or shopkeeper. S. (*khatrī* or *kshatri*).

ښتګري *kkhatgarai*, s.m. The ankle, ankle joint; fetlock, fetlock joint.

ښځونک *kkhadzonak*, s.m. Hermaphrodite, effeminate man.

ښځه *kkhadza* or *kkhidza*, s.f. Woman, wife. a. Female, feminine, feminine gender. A. (*zauja*).

ښخ *kkhakh*, a. Hard, rigid, inflexible, stiff. P. (*shakh*). a. Buried, etc. See خښ.

ښرا *kkharā*, s.f. A curse. See ښيره.

ښروه *kkhorawa*, s.f. The yew tree (*Taxus baccata*). The castor oil tree (*Ricinus communis*). A (*khuroa'*).

ښکار *kkhkār*, s.m. Chase, hunting, sport; game, prey; plunder. P. (*shikār*).

ښکاره *kkhkārah*, a. Clear, manifest, apparent, visible, evident. P. (*āshkār*).

ښکاري *kkhkārī*, s.m. A hunter, fowler, sportsman; a robber. P. (*shikārī*).

ښکالوه *kkhkālwah*, s.m. Conversation, discussion; buzz, hum, murmur (of talking).

ښکته *kkhkata*, ad. Down, below, under. *kkhkatanai*, a. Inferior, lower, under.

ښکر *kkhkar*, s.m. A horn, antler; powder horn.

ښکري *kkhkarai*, s.m. A flat round basket. See شکري *shkarai*.

ښکل *kkhkul*, s.m. A kiss. *kkhkul·kawul*, v.a. To kiss. *kkhkal*, v.a. To draw, pull, tighten; to pen, write; endure, suffer; flay, remove, strip. See کښل.

ښکلول *kkhkulawul*, v.a. To kiss.

ښکلي *kkhkulai*, a. Kissed; handsome, pretty; comely, elegant; agreeable, pleasant. *kkhkalai*, a. Drawn, tight, tense; written; suffered, endured, etc.

ښکنځل *kkhkandzal*, s.m. Abuse, vituperation. P. *kkhkandzal* or *kkhkandzal·kawul*, v.a. To abuse, call bad names, etc. P. (*shikanjīdan*).

ښکول *kkhakawul*, v.a. To move, shake, loosen; slide, slip; push, thrust. *kkhkawul*, v.a. To cause to draw, extract, etc. See ښکل *kkhkal*.

ښکېدل *kkhakedal*, v.n. To fall, glide, slip, slide.

ښکيل *kkhkel*, s.m. A hobble, tether, fetter for the feet of cattle (to prevent their straying); cheat, fraud, imposition, trick. See شکيل.

ښکيه *kkhkiya*, ad. See ښکته.

ښلونه *kkhalūna*, s.f. A whitlow, abscess, boil.

ښندل *kkhandal*, v.a. To bestow, contribute, give, dispense, spend, etc.

ښنزه *kkhanza*, s.f. A boil, abscess, pustule.

ښنګري *kkhangarai*, s.m. Ankle, ankle-joint; fetlock; a cloven hoof.

ښنه *kkhna*, s.f. The hip bone (*os ilium*).

ښوڅه *kkhūtsa*, s.f. Nettlerash, hives.

ښور *kkhor*, s.m. Nest or hive of ants, bees, or wasps, etc.

ښورن *kkhoran*, a. Barren, sterile; nitrous, saline (as land).

ښوروا *kkhorwā*, s.f. Soup, broth. P. (*shorbā*).

ښوررول *kkhorawul*, v.a. To move, agitate, rock, wave to and fro, etc.

ښوره *kkhora*, s.f. Nitre, saltpetre. P. (*shora*). *kkhora-nāk*, a. Barren, sterile, full of nitre.

ښوريدل *kkhoredal*, v.n. To move, undulate, vibrate, wave, swing. P. (*shorīdan*).

ښونه *kkhona*, s.f. The olive tree.

ښوول *kkhowul*, v.a. To show, indicate. See ښيل.

ښوي *kkhwai*, a. Slippery, smooth.

ښوهول *kkhwahawul*, ښويول *kkhwayawul*, } v.a. To slide, slip, or push along (on a smooth surface).

ښوئيدل *kkhwa-edal*, v.n. To slip, slide, glide, fall down. Also ښوهيدل, *kkhwahedal*. P. (*shāfīdan*).

ښه *kkhah* or *kshah*, a. Good, proper, well; healthy, sound; fair, pleasant, etc. in. Well! Good! P. (*khūb*).

ښهر *kkhahr*, s.m. A town, city. P. (*shahr*).

ښي *kkhai* or *kshai*, a. Right, right hand, etc.

ښيره *kkhera* or *kshera*, s.f. Curse, malediction, imprecation, denunciation.

ښيښه *kkhīkkha*, s.f. A bottle, glass, phial. P. (*shīsha*).

ښيګړه *kkhegaṛa*, s.f. Excellence, goodness; value, worth; profit, advantage, benefit.

ښيل *kkhayal*, v.a. To show, point out; teach, instruct. P. (*nishāndan*). Def. in past ten. See ښوول. *kkhayal*, v.a. To reject, repudiate, turn off (as a disobedient son, etc.); to arm, equip oneself. P. (*shāyīdan*).

ښينه *kkhīna*, s.f. Sister-in-law, wife's sister.

ص

ص *ṣwād* is the fourteenth letter of the Arabic and the twenty-fourth of the Pukkhto alphabet. It is generally pronounced like س, and is only found in words adopted from the Arabic.

صاحب *ṣāḥib*, s.m. Master, lord; owner, possessor. A.

صادر *ṣādir*, a. Happened, issued, produced, passed, etc. A.

صاف *ṣāf*, a. Clean, pure, candid, frank, etc. A.

صافي *ṣāfī*, s.f. A filter, strainer.

صبا *ṣabā*, s.m. Morning, dawn; to-morrow; the morning breeze. A. (*ṣabāḥ*).

صبح *ṣubḥ*, s.f. Morning, daybreak, dawn. A.

صبر *ṣabr*, s.m. Endurance, patience. A.

صحاف *ṣaḥḥāf*, s.m. A bookbinder; bookseller. A.

صحبت *ṣuḥbat*, s.m. Companionship, society; picnic, dinner party, company; cohabitation; coition. A.

صحت *ṣiḥḥat*, s.m. Health, integrity, perfection. A.

صحرا *ṣaḥrā*, s.f. A desert, wilderness. A.

صحي *ṣaḥī*, a. Accurate, true, just, certain, perfect, entire. A. (*ṣaḥīḥ*).

صداقت *ṣadāqat*, s.m. Sincerity, truthfulness, candour, friendship. A.

صدقه *ṣadqa*, s.f. Alms, propitiatory offerings, sacrifice. A.

صديق *ṣadīq*, a. Faithful, true, sincere, just. A.

صراف *ṣarrāf*, s.m. A banker, money lender. A.

صرف *ṣirf*, ad. Only, alone; simply, merely,

etc. A. *ṣarf*, s.m. Excess, gain, increase; expense, expenditure, waste. A.

صرفه *ṣarfa*, s.f. Expense, expending; profit, profusion; surplus; waste. A.

صف *ṣaff*, s.m. A line, file, rank, row; series, order, etc. A.

صفا *ṣafā*, a. Clean, clear, pure. A.

صفائي *ṣafā-ī*, s.f. Purity, cleanness; innocence. A.

صفت *ṣifat*, s.m. Attribute, quality; commendation, praise; description; an adjective. A.

صفحه *ṣafḥa*, s.f. Page of a book; face, surface. A.

صفره *ṣafara*, s.f. Name of the second month of the Muḥammadan calendar. A. (*ṣafar*).

صلحه *ṣulḥa*, s.f. Concord, peace; reconciliation, truce, treaty, armistice. A. (*ṣulḥ*).

صلوة *ṣalāt*, } s.m. Benediction, prayer;
صلات *ṣalāt*, } mercy or compassion of God. A.

صندل *ṣandal*, s.m. Sandal wood. A.

صندوق *ṣandūq*, s.m. A box, trunk, chest, casket. A.

صندوقچه *ṣandūqcha*, s.f. Casket, small box.

صنوبر *ṣanobar*, s.m. A fir, pine, conifer. A.

صواب *ṣawāb*, s.m. Virtuous action; rectitude, right. A.

صوبه *ṣūba*, s.f. A province, division of a country. A. *ṣūba-dār*, s.m. Viceroy, provincial governor.

صورت *ṣūrat*, s.m. Appearance, form, face; portrait, countenance; manner; case, condition, state; body, person; the privates. A.

صوفي *ṣūfī*, a. Pious, devout; intelligent, wise. s.m. A philosopher, members of the Sūfī sect. A.

صياد *ṣayād*, s.m. A hunter, fowler, sportsman A.

صيد *ṣaid*, s.m. Game, prey. A.

صيقل *ṣaiqal*, s.m. Cleaning, polishing, scouring, furbishing; a polisher, etc. A.

صيقلگر *ṣaiqal-gar*, s.m. A polisher of swords, knives, etc.

ض

ض *dwād* or *ẓād*, is the fifteenth letter of the Arabic, and the twenty-fifth of the Pukkhto alphabet. It is pronounced like ز, and is only found in words from the Arabic, in which language it has the sound of *d* or *dh*.

ضابط *ẓābit*, s.m. Master, ruler, governor. A.

ضابطه *ẓābiṭa*, s.f. Canon law, rule, regulation. A.

ضامن *ẓāmin*, s.m. Security, sponsor, bail, bond. A.

ضامني *ẓāminī*, s.f. Surety, bail, security.

ضايعه *ẓāy'a*, s.f. Loss, detriment, injury. *ẓāy'ah*, a. Lost, destroyed, spoiled, perished; fruitless, abortive. A. (*ẓāī'*).

ضبط *ẓabt*, s.m. Confiscation; check, control. a. Confiscated, seized. A.

ضحا *ẓuḥā*, s.m. Forenoon, between sunrise and noon; a prayer repeated at that time. A.

ضد *ẓidd*, s.m. Contrary, opposite; enemy, rival; opposition, contrariety. A.

ضرب *ẓarb*, s.m. A blow, thump; coining; stamp; violence; emphasis (in speech). A.

ضرر *ẓarar*, s.m. Damage, detriment, injury; loss, ruin; affliction, distress. A.

ضرور *ẓarūr*, a. Expedient, necessary; urgent, unavoidable. A.

ضرورت *ẓarūrat*, s.m. Necessity, exigence, want; compulsion, force. A.

ضعف *ẓu'f*, s.m. Debility, weakness. A.

ضعيف *ẓa'īf*, a. Weak, feeble, infirm. A.

ضلعه *ẓil'a*, s.f. A district, division of a province. A.

ضماد *z̤amād*, s.m. Embrocation, plaister, A.

ضمانت *z̤amānat*, s.m. Security, bail, surety. A.

ضيافت *z̤iyāfat*, s.m. Banquet, entertainment, feast; invitation, hospitality. A.

ط

ط *t̤oe* is the sixteenth letter of the Arabic and the twenty-sixth of the Pukkhto alphabet. It is only found in words adopted from the Arabic, and has a sound stronger than ت, for which it sometimes changed.

طابوت *t̤ābūt*, s.m. A coffin, bier. A.

طاعت *t̤ā'at*, s.m. Obedience, devotion. A.

طاق *t̤āq*, s.m. An arch, cupola; alcove, shelf. a. Odd, singular, unique, not even. A. *juft-o-t̤āq*, s.m. Odd and even (the game).

طاقچه *t̤āqcha*, s.f. A niche, recess, shelf.

طاقت *t̤āqat*, s.m. Ability, force, power, strength. A.

طاقي *t̤āqī*, a. Arched, arching.

طالب *t̤ālib*, s.m. An enquirer, seeker; student. Asking, demanding. A.

طالع *t̤āli'*, s.m. Appearing, rising (as the sun). A. *t̤āli'-man*, a. Fortunate, prosperous.

طائفه *t̤ā-ifa*, s.f. People, nation, race, tribe; party, band, troop; suite, equipage. A.

طب *t̤ibb*, s.m. Medicine, magic. A.

طبابت *t̤ibābat*, s.m. The practice of medicine. A.

طباق *t̤abāq*, s.m. A kneading dish or platter. A.

طبعه *t̤ab'a*, s.f. Disposition, temperament, nature, quality. A. (*t̤ab'*).

طبق *t̤abaq*, s.m. A dish, plate; leaf; disk; cover; a layer; gold leaf. A.

طبقه *t̤abqa*, s.f. A floor, stage, story; class, order; degree, rank; a shelf, recess. A.

طبل *t̤abl*, s.m. A drum. A.

طبله *t̤abla*, s.f. A small tambourine, small drum; a wooden platter or tray for fruit, etc. A.

طبيب *t̤abīb*, s.m. A physician. A

طبيبي *t̤abībī*, s.f. Profession of a physician, physic. A.

طبيعت *t̤abī'at*, s.m. Nature, disposition, temper; constitution, health; property, quality, essence. A.

طبيله *t̤abela*, s.f. A stable. A.

طرب *t̤rab*, s.m. Hilarity, mirth, joy. A.

طرحه *t̤arḥa*, s.f. Manner, mode. A. (*t̤araḥ*).

طرز *t̤arz*, s.m. Fashion, mode, manner. A.

طرف *t̤araf*, s.m. Side, direction, quarter. A. *t̤araf-dār*, s.m. A follower, partizan. a. Partial, prejudicial. *t̤araf-dārī*, s.f. Favour, assistance; prejudice.

طرفين *t̤arafain*, s.m. Both sides, both parties. A.

طريقه *t̤arīqa*, s.f. Path, way; manner, mode; religion, rite; sect, party; custom, habit. A.

طعام *t̤a'ām*, s.m. Food, victuals; eating. A.

طعامبه *t̤a'āmba*, s.f. Food, victuals.

طعنه *t̤a'na*, s.f. Reproach, disgrace, reproof; scoffing, reviling, taunting. A. (*t̤a'n*).

طغيان *t̤ug̠hiyān*, s.m. Rebellion, sedition; perverseness, insolence. *t̤ug̠hiyānī*, s.f. Excess, overflowing, flood. A.

طفل *t̤ifl*, s.m. Babe, infant. A. *t̤iflī* or *t̤ufūliyat*, s.m. Infancy, childhood. A.

طفيل *t̤ufail*, s.m. Sponger, parasite, glutton. A. ad. Through, by means of, by agency of. A.

طلا *t̤ilā*, s.f. Gold; name of a gold coin, ducat. A.

طلاق *t̤ilāq*, s.m. Divorce, repudiation. A.

طلاي *t̤ilā-ī*, a. Golden, covered with gold. A.

طلب *t̤alab*, s.m. Demand, desire, request; call, summons; enquiry, search; pay, salary, A. *t̤alab-dār*, s.m. A credit dunning, demanding. *t̤alab-gār*, s.m. A seeker, enquirer. a. Desirous. *ṯalab-nāma*, s.f. A summons, citation.

طلبه *ṯalaba*, s.f. A lure, call, etc. for hawks, etc.

طلسم *ṯilism*, s.m. Amulet, charm, spell, talisman; marvel, wonder, prodigy. A.

طمعه *ṯam'a*, s.f. Avidity; desire, longing; avarice, greediness, covetousness. A. (*ṯam'*).

طناب *ṯanāb*, s.m. Tent rope, clothes line, cord, etc. A.

طور *ṯaur*, s.m. Manner, mode; condition, state. A.

طوفان *ṯūfān*, s.m. Deluge, inundation; tempest, storm, hurricane. A. *ṯūfānī*, a. Boisterous, stormy; quarrelsome.

طوق *ṯauq*, s.m. Yoke, collar; necklace; ring for the neck. A.

طول *ṯūl*, s.m. Length. a. Long, lasting. A.

طومار *ṯūmār*, s.m. A book, volume. A.

طهارت *ṯahārat*, s.m. Purity, cleanliness; sancity; purification. A.

طي *ṯai*, s.m. Folding, rolling up. A.

ظ

ظ *zoe* is the seventeenth letter of the Arabic and the twenty-seventh of the Pukkhto alphabet. It is only found in words from the Arabic.

ظالم *ẕālim*, s.m. Oppressor, tyrant. a. Cruel, oppressive, tyrannical. A.

ظاهر *ẕāhir*, a. Manifest, apparent, evident, clear; outward appearance.

ظاهرا *ẕāhirā*, ظاهراً *ẕāhiran*, ad. Outwardly, apparently, publicly, openly, evidently. A.

ظاهري *ẕāhirī*, a. Outward, external, apparent. A.

ظرافت *ẕarāfat*, s.m. Elegance; politeness; wit, humour; polish. A.

ظرف *ẕarf*, s.m. A vase, vessel, jar. a. Witty, ingenious. A.

ظريف *ẕarīf*, a. Witty, jocose; ingenious, clever; elegant, polished, polite. A.

ظفر *ẕafar*, s.m. Victory, triumph. A.

ظلم *ẕulm*, s.m. Oppression, injustice, cruelty, tyranny. A.

ظلمت *ẕulmat*, s.m. Obscurity, darkness. A.

ظن *ẕann*, s.m. Idea, thought, opinion; suspicion, jealousy. A.

ظنّي *ẕannī*, a. Supposed; suspected. A.

ظهر *ẕuhr*, s.m. Mid-day; the time just after the sun has passed the meridian. A.

ع

ع *'ain* is the eighteenth letter of the Arabic and the twenty-eighth of the Pukkhto alphabet. It is a very weak guttural aspirate, articulated by compression of the muscles of the fauces. It varies in sound according to the vowel point by which it is "moved," and in this work is represented by ' placed above and before the vowel by which it is "moved," as *'a*, *'i*, *'u*, etc. It is only found in words derived from the Arabic, and is sometime replaced by ا.

عابد *'ābid*, s.m. A devotee, votary. A.

عاجز *'ājiz*, a. Humble, helpless; hopeless, dejected; exhausted, weak; impotent, powerless. A.

عاجزي *'ājizī*, s.m. Weakness; helplessness; humility.

عادت *'ādat*, s.m. Custom, usage, habit. A. *'ādatī*, a. Habituated, accustomed, inured, addicted.

عادل *'ādil*, a. Just, upright, impartial. A.

عارف *'ārif*, a. Devout, holy; wise, ingenious. A.

عاريت *'āriyat*, s.m. Borrowing, lending (what is itself to be returned). A. *'āriyatī*, a. Borrowed; lent.

عاشق *'ā<u>sh</u>iq*, s.m. A lover. A. *'ā<u>sh</u>iqī*, s.f. Amour, love, courtship.

عاشوره *'ā<u>sh</u>ora*, s.f. The first ten days of the month Muḥarram. A.

عاصي *'āṣī*, s.m. A sinner, rebel. A.

عافيت *'āfiyat*, s.m. Health, safety. A.

عاقبت *'āqibat*, s.m. Conclusion, end; futurity, the future. ad. After all, finally, at last. A.

عاقل *'āqil*, a. Sensible, wise. A.

عالم *'ālam*, s.m. The world, universe; people, mankind, creation; time, state. A. *'ālim*, a. Learned, knowing, wise. A.

عالي *'ālī*, a. Eminent, high, sublime. A.

عام *'āmm*, a. Common, general, public. s.m. The vulgar, public, common people. A.

عامّي *'āmmī*, s.m. A layman; one of the public.

عامل *'āmil*, s.m. Revenue collector, governor, ruler, finance minister. A.

عائد *'ā-id*, a. Happening, occurring; reverting, returning (as money, etc.). A.

عبادت *'ibādat*, s.m. Adoration, divine worship. A.

عبارت *'ibārat*, s.m. Meaning, signification; phrase, style, speech. A.

عبث *'abaṣ*, a. Vain, useless, absurd, idle. ad. In vain, uselessly. A.

عبرت *'ibrat*, s.m. Example, warning. A.

عبور *'ubūr*, s.m. A ferry, ford; crossing, passing over. A.

عتاب *'itāb*, s.m. Anger, displeasure, rebuke, reproach, reprimand. A.

عجائب *'ajā-ib*, a. Wonderful, astonishing. s.m. Wonders, curiosities. A.

عجب *'ajab*, عجيب *'ajīb*, } a. Wonderful, rare, curious. A.

عجز *'ajz*, s.m. Impotence, weakness, helplessness; meekness, humility, submission. A.

عدالت *'adālat*, s.m. A court of justice; equity, justice; law. A.

عداوت *'adāwat*, s.m. Animosity, enmity, hostility, hatred, strife. A.

عدد *'adad*, s.m. Number; item. A.

عدل *'adl*, s.m. Justice, equity. A.

عدم *'adam*, s.m. Nonexistence, nonentity; nothing; privation. A.

عدول *'udūl*, s.m. Refusing, declining. A.

عذاب *'azāb*, s.m. Anguish, torment, pain; torture, punishment. A.

عذر *'uzr*, s.m. Apology, excuse. A. *'uzr·<u>kh</u>wāh*, s.m. Apologist; condoler, sympathizer. P. *'uzr·<u>kh</u>wāhī*, s.f. Apology, excuse; condolence, sympathy. P.

عرس *'urs*, s.m. Oblations, offerings (to a saint); a marriage feast. A.

عرش *'ar<u>sh</u>*, s.m. Firmament; roof; throne. A.

عرصه *'arṣa*, s.f. Area, space; interval, while, time; a plain. A.

عرض *'arẓ*, s.m. Petition, request, representation. A. *'arẓ·begī*, s.m. An officer who presents petitions, letters, etc. (in native courts). T. *'arẓ·dā<u>sh</u>t*, s.m. Statement, written petition. P. *'arẓ·dār*, s.m. A petitioner. P. *'araẓ*, s.m. An accident, casualty; muster of troops. A.

عرضي *'arẓī*, s.f. A memorial, petition; letter from an inferior. A.

عرف *'urf*, a. Known as, alias, commonly called; the late; proper, equitable; goodness, merit; confession. A.

عرفي *'urfī*, a. Notorious, well-known, public. A.

عرق *'arq*, s.m. Essence, juice; spirit; sap; sweat. A.

عروس *'arūs*, s.m. Bridegroom, spouse. A. *'arūsa*, s.f. Bride. *'arūsī*, s.f. Marriage, wedding. A.

عزت *'izzat*, s.m. Grandeur, power; glory; honour, respect. A.

عزلت *'azlat*, s.m. Retirement (from office), dismissal, discharge. A.

عزلتي *'azlatī*, s.m. A hermit, recluse. A.

عزلي *'azlī*, s.f. Abdication, retirement. A.

عزم *'azm*, s.m. Purpose, intention, design. A.

عزيز *'azīz*, a. Dear, beloved, precious. s.m. An esteemed or honoured friend; great man, saint; a nephew; a king of Egypt (the title). A.

عزيزگلوي *'azīz·galwī*, عزيزولي *'azīz·walī*, s.m. Relationship between nephew and uncles.

عزيزي *'azīzī*, s.f. Esteem, respect, friendship.

عسل *'asl*, s.m. Honey. A.

عشر *'ushr*, s.m. Tithe, tenth part. A.

عشرت *'ashrat*, s.m. Enjoyment, pleasure, delight; society, pleasant intercourse, etc. A.

عشق *'ishq*, s.m. Affection, love. A. *'ishq·bāz*, a. Amorous, gallant. P. *'ishq·bāzī*, s.f. Love-making, gallantry. P.

عصا *'aṣā*, s.f. A club, mace, baton, staff. A.

عطا *'aṭā*, s.f. A gift, present; giving. A.

عطار *'aṭṭār*, s.m. A perfumer. A.

عطر *'aṭr*, s.m. Perfume, fragrance, essence. A.

عظيم *'aẓīm*, a. Great, huge, immense; high in dignity. A.

عفريت *'ifrīt*, s.m. Demon, spectre, ghost. A.

عقب *aqab*, ad. After, behind, in rear. A.

عقد *'aqd*, s.m. Agreement, compact, contract; knot; marriage knot; necklace, collar. A.

عقل *'aql*, s.m. Reason, sense; intellect, wisdom; opinion, understanding. A. *'aql·man*, a. Intelligent, wise. P. *'aql·manī*, s.f. Wisdom, intelligence. P.

عقلي *'aqlī*, a. Judicious, rational, sensible, reasonable. A.

عقوبت *'uqūbat*, s.m. Punishment, torture. A.

عقيده *'aqīda*, s.f. Belief, faith, tenet. A.

عكس *'aks*, s.m. Contrary, opposite; reflection, inversion; image, shadow. A.

علاج *'ilāj*, s.m. Cure, remedy; medicine. A.

علاقه *'ilāqa*, s.f. Relation, connection, interest; commerce, correspondence, intercourse. A.

علامت *'alāmat*, s.m. Mark, sign, symptom; emblem, ensign, escutcheon. A.

علاوه *'alāwa*, ad. Besides, in addition. A.

علت *'illat*, s.m. Cause, pretence; dirt, filth; defect, disease. A.

علف *'alaf*, s.m. Grass, hay, fodder. A.

علم *'ilm*, s.m. Knowledge, science. A.

علما *'ulamā*, s.m. The learned, scholars, wise. A.

علمي *'ilmī*, a. Learned, scientific. A.

علي *'alī*, a. Eminent, high, noble. A. *'alī bau·bau*, s.m. A bogy, goblin, scarecrow.

عليحده *'alaiḥidah*, a. Apart, separate, distinct. A.

عليم *'alīm*, a. Learned, wise. A.

عمارت *'imārat*, s.m. Building, edifice; habitation, fortification. A.

عمده *'umdah*, a. Great, noble; choice, excellent. A.

عمر *'umr*, s.m. Age, lifetime. A.

عمل *'amal*, s.m. Action, operation, effect; work, practice. A.

عمله *'amala*, s.f. Officials, staff, subordinates. A.

عملي *'amalī*, a. Practical, artificial. A.

عناب *'unnāb*, s.m. Jujube fruit and tree. A.

عناد *'inād*, s.m. Obstinacy, perverseness, stubbornness. A. *'inādī*, a. Stubborn, obstinate, etc.

عنايت *'ināyat*, s.m. Favour, gift, present. A.

عنقا *'unqā*, s.f. The phœnix. A.

عنقريب *'anqarīb*, ad. Nearly, shortly, soon. A.

عنكبوت *'ankabūt*, s.m. A spider. A.

عود *'ūd*, s.m. Aloes wood; incense. A.

عورت *'aurat*, s.m. The private parts. A.

8

عورته *'aurata,* s.f. A woman, wife.

عوض *'iwaẓ,* s.m. Retribution, recompense, reward; exchange. A.

عهد *'ahd,* s.m. Compact, contract; promise, treaty; conjuncture, season, time; reign, life-time; oath, vow. A.

عهده *'uhda,* s.f. Commission, obligation, agreement; appointment, office, post. A.

عيال *'ayāl,* s.m. Family, children; household, domestics, etc. A.

عيان *'ayān,* a. Clear, visible, manifest. A.

عيب *'aib,* s.m. Blemish, defect, vice; disgrace, fault, sin. A. *'aib-nāk,* a. Defective, faulty.

عيد *'īd,* s.m. Festival, holy day; Easter. A.

عيش *'aish,* s.m. Enjoyment, delight, pleasure. A. *'aish-o-'ashrat,* s.m. Jollity, enjoyment. A.

عين *'ain,* a. Exact, just, very, real, etc. s.m. The eye; sight; essence. A.

عينکه *'ainaka,* s.f. An eyeglass, spectacles. A. (*'ainak*).

غ

غ *ghain,* is the nineteenth letter of the Arabic, and the twenty-ninth of the Pukkhto alphabet. It is a guttural letter, and is pronounced by a compression of the fauces at the time of articulation. It is sometimes used instead of ق, and is itself sometimes replaced by ګ.

غاب *ghāb,* s.m. A dish, plate. A. (*qāb*).

غار *ghār,* s.m. A cave, cavern, pit. A.

غارت *ghārat,* s.m. Devastation, plunder, sack. A.

غارمه *ghārmah,* s.m. Sun's rays; heat of the sun; noonday heat. P. (*garma*).

غارندوني *ghārandūnai,* s.m. A kind of lizard, the iguana.

غاري *ghārai,* s.m. A glutton.

غاړه *ghāṛa,* s.f. The throat, fauces; coast, shore; border, bank, margin; neck of a bottle or jar; joke, pleasantry, fun. *ghāṛa-ghara-ī,* s.f. Embracing, hugging. a. Connected, joined together.

غازي *ghāzī,* s.m. Champion, hero, warrior (for the faith), crescentader. A.

غاښ *ghākkh,* s.m. A tooth.

غاښور *ghākkhawar,* s.m. Having large teeth; a kind of harrow or rake.

غاښي *ghākkhai,* s.m. A prong, pitchfork; crest or ridge of a mountain, pass over a mountain.

غافل *ghāfil,* a. Careless, negligent, thoughtless. A.

غالب *ghālab,* s.m. A form, mould. A. (*qālib*). *ghālib,* a. Excelling, overcoming, superior. ad. Most likely.

غالبوزه *ghālbūza,* s.f. A hornet, wasp.

غال وبول *ghāl-o-būl,*
غال وغول *ghāl-o-ghūl,* } s.m. Clamour, uproar, noise, din.

غالي *ghāla-ī,*
غاليچه *ghālīcha,* } s.f. A rug, small carpet. A.

غانده *ghāndah,* a. Disagreeable, offensive, loathsome, stinking. P. (*gandah*).

غاو *ghāw,* s.m. Noise, din, uproar, tumult.

غاوچي *ghāwchī,* s.m. Doorkeeper, porter.

غائب *ghā-ib,* a. Absent, invisible, concealed. A

غايت *ghāyat,* a. Very, chiefly, extremely. s.m. Extremity, end; filth, ordure, dirt. A.

غبار *ghubār,* s.m. Dust, haze, obscurity, vapour; impurity, foulness. A.

غبرګ *ghbarg,* a. Double, duplex, twofold.

غبغب *ghab-ghab,* s.m. Dewlap, double-chin. P.

غپ *ghap,* s.m. Bark, yelp, snap (of a dog).

غپل *ghapal,* v.a. To bark, snap, yelp, etc.

غپه *ghupa,* s.f. A dip, dive, plunge.

غټ *ghaṭ*, a. Big, bulky, large, stout, great, etc.; great in rank, power, etc. H. (*kaṭṭā*).

غټي *ghaṭai*, s.m. A block, lump, mass, etc.

غڅکي *ghutskai*, s.m. A bullock, ox, bull.

غچ *ghach*, s.m. Hatred, malice, spite, envy. Noise, sound of walking in mud, etc. H.

غچي *ghachī*, s.f. Scissors. See بياتي.

غدر *ghadar*, s.m. Villany, deceit, perfidy. A.

غذا *ghizā*, s.m. Aliment, food, diet. A.

غر *ghar*, s.m. Mountain, hill. S. (*gir*). *ghur*, s.m. Bronchocele, goitre. *gha-ar*, s.m. Leap, bound, jump. Rattle (as of wheels).

غرا *gharā*, s.f. Peal, roar, boom, thunder; roaring, thundering (noise).

غراره *gharāra*, s.f. A large sack. A.

غرانډه *gharānḍa*, s.f. A blaze, flame.

غربت *ghurbat*, s.m. Emigration, travelling; exile, separation from friends. A.

غربه *gharaba*, s.f. A cannon, gun.

غربي *gharabbai*, s.m. Boom, report (of a cannon). A buckle, breastplate, clasp.

غرپ *ghurap*, s.m. A gulp. P.

غرپش *ghurpish*, s.m. Din, clamour, noise, row.

غرڅني *ghartsanai*, a. Mountain, highland, of the hills.

غرڅه *ghartsah*, a. A hill goat; inhabitant of the hills, highland (animal).

غرزنگ *ghurzang*, s.m. A bound, leap. P.

غرض *gharaẓ*, s.m. Aim, object, design, purpose; business, meaning, interest, occasion, use, want; spite, selfishness, hatred. ad. In fine, in short, in a word.

غرغړه *gharghaṛa*, s.f. Gurgling, a gurgle. A. A blaze, flame, fire.

غرغشت *gharghusht*, s.m. Romping, frolic, fun, sport; a play amongst women. *ghurghusht*, s.m. Name of the third son of Kais. *ghurghushtī*, s.m. The Ghurghushtis, clan or tribe of Ghurghusht.

غرغشتي *gharghashtī*, s.f. A kind of peach (*Amygdalus Persicus*).

غرق *gharq*, a. Drowned, sunk, immersed. A.

غرقاب *gharqāb*, s.m. A whirlpool, vortex. P.

غرکمانه *ghur·kamāna*, s.f. A pellet bow. P. (*golā*). P. (*kamān*).

غرگي *ghargai*, s.m. Boulder, rock; stone, pebble; hillock, mound.

غرمه *gharma*, s.f. Noon, mid-day, hottest part of the day. *ṭakanḍa*-, *ṭakanṛa*-, or *ṭakana-ī·gharma*, s.f. Exactly noon, hottest time of the day.

غرند *ghrand*, s.m. The neck, throat, windpipe. P. (*gardan*).

غرندي *ghrandai*, s.m. The hollow over the collar bone.

غرنگ *gharang*, s.m. The creaking of a wheel.

غرنيکه *ghar·nīkah*, s.m. A great grandfather.

غروب *ghurūb*, s.m. The west; setting (of the sun). A.

غرور *ghurūr*, s.m. Pride, vanity. A.

غروړي *ghurūṛai*, s.m. A node, tumour.

غره *gharah*, a. Haughty, arrogant, proud, vain: deceived, misled; cross, stern. A. *ghara*, s.f. Backside, podex. *ghurra*, s.f. First day of the moon; whiteness. A.

غري *gharai*, s.m. The throat. See غرند.

غريابښه *ghuryākkha*, s.f. } A button hole, loop.
غريابښي *ghuryākkhai*, s.m. } See پلوابښه.

غريب *gharīb*, a. Meek, humble; poor; foreign, strange. A.

غريدل *gharedal*, v.n. To chatter, gabble, jabber; to bellow, roar; peal, boom, thunder.

غريز *gharīz*, s.m. Clemency, forbearance. P.

غريو *gharew*, s.m. Noise, hum, murmur; lamentation, groaning, weeping. P.

غړانگه *ghaṛānga*, s.f. A shout, scream, yell; a long neck. *ghaṛānga·war*, a. Longnecked.

غړڅکي *ghuṛutskai*, s.m. A spark. See بڅري.

غړل *gharal*, v.a. To plait, spin, twist, roll; to fold, roll up, envelop. See غښتل.

غړنب *ghurunb*, s.m. Boom, peal, roar, thunder, etc.

غړنبل *ghranbal*, v.n. } To bellow, roar, low;
غړنبيدل *ghranbedal*, } to peal, thunder, boom.

غړند *gharand*, a. Lax, loose; frail, soft, weak; idle, lazy, negligent; tardy, slow; cautious, stealthy, sly.

غړوندي *gharwandai*, s.f. A dog collar, halter, tether for horses; a loop, slip knot; the loop in the letters ټ, ډ, ړ.

غړي *gharai*, s.m. A kind of coarse bread given to the poor; the calf of the leg.

غړيدل *gharedal*, v.n. To growl, snarl; to grate, jar (upon the ear); to blow, wheeze, breathe roughly.

غز *ghaz*, s.m. The Tamarisk tree (*Tamarix Indica*).

غزا *ghazā*, s.f. War against infidels, crescentade. in. Astonishing! A.

غزار *ghuzār*, a. Dropped, fallen, upset.

غزل *ghazal*, s.m. An ode, love song. A.

غزول *ghazawul*, v.a. To lay flat, lay down, prostrate, stretch out (as the arm, leg, etc.).

غزيدل *ghazedal*, v.n. To lie down, lie flat, recline, etc. Also *gazedal*.

غږ *ghag*, s.m. Noise, sound, voice, etc.

غږول *ghagawul*, v.a. To sound, make a noise, etc.

غږيدل *ghagedal*, v.n. To sound, resound, vibrate, etc.

غسل *ghusl*, s.m. Ablution, bathing. A.

غشايه *ghushāyah*, s.m. pl. of غشوئي.

غشو *ghasho*, s.m. A curry comb.

غشوئي *ghushoe*, s.m. Dung of cows and buffaloes.

غشي *ghashai*, s.m. An arrow; spoke of a wheel; pole or shaft of a cart, plough, etc. a. Direct, swift, straight.

غښتل *ghakkhtal*, v.a. To plait, twist; roll, fold, envelop. Def. in pres. ten. See غړل.

غصب *ghasab*, } s.m. Compulsion, force; op-
غضب *ghazab*, } pression, violence; plunder; passion, vengeance, wrath. A.

غصه *ghussa*, s.f. Anger, passion. A.

غفلت *ghaflat*, s.m. Negligence, carelessness. A.

غفور *ghafūr*, a. Merciful, forgiving. A.

غل *ghal*, s.m. A thief, robber. *ghul*, s.m. Dung, excrement, fæces.

غلا *ghlā*, s.f. Robbery, theft.

غلاف *ghilāf*, s.m. A case, cover, sheath. A.

غلام *ghulām*, s.m. A slave. A.

غلانزه *ghulānza*, s.f. Udder, mammary gland.

غلبله *ghalbala*, s.f. Noise, uproar, tumult.

غلبه *ghalaba*, s.f. Advantage, superiority assault; prevalence; strength. A.

غلبيل *ghalbel*, s.m. A colander, sieve; sifting winnowing. P. (*ghirbāl*).

غلت *ghulat*, s.m. Cheat, trick, deceit (a play). *ghulatī*, s.f. Swindling, cheating.

غلط *ghalat*, s.m. Error, mistake. a. Wrong, mistaken. A.

غلغله *ghulghula*, s.f. Tumult, row, disturbance, etc. P.

غلوزه *ghlawza*, s.f. A honey bee. See لوزه.

غلول *ghulawul*, v.a. To deceive, dupe, mislead. H. (*ghūlānā*).

غله *ghalla*, s.f. Corn, grain. A.

غلي *ghalai*, a. Concealed, hidden; silent, still; sneaking, stealthy. *ghulai*, s.m. A whirlpool, eddy, vortex; a bubble.

غليم *ghalīm*, s.m. A robber; enemy. A. (*ghanīm*). *ghalīmī*, s.f. Animosity, hatred, enmity.

غم *gham*, s.m. Anxiety, sorrow, grief. A. *gham-jan*, a. Grieved, sorrowful.

غمّاز *ghammāz*, s.m. Informer, tale-bearer. A. *ghammāzī*, s.f. Backbiting, tale-bearing.

غماشه *ghamāsha*, s f. A gnat, musquito.

غمبه *ghumba*, s.f. A gland, bubo, tumour.

غمزه *ghamza*, s.f. A wink, glance; ogling. A.

غمي *ghamai*, s.m. The stone of a ring; a seal; ferule of a knife handle, etc.

غميدل *ghamedal*, v.n. To fret, chafe, worry; to be overcome, subdued, conquered.

غنا *ghanā*, s.f. Riches, wealth. A.

غنچه *ghuncha*, s.f. A bud, sprout; a bunch. P.

غنډ *ghundi*, a. See غونډ.

غندل *ghandal*, s.f. A sprout, shoot; young shoots of mustard and other plants used as potherbs. *ghandal*, v.a. To disparage, run down, find fault with; to dislike, disapprove, disrelish.

غنډاري *ghunḍārai*, s.m. A noose, snare for birds (formed of a hair loop fixed to a lump of clay); a phlegmon, carbuncle; a disease in cows, etc.

غنډايه *ghunḍāyah*, s.m. A lad, youth, stripling; a boor, clodhopper, country bumpkin.

غنډهاري *ghunḍhārai*, s.m. See غنډاري.

غنزاښه *ghunzākkha*, s.f. A kind of sweet cake made of flour and sugar, fried in butter.

غنزاښي *ghunzākkhai*, s.m. An instrument for separating the seeds of cotton from the fibre.

غنم *ghanum*, s.m. Wheat. P. (*gandum*).

غنه *ghana*, s.f. A thorny bush, branch of a thorny tree. pl. *ghane*, thorns, bramble.

غني *ghanī*, a. Wealthy, rich. A.

غنيمت *ghanīmat*, s.m. Plunder; abundance; good fortune, boon. A.

غنړه *ghanṛa*, s.f. A kind of spider, the tarantula (*Lycosa tarantula*).

غو *gho*, s.m. Copulation, coition.

غوا *ghwā*, s.f. A cow. S. and P. (*gāw*).

غواښكي *ghwākkhkai*, s.m. The notch in the head of an arrow.

غوباړي *ghobāṛai*, s.m. A horsefly, gadfly.

غوبل *ghobal*, s.m. Treading out corn by driving cattle over it; threshing.

غوبني *ghobanī*, s.f. Cowherding, tending cattle.

غوبه *ghobah*, s.m. A cowherd, grazier of cows.

غوپه *ghopa*, s.f. A dive, dip, plunge; dipping, submersion, immersion.

غوټ *ghūṭ*, a. Docked, clipped, cut short.

غوټه *ghoṭa*, s.f. A dip, dive, plunge; dipping, immersion; a clutch, snatch, swoop; a fit, paroxysm, convulsion. A. (*ghoṭā*). *ghūṭa*, s.f. An articulation, joint, knot; band, strap; group, party (of horsemen.)

غوټي *ghūṭai*, a. Docked, cropped, cut short. s.m. A horse with a docked tail, dog with cut ears, man with an amputated limb, tree with the boughs cut off, etc. *ghūṭa-ī*, s.f. A rose-bud, a bud; a globule, drop, bubble; a button, knot, jewelled flower, etc.

غوجل *ghojal*, s.f. A cow-shed, cow-pen.

غوځ *ghwats*, a. Cut, divided, incised.

غوچه *ghūcha*, in. Ho! Hallo! I say!

غور *ghaur*, s.m. Reflection, thought, meditation, care, attention. A.

غوراسكي *ghwarāskai*, s.m. Name of a shrub (*Dodonæa Burmanniana*).

غورزول *ghwarzawul*, v.a. To fling, pitch, project; to cast off, throw away.

غورزيدل *ghwarzedal*, v.n. To palpitate, toss, flutter, bound, etc.

غوره *ghūrah*, s.m. A cotton pod; unripe dates or grapes. P. *ghwarah*, a. Choice, good, excellent, preferable. P. (*gawārah*).

غوړ *ghwaṛ*, s.m. Fat, grease, suet. a. Oily, greasy, fatty, unctuous.

غوړپكه *ghoṛpaka*, s.f. Calamity, accident; event, occurrence; cry of distress.

غوړول *ghwaṛawul*, v.a. To unclose, open (the

eyes); **distend, inflate,** spread. *ghwaṛawul,* v.a. To anoint, grease, oil, lubricate, etc.

غوړي *ghwaṛī,* s.m. Butter, grease, tallow, *ghī.*

غوړيدل *ghwaṛedal,* v.n. To germinate, sprout, grow, expand, spread, open, unfold, etc.

غوړيژه *ghwaṛeja,* s.f. Name of a plant (*Indigofera Gerardiana*).

غوز *ghoz,* s.m. The fat of the kidneys; flatus, wind from the belly. P.

غوزکرکي *ghozakarkai,* s.m. A dung beetle.

غوزه *ghoza,* s.f. Pod, capsule, cocoon, shell, etc. P. (*ghoja*).

غوزي *ghūzai,* s.m. Bosom, embrace, arms; armful; lap. P. (*āghosh*). *ghozai,* s.m. A kind of black beetle.

غوږ *ghwag,* s.m. The ear; screw of a violin. P. (*gosh*).

غوږي *ghwagai,* s.m. A floodgate, lock, sluice; the horn end of a bow; key of a violin; streak of sunlight through clouds.

غوشاک *ghoshāk,* s.m. Fresh cowdung.

غوښت *ghokkht,* s.m. Italian millet (*Panicum Italicum*). Desire, request, want, wish. P. (*khwāst*).

غوښتل *ghokkhtal,* v.a. To solicit, request, desire, wish, want. P. (*khwāstan, khwāh-*).

غوښه *ghwakkha,* s.f. Flesh, meat. P. (*gosht*). *ghwakkha-war,* a. Fleshy, stout, plump.

غوښي *ghokkhai,* s.m. See غوږي.

غوغا *ghoghā,* s.f. Clamour, din, noise, etc. P.

غول *ghūl,* s.m. An imaginary demon of the woods, man-wolf, loup-garou. A. *ghol,* s.m. Party, crowd, gang; corps, troop, company; flock, flight (of birds). H. (*gol*).

غولونکي *gholawunkai,* s.m. A stye on the eyelid.

غوله کمانه *ghola-kamāna,* s.f. See غرکمانه.

غولي *gholai,* s.m. Area, yard, court. *ghola-ī,* s.f. A small party, gang; small flock (of birds).

غوند *ghūnd,* a. Alike, similar.

غوندِ *ghūndi,* / غوندې *ghūnde,* ad. As if, as it were, just as, etc.

غوندي *ghūndai,* s.m. A bag, pannier or sack of goat's hair (for carrying loads upon camels, bullocks, etc.). S. (*gon*).

غونډ *ghūnḍ,* a. Round, globular, circular; plump, squat; lumpy. s.m. A bubo.

غونډري *ghūnḍurai,* s.m. A ball, globe, anything circular or round, a lump.

غونډکۍ *ghūnḍaka-ī,* s.f. Any round projection, knob, or mass; *mons veneris.*

غونډه *ghūnḍa,* s.f. A hillock, small detached hill, a mound; lump of dough; boulder, pebble, etc.

غونډهاري *ghūnḍhārai,* s.m. See غنډاري.

غونډي *ghūnḍai,* a. Dumpy, low, squat, dwarf, short; a venomous spider, tarantula. *ghūnḍa-ī,* s.f. A low mound, hillock; a dumpy or short woman, etc.

غونزيدل *ghūnzedal,* v.n. To creep, crawl.

غونه *ghūna,* s.f. The hair of the skin; pores of the skin; colour of the skin. *ghūna-zīgedal,* v.n. To roughen (as the skin from from cold, etc.), to stand on end (as the hair, etc.), to horripilate.

غوول *ghowul,* v.a. To copulate, have sexual intercourse. P. (*gādan*). Def. in pres. ten. See غيل.

غوئيلنګ *ghwa-e-lang,* s.m. The rope passed between the hind legs of a bullock to fix the packsaddle; a crupper.

غوئيمنډ *ghwa-e-manḍ,* s.m. Stampede of oxen or cattle; footmarks of a herd of cattle; a rush, bolt, stampede. a. Trodden, trampled, crushed (under foot).

غوئيمه *ghwa-ema,* s.f. A cow or buffalo ready for, or seeking the male.

غوئي *ghwa-e,* s.m. A bull; bullock, ox.

غه *ghah,* pr. See هغه.

غيب *ghaib*, a. Absent, invisible, concealed. A.

غيبت *ghībat*, s.m. Slander, detraction, calumny. A. *ghaibat*, s.m. Absence, invisibility. A.

غير *ghair*, a. Different, strange, foreign. ad. except, unless. s.m. A stranger. In composition it denotes negation. A.

غيرت *ghairat*, s.m. Modesty, bashfulness; self-respect; honour, courage; emulation, jealousy, enmity. A. *ghairat·man*, a. or *ghairat·nāk*, a. Bashful; jealous; emulous, etc.

غيره *ghyara*, s.f. The wild donkey, wild ass.

غيږ *gheg*, s.m. The arms, embrace, bosom; an armful; the lap; a wallet. P. (*āghosh*).

غيل *ghayal*, v.a. To copulate. Def. in past ten. See غوول. P. (*gā-īdan*). *ghīl*, s.m. A grove, wood, forest. A.

غيله *ghela*, s.f. A herd or flock of goats and sheep. P. (*galla*).

غينړ *ghenr*, s.m. The penis of a man or beast; *membrum virile*. P. (*ker*).

ف

ف *fe* is the twentieth letter of the Arabic, and thirtieth of the Pukkhto alphabet. It is frequently changed for پ.

فاتحه *fātiha*, s.f. Commencement, exordium; the beginning of the first chapter of the Qurān; it is repeated when praying for the souls of the dead. A.

فاجر *fājir*, s.m. Adulterer, fornicator. A.

فاحش *fāhish*, a. Indecent, obscene. A.

فارسي *fārsī*, a. Persian. P.

فارغ *färigh*, a Disengaged, at leisure. A.

فاسد *fāsid*, a. Depraved, vicious. A.

فاسق *fāsiq*, a. Impious, sinful; fornicator. A.

فاش *fāsh*, a. Apparent, manifest. P.

فاصله *fāṣila*, s.f. Interval, space. A.

فاضل *fāẓil*, a. Abundant; excellent; learned. A.

فاعل *fā'il*, s.m. Agent, actor; doing, making. A.

فاقه *fāqa*, s.f. Starvation; poverty, want. A.

فال *fāl*, s.m. Augury, omen; diet, regimen. A.

فالتو *fāltū*, a. Spare, surplus. H.

فالوده *fālūda*, s f. Name of a sweetmeat; a kind of flummery. P.

فانوس *fānūs*, s.m. A lantern; shade for a lamp. P.

فاني *fānī*, a. Transitory, inconstant. A.

فائده *fā-ida*, s.f. Advantage, benefit, profit. A.

فتحه *fatha*, s.f. Conquest, victory. A.

فتراك *fitrāk*, s.m. Saddle straps; cords fixed to a saddle and used to tie game, etc., to. P.

فتنه *fitna*, s.f. Disturbance, hostility; sedition, strife. A.

فتور *futūr*, s.m. Anarchy, strife, quarrel. A.

فتوی *fatwā*, s.f. Decree, sentence, judgment. A.

فتيله *fatīla*, s.f. A match, wick. A.

فدا *fidā*, s.f. Ransom, sacrifice. A.

فراخ *farākh*, a. Ample, spacious; abundant, cheap; wide, expanded. P.

فرار *farār*, a. Absconding, flight. *farārī*, s.m. A deserter, runaway. A.

فراست *firāsat*, s.m. Sagacity, penetration. A.

فراش *farāsh*, s.m. Valet, bed-maker, chamberlain; carpet spreader. A.

فراغت *firāghat*, s.m. Ease, leisure, repose. A.

فراق *firāq*, s.m. Absence, separation. A.

فراموش *farāmosh*, a. Forgotten. P.

فراوان *farāwān*, a. Abundant, much. P.

فرحت *farhat*, s.m. Pleasure, joy. A.

فرد *fard*, s.m. A list, catalogue, roll; sheet (of paper); individual, one, single. A.

فردا *fardā*, s.f. Morrow, to-morrow. A.

فرزند *farzand*, s.m. A child, issue, progeny. P.

فرسخ *farsakh*, } s.m. A league, parasang;
فرسنګ *farsang*, } four miles. P.

فرش *farsh*, s.m. Flooring, pavement; carpeting; bedding; matting, etc. A.

فرښته *firikkhta*, s.m. An angel. P. (*firishta*).

فرصت *furṣat*, s.m. Ease, convenience, leisure; occasion, opportunity, rest. A.

فرض *farẓ*, s.m. Divine command; obligation, duty, indispensable duty. A.

فرق *farq*, s.m. Difference, distinction. A.

فرقه *firqa*, s.f. A class, tribe, set, sect. A.

فرمان *farmān*, s.m. Command, order; edict, grant, patent. P.

فرمايل *farmāyal*, v.a. To command, order, direct. P. (*farmūdan*).

فرنګي *farangī*, a. European, Frank. P. *farangai*, s.m. A European.

فرياد *faryād*, s.m. Complaint, cry for redress, exclamation, lament. P.

فريب *fareb*, s.m. Deception, trick; fraud, deceit. P.

فريبي *farebī*, a. Impostor, cheat. P.

فريفته *fareftah*, a. Infatuated, charmed, enamoured. P.

فريوان *frewān*, a. See فراوان.

فساد *fasād*, s.m. Mutiny, rebellion; disturbance, tumult, riot. A. *fasādī*, a. Rebellious, mutinous, seditious, etc.

فسق *fisq*, s.m. Adultery; obscenity; iniquity, sin. A.

فصل *faṣl*, s.m. Crop, harvest; time, season; section, chapter. A.

فصيح *faṣīḥ*, a. Eloquent, fluent (in speech). A.

فصيل *faṣīl*, s.m. Breastwork, parapet. A.

فضل *fazl*, s.m. Excellence, virtue; increase, gain; favour, gift, grace. A.

فضول *fuẓūl*, a. Redundant, exuberant; excessive, extravagant. A. *fuẓūlī*, s.f. Excess, redundance, extravagance.

فطر *fiṭr*, s.m. Breaking (a fast). A. *'īdu-l-fiṭr*, s.m. The festival held on the termination of the Ramaẓān. A.

فطرت *fiṭrat*, s.m. Cunning, sagacity; alms distributed on the *'īdu-l-fiṭr*. A.

فعل *f'il*, s.m. Operation, action, work; a verb. A.

فغان *fighān*, s.m. Complaint, lament, wail. in. Alas! P.

فقر *fuqr*, s.m. Poverty, beggary. A.

فقط *faqaṭ*, ad. Merely, simply, only. A.

فقهه *fiqha*, s.f. Theology, jurisprudence. A. (*fiqh*).

فقيه *faqīh*, s.m. A thelogian. A.

فقير *faqīr*, s.m. A beggar, mendicant (religious). A. *faqīrī*, s.f. Beggary, poverty; life of a faqīr.

فكر *fikr*, s.m. Reflection, thought; idea, notion; care, concern; anxiety, solicitude. A.

فلان *falān*, s.m. Penis, *membrum virile*. P.

فلانكي *falānkai*, فلاني *falānai*, } s.m. A certain one, so and so, such a thing, etc. A. (*falāna*).

فلك *falak*, s.m. The heavens, sky; destiny, fate, fortune. A.

فليته *falīta*, s.f. See فتيله.

فليل *fulel*, s.m. A kind of scented hair oil.

فن *fann*, s.m. Science, skill, art. A.

فنا *fanā*, s.f. Frailty, mortality. a. Frail, mortal. A.

فواره *fawāra*, s.f. A jet, spout, fountain, spring. A.

فوت *faut*, s.m. Death. A. *fautī*, a. Dead.

فوج *fauj*, s.m. An army. A.

فوفنا *fū-fanā*, a. Annihilated, destroyed, utterly destroyed, exterminated.

فهرست *fihrist*, s.m. Index; list, inventory. P.

فيصله *faiṣala*, s.f. Decision, decree; sentence, settlement. A. *faiṣal*, a. Decided, settled.

فيض *faiẓ*, s.m. Abundance, plenty; bounty, favour, grace. A.

فيل *fīl*, s.m. An elephant. P

ق

ق *qāf*, is the twenty-first letter of the Arabic, and the thirty-first of the Pukkhto alphabet. With few exceptions it is only found in words from the Arabic.

قاب *qāb*, s.m. A kneading trough; platter, dish, salver. A.

قابض *qābiz*, a. Astringent; seizing, taking. A.

قابل *qābil*, a. Able, clever, skilful, worthy; possible, sufficient. A.

قابله *qābila*, s.f. A midwife.

قابو *qābū*, s.m. Authority, command; will, power; opportunity, possession. T.

قاتر *qātar*, s.m. A mule. P.

قاتل *qātil*, a. Deadly, killing, mortal. s.m. An assassin, murderer. A.

قاتي *qātī*, s.f. See قحط.

قادر *qādir*, a. Powerful, potent. A.

قادري *qādarai*, a. Curtailed, docked, cut off. *qādara-ī*, s.f. A kind of frock or gown worn by the Afghans.

قارغه *qārghah*, s.m. A crow, rook.

قاري *qārī*, s.m. A reader of the Qurān. A.

قاري‌درياب *qārī-dariyāb*, } s.m. The ocean, sea.
قالي‌درياب *qalī-dariyāb*, } A. (*q'ari-daryā*).

قاشوغه *qāshogha*, s.f. A ladle, spoon. P.

قاصد *qāṣid*, s.m. Courier, messenger, postman. A.

قاصر *qāṣir*, a. Defective, impotent; deficient, failing. A.

قاضي *qāzī*, s.m. A judge, lawgiver. A.

قاعده *qā'ida*, s.f. Rule, system; custom, manner. A.

قاغه *qāgha*, s.f. A crow, jackdaw, chough. S. (*kāgā*).

قافله *qāfila*, s.f. A caravan, travelling party. A.

قال *qāl*, s.m. A word, saying, speech. A. *qīl-o-qāl*, s.m. Dispute, altercation, controversy.

قالب *qālib*, s.m. A mould, cast; form, figure, bust, model; the body. A.

قالي *qālī*, s.f. } A carpet, woollen carpet. P.
قالين *qālīn*, s.m. }

قاليچه *qālīcha*, s.f. A rug, drugget, small carpet. P.

قام *qām*, s.m. Family, tribe. See قوم.

قامت *qāmat*, s.m. Stature; figure, form. A.

قانع *qān'i*, a. Satisfied, contented. A.

قانون *qānūn*, s.m. Canon, regulation, statute, rule. A.

قائزه *qā-iza*, s.f. A watering bridle; bit of a bridle. A. (*qā-izī*).

قائل *qā-il*, a. Convinced, acknowledging. A.

قائم *qā-im*, a. Firm, fixed, stable, erect. A.

قبا *qabā*, s.f. A frock, gown, jacket; a quilted coat; cover for a book. A.

قباحت *qabāḥat*, a. Deformity; dishonesty, wrong. A.

قبر *qabar*, s.m. A grave, tomb. A.

قبض *qabz*, s.m. Contraction; costiveness; astringency; receipt; tax, tribute. A.

قبضه *qabza*, s.f. Handle (of a sword, etc.); grip, grasp; possession. A.

قبل *qabl*, First, foremost. ad. Previously, before. A. *qabal*, a. Besieged, invested, surrounded. A. *qibal*, s.m. Power; plenty; presence; on the part of, in respect of. A.

قبله *qibla*, s.f. In front, opposite; altar, temple; worship; father. A.

قبول *qabūl*, s.m. Assent, consent; approbation, favourable reception. a. Accepted, approved, consented. A. A holster.

قبولي *qabūlai*, s.m. A holster, pistol case for saddle. A. (*qubūr*).

قبه *qubba*, s.f. An arch, dome, vault. A.

قبيله *qabīla*, s.f. A family; tribe; wife. A.

قت *qat*, s.m. A fold, layer, plait. *qat-pa-qat*, Fold on fold, layer on layer.

قتار *qatār*, s.m. A line, file, rank, row, series, order. A. (*qaṭār*).

قتاري *qatārai*, s.m. Contention, squabble, foolish talk; a wrangler.

قتره *qatra*, s.f. A drop, minim. A. (*qaṭra*).

قتغ *qatagh*, s.m. Meat, fish, soup, etc., eaten with bread to give it a relish; made dish, entrée. P.

قتال *qitāl*, s.m. Battle, slaughter. A.

قتل *qatl*, s.m. Slaughter, homicide, murder. A.

قتي *qutai*, s.m. A ball for play (made of leather or cotton). *quta-ī*, s.f. A dimple on the cheek. *qutta-ī*, s.f. A powder flask (made of untanned leather). S. (*kuppī*).

قجري *qajarī*, s.f. A kind of saddle cloth made of thick felt (it covers the saddle and the horse's fore and hind quarters as well). P.

قچر *qachar*, s.m. A mule. a. Obstinate, perverse. H. (*khachchar*). s.m. A sneak, knave, rogue, cheat. H. (*kamchor*).

قچي *qichai*, s.m. A band, gang, party.

قحط *qaḥṭ*, s.m. Famine, scarcity, dearth. A.

قد *qadd*, s.m. Height, stature. A.

قدر *qadr*, s.m. Value, worth, price; dignity, importance; degree, measure; quantity, size; destiny, fate. A.

قدرت *qudrat*, s.m. Authority, power; omnipotence. A.

قدرتي *qudratī*, a. Divine. A.

قدغن *qadaghan*, } s.m. Prohibition, injunc-
تتغن *qataghan*, } tion. P.

قدم *qadam*, s.m. Footstep, pace. A.

قديم *qadīm*, a. Ancient, old. A.

قر *qur*, s.m. Rumbling sound in the bowels. *qur-qur*, s.m. Borborygmus. A. (*qarāqar*).

قرابت *qarābat*, s.m. Affinity, kinship, relationship; vicinity, proximity. A.

قرات *qirāt*, s.m. Reading, pronunciation. A.

قرار *qarār*, s.m. Rest, quiet, tranquility; stability, firmness; agreement, engagement; patience, waiting. a. Firm, stable; quiet, tranquil. A.

قراري *qarārī*, s.f. Firmness, stability; rest, ease. a. Firm, stable; quiet, etc.

قران *qurān*, s.m. Name of the book of the Arabian prophet Muḥammad; also called *furqān*.

قراول *qarāwal*, s.m. Advance guard of an army; picquet, vidette, sentinel. T.

قربان *qurbān*, s.m. Sacrifice, oblation, victim; a quiver. A.

قربت *qurbat*, s.m. Relationship; proximity. A.

قرت *qurut*, s.m. A kind of very hard cheese; a ball of compressed and dried curds. *qurut-kānrai*, s.m. A pebble of nodular limestone (so named from the resemblance to a nodule or ball of *qurut*), *kankar*.

قرص *qurṣ*, s.m. An orb, disc; the sun; name of an ornament for the neck (of women).

قرض *qarẓ*, s.m. A debt; loan. A.

قرط *qurṭ*, s.m. A gulp, draught. A.

قرعه *qur'a*, s.f. Lot, wager, drawing lots. A.

قرق *qurq*, s.m. Confiscation, embargo, seizure. A.

قرقره *qarqara*, s.f. A plume of feathers for the head (generally of crane's feathers). A. (*qarqarā*, a crane).

قرقري *qarqarai*, s.m. The gripes in a horse.

قرغيچن *qarghechan*, } a. Benumbed, chilled,
قرقيچن *qarqechan*, } doubled up with cold, etc.

قرمساق *qurramsāq*, s.m. Cuckold; pimp; a term of abuse. P.

قرن *qarn*, s.m. A conjunction of the planets; a century. A.

قرنا *qarnā*, s.f. Clarion, trumpet, horn. A.

قريب *qarīb*, a. Close, near; akin, relative. A.

قرينه *qarīna*, s.f. Analogy, context, likeness, similarity, tenour. A.

قز *qaz*, s.m. Raw silk. P.

قسب *qasab*, s.m. Red silk; small turban.

قسط *qist*, s.m. Instalment, portion, tax. A.

قسم *qism*, s.m. Kind, species, sort; division, part. A. *qasam*, s.m. An oath. A.

قسمت *qismat*, s.m. Destiny, fate, lot; distribution, share; division, portion. A.

قشلاق *qishlāq*, s.m. A hamlet, village; winter quarters of the nomade tribes of western and northern Afghanistan. T. The summer quarters are termed *īlāq*.. T.

قصاب *qaṣṣāb*, s.m. A butcher. A.

قصاص *qiṣāṣ*, s.m. The law of retaliation (as eye for eye, blood for blood, etc.). A.

قصد *qaṣd*, s.m. Intention, purpose, aim, wish. A.

قصداً *qaṣdan*, ad. Purposely, intentionally. A.

قصر *qaṣr*, s.m. Defect, diminution. A.

قصور *quṣūr*, s.m. Defect, failure, omission, want; error, fault; crime, sin. A.

قصه *qiṣṣa*, s.f. Story, tale; relation, narration; dispute, quarrel. A.

قصيده *qaṣīda*, s.f. An ode, poem. A.

قضا *qaẓā*, s.f. Fate, destiny; death, fatality; order, decree, judgment; praying at the appointed time; saying a prayer after the appointed time has passed. A.

قضاق *qaẓẓāq*, s.m. A cossack, robber. T.

قضيه *qaẓiya*, s.f. Contention, litigation, quarrel; calamity, misfortune; death; declaration, proposition. A.

قطب *quṭb*, s.m. North pole; Polar star; axis or spindle of a mill-stone; axis. A.

قطعي *qaṭ'aī*, a. Incontestible, true, fact. ad. Really, truly, fully. A.

قفس *qafas*, } s.m. A cage; latticework. E.
قفص *qafaṣ*, }

قفل *qufl*, s.n. See قلف.

قلا *qalā*, s.f. See قلعه.

قلاب *qullāb*, s.m. A hood for the head of a hawk. A.

قلابه *qulāba*, s.f. A hook, hinge, staple. A.

قلار *qalār*, a. Resting, quiet. See قرار.

قلاش *qalāsh*, a. Cunning, crafty, shrewd.

قلبه *qulba*, s.f. A plough. A.

قلپ *qalp*, a. Adulterated, alloyed; counterfeit (as coin, etc.). A. (*qalb*).

قلعه *qil'a*, s.f. Castle, fort; royal residence. A.

قلعي *qil'aī*, s.f. Tin; sodder. A.

قلف *qulf*, s.m. A lock; bolt. A.

قلم *qalam*, s.m. A pen, reed; graft; cutting of a plant. A.

قلنج *qulinj*, s.m. The colic. A.

قلندر *qalandar*, s.m. A hermit, anchorite, ascetic; a monk who has abandoned the world, family, friends, etc. A.

قلنگ *qulang*, s.m. Revenue, tax.

قمار *qimār*, s.m. Dice, gambling with dice. A. *qimār-bāz*, s.m. A gambler.

قماش *qamāsh*, s.m Manners, foibles; goods, chattels. A.

قمچي *qamchī*, s.f. A horsewhip. T.

قمر *qamar*, s.m. The moon. A.

قمري *qumrī*, s.f. A turtle dove. A.

قميص *qamīṣ*, s.m. Chemise, shirt. A.

قنات *qanāt*, s.m. Walls of a tent; canvas walls used to enclose a space about a tent. A. *qanāt*, s.m. Confectionary, sweetmeats. A. (*qanād*).

قناعت *qanā'at*, s.m. Contentment, tranquility; abstinence. A.

قنج *qanj*, s.m. Deceit, imposture, trick. A.

قند *qand*, s.m. Sugar candy, sugar. A.

قنديل *qandīl*, s.m. Chandelier, lamp. A.

قواعد *quwā'id*, s.m. Regulations, rules; military exercise, drill. A.

قوام *qiwām*, s.m. Essence, extract, syrup. A. *qiwāmī*, a. Ropy, thick, syrupy.

قوت *qūt*, Victuals, aliment, food; subsistence, livelihood. A. *qūt·lā·yamūt*, s.m. Sufficient to sustain life. A. *quwat*, s.m. Strength, vigour; power, authority; faculty, virtue. A.

قوج *qūj*, s.m. A fighting ram. P.

قوچق *qūchaq*, a. Fat, stout, lusty. T.

قوده *qawda*, s.f. A handful, a gripful.

قورمه *qorma*, s.f. A dish of meat stewed up with spices and fruits. P.

قول *qaul*, s.m. Word, saying; contract, promise; agreement, consent. A.

قوم *qaum*, s.m. Nation, people, family, sect, tribe. A.

قوي *qawwī*, a. Powerful, strong, vigorous; solid, firm, stable. A.

قهر *qahr*, s.m. Anger, passion, rage; vengeance, fury; severity, punishment. A.

قهرژن *qahr·ĵan*, } a. Irascible, passionate,
قهرناک *qahr·nāk*, } wrathful, furious.

قهقهه *qahqaha*, s.f. Loud laughter. A.

قي *qai*, s.m. Spewing, vomiting. A.

قياس *qiyās*, s.m. Consideration, judgment, opinion, thought; guess, supposition. A.

قيامت *qiyāmat*, s.m. The last day; resurrection; calamity. a. Wonderful, marvellous. A.

قيد *qaid*, s.m. Bondage, imprisonment; fetter, obstacle; obligation, compact. A.

قيدي *qaidī*, s.m. Prisoner, captive.

قيزه *qaiza*, s.f. See قائزه.

قيل *qīl*, s.m. A word, speech, saying. A.

قيمت *qīmat*, s.m. Price, value. A. *qīmatī*, a. High-priced, expensive: valuable.

قيمه *qīma*, s.f. Minced meat. A.

قينچي *qainchī*, s.f. Scissors. H.

ک

ک *kāf* is the twenty-second letter of the Arabic and the thirty-second of the Pukkhto alphabet. It is pronounced like the English *k*, and is sometimes interchanged with ق.

کَ *ka* is a form of the third person singular and plural of the present tense of the verb کول *kawul*, to do. It is also used as an abbreviated form for که *ka*, and وُ که *wu ka*, which are forms of the imperfect and past tenses, and the imperative mood of that verb. See following word.

کا *kā* is a form of the third person singular and plural of the present tenses, and imperative mood of the verb کول *kawul*, to do.

کابين *kābīn*, s.m. A marriage portion or settlement, wife's portion, dowry. P.

کاتک *kātak*, s.m. Name of the seventh Hindu month: October-November. S. (*kātik*).

کاته *kātah*, s.m. A glance, look; looking.

کاپور *kāpūr*, s.m. Camphor. A. (*kāfūr*).

کاتب *kātib*, s.m. A scribe, writer. A.

کاټي *kāṭī*, s.f. A wooden saddle; stocks for criminals. S. (*kāṭhī*).

کاختي *kākhtī*, s.f. Famine, scarcity, dearth. A. (*qaḥt*).

کاذب *kāzib*, s.m. A liar. a. False. A.

کار *kār*, s.m. Business, profession; action, affair; labour, work. P. *pa·kār*, a. Necessary, useful; required, wanted.

کارد *kārd*, s.m. A knife. P.

کاربښت *kārikkht*, s.m. A wine-press; a vat in which grapes are pressed.

کاروان *kārwān*, s.m. Caravan, travelling party. P.

کاره *kāra*, s.f. A deep basket made of cane or reeds; a kind of millet. (*Paspalum kora*).

کاري *kārī*, a. Effectual, efficacious. P.

کاريز *kārez*, s.m. An aqueduct; subterranean canal for irrigating fields. P.

کاريزه *kārīza*, s.f. Name of a plant, safflower (*Carthamus oxyacantha*). P. (*khārīza*).

کاریګر *kārī·gar*, s.m. Artificer, mechanic, workman; skilful workman. P.

کاړ *kāṛ*, کانړ *kāṉṛ*, s.m. Coarse sand, gravel, shingle.

کاړه *kāṛa*, s.f. Caudle, posset, curdled milk.

کاز *kāz*, s.m. Shears, scissors; den of a wild beast; a cavern or cave used by shepherds as a shelter for their flocks. P. *kāz*, s.m. A wild goose. T. (*qāz*).

کاږل *kāgal*, v.a. To draw, extract, pull out; to write, delineate, sketch. Def. in past ten. See کښل.

کاسب *kāsib*, s.m. Mechanic, artist, artificer. A.

کاسه *kāsa*, s.f. A bowl, cup, goblet. A. *shna·kāsa*, s.f. A rainbow.

کاسير *kāsīr*, s.m. Adulterer, fornicator. *kāsīrī*, s.f. Adultery, fornication.

کاش *kāsh*, s.m. Pommel or bow of a saddle; a small holster or saddle bag.

کاشکي *kāshke*, in. God grant! Would to God! P.

کاشي *kāshī*, s.m. A glazed tile or brick. P. *kāshī·gar*, s.m. Maker of glazed pottery. P. *kāshīn*, s.m. Glazed pottery. P.

کاغ *kāgh*, a. Cunning, clever, acute.

کاغذ *kāghaz*, s.m. Paper. P. *kāghāzī*, s.f. A kind of thin skinned lime. a. Delicate, soft, thin; written, printed; documentary.

کافر *kāfir*, s.m. Unbeliever, infidel. A. *kāfirī*, Name of a people inhabiting Kafiristan, a country of Hindu Kush to the north of Kabul. *kāfirai*, s.m. A man Kafir. *kāfira-ī*, s.f. A Kafir woman.

کافي *kāfī*, a. Enough, sufficient; competent, able. A.

کاک *kāk*, s.m. A biscuit, a hard cake of bread, etc. baked upon heated stones. P.

کاکا *kākā*, s.m. Paternal uncle; term of respectful address to a senior. H. Elder brother. P.

کاکړ *kākaṛ*, s.m. Name of an Afghan clan.

کاکل *kākul*, s.m. A curl, lock, ringlet. P.

کاکنج *kākanj*, s.m. Name of a kind of millet (*Panicum Italicum*).

کاکي *kāka-ī*, s.f. Paternal uncle's wife. H.

کال *kāl*, s.m. A year. P. (*sāl*). *sag·kāl*, This year. *paros·kāl*, or *parcsag·kāl*, Last year. *waṛam·kāl*, Year before last. *lā·waṛam·kāl*, Three years ago.

کالبوت *kālbūt*, s.m. Human body; heart; form, figure, mould, model. P. (*kālbud*).

کالخواهي *kālkhwāhī*, s.f. Good will, good wishes; approbation, choice. P. (*khair·khwāhī*).

کالکوچ *kālkūch*, s.m. A bend, turn, curve, twist.

کالکوچن *kālkūchan*, a. Bent, curved, distorted.

کالکوچکه *kālkūchaka*, s.f. A bend, turn, swerve (as of a hunted hare, fox, etc.).

کالکنډي *kālkunḍai*, s.m. A kind of small edible melon that grows wild.

کالکه *kālaka*, s.f. Cotton in the pod; the cotton plant. *kālak·cho*, s.m. Dry stalks of the cotton plant (used as fuel).

کالي *kālai*, s.m. Article, instrument, tool; garment, dress; ornament, jewel. pl. *kālī*, Apparatus, tools; furniture, clothes, jewelry, etc. P. (*kālā*).

کام *kām*, s.m. Desire, wish. P. *kām·nā·kām*, ad. Willing or unwilling, nolens volens.

کامبوري *kāmbūrai*, s.m. Dry mustard stalks after threshing out the seed.

کامبيله *kāmbela*, s.f. Name of a tree (*Rottlera tinctoria*). H. (*kamīla*).

کامل *kāmil*, a. Complete, perfect; learned. A.

کامياب *kāmyāb*, a. Prosperous, successful. P. *kāmyābī*, s.f. Prosperity, success.

کان *kān*, s.m. A mine, quarry. P. *kān*, s.m. Reed, rush, bullrush (*Panicum spicatum* and *Juncus effusus*).

کانټۍ *kānṭa-ī*, s. f. Book-board, pasteboard.

کانجنړ *kānjanṛ*, s.m. Part of a Persian wheel; the large beam that rests on the side walls, and fixes the central upright pillar of the wheel.

کانډِ *kāndi*, } A form of the third person
کاندي *kānde*, } singular and plural of the present tense of the verb کول *kawul*, to do.

کانګه *kānga*, s.f. Gripes, tenesmus, tormina; violent straining at stool without ejection of matter. H. (*kānkhā*).

کانګي *kāngai*, s.m. Echo, reverberation.

کانه *kāna*, s.f. Calamity, disaster; business, affair; border, margin; frame, edging; a quill feather; upper part of the face. *kānah*, a. Stupid, ignorant, foolish; decayed, rotten at the core. S. (*kānā*).

کاني *kānī*, a. Mineral, fossil. P. *kānai*, a. Blind of one eye. S. (*kānā*). *kānaī*, s.f. Whiskers, hair at the temples; a reed, straw, cane, etc. (used by weavers to spread the warp upon).

کاڼړي *kāṇṛai*, s.m. A stone. P. (*kān*).

کاواک *kāwāk*, a. Demented, insane; awkward, clumsy; hollow, useless; thoughtless; acting as one deprived of self control.

کاه *kāh*, s.m. Straw, stubble. P. *kāh-gil*, s.m. Plaster of mud and straw for walls. P.

کاهښت *kāhakkht*, s.m. Mange, itch; grating, or setting the teeth on edge.

کاهل *kāhil*, a. Indolent, lazy, slow. A. *kāhilī*, s.f. Apathy, indolence, neglect.

کاهن *kāhin*, s.m. Astrologer, magician. A. *kāhinī*, s.f. Astrology, magic, sorcery.

کب *kab*, s.m. A fish.

کباب *kabāb*, s.m. Roasted meat. P. *kabābī*, s.m. A cook.

کبر *kibr*, s.m. Arrogance, pride. A. *kibr-jan*, a. Arrogant, haughty, proud.

کبره *kbara*, s.f. Name of a plant (*Capparis spinosa*). H. (*kabar*).

کبک *kabk*, s.m. A partridge. P.

کبل *kabal*, s.m. Cause, motive, reason. *kabl*, s.m. Name of a grass (*Agrostis linearis*).

کبلي *kablai*, s.m. A fawn, young gazelle; sandpiper, snippet; curlew.

کبي *kabī*, s.f. A halter for a horse; a rope passed over the head and through the mouth, instead of a headstall and bit.

کبير *kabīr*, a. Great, large; senior, full-grown. A.

کپري *kaparai*, s.m. The skull. S. (*khoprī*).

کپړۍ *kupṛa-ī*, s.f. A powder flask of leather; a leathern jar or bottle. S. (*kuppī*).

کپي *kapī*, s.f. See کبي. *kupa-ī*, s.f. See کپړۍ.

کت *kat*, s.m. Catechu. H. (*kath*). *kat*, s.m. A pile, heap; line, series, row.

کتاب *kitāb*, s.m. A book. A. *kitābī*, a. Written; learned, well read.

کتل *katal*, v.a. To look, see, view. H. (*taknā*).

کته *kata*, s.f. A pack-saddle or pad for bullocks, donkeys, etc.

کتي پتي *kitī-pitī*, s.f. Gibberish, nonsense. a. Confused, jumbled (as speech).

کتي لعل *kutī-l'al*, s.m. Name of a plant (*Withiana somniferum*).

کټ *kaṭ*, s.m. A cot, bed, bedstead. S. (*khaṭ*). *kaṭ-kai*, s.m. A small bed, settle, cot. *kaṭ-oṭai*, s.m. A child's bed, cradle.

کټ وټ *kaṭ-waṭ*, a. See کډ.

کټوري *kaṭorai*, s.m. A brass bowl, metal cup. H. (*kaṭorā*).

کټوۍ *kaṭwa-ī*, s.f. An earthenware cooking pot.

کټه *kaṭah*, a. Big, bulky, large. H. (*kaṭṭā*).

کټي *kaṭai*, s.m. A buffalo calf; the straw of pulse (used as fodder).

كثرت *kas̤rat*, s.m. Abundance, excess. A.

كثير *kas̤īr*, a. Abundant, excessive. A.

كخوړه *kats̲oṛa*, s.f. A bag, purse, reticule, wallet.

كخوك *kats̲wak*, s.m. Mild small-pox, chicken-pox.

كجاوه *kajāwa*, s.f. A camel-litter. P.

كجك *kajak*, s.m. Hammer or cock of a gun; a curl or lock of hair worn on the forehead by females.

كجل *kajal*, s.m. Soot, lamp-black. S.

كچ *kac̲h̲*, s.m. Measurement; fault, flaw, error. a. Diminutive, small, less, little. H. (*kac̲h̲c̲h̲ā*). *kuc̲h̲*, s.m. Butter.

كچكول *kac̲h̲kol*, s.m. A bowl or trough of wood used by mendicants to collect contributions in. P.

كچماچو *kac̲h̲māc̲h̲ū*, s.m. Name of a plant (*Solanum nigrum*), deadly nightshade.

كچني *kac̲h̲ana-ī*, s.f. Courtezan, whore, dancing girl. H. (*kanc̲h̲anī*). *kuc̲h̲inai*, a. Small, diminutive, puny.

كچوټي *kac̲h̲oṭai*, a. Diminutive, tiny, wee.

كچه *kac̲h̲ah*, a. Crude, immature, raw; silly, inexperienced; clay-built, slight. H. (*kac̲h̲-c̲h̲ā*).

كداي *kadā-ī*, s.f. A kind of frock, long coat, gown.

كدخدا *kad·k̲h̲udā*, s.m. Head man of a village or family; married man, master. P. *kad·k̲h̲udā-ī*, s.f. Marriage, the office of *kad·k̲h̲udā*.

كدو *kadū*, s.m. Pumpkin, bottle gourd. H.

كډله *kaḍala*, s.f. A cabin, hut, hovel (of reeds, etc.); a hole, pit.

كډه *kaḍa*, s.f. Family, household; migration, flitting, change of residence.

كډهل *kaḍhal*, s.m. Land prepared for sowing rice in.

كډۍ *kaḍa-ī*, s.f. A pit, hole; ditch, trench; the hole under a loom for the weaver's feet when at work.

كر *kar*, s.m. Agriculture, farming; tilling, ploughing, and sowing. P. *ka-ar*, s.m. Thin, watery excrement, looseness of the bowels.

كراسته *krāsta*, s.f. Felt, a thick woollen fabric (unwoven).

كرام *kirām*, a. Venerable, noble, great. A.

كرامت *kirāmat*, s.m. Excellence, nobleness; miracle. A.

كراهت *kirāhat*, s.m. Aversion, disgust. A.

كراهه *kirāha*, s.f. Hire, rent, fare. P. (*kirāya*).

كربوړي *karboṛai*, s.m. A kind of lizard; chameleon.

كرپ *krap*, s.m. A munch, crunch.

كرپندوكي *krapandūkai*, كرپندي *krapandai*, } s.m. Cartilage, gristle.

كرپول *krapawul*, v.a. To crunch, munch; bite, champ, gnaw.

كرت *karat*, s.m. One time, stroke, turn, go. A. *yo·karat*, once. *dre·karata*, thrice, etc. *karāt·marāt*, often, frequently, etc. A.

كرتب *kartab*, s.m. Action, business; practice, exercise; skill; horse exercise. S.

كرتوت *kartūt*, s.m. Work, business, action. S.

كرته *kurta*, s.f. A coat, jacket, tunic. P.

كرټ *kruṭ*, ad. At all, not at all, never, by no means, not in the least.

كرچ *krac̲h̲*, s.m. An old hawk or falcon (one fully trained). *krac̲h̲*, s.m. Sound of a crunch, crash, squash, etc.

كرچوني *krac̲h̲ūnai*, كرچي *krac̲h̲ai*, } s.m. Cartilage, gristle.

كرچي *kric̲h̲ī*, s.f. Name of a plant (*Anthemis nobilis*).

كرخت *karak̲h̲t*, a. Austere, rigid, rough, hard. P.

کردار ***kirdār***, s.m. Conduct, action, deed. P.

کرړي ***kirṛai***, s.m. A cricket. ***kariṛī***, s.m. Name of an Afghan tribe, also called کرلاڼري.

کرسي ***kursī***, s.f. Chair, seat, throne; firmament, heaven. P. ***kursī-nāma***, s.f. Genealogical tree; list of precedence.

کرښمه ***karakkhma***, s.f. Amorous look, wink, ogle, leer. P. (*karashma*).

کرښنه ***karakkhna***, s.f. Carving, drawing, painting, engraving.

کرښه ***karkkha***, s.f. A line, streak, scrawl. scratch, furrow.

کرغ ***kurugh***, s.m. A meadow, pasture.

کرک ***karak***, s.m. A snipe, woodcock. P. ***kark***, s.m. Rhinoceros, rhinoceros hide. P. (*karg*). ***krak***, s.m. A furrow, rut, scratch.

کرکنډه ***karkanḍa***, s.f. A rolling stone; landslip on a hill-side; rock or stone hurled down a hill upon an enemy.

کرکڼړ ***karkanṛ***, s.m. A brake, copse, thicket.

کرکڼړه ***karkanṛa***, s.f. A bramble, brier, thorny bush; the jujube tree (*Zizyphus vulgaris*).

کرکه ***kraka***, s.f. Aversion, disgust. A. (*ikrāh*).

کرل ***karal***, v.a. To till, plough and sow. P. (*kāshtan-kār*).

کرلاڼري ***karlānṛī***, s.m. Name of a tribe of Afghans located in Bājawar.

کرم ***karam***, s.m. Clemency, kindness. A. ***kirm***, s.m. A worm. P.

کرمنګ ***kurmang***, s.m. Pheasant, wild fowl.

کرنډي ***karanḍa-ī***, s.f. A trowel. H. (*karnī*).

کروړ ***karoṛ***, a. Ten millions; a crore. S.

کروړه ***karoṛa***, s.f. A whip, scourge. H. (*koṛā*). ***karwaṛa***, s.f. Blackberry bush and fruit (*Rubus vulgaris*).

کروسند ***krosand***, a. Dry, withered (as wood).

کروه ***kroh***, s.m. A coss; a measure of distance nearly equal to two miles. P.

کره ***karah***, a. Genuine, pure; candid, sincere. S. (*kharā*). ***kara***, s.f. Spade, hoe. ***kara***, ad. With, along with. See سره.

کرهډ ***kurhaḍ***, s.m. Name of a plant used as a potherb (*Chenopedium album*).

کړۍ ***kara-ī***, s.f. A fetter, ring, buckle, link, staple; beam, rafter. H. (*kaṛī*). ***kara-ī***, ad. All, the whole, the entire (day or night). ***kara-ī-wradz***, All day. ***kara-ī-shpa***, All night. ***kure***, in. Begone! Get out! away (to a dog).

کریاب ***kariyāb***, a. Disengaged, idle, unused; clogged, hampered, hindered, obstructed; distressed, helpless, tired.

کریابي ***kariyābī***, s.f. Obstruction, hindrance, impediment, bar, hitch, etc.

کریړه ***kirīṛa***, s.f. Name of a plant (*Capparis aphylla*). S. (*karīl*). Weeds, grass, etc., collected from a ploughed field.

کریړي ***kirīṛai***, s.m. Name of a tree (*Salvadora Persica*).

کریز ***kurīz***, s.m. Moulting (of birds). P.

کریم ***karīm***, a. Merciful, gracious, bountiful. A.

کریهه ***kreha***, s.f. See کراهه.

کریه ***karīh***, a. Abominable, detestable; dirty, filthy. A. ***karya***, s.f. Injunction, charge, command.

کړ ***kuṛ***, s.m. A gurgle, bubbling sound; cackle or cluck of a hen.

کړاونه ***kaṛāwna***, s.f. See کنړاوه.

کړبیزن ***karbezan***, a. Snotty-nosed, sniveller.

کړبیزي ***karbeze***, s.f. (pl. of ***karbeza***, obsolete) Snot, mucus from the nose.

کړپ ***kṛap***, s.m. See کرپ.

کړټي ***kṛaṭai***, s.m. A crease, furrow, crumple, pucker, wrinkle.

کړشپ ***kaṛshap***, a. Toothless, old. ***kaṛshapai***, s.m. A toothless old man.

کړکړي ***kuṛkuṛai***, s.m. A turtle dove.

کړکه ***kuṛaka***, s.f. A clucking hen; a sitting or hatching hen.

کرکۍ *kuṛka-ī*, s.f. A kind of bird trap made of a horn bow and catgut, a gin, springe. *kaṛka-ī*, s.f. A wicket, window, loophole; gate. H. (*khiṛkī*).

کړل *kṛal*, v.a. To do, perform, execute, etc. P. (*kardan*).

کړم *kaṛam*, a. Maimed, halt, crippled, lame.

کړميزې *kaṛmeze*, s.f. Snot. See کړېيزې.

کړوسی *kaṛwasai*, s.m. A great grandson.

کړه *kṛah*, s.m. Act, deed; doing, making.

کړه وړه *kṛah-wṛah*, s.m. Beauty, grace; neatness, tidiness, spruceness; arrangement, order.

کړهي *kaṛahai*, s.m. A caldron, boiler (metal); an iron cooking pot. S. (*kaṛāhī*). *kuṛhai*, s.m. Name of a corn measure, the fourth part of an اوږي *ogai*.

کړڅۍ *kaṛetsa-ī*, s.f. A ladle, iron spoon. H. (*karchhī*).

کړېدل *kaṛedal*, v.n. To be parched, scorched, dried; to be reduced, emaciated; to waste, wither, pine, droop (through sickness or grief). H. (*kuṛhnā*).

کړينګ *kṛīng*, a. Awry, distorted, crooked, twisted. *kṛīng-pṛīng*, a. All awry, all askew.

کږدۍ *kigda-ī*, s.f. A tent made of coarse camlet, or goat's hair cloth (used by nomad Afghans).

کږل *kagal*, v.a. To disapprove, to dislike; find fault with, disparage, run down. P. (*kaj*).

کږلي *kagalai*, a. Calamitous, unlucky; unwelcome.

کږليچ *kaglech*, s.m. A bend, crook, turn.

کس *kas*, s.m. Human being, individual, person; anyone, a man. P. *kas*, s.m. A ravine, gully, dry course of a torrent, passage cut by floods. H. *kus*, s.m. Vulva, vagina. P.

کسب *kasb*, s.m. Trade, occupation, **employment**. A.

کسبت *kisbat*, s.m. An instrument case; huntsman's bag for balls, powder, etc., etc.; a bag or case in which barbers, surgeons, etc., keep their tools. A.

کستيج *kustīj*, s.m. The hole in the hem of a pair of drawers, etc., through which the string passes.

کسکر *kaskar*, a. Burnt, dry, arid, scorched; contracted, shrivelled; withered, frost bitten.

کسل *kasal*, v.a. To see, look. See کتل.

کسوری *kasūrai*, a. Broken spirited, distressed, unequal to, impotent.

کسي *kasai*, s.m. The pupil of the eye.

کشاله *kashāla*, s.f. Dragging, trailing, pulling, etc.

کشپ *kashp*, s.m. A tortoise. P. (*kashaf*).

کشته *kishta*, s.f. A kind of dried plum, used in medicine, and by goldsmiths to clean their metals with. P. *kushta*, s.f. A sublimate of mercury. P. *kushtah*, a. Killed, slain; slaked (as lime, etc.). P.

کشر *kashr*, a. Junior, younger; cadet, subaltern; less, minor.

کشک *kashak*, s.m. Watchman, guard, porter. P.

کشمالو *kashmālū*, s.m. Name of a plant, holy basil (*Ocymum sanctum*).

کشور *kishor*, s.m. The manis or pangolin, scaly ant-eater (*Manis crassicaudata*). *kishwar*, s.m. Country, region, climate. P.

کشي *kashai*, s.m. An only son. *kasha-ī*, s.f. Bar or pig iron; a hoe, mattock. H. (*kasī*).

کښ *kakkh*, s.m. A draw, pull; inhalation, whiff, inspiration; suck. P. (*kash*).

کښت *kikkht*, s.m. A crop, sown field, growing crop. P. (*kisht*). *kukkht*, s.m. A defile, gorge, gap in the hills. (Raverty.)

کښل *kak<u>sh</u>al* or *k<u>ksh</u>al*, v.a. To draw out, extricate, extract, pull, pluck out; to write, draw, sketch, etc. Def. in pres. ten. See کاږل. P. (*ka<u>sh</u>īdan*). *k<u>ksh</u>ul*, s.m. A kiss.

کښلول *k<u>ksh</u>ulawul*, v.a. To kiss.

کښلي *k<u>ksh</u>ulai*, a. Comely, fair, handsome, pretty; kissed.

کښول *kak<u>sh</u>awul* or *k<u>ksh</u>awul*, v.a. To cause to extract, draw, etc. To cause to write, etc. See کښل.

کښه *ka<u>kkh</u>a*, s.f. Brace, tightener, puller.

کښي *ka<u>kkh</u>ai*, s.m. A watchman, guard (over cattle, crops, etc.). P. (*ka<u>sh</u>ak*). *k<u>ksh</u>e*, p. In, within. *pa·k<u>ksh</u>e*, ad. Inside, within.

کښيباسل *k<u>ksh</u>ebāsal*, v.a. To insert, introduce, implant, stick in, stuff in, etc. Def. in past ten. See کښيييستل *k<u>ksh</u>eyastal*.

کښيده *ka<u>kkh</u>eda*, s.f. A kind of needlework, embroidery. P. (*ka<u>sh</u>īda*).

کښيږدل *k<u>ksh</u>egdal*, v.a. To place, set, put down, arrange, dispose, etc. Def. in past ten. See کښيښول.

کښيکښل *k<u>ksh</u>ek<u>ksh</u>al*, v.a. To shampoo (or ښکيښکل *k<u>kh</u>ek<u>kh</u>kal*).

کښيناستل *k<u>ksh</u>enāstal*, v.n. To sit, settle, be seated. P. (*ni<u>sh</u>astan*).

کښينول *k<u>ksh</u>enawul*, v.a. To seat, settle, instal, fix, set down, etc.

کښيوتل *k<u>ksh</u>ewatal*, v.n. To fall into, drop into, enter, descend into, etc.

کښيييستل *k<u>ksh</u>eyastal*, v.a. To insert, introduce, etc. Def. in pres. ten. See کښيباسل *k<u>ksh</u>ebāsal*.

کعبه *k'aba*, s.f. The temple at Mecca. A.

کفارت *kifārat*, s.m. Expiation, atonement, penance. A.

کفايت *kifāyat*, s.m. Enough, sufficiency; economy, thrift. A.

کفر *kufr*, s.m. Blasphemy, infidelity, paganism. A.

کفن *kafan*, s.m. Winding sheet, shroud. A.

ککځ *kak*, s.m. A splinter, straw; treacle, syrup.

ککرۍ *kakara-ī*, s.f. The skull. *kakarai*, s.m. A pup, puppy dog.

ککړ *kakaṛ*, a. Defiled, polluted, stained; a spiritless man. f. *kakaṛa*, Raped, ravished; a whore, strumpet.

ککوي *kakawai*, s.m. Name of a bird.

ککوړه *kakoṛa*, s.f. Name of a plant, bitter gourd.

ککوړي *kakoṛai*, s.m. A kind of biscuit, round cake baked on heated stones; a disk.

کل *kal*, a. Bald, scald headed. P. *kal*, s.m. oil-cake. S. (*khal*). *kull*, a. All, universal; amount, total. A.

کلال *kulāl*, s.m. A potter. P.

کلام *kalām*, s.m. A word, speech; conversation, talk. A.

کلان *kalān*, a. Elder, great; large. P.

کلت *kulat*, s.m. Name of a grain, seed of (*Dolichos biflorus*). S. (*kulthī*).

کلک *klak*, a. Firm, hard; stiff, rigid, etc. P. (*kara<u>kh</u>t*).

کلکل *kalkal*, s.m. Wrangling, quarrelling. H.

کلمه *kulma*, s.f. An entrail, gut; sausage. A. (*qulmā*). *kalima*, s.f. A word, speech; the Muhammadan belief or creed. A.

کلنګ *kulang*, s.m. A long-legged fowl; a crane, heron. P. A pick, pickaxe; a bow; hammer of a gun; dower, furniture of every description which a bride brings to her husband.

کلني *kalanai*, Added to words in composition, denotes the age. Ex. *pīn<u>dz</u>ah·kalanai*, a. Five years old.

کلوټ *kaloṭ*, a. Dark, dark-complexioned.

کلوښته *kalo<u>kkh</u>ta*, s.f. A wisp of straw, floss of silk, curl, tuft, bundle, etc.

کله *kala*, ad. Ever, at any time, sometime;

when? since when? *kala·kala,* Now and then, occasionally, sometimes. *kala·shū·lā·kala,* Since when? how long? *kala,* s.f. The head. P.

كلي *kilai,* s.m. A village. A. (*qil'a*). *kalai,* a. Short-horned, without horns. P. (*kal*). *kala-ī,* s.f. Bunion, callosity, corn. *killī,* s.f. A key. H. *kullī,* s.f. A gargle, gargling. H.

كم *kam,* a. Deficient, less, little, seldom. scanty (in comp.). P. *kum* or *kam,* pr. What? which? See كوم.

كمال *kamāl,* s.m. Perfection, excellence; completion. a. Complete, perfect. A.

كمان *kamān,* s.m. A bow. *kamān·gar,* s.m. A bow-maker. P.

كمانچه *kamāncha,* s.f. Bow of a violin. P.

كماني *kamā-ī,* s.f. Earning, gain, profit, wages. H.

كمبلي *kambala-ī,* s.f. A butterfly.

كمر *kamar,* s.f. A cliff, precipice; steep bank; ridge of a hill, etc.; the waist, loins. P. *kamar·kīsa,* s.f. A waist belt with powder flask, etc., etc. *kamar·band,* s.m. A girdle, waist-belt. P.

كمري *kamarī,* a. Relating to the loins, lumbar; weak in the loins (as a horse).

كمك *kumak,* s.m. Aid, help; reserve of an army. P. *kumakī,* a. Auxiliary. s.m, Assistant, helper.

كمند *kamand,* s.m. A ladder of ropes; halter, lasso, noose; a tethering rope; ringlet or long curl. P.

كمنړ *kamanr,* a. Faded, withered, decayed.

كمنړيدل *kamanredal,* v.n. To droop, decay, wither, fade, etc. H. (*kumhlānā*).

كموده *kamoda,* s.f. A dish of rice boiled with ghee, and flavoured with spices.

كميس *kamīs,* s.m. A shirt. See قميص.

كمين *kamīn,* a. Mean; defective; humble, poor. s.m. A village serf. P.; an ambuscade. A.

كمينه *kamīnah,* a. Humble, meek; abject, base; mean, ignoble. P. *kamīnī,* s.f. Humility, meekness; baseness.

كن *kan* (in comp.), Digger, digging. P. *kun* (in comp.), Actor, doer; doing, acting. P.

كناټي *kunāṭai,* s.m, Buttock, rump. *kunāṭa-war,* a. Broad-buttocked, large rumped.

كنار *kinār,* s.m. Side, edge; bosom, embrace. P.

كنال *kanāl,* s.m. A land measure equal to twenty *marla*; the fourth part of a *jarīb*.

كنايت *kināyat,* s.m. } Allusion, hint, metaphor, sign. A.
كنايه *kināya,* s.f. }

كنټكين *kanṭkīn,* a. Made of thread.

كنج *kunj,* s.m. A corner, nook; grove, bower. P.

كنجك *kunjak,* s.m. } A cowrie, small shell (used as money). (*Cypræa moneta*).
كنجكه *kunjaka,* s.f. }

كنجوغه *kanjogha,* s.f. Saddle straps, cords attached to a saddle (used to tie game, etc.).

كنجي *kunja-ī,* s.f. A key. S. (*kunjī*). A small water jar or ewer (of pottery).

كند *kand,* s.m. A gorge, ravine, dry water-course, excavation. P. *kind,* s.m. A tattered and patched garment worn by dervishes. *kund,* a. Blunt. P.

كنداغ *kundāgh,* s.m. The stock of a gun. P. (*kunda*).

كندره *kandara,* s.f. A fissure, chasm; gully, watercourse, ravine; broken or ravine cut ground. S. (*kandarā*).

كندل *kandal,* v.a. To dig, excavate. P. (*kandan*).

كندو *kandū,* s.m. A corn bin.

كنده *kanda,* s.f. A gully, ravine, watercourse, (cut by floods). P. *kunda,* s.f. Block, log; stock of a gun, ploughshare, etc. P.

كندي *kandai,* s.m. A potsherd, bit of broken pottery; a division, or quarter of a village, parish ward. s. (*khanḍ*). *kunḍī*, s.f. Calendering (cloth). H.

کند *kanḍ*, s.m. Sugar candy. S. (*khanḍ*). Gum. S. (*gond*). *kunḍ*, s.m. A widower.

کندا *kunḍā*, a. Harelipped, having a broken horn.

کنداس *kunḍās*, s.m. A man who has lost, or broken his front teeth; a toothless old man.

کندال *kanḍāl*, s.m. A cup, bowl, basin, etc. (of pottery).

کندتون *kunḍtūn*, s.m. Widowhood.

کندر *kanḍar*, s.m. Ruins of a house or village, broken and decayed walls, ruins; a place haunted by demons. H. (*khanḍar*).

کندک *kanḍak*, s.m. A herd of deer, flock of goats or sheep; a piece of bread.

کندکپړ *kanḍ-kapaṛ*, a. Shattered, smashed, broken to bits, cut to pieces, etc.

کندلي *kanḍala-ī*, s.f. Name of a plant (*Bryonia grandis*). A prickly seed that sticks to the fleece of sheep.

کندو *kanḍaw*, s.m. A notch, dent, gap; dip in a hill, gap in a wall, notch in wood, etc. a. Dented, notched. H. (*khanḍā*).

کندول *kanḍol*, }
کندولي *kanḍolai*, } s.m. See کندال.

کنده *kanḍa*, s.f. The spring or source of a river. *kunḍa*, s.f. A widow. A hook, fish hook, hook of a door, etc. H. (*kunḍā*).

کندۍ *kanḍa-ī*, s.f. See کنړۍ.

کنزل *kanzal*, v.a. See ښکنځل.

کنزله *kunzala*, s.f. Sesame, the plant and seed (*Sesamum orientale*). P. (*kunjad*).

کنزه‌گوته *kanza-gūta*, s.f. The third or ring finger.

کنستل *kanastal*, v.a. To dig, excavate.

کنف *kanaf*, s.m. Brink, edge, margin. A.

کنگال *kangāl*, a. Poor, friendless. S.

کنگخړ *kangakhaṛ*, s.m. Rubbish, sticks, straw, etc. carried down by floods, drift wood.

کنگر *kangar*, s.m. Pumice stone. H. (*khangaṛ*).

کنگره *kangura*, s.f. A pinnacle, turret; battlement, parapet; niched or loopholed wall; porthole; the plume of a helmet; ornaments on a crown. P.

کنگرې *kangarai*, s.m. A puppy. See کوترې.

کنگس *kangas*, s.m. A trip, stumble.

کنگل *kangal*, a. Congealed, frozen; compact, solid, dense. s.m. Ice.

کنگو *kangū*, s.m. Saffron.

کنل *kanal*, v.a. }
کنودل *kanawdal*, } To dig. See کندل.

کنه *kana*, s.f. A dog tick, sheep louse, large tick. The border of a garment, edge of a shawl. P.

کنیزه *kanīza*, s.f. A female servant, housemaid; a concubine. P. (*kanīz*).

کنړ *kanṛ*, s.m. Mucus from the nose, snot.

کنړاوه *kanṛāwa*, s.f. A clog, patten. H. (*khaṛānw*).

کنړه *kanṛa*, c. If not, of course, otherwise, then.

کنړي *kanṛai*, s.m. The warp (in weaving). *kanṛa-ī*, s.f. A wooden cup or bowl.

کواره *kawāra*, s.f. A pannier or basket, used to carry fruit, etc. in. H. (*ganwārā*).

کوب *kūb*, s.m. A hump, hunch. a. Humped. S. (*kub*).

کوبي *kūbai*, s.m. A hunch-back, humped ox or camel, etc. One of the pieces or stops of wood, in the horizontal wheel of a Persian wheel, which catches the cogs of the smaller wheel.

کوپ *kūp*, a. Bowed, stooping, bent, crooked in the back (as from old age).

کوپله *kopla*, s.f. A lark, skylark.

کوت *kawt*, a. Contracted, drawn in, pinched, tucked in, shrunk (as the belly from hunger).

کوتان *kotān*, s.m. A pelican.

کوتاه *kotāh*, a. Brief, short (in comp.). P.

کوتر *kautar*, s.m. A pigeon. P. (*kabūtar*).

کوتري *kūtrai*, s.m. A pup, puppy dog. H. (*kutrū*).

کوتل *kotal*, s.m. A pass over a mountain. P. A led horse. H. *kūtal*, v.a. To cut up, disjoint, divide. H. (*kāṭnā*).

کوتي *kwatai*, s.m. A dimple on the cheek or chin.

کوتي‌لال *kūtī-lāl*, s.m. See کتي‌لعل.

کوټ *koṭ*, s.m. A castle, fort, stronghold, hill fort. S.

کوټخه *koṭakha*, s.f. A cap made to cover the forehead and ears, a travelling cap; a mouth-piece or nosebag for cattle.

کوټک *koṭak*, s.m, Bludgeon, club; a pestle. H. (*kūtak*). The back of the head, occiput.

کوټل *kūṭal*, v.a. To pound, bruise; cudgel, beat, thrash, wallop. H. (*kūṭnā*).

کوټوال *koṭwāl*, s.m. The chief constable of a village or town. H.

کوټه *koṭa*, s.f. A mansion, large house; a chamber room. H. (*koṭhā*). *kūṭah*, s.m. A dog. H. (*kuttā*).

کوټئ *koṭa-ī*, s.f. A factory, warehouse, bank. H. (*koṭhī*). *koṭai*, s.m. The head. *kūtai*, s.m. An ass colt, a young donkey. H. (*khotrā*).

کوثر *kauṣar*, s.m. Name of a well in Paradise. Name of a disease, tetanus, lockjaw; stroke of the wind, or of cold.

کوڅه *kūtsa*, s.f. A lane, street. P. (*kūcha*).

کوڅئ *kotsa-ī*, s.f. See کونځي.

کوچ *kūch* or *koch*, s.m. Migration, a march. P. *kochi*, s.m. A nomade.

کوچټ *kūchaṭ*, a. Small, little, young. P. (*kūchak*). *kūchaṭ-wālai*, s.m. Smallness; childhood.

کوچمال *kūchmāl*, s.m. The leader of a march; conductor of a caravan.

کوچي *kūchai*, s.m. The tendon of the heel (*Tendo Achillis*). H. (*khūnch*). *kūchai*, s.m. An ass colt. *kocha-ī*, s.f. A cloak made of felt. *kochī*, s.m. A nomade.

کودالي *kūdāla-ī*, s.f. A hoe, mattock. S. (*kudālī*).

کودري *kawdarai*, s.m. A potsherd.

کودک *kodak*, s.m. A boy, youth. P.

کودله *kodala*, s.f. Hut, cabin, hovel.

کودن *kawdan*, a. Silly, foolish, imbecile. A.

کودي *kodai*, s.m. A pot, pipkin; potsherd.

کوديک *kawdīk*, s.m. A cooking pot, earthen pot.

کوډ *koḍ*, s.m. A shell, charm. S. (*gadh*).

کوډه *koḍa*, s.f. Sorcery, enchantment; jugglery. *koḍ-gar*, s.m. A sorcerer, magician, conjurer.

کوډئ *kawḍa-ī*, s.f. A cowrie. S. (*kauṛī*). *kūḍa-ī*, s.f. A shed, arbor, temporary hut made of boughs and leaves. S. (*kūṭī*).

کور *kor*, s.m. A house, dwelling, habitation; wife, family. H. (*ghar*). *kwar*, s.m. A wild grape tree, vine. *kor*, a. Blind. P. Border, margin, side. H.

کوربه *korbah*, s.m. Landlord, master of house; host, paterfamilias.

کورته *kūrta*, s.f. A coat, jacket, frock. P.

کورغنډل *korghunḍal*, s.m. Indian cactus, prickly pear.

کورکمان *kūrkamān*, s.m. Turmeric.

کورمانه *kormāna*, s.f. Domestic economy, housewifery, keeping house.

کوروالي *kor-wālai*, s.m. Marital duty, intercourse between husband and wife.

کوره *korah*, a. New, unused. H. (*korā*).

کوري *korai*, s.m. Net for carrying grass, forage, etc. H. (*khārā*). *kūrī*, in. Away! Get out!

کوړ *koṛ*, s.m. Leprosy. S. (*koṛh*).

کوړمه *koṛma*, s.f. Family, household, wife.

کوړه *koṛa*, s.f. A hole made in the ground for playing at marbles. H.

کوړي *kūṛai*, s.m. A measure of corn equal to the fourth part of an اوړي *ogai*. H. (*kuṛā*). *korī*, s.m. A leper. a. Leprous. S. (*koṛhī*).

کوز *kūz*, a. Below, under; low, lower.

کوزکتل *kūz·katal*, v.a. To look down, be sick at stomach, feel nausea.

کوزغالي *kūz·ghālai*, s.m. A dog's basin or eating dish.

کوزه *kūza*, s.f. A gugglet, long-necked water jar.

کوژدن *koĵdan*, کوژدنه *koĵdana*, } s.f. Betrothal, marriage engagement. See غوښتل.

کوژه *koĵa*, s.f. Eating the fast, not keeping the روژه.

کوږ *kog*, a. Bent, crooked, askew. P. (*kaj*).

کوږل *kwagal*, v.a. To endeavour, strive.

کوږووږ *kog·wog*, a. Very crooked, all awry.

کوس *kūs*, s.m. A large drum. P.

کوښښ *kokkhikkh*, s.m. Endeavour, application, zeal. P. (*koshish*).

کوښلي *kūkkhalai*, a. See کښلي *kkshulai*.

کوښه *kokkha*, s.f. A kind of slipper. P. (*kaush*).

کوک *kūk*, s.m. Crying, sobbing. S.

کوکري *kūkarai*, s.m. A puppy dog. S.

کوکړي *kokaṛai*, s.m. A biscuit, bun. See ککوړي.

کوکنار *koknār*, s.m. The poppy plant; the capsule. P.

کوکه *kūka*, s.f. See کوک.

کوکوړي *kokoṛai*, s.m. A large bannock or cake of bread baked upon heated stones.

کوکئ *kūka-ī*, s.f. Name of a tree (*Rhamnus virgatus*). *kokai*, s.m. A boy, lad, child. H. (*khokhā*). *koka-ī*, s.f. The cheek, side of the face; a little girl, female child.

کول *kawul*, v.a. To do, act, perform. *kūl*, a. Cotemporary, peer, of the same age. *kol*, s.m. A pond; a ford, shallow water. A. (*qūl*). *kol*, s.m. See کهول.

کولک *kolak*, s.m. The brow above the forehead; a hole in the roof by way of chimney.

کولنډ *koland*, s.m. A piece of stick used to tether cattle, etc. by the neck or foot; a log of wood attached to the neck of cattle to prevent their straying.

کولي *kolai*, s.m. A helmet, hat. P. (*kulāh*).

کوليار *koliyāṛ*, s.m. Name of a tree (*Bauhinea variegata*). H. (*kachnār*).

کوم *kūm*, pr. What? which? that which. P. (*kudām*).

کومک *komak*, s.m. Aid, help. See کمک.

کومي *kūmai*, s.m. The palate; cleft in the palate.

کونتر *kawntar*, s.m. A pigeon. See کوتر.

کونټي *kūnṭai*, s.m. A shepherd's crook; a stick with a crook at the end.

کونځئ *kontsa-ī*, s.f. The braided or plaited hair at the back of the head of women.

کونسټ *kūnsaṭ*, a. Contracted, shrunk, shrivelled. s.m. Foundation, base, root; stock or stump (as of a tree).

کونکي *kawunkai*, s.m. Actor, agent, doer, performer. *konkai*, a. (for *kamkai*), Diminutive, small.

کونګړي *kūngaṛai*, s.m. A puppy dog.

کونه *kūna*, s.f. Backside, podex, anus. P. (*kūn*). *kūna·starkai*, s.m. A clout, child's napkin.

کوني *kūnī*, s.m. } A catamite.
کونيګي *kūnīgai*, }

کوني *kūnai*, s.m. A dog louse, dog tick. Mortar, lime, whitewash.

کوني کبر *kūnī·kabar*, s.m. A crab.

کوڼ *kūṉr*, a. Deaf. P. (*kar*). *koṉr*, s.m. A tick, dog-louse.

کوه *koh*, s.m. Mountain, hill (in comp.). P.

کوهستان *kohistān*, s.m. Mountain country,

highlands. P. Name of the highland tract north of Swat.

کوهي *kūhai*, s.m. A well. S. (*kūā*).

کوئي *koe*, s.m. Itching, titillation.

کويښل *kwekkhal*, v.a. To write. Def. in pres. ten. See کارل.

کوئي‌کبر *koe-kabar*, s.m. See کوني کبر.

کويلي *koyilai*, } s.m. Pot-scrapings, burnt
کويني *koyinai*, } part of victuals at the bottom of a pot. H. (*khoyā*).

که *ki*, c. If, as, that. P.

کهاره *kahāra*, s.f. A pannier. See کواره.

کهاړه *kahāṛa*, s.f. A ring of rope, straw, etc. used as a target for arrows.

کهالي *kahālī*, s.f. Indolence, laziness; yawning, gaping, stretching. A. (*kāhilī*).

کهتر *kihtar*, a. Junior, minor, less, small. P.

کهربا *kahrubā*, s.f. Amber. P.

کهند *kuhand*, a. Ancient, old. P. (*kuhan*).

کهول *kahol*, s.m. Family, house, tribe.

کهه *kaha*, s.f. Itching; nausea.

کهي *kahai*, s.m. A reed, rush; a kind of clay, ochre. *kaha-ī*, s.f. A pickaxe; axle of a water mill; a ditch, trench.

کيجم *kejam*, s.m. A saddle cloth of felt.

کيدل *kedal*, v.n. To be, to become.

کير *kīr*, s.m. Rice and milk cooked together. S. (*khīr*). *ker*, s.m. *Penis virilis*. P.

کيړي *kīṛai*, s.m. A mole cricket.

کيرئي *kīra-ī*, s.f. The felloe or rim of a wheel.

کيړ *keṛ*, s.m. A screen or wattling made of the twigs of the tamarisk tree; a hedge, paling, etc. of tamarisk twigs.

کيړه *keṛa*, s.f. An iron ring in a plough; twigs or saplings (generally of the tamarisk tree) used in forming the roof of a house. H. (*keṛā*).

کيږدل *kegdal*, v.a. (For کښيږدل or ښکيږدل.) To set, place, put, etc. Def. in past ten. See کيښول.

کيس *kais*, s.m. The name of the great ancestor of the Afghans. He had three sons named Saṛabanṛ, Batanṛ, and Ghurghusht, to whom are traced in three great divisions all the different tribes of Afghans.

کيش *kesh*, s.m. Faith, religion, belief; manner, quality. P. Damask, diaper. H. (*khīs*).

کيښودل *kekkhodal*, } v.a. To place, put, set,
کيښول *kekkhawul*, } etc. Def. in pres. ten.
کيښوول *kekkhowul*, } See کيږدل.

کيښئي *kīkkha-ī*, s.f. A worm, mite, insect.

کيف *kaif*, s.m. Intoxication. A. *kaifī*, a. Intoxicated; intoxicating. s.m. A drunkard, sot.

کيفيت *kaifiyat*, s.m. Condition, state; statement, account; description, remark. A.

کيک *kaik*, s.m. A flea. P.

کيکړ *kīkaṛ*, s.m. Acacia tree. H.

کيل *kīl*, s.m. Furrow, rut, track, scratch. H. (*līk*).

کيلک *kīlak*, s.m. A hobble or fetter for the feet of a horse; a cord or tassel used to tie the scabbard to the sword handle.

کيمخت *kīmukht*, s.m. Shagreen; leather prepared from the hide of the horse or ass.

کيميا *kīmiyā*, s.f. Alchemy, chemistry. A.

کيناستل *kenāstal*, v.n. To sit, sit down, settle, subside. (For ښکيناستل or کښيناستل.)

کيند *kīnd*, s.m. A tattered and patched garment worn by dervishes.

کينول *kenawul*, v.a. To seat, instal, set. (For کښينول or ښکينول.)

کينه *kīna*, s.f. Malice, spite, rancour. P. *kīnawar*, a. Spiteful, revengeful, malicious.

کيڼ *kīṉr*, a. The left hand, left side, left.

گ

گ *gāf*. This letter being unknown in the Arabic is called the Persian kāf. It is the twenty-sixth letter of the Persian, and the thirty-third of the Pukkhto alphabet. It always has the sound of *g* hard as in *gun*. By the Yusufzais and Eastern Afghans it is very generally substituted for ږ *g*.

گاتلي *gātla-ī*, s.f. A bundle, package. H. (*gaṭhrī*).

گاټي *gāṭa-ī*, s.f. A small flat pebble, or bit of pottery set at the bottom of a pipe bowl, to prevent the tobacco getting into the stem. *gāṭai*, s.m. A round pebble, or pallet of dried clay, used to shoot from a sling.

گاډي *gāḍa-ī*, s.f. A cart, waggon. H. (*gāṛī*).

گاډيره *gāḍera*, s.f. Mixed grain, meal of pulses, corn, etc. mixed together; bread of mixed meal.

گازره *gāzara*, s.f. A carrot. S. (*gājar*).

گاگره *gāgra*, s.f. Granite, amygdaloid, trap-rock.

گالل *gālal*, v.a. To keep, preserve; watch over, care for; to finish, complete.

گام *gām*, s.m. A pace, step. P.

گانده *gāndah*, s.m. Future, coming time. P. (*āyanda*).

گانډي *gānḍa-ī*, s.f. The pole or shaft by which a Persian wheel is set in motion, and to which the bullocks are yoked.

گانګوړه *gāngūṛa*, s.f. Snivelling, snuffling, speaking through the nose.

گاڼره *gānṟa*, s.f. Pawn, pledge; jewel, ornament, trinket. S. (*gahnā*).

گاڼري *gānṟa-ī*, s.f. An oil press. H. (*ghānī*).

گاودم *gāwdum*, a. Tapering, like a cow's tail. P.

گاوز *gāwuz*, s.m. Stag, elk. P. (*gawaz*).

گاولي *gāwlai*, s.m. A kind of sandal or slipper made of leather.

گاوميښ *gāwmekkh*, s.m. A buffalo. P. (*gāw-mesh*).

گاونډ *gāwanḍ*, a. Neighbouring, next door.

گاونډي *gāwanḍai*, s.m. A neighbour, parishioner, fellow townsman. S. (*gāonṫī*).

گاه *gāh*, s.m. Time; place (in comp.). P.

گاهر *gāhar*, s.m. A drove of oxen, herd of cows.

گاهو *gāhū*, s.m. Drover, cattle driver.

گاهي *gāhe*, ad. Ever, anytime; once, sometime. P. *gāhe-gāhe*, ad. At times, sometimes, occasionally. P. *gāhī*, s.f. A deep wound or sore.

گايل *gāyal*, a. Wounded. H. (*ghāyal*).

گبر *gabr*, s.m. A fire worshipper, Zoroastrian. P.

گبينه *gabīna*, s.f. Honey; honeycomb. P. (*angabīn*).

گپه *gapa*, s.f. Chatter, prattle, talk. H. (*gap*). A lump or handful of mud.

گپي *gapī*, s.f. A cord used as halter, bit and bridle of rope.

گتکه *gatka*, s.f. Fencing foil. H. (*gadkā*).

گتمه *gutma*, s.f. A button hole or loop; a thimble, thumbstall of leather.

گټ *gaṭ*, s.m. A boulder, rock, stone; a dark and heavy cloud. *guṭ*, s.m. A corner, angle, recess; a hole dug in a wall by burglars.

گټل *gaṭal*, v.a. To acquire, realize, gain; to win, succeed, gain the victory, etc. P. (*yāftan*).

گټمي *guṭma-ī*, s.f. A thimble.

گټه *gaṭa*, s.f. A pebble, stone; advantage, gain, profit.

گټي *giṭa-ī*, s.f. A potsherd, bit of stone; gravel, shingle; urinary calculus, stone in the bladder. *giṭai*, s.m. Pebble, small stone.

گټين *giṭīn*, a. Stony, pebbly, gravelly, shingly.

گځاري *gadzārai*, s.m. Refuse, chaff, stubble.

گڅ *gats*, a. Left, the left side.

گڅي *gatsai*, a. Left-handed.

گچ *gach*, s.m. Lime, cement, mortar. H.

گداي *gadāe*, s.m. A beggar, mendicant. P. (*gadā*). *gadā-ī*, s.f. Begging; beggary, poverty. P.

گدل *gdal*, v.a. To place, set. P. (*hīdan*). See ږدل.

گډ *ga-aḍ*, s.m. A ram, sheep. H. (*gāḍar*). *gaḍ*, a. Mixed, compounded, blended. *guḍ*, a. Halt, lame, crippled, maimed.

گيدړ *gidaṛ*, s.m. A jackal. H. (*gīdaṛ*).

گډندي *gaḍandai*, s.m. A dancer.

گډوډ *gaḍ-waḍ*, a. Higgledy-piggledy, confused, entangled, jumbled. H. (*gaḍ-baḍ*).

گډوري *gaḍūrai*, s.m. A lamb.

گډوزي *gaḍozai*, s.m. A span, the space between thumb and forefinger.

گډول *gaḍawul*, v.a. To mix, compound, combine, etc.; to make dance.

گډون *gaḍūn*, s.m. Intercourse; mixture. Name of a Pathan tribe located on the southern slopes of the Mahaban mountain.

گډه *ga-aḍa*, s.f. An ewe, sheep.

گډهل *gaḍhal*, s.m. A bucket, tub, pail.

گډي *guḍa-ī*, s.f. A lame woman; a doll. H. (*guḍḍā*). *guḍai*, s.m. A lame man, etc. *gaḍa-ī*, s.f, A cushion, pad. H. (*gaddī*).

گډيدل *gaḍedal*, v.n. To dance; to be mixed, confused, blended, etc.

گډيدنه *gaḍedana*, s.f. Dancing; mixing, blending.

گډيدونکي *gaḍedūnkai*, | گډيدوني *gaḍedūnai*, } s.m. A dancer; mixer.

گډيره *gaḍera*, s.f. Mixture; intercourse.

گډيکه *gaḍeka*, s.f. The support of a spinning wheel; the crutch at the side of a sandal.

گذار *guzār*, s.m. A blow, stroke; pass, turn, round, etc. P.

گذر *guzar*, s.m. A ferry, ford, passage. P.

گذران *guzrān*, s.m. Employment, living, livelihood. I.

گړ *ga-aṛ*, s.m. Rumble, rattle, clatter, etc. (as of wheels).

گر *gar* (in comp.), added to words denotes -doer, -maker, -performer. P.

گران *grān*, a. Important, momentous; heavy, weighty; dear, precious; difficult, hard. P. (*girān*). *grānī*, s.f. Dearth, scarcity, dearness of provisions, etc.

گرت *grut*, s.m. Interdigital space (hand or foot); angle between the trunk and branch of a tree. *grut-niwul*, v.a. To hold between the finger and thumb (as a pen, arrow, etc.).

گرد *gird*, a. Circular, round. P. *girdāgird*, a. Round about, all round, on all sides. P. *gard*, s.m. Dust; the globe; fortune. P.

گرداب *girdāb*, s.m. A whirlpool. P.

گردن *gardan*, s.m. The neck. P.

گردني *gardanī*, s.f. A horse cloth. P.

گردون *gardūn*, s.m. A wheel; firmament, heavens; destiny, fortune; a chariot. P.

گردي ليچي *gardai-lechai*, s.m. The arm above the elbow; humerus.

گرز *garz*, s.m. Dust. P. (*gard*). *gurz*, or *gruz*, s.m. A battle-axe, club, mace. P.

گرزندي *ga-arzandai*, | گرزني *ga-arzanai*, } s.m. A reel, spindle; whirligig.

گرزول *ga-arzawul* or *girzawul*, v.a. To turn, change about, turn round, wheel, twirl, etc.

گرزيدل *ga-arzedal* or *girzedal*, v.n. To revolve, spin, turn about, wander, meander, walk about, etc. P. (*gardīdan*).

گرړل *gargal*, v.a. To scratch, claw, scrape (with the nails).

گرکنډه *garkanḍa*, s.f. See کرکنډه.

گرکي *ga-arkai*, s.m. The rattle or rumble of wheels.

گرگ *garg*, s.m. Mange, itch, scab. *gurg*, s.m. A wolf. P.

گرگره *gurgura*, s.f. Name of a tree yielding an edible fruit or berry (*Reptonia buxifolia*).

گرگس *gargas*, s.m. A vulture. P. (*kargas*). *gargas*, s.m. The cavity of the chest, thorax.

گرگه *garga*, s.f. A log, block, stump of a tree.

گرم *garm*, a Hot, warm; active, zealous; fiery, virulent; eager, intent; crowded, thronged. P. *gram*, a. Confuted, convicted; censured, rebuked. *guram*, s.m. A clump of trees; anxiety, mental distress, perturbation.

گرمكه *garmaka*, s.f. A heat spot, vesicle, pustule. pl. *garmake*, Prickly heat (*Lichen tropicus*).

گرمه *garmah*, s.m. A kind of melon. P.

گرمي *garmī*, s.f. Heat, warmth, etc.; the venereal disease. P.

گرنده *garanḍa*, s.f. Name of a shrub and its fruit (*Carissa spinarum*). H. (*karaundā*).

گرو *graw*, s.m. Pawn, pledge. P. (*girau*).

گرول *garawul*, v.a. To scratch, claw, scrape (with the nails).

گرولبي *grolbai*, s.m. Phlegm, mucus or pus from the lungs.

گروه *griwa*, s.f. The collar bone, neck above the collar bone; collar of a garment; button-loop. P. (*girebān*). *guroh*, s.m. A band, troop; people, tribe; party, sect. P.

گروهيدل *grohedal*, To admire, follow; be attracted, captivated; flock to; to fear, respect, revere. P. (*girwīdan*).

گريوان *girewān*, s.m. Collar of a garment; the neck. P. (*girebān*).

گريوه *grewa*, s.f. See گروه *griwa*.

گړ *gaṛ*, A castle, fort. S. (*gaṛh*).

گړدئ *gaṛda-ī*, s.f. The whirl of a spindle.

گړنج *gṛanj*, s.m. A clink, jingle, ring (of money), tinkle (of a bell), etc. *guṛanj*, s.m. A low voice, whisper.

گړندي *gaṛandai*, a. Quick, hasty, precipitate, rash; nimble, swift, fast.

گړنګ *gaṛang*, s.m. Abyss, crater; cavity, shaft, pit. *gṛang*, s.m. Mucus from the nose, snot.

گړوبي *guṛobai*, s.m. Sherbet, eau sucré, sugar and water.

گړونج *gaṛwanj*, s.m. A frame or stand for water jars; a stand, stage, platform. S. (*ghaṛwanchā*).

گړه *guṛa*, s.f. Raw sugar, brown sugar. S. (*guṛ*).

گړئ *gaṛa-ī*, s.f. A measure of time, about twenty-four minutes; a clock, watch. S. (*ghaṛī*). A pond, pool. H. (*gaṛhaī*). A fort, castle. S. (*gaṛhī*).

گز *gaz*, s.m. A yard measure; a ramrod. P.

گزك *gazak*, a. Festered, sloughed, suppurated, mortified (a wound); nipped with cold. P. s.m. Corruption, decay.

گزن *guzan*, s.m. Palsy, paralysis. *guzan-wahalai*, a. Palsied, paralysed.

گږ *gag*, a. Dappled, mottled; hybrid, mongrel.

گستاخ *gustā*kh**, a. Insolent, impertinent, rude, saucy, pert. P. *gustākhī*, s.f. Impertinence, assurance, pertness, etc.

گسه *gasa*, s.f. Rebound, recoil, ricochet; blow, dig, stroke, poke.

گسيا *gasiyā*, a. Abraded, rubbed, frayed. S. (*ghasā*).

گښت *gakkht*, s.m. Patrolling, walking round, strolling, wandering. P. (*gasht*).

گفتار *guftār*, s.m. Discourse, conversation. P.

گفتگوي *guft-goe*, s.m. Conversation, talk, etc. P.

گگر *gagar*, a. Brawny, muscular, stout, strong.

گگړوځه *gagaṛodza*, s.f. A shiver, tremble.

گگشتو *gugushtū*, s.m. A turtle dove, ring-dove. H. (*ghūghū*).

گل *gul*, s.m. A rose; a flower in general. P. A disease of the eye, albugo. Monday. *gil*, s.m. Clay, earth. P.

گلاب *gulāb*, s.m. Rosewater. P. *gulābī*, s.m. A barber.

گلخن *gulkhan*, s.m. A flat slab of stone used

for the flooring of a Turkish bath; a furnace, stove. P.

گلستان *gulistān*, } s.m. A rose bed, flower
گلشن *gulshan*, } garden. P.

گلو *gulū*, s.m. The throat, neck. P. *gilau*, s.m. Name of a plant, called also *kulma·walai* (*Mimosa scandens*). H. (*gīlā*).

گله *gila*, s.f. Complaint, lament, grumble. P. *gila·man*, a. Complaining, grumbling. P. *galla*, s.f. A herd, flock. P.

گلئ *gala-ī*, s.f. Hail. See ږلئ.

گم *gum*, a. Lost, missing, wanting. P.

گمارل *gumāral*, v.a. To consign, entrust, give in charge, commit. P. (*gumārīdan*, *gumāshtan*).

گماشته *gumāshtah*, s.m. Agent, factor. P.

گمان *gumān*, s.m. Doubt, suspicion; imagination, fancy; thought, supposition. P.

گمراه *gumrāh*, a. Erring, astray. P.

گمنز *gamanz*, s.f. A comb. See ږمنز.

گناه *gunāh*, s.m. Crime, fault, sin. P.

گنبته *gunbata*, s.f. An arch, dome, cupola, vault. P. (*gumbad*).

گنج *ganj*, s.m. A granary, market; treasure, store. P.

گنجي *ganjai*, a. Bald, scald headed; a vulture. H. (*ganjā*).

گنجيفه *ganjīfa*, s.f. A pack of cards; game at cards. P.

گند *gand*, s.m. A patchwork garment worn by dervishes. *gind*, s.m. A ball for play. S. (*gend*). *gund*, a. Equal, level, even, on a par; peer, compeer, match. *gundi*, ad. By chance, perhaps, possibly.

گندنه *gandana*, s.f. A leek (*Allium porrum*). P.

گنده *gandah*, a. Fœtid, stinking. P. *gundah*, a. Coarse, thick. P.

گنډ *ganḍ*, s.m. Edging of a garment; an ornamental collar worn by women; edging of clay round a millstone. S. (*ganḍā*). A patchwork coat worn by dervishes.

گنډل *ganḍal*, v.a. To hem, sew, stitch, baste, etc. P. (*nigandan*).

گنډولي *ganḍolai*, s.m. A short sleeved shift or jacket worn by women.

گنډهير *ganḍher*, s.m. Name of a plant (*Rhazzia stricta*).

گنډهيرئ *ganḍhera-ī*, s.f. A joint or segment of sugar cane (cut for convenience of chewing). S. (*ganḍerī*).

گنډي *gunḍī*, s.f. Collar of a dress; edging of a garment; a button loop, button. H. (*ghunḍī*). *gunḍai*, s.m. Refuse ears of corn, straw, etc. left on the threshing-floor. *gunḍe*, ad. By chance, possibly, perhaps.

گنډيري *ganḍerai*, s.m. The oleander or rose-bay (*Nerium odorum*).

گنزه *gunza*, s.f. A crease, crumple, pucker, wrinkle; a comb.

گنس *gans*, a. Stunned, stupefied, deafened. P.

گنكپ *gankap*, s.m. A cut-purse, pickpocket. H. (*gaṭh·kaṭā*).

گنګ *gung*, a. Dumb, mute. P.

گنګري *gungrī*, s.m. Boiled grain of pulse, wheat, etc. Grain steeped in water. S. (*ghūngnī*).

گنګړي *gingaṛai*, s.m. A small bell for the feet of pigeons, hawks, etc. H. (*ghūngrū*).

گنګس *gangas*, s.m. A bend, swerve, turn, twist; narcissus, daffodil.

گنګوسي *gangosai*, s.m. Rumour, report; hum, murmur, whisper; sound of footsteps, talking, etc.

گنه *gunah*, s.m. Sin, crime, fault. P. *gunah·gār*, s.m. A sinner, culprit. *gunah·gārī*, s.f. Sinfulness, guiltiness, criminality. P. *ganna*, s.f. The sugar cane. H. (*gannā*).

گنهر *gunhar*, s.m. Name of a potherb (*Amarantus polygamus*).

گنړ *ga<u>n</u>r*, a. Close, dense, thick, crowded; cloudy. S. (*ghan*).
گنړل *ga<u>n</u>ral*, v.a. To count, reckon; to consider, know. P. (*angārdan*).
گنړني *ga<u>n</u>ranai*, s.m. The womb.
گنړه *ga<u>n</u>ra*, ad. As if, as though; know, reckon.
گواښ *gwā<u>kkh</u>*, s.m. Arbitration, mediation; compromise, settlement.
گواښګرندي *gwā<u>kkh</u>·grandai*, s.m. Intercessor, mediator; negotiator, arbitrator.
گواښل *gwā<u>kkh</u>al*, گواښيدل *gwā<u>kkh</u>edal*, v.n. To pick a quarrel, peck at, irritate, prepare to quarrel; chide, reproach, blame. To mediate, parley, compromise, settle a quarrel. P. (*gawājīdan*).
گوانډي *gawānḍai*, s.m. A neighbour.
گواه *gawāh*, s.m. A witness. P.
گواهي *gawāhī*, s.f. Evidence, testimony. P. *gawāhī·lal*, v.a. To testify, give evidence. *gawāhī·lūnai*, s.m. A witness, testifier.
گوپ *gūp*, s.m. The evening star, Venus; a bank of clouds.
گوته *gūta*, s.f. A finger, toe.
گوټ *gūṭ*, s.m. A corner, angle, nook; a hole dug in a wall by burglars. *gūṭ·mātanul*, v.a. To break into a house through a hole in the wall (as burglars).
گوجر *gūjar*, s.m. A grazier, cowherd. Name of a tribe of Rājpūts dwelling amongst the Eastern Afghans, and mostly occupied as cattle breeders and graziers. S.
گوجي *gūjai*, s.m. A small fresh-water shell; a fir cone.
گودر *gūdar*, s.f. Ford, ferry, passage. P. (*guzar*).
گوډ *goḍ*, s.m. Weeding, thinning plants. S. (*<u>kh</u>od*). *goḍ·kawul*, v.a. To weed.
گوډا *gūḍā*, s.m. A doll, puppet. H.
گوډي *gūḍai*, s.m. A pouch; ear of Indian corn before the grain is formed. *gūḍa-ī*, s.f. A doll, puppet.
گور *gor*, s.m. A grave, tomb. P. *gor·kan*, s.m. A grave-digger. P. *gūr*, a. See گنړ.
گوراگور *gorāgor*, a. Fast, quick.
گورستان *goristān*, s.m. A graveyard. P.
گورکښ *gor·ka<u>kkh</u>*, s.m. Name of an animal found in graveyards, Indian badger.
گورل *goral*, v.a. To see, look, inspect, view, etc. P. (*girāndan*). Def in past tenses. See کتل.
گورم *goram*, s.m. A drove of buffaloes.
گوروان *gorwān*, s.m. A drover, grazier, cattle driver.
گوره خر *gorah·<u>kh</u>ar*, s.m. The wild ass. P. (*gor<u>kh</u>ar*).
گورهنده *gorhanda*, s.f. Rough uneven ground; ravine, chasm, pit, fissure.
گوړۍ *gūṛa-ī*, s.f. Juice or sap of trees.
گوشي *go<u>sh</u>ī*, s.f. Capitation tax on cattle.
گوښه *go<u>kkh</u>a*, s.f. Corner, angle, nook; privacy, retirement; aside, side; cell, closet. P. (*go<u>sh</u>a*).
گوګړ *gogaṛ*, s.m. Sulphur. P. (*gogird*). *gūgaṛ*, a. Aged, old, worn out (man or beast).
گوګل *gogal*, s.m. Cavity of the chest, thorax. *gūgal*, s.m. Name of a gum resin, Indian bdellium. S. *gogil*, s.m. Sulphur. P. (*gogird*).
گوله *gola*, s.f. A mouthful, morsel.
گولۍ *gola-ī*, s.f. A ball, bullet, pill. P. (*golī*).
گوماندو *gūmānḍū*, s.m. Mushroom, toadstool.
گونځه *gūn<u>dz</u>a*, s.f. A crease, wrinkle. See گنځه.
گونګټ *gūngaṭ*, s.m. A dung beetle.
گونګو *gūngū*, s.m. The yellow crocus, saffron.
گونګي *gūngai*, s.m. An owl.
گونه *gūna*, s.f. Colour, face, figure, form; kind, species. P.
گونړ *gū<u>n</u>r*, s.m. A weevil, insect in corn. H. (*ghūn*).

گوهاټه *gohāṭa*, A stack of cowdung (dried and stored for use as fuel).

گوهار *gūhār*, s.m. A drove of oxen or buffaloes.

گوهر *gauhar* or *gūhar*, s.m. A pearl, gem; essence, nature, substance, disposition; intellect, wisdom; lustre of a gem or metal. P.

گوي *goe*, s.m. Dry cowdung; a ball. P.

گويا *goyā*, ad. As if, thus, as one would say, etc. P.

گه *gah*, s.m. Time, place. See گاه.

گهواره *gahwāra*, s.f. A cradle, swing. P.

گهور *gahūr*, a. Dense, shady, umbrageous.

گهي *gahe*, ad. Ever. See گاهي.

گهيځ *gahīdz*, s.m. Dawn, morning.

گياه *giyāh*, s.m. Grass, herbage, weeds. P.

گيدي *gedī*, a. Stupid. P. *gedī-khar*, s.m. Stupid ass.

گيډه *geḍa*, s.f. Belly, abdomen.

گيډي *geḍai*, s.m. A load of wood, grass, etc., for the head. *geḍa-ī*, s.f. A small sheaf of corn, a bundle of grass, faggot of sticks, etc.

گير *gīr*, a. Caught, seized, captured, taken; (in comp.) conqueror, taker, seizer. P. *ger*, a. Surrounded, besieged, enclosed. H. (*gher*).

گيرګه *gīgaka*, s.f. A magpie.

گيسو *gesū*, s.m. A curl, ringlet. P.

گينډي *genḍai*, s.m. A rhinoceros; a shield of rhinoceros hide. S. (*gainḍā*).

گينړني *genṛanai*, s.m. The womb. H. (*ghaṛiyā*).

گيول *gayawul*, } v.a. To interlace, intertwine,
گييل *gayayal*, } wattle, net.

ل

ل *lām* is the twenty-third letter of the Arabic, and the thirty-fourth of the Pukkhto alphabet. It is often substituted for the letters د and ر in words from the Hindi and Persian.

لا *lā*, ad. Even, yet, still, hitherto, otherwise, unless. A particle prefixed to words to denote privation or negation, and equivalent to the English prefixes *im-*, *in-*, *un-*, etc., and the affix *-less*. A.

لابه *lāba*, s.f. Jest, irony, ridicule. P.

لاپه *lāpa*, s.f. Boasting, bragging. P. (*lāf*). *lāp-shap*, a. Proud, arrogant; bragging, boasting.

لات *lāt*, s.m. Name of an idol of the ancient Arabians.

لاټو *lāṭū*, s.m. A shrike, butcher bird; a humming-top; a whip-top. H.

لاجبر *lājbar*, s.m. Lapis lazuli. P. (*lājward*).

لاچي *lāchī*, s.f. Cardamums. H. (*ilāchī*).

لاډو *lāḍū*, s.m. A kind of sweetmeat. H. (*laḍḍū*). A humming-top. H. (*lāṭṭū*).

لار *lār*, s.f. A road, way, path. P. (*rāh*).

لارغه *lārghah*, s.m. Delay, procrastination; lateness, slowness. ad. Ago, formerly. *lire-lārghah*, ad. Long ago, of yore, long since.

لاړل *lāṛal*, v.n. To go, depart, set out. Def. in pres. ten. See تلل *tlal*. P. (*rāh-raftan*.)

لاړه *lāṛa*, s.f. Saliva, spittle. S. (*lār*).

لازم *lāzim*, a. Necessary, urgent; proper, suitable. A.

لاس *lās*, s.m. The hand; the arm. P. (*dast*).

لاسته *lāsta*, s.f. Direction, side, quarter.

لاستي *lāstai*, s.m. Handle, haft, hilt.

لاشوړه *lāshoṛa*, s.f. Name of a tree and its fruit (*Cordia Myxa*). H. (*lāsoṛa*).

لاښ *lākhsh*, s.m. A corpse, carcase. P. (*lāsh*).

لاغر *lāghar*, a. Weak, thin, lean. P.

لافه *lāfa*, s.f. See لاپه.

لاك *lāk*, s.m. Gum lac; sealing wax. S. (*lākh*).

لاکن *lākan*, a. Waxed; covered with wax. *lākin*, c. But, etc. See ليکن.

لاګ *lāg*, s.m. Dealings on credit with a tradesman.

لاگي *lāgī*, s.f. Trade, commerce. s.m. A dealer, customer.

لال *lāl*, a. Red; dumb. P. s.m. A ruby. P. (*l'al*).

لالا *lālā*, in. Master! Sir! H.

لالن *lālan*, s.m. A lover, sweetheart. S.

لاله *lāla*, s.f. A tulip. P. *lāla·gul*, s.m. The corn-poppy.

لالي *lālai*, a. Dear, beloved, darling.

لانبو *lānbo*, s.f. Swimming. *lānbo·zan*, s.m. A swimmer.

لاندِ *lāndi*, } ad. Below, under, beneath, down. *lānde·bānde*, ad. Upside down, topsyturvy, tumbled, jumbled.
لاندي *lānde*, }

لاندي *lāndai*, s.m. Salt meat, sun-dried meat.

لانډئي *lānḍa-ī*, s.f. A kind of snake, *amphisbœna*.

لانډيس *lānḍes*, s.m. Name of a tree and its fruit (*Cassia fistula*).

لانگه *lānga*, s.f. The cord at the foot of a bed, which is used to brace up or tighten the netting. The name of a tree from the wood of which arrows are made.

لانړه *lāṉra*, s.f. Name of a plant (*Salsola kali*); it is burnt for the potash it yields. Spittle, saliva. See لاړه.

لانوده *lānwdah*, a. Wet, damp. Pl. of لوند.

لاونړ *lāwaṉr*, s.m. Caudle, posset.

لاهو *lāhū*, a. Flooded, swept away by a flood, floated down by a river, etc.

لاهه *lāha*, s.f. Alluvium, mud, mire, muddy deposit left by floods.

لاي *lāe*, s.m. Mire, mud. See preceding word.

لائق *lā-iq*, a. Becoming, fit, suitable; proper, deserving, worthy; capable, qualified, expedient. A.

لب *lab*, s.m. The lip; brim, edge; bank, margin; coast, shore. P.

لباس *libās*, s.m. Apparel, clothes, dress; garb. A.

لپ څټ *lap·tsaṭ*, a. Fertile, fruitful (as land).

لپړ *lapaṛ*, a. Coarsely ground, gritty, unevenly mixed, clogged, clotty, lumpy (as food); thick stalks, stringy fibres, etc. mixed with potherbs; stiff, stark.

لپه *lapa*, s.f. The palm held to receive a thing; a handful, palmful. *lapakai*, s.m. The quantity containable in both hands held together. H. (*lapkā*).

لت پت *lat·pat*, a. Soiled, polluted, splashed; trampled, trodden down. etc.

لتاړه *latāṛah*, a. Trodden, trampled; spoiled, ruined.

لته *lata*, s.f. A kick. H. (*lāt*).

لټ *laṭ*, s.m. An axle; axle of a Persian wheel, weaver's loom, etc. A fishing stake, bird springe. a. Dull, indolent, lazy, listless. s.m. A lubber, lazy brute.

لټ پټ *laṭ·paṭ*, a. Tangled, tumbled, confused; soiled, stained; trampled, trodden.

لټول *laṭawul*, v.a. To examine, seek, search, rummage, turn over, investigate, look into, etc. H. (*ṭaṭolnā*).

لټه پير *laṭa·per*, s.m. Romping, frolicking, playing pranks, playing roughly, boisterous play.

لحاف *liḥāf*, s.f. A coverlet, quilt. A.

لحد *laḥad*, s.m. The niche in the side of a grave for the reception of a dead body. A.

لحظه *laḥẓa*, s.f. A moment; glance, look. A.

لد *lid*, s.m. Horse dung. H. (*līd*).

لدن *ladan*, } s.m. Inspiration. *'ilmi·ladūn*, s.m. Inspired knowledge, inherent wisdom. A.
لدون *ladūn*, }

لډر *laḍar*, s.m. A dealer in old clothes, rags, etc. a. Imbecile, foolish, stupid.

لذت *lizzat*, s.m. Flavour, taste; delight, enjoyment. A.

لذيذ *lazīz*, a. Pleasant, savoury. A.

لر *lar*, a. Lower, inferior; subordinate, minor;

conquered, subdued. p. Under, below, beneath. *lar·taraf*, s.m. The losing side, lower side. *liri*, ad. Far, far off, off, away. P. (*dūr*).

لرغونِ *larghūni*, ad. Already, ere now, before, long since, long ago.

لرغوني *larghūnai*, a. Former, pristine, old. *larghūne*, ad. Long ago, formerly, anciently, of old.

لرګي *largai*, s.m. A stick, staff; timber, wood. H. (*lakṛī*). *liragai*, s.m. The lobe of the ear.

لرل *laral*, v.a. To own, have, possess. P. (*dāshtan*, *dār-*).

لره *lara*, A particle used as the sign of the dative case; to, unto, near, with, at; for, for the sake of.

لري *larai*, s.m. The small intestines; bowel, gut. Defeat, discomfiture, loss. *lire*, ad. Off, away; far, far off, distant.

لړ *laṛ*, s.m. A row, bead, string, thread (as of beads, pearls, pots, etc.), H.

لړزه *laṛza*, s.f. A shake, tremor, quiver. P.

لړزيدل *laṛzedal*, v.n. To tremble, shake, shiver, quiver. P. (*larzīdan*).

لړل *laṛal*, v.a. To mix, stir, stir up, combine, stir about. H. (*lahrānā*).

لړم *laṛam*, s.m. A scorpion.

لړمون *laṛmūn*, s.m. The bowels, the internals, the heart, liver, lungs, etc. P. (*darūn*).

لړمه *laṛama*, s.f. Nettlerash, hives, urticaria.

لړوڅتو *laṛo·tsato*, a. Mean, low, vulgar. s.m. A rascal, blackguard, scoundrel, vagabond.

لړه *laṛa* or *la-ara*, s.f. Fog, mist, vapour.

لږ *la-ag* or *lag*, a. Small, little, less; few, scarce. *la-ag·der*, a. More or less, somewhat, a little, few, some.

لږکوټي *la-agkūṭī*, ad. Little; somewhat, few; scantily, slightly.

لس *las*, a. Ten. S. (*das*). *lasam*, a. Tenth.

لستونړي *lastūnṛaï*, s.m. Sleeve of a dress.

لسته *lasta*, s.f. Handle, hilt. P. (*dasta*).

لسره *lasara*, ad. Never, not at all, not a bit.

لشمكه *lashmaka*, لشمكۍ *lashmaka-ī*, s.f. Artful, intriguing, cunning, deceitful (woman); wanton, lewd, shameless (woman).

لشه *lasha*, s.f. Spike, prickle, bristle; sting of an insect; beard or spike of corn, grasses, etc. P. (*nesh*).

لښته *lakkhta*, s.f. A twig, switch, rod, cane.

لښتي *lakkhtai*, s.m. A brook, rivulet, linn, stream. *lakkhta-ī*, s.f. A dancing girl; ear-drop, pendant (of gold or silver). Name of a plant, the root of which is used as a charm by wounded persons to protect them from the evil wishes of their enemies, who, it is believed, by eating some of the root and then breathing upon a wounded man can prevent the healing of his wound, until some of their own spittle be applied to it; visitors to a wounded man are therefore requested to spit on a bit of the root, which is then passed over the wounds. The root is commonly found mixed with those of the madder plant (*majīṭ* or *rodang*) as sold in the shops.

لښکر *lakkhkar*, s.m. An army, multitude. P. (*lashkar*).

لښكي *lakkhke*, ad. Little. See لكوټي.

لطافت *laṭāfat*, s.m. Delicacy, elegance; humour, wit, facetiousness. A.

لطف *luṭf*, s.m. Courtesy, gentleness, kindness. A.

لطيف *laṭīf*, a. Elegant, delicate; agreeable, pleasant; courteous, kind, gracious. A.

لطيفه *laṭīfa*, s.f. A joke, witticism. A.

لعاب *lu'āb*, s.m. Mucilage. A.

لعل *l'al*, s.m. A ruby. P.

لعن *l'an*, s.m. Cursing, damning. A.

لعنت *l'anat*, s.m. Anathema, curse, malediction. A. *l'anatī*, a. Damned, cursed, execrated. A.

لغت *lug̲h̲at*, s.m. Dialect, phraseology; dictionary; word. A.

لغته *lag̲h̲ata*, s.f. A kick. P. (*lagad*).

لغړ *lag̲h̲aṛ*, a. Bare, stripped, naked; poor, destitute. *lūt̲s̲-lag̲h̲aṛ*, a. Bare as a bone, stark naked.

لغز *lag̲h̲z*, s.m. A slip, slide, stumble. A. *lug̲h̲z*, s.m. Enigma, riddle. A.

لغوي *lug̲h̲awī*, a. Linguistic, literal meaning of a word. A.

لفافه *lifāfa*, s.f. Cover, envelope, wrapper. A.

لفظ *lafẓ*, s.m. A word, saying. A.

لقب *laqab*, s.m. Surname, title; nickname. A.

لقمه *luqma*, s.f. A morsel, mouthful. A.

لقوه *laqwa*, s.f. Spasmodic distortion of the face; paralysis of the facial nerve. A.

لقه *luqah*, s.m. A bully, brag.

لک *lak*, a. Stiff, rigid, straight; punctured, bored, pierced. s.m. A lac, a hundred thousand. S.

لکړه *lakaṛa*, s.f. A beam, rafter; pole, staff; barge pole; boat hook. H. (*lakāṛ*).

لکوټي *lakūṭe*, or *lakūṭī*, ad. A little, somewhat, slightly, not much. See لږکوټي

لکوړي *lakoṛai*, s.m. Name of a fruit.

لکه *laka*, s.f. A blemish, blot, spot, stain; the tail (of bird or beast). ad. Like, so, as, thus.

لکه‌لمي *laka-lamai*, s.m. The rump bone, tail bone, coccyx.

لکئ *laka-ī*, s.f. The tail (of bird or beast); a meteor, falling or shooting star.

لګړ *lagaṛ*, s.m. A kind of hawk. H.

لګنړ *laganṛ*, s.m. A washing basin. P. (*lagan*).

لګول *lagawul*, v.a. To attach, fix, join; ascribe, impose, add; place, put, set; employ, engage, use; set to work, etc. S. (*lagānā*).

لګیا *lagiyā*, a. Applied, attached, placed; employed, occupied; intent.

لګیدل *lagedal*, **v.n.** To adjoin, reach, **touch,** apply; **happen**, befall, occur, begin; be occupied, employed etc. H. (*lagnā.*)

لال *lal*, a. Dumb, mute, speechless. P. (*lāl*).

لل *lal*, v.a. To utter, pronounce, say, express. Only used with a few words as, *ganāhī-lal*, v.a. To give evidence, testify, bear witness, etc. *salām-lal*, v.a. To say salām, pay respects.

للم *lalam*, a. Arid, dry, unirrigated (land).

للمي *lalamī*, s.m. Crops entirely dependent on the rains for water, unirrigated crops.

للئ *lala-ī*, s.f. Lullaby, hushaby. *lala-ī-lalos̲h̲a*, Hushaby baby, words intoned to put a child to sleep.

للون *lalūn*, s.m. Weeding, thinning (a field or garden).

لم *lam*, s.m. Tail, end, extremity; fat tail of the Afghan sheep. P. (*dum*). *lamawar*, a. Fat tailed, having a fat tail.

لمبړ *lumbaṛ*, s.m. A fox. H. (*lambar*).

لمبل *lambal*, v.a. To bathe, wash, clean, purify.

لمبه *lamba*, s.f. A blaze, flame.

لمبیدل *lambedal*, v.n. To wash, bathe.

لمڅي *lamt̲s̲ai*, s.m. Felt. P. (*namad*)

لمسول *lamsawul*, v.a. To incite, instigate, urge, prompt, tempt. A. (*lams*).

لمسون *lamsūn*, s.m. Instigation, prompting.

لمغړئ *lamg̲h̲aṛa-ī*, s.f. Contortion, writhe, twist; device, trick, wile; shamming, malingering.

لمن *laman*, s.m. Border, hem, skirt; margin, edge, verge. P. (*dāman*).

لمور *lamawar*, a. Fat tailed (as Afghan sheep).

لنبل *lanbal*, v.a. To bathe. See لمبل.

لنده *linda*, s.f. A bow.

لندي *lindai*, s.m. An archer, bowman. *linda-ī*, s.f. A small bow used by carpenters to work a drill or *barma*; the bow of a fiddle; one of the bones of the forearm; the outer bone of the leg; the hamstrings; any bent or arched twig; guard of a sword; a jet, spout, spurt of water.

لند *land*, a. Brief, short.

لنده *landa*, s.f. Lower end of the spine, sacrum.

لندئي *landa-ī*, s.f. A kind of poetry or verse, with seven or eight syllables to the line. A kind of snake, the head and tail of which are like each other (*amphisbæna*).

لنگ *lang*, a. Lame, crippled. P. *lung*, s.m. A cloth worn over the loins and hips when bathing; a clout worn between the thighs. P.

لنگټئي *lingaṭa-ī*, s.f. Name of a herb (*Heliotropum orientale*).

لنگر *langar*, s.m. An anchor; almshouse; kitchen. P.

لنگري *langarai*, s.m. A shallow metal dish, in which dough is kneaded; a deep bowl of metal or pottery in which snuff, spices, etc. are pounded; mortar. H. (*langrī*).

لنگور *langor*, s.m. A span between the thumb and fore finger.

لنگه *langa*, a. Puerperal, childbed; a puerperal woman, a woman for forty days after childbirth; an animal about to drop its young; an animal suckling its young; a bird hatching or sitting on eggs; with young, breeding, pregnant. *langa·kkhadza*, a puerperal woman. *langa·ghwā*, a milch cow *langa·chirga*, a brood hen. *langa*, s.f. A brace. See لانگه.

لنگئي *lunga-ī*, s.f. A scarf, sash (used as a head dress, or waist band, or worn as a sash over the shoulders). P. (*lūngī*).

لنگيدل *langedal*, v.n. To litter, drop young. P. (*langīdan*).

لو *lū*, s.m. Smoke. P. (*dūd*). *lau*, s.m. Reaping, mowing. P. (*dirau*).

لوار *lwāṛ*, a. Coarse, thick; rough, uneven; boorish, clownish; rude, unpolished.

لواطة *lawāṭat*, s.m. Sodomy. A.

لوال *liwāl*, a. Hungry, peckish; longing, yearning; inclined, hankering. A. (*luwāh*).

لواور *lawā·or*, s.m. A sickle, scythe. See لور *lor*.

لوبان *lobān*, s.m. Benzoin. A.

لوبه *loba*, s.f. Play, fun, frolic, game. A. (*l'ab*).

لوبيا *lobiyā*, A kind of bean (*Dolichos sinensis*).

لوټ *lūṭ*, s.m. Booty, plunder, spoil. S.

لوټه *lūṭa*, s.f. A clod, clod of earth. H. (*londā*).

لوټكي *loṭkai*, s.m. A pot, pipkin (of the kind used on Persian wheels). H. (*loṭā*). A small pillar of baked clay, three of which are used to form a tripod for the support of the iron dish on which cakes of bread are baked.

لوڅ *lūts*, a. Bare, naked, nude. P. (*lūch*). *lūts·lapaṛ*, or *lūts·pūts*, a. Stark naked, bare as a bone, without a shred.

لوڅک *lūtsak*, | لوچک *lūchak*, } a. Alone, destitute, friendless; profligate, vagabond, libertine; having little hair on the body (as a dog, etc.).

لوڅه پوڅه *lotsa·potsa*, s.f. Rolling and tumbling (as a baby on its back); rolling on the ground (as a dog, horse, etc.). H. (*loṭ·poṭ*).

لوح *lauḥ*, s.m. A board or tablet used by school-boys to write upon. A.

لوحه *loḥa*, s.f. A ruler, or scale of iron for drawing lines.

لوخړه *lūkhaṛa*, s.f. A blaze, flame. S. (*lūkh*).

لوخه *lūkha*, s.f. Bulrush (*Pencillaria spicata*); soft rush (*Juncus effusus*). P.

لودل *lawdal*, v.a. To say, express. See لل. Particularly applied to giving evidence, paying respects, etc. P. (*lāwīdan*).

لودي *lodī*, s.m. Name of an Afghan tribe, famous as having furnished emperors of Hindostan.

لور *lor*, s.m. A sickle, scythe. Direction, side. *lūr*, s.f. A daughter. P. (*dukhtar*).

لورایه *lawarāya*, ad. From afar, a long way off. (For لهورایه *la warāya*).

لوري *lorai*, s.m. Direction, quarter, side.

لوړ *lawaṛ*, s.m. A bludgeon, club, baton; a wooden pestle. s. (*loṛhā*). *lwaṛ*, a. Elevated, raised, high; upland, rising, hilly, etc. (ground). *lwaṛa·jawaṛa·zmaka*, High and low-, up and down-, undulating-, uneven-, or broken ground.

لوړول *lwaṛawul*, v.a. To detach, divide, separate, part, sever.

لوړیدل *lwaṛedal*, v.n. To part, separate, fall away.

لوزه *lauza*, s.f. A honey bee.

لوږه *lwuga*, s.f. Hunger. s. (*bhūkh*).

لوږي *lwugai*, a. Hungry, famished. s. (*bhūkhā*).

لوستل *lwustal* or *lūstal*, v.a. To read, learn. P. (*nabistan*, to write).

لوستل *lawastal*, v.a. To bale, empty; disperse, scatter, strew, daub, dash, besmear. Irr. pres. *lawanī*. Past. *lawast:*

لوشل *lwashal*, v.a. To milk (as a cow, etc.) P. (*doshīdan*).

لوښتل *lwukkhtal*, v.n. To part, separate, diverge, fall away, abscond. Def. in pres. ten. See لوړیدل.

لوښي *lokkhai*, s.m. A basin, pan, pot, etc. s. (*lokhar*). Nature, temperament, quality.

لوغزه *lwaghza*, s.f. A milch cow, goat, etc.

لوغړن *lūghaṛan*, a. Charred, smoked, smoke stained.

لوغونه *lawaghūna*, s.f. A milk pail.

لوګري *lau·garai*, s.m. A reaper, mower.

لوګي *lūgai*, s.m. Smoke, vapour, steam.

لولپه *lūlapah*, a. Burnt to ashes, scorched.

لولو *lolo*, s.m. An ornament for the arm or turban.

لولول *lwulawul*, v.a. To cause to read, to teach or learn by reading.

لوله *lola*, s.f. A ball or skein of thread; roll of paper, cloth, etc. P.

لولي *lolai*, s.m. A dancing boy. *lola-ī*, s.f. A dancing girl, prostitute. P. (*lūlī*).

لوم *lūm*, s.m. A net, noose, snare. P. (*dām*). S. (*lūm*),

لومکه *lūmaka*, } s.f. A noose, snare; a bird
لومه *lūma*, } trap of horse-hair nooses.

لون *laun*, s.m. Colour, hue; kind, species. s.

لونبړ *lūnbaṛ*, s.m. A fox. See لمبړ.

لوند *lūnd*, a. (f. *lamda*) Damp, moist, wet. P. (*nam*).

لونډ *lawanḍ*, s.m. A bachelor; widower; adventurer, vagabond, rake. P. (*lawind*).

لونګ *lawang*, s.m. A clove. s. (*laung*). *laung*, s.m. Posset, caudle, boiled milk and sugar.

لونه *lūna*, s.f. An abscess, boil.

لوهار *lohār*, s.m. A blacksmith. s.

لوهاني *lohānī*, s.m. Name of an Afghan tribe, principally occupied as carriers of merchandise between Hindustan and Turkistan. (For *rawānī*, by which name they are sometimes called.)

لوي *loe*, a. Great, large; corpulent, stout; chief, superior; full grown: great in office, rank, etc.

لویدل *lwedal*, v.n. To fall, slip, slide; drop down, fall down, tumble down, etc.

لویشت *lwesht*, s.f. A span between the thumb and little finger. P. (*bihisht*).

لویشتنک *lweshtinak*, } s.m. A pigmy, dwarf;
لویشتینک *lweshtīnak*, } small span; precocious child.

لویګنده *lweganda*, s.f. The temple, space between the ear and eye; fontanelle of an infant.

لوینه *lwīna*, s.f. A net or snare for birds.

لویرند *lwegand*, s.m. A sponger, parasite, toady.

له *la*, A preposition governing the ablative

case; from. A preposition or affix governing the dative case; to, unto.

لهري *laharai*, s.m. A beam, rafter.

لهلپاند *lahlapānd*, a. Scorched, charred. See لولپه.

لياقت *liyāqat*, s.m. Capacity, fitness; ability, skill; merit, worth. A.

ليټي *leṭa-ī*, s.f. Batter, paste, pap. H. (*leṭī*). *leṭai*, s.m. Hard clay, marl.

ليچ *lec͟h*, s.m. Ophthalmia, disease of the eyes.

ليچن *lec͟han*, a. Blear-eyed.

ليچه *lec͟ha*, s.f. The cubit, forearm.

ليچي *lec͟ha-ī*, s.f. The trotters of a sheep, etc.

ليدل *līdal*, v.a. To see, look, perceive. P. (*dīdan*). Irr. Pres. *wīnī*. Past, *līdah*.

ليده *līdah*, s.m. Seeing, sight, vision. P. (*dīdah*).

ليره *līra*, s.f. A shred or strip of cloth. H. (*līr*).

ليري *lera-ī*, s.f. Narrow ridge or edge of a hill.

ليزم *lezam*, a. Confuted, abashed.

ليږل *legdal*, v.a. To march, set out, pack up and depart.

ليږدول *legdawul*, v.a. To load and move off, march.

ليږل *legal*, v.a. To send, despatch, transmit.

ليښل *lekkhal*, v.a. To load, lade; march, set out. Def. in pres. ten. See ليږدل.

ليک *līk*, s.m. A line, mark, ruled line; furrow, rut, scrawl, wheel track. H.

ليکل *līkal*, v.a. To write. S. (*likhnā*).

ليکن *lekin*, c. But, yet, moreover. A.

ليکه *līka*, s.f. A line, furrow. See ليک.

ليمه *lema*, s.f. The pupil of the eye; the eye.

لينده *līnda*, s.f. A bow.

ليندي *līndai*, s.m. A bow. See لندي.

ليندړه *lenḍah*, a. Bald; scald headed.

لينګي *lengai*, s.m. The leg.

ليو *lew*, s.m. Plaster, mud plaster. H.

ليوال *lewāl*, a. Hungry. s.m. Appetite, hunger. See لوال.

ليور *lewar*, s.m. Husband's brother. S. (*dewar*).

ليوني *lewanai*, a. Demented, mad. P. (*dīwānah*).

ليوول *lewawul*, v.a. To plaster, daub, smear.

ليوه *lewah*, s.m. A wolf.

ليه *liyah*, a. Useless, worthless; uncontrolled, dissolute; wanton, lewd. Covered, veiled; noble, exalted. A. *liya*, s.f. The Tamarisk tree. ad. Merely, simply, only.

mīm is the twenty-fourth letter of the Arabic, and the thirty-fifth of the Pukkhto alphabet. It is a labial letter, and is sounded like the English *m*. In words where it is followed by ب it is sometimes changed to ن, as لنبه *lanba*, for لمبه *lamba*, flame. Prefixed to the imperative of a verb it denotes prohibition, being in place of the particle مه *ma*, as مکوه for مه‌کوه *makawā*, don't. It is added to the cardinal numbers to form the ordinals, as لس *las*, ten—لسم *lasam*, tenth.

مِ *mi*, a form of the genitive and instrumental cases, singular number, of the first personal pronoun زه *zah*, I. Also written مي *me*.

ما *mā*, The instrumental case and inflected form of the first personal pronoun زه.

مابوب *mābūb*, a. Beloved. See محبوب.

ماپښين *māpakkhīn*, or *māpakshīn*, s.m. Afternoon; afternoon prayers. P. (*namāz-peshīn*).

مات *māt*, a. Broken, cracked; beaten, dispersed; torn, lacerated. P.

ماتول *mātawul*, v.a. To break, burst open, smash; to break in upon, disperse, beat, etc.

ماته *māta*, s.f. Prey, quarry. S. (*mārā*).

ماتيدل *mātedal*, v.n. To break, burst, crack.

ماټس *māṭus*, s.m. A bump, swelling (from a blow).

ماچي *māc͟he*, s.f. (pl. of *māc͟ha*) Vermicelli.

ماخستن *mā<u>kh</u>ustan*, s.m. Bedtime, evening; bedtime prayers. P. (*namāz·<u>kh</u>uftan*).

مادہ *māda*, s.f. Article, clause; matter, subject. A. (*mādda*). *māda*, s.f. Female. a. Feminine. P.

مادیان *mādiyān*, s.f. A mare. P.

مادین *mādīn*, s.f. A female. P.

مار *mār*, s.m. A serpent, snake. P.

مارج *mārij*, s.m. A flame of fire. A.

مارجړي *mār·jaṛai*, s.m. Name of a bulbous root used as a remedy for snake bites.

مارغه *mār<u>gh</u>ah*, s.m. Pl. of مرغه which see.

ماړي‌هاړي *māṛe·hāṛe*, in. Exclamation of complaint, dear me! oh dear!

مازدگر *māzdigar*, s.m. Afternoon; evening; afternoon prayers. P. (*namāz dīgar*).

مازو *māzū*, s.m. A gallnut. P.

ماسپښين *māspak<u>kh</u>īn*, s.m. See ماپښين.

ماسته *māstah*, s.m. Curds, curds and whey.

ماسختن *mās<u>kh</u>utan*, s.m. See ماخستن.

ماسوا *mā·siwā*, ad. Besides, moreover. A.

ماسه *māsa*, s.f. Name of a weight equal to twelve grains. H.

ماسئ *māsa-ī*, s.f. Leather socks worn inside the shoes, and not removed in the house.

ماش *mā<u>sh</u>*, s.m. Name of a kind of pulse or bean (*Phaseolus Max*). S. *girgirah·mā<u>sh</u>*, s.m. Bean meal.

ماشله *mā<u>sh</u>ala*, } s.f. A skein, hank of thread
ماشوړه *mā<u>sh</u>oṛa*, } or silk.

ماشوق *mā<u>sh</u>ūq*, s.m. A lover. See معشوق.

ماشوم *mā<u>sh</u>ūm*, s.m. An infant. See معصوم.

ماشي *mā<u>sh</u>ai*, s.m. A musquito, gnat.

ماښام *mā<u>kkh</u>ām* or *mā<u>ksh</u>ām*, s.m. Evening. P. (*namāz <u>sh</u>ām*).

ماغزه *mā<u>gh</u>zah*, s.m. The brains (pl. of مغز which see).

ماکو *mākū*, s.m. A weaver's shuttle. S. (*mākho*). Name of an Afghan clan.

مال *māl*, s.m. Property, wealth; effects, goods; cattle, merchandise. A. *māl* (in comp.), Rubbing, rubber. P. *ma-āl*, s.m. End, issue. A. *<u>kh</u>air·ma-āl*, s.m. A happy issue.

مالدار *māl·dār*, a. Wealthy, rich in cattle, etc. Owner of cattle; cattle grazier.

مالت *mālat*, s.m. A division, quarter, parish, ward. A. (*muḥalla*).

مالش *māli<u>sh</u>*, s.m. Polishing, rubbing, friction. P.

مالك *mālik*, s.m. Master, owner, proprietor. P.

مالکنډئ *mālkunḍa-ī*, } s.f. Name of a plant,
مالکنړئ *mālku<u>nr</u>a-ī*, } caltrops (*Tribulus terrestris*).

مالګه *mālga*, s.f. Salt.

مالګبه *mālgbah*, s.m. Collector of salt, dry salter.

مالګين *mālgīn*, a. Salt, saline.

مالګينړي *mālgī<u>nr</u>ai*, s.m. A game played by boys.

مالوچ *mālū<u>ch</u>*, s.m. Picked cotton, carded cotton.

ماله *māla*, s.f. A weaver's brush; clod crusher; rubber. P.

ماما *māmā*, s.m. Maternal uncle. S.

مامن *māman*, Place of security, asylum. P.

مامور *māmūr*, a. Established, ordered, fixed. S.

ماموله‌که *māmūlaka*, s.f. A water-wagtail. A. (*māmolā*).

ماموئ *māmū-ī*, s.f. A dried apricot, with the kernel preserved inside it.

مامي *māmī*, s.f. Aunt, maternal uncle's wife.

مانجي *mānjī*, s.m. A marriage guest of the the bridegroom. H. (*mānjhā*, wedding feast).

ماندړه *māndara*, s.f. A tent rope; a heart string, one of the *cordæ tendineæ*.

مانده *māndah*, a. Weary, fatigued, tired. P. *mānda*, s.f. A heart string, tendinous cord of the heart.

ماندينه *māndīna*, s.f. A female. P (*mādīn*).

مانع *mān'i*, s.m. Forbidder, preventer; obstacle, hindrance. A.

مانگي *māngai*, }
مانړگي *mān̲rgai*, } s.m. A boatman, sailor. H. (*mānjhī*).

مانموله *mānmola*, s.f. Name of a potherb.

مانه *māna*, }
مانړه *mān̲ra*, } s.f. Blame, complaint; murmur, lament.

مانړو *mān̲rū*, s.m. A kind of wild sloe or plum; the name of a herb used in medicine.

مانړي *mān̲rai*, s.m. Estrangement, misunderstanding; umbrage, pique. *mān̲ra-ī*, s.f. Edifice, building; pile, storied house.

مانړيگر *mān̲rī-gar*, a. Annoyed, piqued, displeased, estranged.

ماولي *mānlai*, s.m. The piece of wood, in the centre of the upper millstone, through which the pivot of the lower one passes.

ماه *māh*, s.m. The moon (in comp.); month. P.

ماهي *māhai*, s.m. A fish. P. (*māhī*).

مائچي *mā-ic̲he*, s.f. Vermicelli. See ماچي.

مائل *mā-il*, s.m. Propensity, inclination, tendency. A.

مائلان *mā-ilān*, a. Partial, biassed, inclined. A.

مايه *māya*, s.f. Capital, stock; leaven, ferment; rennet. P. *māyah*, s.m. A double humped camel. P.

مباح *mubāḥ*, s.m. An indifferent action, an action neither ordained nor prohibited in the law. A.

مباد *mabādā*, in. God forbid! lest! be it not! P.

مبارك *mubārak*, a. Fortunate, happy; holy. in. Hail! welcome! A. *mubāraki*, s.f. Congratulation, happiness. A.

مبالغه *mubālig̲ha*, s.f. Hyperbole, exaggeration. A.

مبتدي *mubtadī*, s.m. Tyro, novice, beginner; beginning. A.

مبتلا *mubtilā*, a. Captivated, fascinated; involved in trouble, distracted. A.

مبلغ *mublag̲h*, s.m. A sum, ready money; much, many. A.

مبهم *mubham*, a. Ambiguous, occult, unknown, secret. A.

متره *matra*, s.f. Posset, sillabub, curdled milk; dregs, sediment, refuse. *matrah*, a. Rare, scarce.

متصل *mutaṣṣil*, a. Contiguous, close, adjoining. A.

متعلق *mut'alliq*, a. Concerning, relative; belonging to. A.

متفرق *mutafarriq*, a. Separate, distinct; dispersed. A.

متفق *mutaffiq*, a. United, agreeing; accomplice. A.

متل *matal*, s.m. Proverb, adage; fable, saying. A. (*maṣal*).

متن *matan*, s.m. Middle or text of a book. A.

متوجه *mutawajjah*, a. Facing, turning; attending, favouring. A.

متولي *mutawallī*, s.m. Superintendent or treasurer (of a mosque). A.

مته *matah*, s.m. A wild boar.

متيازه *mitiyāza*, s.f. Urine. S. (*mūt*).

مټ *ma-aṭ*, s.m. The arm; fore limb of an animal.

مټ *maṭ*, s.m. Celerity, dispatch; deep dust on a road; a kind of earthenware pot. *muṭ*, s.m. The fist, closed hand. H. (*muṭh*).

مټاك *maṭāk*, s.f. A walnut with a hard shell.

مټاكه *maṭāka*, s.f. A bump, swelling from the sting of a bee, etc.; nettlerash; ball of a pellet-bow; kind of hard walnut.

مټر *muṭar*, s.m. Dolt, fool, piss-a-bed. S. (*mūtr*).

مټكي *maṭkai*, s.m. Bracelet, ornament for the arm. A large earthen jar. H. (*maṭkā*).

مټه *maṭa*, s.f. Clay, marl, greasy earth. S. (*maṭṭī*). *maṭah*, a. Lazy, stubborn, obstinate.

متي *muṭai*, s.m. The fist; handle, hilt. s. (*muṭhī*). *muṭa-ī*, s.f. A bow for cleaning cotton; the club with which it is worked. Handle of a plough, hilt of a sword, etc.

متياي *miṭiyā-ī*, s.f. A sweetmeat; confectionary. H. (*miṭhā-ī*),

متيز *maṭīz*, s.m. A man who has eloped with another's wife or daughter.

متيزه *maṭīza*, s.f. A woman who has eloped with a man to whom she is not married; elopement, running away (of lovers).

مثال *mis̤āl*, s.m. Metaphor, allegory; likeness, simile; parable, saying. A.

مثقال *mis̤qāl*, s.m. Name of a weight equal to fifty-four grains (Troy). A.

مثل *mas̤al*, s.m. A proverb. See متل.

مثلاً *mas̤lan*, ad. For example; *e.g.*; *i.e.*; *viz*. A.

مجاور *majāwar*, s.m. A verger, sweeper at a mosque or shrine. A.

مجرا *mujrā*, s.f. Premium, allowance; deduction, retrenchment. A.

مجرب *mujarrab*, a. Proved, tried; skilled, expert. A.

مجرد *mujarrad*, a. Alone, single; unmarried. A.

مجرم *mujrim*, a. Sinful, criminal. s.m. culprit. A.

مجلس *majlis*, s.m. Assembly, congregation; meeting, party. A.

مجمر *majmir*, s.m. A chafing dish, incense dish. A.

مجمل *mujmal*, s.m. Abstract, summary. A.

مجنون *majnūn*, a. Insane, love mad, P.

مڅوڅکي *maṯsoṯskai*, s.m. See مچڇکي.

مچ *mac̱h*, s.m. A fly; the sight at the muzzle of a gun.

مچڇکي *mac̱hic̱hkai*, s.m. Name of a plant used in medicine.

مچک *mac̱hak*, s.m. A shepherd's crook.

مچمچي *mac̱hmac̱hai*, s.m. A honey bee.

مچلوغزه *mac̱haloghza*, } s.f. A sling (for throwing stones).
مچوغنه *mac̱hoghana*, }

مچه *mac̱ha*, s.f. A kiss. H. (*mac̱hhī*).

مچۍ *mac̱ha-ī*, s.f. A bee.

محافظت *muḥāfiz̤at*, s.m. Custody, care, protection. A.

محال *maḥāl*, a. Absurd, impossible. A.

محبت *muḥabbat*, s.m. Affection, love. A.

محبوب *maḥbūb*, a. Loved, beloved. A.

محتاج *muḥtāj*, a. Needy, indigent, necessitous. A.

محتسب *muḥtassib*, s.m. A censor. A. An official who parades the streets armed with a thong, sees that the faithful duly perform their prayers and repeat the belief, etc. A.

محراب *miḥrāb*, s.m. The alcove or closet in a mosque, in which the priest, facing Mecca, performs prayers before the congregation. A.

محرم *muḥarram*, a. Sacred, forbidden. A.

محرمه *muḥarrama*, s.f. Name of the first month of the Muḥammadan calendar.

محروم *maḥrūm*, a. Forbidden, prohibited; deprived, excluded. A.

محصول *maḥṣūl*, s.m. Custom, excise, duty, tax.

محض *maḥz̤*; a. Pure, simple. ad. Purely; solely. A.

محفوظ *maḥfūz̤*, a. Secure, protected. A.

محکم *muḥkam*, a. Firm, strong. secure. ad. Firmly. A.

محکمه *muḥkama*, s.f. A court of justice. A.

محل *maḥall*, s.m. Place, house, abode; time. A.

محله *muḥalla*, s.f. A district, parish, ward; place, building, edifice. A.

محمد *muḥammad*, a. Praised. s.m. Name of the Arabian prophet. A.

محنت *miḥnat*, s.m. Labour, toil, trouble; wages, hire; affliction, difficulty, misfortune. A.

مخ *ma<u>kh</u>*, s.m. Face, front, surface; civility, kindness, courtesy. s. (*mu<u>kh</u>*). *ma<u>kh</u>ā-ma<u>kh</u>*, ad. Face to face, opposite.

مخالف *mu<u>kh</u>ālif*, a. Adverse, opposed, contrary. A.

مخالفت *mu<u>kh</u>ālifat*, s.m. Opposition, contrariety. A.

مخبر *mu<u>kh</u>bir*, s.m. A spy, reporter, informer. A.

مختار *mu<u>kh</u>tār*, s.m. A free agent, attorney. a. Absolute, independent; chosen, selected. A.

مختصر *mu<u>kh</u>taṣir*, a. Abridged. s.m. Compendium, abstract, epitome. A.

مختلف *mu<u>kh</u>talif*, a. Discordant, diverse. A.

مخسره *ma<u>kh</u>sara*, s.f. Jesting, joking. See مسخره.

مخرني *ma<u>kh</u>ranai*, s.m. A kind of plum, apricot.

مخفي *ma<u>kh</u>fī*, a. Secret, concealed, hidden. A.

مخلص *mu<u>kh</u>liṣ*, a. Sincere, true (friend). A. *mu<u>kh</u>laṣ*, s.m. Asylum, refuge. A.

مخلوت *ma<u>kh</u>lūt*, a. Mixed, combined, confused. A.

مخلوق *ma<u>kh</u>lūq*, s.m. Creature, created being. a. Created. A.

مخور *ma<u>kh</u>awar*, a. Polite, courteous, civil, kind.

مخه *mu<u>kh</u>a*, s.f. A butt for arrows, archery butt. *ma<u>kh</u>a*, s.f. Direction, side, way.

مخي *ma<u>kh</u>ai*, a. Equal, even, par. s.m. compeer, peer, equal, clansman.

مدار *madār*, s.m. Affability, complaisance, favour, politeness, kindness. A. (*mudārā*).

مدام *mudām*, ad. Always, continually, ever. A.

مدت *muddat*, s.m. Time, space, long time. A.

مدد *madad*, s.m. Aid, help, succour. A.

مدرس *mudarris*, s.m. Professor, teacher, head of a college. A.

مدرسه *madrassa*, s.f. College, university, school. A.

مدعا *mudd'ā*, s.f. Desire, wish; object, view. A.

مدعي *mudda'ī*, s.m. A plaintiff, claimant, prosecutor; enemy. A. *mudda'ī-alaihi*, s.m. A defendant. A.

مذكور *maẕkūr*, a. Aforesaid, mentioned. s.m. Discourse, mention, conversation. A.

مذمت *maẕamat*, s.m. Abuse, contempt. A.

مذهب *maẕhab*, s.m. Religion, sect. A.

مذي *maẕa-ī*, s.f. Mucus from urethra or vagina. A.

مراد *murād*, s.m. Desire, wish; purport, design. A.

مرانده *marānda*, s.f. A tent rope. See ماندره.

مراوه *mrāwa*, s.f. The part of a Persian wheel which supports one of the troughs.

مربي *murabbī*, s.m. Tutor; guardian; patron. A.

مرت *murt*, s.m. A kind of wormwood; a powder applied to the private parts of infants.

مرتبه *martaba*, s.f. Degree, office, rank; class, order; time, turn. A.

مرتد *murtadd*, s.m. Apostate, renegade. A.

مرجان *marjān*, s.m. Coral. P.

مرجيونړه *marjīwa<u>n</u>rah*, s.m. Coral diver, pearl diver. s. (*marjīyā*).

مرچ *mra<u>ch</u>*, s.f. Pepper. s. (*mir<u>ch</u>*). *sra-mra<u>ch</u>*, s.f. Red pepper, capsicum.

مرد *mard*, s.m. A man; a male. P.

مردار *murdār*, a. Polluted, filthy, foul; ugly. s.m. Carrion, offal, pollution. P.

مردانه *mardānah*, a. Manly, brave. P.

مردرو *mard-rau*, s.m. Parapet, breastwork. P.

مردك *mardak*, s.m. A ball, cannon ball.

مردكه *mardaka*, s.f. } A bullet, pellet, bolus;
مردكي *mardakai*, s.m. } a marble, pebble.

مردم *mardum*, s.m. Man, mankind; people, the world. P.

مردود *mardūd*, a. Outcast, reprobate, rejected. A.

مرده *murdah*, a. Dead. s.m. A corpse. P.

مردي *mardī*, s.f. Manliness, bravery; virility, semen. P.

مرسته *mrasta*, s.f. Partiality, favour; help, aid, assistance.

مرسل *mursal*, s.m. Messenger; prophet. A.

مرسله *mursila*, s.f. Epistle, missive. A.

مرشد *murshid*, s.m. Guide, teacher, director (religious); monitor, instructor. A.

مرصع *murassa'*, a. Jewelled, gilt. A.

مرض *maraz*, s.m. Disease, sickness. A.

مرضي *marzī*, s.f. Will, pleasure. A. *marazī*, a. Sick, diseased. A.

مرغ *mragh*, s.m. A large stone used in the exercise of "putting the stone."

مرغچچي *marghachichai*, s.m. Name of a grain used to make necklaces, etc.; Job's tears, seeds of *Coix lachryma*.

مرغړي *margharai*, s.m. A tumour, glandular swelling.

مرغلره *marghalara*, s.f. A pearl.

مرغمي *marghumai*, s.m. A kid. See ورغومي.

مرغه *marghah* (pl. *mārghah*), s.m. A bird. P. (*murgh*). *margha*, s.f. A kind of grass (*Milium filiforme*). P. (*margh*).

مرغۍ *margha-ī*, s.f. A little bird, any small bird.

مرکنډۍ *markanda-ī*, s.f. The throat, neck; windpipe and gullet.

مرګ *marg*, s.m. Death, decease, demise. P.

مرګوټي *margotai*, s.m. Paroxysm of death, death struggle, death.

مرله *marla*, s.f. A land measure equal to four and a half yards square.

مروت *marwat*, s.m. A coil, twist; screw. *marwat*, s.m. Name of a district between the Indus and Sulaiman mountains; name of the tribe inhabiting Marwat. *muruvat*, s.m. Urbanity, generosity; fortitude, manliness. A.

مرور *marawar*, a. Displeased, offended, piqued.

مروري *marorī*, s.f. Name of a plant (*Helicteres isora*). H.

مروړ *maror*, s.m. Convolution, turn, twist. H.

مرهم *marham*, s.m. A plaister, ointment, salve. A.

مرۍ *mara-ī*, s.f. The neck, throat, gullet and windpipe; a bead; a charm.

مريد *murīd*, s.m. Disciple, follower. A.

مريض *marīz*, a. Diseased, sick. A.

مرينړه *marīnra*, s.f. Patch of a field left uncut, work left unfinished.

مرئي *mra-e*, s.m. A slave, bondsman.

مړ *mur*, a. Dead, lifeless, defunct. P. (*murd*). *mur·kawul*, v.a. To kill, deprive of life, put out (as fire, etc.).

مړام *mrām*, } a. Decayed, withered, faded.
مړاو *mrāw*, }

مړانه *marāna*, s.f. Bravery, heroism, manliness. P. (*mardānah*).

مړځپن *martsapan*, a. Faded, withered, decayed.

مړد *mard*, s.m. A saint, religious guide.

مړشومه *mur·shūma*, s.f. Food sent by friends and relatives to the house of a deceased person on the day of death.

مړز *mraz*, s.f. A quail.

مړغونه *maraghūna*, s.f. Bitter apple, colocynth (*Citrullus Colocynthis*).

مړغيچن *marghechan*, a. Faded, withered; frost bitten, nipped by cold. See مړځپن.

مړل *mral*, v.n. To die. P. (*murdan*).

مړني *maranai*, a. Brave, daring, manly. s.m. A hero. P. (*mardānah*).

مړوښه *marokkha*, s.f. A married woman, woman under coverture, wife.

مړوند *marwand*, s.m. The wrist, wrist joint.

مړونډۍ *marwanda-ī*, s.m. Name of a shrub (*Vitex negundo*).

مړه *marah*, } in. Man! Sir! Master! Sirree! P. (*mard*).
مړي *marai*, }

مړي *murai*, a. Dead, lifeless. s.m. A corpse,

dead body. *maṛa-ī*, s.f. A morsel, mouthful.

مزاج *mizāj*, s.m. Constitution, temperament, habit, disposition, temper, nature. A.

مزاخ *mazākh*, s.m. A joke, jest; ridicule. A.

مزد *muzd*, s.m. Hire, salary, wages; perquisite, premium; corn taken by a miller as the price of grinding. P. *mazdah*, s.m. A miller.

مزدگري *muzd·garai*, s.m. A miller.

مزدور *mazdūr*, s.m. A labourer, workman. P. *mazdūrī*, s.f. Labour, work; hire, wages. P.

مزري *mzarai*, s.m. A leopard, panther; tiger.

مزكه *mzaka*, s.f. Earth, ground, land, soil.

مزل *mazal*, s.m. A stage. See منزل.

مزه *maza*, s.f. Flavour, relish, taste; delight, enjoyment, pleasure. P. (*mazā*).

مزي *mazai*, a. Powerful, strong. s.m. Cord, twine, thread, string; edging or piping of a dress.

مږ *mag*, s.m. A ram. S. (*mekh*).

مږك *magak*, s.m. A rat.

مږكوړي *magakūṛai*, s.m. A mouse, young rat.

مږل *mugal*, v.a. To rub. Def. in past ten. See مښل.

مږه *magah*, s.m. A rat. P. (*mūsh*).

مس *mis*, s.m. Copper. P. *mas*, s.m. A cup for collecting lamp-black.

مسافر *musāfir*, s.m. A traveller, stranger. A.

مست *mast*, a. Drunk, intoxicated; proud, wayward; wanton, sensual. P.

مستك *mastak*, s.m. Name of a weed, darnel, tares. Name of a resin, mastick. A. (*maṣtakī*).

مسجد *masjid*, s.m. A mosque, house of prayer. A.

مسحه *masḥa*, s.f. Anointing; wiping. A. (*masḥ*).

مسخراچي *maskharāchī*, s.m. A buffoon, jester, clown. P.

مسخره *maskhara*, s.f. Drollery, jesting. P.

مسرف *musrif*, a. Prodigal, extravagant. A.

مسكن *maskan*, s.m. Abode, dwelling. A.

مسكي *muskai*, s.m. Laughing, smiling; simper, smile. H. (*muskān*).

مسل *musal*, v.n. To simper, smile.

مسله *masala*, s.f. Proposition, question; a precept of Muhammad. A.

مسند *masnad*, s.m. A throne. A.

مسواك *miswāk*, s.m. A toothbrush. A.

مسي *masa-ī*, s.f. An ornament for the head.

مسيدل *musedal*, v.n. To simper, smirk, smile.

مسين *misīn*, a. Made of copper or brass, brazen. P.

مسينه *misīna*, s.f. A set of copper pots and pans.

مشابه *mushābih*, a. Resembling, like. A.

مشابهت *mushābihat*, s.m. Resemblance, likeness, conformity. A.

مشاته *mushāta*, s.f. An ugly face, cross look.

مشاد *mushād*, a. Ugly, cross-looking.

مشال *mashāl*, s.m. A torch. A. (*mash'al*).

مشت *musht*, s.m. A fist, closed hand. P.

مشته *mushta*, s.f. A cotton carder's beetle or club.

مشر *mashar*, a. Elder, senior, chief.

مشرف *musharraf*, a. Honoured, exalted. A.

مشرق *mushriq*, s.m. The east. A.

مشرك *mushrik*, s.m. An infidel. A.

مشغول *mashghūl*, a. Busy, occupied, employed. A.

مشغولا *mashghūlā*, s.f. Business, occupation; pastime, recreation.

مشفق *mushfiq*, s.m. Friend, companion. a. Kind, merciful, obliging. A.

مشق *mashq*, s.m. Copy, exercise, example. A.

مشقاب *mashqāb*, s.m. A trencher, kneading dish. T.

مشقت *mushaqqat*, s.m. Labour, pains, trouble, toil. A.

مشک *mashk*, s.m. A leather sac for holding water. P. *mushk*, s.m. Musk. P.

مشکار *mushkār*, s.m. A falconer; chief huntsman. P. (*mīr·shikār*).

مشکل *mushkil*, a. Difficult. A.

مشکنډۍ *mushkunḍa-ī*, s.f. A pod or bag of musk.

مشکنړه *mashkanṛa*, s.f. A glass bead.

مشکي *mushkai*, a. Musk-coloured, dark brown.

مشکین *mushkīn*, a. Musky, smelling of musk.

مشوانړۍ *mashwānṛa-ī*, s.f. An inkstand. H. (*mīsiyānī*). *mashwānṛī*, s.m. Name of an Afghan clan.

مشورت *mashwarat*, s.m. Consultation, counsel, advice. A.

مشه *masha*, s.f. The priming pan of a gun.

مشهور *mashhūr*, a. Notorious, celebrated, famous, well known, published. A.

مښل *mukkhal*, v.a. To rub, polish; anoint, lubricate. Irr. Pres. *mugī*. Past. *mukkhah*. P. (*mushtan*).

مښوکه *makkhūka*, s.f. Beak, bill of a bird.

مصاله *maṣāla*, s.f. Spice, seasoning. A. (*maṣālah*).

مصرف *maṣraf*, s.m. Cost, expenditure. A. *muṣrif*, a. Prodigal, extravagant. A.

مصروف *maṣrūf*, a. Expended; changed. A.

مصلحت *maṣlaḥat*, s.m. Advice, consultation, counsel; convenience, expedience. A.

مصله *maṣalla*, s.f. A carpet used to pray on. A.

مصیبت *muṣībat*, s.m. Adversity, calamity, disaster, misfortune. A.

مضبوط *maẓbūt*, a. Firm, fixed, strong. A.

مضر *muẓirr*, a. Hurtful, pernicious. A.

مضمون *maẓmūn*, s.m. Meaning, sense. A.

مطابق *muṭābiq*, a. Agreeable, conformable, suitable. A.

مطالعه *muṭāl'a*, s.f. Contemplation, consideration; reading, study. A.

مطبوع *maṭbū'*, a. Acceptable, worthy; innate, natural. A.

مطرب *muṭrib*, s.m. A musician. A.

مطلب *maṭlab*, s.m. Desire, wish; aim, object; meaning, purport. A.

مطلق *muṭlaq*, a. Absolute, supreme. ad. Entirely, wholly, altogether. A.

مطلوب *maṭlūb*, a. Wanted, required. A.

مظلوم *maẓlūm*, a. Injured, oppressed; mild, gentle. A.

معاش *m'āsh*, s.m. Living, livelihood, subsistence. A. *m'āsharat*, s.m. Conversation, society, living together. A.

معاف *mu'āf*, a. Absolved, exempted, forgiven. A. *mu'āfī*, s.f. Exemption, immunity; rent free lands A.

معالجه *mu'ālija*, s.f. Cure, remedy; healing. A.

معاملت *mu'āmalat*, s.m. } Affair, transaction, business. A.
معامله *mu'āmala*, s.f.

معتبر *mu'tabar*, a. Trustworthy, reputable, confidential, respectable. A.

معتدل *mu'tadil*, a. Temperate, moderate. A.

معتقد *m'utaqid*, s.m. A believer, faithful person. a. Confiding, believing, trusting. A.

معتقف *m'utaqqif*, a. Devout, pious. A.

معجزه *m'ujiza*, s.f. A miracle. A. (*m'ujiz*).

معجون *m'ajūn*, s.m. Confection, electuary. A.

معدوم *m'adūm*, a. Abolished, non-existent. A.

معده *m'ida*, s.f. Stomach. A.

معذور *m'azūr*, a. Excused, disappointed. A.

معرفت *m'arifat*, s.m. Knowledge; account, cause, reason. p. By, through, by means of. A.

معرکه *m'arika*, s.f. Assembly or convocation of arbitrators to settle disputes between warring tribes. A.

معروف *m'arūf*, a. Known. A.

معشوق *m'ashūq*, s.m. A loved man; lover. A. *m'ashūqa*, s.f. A mistress, sweetheart.

معصوم *m'aṣūm*, s.m. An infant, babe. a. Innocent, simple; defended, preserved. A.

معطل m'aṭṭal, a. Idle, neglected, **unemployed**; suspended from office, disengaged. A.

معقول m'aqūl, a. Just, proper, **reasonable**. A.

معلوم m'alūm, a. Known; notorious, distinguished; apparent, evident. A.

معمار m'imār, s.m. A builder; mason. A.

معمور m'amūr, a. Full, stocked; cultivated; happy. A.

معمول m'amūl, a. Customary, practised. A.

معنا m'anā,) s.f. Meaning, signification,
معني m'anī,) sense. A.

معهود m'ahūd, a. Agreed, determined, fixed, promised. A.

معين mu'aiyan, a. Appointed, established, certified, fixed. A.

مغاك mughāk, s.m. A pit. P.

مغانه mghāna, s.f. The groin, inside of thigh.

مغرب maghrib, s.m. The west. A.

مغرور maghrūr, a. Arrogant, proud, haughty. A.

مغز maghz, s.m. Brain, marrow, pith. P.

مغزن maghzan, a. Powerful, strong.

مغزي maghzī, s.f. Border, edging. P.

مغلوب maghlūb, a. Conquered, overcome. A.

مغيلان mughīlān, s.m. Acacia tree. A.

مفاجات mafājāt, s.m. Sudden death. A.

مفارقت mufāriqat, s.m. Absence, separation. A.

مفاصله mafāṣila, s.f. Interval, distance. A.

مفت muft, ad. Gratis, for nothing. A.

مفتاح miftāḥ, s.m. A key. A.

مفتي muftī, s.m. A lawgiver, chief justice. A.

مفرد mufrad, a. Alone, solitary, single. s.m. The singular number. A.

مفسد mufsid, s.m. Rebel, seditious person; evil-doer, michief maker. A.

مفصل mufaṣṣal, a. Detailed, distinct; full, ample. ad. Fully, distinctly. A.

مفلس muflis, a. Destitute, poor.

مفيد mufīd, a. Profitable, salutary. A.

مقابل muqābil, a. Confronting, opposite; comparing, matching, equalling. A.

مقابله muqābala, s.f. Comparison, matching; opposition, contending. A.

مقاتله muqātila, s.f. Slaughter, carnage. A.

مقال maqāl, s.m. Speech, discourse, talk. A.

مقام muqām, s.m. Abode, dwelling; mansion, place; stage, resting place. A.

مقبره maqbara, s.f. A tomb, sepulchre, mausoleum. A.

مقبول maqbūl, a. Acceptable, agreeable; accepted. A.

مقتدي muqtadī, s.m. Imitator, follower. A.

مقتول maqtūl, a. Killed, slain. A.

مقدار miqdār, s.m. Measure, quantity. A.

مقدس muqaddas, a. Consecrated, holy. A.

مقدم muqaddam, a. Prior, antecedent; chief, leader. A.

مقدمه muqaddama, s.f. Preamble, preface; affair, matter business; cause (in law). A.

مقدور maqdūr, s.m. Ability, power, possibility. A.

مقرر muqarrar, a. Fixed, established, certain; unquestionable, infallible. ad. Certainly, positively. A.

مقسوم maqsūm, a. Distributed, divided. A.

مقصد maqṣad, s.m. Design, purpose, wish, aim. A.

مقعد muq'ad, s.m. The hips; anus, podex. A.

مقل muql, s.m. Fruit of the dwarf palm. A.

مقوي muqawwī, a. Strengthening, tonic. A.

مقيش muqqaish, s.m. Brocade. A.

مقيم muqīm, a. Constant, fixed, stable. s.m. Resident, dweller, lodger. A.

مكار makkār, a. Deceitful, insidious. s.m. Cheat, hypocrite, impostor. A.

مكاري makkārī, s.f. Hypocrisy, imposture, roguery. A.

مكان makān, s.m. Place, station. A.

مكتب maktab, s.m. A school. A.

مکر *makr*, s.m. Deceit, evasion, fraud. A.

مکرر *mukarrar*, a. Repeated, reiterated. A.

مکروه *makrūh*, a. Odious, hateful, disgusting. A.

مکنړه *makanṛa*, s.f. The wooden catch which fixes the upright pillar of a Persian wheel to the cross-beam.

مکيز *makez*, s.m. Pretence, coquetry.

مگر *magar*, c. Except, but, otherwise, only, moreover, unless. P. s.m. A crocodile, alligator. S.

مگهر *maghar*, s.m. A stone used in a game like pitch and toss, ducks and drakes, etc.; a stone used in the exercise of "putting the stone."

مل *mal*, s.m. Associate, comrade, chum. S. (*mel*).

ملا *mlā*, s.f. The loins, waist. *mullā*, s.m. Schoolmaster, doctor, scholar, learned man. A.

ملاتړ *mlā·taṛ*, s.m. Armed retainer, henchman; mercenary soldier; reserve of an army; aid, succour, support. a. Armed, accoutred, having the loins girded.

ملاچرگک *mullā·chargak*, s.m. The hoopoe.

ملاح *mallāḥ*, s.m. Boatman, sailor. A.

ملاحظه *mulāḥiza*, s.f. Consideration, contemplation, notice, regard; looking at, A.

ملازم *mulāzim*, s.m. Attendant, servant. a. Attentive, diligent. A.

ملاست *mlāst*, a. Reclining, lying down.

ملاستل *mlāstal*, v.n. To recline. See څملاستل.

ملاقات *mulāqāt*, s.m. Interview, meeting; visiting. A.

ملال *malāl*, a. Dejected, sad; drooping, faded. s.m. Languor; grief, sadness. A.

ملامت *malāmat*, s.m. Blame, censure, rebuke. a. Reproved, censured. A. *mulāmatī*, a. Reprehensible, blameable. A.

ملتوي *muitawī*, a. Protracted, delayed. s.f. Delay, procrastination. A.

ملخ *mlakh*, s.m. A locust. P. (*malakh*).

ملعون *mala'ūn*, a. Cursed, execrated. A.

ملخوزه *malkhoza*, s.f. Name of a potherb, fenugreek (*Trigonella fœnugræcum*).

ملک *mulk*, s.m. Country, kingdom, region. A. *malik*, s.m. Chief, master, king. A. *milk*, s.m. Possession, property, right. A. *malak*, s.m. An angel. A.

ملکه *malaka*, s.f. An angel. *malika*, s.f. Queen, empress, mistress, wife of a *malik*.

ملکي *malikī*, s.f. Office or duty of malik. *mulkī*, a. Civil, political, relating to the country or empire. *milkī*, s.m. A farmer, land-holder. A.

ملگري *mal·garai*, s.m. Associate, comrade, chum.

ملگرتيا *malgar·tiyā*, } s.f. Friendship, companionship association, etc.
ملگيري *malgīrī*, }

ململ *malmal*, s.m. Muslin. H.

ململه *malmah*, a. Enamelled, glazed, gilded; coated, covered. A. (*mulamm'ā*).

ملنډه *malanda*, s.f. A joke, jest.

ملنډي *malandai*, s.m. Buffoon, jester, clown.

ملنگ *malang*, s.m. An ascetic, hermit. H.

ملنگان *malangān*, s.m. Name of a grass (*Cyperus elatus*). H. (*malanga*).

ملو *malaw*, s.m. A sac or bag in which loads are packed previous to loading,

ملوب *malob*, s.m. Blood and water.

ملوک *malūk*, a. Delicate, handsome.

ملول *malūl*, a. Faded; sad. See ملال.

ملونه *mlūna*, s.f. Bridle, reins and bit. P. (*dahāna*).

مله *mala*, s.f. Name of a grass.

ملهم *malham*, s.m. Ointment, salve. P.

ملي *malai*, a. Emasculated, castrated (by crushing the testicles). H. (*malā*).

مليا *miliyā*, a. Encountering, meeting. S. (*milā*).

ممانعت *mumāni'at*, s.m. Prohibition, hindrance. A.

ممانړه *mamāṉra*, s.f. Name of a tree (*Sageretia oppositifolia*).

ممتاز *mumtāz*, a. Eminent, illustrious, exalted. A.

ممريز *mamrez*, s.m. A spur. P. (*mahmez*).

ممکن *mumkin*, a. Possible. A.

مملکت *mumlakat*, s.m. Empire, dominion. A.

مملوک *mamlūk*, a. Possessed, in one's power. s.m. A Mameluke, captive, slave. A.

من *man*, s.m. Name of a weight. The *man* of Tabriz, used in Western Afghanistan, is equal to eight pounds (avoirdupois); that of Peshawur is equal to eighty pounds. A.

منا *manā*, s.f. A raised platform or stage for watching a field from.

منات *manāt*, s.m. Name of an idol of the ancient Arabians. A.

مناجات *munājāt*, s.m. Prayers, supplications. A.

منادي *munādī*, s.f. Proclamation. A.

مناره *munāra*, s.f. A minaret, turret. A.

مناسب *munāsib*, a. Convenient, proper, fit. A.

مناسبت *munāsibat*, s.m. Expediency, propriety, fitness; comparison, connexion, relation. A.

منافق *munāfiq*, s.m. Atheist, heretic; hypocrite; enemy. A.

منال *manāl*, s.m. Substance, wealth. A.

منبر *minbar*,
ممبر *mimbar*, } s.m. A pulpit. A.

منّت *minnat*, s.m. Entreaty, supplication, obligation, favour. A.

منتر *mantar*, s.m. Charm, spell, philter. S.

منتظر *muntazir*, a. Expecting, looking for. A.

منځ *manḏz*, s.m. Centre, middle. ad. Between, atwixt.

منځګري *manḏz-garai*, s.m. Mediator, go-between.

منځوي *manḏzwai*, a. Central, medial.

منج *manj*, s.m. A bed, bedstead. S. (*manjā*). *munj*, s.m. Name of a grass from which ropes are made (*Saccharum munja*). S. (*mūnj*).

منجقي *manjaqai*, s.m. Clitoris.

منجله *manjala*,
منجيله *manjīla*, } s.f. A ring of grass or rags, used as a stand for round bottomed vessels, or as a pad for the head to support a load, etc.

منحصر *munḥaṣir*, a. Besieged, surrounded. A.

من *man*,
مند *mand*, } m. A possessive particle added to nouns and adjectives to denote endowment or possession. P.

منډانړو *manḍāṉṟū*, s.m. A churning stick; rolling pin. H. (*manthanī*). Name of a plant.

منډري *manḍrai*, a. Short, squat, little. H. (*mandarā*). *mundarai*, s.m. An ear-ring. H. (*mundrā*).

منډو *manḍaw*, s.m. The withers of a horse, etc. H. (*mondhā*). Mustard seed.

منډ *manḍ*, s.m. Footprint, footmark; footstep; the stump of a tree.

منډر *munḍar*, s.m. The stump of a tree.

منډر *manḍar*,
منډن *manḍan*,
منډنړ *manḍaṉṟ*, } s.m. Name of one of the two great divisions of the Yūsufzai tribe, located on the Sama or Yūsufzai plain.

منډل *manḍal*, v.a. To cram, stuff, thrust, or force in; to knead the limbs, shampoo.

منډو *manḍaw*, s.m. An arbour; porch, verandah, shed. H. (*manḍwā*).

منډوس *manḍos*, s.m. A play ball. A cloth tied over the head and under the chin; a small turban. H. (*munḍāsā*).

منډه *manḍa*, s.f. A pace, step; race, run, course. *manḍa-wahal*, v.a. To stamp with the foot. *manḍe-wahal*, v.a. To run, race.

منډهي *manḍha-ī*, s.f. A market. H. (*manḍī*).

منډي *munḍai*, s.m. The innermost of two

bullocks treading corn, or working a Persian wheel. A pollard, or lopped tree; a man who has lost a limb; a short, squat person.

منزل *manzil*, s.m. A day's journey, stage. A.

منزلت *manzilat*, s.m. Dignity, rank. A.

منسوخ *mansūkh*, a. Abolished, cancelled. A.

منشا *manshā*, s.f. Beginning, origin, source. A. *munshā*, s.f. Intention, meaning, wish. A.

منشي *munshī*, s.m. Secretary, writer, clerk. A.

منصب *manṣab*, s.m. Dignity, office. A.

منصف *munṣif*, s.m. Arbitrator, judge, umpire. a. Equitable, just. A. *munṣifī*, s.f. Arbitration, judgment; decision, justice. A.

منظور *manẕūr*, a. Approved, accepted, chosen; seen, looked at. A.

منعه *man'a*, s.f. Refusal, prohibition. A. (*mana'*).

منكر *munkir*, s.m. Denying, rejecting. A.

منگ *mung*, pr. We. See مور.

منگار *mangār*, s.m. A viper. See منگور.

منگاره *mangāra*, s.f. A scratch with the nails.

منگر *mangar*, c. But, etc. See مگر. s.m. Name of the eighth Hindu month, October-November. S. (*aghan*).

منگري *mangarai*, s.m. A viper, a small venomous snake.

منگز *mangaz*, s.f. A hair comb, a comb.

منگنړ *manganṛ*, s.m. A bug.

منگور *mangor*, s.m. A viper. See منگري.

منگول *mangūl*, s.f. The hand, claw, paw.

منگه *munga*, pr. One of the plural oblique forms of the first personal pronoun زه; us.

منگي *mangai*, s.m. An earthenware pitcher for water. *mangoṭai*, s.m. A small pitcher.

منل *manal*, v.a. To obey, submit, yield, comply, attend; accept, believe, agree, confess. S. (*mānnā*).

منه *manah*, s.m. An arbour, shed (of boughs and leaves).

مني *manai*, s.m. Autumn, autumn harvest. *manī*, s.f. Semen, sperma genitale. A. Egoism, egotism. P. *munai*, s.m. A sage; a devout, pious, or holy man. S. (*munī*)

منړه *manṛa*, s.f. An apple.

مو *mo*, pr. A form of the genitive and instrumental cases plural of the second personal pronoun تۀ. *mū*, pr. A form of the genitive and instrumental cases plural of the first personal pronoun زه. *mū*, s.m. Fat, grease, tallow, suet. The hair (in comp.). P.

مواجب *muwājib*, s.m. Pension, salary. A.

موړه *muwaṛa*, s.f. An instrument for cleaning cotton.

مواس *muwās*, s.m. Backbiter, tell-tale; rebel, mischief maker. *mawās*, s.m. Asylum, protection, refuge. H.

موافق *muwāfiq*, a. Apt, agreeing, conformable, like, consonant, suitable. A.

موافقت *muwāfiqat*, s.m. Analogy, conformity, etc.

موت *maut*, s.m. Death. A.

موټ *moṭ*, s.m. Name of a pulse (*Phaseolus aconitifolius*). H. (*moṭh*). *mūṭ*, s.m. The hand closed, fist; a handful; handle, hilt. S. (*muṭh*).

موج *mauj*, s.m. A wave, billow. A.

موجب *mūjib*, s.m. Cause, motive, reason. A.

موجود *maujūd*, Present; existing. A.

موچنړه *mochanṛa*, s.m. A cobbler's wife; a shoe.

موچي *mochī*, s.m. A cobbler, leather worker. H.

موده *mūda*, s.f. Appointed time, season.

موذن *muwazzin*, s.m. Public crier to prayers. A.

موذي *mūzī*, a. Pernicious, hurtful, noxious. A.

مور *mor*, s.m. A mother. (pl. *mainde*). P. (*mādar*). *mor*, s.m. A peacock. S. *mor*, s.m. An ant. P.

مورانۍ *morāna-ī*, s.f. Ferule of a knife handle.

مورچنگ *morchang*, s.m. A Jew's harp. P.

مورچه *morcha*, s.f. A battery, redoubt; rust. P.

مورگني *mor·ganai*, s.m. A relative by the mother's side.

مورگه *morga*, s.f. Brim, edge, rim, margin, border, etc.

مورني *moranai*, a. Of the same mother by different fathers.

موروث *maurūs*, a. Hereditary. A.

موري *mora-ī*, s.f. A drain, gutter, waterpipe. H. (*morī*).

موړ *moṛ*, a. Sated, satisfied, surfeited; comfortable, well off, in easy circumstances.

موړه *moṛa*, s.f. A pad, cushion for the back of a baggage animal. A stool. H. (*moṛhā*).

موز *mauz*, s.m. A plantain, A.

موزه *moza*, s.f. A boot; a stocking. P.

موږ *mūg*, pr. A plural form of the first personal pronoun زه. Also written منږ.

موږي *mogai*, s.m. A peg, stake, tent peg.

موسم *mosim*, or *mausim*, s.m. Season, time. A.

موسي *mosa-ī*, s.f. A stone used in a game like pitch and toss.

موش *mūsh*, s.m. A rat; a mouse. P.

موصوف *mauṣūf*, a. Described; celebrated, praised. A.

موضع *mauẓ'a*, s.f. District, place, village. A.

موقع *mauq'a*, s.f. Contingency, occurrence; proper, fit, suitable. A.

موقوف *mauqūf*, a. Deferred, postponed; relinquished, stopped; dependent. A.

موک *mok*, s.m. A bribe.

مولا *maulā*, s.m. God; judge, lord, master. A.

مولي *molai*, s.m. A wooden pestle; stump of a tree. *mūla-ī*, s.f. A radish. S. (*mūlī*).

موم *mom*, or *mūm*, s.m. Wax. P.

مومن *momin*, a. Believing, orthodox, faithful. A.

مومیائي *momyā-ī*, s.f. Name of a waxy substance found in caves, and used as a remedy for fractures, bruises, and sprains; mummy wax. P.

موندره *mūndra*, s.f. A ring, ear-ring, finger ring. S. (*mūndrī*).

موندل *mūndal*, v.a. To find, get, obtain, procure, gain, acquire, etc.

موندي *mūndai*, s.m. A goat or ram with short ears or horns, or without horns.

مونډ *mūnḍ*, s.m. Root of a tree, germ of a plant; source, origin, cause; germ, nucleus, radix.

مونز *mūnz*, s.m. Prayer. See نمونځ.

مونګ *mūng*, pr. See منګ or موږ.

مونړي *mūnṛai*, s,m. A plug of rags, etc. used to stop the hole of a cistern or tank.

مويښي *mawekkhe*, s.f. (pl.). Hemorrhoids, piles; *pruritus ani*.

مه *ma*, ad. of prohibition used with the imperative mood; no, don't.

مهار *muhār*, s.m. A bridle, reins; the nose peg and string by which a camel is led. P.

مهال *mahāl*, s.m. Delay, respite, pause. A.

مهتابي *mahtāba-ī*, s.f. A kind of firework. P.

مهتر *mihtar*, s.m. A chief, prince; a groom. P.

مهتمم *muhtammim*, s.m. A superintendent, factor. a. Thoughtful, anxious. A.

مهجور *mahjūr*, a. Forsaken, left; separated, cut off. A.

مهر *mahr*, s.m. Marriage portion, settlement. A. *muhr*, s.m. A seal; gold coin equal to sixteen rupees. P. *mihr*, s.m. Affection, kindness. P.

مهرباش *mihrbāsh*, } a. Indulgent, friendly,
مهربان *mihrbān*, } kind, favouring. P.

مهربانګي *mihrbāngī*, } s.f. Favour, friendliness,
مهرباني *mihrbānī*, } kindness. P.

مهرکن *muhr·kan*, s.m. A seal engraver. P.

مهره *muhra*, s.f. A shell; a rubber for smoothing paper, etc. P.

مهري *muhrī*, a. Sealed, stamped. s.f. A gutter, drain, water-pipe. P.

مهلت *muhlat*, a. Deferring, retarding; laziness, indolence; leisure, time. A.

مهلك *muhlik*, a. Deadly, killing, mortal. A.

مهم *muhimm*, a. Important, momentous. s.m. Risk, hazard, danger. A.

مهمان *mihmān*, s.m. A guest, stranger. P.

مهماني *mihmānī*, s.f. Hospitality, entertainment.

مهمند *mahmand*, s.m. Name of an Afghan tribe.

مهميزه *mahmeza*, s.f. A spur. P. (*mahmez*).

مهنړه *mahanṛah*, s.m. A boatman, sailor.

مهي *mahai*, s.m. A fish. P. (*mahī*). *mahe*, s.f. (pl.). A kind of pulse (*Phaseolus max*).

مهيرگه *maherga*, s.f. Epilepsy. See ميرگي.

مهين *mahīn*, a. Fine, subtle, thin. P.

مهينه *mahīnah*, a. Foregoing, preceding, prior; elder, first-born; early sown crops. ad. Before, ere now, previously.

مي *me*, pr. A form of the genitive and instrumental cases singular of the first personal pronoun زه. See م. *mai*, s.m. Wine, spirits. P.

ميا *miyā*, s.m. Title of a religious class; a friar; master, sir. H. (*miyān*).

مياشت *myāsht*, s.f. A month; new moon.

ميان *miyān*, s.m. The loins, middle, waist; sheath, scabbard. p. Between, betwixt. P.

ميانه *miyāna*, s.f. Name of the eleventh Afghan month, between the festivals of Ramazān and Qurbān. P. *miyānah*, a. Middling, medium, medial. P.

ميتل *mītal*, v.a. To piss, make water.

ميچ *mech*, s.m. Measure, scale; measurement, reckoning. P. *mech-kawul*, v.a. To measure.

ميچن *mechan*, s.f. A handmill. A. (*mījan*).

ميخ *mekh*, s.m. A bolt, peg, tent peg. P.

ميخچو *mekhchū*, s.m. A nail, pin, spigot.

ميدان *maidān*, s.m. Area, field, plain; field of battle; parade ground; race course. P.

ميده *maidah*, s.m. Meal, flour, fine meal. P.

مير *mīr*, s.m. Chief, leader; a title given to Sayads. P.

ميرات *mīrāt*, }
ميراث *mīrāṣ*, } s.m. Heritage, patrimony. A.

ميراثي *mīrāṣī*, a. Inherited, hereditary. s.m. Name applied to a class of bards, improvisatores, or singers.

ميرڅمن *mīrtsaman*, a. Deceitful, false, lying; hateful, vile, odious.

ميرڅي *mīrtsī*, s.f. Woe, distress, trouble; malice, spite, enmity; pique, umbrage.

ميرخانۍ *mīrkhāna-ī*, s.f. A kind of turban; a kind of fine cloth. P.

ميرزا *mīrzā*, s.m. Grandee, noble, prince; title given to a secretary or scribe. P.

ميرسنگ *mīr-sang*, s.m. A conch, a large shell used as a trumpet by hammām keepers, to announce the opening of the baths. S. (*sankh*).

ميرگنج *mīr-ganj*, s.m. A kind of vulture; the royal vulture. P.

ميرگي *mergai*, s.m. Epilepsy. H. (*mirgī*).

ميرمن *merman*, s.f. Lady, matron, madam, mistress, hostess.

ميره *maira*, s.f. Mother-in-law, stepmother. S. (*maibhā*). A desert, open plain.

ميړه *meṛah*, s.m. Husband, lord, master, owner.

ميز *mez*, s.m. A table. P. *mezmān*, s.m. A guest. P.

ميزان *mīzān*, s.m. Balance, pair of scales; metre, measure; addition. P.

ميزر *maizar*, s.m. A veil of fine muslin worn by women.

ميزري *maizarai*, }
ميځري *maidzarai*, } s.m. The dwarf palm (*Chamærops Richiana*).

ميږ *meg*, s.f. An ewe. P. (*mesh*).

ميږتون *megatūn*, s.m. An ant's nest.

ميږي *megai*, s.m. An ant, the black ant.

ميسر *muyassar*, a. Procurable, obtainable. A.

ميشت *mesht*, a. Settled, abiding, residing.

ميشته *meshta*, s.f. Abode, residence, dwelling. A. (*m'aīshat*). *meshta-kawul*, v.a. To inhabit, colonize.

ميښ *mekkh*, s.m. A bull buffalo, buffalo. S. (*mahish*).

ميښبه *mekkhbah*, s.m. A buffalo grazier; owner of buffaloes.

ميښميښ *mīkkhmīkkh*, a. Sick at stomach, nauseated; disappointed, chagrined.

ميعاد *miy'ād*, s.m. Time or place of a promise. A.

ميل *mīl*, s.m. A bodkin, needle, skewer; the barrel of a gun; a horse that stands on its hind legs. P. *mail*, s.m. Dirt, rust, scum. S. *mai-l*, s.m. Partiality, desire, fondness, inclination. A.

ميلان *mai-lān*, a. Inclined, partial, biassed, bent on. A.

ميلمستيا *melmastiyā*, s.f. Hospitality, entertainment.

ميلمه *melmah*, s.m. A guest, visitor. P. (*mezmān*).

ميلو *melū*, s.m. A bear. H. (*mallū*).

ميله *mela*, s.f. A fair; picnic; concourse of people gathered together for religious or commercial purposes. S. (*melā*).

ميمي *meme*, in. The bleating of sheep, kids, etc.; the call of a child for the mother's breast. S.

مين *mayan*, a. Fond of, loving, in love. s.m. A lover. A. (*mail*).

مينا *mainā*, s.f. Name of a bird (*Graculus Indicus*).

مينځ *myanḏz*, a. Midst. See منځ.

مينځل *mīndzal*, v.a. To wash. P. (*misīdan*). See وينځل.

ميناجور *mīnjawar*, s.m. A sweeper at a mosque or shrine. A. (*mujāwir*).

ميندہ *mīndah*, s.m. A male kept for breeding purposes; bull, ram, etc.

مينه *mīna*, s.f. Affection, love; partiality, regard. *mena*, s.f. Building, habitation, house.

ميو *miyaw*, s.m. The mew of a cat.

ميوه *mewa*, s.f. Fruit in general; raisins. P.

مئي *ma-ī*, s.f. Name of a kind of pulse (*Phaseolus radiatus*).

ن

ن *nūn* is the twenty-fifth letter of the Arabic, and the thirty-sixth of the Pukkhto alphabet. It is a dental letter, and has the sound of the English *n*. It is added to some nouns to transform them to adjectives, as پم *pam*, mange; پمن *paman*, mangy. Added to the Aorist and Future tenses of verbs it denotes certainty or belief, as کوي *kawī* (he does), کوين *kawīna* (he surely does). It is also used as an adverbial prefix of negation instead of نه *na*, as منل *manal* (to obey), نمنل *namanal* (to disobey).

نا *nā*, No, not; a negative particle prefixed to nouns, participles, and adjectives, has the same meaning as the English prefixes *dis-*, *in-*, *un-*, etc. as ناپاك *nāpāk* (unclean), ناقلار *nāqalār* (discomposed), ناراست *nārāst* (unfair), etc.

ناب *nāb*, a. Pure, genuine. P.

نابړ *nābaṛ*, } a. Clumsy, sturdy, stout; huge,
ناپړ *nāpaṛ*, } gigantic, immense.

ناتار *nātār*, s.m. Plunder, devastation, destruction.

ناتکي *nātka-ī*, s.f. Individuality, oneness, unity.

ناجو *nājū*, s.m. A pine, fir tree. P.

ناڅاپه *nātsāpa*, ad. Suddenly, unawares.

ناچ *nāch*, s.m. A dance. S.

ناخن *nākhun*, s.m. A nail (of finger or toe). P.

ناخنه *nākhuna*, s.f. A disease of the eye, pterygium. P.

نادان *nādān*, a. Ignorant, simple. P. *nādānī*, s.f. Ignorance, stupidity.

نادر *nādir*, a. Exquisite, choice, rare. A.

نار *nār*, s.m. A shoot, sprout. Fire, hell. A. A pomegranate. P.

نارنج *nāranj*, s.m. An orange. P.

نارو *nārū*, s.m. Guinea worm, dracunculus. H.

ناره *nāra*, s.f. A shout, call. See نعره.

نارينه *nārīnah*, a. Male, masculine; manly, bold, brave. P. (*narīnah*).

ناري *nārai*, s.m. Food, refreshment. See نهاري.

ناړ *nāṛ*, s.m. A shoot, sprout; stalk, stem, stubble. H.

ناړه *nāṛa*, s.f. Stalk or stem of a grass or herb.

ناړي *nāṛai*, s.m. Rope made of strips of raw hide.

ناز *nāz*, s.m. Blandishment, coquetry; elegance, gracefulness; fondling, soothing; consequential airs, pride. P.

نازک *nāzak*, a. Delicate, elegant; fragile, tender; light, thin. P.

نازکه *nāzaka*, s.f. A doll; mistress.

نازل *nāzil*, a. Descending, alighting, dismounting; befalling, occurring. A.

نازله *nāzila*, s.f. Calamity, misfortune. A.

نازنين *nāznīn*, a. Delicate, lovely. P.

نازول *nāzawul*, v.a. To fondle, pamper, spoil (as a child).

نازيدل *nāzedal*, v.n. To coquet, assume consequential airs.

ناست *nāst*, a. Seated, sitting.

ناسره *nāsarah*, a. Alloyed, counterfeit, impure; false (as coin), etc. P.

ناسوت *nāsūt*, s.m. Humanity, human nature. A.

ناسور *nāsūr*, s.m. Sinus, fistula. A.

ناسولت *nāsolaṭ*, a. Uncircumcised. A. (*nāsunnat*).

ناشپاتي *nāshpātai*, s.m. A pear. P.

ناشته *nāshta*, s.f. Breakfast, luncheon. P. (*nāshtā*).

ناښنده *nākkhanda*, ناښنه *nākkhana*, } s.f. Impropriety, wrong.

ناصح *nāṣiḥ*, s.m. Adviser, counsellor, monitor. A.

ناطق *nāṭiq*, s.m. Speaking, a speaker. A.

ناظر *nāẓir*, s.m. Observing, seeing; inspector, supervisor; an officer in judicial courts, sheriff. A.

ناظم *nāẓim*, s.m. Governor, ruler; arranger, composer. A.

ناغه *nāgha*, s.m. Mulct, fine, poundage; respite, adjournment. *nāghah*, a. Vacant, empty, void; unemployed, out of use. T.

ناف *nāf*, s.m. The navel. P.

نافه *nāfa*, s.f. A musk pod. P.

نافع *nāfi'*, a. Advantageous, profitable, useful. A.

ناقص *nāqiṣ*, a. Deficient, imperfect. A.

ناقل *nāqil*, s.m. A reciter, reporter. A.

ناک *nāk*, s.m. A pear. P. m. A particle added to nouns to denote endowment or possession, and corresponding with the English affix *-ful*, as *gham-nāk* (woeful), *qahr-nāk* (wrathful), *sharm-nāk* (bashful), etc.

ناکار *nākār*, a. Useless. See نکاره.

ناکه *nāka*, s.f. An alligator. S. (*nākā*).

ناګاه *nāgāh*, ad. Suddenly, unawares, unexpectedly, all at once. P.

ناګمان *nāgumān*, ناګهان *nāgahān*, } a. Abrupt, sudden, unexpected. ad. Unawares, by surprise. P.

نال *nāl*, s.m. A horse shoe. See نعل.

نالش *nālish*, s.m. Complaint, lament, growl, grumble. P.

نالہ *nāla*, s.f. A canal, stream, rivulet; gutter, drain, watercourse; weeping, lamentation. P.

نالي *nālī*, s.f. A quilt, etc. See نهالي.

نام *nām*, s.m. Name (in comp.). P.

ناموس *nāmūs*, s.m. Renown, fame, reputation; disgrace; female part of a family. A.

نامه *nāma*, s.f. Book, letter; treatise, writing. P.

نامور *nāmwar*, } a. Celebrated, famous, renowned. P.
نامير *nāmer*,

نان *nān*, s.m. Baked or leavened bread. P.

نانګه *nānga*, s.f. A blackberry.

نانوائي *nānwā-ī*, s.m. A baker. P.

ناور *nāwar*, s.m. A reservoir, pond, tank, cistern.

ناوک *nāwak*, s.m. An arrow; tube, pipe; bee's sting. P.

ناوکي *nāwaka-ī*, s.f. A doll, plaything. *nāwakai*, s.m. An arrow; name of a plant (*Jasminum revolutum*).

ناوه *nāwa*, s.f. A canal, gutter; a tube, pipe; a long barrelled gun.

ناوي *nāwe*, s.f. A bride.

ناويات *nāwiyāt*, a. Rare, choice, matchless, peerless.

ناويت *nāwiyat*, s.m. Honeymoon, bridal state.

نائي *nā-ī*, s.m. A barber. S. *nāe*, s.m. A reed, pipe; flute. P.

نائب *nā-ib*, s.m. Deputy, lieutenant. A.

نايک *nāyak*, s.m. Chief, leader, master, patron. S.

نايړه *nāyanṛa*, s.f. A barber's wife.

نبات *nabāt*, s.m. Sugar. P. A herb, grass. A.

نبض *nabẓ*, s.m. The pulse (at the wrist). A.

نبي *nabī*, s.m. A prophet. A. *nabūwat*, s.m. Prophecy, prophetship. A.

نتکي *natka-ī*, s.f. A small ring worn in the nose by women. H.

نتل *natal*, v.a. To despoil, plunder, sack, ravage, etc.

نته *nata*, s.f. A ring worn in the nose by women; the peg of wood in a camel's nose. S. (*nath*).

نتيجه *natīja*, s.f. Consequence, result, issue; reward, retribution. A.

نټ *naṭ*, s.m. Name of a caste of Indians who are jugglers, tumblers, ropedancers, etc. A cheat, rogue, knave. S.

نثار *niṣār*, a. Scattering, strewing. A.

نجات *najāt*, s.m. Escape, flight; salvation. A.

نجار *najjār*, s.m. A carpenter. A.

نجاست *najāsat*, s.m. Filth, impurity, dirt, offal. A.

نجتل *njatal*, v.a. To implant, imbed, stick into, thrust. Irr. Pres. *njanī*; Past, *njātah*.

نجس *najis*, a. Nasty, dirty; filthy, foul. A. *najas*, s.m. Dirt, dung, filth, ordure. A.

نجوم *najūm*, s.m. Astrology, astronomy. A. *najūmī*, s.m. Astrologer, fortune-teller. A.

نجيب *najīb*, s.m. A kind of soldier, guardsman. a. Noble, excellent. A. *najīb-zādah*, s.m. A nobleman.

نڅا *natsā*, s.f. Waving, shaking; bounding, dancing. S. (*nachā*).

نڅي *natsa-ī*, s.f. Cord, twine. See انڅي.

نچور *nichor*, s.m. A squeeze, wring. H.

نچورول *nichorawul*, v.a. To squeeze, wring, rinse.

نچه *nicha*, s.f. A weaver's reel; tube of a smoking apparatus or ḥuqqa. P. (*necha*).

نخالس *nakhālas*, a. Genuine, pure, unmixed. A. (*nikhālaṣ*).

نخره *nakhra*, s.f. Coquetry, pretence, artifice; trick, sham; joke, pleasantry. P. A hole, fissure, crevice. See رخنه.

نخره باز *nakhra-bāz*, s.m. An affected person. *nakhra-bāza*, s.f. A coquette. P.

نخښ *nukhakkh*, s.m. A flesh-hook, an iron hook used to draw meat out of a pot.

نخښه *nakhkkha*, s.f. A plan, chart. See نښه.

نخل *na<u>kh</u>l*, s.f. A date tree, palm tree. A.
na<u>kh</u>listān, s.m. A palm or date grove.
نخوت *na<u>kh</u>wat*, s.m. Pomp, pride. A.
نخود *nu<u>kh</u>ūd*, s.m. A kind of pulse (*Cicer arietinum*). P.
ندا *nidā*, s.f. Voice, sound; call, shout. A.
نداپ *naddāp*, | نداف *naddāf*, } s.m. A cotton carder, cotton dresser. A.
ندامت *nadāmat*, s.m. Contrition, regret. A.
ندرور *ndror*, s.f. pl. *ndrende*, Sister-in-law, husband's sister. S. (*nand*).
نديم *nadīm*, s.m. A courtier; intimate friend. A.
نذر *nazr*, s.m. A gift, present, offering. A.
نذرانه *nazrāna*, s.f. A present offered or received when people of rank meet, or pay their respects to a prince; tribute; fees paid to Government for grants of land, office, etc. A.
نر *nar*, a. Male, masculine; manly, bold. P.
نرخ *nir<u>kh</u>*, s.m. Tariff, price current, rate. P.
نرسوي *narsawai*, s.m. A kind of wild pomegranate. a. Sun-burnt, scorched by the sun.
نركښ *narka<u>kkh</u>*, s.m. A mountain ram; leader of a herd.
نركوښ *narko<u>kkh</u>*, s.m. A fish-hook; a hook used to gather fruit from the tree. See نخښ.
نرگس *nargis*, s.m. The narcissus. P.
نرلوخ *narlū<u>kh</u>*, s.m. The bulrush. See لوخه.
نرم *narm*, a. Soft, tender; easy, gentle, silly. P.
نرمئي *narma-ī*, s.f. The lobe of the ear.
narmī, s.f. Softness; mildness; silliness. P.
نرناحق *nar-nāhaqq*, ad. Entirely unjust, altogether wrongfully, without cause, illegally. P. (*bar-nāhaqq*).
نري *narai*, a. Fine, narrow, thin, slender.
نړا *naṛā*, s.f. A bellow, bray, roar, low, shout. A. (*n'ara*).

نړل *naṛal*, v.a. To bray, roar, bellow; call, shout.
نړول *naṛawul*, v.a. To raze, demolish, knock down, level, overthrow (as walls, etc.).
نړئي *naṛa-ī*, s.f. World, universe, globe.
نړيدل *naṛedal*, v.n. To crumble, fall down, tumble, fall to ruin, subside (as walls, etc.).
نزاكت *nazākat*, s.m. Delicacy, neatness, elegance. P.
نزله *nazla*, s.f. Defluxion of humours; catarrh. A.
نزدي *nizde*, | نژدي *niĵde*, } ad. Close, near, adjacent, contiguous. P. (*nizd*).
نژديكي *niĵdekī*, ad. Closeness, nearness, contiguity.
نږي *ngai*, s.m. A sneeze.
نږور *ngor*, s.f., pl. *ngende*, Son's wife, daughter-in-law.
نس *nas*, s.m. Abdomen, belly; concupiscence, lust; a sinew, tendon; nerve, vein. A.
نسب *nasab*, s.m. Genealogy, lineage. A.
نسبت *nisbat*, s.m. Affinity, relation; reference, respecting, regarding. A.
نسخه *nus<u>kh</u>a*, s.f. Prescription, recipe; exemplar, copy, model; book, letter, writing. A.
نسرين *nasrīn*, s.m. A wild rose. P.
نسغ *nasa<u>gh</u>*, s.m. Boring, piercing (as the nose, ears, etc.). A. Order; execution, torture. P. (*nasaq*).
نسكور *naskor*, a. Inverted, upside down.
نسل *nasal* or *nasl*, s.m. Breed, descent, family, origin, pedigree, race. A.
نسوار *naswār*, s.m. Snuff. S. (*nās*).
نسيم *nasīm*, s.m. A breeze, gentle air, zephyr. A.
نسيه *nasiya*, s.f. Credit, money promised. P.
نشان *ni<u>sh</u>ān*, s.m. A mark, sign; scar; butt; family arms; ensign, standard. P.
نشتر *na<u>sh</u>tar*, s.m. A lancet. P.

نشته *nishta,* Negative form of شته, Is not. P. (*nest*).

نشست *nishast,* s.m. Sitting, seated (in comp.). P.

نشم *nashm,* s.m. Deceit, craft, artfulness; lewdness, wantonness, extravagance, luxury.

نشمي *nashmī,* a. Luxurious, extravagant; lewd, wanton; crafty, artful.

نشه *nasha,* s.f. Intoxication. A. (*nashā*).

نشيب *nasheb,* s.m. Declivity; hollow. P.

نښان *nikkhān,* s.m. Mark, sign. See نشان.

نښاني *nikkhānī,* s.f. A keepsake, token, sign.

نښتر *nakkhtar,* s.m. A pine tree, conifer.

نښتل *nkkhatal* or *nkshatal,* v.n. To hitch, catch, stick, be caught, entrapped; to cling, cleave to, etc. P. (*nishākhtan, nashlīdan*).

نښتيځل *nakkhtedzal,* v.a. To squeeze, wring, strain.

نښلول *nkkhlawul,* v.a. To obstruct, catch, stop, jam, hitch, entrap.

نښه *nakkha* or *naksha,* s.f. Mark, sign, token; emblem, device; banner, flag, standard; target, butt. A. (*naqsha*).

نصب *naṣb,* s.m. Fixing, establishing, planting. A.

نصف *niṣf,* a. Half. A.

نصيب *naṣīb,* s.m. Destiny, fate, lot. A.

نصيحت *naṣīḥat,* s.m. Admonition, counsel, advice. A.

نطفه *nutfa,* s.f. Seed, sperm; semen. A.

نظام *niẓām,* s.m. Arrangement, order; custom, habit, constitution: sovereign, ruler. A.

نظر *naẓar,* s.m. Sight, vision; look, glance; regard, observation. A.

نظم *naẓm,* s.m. Poetry, verse. A.

نعره *n'ara,* s.f. Bawl, shout, call; noise, clamour. A.

نعل *n'al,* s.m. A horse shoe; ferrule of a scabbard. A.

نعمت *n'imat,* s.m. Favour, benefit; delight, joy; affluence, ease, wealth. A.

نغاره *naghāra,* s.f. A kettle drum. A. (*naqara*).

نغاړل *nghāṛal,* v.a. To fold, envelop, wrap, roll up.

نغري *ngharai,* s.m. A fire-place.

نغړدل *nghaṛdal,* v.a. To swallow, gulp.

نغښتل *nghakkhtal,* v.a. To foll, wrap, roll, etc. Def. in pres. ten. See نغاړل.

نغلاند *naghlānd,* a. Hungry.

نغم *nagham,* s.m. A mine, tunnel. P.

نغمه *naghma,* s.f. Melody, music, song. A.

نغوتل *nghwatal,* v.a. To attend, listen, give ear, etc. Irr. Pres. *nghwagī.* Past, *nghwat.*

نغوښيدل *nghwakkhedal,* v.n. To crawl, creep.

نغي *nughai,* s.m. Brand, scar, cicatrix; cutting off the nose, ears, etc.

نفاق *nifāq,* s.m. Enmity, disagreement; hypocrisy, fallacy. A.

نفر *nafar,* s.m. A person, individual; servant, groom. A.

نفرت *nafrat,* s.m. Abomination, aversion; flight, terror. A.

نفرين *nafrīn,* s.m. Malediction, curse, imprecation. P. Detestation, aversion. A.

نفس *nafas,* s.m. Respiration, breath; moment, minute. A. *nafs,* s.m. Spirit, substance, soul; sensuality, concupiscence; lust, desire; envy, pride; vice; gravity; sperm; penis. A.

نفساني *nafsānī,* a. Carnal, sensual, lustful; luxurious. A.

نفعه *naf'a,* s.f. Profit, advantage, gain. A. (*nafa'*).

نفقه *nafaqa,* s.f. Necessary expenses of living (food, clothing, and lodging). A.

نقاب *niqāb,* s.m. A veil. A.

نقاش *naqqāsh,* s.m. A draftsman, sculptor, painter; carver, engraver. A.

نقب *naqb,* s.m. Tunnel, mine, gallery;

burrow; excavation. A. *naqb·zan*, s.m. A miner, excavator; burglar. *naqb·zanī*, s.f. Funnelling; housebreaking by digging through the walls.

نقد *naqd*, s.m. Cash, ready money. A.

نقره *nuqra*, s.f. Silver. A.

نقش *naqsh*, s.m. Carving, painting, embroidering, etc. A.

نقشه *naqsha*, s.f. Map, pattern, model, plan, etc. A.

نقصان *nuqṣān*, s.m. Blemish, defect; injury, loss, damage, etc. A.

نقطه *nuqṭa*, s.f. A spot, dot, point. A.

نقل *naql*, s.m. Fable, anecdote; history, tale; copying, imitating, transcribing; copy; change of place, migration. A.

نکاح *nikāḥ*, s.m. Marriage, matrimony, wedlock. A.

نکاره *nakārah*, a. Useless, worthless; invalid. P.

نکته *nukta*, s.f. A subtle point, mystical meaning. A.

نکریزه *nakrīza*, s.f. Name of a plant (*Lawsonia inermis*), the henna plant. pl. *nakrīze*, Henna leaves; the dye obtained from them.

نکس *nakas*, a. Abject, mean; friendless, poor. P. (*nākas*).

نکیر *nakīr*, s.m. Name of an angel. *Munkir Nakīr*, The names of two angels who examine the spirits of the dead in the grave. A.

نګار *nigār*, s.m. Effigy, picture, idol. P.

نګاه *nigāh*, s.m. A look, glance, sight; observing, watching; custody, care. P. *nigāh·bān*, s.m. Guard, keeper. P.

نګښي *ngakkhai*, s.m. A plaited lock of hair on the temple or forehead (of women).

نګوبي *ngūbai*, s.m. Pommel of a saddle.

نګولي *ngolai*, s.m. Meat, fish, etc., eaten with bread or rice as a relish, a made dish, entrée.

نګون *nigūn*, a. Inverted; hanging downwards. P.

نل *nal*, s.m. A reed; tube, pipe, spout. S.

نله *nala*, s.f. Urinary passage, urethra. S. (*nalā*).

نم *nam*, a. Damp, moist, wet. P. *nam*, a. The ninth. P. (*naham*).

نماز *namāz*, s.m. Prayer. See نمونځ.

نمازل *nmāzal*, v.a. } To rear, sustain, support,
نمانځل *nmāndzal*, } bring up, cherish, nourish; to pamper, spoil. P. (*nawāzīdan*).

نماښام *nmākkhām*, s.m. Evening. See ماښام.

نمد *namad*, s.m. Felt, unwoven woollen stuff. P.

نمر *nmar*, s.m. The sun, sunshine.

نمري *nmarī*, s.m. (pl.) Clothes, garments, dress.

نمړ *numaṛ*, ad. Before, formerly. a. Prior, first; fixed, determined; betrothed, engaged; promised, pledged; bespoken.

نمړي *numaṛai*, a. Former, preceding, etc. *nmaṛa-ī*, s.f. A morsel. See نوړئ.

نمسي *nmasai*, s.m. A grandson. P. (*nawāsa*). *nmasa-ī*, s.f. A granddaughter. P. (*nawāsī*).

نمک *namak*, s.m. Salt (in comp.) P.

نمله *namla*, s.f. A felt pad for a saddle. P. (*namda*).

نمود *namūd*, s.m. Guide, index; display, show. P.

نمودار *namūdār*, a. Conspicuous, famed, noted. s.m. Specimen, model, sample; proof; index. P.

نمونځ *nmūndz*, s.m. Prayer. P. (*namāz*).

نمونه *namūna*, s.f. Pattern, specimen, sample. P.

نن *nan*, ad. To-day. *nan·wradz*, This day, to-day. *nan·shpa*, This night, to-night. *nan·ṣabā*, To-day or to-morrow, in these days, in a day or two.

ننباسل *nanabāsal*, v.a. To insert, etc. Def. in past ten. See ننیستل.

ننداره *nandāra*, s.f. Sight, spectacle, show; glance, look, inspection. P. (*nanūdārī*).

ننډرور *nandror*, s.f. Husband's sister. See ندرور.

ننزړه *nanzaṛah*, s.m. Tar, pitch.

ننکه *nanaka*, s.f. A vesicle, pustule.

ننکئ *nanaka-ī*, s.f. Small pox.

ننګ *nang*, s.m. Honour, reputation; disgrace. P. *nang-o-nāmūs*, Honour, disgrace. P.

ننګو *nangū*, s.m. A span; the space between the thumb and forefinger.

ننګيالي *nang-yālai*, a. Honourable, reputable.

نننی *nananai*, a. Hodiernal, of to-day.

ننواته *nanawātah*, s.m. Entrance, admission; refuge, shelter, asylum.

ننوتل *nanawatal*, v.n. To enter, go in, intrude; to take refuge, seek protection from another.

ننه *nana*, ad. Inside, within.

ننیستل *nanayastal*, v.a. To insert, introduce, draw in, retract, conduct, or lead in, etc. Def. in pres. ten. See ننباسل.

نو *naw*, s.m. Moisture, dampness. P. (*nam*). *nau*, a. Fresh, new, young. P. *nū*, s.m. The navel.

نواب *nawāb*, s.m. A chief, governor of a province. A.

نواحي *nawāhī*, s.f. Environs; territories. A.

نواره *nawāra*, s.f. Cultivation, habitation, population.

نوار *niwāṛ*, s.m. Broad tape. H.

نواړي *niwāṛai*, s.m. The tape or lacing of a pair of trousers; the hem in which the tape passes.

نواز *nawāz* (in comp.), Cherishing. P.

نوازش *nawāzish*, s.m. Favour, patronage. P.

نوبت *nobat*, or *naubat*, s.m. Period, time, turn; opportunity, occasion; accident; occurrence; degree, pitch; keeping watch; relieving guard; musical instruments sounded at the gate of a great man's house, or at the market place, etc., at fixed intervals. A.

نوبهار *nau-bahār*, s.m. Spring, early spring. P.

نوڅئ *nūtsa-ī*, s.f. Pliers, forceps, pincers. H. (*nochī*).

نور *nor*, a. Other, another, different, more. ad. Besides, moreover, also, likewise. H. (*aur*). *nūr*, s.m. Light, splendour. P. *nwar*, s.m. The sun. See نمر.

نوراني *nūrānī*, a. Bright, light, clear. P.

نوروز *nau-roz*, s.m. New year's day of the Persian calendar. P.

نوري *nwarī*, s.m. Old clothes. See نمري.

نوړز *nwaṛaz*, s.f. A quail.

نوړئ *nwaṛa-ī*, s.f. A mouthful, morsel; food. P. (*nihārī*).

نوړيدل *nwaṛedal*, v.n. To peel, excoriate, strip off.

نوږد *nogd*, } s.m. Genus, kind, source, origin.
نوږي *nogai*, } A. (*nau'*).

نوس *naus* or *naws*, s.m. Spirit, soul; self; lust, sensuality. A. (*nafs*).

نوسي *nwasai*, s.m. Grandson. See نمسي.

نوعه *nau'a*, s.f. Species, kind; manner, mode. A.

نوک *nūk*, s.m. A nail (toe or finger); claw (of an animal or bird). S. (*nakh*).

نوکاره *nūkāra*, s.f. A scratch, claw, scrape; clawing, scratching.

نوکر *nokar*, s.m. A servant. P. *nokarī*, s.f. Service.

نول *nūl*, s.m. Grief, sorrow, affliction. P. (*nāla*).

نولس *nolas*, a. Nineteen. *nolasam*, a. Nineteenth.

نولي *nolai*, s.m. A weasel, mongoose. S. (*newlā*).

نوليدل *nūledal*, v.n. To fret, pine, grieve, sorrow.

نوم *nūm*, s.m. Name; reputation, fame;

honour, character. s. (*nām*). *nūm*, s.m. The navel.

نوماندي *nūmāndai*, a. Named, called, yclept.

نومد *nūmd*, a. Damp, wet. See لوند.

نومړي *nūmaṛai*, a. Named, called; famed, celebrated; eminent, great.

نوميد *naumed*, a. Hopeless, without hope. P.

نوند *nūnd*, a. Damp, wet. See نومد.

نونکۍ *nūnaka-ī*, s.f. A furuncle, boil, pustule. See ننکۍ.

نوي *nawai*, a. New, fresh; unused; young, late, modern. P. (*nau*). *nawai*, s.m. The inside one of a drove of oxen treading corn. *nawe*, a. Ninety. *nūe*, s.f. Mother's brother, maternal uncle.

نه *nuh*, a. Nine. *na*, ad. Nay, no. Negative particle. Neither, nor, not.

نهاد *nihād*, s.m. Habit, nature, quality. P.

نهار *nahār*, a Fasting. P.

نهاري *nahārai*, s.m. Breakfast, luncheon, forenoon meal, refreshment. P.

نهال *nihāl*, s.m. A sapling, shoot, sprout, seedling. P.

نهالي *nihālī*, s.f. A cushion, mattress; quilt, coverlet; sapling, seedling, sucker.

نهان *nihān*, a. Concealed, hidden. P.

نهايت *nihāyat*, a. Extreme, excessive. ad. Extremely. s.m. Extremity, limit; excess. A.

نهر *nahr*, s.m. A canal, stream, rivulet. A. *nahar*, a. Fasting, unfed. P.

نهنګ *nahang*, s.m. A whale, leviathan, crocodile. P.

نهوه *nahwa*, s.f. Refusing food, fasting.

نهه *naha*, s.f. Tuesday.

نهيه *nahiya*, s.f. Prohibition; interdict. A. (*nahī*).

ني *nai*, s.m. A reed, tube; flute, pipe. P.

نيا *niyā*, s.f. A grandmother.

نياز *niyāz*, s.m. Petition, supplication; indigence, poverty; a thing dedicated. P. *niyāz-man*, a. Indigent, suppliant. *niyāzī*, s.m. Lover, friend. Name of a Pathan tribe.

نياګانه *niyāgāna*, s.f. A mother's family or relations.

نيام *niyām*, s.m. Sheath, scabbard; bandage for a broken limb; plough tail or handle. P. (*miyān*).

نياو *niyāw*, s.m. Right, equity, justice. S.

نيايه *niyāyah*, s.m. Maternal uncle.

نيبو *nībū*, s.m. A lemon, citron. S.

نيت *niyat*, s.m. Purpose, intention, design; will, desire, wish. A.

نيټه *neṭa*, s.f. Bargain, contract; promise, engagement; appointed time; season.

نيرنګ *nairang*, s.m. Deceit, evasion, fraud; magic, sorcery; miracle, novelty. P.

نيره *nīra*, s.f. A cobbler's awl.

نيز *nīz*, s.m. Deluge, inundation, flood; drift wood, rubbish, etc. carried by floods. ad. Also, again, likewise. P.

نيزه *neza*, s.f. A spear, lance. P.

نيستي *nestī*, s.f. Non-existence. P.

نيشتر *neshtar*, s.m. A lancet, fleam. See نشتر.

نيښ *nekkh*, s.m. A prickle; sting of an insect; puncture, prick; tusk of a camel, dog, etc. P. (*nesh*).

نيغ *negh*, a. Straight, stiff, upright, erect.

نيک *nek*, a. Moral, honest; good; lucky. P. *nayak*, s.m. See نايک.

نيکوکار *nekokār*, a. Righteous, honest, moral. P.

نيکه *nīkah*, s.m. Paternal grandfather, ancestor.

نيکي *nekī*, s.f. Piety, virtue, goodness, morality. P.

نيل *nīl*, s.m. Indigo; blue. S.

نيلاب *nīlāb*, s.m. The river Indus. Name of a town on the Indus below Attak.

نيلم *nīlam*, s.m. A sapphire. S.

نيلي *nīlai*, s.m. A grey horse. P.

نیم ***nīm,*** a. Half. P. *nīma·khwā,* a. Immature, crude, unripe; changeable, fluctuating; bootless, unavailing.

نیمایه ***nīmāyah,*** s.m. A half, one half.

نیمبولۍ ***nīmbola-ī,*** s.f. A necklace of gold and glass beads (worn by women). H.

نیمتنی ***nīmtanai,*** s.m. A vest, waistcoat, jacket.

نیمګړی ***nīmgaṛai,*** a. Unfinished, incomplete.

نیمچه ***nīmcha,*** s.f. A short sleeved fur coat. *nīmchah,* a. Hybrid, mongrel. s.m. Name applied to certain tribes of Kafiristanis who have become converts to Islām.

نیمی ***nīmai,*** s.m. A half, moiety.

نینزکه ***nenzaka,*** s.f. See نازکه.

نینکه ***nenaka,*** s.f. Name of a bird, the tomtit.

نینی ***nīne,*** s.f. (pl.) Parched grain.

نیوز ***niyūz,*** s.m. Flood, torrent, inundation. *niyūz·wṛai,* a. Drift wood, rubbish carried by floods.

نیول ***nīwul,*** v.a. To catch, lay hold of, take, capture, seize. Irr. Pres. *nisī.* Past, *nīwah.*

ڼ

ڼ or **نړ** ***ṛūn,*** This compound letter is peculiar to the Pukkhto alphabet, of which it is the thirty-seventh in number. It has a peculiar sound formed by a combined pronunciation of the component letters; the sound of the *n* is nasal, and that of the *r* full and rolling as pronounced by a Frenchman. By some tribes this letter is pronounced as *n* doubled or emphatic, as *rannā* for *ranṛā, gann* for *ganṛ,* etc. This letter does not occur at the commencement of any word in the Pukkhto language.

و

و ***wāw,*** is the twenty-sixth letter of the Arabic and the thirty-eighth of the Pukkhto alphabet. As a consonant it has the sound of *w,* and is sometimes interchanged with ب. As a vowel it has the sound of *o-, ū-,* and *au,* as is explained in the Grammar.

وَ ***wa,*** c. A copulative conjunction used to connect words and sentences; and, also. P. A particle used as the sign of the vocative case. A particle used with signs of the dative case.

وُ ***wu,*** A particle prefixed to the aorist, future, and perfect tenses, and imperative mood of verbs; it corresponds to the ب similarly used in the Persian, and like that letter is also sometimes rejected as redundant.

وِ ***wi,*** An abbreviated form of the third person singular, perfect tense of the verb ویل *wayal,* To speak.

وابسته ***wābastah,*** a. Related, connected, bound. s.m. An adherent, dependent. P.

واپس ***wāpas,*** ad. Again, back, return. P.

واته ***wātah,*** s.m. Exit, issue, coming out.

واټ ***wāt,*** s.f. A road, path. S. (*bāṭ*).

واټن ***wātan,*** s.m. Distance, interval, space.

واج ***wāj,*** s.m. Barter, exchange, trading in kind.

واجب ***wājib,*** a. Expedient, fit, necessary, proper; worthy, just, reasonable. A.

واحد ***wāḥid,*** a. One, single, sole. A.

واخ ***wākh,*** in. Alas! sorrow! woe!

واده ***wādah,*** s.m. Marriage, wedding; marriage festival. *wāda,* s.f. Agreement, promise, vow. A. (*w'ada*).

وار ***wār,*** s.m. Turn, time, period. P. A blow, stroke; attack, assault. H. Leisure, rest. S. *wār,* A particle added to nouns to denote similitude or endowment. P.

وارث *wāris̤*, s.m. Heir, owner, lord. A.

واريزه *wārīza*, s.f. Intermittent fever.

واړه *wāṛah*, a. All, the whole. ad. Wholly.

واز *wāz*, a. Open, ajar, gaping. P. Fat, blubber.

وازده *wāzda*, } s.f. Fat, blubber.
وازګه *wāzga*, }

وازه *wāza*, s.f. A fathom, stretch of both arms extended; stride of a horse.

واژګون *wāǰgūn*, a. Inverted, upside-down. P.

واسطه *wāsṭa*, s.f. Account, cause, sake, reason. A. *wāsiṭa*, s.f. Agency, medium, means. A

واسيکه *wāsīka*, ad. Immediately, now, at once.

واښ *wākkh*, s.m. } Rope or cordage made of
واښکي *wākkhkai*, } goat's or camel's hair.

واښه *wākkhah*, s.m. Fodder, grass, hay; herbage, pasture.

واصل *wāṣil*, a. Arrived, met; coupled, joined. A.

واعظ *wā'iẓ*, s.m. Preacher, lecturer. A.

واف *wāf*, s.m. Nightingale; songster. P.

واقع *wāq'i*, s.m. Befalling, happening, occurring; appearing. A.

واقعه *wāq'ia*, s.f. Event, occurrence, incident.

واقعي *wāq'ī*, a. Proper, right, true. ad. Truly, actually, really. A.

واقف *wāqif*, a. Acquainted, conversant. A.

واك *wāk*, s.m. Authority, command; choice, will; power, force. P.

واګه *wāga*, s.f. A bridle, rein. H. (*bāg*).

وال *wāl*, } A particle added to nouns to denote
والا *wālā*, } resident, inhabitant; agent, owner, keeper, etc. H. Ex. *buner-wāl*, A resident of Buner. *hotī-wālā*, A townsman of Hoti.

والا *wālā*, a. Dignified, sublime, high. A. s.f. A kind of silk, sarcenet. P.

والد *wālid*, s.m. A father. A.

والده *wālida*, s.f. A mother. A.

والدين ***wālidain***, s.m. Both parents. A.

واله *wāla*, s.f. Rivulet, canal, stream.

والي *wālī*, s.m. A chief, ruler, prince. A. *wālai*, s.m. An earring. S. (*bālī*). *wālai*, m. A particle affixed to nouns and adjectives to denote endowment or possession, as, *plan* (wide), *plan-wālai* (wideness). H. (*wālā*).

وام *wām*, s.m. Debt, credit, loan; borrowing, lending. P.

وانړه *wānṛa*, s.f. A pile of grain mixed with the husk and chaff as trodden out on the threshing floor, a pile of grain, husk and chaff before winnowing.

واورا *wāwrā*, s.f. A kind of vulture.

واوره *wāwra*, s.f. A flake of snow. pl. *wāwre*, Snow. P. (*barf*).

واويلا *wāwailā*, s.f. Wail, lament, bewailing. A.

واه *wāh*, in. Bravo! well done! excellent. P.

واهمه *wāhima*, s.f. Fancy, imagination. A.

واي *wāe*, in. Alas! woe! woe to you! A.

وبا *wabā*, s.f. Plague, pestilence, epidemic, disease. A.

وبال *wabāl*, s.m. Sin, crime, fault. A.

وبلته *wabulta*, } ad. Together, one with
وبله *wabla*, } another.

وبله باندي *wabla-bānde*, ad. One above another, before and behind, in layers, in folds, together, etc.

وپار *wapār*, s.m. Trade, traffic, commerce. S. (*baipār*).

وپاري *wapārī*, s.m. A merchant, trader.

وت *wat*, s.m. Interval, gap; gorge, defile; pass. *wit*, a. See ويت.

وتر *watar*, a. Watered, saturated, irrigated (field). *witar*, s.m. A voluntary prayer not enjoined by the *farẓ* nor the *sunnat*.

وتراوي *watrāwī*, a. Unaccented, without harmony (as poetry).

وتل *watal*, v.n. To issue, emerge, come out, go forth; to exude, ooze.

وټه *waṭa*, s.f. Discount, exchange; defect, deficiency; injury, blemish. H. (*baṭṭā*).

وجاړ *wujāṛ*, a. Desolate, ruined, waste. H. (*ujāṛ*).

وجاړي *wujāṛai*, s.m. Wilderness, desert, wild.

وجلل *wajlal*, v.a. To kill, slay, put to death. Irr. Pres. *wajnī*; Past. *wājah*.

وجود *wujūd*, s.m. Body, being, substance; penis. A.

وجه *waja*, s.f. Nape, occiput, depression at the back of the neck. *wuja*, s.f. A nerve, vein, tendon, sinew.

وجهه *wajha*, s.f. Cause, reason; manner, way; appearance, visage. A.

وڅکه *wutska*, s.f. A raisin; a kind of raisin without pips.

وچ *wuch*, a. Arid, dry; parched, withered; sapless; without milk, etc.

وچکول *wuchkūl*, } A castrated ram, wether.
وچکولي *wuchkūlai*, }

وچکۍ *wuchaka-ī*, s.f. A burning fever.

وچولي *wuchwulai*, s.m. The forehead, brow.

وحش *waḥsh*, s.m. A wild beast. A.

وحشت *waḥshat*, s.m. Fear, fright; solitude, desert, wild, waste. A.

وحشي *waḥshī*, a. Fierce, savage, ferocious, wild. A.

وخ *wakh*, in. Ugh! Oh! Heigh ho!

وخت *wakht*, s.m. Time, season. A. (*waqt*).

وداع *widā'*, s.m. Adieu, farewell. A.

ودان *wadān*, a. Cultivated, inhabited; peopled, prosperous. *wadānī*, s.f. Prosperity, plenty; cultivation, population. P. (*ābādān*).

ودانول *wadānawul*, v.a. To cultivate, populate, people, colonize.

ودانيدل *wadānedal*, v.n. To flourish, prosper.

ودرول *wudrawul*, v.a. To erect, set up, pitch (as a tent, etc.); prop, support; to stop, stay, halt.

دريدل *wudredal*, v.n. To stand, stand up, stand still; arise, get up; stay, abide, halt, stop.

ودول *wadawul*, v.a. To marry, give in marriage, take in marriage.

ويدل *wadedal*, v.n. To be married, taken or given in marriage.

وډ *waḍ*, a. Fallow land, land from which the crop has been gathered.

ور *war*, s.m. A door, gate. P. (*dar*). *war*, m. A particle added to nouns to denote possession or endowment, as *dzān* (life), *dzānwar* (an animal). P. *war*, The pronominal dative affix, singular, of the third personal pronoun, as *war-dza*, go to him.

ورا *wrā*, s.f. A marriage procession; party of women who conduct the bride to the house of the bridegroom. S. (*barāt*). *warā*, ad. Afar, far off, yonder; beyond, besides. A.

ورابانړي *wrā-bāṉrai*, s.m. A male member of the *wrā*, or marriage procession; guest at a wedding feast.

وراثت *wirāsat*, s.m. Heritage, heirship. A.

وراڅه *wrādza*, s.f. A species of louse which infests camels, sheep, dogs, etc.

وراره *wrārah*, s.m. Brother's son, nephew. *wrāra*, s.f. A woman whose brother is dead.

وراشه *wrāsha*, s.f. Language, dialect. H. (*bhāshā*).

وران *wrān*, a. Destroyed, ruined, spoiled; desolate, deserted, waste. P. (*wairān*). *wrānī*, s.f. Desolation, ruin; spoiling, ruining.

ورايه *warāya*, ad. Far, far away; beyond, yonder. *la-warāya*, From afar.

وربوز *wurbūz*, s.m. The snout, muzzle.

ورتګ *wartag*, s.m. Outset, departure, exit.

ورتول *wratawul*, v.a. To fry, grill, roast, broil.

ورتيدل *wratedal,* v.n. To fret; be broiled, fried.
ورت *wraṭ,* s.m. A gush or flood of tears.
ورځ *wradz,* s.f. A day; daytime. P. (*roz*).
ورځني *wardzane,* / ورچني *warchane,* ad. Outside, without (the house).
ورځه *wrudza,* s.f. The eyebrow.
ورخ *warkh,* s.m. / ورخه *warkha,* s.f. A small hole or passage in the side of a watercourse to let out the water for irrigation of fields, etc.
ورخاري *warkhāṛai,* s.m. Name of a potherb purslain (*Portulaca oleracea*). A disease of goats and sheep, murrain.
ورخته *warkhata,* ad. Firstly, in the first place.
ورخړه *warkhaṛa,* s.f. Rubbish, litter, sweepings.
ورد *wird,* s.m. Reading the Qurān at certain fixed times; daily use, practice, task. A.
وررول *wraṛawul,* v.a. To tear, rend, lacerate.
ورريدل *wraredal,* v.n. To tear, be torn, rent, etc.
ورزيدل *warzedal,* v.n. To fly (as a bird).
ورژل *warĵal,* v.a. To chop, mince. Pres. *warĵanī.* Past. *wārĵah.*
ورژې *wriĵe,* s.f. (pl.) Rice (the grain). A. (*aruz*).
ورږ *wrag,* s.m. Mane of a horse, etc.
ورږه *wraga,* s.f. A flea. *wargah,* s.m. Biestings, the first milk after calving or kidding.
ورستو *wrusto,* ad. After, behind, astern.
ورستول *warastawul,* v.a. To send. See آستول.
ورسته *wrustah,* s.m. The rear, stern.
ورستي *wrustai,* / ورستني *wrustanai,* a. Hinder, posterior, rear, hindmost, rearmost, backmost.
ورستيدل *wrastedal,* v.n. To decay, rot, putrefy, stink.
ورسركول *warsarkawul,* v.a. To give freely or liberally.
ورشو *warsho,* s.f. A grass plot, lawn, meadow.
ورطه *warṭa,* s.f. A labyrinth, maze; whirlpool, vortex. A.

ورغانړي *warghānṛai,* s.m. A paste of butter and flour used to anoint newborn babes and puerperal women with.
ورغلل *waraghlal,* v.n. To arrive at, go to, set out to, depart. Irr. Pres. *wardzam.* Past, *warāghlam.* See راغلل.
ورغومي *warghūmai,* s.m. A young kid.
ورغوي *warghawai,* s.m. The palm, sole.
ورق *warq,* s.m. A card, leaf of a book. A.
ورک *wruk,* a. Lost, mislaid; wasted.
ورکړل *warkṛal,* / ورکول *warkawul,* v.a. To give, present, bestow, grant (to another).
ورکول *wrukawul,* v.a. To lose, mislay; squander, waste. H. (*lukānā*).
ورکه *wruka,* s.f. Deprivation, loss; wasting.
ورکيدل *wrukedal,* v.n. To be lost, to wander, stray; to be mislaid, forgotten.
ورګ *warg,* s.m. The fleece of a sheep. *wrag,* s.m. The mane of a horse, etc.
ورله *warla,* a. Big with young, pregnant.
ورم *waram,* s.m. Swelling, tumour. a. Swelled, tumefied, inflated. A.
ورمارګه *warmārgah,* / ورماګه *warmāgah,* s.m. An eruption of boils on the face (of children).
ورميږ *warmeg,* s.m. The nape, the neck.
ورندار *wrandār,* s.f. Brother's wife, sister-in-law.
وُرنيکه *wa-arnīkah,* s.m. A great grandfather on the father's side; an ancestor.
ورو *wro,* ad. Gently, slowly.
وروځه *wrūdza,* s.f. The eyebrow. See ورځه.
ورور *wror,* s.m. A brother. P. (*barādar*). *wrorī,* s.f. Fraternity, brotherhood.
وروست *wrost,* a. Rotten putrid, decayed.
ورون *wrūn,* s.m. The thigh. P. (*rān*).
ورهول *warhawul,* v.a. To liberate, release, set free, save. P. (*rahānīdan*).
ورهيدل *warhedal,* v.n. To escape, become free. P. (*rahīdan*).

وري *wrai*, s.m. A lamb. P. (*barra*). *warai*, s.m. A bundle or load for the head; one of the packs of a camel's or bullock's load.

وريت *wrīt*, a. Broiled, grilled, roasted, fried.

وريځ *waryadz*, } s.f. A cloud.
وريځه *waryadza*, }

وريدل *wuredal*, v.n. To rain, drizzle, shower.

وريره *wrera*, s.f. Brother's daughter, niece.

وريشل *wreshal*, v.a. To spin, twist.

وريښم *wrekkham*, s.m. Silk. P. (*resham*).

وړئيزه *wra-eza*, s.f. Bridesmaid, female guest at a wedding.

وړ *wa-aṛ*, a. Successful, victorious, winning. P. (*burd*): H. (*war*). *waṛ*, s.m. Scab, crust of a sore; miscellany, mass, bits of gold and silver mixed together. *wuṛ*, a. Small. P. (*khurd*). See ووړ.

وړاندِ *wṛāndi*, } ad. Ahead, in front, before, foremost.
وړاندې *wṛānde*, }

وړاندي *wṛāndai*, a. Prior, preceding, foremost. s.m. The front, bow, prow, advance, van.

وړانديني *wṛāndīnai*, a. Foremost, prior, first.

وړانه *wa-aṛāna*, Success, winning, gaining. *wa-aṛāna-pa-aṛāna*, Winning and losing.

وړل *wṛal*, v.a. To bear, support, carry, convey, remove, take away; endure, put up with, etc. (only used with reference to inanimate objects). Def. in past ten. See يوسل. P. (*burdan*).

وړم *waṛam*, ad. Last but one (applied only to times and seasons). *waṛam-kāl*, The year before last. *waṛama-shpa*, The night before last. *la-waṛama-wradz*, Three days ago.

وړمبې *wṛumbe*, ad. Firstly, in the first place.

وړمبي *wṛumbai*, } a. First, principal, foremost, chief.
وړمبني *wṛumbanai*, }

ووړکي *wṛūkai*, a. Tiny, small, wee.

ووړول *wuṛawul*, v.a. To powder, pulverize, grind, triturate.

ووړونبې *wṛūnbe*, ad. See وړمبې.

ووړه *wuṛah*, s.m. Flour, meal, powder.

ووړي *wuṛai*, s.m. Summer. *wṛai*, ad. Removed, carried away; borne, endured. *waṛa-ī*, s.f. Wool, fleece. *ūṛai*, m. A particle affixed to nouns to denote smallness, as *chirg* (a cock), *chirgūṛai* (a cock chicken).

وز *wuz*, s.m. A he-goat; mountain goat. P. (*buz*).

وزر *wazr* or *wazar*, s.m. The wing of a bird or insect; fin of a fish. P. (*bāzū*).

وزګار *wuzgār*, a. Unemployed, unused, unoccupied; idle, inactive, at leisure.

وزګري *wuzgarai*, s.m. A young goat.

وزمه *wazma*, s.f. The charge of a gun.

وزن *wazn*, s.m. Measure, weight; metre (of verse); esteem, reputation. A.

وزير *wazīr*, s.m. A minister of state, prime minister. A.

وزيري *wazīrī*, s.f. The office of Wazīr. s.m. Name of a Pathan tribe, the Wazīrīs.

وزيمه *wazema*, s.f. An ewe or goat seeking the male, in heat.

وژل *waĵal*, } v.a. To kill, slay. See وجلل.
وژلل *waĵlal*, }

وژه *wuĵa*, s.f. A nerve, vein, sinew.

وږم *wagm*, s.m. } Breath, vapour, exhalation, steam.
وږمه *wagma*, s.f. }

وږمکۍ *wagmaka-ī*, } s.f. The moon.
وږمۍ *wagma-ī*, }

وږي *wugai*, a. Hungry, famished. *wagai*, s.m. An ear of corn, grasses, etc.

وس *was*, s.m. Endeavour, attempt, trial; ability, power, force; advantage; opportunity; authority. s. (*bas*).

وسته *wasta*, s.f. A pond, pool.

وسک *waska*, } ad. As, as if, as it were. Finally, then, therefore.
وسکه *waska*, }

وسله *wasla*, s.f. Arms, accoutrements, weapons; tools, implements. A. (*silāḥ*).

وسمه *wasma*, s.f. Leaves of the Indigo plant, used as a dye for the hair. A.

وسواس *wiswās*, s.m. Apprehension, suspense, doubt, hesitation; distraction of mind; temptation of the devil. A. *wiswāsī*, a. Apprehensive, distracted; perplexing, causing doubt or suspense.

وسوسه *waswasa*, s.f. Temptation; suspense. A.

وسه *wasa*, s.f. A summer shower, summer rain.

وسيله *wasīla*, s.f. Affinity, conjuncture, cause, medium, means; prop, support, patronage. A. *wasīla-dār*, s.m. Client, defendant.

وشته *washta*, s.f. A joke, jest; joking.

وښتي *wakkhte*, s.f. (pl.). An inferior kind of rice.

وښخور *wakkhkhor*, s.m. An herbivorous animal, grass eater.

وښکل *wukkhkal*, v.a. To pull. See وکښل.

وښي *wakkhai*, s.m. A bracelet.

وصال *wiṣāl*, s.m. Meeting, interview; death. A.

وصف *waṣf*, s.m. Encomium, praise. A.

وصول *wuṣūl*, s.m. Arrival, acquisition; juncture. A.

وصيت *waṣiyat*, s.m. A will, making a will; precept, mandate. A.

وضو *wuẓū*, s.m. A form of purification by ablution before prayer. A.

وطن *waṭan*, s.m. Birthplace, home, native country. A.

وطواط *waṭwāṭ*, s.m. A kind of swallow; a bat; a languid man, timid man. A.

وطي *waṭī*, s.f. Copulation, coition. A.

وظيفه *waẓīfa*, s.f. Pension, stipend, salary; religious duty, task. A.

وعظ *w'aẓ*, s.m. Sermon, lecture; admonition. A.

وغه *wagha*, s.f. A long red worm; a kind of intestinal worm.

وغيره *waghaira*, ad. And so forth, and the rest, et cetera, etc.

وفا *wafā*, s.f. Fidelity, sincerity. A.

وقار *wiqār*, s.m. Dignity, estimation; constancy, steadiness; mildness, modesty; honour, reputation. A.

وقت *waqt*, s.m. Time, season. A.

وقف *waqf*, s.m. Endowment, foundation, legacy for pious purposes. A.

وقوف *wuqūf*, s.m. Sense, understanding; experience, information. A.

وکښل *wukkshal*, v.a. To draw. See کښل.

وکيل *wakīl*, s.m. Attorney, agent; delegate. A. *wakālat*, s.m. Commission, embassy, agency. A.

وګړي *wagaṛai*, s.m. A creature, man, human being.

ول *wal*, s.m. A coil, curl, twist, etc. H. (*bal*). *wul*, A particle added to nouns and adjectives to form the infinitive mood of active verbs. *wal*, s.m. Cheapness. See ويل *wel*.

ولاړ *wulāṛ*, a. Erect, upright, standing.

ولاړِ *wulāṛi*, } ad. A short time, brief interval,
ولاړي *wulāṛe*, } somewhat, slightly.

ولايت *wilāyat*, s.m. Abroad, foreign country. A. *wilāyatī*, s.m. A foreigner. a. Foreign.

ولل *wlal*, v.a. To wash.

وله *wala*, s.f. A canal, watercourse, stream; a cane, reed; willow tree. *wula*, s.f. Root of a plant. *wlah*, s.m. Washing. *wala*, p. To, unto; sign of the dative case.

ولِ *wali*, } ad. But, besides, yet, however. A.
ولي *wale*, } (*walek*). Why? wherefore?

ولي *walī*, s.m. Lord, prince, master. A. *wilī*, a. Melted. See ويلي.

وليشت *wlesht*, s.m. A span. See لويشت.

وند *wand*, s.m. A bank, dyke, embankment. P. (*band*).

وندر *wandar*, s.m. A tethering rope with

several loops for the feet of goats, sheep, etc.

وندني *wandanai*, s.m. A bandage, binder, wisp of straw used to tie up a sheaf of corn, etc.

وندیار *wandyār*, s.f. Brother's wife. See ورندار.

وند *wanḍ*, s.m. A field, estate, farm, parcel of land.

ونډه *wanḍa*, s.f. Division, portion, quota, share.

ونګره *wangara*, s.f. Pond, pool, lake.

ونه *wana*, s.f. A tree, shrub.

وو *wo*, s.m. Air, wind; rheumatism. P. (*bād*).

وودل *wūdal*, v.a. To weave, plait, braid.

وودہ *wūdah*, a. Asleep, sleeping.

ووړ *wor*, a. Diminutive, minute, small, wee.

ووړکي *woṛkai*, or *woṛukai*, s.m. A little one, child.

ووړوکي *woṛūkai*, a. Minute, tiny, very small.

ووته *wūna*, s.f. A kind of Damascened sword.

وهل *wahal*, v.a. To beat, hit, strike, wallop, baste.

وهلندي *wahlandai*, a. Wavy, tortuous, meandering, serpentine, winding.

وهم *wahm*, s.m. Idea, fancy, conjecture; anxiety, dread. A. *wahmī*, a. Fanciful, flighty, etc.

وهوه *wahwah*, in. Bravo! well done!

وهویله *wahwaila*, s.f. Lament. See واویلا.

وهیر *waher*, a. Forgotten.

ویاړ *wiyāṛ*, s.m. Vanity, conceit; envy, jealousy.

ویاړل *wiyāṛal*, v.a. To boast, exult, chuckle.

ویت *wīt*, a. Ajar, open, gaping; pert, saucy; mischievous, wanton.

ویتکي *wītakai*, s.m. A mischievous, pert, precocious, forward, etc. child.

ویته *wīta*, s.f. Impudence, precocity, pertness, etc.

ویخ *wekh*, s.m. Root of a tree; foundation, root; origin, source. P. (*bekh*).

ویر *wīr* or *vīr*, s.m. Mourning, lamentation; beating the breast. P. *wīr-ĵalai* or *wīra-ĵalai*, s.m. A mourner, lamenter.

ویران *wairān*, a. Desolate, ruined, waste. P. *wairāna*, s.f. A desert, wilderness, solitude. *wairānī*, s.f. Desolation, ruin. P.

ویره *wera*, s.f. Fear, fright, alarm. *werawul*, v.a. To frighten, terrify, alarm.

ویریدل *weredal*, v.n. To fear, be afraid.

ویړ *wīṛ*, a. Open, distended, spread out, expanded.

ویړول *wīṛawul*, v.a. To strew, spread out, scatter, etc.

ویړیدل *wīṛedal*, v.n. To expand, open out, blossom, etc.

ویړیا *weṛiyā*, ad. Free, gratis, for nothing.

ویزار *wīzār*, a. Angry, displeased, chagrined, vexed. P. (*bezār*). *wīzārī*, s.f. Anger, displeasure.

ویسا *wīsā*, s.f. Faith, belief; trust, reliance.

ویساک *wīsāk* or *waisāk*, s.m. Name of the first Hindu month, April-May. S. (*baisākh*).

ویش *wesh*, s.m. Division, distribution; lot, share.

ویشتل *wīshtal*, v.a. To cast, hurl, throw; discharge, propel, shoot. Pres. *wuli*. Past, *wīsht*.

ویشل *weshal*, v.a. To distribute, divide, allot; sift, separate.

ویشله *weshala*, s.f. A kind of unleavened bread, a pancake.

ویښ *wīkkh*, a. Awake, waking, vigilant.

ویښته *wekkhtah*, s.m. Hair, a hair.

ویل *wayal*, v.a. To say, speak, talk, tell. *wel*, s.m. Cheapness, low price. H. (*wārā*).

ویلني *welanai*, s.m. Herb mint, peppermint. P. (*pedīna*).

ویله *wela*, s.f. A brook, small stream, rivulet.

ويلي *wīlī*, a. Fused, melted; liquefied, thawed. H. (*pighlā*).

وينا *wainā*, s.f. A lament, wail; dirge, funeral song; conversation, speech, talk.

وينځل *wīndzal*, v.a. To wash, cleanse, purify.

وينځه *wīndza*, s.f. A bondmaid, slave girl.

وينه *wainah*, s.m. The white ant.

ويني *wīne*, s.f. (pl.). Blood.

ويي *wayai*, s.m. A word, saying; talk, speech.

ه *hā* or *he* is the twenty-seventh letter of the Arabic and the thirty-ninth of the Pukkhto alphabet. It is sometimes substituted for ح, and by some hill tribes is used instead of خ and ښ. At the end of a word it is either "perceptible" or aspirated (*hāe-ẓāhir*), or it is "imperceptible" or unsounded (*hāe-khafī*). Words ending in the former are of the masculine gender, and those ending in the latter are of the feminine. *Hāe-khafī* is added to nouns, adjectives, etc. ending in a consonant for the formation of their feminines. Adjectives ending in *hāe-ẓāhir* form their feminines by changing it to *hāe-khafī*, and this letter itself is often dropped and replaced by the short vowel َ (*zabar*), especially in poetry. At the end of Arabic words it is generally written with a couple of dots over it (ة) and pronounced as ت.

ها *hā*, s.f. An egg (of bird, insect, reptile, etc.); the testicle. *hā*, ad. Aye, yes. See هو. *hā*, in. Lo! Behold!

هاتنړه *hātanṛa*, s.f. An elephant. s. (*hāthnī*).

هاتي *hātī*, s.m. An elephant. s. (*hāthī*).

هادي *hādī*, s.m. Director, leader, guide. A.

هار *hār*, s.m. Necklace, garland, wreath; herd, flock, drove (of cattle). s. *hār*, A particle affixed to nouns, denoting sound, to form their plurals, as *shṛang* (a jingle). *shṛangahār*.

هاړ *hāṛ*, s.m. Name of the third Hindu month, June-July. s. (*asāṛh*).

هاړه هوړه *hāṛa-hūṛa*, s.f. Clamour, noise, tumult.

هاړي *hāṛe*, s.f. (pl.) Entreating, coaxing, wheedling.

هاله *hāla*, s.f. A halo or circle round the moon. P. *hāla*, ad. Then, at that time.

هامون *hāmūn*, s.m. A desert, plain. P.

هانډئ *hānḍa-ī*, s.f. A cooking pot, stewpan. s. (*hānḍī*). *hānḍa-i-wāl*, s.m. A messmate, pot companion. H.

هاها *hāhā*, s.f. Laughter, laughing loudly. A.

هاهو *hāhū*, s.m. Noise, din, tumult; fame, report, rumour. H. (*hūhā*).

هاي *hāe*, in. Alas! Woe! s. *hāe-hāe*, Alas, alas! Dear, oh dear! *hāe-hūe*, Ah me! Woe, woe! *hā-ī*, pr. See following word.

هايه *hāyah*, pr. An emphatic form of the proximate demonstrative pronoun; this, this very.

هبته *habatah*, a. Worthless, useless, spoiled. A. (*ḥabaṭah*).

هبه *hiba*, s.f. A bequest, gift. A.

هبډبه *hāba-ḍaba*, s.f. Name of a disease, croup.

هپ دپ *hap-dap*, a. Hasty, quick, rash. ad. Suddenly, all of a heap, quickly. H. (*hap-jhap*).

هپه *hapa*, s.f. Help, succour, rescue; reprisal, foray, raid, incursion.

هته *hata*, s.f. Beam of a weaver's loom; the cubit, forearm.

هتيات *hatiyāt*, s.m. Foresight, caution, care. A. (*iḥtiyāṭ*).

هتيار *hatiyār*, s.m. Apparatus, arms; implement, tool. s. (*hathyār*).

هت *haṭ*, s.m. Obstinacy, perversity, stubbornness. S. a. Erect, standing; stationary, stock-still.

هټال *haṭāl*, a. Prevented, stopped, driven back, repelled, hindered. H.

هټالول *haṭālawul*, v.a. To hinder, prevent, repel, push back, etc. H. (*haṭānā*).

هټكي *haṭkai*, s.m. Hiccough. H. (*hichkī*).

هټه *haṭah*, a. Active, stout, vigorous. H. (*haṭā*).

هټئ *haṭa-ī*, s.f. A chandler's shop, market. S.

هجر *hijr*, s.m. Absence, separation. A.

هجران *hijrān*, s.m. Separation (from friends, etc.).

هجرت *hijrat*, s.m. Flight; the flight of Muḥammad from Mecca to Medina; the date or era of that event. *hijrī*, s.f. The Muḥammadan era. A.

هجره *hujra*, s.f. A kind of inn or hostelry for the reception of travellers and visitors, free of expense; there is always one of these buildings in each quarter of a village amongst the Yusufzais and Eastern Afghans generally. The *hujra* is also used as a town-hall and vestry-room; also as a club or place of common resort for the men of the quarter in which it is situated.

هجړي *hijṛai*, s.m. An eunuch, hermaphrodite. H. (*hijṛā*).

هجكي *hijgī*, s.f. Spelling. A. (*hajī*).

هڅ *huts*, a. Infatuated, mad. H. (*huch*).

هڅه *hatsa*, s.f. Labour, trouble, toil; desire, inclination, wish.

هچ *hich*, ad. Nothing. See هيڅ.

هدايت *hidāyat*, s.m. Guidance, direction. A.

هدف *hadaf*, s.m. A butt, target, mark. A.

هدهد *hudhud*, s.m. The hoopoe. A.

هديره *hadera*, s.f. Area, enclosure; graveyard.

هديه *hadiya*, s.f. A present to a teacher, schooling fee. A.

هډ *haḍ*, s.m. A bone; centre or hard part of fruit, etc. S. (*haḍḍī*). Ancestry, lineage; greatness, nobility.

هډو *haḍo*, ad. Never, not at all, no such thing. in. I say! a term of familiarity or affection.

هډور *haḍawar*, a. Bony, strong.

هډوكي *haḍūkai*, s.m. A bone, stone of fruit.

هډي *haḍai*, s.m. Bone spavin; a node; tongue bone; tonsil. S. (*haḍḍā*)

هر *har*, s.m. A rogue, wag. S. *har*, s.m. Bray of an ass. *har*, a. Every, each, any (in comp.). P. *har-wakht*, Each time. *hara-wradz*, Every day.

هراس *hirās*, s.m. Fear, terror. P.

هراول *harāwul*, s.m. Advanced guard of an army. T.

هراند *harānd*, a. Fearful, timid.

هرتال *hartāl*, s.m. Orpiment. S.

هرټ *haraṭ*, s.m. A Persian wheel for drawing water from a well. H.

هرځائي *hardzā-ī*, s.m. Vagabond, wanderer, rascal.

هرج *harj*, s.m. Interruption, delay; tumult, sedition. A.

هرزه *harzah*, a. Nonsensical, frivolous. *harza*, s.f. A trifle, bagatelle, absurdity. P.

هركاره *harkārah*, s.m. A courier, messenger; emissary, spy; man of all work. P. *harkāra*, s.f. An iron spoon, a large ladle.

هرگاه *hargāh*, ad. Whenever, wherever. P.

هرگز *hargiz*, ad. Ever, never. P.

هرگوره *hargora*, ad. At least, at all events, by all means; wholly, altogether, entirely.

هرئ *hira-ī*, s.f. Excuse, pretence, shift, plea. A. (*ḥīla*).

هريړه *hareṛa*, s.f. Name of a nut used in medicine, and as a dye, myrobalan (*Terminalia chebula*).

هرپئ *harpa-ī*, s.f. A casket, small box.

هزاره *hazārah*, s.m. Name of a Tartar tribe

who possess the hill country between Kabul and Herat.

هزم *hazm*, s.m. Digestion. A. (*hazm*)

هژدات *haĵdāt*, s.m. Bell metal, bronze, brass. S. (*aĵdhāt*).

هسار *hisār*, s.m. A castle, fort. A. (*hiṣār*). Difficulty, embarrassment. a. Enclosed, surrounded, besieged.

هسارول *hisārawul*, v.a. To enclose, surround, besiege; stop, prevent, keep.

هساريدل *hisāredal*, v.n. To be besieged, en-enclosed, etc., to stick, stop, be stuck, clogged, etc.

هسپه *haspa*, s.f. Erysipelas; quinsy; purpura. *haspa·buṭai*, s.m. Name of a plant used as a remedy for *haspa* (*Indigofera sp.*).

هستي *hastī*, s.f. Being, existence. P.

هسک *hask*, a. High, lofty, tall. p. Above, aloft. *hisk*, s.m. Lottery, hazard, chance; drawing lots, lot.

هس *hasi*, } ad. As, thus, in like manner,
هسي *hase*, } likewise, therefore.

هښمه *hakkhma*, s.f. An April shower, a spring shower soon passing away (of rain).

هغومبره *haghombra*, ad. So much, that much.

هغه *haghah*, pr. The third personal pronoun; he, she, it. The remote demonstrative pronoun; that. A. (*hazā*).

هفته *hafta*, s.f. A week. P.

هک پک *hak·pak*, a. Aghast, confounded, confused. H. (*hakkā·bakkā*).

هگي *haga-ī*, s.f. An egg. See ها.

هل *hal*, s.m. Handle of a plough; a plough. S.

هلاک *halāk*, s.m. Perdition, ruin, death. a. Dead, killed; annihilated, lost, ruined. A.

هلاکت *halākat*, s.m. Perdition, death.

هلاکي *halākī*, s.f. Ruination, destruction A.

هلال *hilāl*, s.m. The new moon; the first and last two or three days of the moon. A. *halāl*, a. Lawful, etc. See حلال.

هلاهل *halāhal*, s.m. Deadly poison. S.

هلته *halta*, ad. } There, yonder, thither, in
هلته کي *halta·ke*, } that place, over there.

هلک *halak*, s.m. A boy, lad, youth. a. Small, little; slight, mean; debased, cheap; easy, soft; silly, useless. H. (*halkā*).

هلکت *halakat*, s.m. } Boyhood, youth.
هلکوالي *halak·wālai* }

هلکينه *halkīna*, s.f. Infancy, childhood.

هلم *halam*, s.m. Cress, water cress (*Lepidum sativum*). H. (*hālim*).

هلواک *halwāk*, a. Fast, swift, quick, fleet, rapid.

هله *halla*, s.f. Charge, attack, onset, assault; riot, uproar, tumult. A. *hala*, ad. Then, at that time.

هلي *hale*, ad. Here, hither, in this place.

هم *hum*, c. Also, even, likewise. P. (*ham*) (in comp.). Together, with, same, equal, etc. as *hum·kār*, s.m. A fellow workman. *hum·wazn*, Of equal weight. *hamm*, s.m. Solicitude, anxiety, care. A.

هماي *humāe*, s.m. Phœnix, bird of happy omen. P. (*humā*).

همت *himmat*, s.m. Bravery, courage; resolution, spirit. A.

همتناک *himmat·nāk*, } Resolute, daring, bold,
همتي *himmatī*, a. } courageous.

همراه *hamrāh*, s.m. Companion, fellow-traveller. p. Along with, together. P.

همسا *hamsā*, s.f. A mace, stick. See امسا.

همگي *hamagī*, } a. All, the whole. P.
همه *hamah*, }

همياني *hamiyānī*, s.f. A purse. P.

هميشه *hamesha*, a. Perpetually, always. P.

هنج *hanj*, s.m. } Assafœtida. S. (*heng*).
هنجه *hanja*, s.f. }

هند *hind*, s.m. India, Hindustan.

هنداره *hindāra*, s.f. A mirror, looking glass.

هندكو *hindko*, s.f. The language of the Indians.

هندكي *hindkī*, s.m. The Indians; name of an Indian tribe (converts to Islam), settled in parts of the Peshawar valley and surrounding hills. *hindkai*, s.m. An Indian (Mussulman). *hindka-ī*, s.f. An Indian woman.

هندو *hindū*, s.m. A Hindu; a pagan, idolater.

هندوبار *hindūbār*, s.m. A place where Hindus dwell or meet; dealings with a Hindu.

هندوستان *hindūstān*, s.m. India, Upper India, the country of the Hindus.

هندوګي *hindūgai*, s.m. A term of abuse. A Hindu grocer, grain dealer.

هندوانه *hindwāna*, s.f. A water melon. P.

هندوانړي *hindwānṛa-ī*, } s.f. A Hindu woman.
هندوه *hindawa*, }

هنډه *hunḍah*, s.m. A wolf. H. *hanḍa*, s.f. Ambition, desire, wish; fancy; want. *hinḍah*, s.m. A stallion, bull, male kept for breeding purposes.

هنډي *hunḍa-ī*, s.f. Bill of exchange, money order. S. (*hunḍī*).

هنر *hunar*, s.m. Art, skill; virtue, quality. P. *hunar-man*, a. Clever, ingenious. P.

هنس *hans*, s.m. A goose, swan. S. (*hāṅs*).

هنګام *hangām*, s.m. Period, time, season. P.

هنګامه *hangāma*, s.f. Mob, crowd, assembly; uproar, riot, tumult; assault, onset. P.

هنوز *hanoz*, ad, Yet, hitherto, still. P.

هنړ *hanṛ*, s.m. Neigh of a horse, bray of an ass.

هنړهنړيدل *hanṛ-hanṛedal*, v.n. To neigh, bray. H. (*hinhinhānā*).

هو *ho*, ad. Aye, yea, yes. S. (*hāṅ*). in. Halloa! ho! S. Hurrah! An exclamation used when rushing on an enemy in battle.

هوا *hawā*, s.f. Wind, atmosphere, air; lust, desire; affection, love; pride, conceit. A. *hawā*, in. Dear me! Ah! Alas! See هاي.

هوار *hawār*, a. Even, smooth; level, flat; fit, proper; gentle, docile. P. (*hamwār*).

هوباره *hūbārah*, s.m. A kind of bustard. A.

هوبهو *hūbahū*, ad. Exactly, perfectly, quite. A.

هوده *hūda*, s.f. Charming, exorcising, mesmerising (by breathing). Appointment, office, post, business. A. (*'uhda*). *hauda*, s.f. A litter or sedan used by women when they travel; a seat or stage placed on the back of an elephant. A.

هوډ *hoḍ*, s.m. The contrary, opposite.

هوډه *hoḍa*, s.f. Perversity, obstinacy.

هوډي *hoḍai*, a, Stubborn, perverse, wayward; opposed, opposite. s.m. Name of a hill opposite Attak (on the Indus), on the top of which are some Buddhist ruins.

هور *hor*, s.m. Time, season. Fire. A deer.

هور *hūri*, } ad. There, thither, over there.
هوري *hūre*, }

هوږه *hūga*, s.f. Garlic.

هوس *hawas*, s.m. Lust, concupiscence; ambition, desire; curiosity. A. *hawas-nāk*, a. Sensual, ambitious, etc.

هوسا *hosā*, a. Refreshed, recruited; untired, unwearied; idle, lazy. P. (*hoshā*). *hosā-kawul*, v.a. To recruit, rest, refresh, repair, refit, etc.

هوسي *hosai*, s.m. A deer, gazelle. P. (*āhū*).

هوښ *hokkh*, s.m. Sense, understanding; mind, soul; judgment. P. (*hosh*).

هوښيار *hokkhyār*, a. Intelligent, sensible, wise; cautious, discreet, prudent.

هوښيارتيا *hokkhyār-tiyā*, } Intelligence, discretion, prudence.
هوښياري *hokkhyārī*, s.f. }

هوک *hūk*, a. Flooded, inundated, sunk.

هوکلي *hokla-ī*, s.f A large wooden pestle.

هوکه *haukah*, a. Fatigued, tired, weary

هوکي *hokai*, s.m. Assent, consent, saying "yes"; consent of parents to marriage of a daughter.

هول *hūl*, s.m. Bolt or bar of a door. *haul*,

s.m. Horror, fear, terror. A. *haul·nāk*, a. Terrible, awful, dismal, fearful.

هومره *homra*, } ad. So much, that much,
هونبره *honbra*, } this much.

هونړا *honṛā*, s.f. A kind of trap for catching birds; the perch placed over the trap.

هوي *hūe*, in. Alas! See هاي.

هويدا *hawīdā*, a. Evident, manifest, clear. P.

هويه *hoya*, s.f. An egg.

هه *hah*, in. Indeed! Really! Oh ho! Halloa!

هي *hai*, in. Alas! Dear me! *hai·hai*, in. What a pity! Dear me! Wonderful! Strange!

هيات *hayāt*, s.m. Form, aspect, visage, face. A.

هيبت *haibat*, s.m. Panic, terror, awe. A. *haibat·nāk*, a. Terrific, awe-inspiring, fearful.

هيڅ *hets*, ad. Nothing, nought, none. P. (*hech*). *hets·tsok*, Nobody. *hets·shai*, Nothing.

هيچرِ *hechari*, } ad. Never, at no time.
هيچري *hechare*, }

هيچرته *hecharta*, ad. Nowhere.

هير *her*, a. Forgotten, omitted, lost to memory.

هيرړي *herṛai*, s.m. A sheep of the long-tailed breed. H. (*bheṛā*).

هيرقطار *hīr·qaṭār*, s.m. Indian file, one behind the other, filing along.

هيړ *heṛ*, s.m. Time, season, period. H. (*pher*).

هيړه *heṛa*, s.f. Turn, time. ad. Once, one time. *yawa·heṛa*, Once. *dwa·heṛa*, Twice, etc.

هيړي *heṛai*, s.m. A sheep. See هيرړي.

هيز *hīz*, s.m. Hermaphrodite. P.

هيزگي *hezgī*, s.f. Spelling. See هجکي.

هيسته *hīsta*, ad. Here, hither. *rāhīsta*, Near me. *darhīsta*, Near thee, *warhista*, Near him, her, it, etc.

هيښ *hekkh*, a. Amazed, confounded, perplexed.

هيضه *haiẓa*, s.f. Cholera morbus. A.

هيغ *hegh*, a. Stiff, straight. See ميغ.

هيكل *haikal*, s.m. An ornament for the neck; face, figure, form, person; palace, temple. A.

هيل *hel*, s.m. Cardamoms. A. (*elā*).

هيله *hīla*, s.f. Subterfuge, trick. See حيله.

هيلئ *hīla-ī*, s.m. A duck, water fowl.

هينګ *heng*, s.m. A groan, moan, sigh.

هيواد *hewād*, s.m. Country, region, clime.

هيون *hayūn*, s.m. A horse; camel. P.

هيهات *haihāt*, a. Lamenting, wailing. A. in. Alas! Begone!

ي

ي *yā* or *ye* is the twenty-eighth letter of the Arabic and the fortieth and last of the Pukkhto alphabet. When used as a consonant it has the sound of *y*, if moved by a vowel (*mutaḥarrik*), and of the French *e* or English *ey* (as in *they*), if quiescent or unmoved (*sākin*). When used as a vowel it has the sound of *ī* (*yāe·m'arūf*), or *e* (*yāe·majhūl*) if preceded by the short vowel *kasra* ـِ, and of the diphthong *ai*, if preceded by the short vowel *fatha* ـَ (*yāe·sākin·māqabl·i·maftūḥ*), as is explained in the Grammar. *Yāe·m'arūf*, preceded by *hamza* ـٔ has the sound of *a-ī*. (*yāe·m'arūf māqabl·i·hamza·i·khafi·i·maksūr*), and is the termination of a number of feminine nouns, both in the singular and plural. In Pukkhto the vowel sounds *yāe·m'arūf* (*ī*), *yāe·majhūl* (*e*), and *yāe·m'arūf māqabl·i·hamza* (*a-ī*) are often dropped and replaced by the short vowel *kasra* ـِ.

يا *yā*, c. Either, or, whether. P. in. Oh! Vocative particle. Oh! Halloa! A.

ياب *yāb* (in comp.). Finding, obtaining. P. *kam·yāb*, a. Scarce. P.

یابو **yābū**, s.m. A pony. H.

یاد **yād**, s.m. Recollection, memory. P. *yādawul*, v.a. To remind, mention, call to mind. *yādedal*, v.n. To recollect, remember, recur.

یار **yār**, s.m. Paramour, lover, friend; comrade, companion, assistant. P. *yārī*, s.f. Friendship.

یاستي **yāsta-ī**, You are; a form of the second person plural present tense of the defective verb *yam*, I am.

یاسمین **yāsmīn**, s.m. Jasmine. P.

یاغي **yāg͟hī**, a. Mutinous, rebellious. s.m. A rebel, mutineer. A. (*bāg͟hī*).

یاغیگر **yāg͟hī·gar**, s.m. A mutineer, rebel. *yāg͟hī·garī*, s.f. Mutiny, rebellion; sedition, revolt.

یافت **yāft**, s.m. Earnings, perquisites. P.

یاقوت **yāqūt**, s.m. A ruby. A.

یال **yāl**, s.m. The mane of a horse, etc. P.

یاور **yāwar**, a. Aiding, helping, friendly. s.m. Coadjutor, assistant; companion, friend. P. *yāwarī*, s.f. Help, succour, aid.

یاوره **yāwara**, s.f. A bigbellied mare, ass, etc.

یاوه **yāwah**, a. Vain, absurd, futile; ruined, lost. P. *yāwa·goe*, s.m. A talker of nonsense.

یاهو **yāhū**, s.m. Jehovah. A.

یبل **yabl**, a. Barefooted. See ابل.

یتیم **yatīm**, s.m. An orphan. A.

یخ **yak͟h**, a. Cold, frigid; cooled, damped; satiated; slaked, subsided. s.m. Cold; ice. P.

یخني **yak͟hnī**, s.f. Coldness, frigidity, chilliness; cold, chill; gravy, jelly. P.

یراق **yarāq**, s.m. Arms, accoutrements, weapons. T.

یرړي **yarṛai**, s.m. A sheep. See هیرړي.

یرز **yarz**, s.m. Ability, skill, fitness, capacity; merit, worth; propriety, expediency; consistency, congruity.

یرزن **yarzan**, a. Expedient, fit, worthy, suitable.

یرغمال **yarg͟hamāl**, s.m. A hostage. P.

یرغه **yarg͟hah**, a. Ambling. s.m. An ambler, an ambling horse or mule; a horse or mule with the ears slit. P.

یرمن **yar·man**, a. Timid, timorous, nervous, fearing, shy.

یره **yara**, s.f. Fear, fright. ad. Really, truly, yes, indeed, verily. P. (*āre*).

یزد **yazd**, } s.m. God. P.
یزدان **yazdān**, }

یږ **yag**, s.m. A bear.

یږه **yaga**, s.f. A she bear. A kind of ulcer.

یساول **yasāwul**, s.m. A mace bearer; equerry, mounted attendant on a man of rank. P.

یستل **yastal**, v.a. To eject, expel, pick out, extract, produce, etc. Def. in pres. ten. See باسل.

یشم **yas͟hm**, s.m. Jasper, jade, agate. P.

یشند **yas͟hand**, a. Boiling, effervescing.

یشنا **yas͟hnā**, s.f. Ebullition, effervescence.

یشول **yas͟hawul**, v.a. To boil, cook, stew.

یشیدل **yas͟hedal**, v.n. To boil, bubble, ferment, effervesce. P. (*jos͟hīdan*). See ایشیدل.

ییښل **yak͟hk͟hal**, v.a. To put, place, set, deposit, etc. P. (*s͟hāndan*). Applied to inanimate objects. Def. in pres. ten. See ږدل.

ییښودل **yak͟hk͟hodal**, } v.a. To place, put, set.
ییښول **yak͟hk͟hawul**, } See ایښودل.

ییښي **yak͟hk͟hai**, a. Placed, put, set.

یعني **y'ane**, ad. Namely, that is to say, viz., i.e. A.

یغمه **yag͟hma**, s.f. Plunder, booty, spoil. P.

یقین **yaqīn**, a. Certain, sure, true, real. ad. Certainly, surely, truly. A. *yaqīnī*, s.f. Reality, certainty. a. Certain, sure, real.

یقیناً **yaqīnan**, ad. Assuredly, certainly, A.

یک **yak**, a. One (in comp. only). P. *yak·dil*, a. Of one mind, unanimous. *yak·lak͟hta*, ad. All at once, suddenly.

یکلنگه **yak·linga**, s.f. A lever used to draw water from a well. P. See ډنګلي.

يکشمبه *yak·shamba*, s.f. Sunday. P.

يکلائي *yaklā-ī*, s.f. A mantle of a single layer of cloth. P.

يکه *yakah*, a. Unique, single, alone, sole; a one-horse chaise. P.

يکي *yakī*, s.f. Name of a small copper coin.

يګان *yagān*, a. Single, unique. P.

يګانګي *yagānagī*, s.f. Singleness, uniqueness; unanimity, concord, unity. P.

يګانه *yagānah*, a. Single, sole; unanimous, agreed. P.

يګه *yaga*, s.f. A kind of corroding ulcer; a disease affecting the tail of a horse, melanosis; cancer; a she bear. See يږه.

يل *yal*, s m. Hero, champion. P.

يلغر *yalghar*, s.m. Foray, raid, incursion. E.

يله *yalah*, a. Free, liberated; wandering, vagabond. *yala*, s.f. A bog, marsh, morass.

يم *yam*, s.m. The ocean, sea. A. *yam*, I am, the first person singular present tense of the defective verb "to be" (inf. wanting).

ينګ *yang*, s.m. Conduct, behaviour; manner, mode, way.

يو *yo*, a. One; a, an. P. (*yak*).

يواځې *yawādzai*, a. Alone, single, solitary. ad. Separately, alone, apart.

يواڼ *yawād*, s.m. Country, region. See هيواد.

يور *yor*, s.f. Husband's brother's wife. pl. *yūnre*.

يورش *yūrish*, s.m. Assault, charge; invasion. P.

يوز *yūz*, s.m. A lynx; panther. P.

يوسپزي *yūsupzī*, s.m. Name of a powerful clan of Afghans, the Yūsufzais.

يوستوي *yawastawai*, a. Single, without fold or lining (as a garment).

يوسفزي *yūsufzī*, s.m. See يوسپزي.

يوسل *yosal*, v.a. To bear, carry, support, put up with, endure (applied only to inanimate objects). Irr. Pres. *yosī*. Past. *yowaṛ*. See وړل.

يوم *yūm*, s.m. A shovel, spade (with a bar of wood fixed above the blade as a rest for the foot in shoving it into the ground). *yaum*, s.m. A day. A.

يون *yūn*, s.m. Pace, step; gait, carriage; custom, habit; moving, passing.

يوه *yawa*, يويه *yoya*, s.f. A plough. *yawe* or *yiwe*, pl. Ploughing, tilling.

ييښل *yekkhal*, v.a. To put, set: See ينبل.

ييم *yīm*, s.m. A shovel. See يوم *yūm*.

يه *ya*, ad. No, not. P.

ئي *e*, A form of the Genitive and Instrumental cases, singular and plural of the third personal pronoun هغه, His, her's, it's, their's, etc. He, she, it, they.